Professional Issues in Therapeutic Recreation

On Competence and Outcomes

Norma J. Stumbo, Ph.D., CTRS™
Editor

Sagamore Publishing
Champaign, Illinois

Publishers: Joseph J. Bannon/Peter Bannon
General Manager: M. Douglas Sanders
Director of Production: Susan M. Davis
Cover Design: Jose Barrientos
Interior Design: Michelle R. Dressen

Library of Congress Catalog Card Number: 2009927829
ISBN: 978-1-57167-535-4
Printed in the United States.

10 9 8 7 6 5 4 3 2 1

Sagamore Publishing, L.L.C.
804 North Neil Street
Champaign, IL 61820
www.sagamorepub.com

Contents

Preface

The gestation period for this book was unusually long. I'm not sure whether that was due to the book's new organization, the authors' complexity of thoughts that took time to harness, or just the fact that 30 chapters is a large collection of manuscripts to bring to fruition. But as I look at the final product, I am very proud and honored to have been a part of this adventure.

Like the first edition, this second effort has four major sections: Introduction, Education, Practice, and Research. It is clear that these divisions are largely arbitrary, as every practice issue affects every research issue, every education issue affects every practice issue, and on and on. However, books need an organizational layout, and these divisions appear to make sense.

Five new chapters have been added to the Introduction section. The first chapter on competencies and outcomes by the editor updates this information from the first edition. Kari Kensinger provides an overview of how the history of the profession affects current issues. The impact of world demographics is outlined by Jerome Singleton, while Marieke Van Puymbroeck and Heather Porter discuss the World Health Organization's International Classification system. Heewon Yang closes out the first section with a look at how therapeutic recreation is evolving worldwide. In comparison to the first edition, which only had one chapter in the first section, these new chapters will help us broaden our lenses from which to examine other issues.

In the second section on Education issues, Nancy Navar provides a thoughtful review of therapeutic recreation education and sets the tone for this section. An updated profile of therapeutic recreation curricula in the U.S. is provided. Marcia Carter and Ramon Zabriskie update their chapter on educational program accreditation, while Peggy Holmes-Layman and John Pommier do the same for undergraduate internship requirements. Again, two perspectives chapters are provided, one by Jean Folkerth on support courses, and one by Terry Kinney, Jeff Witman, Janet Sable, and Judy Kinney, on a proposed model program for undergraduate curricula.

Several new chapters appear in the Practice section. Sharon Nichols leads off this section with an update on whether the profession is an art, science, or magic. Jo Ellen Ross and Candy Ashton-Shaeffer update their chapter on therapeutic recreation practice models as well. Ray West authors a new chapter on evidence-based practice. A fresh look at clinical practice guidelines is offered by Nancy Richeson, Suzanne Fitzsimmons, and Linda Buettner. An updated look at client assessment is also provided. Sharon Nichols and Mary Ann Keogh Hoss give us a fresh perspective on ethics. G.T. Thompson and John Shank furnished contemporary views of reimbursement and legislation issues, respectively.

Another new addition is Peg Connolly's chapter on verifying professional competence. Susan Hutchinson sheds light on the complexities of client-professional relationships in a new chapter. Norma Stumbo and Mary Ann Keogh Hoss outline a number of parallel issues between higher education and health care. Closing this section, Charles Bloom provides a perspective chapter on the transitions that must occur when maturing from a student to a professional.

The last section on Research issues contains five updated chapters from the first edition. Leandra Bedini discusses the state of the art in therapeutic recreation research, while Linda Caldwell reminds us of the importance of using theory as a foundation for research activities. Mark Widmer provides new insights on ways to conduct outcome research. Bryan McCormick and Youngkhill Lee take a different perspective on evidence-based practice and practice-based research. The last chapter on the absolute necessity for clinical research in therapeutic recreation is authored by George Patrick.

In all, these 29 chapters represent some of the most gifted and talented minds in the profession. I'll reiterate from the first edition: "There are two celebratory events in the making of a book: first, when an agreement is signed signaling a new adventure full of learning and anticipatory excitement, and second, when that adventure is complete and the manuscript is relinquished to the publisher. Luckily, on the road of this particular journey, I had the opportunity to work with some of the most gifted, talented minds in the profession. I'd like to thank each of the chapter authors for creating such beautiful capsules of thought-provoking material. I can only hope the readers will learn as much as I did. It was a pleasure to work with both old and new friends. The profession of therapeutic recreation is well-served by such dedicated, intelligent, and wonderful human beings." Thank you all for making this a great edition and addition to our literature.

I'd also like to acknowledge the two individuals at Sagamore Publishing who were instrumental in keeping the wheels under this project: Jose Barrientos and Doug Sanders. Rewards in heaven await those with such patience.

I'd also like to thank my sisters, Barbara A. Busch and Nancy L. Lockett, for recently helping me celebrate my life and retirement. I can only aspire to such grace and goodness when I reach their ages (ha ha). And a special thanks to Randy Duncan, my song and dance man.

Norma J. Stumbo
Editor

Section I
Introduction

Section I
Introduction

CHAPTER 1

On Competencies and Outcomes in Therapeutic Recreation

Norma J. Stumbo, Ph.D., CTRS™
Education Associates

Ensuring that healthcare professionals attain and maintain competence is a complex task that is clearly related to their ability to design and deliver quality services that produce wanted client outcomes (Swankin, LeBuhn, & Morrison, 2006). Professional competence is tightly interwoven with service quality. This applies to all healthcare professions, including therapeutic recreation.

One purpose of this text is to help therapeutic recreation professionals and students explore some of the issues related to professional competence and quality service delivery. This implies two broad sets of inquiry. First, how do we ensure our worth—that is, how do we provide proof of professional competence? And second, how do we prove our value—that is, how do we provide proof of our service outcomes? While the aim of this text is not to provide definitive answers to these questions, we hope at least to surface the right questions that spark further debate and inquiry. This chapter embarks on that task by reviewing recent literature on professional competence and service outcomes in order to set the stage for the remaining chapters. This chapter first explores the notion of professional competence before examining concepts related to service outcomes.

How Do We Define the Profession?

Dower, O'Neil, and Hough (2001) authored an interesting treatise on questions to be asked of "emerging" healthcare professions. Among their lengthy list, are these questions that have great relevance to the profession of therapeutic recreation:
- What does the profession do, and how does it provide care? Is there a professional consensus document describing the profession?
- Is the profession best described as a complete system that includes a range of modalities and therapies? If not, would it be better described as a modality that could be provided by members of different professions? If it is a system, what characterizes it as a system? If it is a modality, what systems and professions employ it?

- How is the profession different from/similar to other healthcare professions, systems, and modalities? What is the value that this profession adds to healthcare? How does the profession promote good health?
- How does the profession fit into the larger health picture? For what range of conditions and health concerns do members of the profession treat/provide care for/advise? For what range of conditions and health concerns do members of the profession decline to offer care/refer to other providers?
- How does the profession fare when held up to a progressive, normative set of goals for health professional such as that developed by the Pew Health Professions Commission? How does the profession measure up to other external norms regarding such issues as risk management or disease prevention?

It is clear that the collective answers to these questions become important for defining the scope of the profession and its future directions. How does therapeutic recreation define and measure professional competence? How do these definitions and measurements impact how we determine and defend service outcomes? Is there consensus on these answers? If not, is it possible to arrive at consensus or, minimally, some mutual agreements?

What is Professional Competence?

Greiner and Knebel (2003), in a publication on behalf of the Institute of Medicine, noted that there are five core competencies that all healthcare professionals should possess, regardless of their discipline, to meet the needs of the 21st-century healthcare system. These include:

- Ability to provide patient-centered care; e.g., providing culturally relevant care; coordinating continuous care; and advocating health, wellness, and quality of life;
- Ability to work in interdisciplinary teams that cooperate, collaborate, and integrate services to ensure care is continuous and reliable;
- Ability to uptake and utilize evidence-based practice through the integration of best practices, clinical expertise, and patient preferences;
- Ability to implement quality assessment and quality improvement; e.g., designing and evaluating whether systems and processes of care are improving quality; and
- Ability to utilize informatics; e.g., using information technology to communicate, manage data, and reduce error.

Epstein and Hundert (2002) defined professional competence as "the habitual and judicious use of communication, knowledge, technical skills, clinical reasoning, emotions, values, and reflection in daily practice for the benefit of the individual and community being served" (p. 226). They reviewed 195 studies and noted that professional competence for physicians reflected seven dimensions as noted in Figure 1.1. With the exception of technical skills, it appears that this list also applies to therapeutic recreation specialists.

Of course, the "content" of therapeutic recreation competencies is missing from these lists, but is delineated in documents such as the National Council for Therapeutic Recreation Certification's *2007 Job Analysis*. Both the content and dimensions of competence are

---

Figure 1.1
Dimensions of Professional Competence
(Epstein & Hundert, 2002, p. 227)

- Cognitive
  - Core knowledge
  - Basic communication skills
  - Information management
  - Applying knowledge to real-world situations
  - Using tacit knowledge and personal experience
  - Abstract problem-solving
  - Self-directed acquisition of new knowledge
  - Recognizing gaps in knowledge
  - Generating questions
  - Using resources (e.g., published evidence, colleagues)
  - Learning from experience
- Technical
  - Physical examination skills
  - Surgical/procedural skills
- Integrative
  - Incorporating scientific, clinical, and humanistic judgment
  - Using clinical reasoning strategies appropriately (hypthetico-deductive, pattern-recognition, elaborated knowledge)
  - Linking basic and clinical knowledge across disciplines
  - Managing uncertainty
- Context
  - Clinical setting
  - Use of time
- Relationship
  - Communication skills
  - Handling conflict
  - Teamwork
  - Teaching others (e.g., patients, students, colleagues)
- Affective/Moral
  - Tolerance of ambiguity and anxiety
  - Emotional intelligence
  - Respect for patients
  - Responsiveness to patients and society
  - Caring
- Habits of Mind
  - Observations of one's own thinking, emotions, and techniques
  - Attentiveness
  - Critical curiosity
  - Recognition of and response to cognitive and emotional biases
  - Willingness to acknowledge and correct errors

---

important factors in determining a professional's ability to adequately design and deliver services to constituents. That is, a professional's competence is closely related to his or her ability to provide high-quality services that help the client achieve desired and meaningful outcomes.

A notable assertion made by Swankin et al. (2006) is that too often in healthcare, a profession is too narrowly focused on the initial assignation of competence and fails to periodically assess the professional's updated knowledge, skills, and clinical performance, his or her need for a methodical improvement plan based on that assessment, and his or her continued demonstration of continued competence. They believe that continuing *education* requirements be abandoned in favor of stringent professional *development* plans that require routine periodic assessments, personal improvement plans, extensive record-keeping, and continual monitoring and evaluation of professional competence.

To what degree are professional competence and quality service provision related? Buettner and Fitzsimmons (2007) noted, "The individual recreation therapist has a considerable impact on outcomes, both in research and in practice settings. Being the best clinician possible is, therefore, important in advancing evidence-based practice" (p. 16). Do you agree that ensuring our worth as healthcare professionals through evidence of continued competence is closely related to proving our value as a profession in delivering sought-after client outcomes? If a professional's competence is not adequately and continually monitored, are clients put at risk? How does therapeutic recreation fare in establishing and continually measuring professionals' competence with relation to high-quality practice? The next section will explore the definitions and parameters of client outcomes and their relationship to evidence-based practice.

What are Client Outcomes?

The ability of the professional to designate and deliver services that produce predictable, meaningful, and important client outcomes is of paramount importance to administrators, clinicians, and healthcare consumers alike (McGrath & Tempier, 2003). Conceptualizing and managing service quality is important to all healthcare stakeholders. "It is important that the primary focus of any quality-management system be improved quality of care and treatment effectiveness, with cost-effectiveness a welcome and likely companion" (McGrath & Tempier, p. 469). Central to quality healthcare is the concept of client outcomes.

A number of authors have emphasized that outcomes are the documentable changes in client behavior, skills, and/or attitudes that can be attributed to active participation in the therapeutic recreation intervention program (Dunn, Sneegas, & Carruthers, 1991; Stumbo & Peterson, 2009; Shank & Kinney, 1991; Stumbo, 1996). The following represent definitions of client outcomes located in the healthcare literature:

- The (change in a) state or situation that arises as a result of some process of intervention (Wade, 1999, p. 93)
- Refers to change in a client's status over time (McCormick & Funderburk, 2000, p. 10)
- Outcomes are reported as changes in the score between two points of time on individual level standardized instruments (Blankertz & Cook, 1998, p. 170)

- The results of performance (or non-performance) of a function or process(es) (Joint Commission on Accreditation of Healthcare Facilities, 1995; p. 717)
- Outcomes are the observed changes in a client's status as a result of our interventions and interactions, whether intended or not. Outcomes are the complications, adverse events, or short- or long-term changes experienced by our clients and represent the efforts of our care. Outcomes can be attributed to the process of providing care, and this should enable us to determine if we are doing for our clients that which we purport to do (Shank & Kinney, 1991, p. 76)
- Client outcomes are the results or changes in the client that result from participation and involvement in services, and, therefore, need to be clarified and targeted before any intervention or service is conceptualized or designed (Stumbo & Peterson, 2009, p. 469)
- The direct effects of service upon the well-being of both the individual and specified populations; the end result of medical care; what happened to the patient in terms of palliation, control of illness, cure, or rehabilitation (Riley, 1991, p. 58)
- Clinical results (Scalenghe, 1991, p. 30)

The majority of these definitions concur that outcomes represent the differences in the client from the beginning compared to the end of treatment (and perhaps beyond). Of course, most clinicians are hopeful that client changes or outcomes are positive (in the desired direction of treatment) and result directly from active participation within treatment services. In all cases, outcomes must be targeted prior to the intervention and must be measurable.

Because client outcomes are so complex and multifaceted, many authors have attempted to classify them into broader health and functional outcome categories. These categories help professionals communicate client needs across disciplines and help individual professionals make sure their services contribute to the overall health and functioning of the clients served. In general, healthcare outcomes can be divided into five overall categories: (a) clinical status, (b) functional status, (c) well-being or quality of life, (d) satisfaction, and (e) cost/resource consumption (Hendryx, Dyck, & Srebnick, 1995; Johnson, 1993; McGlynn, 1995; McGrath & Tempier, 2003).

Clinical status may include measurements of psychopathology, symptomatology, short-term changes in symptoms, or severity of problems or syndromes targeted by services (Hendryx et al., 1995; McGlynn, 1995). McCormick and Funderburk (2000) cited Granger (1984) and Ware (1997) to describe clinical status as changes that are measured at the organ level, such as blood pressure, temperature, white blood cell count, respiration, and fitness.

Functional status includes the ability to fulfill social and role functions that reflect broad long-term effects after services have ended and that tend to reflect a person's or family's ability to lead a successful, productive, and satisfying life. Examples include ADLs; leisure lifestyle, life and self-care skills; safety; stability of living environment; relationship abilities, such as marriage, parenting, and sibling interactions; school or employment status; and engagement in at-risk behaviors (Granger, 1984; Hendryx et al., 1999; Mason, 2000; McCormick & Funderburk, 2000; Tully & Cantrill, 1999; Ware, 1997).

Well-being or Quality of Life includes the personal or subjective definition of well-being for the individual. It may involve relative assessment of satisfaction with living conditions, work or school, leisure, finances, and whether basic and fundamental needs are met (Hendryx et al., 1999; Mason, 2000; McCormick & Funderburk, 2000; Russo, Roy-Brune, Jaffe, & Ries, 1997).

Satisfaction measures usually target satisfaction with services received. These assessments may help to determine the patients' opinions whether care is accessible, affordable, effective, and professional (Hendryx et al., 1999; Mason, 2000; McCormick & Funderburk, 2000; Mordock, 2000).

Costs and resource consumption balance the need to reduce costs with unfavorable impacts on the quality of care (Johnson, 1993).

Healthcare in general and each profession specifically work in tandem to identify overall trends in outcomes. In the last twenty years or so, healthcare has moved from solely measuring improvement in functional abilities, to health, then to quality of life. As each wave sends ripples throughout the system, professions must respond by honing their ability to identify and measure appropriate and corresponding outcomes.

Of course, outcomes are only as good as the systems put in place to measure and document them. This effort is called *outcome measurement*. Outcome measurement reflects efforts to document changes in the clients' clinical status, functional status, well-being or quality of life, satisfaction, and cost or resource consumption that result from a particular set of services. As mentioned previously, healthcare is currently moving toward an emphasis on quality of life.

Two parallel decisions must be weighed: what outcomes to measure and how to measure them. Measurement simply refers to the quantification of data in some way, either in absolute terms or in relative terms. "Thus, in order to evaluate the outcome of a process, one has to decide and specify what the rehabilitation process is trying to achieve. It is only sensible to measure those factors that the process will or might affect. The measure chosen should focus on the intended area(s) of concern and, as far as possible, should not cover any other extraneous areas" (Wade, 1999, p. 93). Outcome measurement is the "how" after the "what" of outcomes has been determined (Granello, Granello, & Lee, 1999).

More recently, McGrath and Tempier (2003) concurred with the five categories of client outcomes (clinical status, functional status, quality of life, satisfaction, and cost) suggested by Hendryx et al. (1999), Johnson (1993), and McGlynn (1995). In addition, McGrath and Tempier suggested a number of criteria for outcome measuring assessing these five areas: (a) be widely accepted, (b) be comprehensive, (c) be suitable or meaningful, (d) be sensitive to change, (e) be psychometrically sound, (f) be statistically amenable, (g) and be practical or actionable.

Knowledge of the five client outcome categories (the "what") and outcome measurement (the "how") is an important stepping-stone in providing quality care. "In a climate of fiscal restraint and healthcare cutbacks, patient needs may not be met, or they may be met inadequately. Without evaluation, one cannot determine whether or to what extent patient needs are met, what patients' changing needs are over time, and how best to respond to these needs" (McGrath & Tempier, 2003, p. 471). A tandem effort to improve healthcare quality is evidence-based practice.

Why are Outcomes Important?

Quite simply, specifying outcomes is a minimal expectation of human services. "Healthcare professionals and agencies are expected to demonstrate that the care they provide does make a difference for the population receiving care" (Ray, 1999, p. 1017). Ray suggested that healthcare professionals be asked about the evidence that they can provide that their service improves, maintains, or promotes the health and/or quality of life of clients. She further suggested that answering this question well depends on the degree to which professionals use evidence (that is, research) to support their service design and delivery.

Interestingly, Kelly (2003) suggested that specifying outcomes might be important because "that which is measured tends to get better" (p. 254). When clinicians pay close attention to the designation of outcomes, they might also be more careful in their design and delivery of programs to clients. By focusing on and measuring the degree of treatment effectiveness, the professional is likely to improve service delivery to clients.

Outcome research or outcome measurement concerns the generation and use of data to evaluate care provided to clients, while evidence-based practice then utilizes this research evidence to make decisions about how services are designed and delivered. Professionals should be able to provide substantiated proof (or evidence) that services are effective, efficient, and lead to valued outcomes. When research results are used as the foundation of practice, services provided to clients are more likely to be of higher quality.

What is the Relationship between Outcomes and EBP?

Evidence-based medicine or practice means that the services delivered to clients should be based on the best available scientific evidence of treatment efficacy or effectiveness (Adams & Titler, 2007; Buettner & Fitzsimmons, 2003, 2007; Linde, 1999; Margison et al., 2000). This means that interventions should be designed and delivered using research evidence to implement "best practices." Evidence-based interventions are created and delivered based on the best available information on moving clients toward desired outcomes in the most effective and efficient way possible.

The evidence-based concept is highly favored by power holders in government and healthcare organizations because of its capability to a) advance quality of care and services recreation therapists provide, b) have fewer variations in recreation therapy practice, c) provide cost savings that flow from appropriate and timely recreation therapy intervention use, and d) improve health outcomes in general (Buettner & Fitzsimmons, 2003, p. ii).

While we may think that therapeutic recreation has little quality research concerning most interventions, Petticrew (2003) and Regan (1998) reminded all healthcare professionals that "best available" is an important clause in that few, if any, professions have enough clear cut research evidence to provide the singular source of decision making. Clinical judgment, expertise, and prior experience all become additional sources to research results (Wittink, Nicholas, Kralik, & Verbunt, 2008).

Effectiveness characterizes how an intervention works under everyday circumstances in routine clinical practice (Aral & Peterman, 1998; Powe, 1996). "The effectiveness of an intervention is the impact an intervention achieves in the real world, under resource constraints, in entire populations, or in specified subgroups of a population. It is the improvement in a health outcome achieved in a typical community setting" (Aral & Peterman, 1998, p. 3). Effectiveness studies attempt to address the degree to which clients improve under treatment as it is actually practiced in the field (i.e., with fewer controls and manipulations than in efficacy research designs) (Granello et al., 1999).

Efficacy characterizes how an intervention performs under ideal or more controlled circumstances (Aral & Peterman, 1998; Powe, 1996). "Efficacy is the improvement in health outcome achieved in a research setting, in expert hands, under ideal circumstances" (Aral & Peterman, 1998, p. 3). It usually requires randomization to treatment and control groups, and a specific intervention for the treatment group—that usually has met criteria for a single diagnosis (Granello et al., 1999).

The purpose of evidence-based practices is to reduce wide and unintended fluctuations in practice using the best, cumulated evidence possible to inform and enlighten service delivery. Evidence-based practice improves the predictability and causality of service outcomes and provides regulators, payers, and consumers increased assurance of quality care.

Evidence-based practice, in the largest sense, involves four distinct actions of the part of the healthcare professional:
1. Production of evidence through research and scientific review
2. Production and dissemination of evidence-based clinical guidelines
3. Implementation of evidence-based, cost-effective practice through education and management of change, and
4. Evaluation of compliance with agreed practice guidance and patient outcomes— this process is called *clinical audit* (Belsey & Snell, 2001).

That is, through evidence-based service delivery, each practitioner should feel confident that she or he is providing the best possible care that is known to produce the most desirable, intended, and meaningful outcomes. Evidence must be gathered through well-designed and meaningful research efforts with client groups and be applicable to daily practice. In the literature, evidence-based practice also is termed *empirically validated treatment, empirically supported treatment, empirically evaluated treatment, empirical practice, research-based practice, research utilization, evidence-based treatment,* and *evidence-based healthcare* (Chambless & Ollendick, 2001; Denton, Walsh, & Daniel, 2002; Evidence-Based Medicine Working Group, 1992; Kendall, 1998; Lee & McCormick, 2002). Below is a collection of definitions of evidence-based practice found in the healthcare literature.
- The aim of evidence-based healthcare is to provide the means by which current best evidence from research can be judiciously and conscientiously applied to the prevention, detection, and care of health disorders (Haynes & Haines, 1998, p. 273)
- Process of systematically reviewing, appraising, and using clinical research findings to aid in the delivery of optimum clinical care of patients (Belsey & Snell, 2001)
- Evidence-based healthcare extends the application of the principles of evidence-based medicine (see below) to all professions associated with healthcare, including

purchasing and management (Sackett, Rosenberg, Gray, Haynes, & Richardson, 1996)

- Evidence-based medicine is the conscientious, explicit, and judicious use of current best evidence in making decisions about the care of individual patients. The practice of evidence-based medicine means integrating individual clinical expertise and our patients' own values and expectations with the best available external clinical evidence from systematic research (Sackett et al., 1996)

- Evidence-based healthcare is, at its simplest, the idea that care that health professionals provide should be based as closely as possible on evidence from well-conducted research into the effectiveness of healthcare interventions, thereby minimizing the problems of underuse, overuse, and misuse (Walshe & Rundall, 2001, p. 431)

- The ability to track down, critically appraise (for its validity and usefulness), and incorporate this rapidly growing body of evidence into one's clinical practice has been named "evidence-based medicine" (Sackett et al., 1996)

- Placing the clients' benefits first, evidence-based practitioners adopt a process of lifelong learning that involves continually posing specific questions of direct practical importance to clients, searching objectively and efficiently for the current best evidence related to each question and taking appropriate action guided by evidence (Gibbs, 2003, p. 6)

- The collection, interpretation, and integration of valid, important, and applicable patient-reported, clinician-observed, and research-driven evidence. The best available evidence, moderated by patient circumstances and preferences, is applied to improve the quality of clinical judgments and facilitate cost-effective healthcare (Tanner, 1999, p. 99)

- Reliance on current scientific evidence to reach medical decisions (Timmermans & Angell, 2001)

As such, evidence-based practice involves the systematic collection of data, over time, through near-patient research studies as well as the clinician's reflective approach in applying this information in daily work with clients. According to Pruett, Swett, Chan, Rosenthal, and Lee (2008), evidence-based practice can be defined as:

A total process beginning with knowing what clinical question to ask, how to find the best practice, and how to critically appraise the evidence for validity and applicability to the particular care situation. . . . The best evidence then must be applied by a clinician with expertise in considering a patient's unique values and needs. The final aspect of the process is evaluation of the effectiveness of care and the continual improvement of the process (p. 57).

Timmermans and Angell (2001) noted that evidence-based clinical judgment has five important characteristics. Evidence-based clinical judgment: (a) is neither solely evidence nor judgment, (b) requires understanding of the requirements to make a satisfactory clinical decision, (c) increases with opportunity and practice, (d) reduces but does not eliminate clinical uncertainties, and (e) is currently grounded in a Western, allopathic, and professionalized approach to medicine.

King and Teo (2000), while addressing nurses, stated that evidence-based practice might help close the gap between research and practice. "The foundation of evidence-based practice de-emphasizes decision making based on opinion, custom, or ritual . . . Rather, emphasis is placed on applying the best available research findings to specific clinical situations" (p. 597).

For evidence-based practice to advance, better and high-quality evidence from patient-based research is needed, along with more and better ways to incorporate and use this evidence in everyday practice (Bliss-Holtz, 1999; Deaton, 2001; Richardson, 1997). Rosenberg and Sackett (1996) and Sackett and Haynes (1995) wrote that evidence-based practice can actually be accomplished in three ways: (a) through learning the five steps of evidence-based practice, (b) seeking evidence collected by others, and (c) adopting protocols written by others who have done evidence-based practice research. The ultimate expectation of evidence-based service delivery is improved, informed, and more standardized healthcare for all clients. "Bridging gaps between evidence and practice is central to ensuring that beneficial interventions are used appropriately and harmful interventions are avoided" (Brockelhurst & McGuire, 2005, p. 38).

Although originating in medicine, evidence-based practice has "permeated" social and behavioral professions as well (Pruett et al., 2008, p. 56). This is certainly the case for therapeutic recreation. Stumbo and Peterson (2009) remarked:

> It is clear that evidence-based practice, because it improves the likelihood of clients achieving the desired outcomes in the most direct and potent manner, is here to stay. Therapeutic recreation specialists who use evidence-based practice will shorten their overall preparation time and heighten their ability to reach meaningful client outcomes (p. 83).

Hopefully, therapeutic recreation specialists can embrace outcome measurement and evidence-based practice beyond just fiscal or management mandates and agree that delivering the best possible services to clients, based on the best available research evidence is more effective and will lead client to better outcomes. It's not just the smart thing to do, it's the right thing to do.

What are the Benefits to Defining and Measuring Outcomes?

The benefits of evidence-based and standardized intervention programming are wide ranging. Below are some of the professional benefits of evidence-based and standardized practice as noted by Stumbo (2003):

- Provides reasonable guarantee to client and others that programs are designed and delivered for a specific purpose;
- Helps specialist focus on meeting client needs rather than providing programs without purpose;
- Ensures relative consistency of treatment from client to client, day to day, specialist to specialist;

- Groups clients into programs based on need rather than convenience;
- Helps determine content of client assessments;
- Provides direction for content of client documentation;
- Aids in producing predictable client results from programs;
- Allows better data collection about program efficacy in meeting the needs of clients;
- Increases communication between therapeutic recreation specialists throughout the country, as well as with other disciplines; and
- Provides explanation of therapeutic recreation services to auditing groups such as third-party payers, accrediting bodies, and administrative policy makers.

These benefits can be divided into areas regarding the program, the clients, therapeutic recreation specialists, and external (to therapeutic recreation) audiences. Benefits to the overall therapeutic recreation program result as close attention is paid to the planning, selecting, and designing of programs to meet a specific purpose or area of client need. This requires systematic forethought and diligence on the part of the therapeutic recreation specialist as well as a reasonable knowledge of research evidence and theories related to intervention.

Benefits to clients stem from the systematic and purposeful planning that must take place with evidence-based practice and protocols. Clients can be reasonably assured that there is a specific purpose, implementation plan, and predicted outcomes that remain the focus of the program. Clients are more guaranteed that there is a desirable end result of participation in the program. For many clients, this assurance results in increased motivation to participate actively in the programs described in the protocol.

Benefits to therapeutic recreation specialists are many. Knowing that programs have a defined purpose and targeted outcomes helps the specialist implement and evaluate them with more confidence and uniformity. Program delivery becomes standardized rather than haphazard, as does professional terminology.

Another benefit then becomes the ability to better communicate and market therapeutic recreation services to outside constituents. This may include other disciplines, healthcare administrators, external accrediting bodies, insurance companies, and clients themselves. The ability to provide consistent, high-quality, and predictable client care is essential in this era of accountability. Shorter lengths of client stay support more predictable timelines for intervention, and both evidence-based practice and use of clinical guidelines allow therapeutic recreation specialists to be more responsive in this area. These efforts form the foundation of common practices that move the profession toward greater accountability.

What are the Barriers to Defining and Measuring Outcomes?

There is no doubt about it: Outcome measurement in healthcare is difficult (Greenhalgh, Long, Brettle, & Grant, 1998; Greenhalgh & Meadows, 1999). Beyond problems with the psychometric properties of outcome measures such as lack of validity and reliability [see for example, Bilsker and Goldner (2002), Deaton (2001), Goldsmith, Bankhead, and Austoker (2007), and Greenhalgh et al. (1998) for interesting discussions], social and behavioral science professions have added tribulations.

Wittink et al. (2008) noted that nonpharmacological treatment is usually complex and difficult to standardize, partially because treatment is being adjusted even as it is being carried out. They discussed the field of pain management as an example of a specialty that uses performance-based measures (such as standing or sitting tolerance), external criterion measures (such as return-to-work variables) and various self-reported measures (such as pain quality, mood, degree of disability, and the like), but still often fails at measuring outcomes of treatment due to the lack of normative measures against which each client's scores can be compared. As such, "effect" of treatment cannot be measured explicitly enough to declare the treatment either a success or a failure.

Likewise, Chronister, Chan, da Silva Cardoso, Lynch, and Rosenthal (2008), Johnson, Dow, Lynch, and Hermann (2006), and Pruett et al. (2008) have noted extensive difficulties in defining and measuring outcomes in rehabilitation counseling. They noted that rehabilitation counseling calls for a diversity of job functions performed over a wide range of settings, with diverse groups of clients, using various intervention approaches, with sometimes dissimilar philosophies. Zlotnik and Galambos (2004) noted similar problems in social work and called for professionals to concentrate efforts on high-quality program evaluations and intervention studies, using more sophisticated designs with multiple sites and multiple populations.

Clearly, therapeutic recreation is not the only profession that has few, if any, significant outcome studies. It is difficult to get traction on this important effort. But if not now, then when? If not you, then who?

Discussion Questions

1. In comparison with other professions with which you are familiar, how does therapeutic recreation fare in terms of being well-defined and coherent?

2. What other foundational professional competencies would you add to the lists provided in this chapter? Prior to looking at the newest NCTRC Job Analysis, construct a list of professional competencies for therapeutic recreation. How does your list compare to NCTRC and other students in your class?

3. What is the relationship of professional competence to client outcomes? If a therapeutic recreation specialist is not able to well define and measure client outcomes prior to designing and delivering the service, what does this say about his or her competence? How does this compare to other health professionals, such as surgeons, physical therapists, and acupuncturists?

4. What are typical client outcomes for therapeutic recreation? Which of the five major areas of outcomes listed in this chapter do most therapeutic recreation outcomes fall into? Is there professional consensus on which client outcomes are important? On how to measure them and report their achievement?

5. What is the relationship of client outcomes to evidence-based practice? Why has evidence-based practice become so popular in healthcare? What are the advantages of evidence-based healthcare to clients? How well does therapeutic recreation use available evidence (i.e., research) to develop programs for client involvement? What would be the consequences if therapeutic recreation specialists were more involved in evidence-based practice?

6. How will professional competence, client outcomes, and evidence-based practice impact therapeutic recreation in the near future? What does therapeutic recreation need to do to ensure its future? What role will you play?

References

Adams, S., & Titler, M. G. (2007). Strategies for promoting development of evidence-based practice in an allied health profession. *Annual in Therapeutic Recreation, 15,* 1-11.

Aral, S., & Peterman, T. A. (1998). Do we know the effectiveness of behavioral interventions? *Lancet, Supplement STD's, 351*(9119), 33-37.

Belsey, J., & Snell, T. (2001). *What is evidence-based medicine?* Retrieved November 9, 2002 from http://www.evidence-based-medicine.co.uk/

Bilsker, D., & Goldner, E. M. (2002). Routine outcome measurement by mental health-care providers: Is it worth doing? *The Lancet, 360,* 1689-1690.

Blankertz, L., & Cook, J. A. (1998). Choosing and using outcome measures. *Psychiatric Rehabilitation Journal, 22*(2), 167-174.

Bliss-Holtz, J. (1999). Editorial: The fit of research utilization and evidence-based practice. *Issues in Comprehensive Pediatric Nursing, 22,* iii-vi.

Brocklehurst, P., & McGuire, W. (2005). ABC of preterm birth: Evidence-based care. *British Medical Journal, 330,* 36-38.

Buettner, L., & Fitzsimmons, S. (2003). *Dementia practice guideline for recreation therapy: Treatment of disturbing behaviors.* Alexandria, VA: American Therapeutic Recreation Association.

Buettner, L., & Fitzsimmons, S. (2007). Introduction to evidence-based recreation therapy. *Annual in Therapeutic Recreation, 15,* 12-19.

Chambless, D. L., & Ollendick, T. H. (2001). Empirically supported psychological interventions: Controversies and evidence. *Annual Review of Psychology, 52,* 685-716.

Chronister, J. A., Chan, F., da Silva Cardoso, E., Lynch, R. T., & Rosenthal, D. A. (2008). The evidence-based practice movement in healthcare: Implications for rehabilitation. *Journal of Rehabilitation, 74*(2), 6-15.

Deaton, C. (2001). Outcomes measurement and evidence-based nursing practice. *Journal of Cardiovascular Nursing, 15*(2), 83-86.

Denton, W. H., Walsh, S. R., & Daniel, S. S. (2002). Evidence-based practice in family therapy: Adolescent depression as an example. *Journal of Marital and Family Therapy, 29*(1), 39-45.

Dower, C., O'Neil, E. H., & Hough, H. J. (2001). *Profiling the professions: A model for evaluating emerging health professions.* San Francisco: Center for Health Professions, University of California, San Francisco.

Dunn, J. K., Sneegas, J. J., & Carruthers, C. A. (1991). Outcomes measures: Monitoring patient progress. In B. Riley (Ed.), *Quality management: Applications for therapeutic recreation* (pp. 107-115). State College, PA: Venture.

Epstein, R. M., & Hundert, E. M. (2002). Defining and assessing professional competence. *Journal of the American Medical Association, 287*(2), 226-235.

Evidence-based Medicine Working Group. (1992). Evidence-based medicine: A new approach to teaching the practice of medicine. *Journal of the American Medical Association, 268,* 2420-2425.

Gibbs, L. (2003). *Evidence-based practice for the helping professions: A practical guide.* Pacific Grove, CA: Brooks/Cole.

Goldsmith, M. R., Bankhead, C. R., & Austoker, J. (2007). Synthesizing quantitative and qualitative research in evidence-based patient information. *Journal of Epidemiology and Community Health, 61,* 262-270.

Granello, D. H., Granello, P. F., & Lee, F. (1999). Measuring treatment outcomes and client satisfaction in a partial hospitalization program. *Journal of Behavioral Health Services and Research, 26*(1), 50-63.

Granger, C. V. (1984). A conceptual model for functional assessment. In C. V. Granger, & G. E. Gresham (Eds.), *Functional assessment in rehabilitation medicine.* (pp. 14-25). Baltimore, MD: Williams and Wilkins.

Greenhalgh, J., Long, A. F., Brettle, A. J., & Grant, M. J. (1998). Reviewing and selecting outcome measures for use in routine practice. *Journal of Evaluation in Clinical Practice, 4*(4), 339-350.

Greenhalgh, J., & Meadows, K. (1999). The effectiveness of the use of patient-based measures of health in routine practice in improving the process and outcomes of patient care: A literature review. *Journal of Evaluation in Clinical Practice, 5*(4), 401-416.

Greiner, A. C., & Knebel, E. (2003). (Ed.). *Health professions education: A bridge to quality.* Washington, D.C.: Institute of Medicine.

Haynes, B., & Haines, A. (1998). Barriers and bridges to evidence-based clinical practice. *British Medical Journal, 317,* 273-276.

Hendryx, M. S., Dyck, D. G., & Srebnick, D. (1999). Risk-adjusted outcome models for public mental health outpatient programs. *Health Services Research, 34*(1), 171-195.

Johnson, D. E. L. (1993). Scott and White measure "quality of health" in outcomes studies. *Healthcare Strategic Management, 11*(3), 7-9.

Johnson, E. K., Dow, C., Lynch, R. T., & Hermann, B. P. (2006). Measuring clinical significance in rehabilitation research. *Rehabilitation Counseling Bulletin, 50*(1), 35-45.

Joint Commission on Accreditation of Healthcare Organizations. (1995). *1996 Comprehensive Accreditation Manual for Hospitals.* Oakbrook Terrace, IL: Author.

Kelly, T. A. (2003). Clinical outcome measurement: A call to action. *Journal of Psychology and Christianity, 22*(3), 254-258.

Kendall, P. C. (1998). Empirically supported psychological therapies. *Journal of Consulting and Clinical Psychology, 66,* 36.

King, K. M., & Teo, K. K. (2000). Integrating clinical quality-improvement strategies with nursing research. *Western Journal of Nursing Research, 22*(5), 596-608.

Lee, Y., & McCormick, B. P. (2002). Toward evidence-based therapeutic recreation practice. In D.R. Austin, J. Dattilo, & B. P. McCormick (Eds.), *Conceptual foundations for therapeutic recreation* (pp. 165-184). State College, PA: Venture.

Linde, M. (1999). Theory and practice in the management of depressive disorders. *International Clinical Psychopharmacology, 14,* S15-S25.

Margison, F. R., Barkham, M., Evans, C., McGrath, G., Clark, J. M., Audin, K., et al. (2000). Measurement and psychotherapy: Evidence-based practice and practice-based evidence. *British Journal of Psychiatry, 177,* 123-130.

Mason, M. M. (2000). Meeting the challenges of data collection in outcome systems. *Education and Treatment of Children, 23*(1), 75-95.

McCormick, B. P., & Funderburk, J. (2000). Therapeutic recreation outcomes in mental health practice. *Annual in Therapeutic Recreation, 9,* 9-20.

McGlynn, E. A. (1995). Quality assessment in reproductive health services. *The Western Journal of Medicine, 163*(3), 19-27.

McGrath, B. M., & Tempier, R. P. (2003). Implementing quality management in psychiatry: From theory to practice—Shifting focus from process to outcome. *Canadian Journal of Psychiatry, 48*(7), 467-474.

Mordock, J. B. (2000). Outcome assessment: Suggestions for agency practice. *Child Welfare, 79*(6), 689-710.

Petticrew, M. (2003). Why certain systematic reviews reach uncertain conclusions. *British Medical Journal, 326,* 756-758.

Powe, N. R. (1996). Measuring effectiveness and outcomes of interventions for renal disease. *Current Opinion in Nephrology and Hypertension, 5*(3), 230-235.

Pruett, S. R., Swett, E. A., Chan, F., Rosenthal, D. A., & Lee, G. K. (2008). Empirical evidence supporting the effectiveness of vocational rehabilitation, *Journal of Rehabilitation, 74*(1), 56-63.

Ray, L. (1999). Evidence and outcomes: Agendas, presuppositions, and power. *Journal of Advanced Nursing, 30*(5), 1017-1026.

Regan, J. (1998). Will current clinical effectiveness initiatives encourage and facilitate practitioners to use evidence-based practice for the benefit of their clients? *Journal of Clinical Nursing, 7,* 244-250.

Richardson, W. S. (1997). Evidence-based diagnosis: More is needed. *Evidence-Based Medicine, 3,* 5.

Riley, B. (1991). Quality assessment: The use of outcome indicators. In B. Riley (Ed.), *Quality management: Applications for therapeutic recreation* (pp. 53-67). State College, PA: Venture.

Rosenberg, W. M., & Sackett, D. L. (1996). On the need for evidence-based practice. *Therapie, 51*(3), 212-217.

Russo, J., Roy-Byrne, P., Jaffe, C., & Ries, R. (1997). The relationship of patient-administered outcome assessments to quality of life and physician ratings: Validity of the BASIS-32. *Journal of Mental Health Administration, 24*(2), 200-214.

Sackett, D. L., & Haynes, R. B. (1995). On the need for evidence-based medicine. *Evidence-based Medicine, 1,* 5.

Sackett, D. L., Rosenberg, W. M., Gray, J. A., Haynes, R. B., & Richardson, W. S. (1996). Evidence-based medicine: What it is and what it isn't. *British Medical Journal, 312,* 71-72.

Scalenghe, R. (1991). The Joint Commission's "Agenda for change" as related to the provision of therapeutic recreation services. In B. Riley (Ed.), *Quality management: Applications for therapeutic recreation* (pp. 29-42). State College, PA: Venture.

Shank, J. W., & Kinney, W. B. (1991). Monitoring and measuring outcomes in therapeutic recreation. In B. Riley (Ed.), *Quality management: Applications for therapeutic recreation* (pp. 69-88). State College, PA: Venture.

Stumbo, N. J. (1996). A proposed accountability model for therapeutic recreation services. *Therapeutic Recreation Journal, 30*(4), 246-259.

Stumbo, N. J. (2003). The language of quality healthcare. *American Journal of Recreational Therapy, 2*(3), 33-40.

Stumbo, N. J., & Peterson, C. A. (2009). *Therapeutic recreation program design: Principles and procedures* (5th ed.). San Francisco: Benjamin Cummings.

Swankin, D., Lebuhn, R. A., & Morrison, R. (2006). *Implementing continuing competency requirements for healthcare practitioners.* Washington, D.C.: AARP.

Tanner, C. A. (1999). Evidence-based practice: Research and critical thinking. *Journal of Nursing Education, 38*(3), 99.

Timmermans, S., & Angell, A. (2001). Evidence-based medicine, clinical uncertainty, and learning to doctor. *Journal of Health and Social Behavior, 42*(4), 342-359.

Tully, M. P., & Cantrill, J. A. (1999). Subjective outcome measurement: A primer. *Pharmacy World and Science, 21*(3), 101-109.

Wade, D. T. (1999). Editorial: Outcome measurement and rehabilitation. *Clinical Rehabilitation, 13,* 93-95.

Walshe, K., & Rundall, T. G. (2001). Evidence-based management: From theory to practice in healthcare. *The Milbank Quarterly, 79*(3), 429-457.

Ware, J. E., Jr. (1997). Healthcare outcomes from the patient's point of view. In E. J. Mullen, & J. L. Magnabosco (Eds.), *Outcomes measurement in human services* (pp. 44-67). Washington, D.C: National Association of Social Workers.

Wittink, H., Nicholas, M., Kralik, D., & Verbunt, J. (2008). Are we measuring what we need to measure? *The Clinical Journal of Pain, 24*(4), 316-324.

Zlotnik, J. L., & Galambos, C. (2004). Evidence-based practices in healthcare: Social work possibilities. *Health & Social Work, 29*(4), 259-261.

CHAPTER 2

TR Past, Present, and Future: A Historical Analysis of Issues in Therapeutic Recreation

Kari Kensinger, Ph.D., CTRS™
Grand Valley State University

The year is 2009. It is the era to be known in history as the "information age." In the "information age," students can be found blogging on Facebook or MySpace for hours. What may look like seemingly obsessed fans of *Lost*, *Grey's Anatomy*, or *American Idol*, are actually Therapeutic Recreation (TR) nerds who are "stoked" or "pumped up" about a given topic they recently learned about in school. While simultaneously obtaining information about popular culture, several TR nerds from Generation X, the Echo Boomers, and the Millennial Generation can be seen occasionally rummaging through the archives of *Hospital Recreation*, and reading Elliott Avedon's 1974 textbook while studying for a kinesiology exam, and asking the more experienced professional "who was Bernie Thorn?"

Meanwhile, the people who knew Bernie Thorn, those who used Avedon's book, and those who thought we needed to move beyond *Hospital Recreation* are debating topics at conferences and on listservs. Should ATRA be called ARTA? Should TR education be aligned with allied health, or should it be aligned with parks and recreation? What are the minimum competencies that we need in order to practice TR? Should we have additional certifications? Do we really need two professional organizations, and what should be the function of each? How can TR become more acceptable and reimbursable? As these questions are debated, some from the "old school" are becoming tired and frustrated. Will they find answers to these questions in their lifetime, or will they pass these problems on to future generations?

Likewise, while attempting to understand the history of TR, many TR nerds on MySpace and Facebook wonder: Why are we still debating TR/RT? Why do we still have two professional organizations? Why don't we just move on? Therefore, the TR nerd is blogging about how can we make TR part of popular culture and how can we be "united not divided." One MySpace blog states, "We are not about one professional organization or the other, but rather we are about educating people about TR."

The issues that we face today are not so different from the issues that faced the profession 30 years ago. At times, it may seem as though TR has made little progress. At times, it may seem as though TR is polarized. At times, it may seem as though the profession may die. Yet, it should be noted that our profession continues to survive, and despite the odds, our profession has made great strides due to the passion, commitment, and dedication of a few individuals. This chapter will explore the history of TR so that we as "young professionals" can understand the current issues and shape the future of TR.

Professionalization

When any TR scholar, student, or professional reviews the literature of the last 40 years, several themes emerge that are related to the trends and issues of our profession. The overarching theme or the thread that connects most of our professional issues is the concept of professionalization. It seems that over time, most discussions about professionalization begin with the question: "To what extent is TR a profession?" (Navar, 2001; Reynolds & O'Morrow, 1985). Are we a distinct profession, or are we a branch of some other profession? If we are a branch of some other profession, what is that other profession? The quest to emerge as a profession launched the development of professional organizations, scholarly journals and textbooks, academic programs, certification, codes of ethics, standards of practice, and best practices. All of this has been accomplished despite controversy and polarization.

The Origins of the Profession

When did TR first emerge as a profession? For years, the answer to this question has been debated, and some may consider the failure to reach consensus on this issue as a hindrance to the growth of our profession. The origins of TR can be traced to a variety of disciplines (e.g., education, philosophy, prostitution, medicine, nursing, social work, recreation).

Although the principles and ideas associated with TR practice were present in ancient civilizations (Avedon, 1974), it is unclear as to when TR began to emerge as a profession. Peterson (1989) suggested that one of the first steps to becoming a profession involved the "recognition and acknowledgment" that the profession makes a "significant contribution to the needs of the people." If this is indeed the case, perhaps the origins of our profession emerged when other disciplines began to recognize the value of the purposeful use of recreation. Avedon (1974) suggested that physicians such as Philippe Pinel and W.A.F. Browne began to recognize the value of recreation in treatment in the middle of the 19th century when the re-humanization of institutions started to occur. During this same time period, Florence Nightingale was introducing the purposeful use of recreation in nursing (James, 1998a). Also, during the 19th century, the purposeful use of recreation was also being recognized in "schools for the blind" (Avedon, 1974). Likewise, the purposeful use of recreation was utilized in the social reform movements during the late 1800s and early 1900s with the emergence of the playground movement and development of the social work professions (Reynolds & O'Morrow, 1985).

It could also be argued that our profession began when the first people were hired specifically to provide recreation for "special populations." Perhaps our origin was in the military hospitals of the 1920s or when the first textbooks were written by psychologists in the 1930s (Avedon, 1974). Some might suggest that TR began to be a profession when a group of "like-minded" individuals gathered together to promote a common cause in a professional organization. The first professional organization emerged from the parks and recreation movement in 1948 (Avedon, 1974; Frye & Peters, 1972; James, 1998b).

The eclectic nature of the profession has brought an understanding of vast theoretical and conceptual frameworks (e.g., systems theory, ecological viewpoint, normalization, mainstreaming, self-determination, person-centered planning, and constraints) which not only helps professionals understand the diverse needs of clients served but also fosters interdisciplinary collaboration with colleagues in myriad disciplines. It has been argued, however, that the diverse nature of the profession has hindered the ability for our profession to excel, specialize, or compete in any specific environment (e.g., healthcare, education, and recreation). The differences of opinions and the schools of thought within the profession first became evident via professional organizations.

Professional Organizations

According to James (1998b), the Hospital Recreation Section (HRS) of the American Recreation Society (ARS) was founded in 1948. Reynolds and O'Morrow (1985) credit this organization with developing standards for higher education in "Recreation Therapy." Reynolds and O'Morrow also indicate that this organization sponsored institutes on hospital recreation at various university campuses.

Shortly thereafter, the Recreation Therapy Section (RTS) of the American Association of Health, Physical Education, and Recreation (AAHPER) was founded in 1952 (James, 1998b). James (1998b) suggested that several of these individuals worked for the department of veteran's affairs (VA). According to Frye and Peters (1972), the members of the organization came into the profession via the physical education route. Accordingly, Frye and Peters suggested that benefits of being a member of RTS included opportunities to network with the teaching profession, "recreation therapy" articles in the *Journal of Health, Physical Education, and Recreation,* and "recreation therapy" sessions at national and district meetings.

In February of 1953, the National Association of Recreation Therapists (NART) was formed. According to Cox and Dobbings (1970), most of the members of NART were members of the HRS who worked in state hospitals and schools who felt that their needs were not being met. Cox and Dobbings suggested that NART members worked diligently to develop education and training standards and to establish a journal entitled *Recreation for the Ill and Handicapped.*

In November of 1953, HRS, RTS, and NART formed the Council on Advancement of Hospital Recreation (CAHR). Each organization selected a few representatives to send to CAHR meetings. The formation of CAHR allowed for the three organizations to co-exist, yet promoted the advancement of the profession (Cox & Dobbins, 1970). While setting aside philosophical differences, the members of CAHR were able to initiate the first registration process in our profession. In 1956, CAHR established a program of "National Voluntary Registration for Hospital Recreation Personnel" (Frye & Peters, 1972).

Discussions began in 1958 regarding the potential merger of the HRS, RTS, and NART (Cox & Dobbins, 1970; Frye & Peters, 1972). In 1965, these three organizations joined other organizations to form the National Recreation and Park Association (NRPA). According to Austin and Hunnicutt (1978), "in 1966, the National Therapeutic Recreation Society (NTRS) was established as a branch of NRPA" (p. 5). During the first decade and a half, NTRS made significant progress in adding to the professional body of knowledge via professional meetings and publications. Likewise, NTRS further developed credentialing, professional standards, legislation, standards for external accrediting bodies, third-party reimbursement, and accreditation in higher education (Austin & Hunnicutt, 1978; Hunnicut, 1978; Peterson, 1984).

As a united profession, much was accomplished during the first 12 years of NTRS, but troubles soon emerged. For the first 18 years, NTRS represented the "professional needs of those individuals who work with special population in community and clinical settings," but in 1984, questions regarding NTRS's capacity "to respond to the increasing demands for professional action in the arena of healthcare systems" surfaced (Peterson, 1984, p. 11). According to Peterson, NTRS did not have "control of its own resources, nor is it accountable directly to its own membership" (p. 13). Peterson discussed the feasibility of establishing a new organization that could "address the unique needs" of those therapeutic recreation personnel who worked in clinical settings. In 1984, the American Therapeutic Recreation Association was established.

According to Van Andel (n.d.), ATRA's interim board had a vision for a professional organization that:

1. Is accountable to the membership;
2. Has a decentralized organizational structure that emphasizes responsiveness to membership needs versus organization expediency;
3. Provides services that are founded on a data-based operational system that is in touch with what is happening in the field;
4. That provides the highest quality services available;
5. Uses strategic planning versus crisis management;
6. Develops and promotes networking with other healthcare agencies and professional organizations; and
7. Focuses on promoting the value of the therapeutic recreation process within the healthcare delivery system (p. 2).

Since 1984, the two professional organizations (NTRS and ATRA) have co-existed. Both ATRA and NTRS attempt to serve therapeutic recreation personnel who work in both clinical and community-based settings. In 1998, a resolution was passed to form the alliance for therapeutic recreation (James, 1998b). This alliance allowed for NTRS and ATRA to collaborate in order to advance the profession. The alliance led to a joint task force on higher education, which sponsored a Therapeutic Recreation Educator's Conference (TREC) in 2004. Furthermore, the alliance promoted communication between the two organizations in respect to legislation and state recognition, among other things. Despite efforts to be united on key issues, politics, and philosophical positions continue to prevent the profession from advancing. The joint task force was disbanded in the fall of 2004.

Philosophical Differences

Since the 1950s, physicians, psychiatrists, and therapeutic recreation personnel have debated the philosophy of therapeutic recreation. According to Frye and Peters (1972), throughout the 1950s and 1960s the predominant philosophical dilemma centered around the question "Is recreation therapy?"

Is Recreation Therapy?

While most in the 1950s and 1960s agreed that recreation was important in the lives of patients, the therapeutic value of recreation was debated. For example, Meng (1960) raised the question, "Is the recreator a therapist or therapeutic agent?" Haun (1966) suggested that while recreation did not cure, it did augment and maximize the therapeutic outcomes. Haun also suggested that leisure deficits could also be problematic for human functioning. Furthermore, Martin Meyer (1962) stated:

> It is during the treatment of an illness, when all the forces of scientific medicine are applied, that recreation, whenever specifically indicated, is utilized as therapy. It may be applied to attack specific problems, such as anxiety. Or more generally in the relief of pain or the maintenance of morale and the desire to get well. (p. 23)

In the 1980s, this debate continued in hopes of answering the question: "Is TR a means to an end or an end to a means?" (Howe-Murphy & Halberg, 1987; Lee, 1987; Mobily, 1985a, 1985b, 1987; Mobily, Weissinger, & Hunnicutt, 1987). This philosophical dilemma coupled with the demands of a society concerned with accountability (especially in healthcare) prompted researchers to identify therapeutic benefits and outcomes associated with the delivery of therapeutic recreation services. Coyle, Kinney, and Shank (1993) highlighted the external factors that influenced the profession's research agenda, stating:

> Beyond our own professional duty to advance our body of knowledge through research, there are several outside groups pressing for definitive evidence that TR interventions are cost effective and will result in necessary and desirable outcomes. Accreditation bodies, such as the Joint Commission on Accreditation of Healthcare Organizations (JCAHO), are mandating an outcome focus in all quality-improvement efforts. Also in response to the unacceptably high costs of healthcare, the U.S. Congress has charged several federal agencies with the responsibility to determine the effectiveness of healthcare practices. (p. 301)

Much research has been conducted that identified the therapeutic benefits of recreation participation. According to Frye and Peters (1972), in 1962, Joseph B. Wolffe found that 50% of over 200 individuals with cardiovascular disease who participated in recreation therapy reduced the need for medication. Likewise, there was a 35% reduction in the need for sedatives and tranquilizer use among his patients with neurocirculatory asthenia.

In 1989, Temple University hosted a conference to identify the efficacy research needs of our profession. In 1991, Coyle, Kinney, Riley, and Shank published the findings of this conference in *The Benefits of Therapeutic Recreation: A Consensus View*. Since that time, a more concentrated effort to develop best practices based on research has emerged, such as those outlined in Buettner and Fitzsimmons' (2003) *Dementia Practice Guidelines for Recreational Therapy*. Hopefully, by now, the question: "Is recreation therapy?" can be a moot point, because there are several other philosophical questions that continue to haunt the discipline.

What is TR?

In 1981, Lee Meyer identified the philosophical positions that were commonly held in the field of therapeutic recreation. This study identified four divergent views related to the purpose of TR including:

- To provide recreative experiences (the recreation view);
- To treat, change, or otherwise ameliorate the effects of illness or disability (the therapy view);
- To enhance the therapeutic effects of the recreative experience (the therapeutic view); and
- To eliminate leisure barriers, provide leisure skills and attitudes, and enable leisure functioning and the recreative experience (the service continuum view). (p. 9)

The membership of NTRS considered these philosophical positions when adopting a position statement in 1982. Similar viewpoints were also considered when ATRA formed its definition statement (West, 1988). When both ATRA and NTRS adopted philosophical positions, the vast majority of people agreed on the broadest definitions of the profession. Our purpose became all encompassing, and our roles involved therapist, educator, and facilitator. We are considered to be recreators, recreation therapists, and therapeutic recreation specialists.

Halberg and Howe-Murphy (1985) commented on the adoption of the NTRS philosophical position, stating:

> At the time of the adoption (1981) of the Philosophical Position Statement and its eventual publication and dissemination (1982), the profession appeared to be ready to stabilize philosophically. However, agreement as to the mission and purpose of the field did not last long. Additionally, the continuum model represented more of an operational paradigm than a philosophy. That is, it identified the dimensions (e.g., freedom/obligation, role of client/therapist, purpose of service) and parameters of practice but did not set out a true philosophy of service. (p. 11)

Halberg and Howe-Murphy concluded: "the therapeutic recreation field is at a major crossroad. The decisions which must be made will determine the basic identity and methods of operation in the profession" (p. 7). Similarly, Peterson (1989) commented:

> The inability or unwillingness of the profession to take a stand on philosophical content issues appears to be a major stumbling block in recognition, acceptance, and marketing of the field as a legitimate profession. The profession needs to resolve its own long-standing debate on philosophy. Until this resolution occurs, it is highly

unlikely that full professional acceptance can, will, or should be awarded. A united front, a commonly accepted and supported approach is imperative. (p. 22)

Several years later, Compton (1997) suggested that as we moved to year 2000 and beyond, we needed to adopt a clear philosophy.

Yet, under the auspices of these broad definitions, much has been accomplished. Professionals in both NTRS and ATRA have been able to establish and revise standards of practice and codes of ethics. Members of both organizations have represented the profession to CARF and the Joint Commission. Members of both organizations have monitored external trends that shape society's view of health and wellness such as the Healthy People 2010 initiative and the classification system of World Health Organization. Members of both organizations, have advocated on behalf of the profession in the areas of public policy and reimbursement. Both organizations have representation in the areas of wheelchair sports and accessible golf. The similarities between both organizations have been noted. In fact, at the 2006 meeting of NTRS, a panel of leaders in the profession were asked to talk about the future of NTRS (McKenney, Sylvester, Beck, & Zuniga, 2006). Some questioned why we needed two organizations doing the same thing. It was suggested that if NTRS was to continue to exist, it would need to define its specific niche. Furthermore, the members of NTRS need to determine how TR fits into the mission of NRPA.

One also must question why we have two professional organizations, when according to the Department of Labor, there are approximately 40,000 people who work in the field of therapeutic recreation. According to the National Council for Therapeutic Recreation Certification (NCTRC), there are approximately 15,000 people who are certified. Nearly 4,000 are members of a professional organization, and most people who are active are members of both organizations (NTRS and ATRA). With a large number of active members in both organizations retiring in the near future, can we continue to support two organizations that similarly promote a broad scope of practice? As this chapter goes to print, the numbers in the professional organizations continue to decline. The decline in membership has seen ATRA move its national office back to Hattiesburg, Mississippi, to be run by an external management company.

Although the broad scope of practice has been adopted by both NTRS and ATRA, polarization still occurs, and many professionals advocate the need to have a more narrow focus. It is apparent now, 10 years later, that the profession has not agreed on nor adopted a clear philosophy of TR. Instead, the number of service models continue to increase (Ross & Ashton-Schaeffer, 2001). This question of philosophy continues to emerge as a pressing issue, but must it be resolved before the profession can move forward? Must it be resolved for the profession to survive?

At the 2007 ATRA Annual Conference in Orlando, Florida, a motion was made on behalf of a group of professionals to change the name of ATRA from the American Therapeutic Recreation Association to the American Recreation Therapy Association (ARTA). This motion was withdrawn, because it was suggested by many that our efforts at that time should be focused on the current legislative endeavors. The topic has been debated several times in the history of the organization. In 1992, Russoniello (believing that recreation therapy originated in the medical fields) felt that it was morally and ethically imperative that our profession return to our roots and use terminology that is consistent with practice. Skalko et al. (n.d.) suggested that a name change would help market the profession to healthcare providers and policy makers who demand treatment services. Skalko et al. urged the profession to adopt terminology consistent with the occupational responsibilities of the constituents. In opposition to this position, a document entitled *10 Reasons to Retain the Title "Therapeutic Recreation"* circulated around ATRA (Anonymous, 1994). This document argued that:

1. TR was currently reimbursable despite the name of the profession;
2. TR is included in the credential of a Certified Therapeutic Recreation Specialist (CTRS), which has "brought our profession much prestige;"
3. TR is aligned with prevention and includes more than a disease-based approach;
4. TR is more than just recreation for people with disabilities, but rather represents a continuum of services;
5. TR needs to be one united profession more than it needs to adopt one unified philosophy;
6. Healthcare reform is calling for services that are inclusionary, offering a continuum of services that include prevention, acute care, and post acute care that are consistent with the current practices of TR;
7. Appropriate cost-effect interventions occur within TR, but more research is needed regardless of name change;
8. Time and energy are taken away from critical issues when we debate the title of the profession;
9. RT is used for respiratory therapy, and CARF and JCAHO are more concerned with our competency and performance than our name;
10. The majority of members are concerned about keeping jobs rather than narrowing scope of service to treatment. (p. 1)

In 2007, the TR/RT debate is not just highlighted in the ATRA/ARTA name change debate but is also debated as the profession attempts to develop curriculum standards. As TR educators explore options for a TR-specific accreditation, the scope of TR continues to be questioned. Is TR an option of the leisure services industry? Or is TR an allied health profession? Some have suggested that before the profession can advance in this area, we need to, once and for all, have one specific purpose statement for TR.

Philosophical Dilemma: Has It Hindered Our Progress?

Since the 1950s, our profession has debated our philosophy. During this same time frame, the profession has made great strides. Academic programs emerged, and as these programs developed, so, too, did the body of knowledge. Thinking back to the 1970s, there were a handful of TR books. Now there are several. Since the 1970s, several individuals have emerged as leaders. They have conducted research and trained generations of future practitioners. There have been great practitioners who have built TR dynasties in hospitals that reached thousands of consumers, while defining competencies and outcomes. Although these leaders had differing philosophies, they ensured that TR was at the table in healthcare and that recreation was included in accessibility standards. They did so on behalf of the consumer.

Many in TR have identified the establishment of NCTRC as being a key historical event in our profession's history. In 1981, when NCTRC was established as an independent entity, it was done to protect the consumer. As the result of those efforts, minimum competencies have been identified, and our practice has been further defined. NCTRC continues to market the profession and the credential to the consumer and in doing so ensures some degree of competence that is based on a systematic approach.

Malik (2001) suggests that this systematic approach can occur regardless of setting and enables the profession to reach a diverse clientele via myriad techniques. It is this broad scope of practice that enables us to provide services across a continuum of care, linking what occurs in hospitals to what occurs in homes, schools, and communities. Perhaps the diverse nature of our services is our greatest strength. If there are mass layoffs in hospitals, we can survive in parks and recreation. When the tax base is weak and parks and recreation are cut, we can thrive in fee-for-service home health markets.

Summary

Despite philosophical differences, TR has emerged as a profession. People who believe in the value of TR have advocated on behalf of the consumer and have made the profession that which it is today. These professionals have learned how to navigate the public policy and healthcare arenas in order to monitor trends and increase advocacy. They continue to monitor the trends and issues that affect our service delivery. What the profession needs is for the great minds to pass their expertise down to the new generations—and, in turn, the new generation needs to accept the challenge. Brasile often said we all can be "pioneers in our profession."

Since the 19th century, we have had several pioneers who sought to fight illness, disability, and societal problems using recreation. These pioneers came together to form numerous professional organizations based on the belief that TR was a valuable service. As such, these pioneers established academic programs in TR, wrote textbooks, and conducted research. They developed standards of practice and codes of ethics.

Today, there continue to be pioneers who explore new ways to offer services and monitored and influenced public policy. In 2007, we strive to make history via the ATRA Medicare Project (H.R. 4248), New Hampshire's licensure bill, and TR education reform. If we want the profession to exist for another 50 years, as young professionals we need to step up to the plate. We need to join the leaders and make a difference. It is up to us to decide whether or not we want one professional organization or two. It is up to us to decide whether or not we should be our own profession or a branch of a larger profession. It is up to us to decide whether or not we can survive without a common philosophy or operate using some guiding principles. Will we let our past prevent us from imagining our future?

Discussion Questions

1. Are we a distinct profession, or are we a branch of some other profession? What makes us a distinct profession? And, if we are a branch of some other profession, what is that other profession?

2. Have we answered the question, "Is recreation therapy?" Does recreation cure anything, and if so, what? If not, what has our efficacy research demonstrated?
3. Should we be one united profession with multiple philosophies, or should we have one, unified philosophy?
4. Identify what you think some of the important milestones have been in TR.
5. What will you do to be a "pioneer" in our profession?

References

Anonymous. (1994). *10 reasons to retain the title "Therapeutic Recreation."* An unpublished manuscript.

Austin, D., & Hunnicutt, B. K. (1978). National therapeutic recreation society: The first twelve years. *Therapeutic Recreation Journal, 12*(3), 4-12.

Avedon, E. M. (1974). *Therapeutic recreation service: An applied behavioral approach.* Englewood Cliffs: Prentice-Hall.

Buettner, L., & Fitzsimmons, S. (2003). *Dementia practice guideline for recreational therapy: Treatment of disturbing behaviors.* Alexandria, VA: American Therapeutic Recreation Association.

Coyle, C. P., Kinney, W. B. Riley, B., & Shank, J. W. (Eds.). (1991). *Benefits of therapeutic recreation: A consensus view.* Ravensdale, WA: Idyll Arbor, Inc.

Coyle, C. P., Kinney, W. B., & Shank, J. W. (1993). Trials and tribulations in field-based research in therapeutic recreation. In M. J. Malkin, & C. Z. Howe (Eds.), *Research in therapeutic recreation: Concepts and methods* (pp. 207-232). State College, PA: Venture.

Compton, D. M. (1997). Where in the world are we going? Armageddon and utopia revisited. In D. M. Compton (Ed.), *Issues in therapeutic recreation: Toward the new millennium* (pp. 39-50). Champaign, IL: Sagamore.

Cox, C. L., & Dobbings, V. (1970). Before the merger: The national association of recreation therapists (1953-1967). *Therapeutic Recreation Journal, 4*, 3-8.

Frye, V., & Peters, M. (1972). *Therapeutic recreation: Its theory, philosophy, and practice.* Harrisburg, PA: Stackpole.

Halberg, K. J., & Howe-Murphy, R. (1985). The dilemma of an unresolved philosophy in therapeutic recreation. *Therapeutic Recreation Journal, 19*(3), 7-16.

Haun, P. (1966). *Recreation: A medical viewpoint.* New York: Teachers College Press.

Howe-Murphy, R., & Halberg, K. J. (1987). Evolution of a philosophy in therapeutic recreation: An essential and continual quest. *Therapeutic Recreation Journal, 21*(2), 79-80.

Hunnicutt, B. K. (1978). A rejoinder to the twelve-year history of the NTRS. *Therapeutic Recreation Journal, 12*(3), 15-19.

James, A. (1998a). Recreation therapy: A history of concern, Part I 1855-1946. *Annual in Therapeutic Recreation, 7*, 83-90.

James, A. (1998b). The conceptual development of recreational therapy. In F. M. Brasile, T. K. Skalko, & j. burlingame (Eds.), *Perspectives in recreational therapy: Issues of a dynamic profession* (pp. 7-38). Ravensdale, WA: Idyll Arbor.

Lee, L. L. (1987). A panic attack in therapeutic recreation over being considered therapeutic. *Therapeutic Recreation Journal, 21*(2), 71-78.

Malik, P. B. (2001). Perspective: Therapeutic recreation is a process not a place. In N. J. Stumbo (Ed.), *Professional issues in therapeutic recreation: On competence and outcomes* (pp 287-302). Champaign, IL: Sagamore.

McKenney, A., Sylvester, C., Beck, T., & Zuniga, S. *Purpose, passion, progress: Celebrating 40 years of NTRS: Preserving our past as the National Therapeutic Recreation Society while embracing opportunities for change.* A paper presented at the National Recreation and Park Association Congress, Seattle, WA, October 10, 2006.

Meng, R. W. (1960). The recreator: Therapist or therapeutic agent? *Recreation, 53,* 360-1.

Meyer, L. E. (1981). Three philosophical positions of therapeutic recreation and their implication for professionalization and NTRS/NRPA. *Therapeutic Recreation Journal, 15*(2), 7-16.

Meyer, M. W. (1962). The rationale of recreation as therapy. *Recreation in Treatment Centers, 1,* 23-26.

Mobily, K. E. (1985a). A philosophical analysis of therapeutic recreation: What does it mean to say "we can be therapeutic?" Part I, *Therapeutic Recreation Journal, 19*(1), 14-26.

Mobily, K. E. (1985b). A philosophical analysis of therapeutic recreation: What does it mean to say, "We can be therapeutic?" Part II, *Therapeutic Recreation Journal, 19*(2), 7-14.

Mobily, K. E., Weissinger, E., & Hunnicut, B. K. (1987). The means/ends controversy: A framework for understanding the value potential of TR. *Therapeutic Recreation Journal, 21*(3), 7-13.

Mobily, K. E. (1987). A quiescent reply to Lee. *Therapeutic Recreation Journal, 21* (2), 81-83.

Navar, N. H. (2001). Keynote: Thoughts on therapeutic recreation education. In N. J. Stumbo (Ed.), *Professional issues in therapeutic recreation: On competence and outcomes* (pp. 23-36). Champaign, IL: Sagamore.

Peterson, C. A. (1984). A matter of priorities and loyalties. *Therapeutic Recreation Journal, 18*(2) *11-16.*

Peterson, C. A. (1989). The dilemma of philosophy. In D. M. Compton (Ed.), *Issues in therapeutic recreation: A profession in transition* (pp. 21-33). Champaign, IL: Sagamore.

Reynolds, R. P., & O'Morrow, G. R. (1985). *Problems, issues and concepts in therapeutic recreation.* Englewood Cliffs, NJ: Prentice Hall.

Ross, J. E., & Ashton-Schaeffer, C. (2001). Therapeutic recreation practice models. In N. J. Stumbo (Ed.), *Professional issues in therapeutic recreation: On competence and outcomes* (pp 159-188). Champaign, IL: Sagamore.

Russoniello, C. V. (1992). *Recreational therapy: An ethical imperative.* A paper presented to the ATRA Annual Conference in Breckenridge, Colorado.

Skalko, T., Russoniello, C., Grote, K., Rhodes, M., Olsson, R., & West, R. (n.d.) An unpublished manuscript. A note on the title "Recreational Therapy".

Van Andel, G. (n.d.) ATRA History an abbreviated history: A personal perspective Retrieved on March 1, 2007 at www.atra-tr.org.

West, R. (1988). Definition of therapeutic recreation: A prospective from key publics. *ATRA Newsletter, 4*(3), 25-27.

CHAPTER 3

World Demographics and Their Implications for Therapeutic Recreation

Rebecca Genoe, Ph.D.
University of Waterloo

Jerome Singleton, Ph.D., CTRS™
Dalhousie University

What contribution can we make to the common good? Unquestionably, our contribution must be grounded in play and leisure. Any therapeutic intervention we can facilitate can only have a meaning in terms of leisure, and leisure today can only be understood in light of global changes in technology, population growth, and the labor force (Lahey, 1998, p. 19).

We reside in a changing world. World demographics are shifting for a number of reasons. Primarily, these shifts are due to an aging population (Myers, 1997). In addition to population aging, world demographics are changing as a result of migration. Therapeutic recreation specialists must be flexible and adaptable in order to meet the needs of an increasingly older and culturally diverse population with varying attitudes and assumptions about both disability and leisure. As our world changes, therapeutic recreation specialists must consider cultural and cohort differences and divergent perceptions of aging, disability, and leisure. In the first section of this chapter, we will describe global population aging. The second section will address migration and the impact of globalization on North American society. Third, we will explore how rates and experiences of disability can vary across the world. Finally, implications of changing world demographics for therapeutic recreation practice are discussed.

Population Aging

A population is considered to be aging when "future populations will have a higher proportion of the population in older age groups than they do today" (Cheal, 2000, p. S110). Population aging is the result of decreased fertility rates, as well as decreased mortality rates

(Bloom & Canning, 2006). As a result of population aging, 10% of the population was over age 60 at the end of the 20th century. By 2050, 20% of the population will be over age 60 (Palacios, 2002). The largest growing segment of the population consists of the oldest old: those aged 80 and older (Bloom & Canning, 2006; Myers, 1997). Population aging is in part due to medical advances that have limited the number of deaths due to acute illness or accidents.

Population aging occurs at different rates in various regions of the world (Bloom & Canning, 2006; Myers, 1997). While population aging is occurring for developed nations, developing nations are different (see Figure 3.1). Bloom and Canning (2006) indicated that developing nations (all regions of Africa, Asia [excluding Japan], Latin America, and the Caribbean plus Melanesia, Micronesia, and Polynesia) are expanding more rapidly than developed nations (all regions of Europe plus North America, Australia, New Zealand, and Japan) and are using more resources as life expectancy is increased. Life expectancy varies within the global community. In developed countries such as Australia and Canada, life expectancy is 78 years for men and 83 years for women, while life expectancy in Nigeria is 45 for men and 46 for women (World Health Organization Statistics, 2007).

Figure 3.1
**Percentage of the population comprised of seniors
in selected countries, 2005**

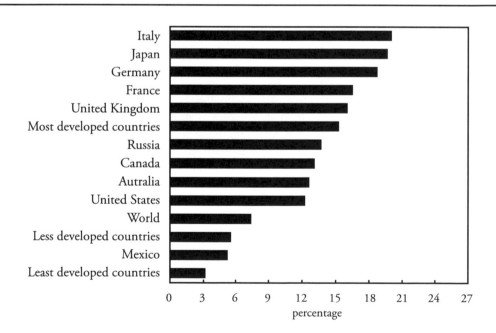

Sources: Statistics Canada, 2001 Census of Canada and World Population Prospect: The 2004 Revision population database, United Nations Population division.

Gender can have an impact on our aging population as well. Since women have a longer life expectancy than men, a higher proportion of the oldest old are women (Myers, 1997). As such, more women than men are likely to be widowed. Widowed women are less likely to receive a pension (Lopata, 1979, 1997); thus, unattached women have lower average incomes than both unattached men and older couples (Statistics Canada, 2007). While gender is important to consider when thinking about population aging, we know little about older men's experiences of aging, especially among the oldest old (Genoe & Singleton, 2006).

In North America, the population is rapidly aging, largely due to the aging of the baby boom generation. Baby boomers were born between 1946 and 1965, and the first of the boomer generation will be turning 65 in 2011. They are currently the largest portion of individuals entering into retirement, which will have a huge impact in relation to shortage of labor in Europe and North America, the elimination of mandatory retirement due to labor shortages and economics, and changes to the pension systems. The baby boomers have the most impact on global society. Demographers have followed this generation as they have influenced the development of grade schools, high schools, post-secondary education, and employment opportunities. The baby boomers will continue to have an impact on aging and how we provide services to older adults. This population has been redefining what it means to be old. How will this generation influence TR service delivery? What impact will the aging boomer have on the experiences of aging and disability for future generations, such as Generation X (1960 – 1980) and Generation Y (1970-1990)?

World Migration

Now that we have explored global population aging, we turn to discussion of another aspect of changing demography—world migration. Over the next 45 years it is expected that 22 million individuals will migrate from developing nations to developed nations each year (Bloom & Canning, 2006). Persons who are migrating from developing nations can be divided into two groups: persons who are immigrants and persons who are refugees. Persons who are immigrating leave the country voluntarily for other opportunities in developed nations. Individuals who are refugees leave their country due to oppression or war (Kensinger, Gearig, Boor, Olson, & Grass, 2007). The movement of individuals between the developing and developed nations will have an impact on both societies (Bloom & Canning, 2007; Bolla & Dawson, 1990; Fox, 1994, 2006; Karlis, 1990).

As discussed above, people migrate from undeveloped to developed nations, and this has an impact on population aging. We need to think about cultural differences as older people move from one country to another. The United States is an example of shifting migration, as it is expected that by the year 2050, 24.4% of the population will be Hispanic or Latino (Shrestha, 2004). In Canada, about 29% of persons age 65-74 and 28% of those aged 75-84 are immigrants (Statistics Canada, 2007). Immigrants to Canada have different experiences than those who are born in Canada. They did not have the same labor market experiences when they were younger; they may have been required to learn a new language during adulthood. Those who immigrate closer to retirement are often not eligible for pension benefits and may have had less time to save for retirement (Statistics Canada,

2007). How will migration impact the current and future aging population? How will it affect therapeutic recreation service delivery for a culturally diverse aging population?

Persons with Disabilities

World demography changes will have an impact on both the experience and incidence of disability. For example, we can expect greater numbers of older adults who experience one or more disabilities or chronic illnesses (Fujiura, Park, & Rutkowski-Kmitta, 2005; Lewis, 2002; Restrepo & Rozental, 1994; WHO, n.d). Adaptations to their lifestyles or activities of daily living may be required in order to maintain quality of life while living with the symptoms or conditions resulting from one's disability or chronic illness.

The World Health Organization (WHO) indicated that increasing incidents of disability are an interaction of "population growth, aging, chronic conditions, injuries at home and work, birth defects, AIDS, environmental change, malnutrition and other causes related to poverty" (WHO, n.d.). The World Health Organization reports that approximately 10% of the world's population (600 million people, including about 200 million children) are living with some form of mental, physical, or intellectual disability (WHO, n.d.).

Currently there is no agreement on definitions of disability, and there is minimal comparable information on the incidence, distribution of, and trends of disability impairments. Persons with disabilities are not a homogeneous group. In general, persons with disabilities can be divided into two groups: persons born with disabilities and persons who acquire disabilities due to a trauma (e.g., such as a person with a traumatic brain injury), war, or chronic condition. Each society will have differing perspectives on persons with disabilities (Mobily & Ostiguy, 2004).

While approximately 10% of the global population has a disability, these statistics vary from country to country. Persons with disabilities are often excluded from educational and employment opportunities. The United Nations (2006, p. 1) fact sheet briefly summarizes the issues that persons living with disabilities face:

- In countries with life expectancies over 70 years, individuals spend on average about eight years, or 11.5% of their life span, living with disabilities.
- Eighty percent of persons with disabilities live in developing countries, according to the UN Development Programme (UNDP).
- Disability rates are significantly higher among groups with lower educational attainment in the countries of the Organization for Economic Cooperation and Development (OECD), says the OECD Secretariat. On average, 19% of less educated people have disabilities, compared to 11% among the better educated.
- The World Bank estimates that 20% of the world's poorest people are disabled and tend to be regarded in their own communities as the most disadvantaged.
- Women with disabilities are recognized to be disadvantaged, experiencing exclusion on account of their gender and their disability.
- According to UNICEF, 30% of street youths are disabled.

The United Nations has recommended guidelines for countries to consider for the equalization of opportunities for persons with disabilities (United Nations, 1993).

The United Nations document identifies 22 rules that governments should consider in developing policies to address inequities for persons with disabilities. These rules are divided into three sections: a) preconditions of equal opportunity (awareness raising, medical care, rehabilitation to support services); b) target areas for equal participation (accessibility, education, employment, income, family life and personnel integrity, culture, recreation, and sports and religion); and c) implementation measures (information and research, policy-making and planning, legislation, economic policies, coordination of work, organizations of persons with disabilities, personnel training, national monitoring and evaluation of disability programmes in the implementation of the rules, technical and economic cooperation, international cooperation). Rule 11 (United Nations, 1993, p. 4) outlines the guidelines for recreation and sports:

- States should initiate measures to make places for recreation and sports, hotels, beaches, sports arenas, gym halls, etc., accessible to persons with disabilities. Such measures should encompass support for staff in recreation and sports programs, including projects to develop methods of accessibility, and participation, information, and training programs.
- Tourist authorities, travel agencies, hotels, voluntary organizations, and others involved in organizing recreational activities or travel opportunities should offer their services to all, taking into account the special needs of persons with disabilities. Suitable training should be provided to assist that process.
- Sports organizations should be encouraged to develop opportunities for participation by persons with disabilities in sports activities. In some cases, accessibility measures could be enough to open up opportunities for participation. In other cases, special arrangements or special games would be needed. States should support the participation of persons with disabilities in national and international events.
- Persons with disabilities participating in sports activities should have access to instruction and training of the same quality as other participants.
- Organizers of sports and recreation should consult with organizations of persons with disabilities when developing their services for persons with disabilities (United Nations, 1993).

Countries such as Canada (Human Resources and Social Development Canada, 2007), Japan (Annual Report on Government Measures for Persons with Disabilities, 2005), New Zealand (New Zealand Disability Strategy, 2007), and the United States (U.S. Department of Health and Human Services, 2003) have formulated policies related to persons with disabilities. The strategies and policies that are developed by each of the nations reflect the norms and values of the society (W.H.O. National Policy Documents, n.d.). The issues confronting persons with a disability in a global society are complex, ranging from access to employment to access to recreation and sport. The International Classification of Functioning, Disability and Health (ICF) is a process that may assist in collecting data internationally to examine trends globally in regard to prevention, management, and rehabilitation of persons with disabilities (WHO, n.d.). Furthermore, issues related to aging and disability need to be placed within the culture and gender of the individual (Fox,

1994, 2006; Karlis, 1990; Iwasaki, Nishino, Onda, & Bowling, 2007). As persons move between developing and developed nations, they bring with them their culture, which has its own way of defining and experiencing illness and disability.

Implications for Therapeutic Recreation Practice

Population aging, migration from developing to developed countries, and increased incidence of disability have implications for therapeutic recreation practice. As more people migrate to developed countries, therapeutic recreation specialists will have a role to fulfill in meeting the needs of a culturally diverse, aging population. Furthermore, these older adults will be dealing with multiple and complex disabilities in a global society. As adults move from one country to another, they bring with them their cultures' perceptions of aging and disability. These perceptions shape the individual's experience of living with a disability or increased age (WHO, n.d.). Each society will have differing perspectives on persons with disabilities (Mobily & Ostiguy, 2004). They also bring with them their perceptions of leisure (Gibson, 2006; Iwasaki et al., 2007). The concept of leisure has often been criticized for being androcentric and Eurocentric (Henderson, Bialeschki, Shaw, & Freysinger, 1996). Iwasaki et al. (2007) indicates that the term "leisure" should be placed within the social and culture context of the person.

Now that we've explored some ways in which world demography is changing, let's consider the interactions between aging, disabilities, migration, and therapeutic recreation. If we use the analogy of a rope, we can see how each of these factors (small, breakable threads) twist together to create a complex system (a strong, unbreakable rope). Each of these concepts is defined within a person's culture and society. Scholars have developed frameworks to understand the interactions between societies' norms and persons' activity involvement during the last 30 years (Bronfenbrenner, 1979, 1989; WHO, 2001). Below we will explore two such models and consider their impacts for therapeutic recreation. These models consider how the complexities of family structures, group norms, social structures of the society, and policy of the society impact the older adult who has a disability in relation to perception of a person's abilities. The Ecological Model (Bronfenbrenner, 1979) and the International Classification of Functioning, Disability and Health (ICF) (WHO, 2001) include various layers of an individual's environment to determine how he or she is affected by his or her particular societal norms.

The Ecological Model
Bronfenbrenner's (1979) model is comprised of four layers that represent the extended surroundings of an individual. These include: macrosystem, exosystem, mesosystem, and microsystem. The macrosystem refers to the societal norms, government policies, and structures that influence human behavior. The exosystem can be conceptualized as the facilities or structures that are interactive with the persons (such as school, work, hospitals, rehabilitation centers) that deliver services that have been developed by government policies. The mesosystem could be interpreted as the classroom the person sits in, the office the person works in, or the rehabilitation program the person participates in. The microsystem refers to the person, his or her family, siblings, and relatives. Bronfenbrenner (1979) provided the analogy of "a set of nested structures, each inside the next, like a set of Russian dolls"

(p. 3) to illustrate how the various levels are interactive with each other. Bronfenbrenner (1979) stated that "behavior evolves as a function of the interplay between person and environment" (p. 16). Bronfenbrenner's model suggested that it is essential to recognize how a person has been socialized, and the importance of considering every aspect of the environment that influences the individual's behavior. Therapeutic recreation specialists can draw upon the Ecological Model to understand how social norms, service delivery structures, governmental policies, work environment, and family situation impacts their experience and perceptions of leisure.

ICF's Biopsychosocial Model

Similar to Bronfenbrenner's model, the International Classification of Functioning, Disability, and Health (ICF) places the individual within his/her social and cultural context through a biopsychosocial model to examine the interactions of health and social conditions on a person with a disability. The ICF focuses on how people live with health conditions and how functioning can be enhanced for the person so he or she can lead a productive life. The indicators used within the ICF have implications for healthcare providers and policy makers in relation to the rights of individuals and groups. This model focuses on the health condition (disorder or disease), participation in their communities (learning and applying knowledge, mobility, major life areas, etc.), physical (body functions and structure), and contextual factors (environmental or personal) of the person within his or her society (WHO, 2001, p. 18).

In this model, the term *activity* is neutral and should be defined within the culture and cohort of the individual. Each cohort across the life course will define the activity within their own cultural norms. A person born in 1930 will think about activity differently from a person who was born in 1990, since they have different life experiences. Terminology used to describe the biopsychosocial model should be framed within the individual's society;

Figure 3.2
International Classification of Functioning, Disability, and Health (ICF).

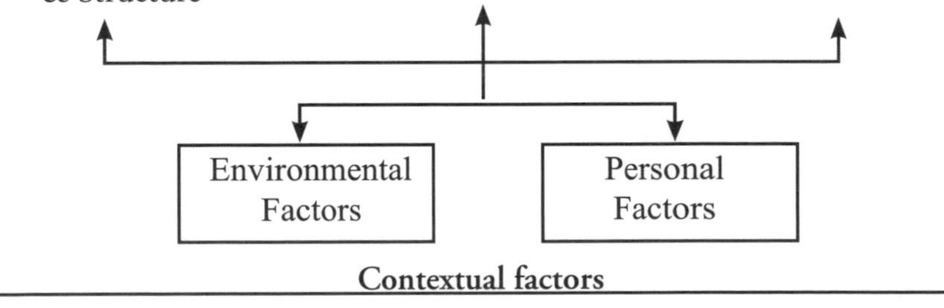

therefore terminology used in a developed society versus a developing society may differ. An activity such as hockey is valued in Canada but may not be valued in another country. Therapeutic recreation professionals need to be aware that the term "leisure" may not be relevant to individuals who have immigrated to their country. The therapeutic recreation professional needs to be aware of cultural norms that may impact on their interactions with immigrants (Anderson & Stone, 2005, Gladwell & Stone, 2005; Kensinger et al., 2007).

Both the Ecological Model (Bronfenbrenner, 1979), and the International Classification Functioning, Disability, and Health (WHO, 2001) model illustrate that a person is affected by the society in which he/she resides. These models provide a framework for understanding the interaction of the person within a societal context yet recognizes that each generation differs due to the values and social structure they are born.

Summary

The global society is aging (Leitner & Leitner, 2004). As a result, people are more likely to experience one or more chronic illnesses and/or disabilities in later life (Lewis, 2002). How individuals age is influenced by the context of their culture, economic resources of the society, and how persons with disabilities are viewed within their society. Bronfenbrenner's Ecological Model (1979) and the International Classification of Functioning, Disability, and Health (ICF) (WHO, 2001) models provide a framework for understanding therapeutic recreation service provisions for persons who are older and/or with a disability (Howard, Nieuwenhuijsen, & Saleeby, 2008; Howard, 2007; Howard, Browning, & Lee, 2007).

Placing the person within the societal norms, culture, and government policies enables the therapeutic recreation professional to understand that individuals who are aging or have a disability from non-Western societies may have differing challenges in relation to access and inclusion in activities across the life course.

Today's global society is fluid. Migration will impact both the society that the individual leaves and the society that he or she enters into. Therapeutic recreation professionals in North America must be aware of the norms and values of immigrants/refugees who migrate to North America. Professionals in other countries such as Japan, Korea, Australia, and New Zealand need to appreciate that their values and beliefs should not be superimposed upon the immigrants/refugees who enter their countries (Allison, 1988; Allison & Geiger, 1993; Bolla & Dawson, 1990; Fox, 1994, 2006; Iwasaki, Nishino, Onda, & Bowling, 2007; Karlis, 1990; Manzenreiter & Horne, 2006; Ng, 1996; Tirone & Shaw, 1997; Tsai, 2006; Rowe, 2006; Ujimoto, 1991).

How will shifting demographics impact on therapeutic recreation service delivery? Therapeutic recreation professionals need to be aware of:
a) the diversity of the people they serve, both within and between particular population groups (Fox, 1994, 2006; Karlis, 1990; Iwasaki et al., 2007; Ujimoto, 1991);
b) that one's age, gender, race, culture, and socioeconomic status can have an impact on how they view both leisure and therapeutic recreation (Kelly, 1989; McPherson, 1983; Zuzanek & Smale, 1999);
c) that the therapeutic recreation assessment process they use should be based upon the culture and ideological principles of the people they serve (Bolla & Dawson,

1990; Fox, 1994, 2007; Karlis, 1990; Leitner & Leitner, 2004; Gladwell & Stone, 2005; Iwasaki et al., 2007)

d) that the term "leisure" may or may not exist within the population they serve (Iwasaki et al., 2007; Leitner & Leitner, 2004).

Students entering into the field of therapeutic recreation need to be cognizant that there is no single definition for the delivery of therapeutic recreation services for persons with disabilities in a global society. Differing terms have emerged to describe therapeutic recreation such as Diversional Therapy (Australia and New Zealand), Chyrio recreation (Korea), Fukushi recreation (Japan), Arts and Crafts (Finland) and Therapeutic Recreation (United States and Canada) and reflect the society values and social structures for services for persons who are aging or with a disability (Stumbo & Singleton, 2007; Patterson, 2007; Hitoshi, Hiroaki, Naomi, & Joseph, 2007; Pegg, & Darcy, 2007; Aho, 2007; also see Yang & Malkin, Chapter 6). Within North America, persons providing services for persons with disabilities have been called Activity Directors, Leisure for Special Populations, Recreation Therapists, Therapeutic Recreationists, and Recreation Integrators. Although the terminology differs, they all have the common goal of enhancing the abilities of persons to participate in leisure independently. The title or label provided by various cultures to describe service delivery for persons with a disability reflect the social constructs (government policies, ideological and social frameworks that govern a person's perceptions of ability) of the society of the aged or persons with a disability resides.

To understand how services have emerged in differing cultures, Bronfenbrenner's (1979) analogy of the nested Russian dolls is appropriate. It is the interaction of the societal, institutional, and family values that are nested within each other, within each cohort that influences the perception of a person with a disability or an old adult in differing societies. Therapeutic recreation services for a global aging population will vary depending on how therapeutic recreation is defined (see Chapter 6), how the society views elders and persons with disabilities, and how the term "leisure" is defined (Iwasaki et al., 2007).

Discussion Questions

1) How do shifting global demographics influence persons with disabilities?
2) What theoretical models can assist in understanding context of persons with a disability and aging population in a global society?
3) What guidelines have been developed by the United Nations for Recreation and Sport?
4) How can therapeutic recreation professionals respond to shifting global society's migration (immigration/refugee)?
5) How do shifting demographics affect therapeutic recreation service delivery in North America?

References

Aho, J. (2007). Therapeutic recreation in Finland, *Therapeutic Recreation Journal*, *41*(2), 141-147.

Allison, M. T. (1988). Breaking boundaries and barriers: Future directions in cross-cultural research. *Leisure Sciences, 10*(2), 247-259.

Allison, T. M., & Geiger, W. C. (1993). Nature of leisure activities among the Chinese-American elderly. *Leisure Sciences, 15*(4), 309-319.

Anderson, D., & Stone, C. (2005, Spring, 2005). Cultural competencies of park and recreation professionals: A case study of North Carolina. *Journal of Park & Recreation Administration, 23*(1), 53-74.

Annual Report on Government Measures for Persons with Disabilities Japan, Retrieved Feb 27, 2007 http://www8.cao.go.jp/shougai/english/index-e.html

Bloom, D. E., & Canning, D. (2006). Global Demography: Fact, Force and Future, The WDA-HSG Discussion Paper Series on Demographic Issues, No. 2006/1, World Demographic Association, Retrieved Feb 20, 2007, from http://www.wdassociation.org/ulfs/documents/WDA-HSG-DP2006-1_Bloom_Canning.pdf

Bolla, P., & Dawson, D. (1990). Meeting the recreation needs of ethnic communities. *Recreation Canada, 48*(4), 10-15.

Bronfenbrenner, U. (1979). *The ecology of human development: Experiments by nature and design.* Cambridge, MA: Harvard University Press.

Bronfenbrenner, U. (1989). Ecology systems theory. *Annals of Child Development, 6*, 187-249.

Cheal, D. (2000). Aging and demographic change. *Canadian Public Policy, 26*(2), 109-122.

Fox, K. M. (2006). Leisure and indigenous peoples. *Leisure Studies, 25*(4), 403-409.

Fox, K. M. (1994). The power and promise of leisure based on diversity. *Recreation Canada, 52*(1), 23-25.

Fujiura, G., Park, H., & Rutkowski-Kmitta, V. (2005). Disability statistics in the developing world: A reflection on the meaning of our numbers. *Journal of Applied Research in Intellectual Disabilities, 18*, 295-304.

Genoe, R., & Singleton, J. (2006). Older men's leisure experiences across the life span. *Topics in Geriatric Rehabilitation, 22*(4), 348-356.

Gibson, H. J. (2006). Leisure and later life: Past, present and future. *Leisure Studies, 25*(4), 397-401.

Gladwell, N., & Stone, C. (2005, August). An examination of multicultural awareness and sensitivity of recreation, parks, and tourism educators. *Schole: A Journal of Leisure Studies & Recreation Education, 20*, 71-89.

Henderson, K. A., Bialeschki, M. D., Shaw, S. M., & Freysinger, V. J. (1996). *Both gains and gaps: Feminist perspectives on women's leisure.* University Park, PA: Venture.

Hitoshi, J. N., Hiroaki, C., Naomi, Y., & Joseph, G. (2007). Therapeutic recreation in modern Japan: Era of challenge and opportunity. *Therapeutic Recreation Journal, 41*(2), 119-131.

Howard, D., Nieuwenhuijsen, E., & Saleeby, P. (2008, June 30). Health promotion and education: Application of the ICF in the U.S. and Canada using an ecological perspective. *Disability & Rehabilitation, 30*(12/13), 942-954.

Howard, D. (2007, December). Leisure and the World Health Organization. *World Leisure Journal, 49*(4), 237-238.

Howard, D., Browning, C., & Lee, Y. (2007). The International Classification of Functioning, Disability, and Health: Therapeutic recreation code sets and salient diagnostic core sets. *Therapeutic Recreation Journal, 41*(1), 61-81.

Human Resources and Social Development Canada. Government of Canada. Retrieved May 30, 2007, from *http://www.hrsdc.gc.ca/en/gateways/individuals/audiences/pd.shtml*

Iwasaki, Y., Nishino, H., Onda, T., & Bowling, C. (2007). Leisure research in a global world: Time or reverse the Western domination in leisure research. *Leisure Sciences, 29,* 1-5.

Karlis, G. (1990). Aged immigrants: Forgotten clients in the provision of recreation services. *Recreation Canada, 48*(4), 36-40.

Kelly, J. R. (1989). Leisure behaviors and styles: Social, economic, and cultural factors. In *Understanding leisure and recreation* (pp. 89-108). USA: Venture.

Kensinger, K., Gearig, J., Boor, J., Olson, N., & Grass, T. (2007). A therapeutic recreation program for international refugees. *Therapeutic Recreation Journal, 41*(2), 148-158.

Lahey, M. (1998). Developing a global perspective in therapeutic recreation. *Journal of Leisurability, 25*(2), 14-19.

Leitner, M. J., & Leitner, S. F. (2004). *Leisure in later life*. New York: The Haworth Press.

Lewis, C. (2002). *Aging: The healthcare challenge* (4th ed.). Philadelphia: F. A. Davis.

Lopata, H. Z. (1979). *Women as widows*. New York: Elsevier.

Lopata, H. Z. (1997). Current widowhood: Myths and realities. *Journal of Leisure Research, 29*(1), 137-140.

Manzenreiter, W., & Horne, J. (2006). Leisure and culture in Japan. *Leisure Studies, 25*(4), 411-415.

McPherson, B. D. (1983). *Aging as a social process*. Toronto: Butterworths.

Mobily, K., & Ostiguy, L. J. (2004). *Introduction to therapeutic recreation: U.S. and Canadian perspectives*. State College, PA: Venture.

Myers, G. (1997). Emerging demographic changes in an aging world: An overview. *World Congress of Gerontology*. Adelaide, Australia, p. 66-68.

New Zealand Disability Strategy. Retrieved February 22, 2007, from www.odi.govt.nz/nzds

Ng, P. P. T. (1996). Leisure and social change in Hong Kong. *Society and Leisure, 19*(1), 91-113.

Palacios, R. (2002). The future of global aging. *International Journal of Epidemiology, 31,* 786-791.

Pegg, S., & Darcy, S. (2007). Sailing on troubled waters: Diversional therapy in Australia. *Therapeutic Recreation Journal, 41*(2), 132-140.

Patterson, I. (2007) Changes in the provision of leisure services for people with disabilities in Australia, *Therapeutic Recreation Journal, 41*(2), 108-118.

Restrepo, H., & Rozental, M. (1994). The social impact of aging populations: Some major issues. *Social Science and Medicine, 39*(7), 1323-1338.

Rowe, D. (2006). Coming to terms with leisure and globalization. *Leisure Studies, 25*(4), 423-436.

Shrestha, L. B. (2004). The changing demographic profile of the United States, CRS Report for Congress, Retrieved June 4 2007 from http://www.fas.org/sgp/crs/misc/RL32701.pdf

Statistics Canada. (2007). A Portrait of Seniors in Canada, Retrieved June 27, 2008 from http://www.statcan.ca/english/freepub/89-519-XIE/89-519-XIE2006001.htm

Stumbo, N., & Singleton, J. (2007). Introduction to special issue globalization of therapeutic recreation. *Therapeutic Recreation Journal, 41*(2), 106-107.

Tirone, S. C., & Shaw, S. M. (1997). At the center of their lives: Indo Canadian women, their families and leisure. *Journal of Leisure Research, 29*(2), 225-244.

Tsai, C. L. (2006). The influence of Confucianism on women's leisure in Taiwan. *Leisure Studies, 25*(4), 469-476.

Ujimoto, K. V. (1991). Ethnic variations in the allocation of time to daily activities. *Society and Leisure, 14*(2), 557-573.

United Nations. (2006). Convention on the Rights of Persons with Disabilities, Some Facts about Persons with Disabilities, Retrieved February 22, 2007, http://www.un.org/disabilities/convention/facts.html

United Nations, Human functioning and disability, Retrieved February 22 2007, from www.unstats.org/unsd/demographic/sconcerns/disability/default.htm/

United Nations Standard Rules on the Equalization of Opportunities for Persons with Disabilities (1993), Retrieved February 22 2007, http://www.un.org/esa/socdev/enable/dissre04.html

U.S. Department of Health and Human Services. (2003). New Freedom Initiative. Retrieved February 22, 2007 from www.hhs.gov/newfreedom

World Health Organization. National Policy Documents, Retrieved Feb 27, 2007 from http://www.who.int/disabilities/policies/documents/en/

World Health Organization. World report on disability and rehabilitation (n.d). Concept Paper. Retrieved Nov. 30, 2006 from www.who.int/disabilities/introduction/en/index.html

World Health Organization. Press release, April 17, 2002. Retrieved February 22, 2007, from http://www.who.int/mediacentre/news/release/release27/en/2007

World Health Organization. (2001). International classification of functioning, disability and health. Geneva, Switzerland: World Health Organization.

World Health Organization National Policy Documents (n.d), Retrieved Feb 27, 2007 http://www.who.int/disabilities/policies/documents/en/

World Health Organization Statistics. (2007). A guide to statistical information at W.H.O. Retrieved February 22, 2007 http://www.who.int/whosis/en/

World Health Organization. International Classification of Functioning, Disability and Health. Geneva: World Health Organization, 2001. Available from: http://www.who.int/classifications/icf/site/intros/ICF-Eng-Intro.pdf

Zuzanek, J., & Smale, B. J. A. (1999). Life cycle and across the week: Allocation of time to daily activities. In W. E. Pentland, A. S. Harvey, M. P. Lawton, & M. A. McColl, (Eds.), *Time use research in the social* sciences (pp. 127-154). New York: Kluwer Academic.

CHAPTER 4

The Role of the International Classification of Functioning, Disability, and Health (ICF) in Therapeutic Recreation Practice, Research, and Education

Marieke Van Puymbroeck, Ph.D., CTRS™, CRC
Indiana University

Heather R. Porter, M.S., CTRS™
Temple University

Bryan P. McCormick, Ph.D., CTRS™
Indiana University

Jerome Singleton, Ph.D., CTRS™
Dalhousie University

The ICF's Impact on Therapeutic Recreation

Models of disability, health, and functioning have proliferated over the past four decades. In order to appreciate the most recent model of health and functioning, a brief history of the existing models will be presented. The original disability model was developed by Nagi (1965). This linear model included components of active pathology, impairment, functional limitation, and disability. Due to its linearity, the model assumed that if an active pathology is present, an eventual decrease in performance (labeled disability) in life-sustaining activities would occur.

The International Classifications of Impairment, Disabilities, and Handicaps (ICIDH) was developed by the World Health Organization (WHO) for trial purposes in 1980 to describe the consequences of health conditions. This model described three separate concepts of disease and health: impairments, disabilities, and handicaps. The model was criticized for a lack of cross-cultural applicability and did not receive international support (Stucki, 2005).

A later model that sought to provide a classification of health was developed by the National Center for Medical Rehabilitation Research (NCMRR). The NCMRR model was developed in 1993 to guide outcome measurement and research. The NCMRR model was also a unidirectional, linear approach to explaining how the course of a disease or pathology impacted the individual but acknowledged that societal limitations (social policies or barriers) further limited one's full participation in society. That is, society may impose a disability upon a person with a medical condition. While this model was an improvement over previous classification schemes, there were still inherent flaws.

The ICIDH was revised in an ongoing process from 1997-1999 and was renamed the International Classification of Functioning, Disability, and Health (called the ICF for short). The ICF has been designed and tested over seven years in over 50 countries to ensure cross-cultural applicability (WHO, 2001). The "overall aim…[of the ICF] is to provide a unified and standardized language and framework for the description of health and health-related states" (WHO, p. 1). The 54th World Health Assembly (the governing body of the WHO) (2001) endorsed the ICF as the international standard for examining individual, societal, and environmental factors that influence health.

The ICF is reflective of the change in perspective in medicine and allied health away from the traditional medical model (that focused on disability as a characteristic requiring intervention from a health profession to fix the problem) and toward more holistic models of health and well-being. The ICF "encourages the health-care community to shift from exclusively using diagnostic labels to painting a more complete picture of the world's health status by describing behavioral aspects of chronic diseases…" (Stambor, 2006, p. 42). In addition to the influence of biological processes and psychological influences, the ICF has been influenced by the social model of disability. Social models of disability posit that individuals experience disability as a result of their interaction with barriers in their environment, such as stairs. Therefore, the ICF is considered a biopsychosocial model. The term "biopsychosocial" is reflective of the interaction between biological, psychological, and social environments of the individual (Bickenbach, Chatterji, Badley, & Üstün, 1999).

Models of functioning, such as the ICF, provide a basis for clinical practice, professional education, and research. In terms of clinical practice, the ICF is intended to guide "needs assessment, matching interventions to specific health states, rehabilitation, and outcome evaluation" (Stucki et al., 2002, p. 281). Although the ICF may be relatively new to therapeutic recreation (TR) services, there are existing examples of its inclusion in TR practice models (e.g., burlingame, 1998), intervention programs (e.g., Sable & Gravnik, 2005), and clinical practice (e.g. burlingame & Blaschko, 2002; Porter & burlingame, 2006; Shank & Coyle, 2002). Further, a recent edition of the *Therapeutic Recreation Journal* included an introduction to the ICF model (Porter & Van Puymbroeck, 2007) and salient code sets for TR practice (Howard, Browning, & Lee, 2007). The American Therapeutic Recreation Association (ATRA) (2005) has affirmed support for the ICF stating,

> the concepts and terminology of the ICF are compatible with recreational therapy practice. ATRA supports the use of ICF language and terminology in recreational therapy practice guidelines, standards of practice, curriculum development,

public policy, international relations, and research. ATRA also acknowledges the significance of the use of the ICF classification and coding system as a vehicle to clarify and enhance practice and research in recreational therapy (para. 2).

Further, ATRA has developed a committee dedicated to representing the interests of the field in regard to ICF development and to assist practitioners, educators, and researchers in implementing the ICF in their practice. Members from this committee and TR practitioners have been involved in field trials of the health profession coding manual that is being developed by the American Psychological Association. The National Therapeutic Recreation Association voted in 2008 to support the ICF, stating in their position statement:

> The National Therapeutic Recreation Society (NTRS) acknowledges the International Classification of Functioning, Disability, and Health (ICF), published by the World Health Organization, as compatible with therapeutic recreation services. The NTRS supports the use of the ICF terminology in therapeutic recreation standards of practice, curriculum development, public policy, and supports the ICF as a classification and coding system to serve as a means for guiding and improving research in therapeutic recreation. (personal communication, Alexis McKenney, June 19, 2008)

These developments are promising and appear to reflect an increasing recognition of the value of the ICF in TR practice. Therefore, the purpose of this chapter is to introduce the ICF classification to the field of TR and to raise issues related to the use and implementation of this model in practice, research, and education.

The ICF Model

According to the WHO (2001), the ICF model has four primary purposes. These are:
- To provide a scientific basis for understanding and studying health and health-related states, outcomes, and determinants;
- To establish a common language for describing health and health-related states in order to improve communication between different users, such as healthcare workers, researchers, policy-makers, and the public, including people with disabilities;
- To permit comparison of data across countries, healthcare disciplines, services, and time;
- To provide a systematic coding scheme for health information systems (p. 5).

The ICF has two parts, each consisting of two components (see Figure 4.1). The first part is functioning and disability, with the components of (a) body functions and structures, and (b) activity and participation. The second part of the ICF is contextual factors, with the components of (a) environmental factors and (b) personal factors (WHO, 2001). The model has double-headed arrows, which indicates that the relationships between the constructs are dynamic. Unlike the Nagi and NCMRR models, the ICF does not assume that the ultimate consequence of a disease or disability is disablement; rather the ICF allows that an intervention at any stage in the model may influence the other constructs. This is important for fields, such as TR, that aim to improve the quality of life for individuals with

---

Figure 4.1
International Classification of Functioning, Disability, and Health (ICF).

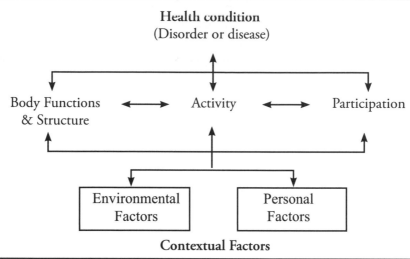

From: World Health Organization. (2001). International classification of functioning, disability, and health. *Geneva, Switzerland: World Health Organization, p. 18. Copyright 2001 from the World Health Organization. Reprinted with permission.*

a variety of health conditions as these fields use therapeutic interventions after the change in health condition to improve or restore well-being.

For clarification purposes, it is necessary to provide definitions of the terms that appear in the ICF Model. Please see Table 4.1 for the relevant descriptions. The terminology in the ICF is distinct from traditional healthcare terminology. These distinctions are very important, as the primary use of the ICF in healthcare practice will include assigning codes to the concepts in the model.

Coding the ICF

It is anticipated that healthcare professionals will begin using the ICF in clinical practice in the near future due, in part, to the growing interest in obtaining functional data. It is important to note that the ICF is a classification system, not an assessment tool. Consequently, therapists will use their own methods and tools for assessment and relate those findings to ICF scaling to determine the ICF code score. Coding the ICF is a complex task at first glance. Only those codes relevant to the purpose of the session are coded, and it is understood that the person's "snapshot" of functioning will be different at different times due to contextual factors (e.g., the person is more alert in the morning than in the afternoon). This is one of the primary reasons that contextual factors are part of the ICF, as explained later.

To understand how to code the ICF, recreational therapists (RTs) must first understand its organization. A brief and basic introduction to coding each of the ICF components is

---

Table 4.1
Definitions of ICF key concepts and terms

Definitions

In the context of health:

Body functions are the physiological functions of body systems (including psychological functions).

Body structures are anatomical parts of the body such as organs, limbs, and their components.

Impairments are problems in body function or structure such as significant deviation or loss.

Activity is the execution of a task or action by an individual.

Participation is involvement in a life situation.

Activity limitations are difficulties an individual may have in executing activities.

Participation restrictions are problems an individual may experience in involvement in life situations.

Environmental factors make up the physical, social, and attitudinal environment in which people live and conduct their lives.

From: World Health Organization. (2001). International classification of functioning, disability, and health. Geneva, Switzerland: World Health Organization, p. 10. Copyright 2001 from the World Health Organization. Reprinted with permission.

provided below. For detailed coding information, refer to Porter and burlingame (2006) *Recreational Therapy Handbook of Practice: ICF-Based Diagnosis and Treatment.*

Body Structures (BS)

The codes in this section all begin with the letter "s" and reflect the anatomical parts of the body (e.g., structure of the brain, structure of the inner ear, structure of the heart). BS has three qualifiers to describe the extent of the impairment, the nature of the change (e.g., deviating position), and the location of the impairment. Although the RT will rarely code this section, therapists will need to know what each qualifier represents and how it is scored to be able to "read" a written code by another health professional.

Body Functions (BF)

The codes in this section all begin with the letter "b" and reflect the physiological and psychological functions of the body. Many of the codes in this section fall within the scope of TR practice (e.g., temperament and personality functions, attention functions, exercise tolerance functions, muscle endurance functions). BF has one qualifier to describe the level of *impairment* that a person has with a body function.

Activities and Participation (A&P)

The codes in this section all begin with the letter "d" and reflect activities that people commonly perform in real life (e.g., carrying out a daily routine, handling responsibilities, starting a conversation, climbing, managing diet and fitness, preparing meals, taking care of animals, forming relationships, play, crafts). Meaningful activity is at the heart of this section and is the basis of TR practice.

Coding A&P is a bit more difficult than the previous sections, and for this reason, it is unable to be fully described in this chapter. A&P has four qualifiers. There are two *capacity* qualifiers that relate to activities and activity limitations in the ICF, and describe an individual's ability to perform an activity in a standard environment (WHO, 2001). A standard environment is "one that is most common and appropriate for testing that particular activity given the individual's functioning and health situation" (Porter & Van Puymbroeck, 2007). An example of an intervention in a standard environment could be testing a client's attention functions in a quiet, non-distracting environment, such as a private therapy room. RTs who work in healthcare will use the capacity scores for inpatient evaluations and in-house treatment sessions.

There are also two performance qualifiers that describe an individual's ability to participate in his/her real life situations. RTs will score performance qualifiers when conducting community integration assessments or assessing any other involvement in a person's life setting/situation (e.g., community recreation).

Environmental Factors (EF)

The codes in this section all begin with the letter "e." EFs are things in the environment that facilitate or hinder a person's health and functioning. These include equipment, attitudes of others, and social policies. EFs can be attached to A&P codes to reflect their effect on a specific activity or participation.

Personal Factors (PF)

The ICF recognizes that personal factors, such as gender and coping styles, affect a person's health and functioning, but due to the large social and cultural variance, they are not currently included in the ICF.

While coding the ICF may be confusing initially, the implementation of the ICF model in healthcare practice has many implications for TR practice.

Application of the ICF in TR Practice

It is expected that the ICF will be utilized in fields in the very near future. Jerome Bichenbach, a leader in ICF research and use, stated:

> There are strong indications in many parts of the world, including the United States, that functional information will soon be required of clinicians by payers... in part because of a realization that functional status information is a far better predictor of health-system usage than diagnostic information. (as cited in Holloway, 2004, p. 32)

The use of the ICF to assess functional status is realistic because it is multi-component and holistic. That is, many components of the model influence functionality, and using the ICF to assess functional status will require a holistic examination of the individual and his/her environment.

The use of the ICF in TR practice can be most clearly seen in its relationship to practice models. burlingame (1998) provided one of the first examinations of TR practice models in comparison to an international model of health and disability. Although burlingame used the ICIDH, many of her original points are relevant to the ICF as well. Among criticisms noted by burlingame was the fact that many existing practice models used domains in the conceptualization of practice (e.g., cognitive, social, etc.) that are not typically used by other disciplines. She also noted the problematic nature of the use of leisure as a domain citing the fact that the domain of leisure referenced an area of practice as opposed to an area of function. Although the use of leisure as a domain was problematic in the use of the ICIDH, the ICF includes a chapter related to social, civic, and community functioning that recognizes recreation and leisure as an important aspect of functioning.

The ICF may enhance TR practice through improved inter-professional communication (Allan, Campbell, Guptill, Stephenson, & Campbell, 2006). Through the adoption of the ICF's framework and terminology related to health, disability, and functioning, all members of an interdisciplinary team can "speak the same language." Thus, RTs can articulate clients' abilities, resources, and needs using the same framework and language as other service providers. As noted by burlingame (1998) above, the use of discipline specific terminology, such as "cognitive domain," limits RTs' abilities to communicate with disciplines that do not use a domain-based language. The adoption of terms related to body functions and structures, activity and participation, and personal and environmental factors will increase RTs' abilities to express themselves clearly to other members of a multidisciplinary team. The case study at the end of this chapter provides an example of how the ICF may improve inter-professional communication.

If RTs in practice do not adopt ICF terminology, they will be behind other disciplines that are also working to incorporate the terminology into their practice (e.g., physical therapy, occupational therapy, psychology, and speech therapy). Further, in practice, the ICF requires a more holistic approach to assessment and treatment planning. For example, using the ICF as our guide, evaluating if a client could be independent at home would mandate the inclusion of personal and environmental factors in the determination of a person's level of independence (e.g., a person has moderate difficulty and the spouse is able to provide the assistance needed, thus there is no residual difficulty and the person is noted as having no difficulty). This is a different way to conceptualize treatment and planning and will require some practice to be able to implement these changes.

Although the ICF presents a number of advantages to practice, it is not without some difficulties. For example, one of the challenges to implementing the ICF has been the difficulty and time-consuming nature of coding the ICF (Schuntermann, 2005). Although a complete coding of each client seems prohibitive, the development of core sets related to specific health conditions (e.g., Cieza et al., 2004) has identified specific codes most relevant to those conditions. These core sets have been developed through a process of international collaboration, coordinated by the World Health Organization. At present, 12 core sets have been developed related to chronic health conditions, and additional core sets are in development. For a list of the existing and developing core sets, see Table 4.2. Furthermore, the Department of Health and Human Services, the Centers for Medicare and Medicaid

---

Table 4.2
Core Sets Related to Health Conditions

Existing Core Sets for Chronic Conditions	Core Sets in Development
• Low back pain	• Acute & Post-acute Core Sets
• Osteoarthritis	• Spinal Cord Injury
• Osteoporosis	• Multiple Sclerosis
• Rheumatoid arthritis	• Psoriasis or Psoriatic Arthritis
• Stroke	• Ankylosing Spondylitis (a chronic inflam-
• Chronic widespread pain	mation of the spine and the sacroiliac joints)
• Depression	• Lupus Erythematodes (SLE) and Systemic
• Obesity	Sclerosis (SSc)
• Obstructive pulmonary diseases	• Malignant tumors of the upper aero-
• Chronic ischemic heart disease	digestive-tract
• Diabetes mellitus	• Bipolar disorder
• Breast cancer	• Head and Neck Cancer
	• Sleep
	• Traumatic Brain Injury
	• Visual Impairment

Source: ICF Research Branch of WHO CC FIC. (2006, December 15). Research Projects. Retrieved June 4, 2008 from http://www.icf-research-branch.org/research/reaserchprojects.htm.

Services, and insurance companies in the United States do not currently mandate use of the ICF, thus limiting its current use in practice (Stambor, 2006).

Another area of criticism that has been raised in the implementation of the ICF is that it does not directly provide any means for the collection of subjective perspectives of the individual's health condition (Hemmingsson & Jonsson, 2005; Ueda & Okawa, 2003). Specifically, the challenge has been that clients' perceptions of their health conditions and functioning are not directly captured in the ICF. Although satisfaction was proposed as a qualifier to the participation element of the ICF, it was not included in the final ICF model (Ueda & Okawa, 2003). Given that two people with the same functional health status may perceive their statuses with different levels of satisfaction and meaning, the absence of a means to capture this in the ICF is a noted weakness.

While there are currently no mandates for the use of the ICF in practice, practitioners who do not adopt ICF terminology and constructs in their practice will be at a disadvantage as the ICF is implemented in facilities. The use of ICF terminology permits comparison of the same constructs across disciplines, improving the communication of the team.

ICF in TR Research

In addition to the opportunities that the adoption of the ICF offers in TR practice, it also provides an "international language for policy development and research" (Shank & Coyle, 2002, p. 35). One way that the ICF can advance research is through the use of the ICF as a framework for clinical research. For example, Threats (2007) asserted that the ICF could be used as a framework for guiding the development of assessment related to access for persons with acquired aphasia. A similar framework could be used in the development of TR practice in such areas as community integration or community functioning including leisure functioning. For example, Van Naarden Braun, Yeargin-Allsopp, and Lollar (2006) used the ICF as a framework for examining the influence of impairments, activity limitations, and adult social roles on leisure activity among young adults with developmental disabilities.

Funding sources (e.g., Centers for Disease Control and Prevention, National Center for Medical Rehabilitation Research, National Institutes of Health) are increasingly interested in multidisciplinary research as well as research that reflects the ICF. Researchers who utilize the ICF as a foundation or to test specific portions of the ICF are being increasingly funded by these large agencies. Other researchers are being funded to develop code sets for specific diseases. Using the ICF as a framework in multidisciplinary research allows all research team members to speak the same language, with all members understanding words that have cross-disciplinary relevance as opposed to discipline-specific relevance (e.g., participation vs. leisure education).

Finally, the ICF provides a framework for cross-cultural research. Since the ICF is developed as a culturally neutral approach to health, disability, and functioning, it does permit the comparison across disparate groups in examining functioning. If TR is to expand internationally, the ability to conduct cross-cultural research and communicate with other cultures about the same constructs, the use of consistent terminology will be important.

If researchers choose not to adopt the ICF in their research, they may not be scored as competitively as researchers who use the ICF as a foundation. This is in part due to the overwhelming support the ICF has received from the international health-related community (e.g., the United Nations, the World Health Assembly, the Disabled Peoples' International, the World Bank, the National Council on Disability, the International Society of Physical and Rehabilitation Medicine, and the Centers for Disease Control and Prevention).

ICF in TR Education

As noted, the ICF provides opportunities for improving practice, articulation of research in therapeutic recreation, and inter-professional communication. At the same time, the inclusion of the ICF in TR education presents additional opportunities and challenges.

Opportunities

Peterson and Rosenthal (2005) stated that the developmental history of the ICF provides a good framework for introducing the evolution of rehabilitation services from a disease-driven medical model to a biopsychosocial model of functional outcome. Furthermore, the ICF reflects concepts and assumptions consistent with holistic values and philosophies of inclusion, dignity, and worth of people with disabilities. Such person-centered values and holistic approaches are quite consistent with the developmental history of therapeutic recreation (Austin, 2005/2006).

In addition to providing an overall model for presentation of the evolution of views of disabling conditions, the ICF also can be used in the instruction of key elements of TR practice. For example, Homa and Peterson (2005) presented an example of the use of the ICF in teaching client assessment in rehabilitation counseling. They identified that the assessment process is one in which practitioners are confronted with volumes of information from a variety of sources, from which they must create a conceptualization of the client and subsequent care. The value of the ICF is that it provides an integrated framework, in the terms of body functions, body structures, and activity and participation, that can be used to identify, organize, and interpret information about the client. In addition, as characterized by the ICF model (Figure 4.1) functioning is the result of the interplay of a variety of personal and environmental factors. According to Homa and Peterson, the ICF model "helps to prevent students from assuming a linear and static perspective of client functioning and helps them to conceptualize the dynamic interplay of these variables" (p. 120).

The ICF also provides a potential structure for instruction on planning care. The use of qualifiers, particularly in the areas of activity and participation, provides an educational tool for the identification of potential areas of intervention. As noted previously, the activities and participation domains can be qualified in terms of capacity (what an individual can do with or without assistance in a standard environment) and performance (what an individual does do in his or her typical environment with and without assistance). Gaps between capacity and performance can be used as guides to highlight areas in which intervention is needed (Homa & Peterson, 2005). As well, when identified, gaps are considered in relation to environmental factors, it provides guidance on what forms of intervention may be needed to improve functional performance.

TR educators have the opportunity to use the first textbook on the ICF, and it happens to be TR-specific (e.g., *Recreational Therapy Handbook of Practice: ICF-Based Diagnosis and Treatment*). This seminal textbook provides educators the means to teach disability specific constructs using the ICF terminology.

Challenges

One of the challenges educators face related to the ICF is that the main body that credentials professionals within the profession does not reflect the ICF structure. For example, the National Council for Therapeutic Recreation Certification™ noted one of the job tasks of the therapeutic recreation specialist in the area of assessment is the task of interviewing "the person served and relevant others to assess physical, social, emotional, cognitive, leisure, and lifestyle needs and functioning" (NCTRC™, 2005, p. 3). This approach using domains such as physical, social, cognitive, etc., is in contrast to the ICF model that characterizes functioning in terms of structures, functions, activities, participation, and the environment. Although functioning in such domains can be "mapped" according to relevant ICF codes, it may provide some difficulty to teach both classifying systems.

This integration of the ICF into TR education presents even greater challenges when one considers the required areas of knowledge specified by the NCTRC™ and how these areas of knowledge are generated. The first challenge faced in education is to provide a curriculum that will prepare students in the stated areas of knowledge, which at present does not include the ICF. It has been shown that accreditation and credentialing standards changes represent one of the greatest influences on curriculum change in TR (Stumbo, Carter, & Kim, 2004). Thus if certification standards do not reflect the ICF, there may be little impetus for providing such education. As noted above, the way in which the NCTRC™ knowledge areas are generated also provides some obstacles. Knowledge areas are generated through a process of job task analysis in which an analysis of current practices provides the basis for the identification of requisite knowledge. Thus, if a concept is not used in current practice, it does not become identified as part of required knowledge for the profession. Given that certification standards influence curriculum, if the ICF is not specified as required knowledge, it is not likely to be included in pre-professional education. Finally, unless the ICF is included in pre-professional education, it seems unlikely that it would become part of practice.

Summary

As with any classification framework, the ICF continues to be refined as it is implemented in practice, research, and education. Although there are some noted criticisms, the main advantages of the ICF for RTs and allied health professionals are that it provides a common framework of communication and can provide a basis for practice models and cross-disciplinary research. The ability to distinguish between activity and participation, gather functional data in both standard and real life settings, and show the effects of environmental factors will also prove to be useful in community integration interventions and research. The failure of TR practitioners, educators, and researchers to integrate the ICF into their daily work will likely lead to our field falling behind fields that have adopted the ICF and are striving to incorporate the ICF systemically into their field. It is the responsibility of all in our field to ensure that we stay at the cutting edge of ICF implementation.

Case Study

Below is an example of how the ICF could facilitate communication among different care settings and among therapy disciplines.

Joe Smith, a 20-year-old male, sustained a complete T6 spinal cord injury from a skiing accident and was admitted to an inpatient rehabilitation center. During his first day, initial evaluations were completed by recreational therapy, occupational therapy, physical therapy, and psychology. Each therapy utilized multi-modal evaluation tools such as interview, clinical observation, and standardized assessments. In addition to discipline-specific documentation procedures, each therapy recorded Joe's impairments, activity limitations, and participation restrictions using the ICF. Some of the ICF codes that each discipline used overlapped. These include: d465 Moving Around Using Equipment; d175 Solving Problems; and d240 Handling Stress and Other Psychological Demands. Although all of the evaluations occurred within a standard testing environment, Joe's level of difficulty varied during each evaluation due to many variables, including: level of fatigue (tired later in the day); context of the situation (supportiveness of the environment for the task); approach of the therapist (stern verses understanding); and Joe's emotions (intensity and type of emotion during the session). Although environmental factor codes can be tied to the above activities to show their impact, the detail of the variables described by the therapists cannot be reflected using the ICF. Consequently, the therapists documented these variables within their discipline notes.

Other environmental factors however, were reflected using the ICF. Physical therapy noted that Joe's mother (e310) was a barrier to Joe's ability to use his wheelchair (d465 Moving Around Using Equipment). She was trying to be helpful but was impeding his progress. Within recreational therapy, Joe expressed that he did not want to go back to college (d830 Higher Education) because he didn't want his friends "looking" at him and making negative judgments about him (e420 Individual Attitudes of Friends). Occupational therapy noted that leg straps (e1151 Assistive Products and Technology for Personal Use in Daily Living) were made and contributed to his improved ability to transfer (d420 Transferring Oneself). And finally, psychology noted that Joe's girlfriend (e320 Friends) provided positive and healthy adjustment support (d240 Handling Stress and Other Psychological Demands) for Joe.

Using the ICF in team conference allowed therapists to compare their findings and share environmental factors that hindered or facilitated Joe's progress. From this discussion, recreational therapy decided to include both Joe's mother and girlfriend in community integration training. Psychological counseling was offered to Joe's mother to provide emotional support. The team also agreed to educate Joe's mother whenever appropriate about the importance of Joe doing things for himself. Psychology recommended for the team to take a cognitive behavioral approach when Joe verbalized distorted thoughts (e.g., "What makes you think that ALL your friends think poorly of you?").

After community integration training, it was clear that the disparity of scores within capacity and performance varied greatly in many of the areas that had been addressed by the therapies during Joe's rehab stay. Particularly, Joe's capacity scores for wheelchair skills, problem solving, and handling stress were much higher than his performance in the community. Although Joe's ability to self-rationalize distorted thoughts had improved, the perceived attitudes of other people in the community (e445 Individual Attitudes of Strangers) hindered Joe's ability to independently problem solve. Accessibility issues (e150 Design, Construction, and Building Products and Technology of Buildings for Public Use) and wheelchair performance abilities (able to bump up a 2" curb only) also contributed to lower scores. With minimal prompting, Joe's mother was able to reduce the level of assistance she provided to Joe and encouraged his independence. Joe's girlfriend was also very encouraging.

Overall, with the help of his mother and girlfriend, however, there was no residual difficulty left unattended. The recreational therapist recorded both performance qualifiers for each ICF activity addressed within the session. The performance with assistance reflected that Joe had no residual difficulty, but if the assistance were not available, Joe would have moderate difficulty. If the recreational therapist did not score performance without assistance, it would appear from the ICF codes that Joe had no problems with these tasks. The problem with this type of coding is that assistance is not always available and provided (e.g., when his girlfriend is not with him). Scoring performance without assistance would show the reader the worst-case scenario. Somewhere between these two scores is probably where true reality lies.

The recreational therapist shared the results of the training session with the team who compared the participation scores with their capacity scores of the same skills. In response to Joe's performance, psychology was able to justify extra sessions to work on adjustment issues. Physical therapy taught the client how to instruct another person (in case his mother/girlfriend was not around) on how to bump his wheelchair up and down a curb if greater than two inches. To reduce the gap between capacity and performance, the team re-allocated therapy hours to increase the number of hours for community integration training.

At discharge, Joe's average level of difficulty with community activities was minimal without assistance. The team recommended an outpatient day treatment program that focused on community skills development. Discharge ICF code scores were sent to the program. Because they, too, used the ICF, they understood how to interpret the code scores and were well prepared prior to Joe's admission to the program to meet his needs. The ICF codes revealed that Joe's mother could be overly helpful at times affecting his ability to progress, so they were able to pre-plan the best approach prior to Joe's arrival. The discrepancy in Joe's capacity and performance scores helped to persuade Joe's insurance company to cover the cost of the program. Also, since the day treatment program has been tracking ICF scores over the last few years along with interventions rendered and outcomes, they have been able to identify patterns that also helped to substantiate the benefits of the program.

Discussion Questions

1. Discuss how terminology in the ICF can be incorporated into national TR standards.
2. How can professionals begin to incorporate the ICF into TR practice?
3. Discuss ideas for using the ICF as a framework for TR research.
4. What steps need to be undertaken to incorporate the ICF into TR education?
5. What are the major barriers to TR specialists using the ICF in practice?
6. What are the major barriers to TR educators using the ICF in education?
7. What would facilitate the full adoption of the ICF?

References

Allan, C. M., Campbell, W. N., Guptill, C. A., Stephenson, F. F., & Campbell, K. E. (2006). A conceptual model for interprofessional education: The International Classification of Functioning, Disability and Health (ICF). *Journal of Interprofessional Care, 20*(3), 235-245.

American Therapeutic Recreation Association. (2005). News release: ATRA affirms support for ICF. Retrieved May 24, 2007 from http://www.atra-tr.org/docs/ATRAICFsta tementNewsrelease.pdf.

Austin, D. R. (2005/2006). The changing contextualization of therapeutic recreation: A 40-year perspective. *Annual in Therapeutic Recreation, 14,* 1-11.

Bickenbach, J. E., Chatterji, S., Badley, E. M., & Üstün T. B. (1999). Models of disablement, universalism, and the international classification of impairments, disabilities ,and handicaps. *Social Science and Medicine, 48,* 1173-1187.

burlingame, j. (1998). Clinical models of practice. In F. Brasile, T. K. Skalko, & j. burlingame (Eds.), *Perspectives in recreational therapy: Issues of a dynamic profession* (pp. 83-106). Ravensdale, WA: Idyll Arbor.

burlingame, j., & Blaschko, T. M. (2002). *Assessment tools for recreational therapy and related fields* (3rd ed). Ravensdale, WA: Idyll Arbor.

Cieza, A., Ewert, T., Ustun, T. B., Chatterji, S., Kostanjsek, N., & Stucki, G. (2004). Development of ICF core sets for patients with chronic conditions. *Journal of Rehabilitation Medicine, Suppl. 44*, 9–11.

Hemmingsson, H., & Jonsson, H. (2005). An occupational perspective on the concept of participation in the International Classification of Functioning, Disability and Health: Some critical remarks. *American Journal of Occupational Therapy, 59*(5), 569-576.

Holloway, J.D. (2004). A new way of looking at health status. *Monitor on Psychology, 35*(1), 32.

Homa, D. B., & Peterson, D. B. (2005). Using the International Classification of Functioning, Disability, and Health (ICF) in teaching rehabilitation client assessment. *Rehabilitation Education, 19*(2-3), 119-128.

Howard, D., Browning, C., & Lee, Y. (2007). The International Classification of Functioning, Disability, and Health: Therapeutic recreation code sets and salient diagnostic core sets. *Therapeutic Recreation Journal, 51*(1), 61-81.

Nagi, S. Z. (1965). Some conceptual issues in disability and rehabilitation. In M. B. Sussman (Ed.), *Sociology and rehabilitation* (pp. 100-113). Washington, DC: American Sociological Association.

National Council for Therapeutic Recreation Certification. (2005). *Certification standards part V: NCTRC™ national job analysis.* New York: Author.

Peterson, D. B., & Rosenthal, D. A. (2005). The International Classification of Functioning, Disability, and Health (ICF): A primer for rehabilitation educators. *Rehabilitation Education, 19*(2-3), 81-89.

Porter, H. R., & burlingame, j. (2006). *Recreational therapy handbook of practice: ICF-based diagnosis and treatment.* Enumclaw, WA: Idyll Arbor.

Porter, H. R., & Van Puymbroeck, M. (2007). Introduction of the International Classification of Functioning, Disability, and Health to therapeutic recreation practice. *Therapeutic Recreation Journal, 51*(1), 47-60.

Sable, J., & Gravnik, J. (2005). The PATH to community for people with disabilities: A community-based therapeutic recreation service. *Therapeutic Recreation Journal, 39*(1), 78-87.

Schuntermann, M. F. (2005). The implementation of the International Classification of Functioning, Disability and Health in Germany: Experiences and problems. *International Journal of Rehabilitation Medicine, 28*(2), 93-102.

Shank, J., & Coyle, C. (2002). *Therapeutic recreation in health promotion and rehabilitation.* State College, PA: Venture Publishing.

Stambor, Z. (2006). Changing 's focus. *American Psychological Association Monitor on Psychology, 37*(1), 42.

Stucki, G. (2005). International Classification of Functioning, Disability, and Health (ICF): A promising framework and classification for rehabilitation medicine. *American Journal of Physical Medicine and Rehabilitation, 84*(10), 733-740.

Stucki, G., Cieza, A., Ewert, T. Kostanjsek, N., Chatterji, S., & Ustun, T.B. (2002). Application of the International Classification of Functioning, Disability, and Health (ICF) in clinical practice. *Disability and Rehabilitation, 24*(5), 281-282.

Stumbo, N. J., Carter, M. J., & Kim, J. (2004). 2003 national therapeutic recreation curriculum study part A: Accreditation, curriculum and internship characteristics. *Therapeutic Recreation Journal, 38,* 22-52.

Threats, T. (2007). Access for persons with neurogenic communication disorders: Influences of personal and environmental factors of the ICF. *Aphasiology, 21*(1), 67-80.

Ueda, S., & Okawa, Y. (2003). The subjective dimension of functioning and disability: What is it and what is it for? *Disability and Rehabilitation, 25*(11–12), 596 – 601.

Van Naarden Braun, K., Yeargin-Allsopp, M., & Lollar, D. (2006). Factors associated with leisure activity among young adults with developmental disabilities. *Research in Developmental Disabilities, 27,* 567–583.

World Health Organization. (2001). *International classification of functioning, disability, and health.* Geneva, Switzerland: author.

CHAPTER 5

Multicultural Diversity and Competence in Therapeutic Recreation

Charlsena F. Stone, Ph.D., LRT/CTRS
The University of North Carolina at Greensboro

Fortunately, the time has long passed when people liked to regard the United States as some kind of melting pot, taking men and women from every part of the world and converting them into standardized, homogenized Americans. We are, I think, much more mature and wise today. Just as we welcome a world of diversity, so we glory in an America of diversity—an America all the richer for the many different and distinctive strands of which it is woven (Hubert Humphrey, 1967, para. 1).

Humphrey's 41-year-old quote reflects how many Americans feel about the issue of diversity; however, significant attitudinal, policy, and practice barriers still restrain a number of minority groups from receiving equitable services. The subject of cultural competence has recently emerged as part of a strategy to reduce disparities in access to and the provision of quality health and human services. Since this is an up-and-coming issue, efforts to define and implement the principles of cultural competence in therapeutic recreation (TR) are ongoing. To provide a framework for discussion and examples of practical approaches to cultural competence, this chapter will provide current definitions of cultural competence and multiculturalism and identify the need for culturally competent service provision in TR. The chapter will also explore diversity issues related to TR education and TR practice as well as offer practical strategies to develop and enhance cultural competence of therapeutic recreation specialists (TRSs).

Changing Demographic Statistics in America

The demographics in the United States have changed and are projected to continue to become more culturally diverse. The U.S. Census Bureau (2000) identified approximately 20 percent of the total U.S. population as racial or ethnic minorities and predicted that percentage to increase to 40 percent by 2030. The 2000 Census also counted a total of 72.3 million families in America and found that 28.9 percent of them (about two in every seven families) reported having at least one member with a disability (U.S. Census Bureau, 2005). Additionally, the Administration on Aging (2007) reported that persons 65 years or older numbered 36.8 million in 2005. They represented 12.4 percent of the U.S. population in 2000, or about one in every eight Americans. They projected the older adult population will grow to be 20 percent of the total population by 2030. According to the Institute for the Future (2003), this dramatic demographic shift is occurring due to the aging baby boomers, the increase in racial and ethnic minorities, the increased disparities between the rich and the poor, and the challenge of disease. With these and many other demographic changes has come an increased demand for culturally sensitive and competent therapeutic recreation services.

What is Cultural Competence?

As a result of these changing demographics, cultural competence has become a commonly discussed concept among scholars and practitioners. However, the area of cultural competence in general suffers from a lack of agreed-upon definition, and what constitutes a culturally competent professional is also unclear. Not even the term "cultural competence" is universally accepted. Experts speak of cultural awareness, cultural diversity, cultural sensitivity, and other concepts (Fortier, 1999). Cultural competence is defined as a "continuous, developmental process of pursuing cultural awareness, knowledge, skills, encounters, sensitivity, and linkages among services and people" (Smith, 1998, p. 8). Cultural competence in healthcare, however, describes the ability of systems to provide equitable care to patients with diverse values, beliefs, and behaviors, including tailoring delivery to meet patients' social, cultural, and linguistic needs (Betancourt, Green, & Carrillo, 2002). Cultural competency implies that therapeutic recreation specialists and agencies are responsive to the cultural differences of their clients and that diversity is valued and acknowledged by their efforts to meet their clients' needs.

Holland (1997) described multiculturalism as a concept that implies that appropriate consideration be given to physical and emotional disabilities, ethnic and racial cultural diversity, as well as poverty and native languages. The concept of multiculturalism includes issues such as racism, sexism, ableism, anti-Semitism, classism, heterosexism, and homophobia. Multicultural competence is a unique category of awareness, knowledge, and skills that enables a system, agency, or professional to work effectively in cross-cultural situations (Harris-Davis & Haughton, 2000). Multicultural competence, according to Sylvester, Voelkl, and Ellis (2001), means becoming a professional who is capable of helping people from different cultures meet their needs and achieve well-being as they understand it. Clearly, it is crucial for therapeutic recreation specialists to achieve multicultural competence as we attempt to meet the needs and expectations of the diverse groups that we serve. However, before addressing strategies useful to enhance multicultural competence in TR, it is essential to identify and examine barriers that currently exist that reduce TRSs' ability to provide culturally competent services.

Barriers to Culturally Competent Care in Therapeutic Recreation

America's increasing cultural diversity and issues of race, ethnicity, socioeconomic status, gender, sexual orientation, age, religion, and physical or mental disabilities complicate the ability of therapeutic recreation specialists to deliver effective client-centered care. Barriers among clients or patients, therapeutic recreation specialists (TRSs), and the U.S. healthcare system or human service system in general that potentially could affect quality and contribute to disparities in care for minorities include: (a) lack of diversity in leadership and workforce of therapeutic recreation, (b) systems of care that are poorly designed to meet the needs of diverse populations, and (c) poor communication between TRSs and clients of different racial, ethnic, or cultural backgrounds (Betancourt, Green, & Carrillo, 2002). According to Donini-Lenhoff and Hedrick (2000), "ignorance of cultural issues, lack of knowledge, language differences—whether on the part of the caregiver or that of the patient—all serve as barriers to access to a uniform standard of healthcare for every American" (p. 241). Competent use of language and effective communication are crucial to an effective relationship between TRSs and their clients or patients.

Cooke (2004) also spoke of barriers that exist for therapeutic recreation specialists serving such a diverse group of clients. She stated that many providers do not understand that different cultures view authority, pain, wellness and illness, home remedy, and seeking help differently. Some may view medical providers as the authority figure, while others view their family members as the decision makers. Still others may not seek help for their problems because of transportation, accessibility, or safety issues. These and other barriers can potentially impact minorities' "movement toward or away from seeking medical attention" (Cooke, 2004, p. 27). Cooke (2004) asked a couple of very important questions, including, "What does diversity mean, and why is it important?" "What can the recreation therapy profession do to address the issues related to diversity in the groups that we serve and within our own ranks?" (p. 25). An additional question she asked is, "What can TR educators do to prepare TR students to deliver culturally competent services?"

Diversity Issues and Efforts Related to TR Education

Many therapeutic recreation specialists, administrators, and educators are beginning to recognize the importance of eliminating these barriers and addressing Cooke's questions. For example, TR accrediting agencies are developing educational standards that address cultural competence, and recreation and park professional associations are developing strategies and implementing initiatives to "create a citizen and professional membership reflective of America's diverse population" (NRPA Vision 2010 Strategic Plan, 2001). Additionally, the TR certification agency has identified cultural diversity as a required functional knowledge domain for TRSs to possess in order to provide competent care. First, we will examine how TR accrediting agencies are addressing this very important issue, and then we will examine national TR certification standards relative to cultural competence.

Program Accreditation Efforts in TR Related to Diversity

Accreditation is a process by which an institution, agency, organization, or program is certified as meeting or exceeding specific standards or competencies (see Chapter 9). Zabriskie

(1998) described two forms of accreditation, including institutionalized accreditation and specialized accreditation. Institutionalized accreditation examines the entire institution to confirm that the institution fulfills its mission and is equal to comparable institutions in quality. Specialized accreditation applies to a particular occupational field where there is a recognized professional degree at either the baccalaureate or graduate levels. Therapeutic recreation is recognized by the National Recreation and Park Association/American Association for Leisure and Recreation (NRPA/AALR) Council on Accreditation as a specialty area, and NRPA/AALR accredits institutions of higher education in therapeutic recreation. The Council approved a new professional standard in TR in October 1999 related to multiculturalism. Specifically, Standard 9D.03 states that therapeutic recreation professionals must possess an "understanding of the significance of multiculturalism in therapeutic recreation" (NRPA/AALR, 2004, p. 21). Thus, every accredited TR curriculum is expected to provide primary coverage in at least one course that meets this standard.

Certification Efforts in TR Related to Diversity

The National Council for Therapeutic Recreation Certification™ (NCTRC™) establishes evaluative standards for certification and recertification of professions, grants certification to individuals who voluntarily apply and meet established criteria, and monitors adherence to these standards by certified therapeutic recreation specialists. In 2007 NCTRC™ completed its third Job Analysis study and developed important tasks and knowledge areas deemed necessary for competent practice in TR. One of the required functional knowledge domains for TRSs to possess is knowledge of diversity factors, such as social, cultural, educational, language, spiritual, financial, age, attitude, and geographic location (NCTRC, 2007).

Remaining Accreditation and Certification Issues in TR Related to Diversity

Regardless of these TR curricular requirements, TRSs have limited exposure and training in areas needed to provide them with these required knowledge and skill areas (Lee & Skalko, 1996; Peregoy & Dieser, 1997; Stone, 2003). Sheldon and Dattilo (1997) reviewed professional journals and textbooks in TR and found a limited number of references to ethnic, racial, religious, or other dimensions of cultural diversity that could indicate a lack of importance or value on diversity issues in TR. They further stated that references that were made often assumed the reader understood multicultural diversity language, which may not be the case for many TR professionals.

Dieser and Peregoy (1998) indicated more than one-half of all graduate-level park and recreation programs do not have multicultural program requirements. Of the 40 programs surveyed, only 13 (32.5%) had curriculum requirements regarding issues of service for individuals from different cultural backgrounds. More recently, Blair and Coyle (2005) used a stratified random sample of CTRSs provided by NCTRC™ (N=156) and found 41 percent of those surveyed had not taken any multicultural courses (n=64), and 39 percent had taken only one multicultural course (n=61). Similarly, they found almost 58 percent of TRSs had not attended any multicultural workshops (n=90), and almost 20 percent had attended only one multicultural workshop (n=31). Not only are few TR students being trained in multiculturalism, but TR educators themselves have typically not received multicultural training in their professional education.

Stone and Gladwell (2004) found that of a random sample of 33 TR educators that were nationally surveyed, only 40 percent had taken two or more multicultural courses during their academic training (n=13). So the question becomes, how can aspiring TR professionals acquire the multicultural knowledge required by our accrediting bodies? And why is this requirement not being enforced more fully?

Many therapeutic recreation program personnel in higher education would respond that multicultural information is infused into other courses offered in their program. Blair and Coyle (2005) reported that 55 percent of TR higher education programs infused multicultural information into other courses. This begs the question, however, is it conceivable that sufficient multicultural knowledge and skills can be acquired simply by being infused into other required courses such as Assessment in TR or Facilitation Techniques in TR? Also, what does "infused" mean? Does the instructor talk about diversity for one class period, or is everything covered throughout the semester presented with issues, challenges, and diverse examples for the students to integrate into their knowledge and attitude base?

Professional Associations' and Publication Efforts in TR Related to Diversity

Therapeutic recreation professional associations have also made formal commitments that support multiculturalism. Both the American Therapeutic Recreation Association (ATRA) and the National Therapeutic Recreation Society (NTRS) have developed education and training resources—including books, videos, and articles in professional journals—to help TR programs and practitioners comply with educational standards and guidelines. ATRA published *Diversity: Case Studies in Healthcare* (Getz, Hironaka-Juteau, & Melcher, 2005) and *Guidelines for Competency Assessment and Curriculum Planning for Recreational Practice* (West, Kinney, & Witman, 2008). Getz, Hironaka-Juteau, and Melcher (2005) presented case studies in healthcare to provide therapeutic recreation specialists the ability to reflect on, develop, and enhance their cultural competencies. The new *Guidelines for Competency Assessment and Curriculum Planning for Recreational Therapy Practice* (West, Kinney, & Witman, 2008) specifies such competencies as "Ability to apply knowledge of multicultural considerations when implementing treatment." (p. 14)

The *Standards for the Practice of Therapeutic Recreation and Self-Assessment Guide* (ATRA, 2007a) was developed by ATRA to provide a comprehensive set of practice guidelines for the field of therapeutic recreation. Within these practice guidelines are standards related to diversity in the following areas:

- generating "culturally appropriate baseline data" through the assessment process (Standard 1.1.2 - p. 9);
- including treatment planning goals reflective of the cultural background and values of the patient/client (Standard 2.1.4);
- incorporating "strategies and interventions that are sensitive to the cultural values and beliefs of the clients" (Standard 2.2.3, p. 11);
- implementing intervention strategies appropriate to "diagnostic and individual characteristics to age, cultural and socioeconomic factors" (Standard 3.1.2.2, p. 13); and
- having recreation and play facilities, equipment and activities that are "available, accessible and appropriate to patient's/client's needs, abilities/disabilities, and cultural differences/similarities (Standard 6.1.2, p. 19).

The board of directors of ATRA approved a Statement on Diversity in March 2006 that reflects the association's ongoing commitment to advancing diversity within TR. The association promotes "diverse and inclusive participation by its leaders, members and affiliates" and "works to educate its membership about diversity issues" (ATRA, 2006). The American Therapeutic Recreation Association's Office of Advocacy has a diversity team whose charge is to examine the diversity needs of its membership as it relates to their direct practice and to provide educational strategies to assist members in their practice. The Diversity Team works with the treatment networks, and other teams such as those for the Clinical Practice Guidelines, Academic Affairs, Standards of Practice, and Research to "identify and facilitate methods of integrating diversity issues into planning documents and delivery of service guidelines" (ATRA, 2007b).

> ATRA is beginning to "put its money where its mouth is" with strategies to support their diversity efforts. ATRA's Award Team recently announced the establishment of the Linda Levine Madori Single-Parent Scholarship. This scholarship was developed to defray the costs associated with attending the ATRA annual conference for two individuals each year. Any single parent who is also a member of ATRA, either student or professional, is eligible to apply for this scholarship. Information concerning this scholarship can be accessed on ATRA's website at http://atra-online.com/cms/index.php?option=com_content&task=view&id=52 &Itemid=29 (ATRA, 2008).

The National Recreation and Park Association (NRPA), the parent organization to NTRS, has also begun to address the issue of cultural competency. In May 2003, the NRPA Board of Trustees revised the nondiscrimination statement in the NRPA bylaws to be more inclusive:

> The National Association and its branches and affiliates does not discriminate on the basis of race, disability, religion, color, national origin, age, sex, covered veterans status, marital status, personal appearance, sexual orientation, family responsibilities, political affiliation, source of income, place of business or residence, pregnancy, childbirth, or any other unlawful basis. This policy is in compliance with Title VII of the Civil Rights Act, the Americans with Disabilities Act, and the Age Discrimination in Employment Act. (NRPA, 2003)

The NRPA Board of Trustees also adopted the following statement:

> We believe that NRPA's Board of Trustees should be reflective of the NRPA membership and the United States diverse population. Our intention is be as inclusive as possible. Every effort should be made to ensure representation of historically underrepresented groups such as women and racial and ethnic minorities on the Board of Trustees and its Executive Committee. (NRPA, 2003)

NRPA is also beginning to "put its money where its mouth is" with strategies to support its strategic plan, such as allocating financial resources to support its new vision. It has developed the NRPA Diversity Scholarship, which is designed to provide professionals, citizens, and students of ethnic minorities with the opportunity to attend the NRPA Congress and Exposition. The goal of this scholarship is to encourage attendance by members of ethnic minorities who would not otherwise be able to attend. NRPA provides up to four professional or citizen complimentary full-package registrations and four student full-package registrations through this scholarship program. Information concerning this scholarship program can be accessed on NRPA's website (NRPA, 2006). It is interesting, however, that only ethnic minorities are eligible for this scholarship, especially considering the nondiscrimination statement in the NRPA bylaws that includes other dimensions of diversity, including not only race, but also disability, religion, age, sex, marital status, and sexual orientation to name just a few.

Publications on the topic of cultural diversity and multicultural competency in therapeutic recreation are also appearing more often in journals, such as the *Therapeutic Recreation Journal, American Journal of Recreational Therapy, Annual in Therapeutic Recreation, Journal of Park and Recreation Administration, SCHOLE, and Parks and Recreation.*

The codes of ethics of both ATRA and NTRS address the importance of cultural competency in therapeutic recreation as well. According to Principle 3 (Justice) of The *ATRA Code of Ethics* (ATRA, 2001):

> Therapeutic recreation personnel are responsible for ensuring that individuals are served fairly and that there is equity in the distribution of services. Individuals receive service without regard to race, color, creed, gender, sexual orientation, age, disability/disease, social and financial status.

Principle II: The Obligation of the Professional to the Individual (C. 2. Cultural Beliefs and Practices) of the *NTRS Code of Ethics* (NTRS, 2001) states:

> Professionals respect cultural diversity and provide services that are responsive to the cultural backgrounds and needs of clients. They use "person-first" language to acknowledge and honor individual uniqueness above any disability, illness, impairment, or condition.

Under Principle VI: The Obligation of the Profession to Society (B. Equality) of the *NTRS Code of Ethics* (NTRS, 2001):

> The profession is committed to equality of opportunity. No person shall be refused service because of race, gender, religion, social status, ethnic background, religious preference, or sexual orientation. Therapeutic recreation specialists support affordable healthcare services to persons currently without coverage or the means to pay for services. Additionally, they are committed to pro bono work that offers some relief for those unable to pay.

Remaining Professional Association and Publication Issues in TR Related to Diversity

Although the national TR professional associations are supporting diversity through many of these efforts, the question becomes "is this information being integrated in pre-service training, in-service training, and continuing education activities, or is it purely policy development?" It is unclear whether or how often these resources are being used as required texts or as supplemental guides by TR educators. It is also unclear to what extent they are being utilized by TR specialists. Therapeutic recreation specialists and students are in the position to move beyond policy development to reach a point where procedures can be implemented to address diversity issues. For example, TR students and professionals should be encouraged to join existing diversity teams or committees within our professional organizations. When these teams or committees do not exist, TR students and professionals must be willing to start them.

Diversity Issues Related to Therapeutic Recreation Practice

Now that we have examined diversity issues related to TR education, it is critical to explore the issue from the TR practice perspective. One of the major diversity issues with respect to therapeutic recreation practice is the lack of diversity among professionals working in the field. The National Council for Therapeutic Recreation Certification™ (2007) conducted a comprehensive study of Certified Therapeutic Recreation Specialists™ (CTRSs™) in order to create a demographic profile of CTRSs™ in the United States. The results substantiate the lack of diversity in our field with respect to race/ethnicity and gender. NCTRC™ reported only 15 percent of a national sample of 979 CTRSs™ were male and only 10 percent racial or ethnic minority. Nearly 60 percent of the CTRSs™ were between 23 and 39 years of age (n=587). NCTRC™'s study reveals that our profession is comprised mainly of young, Caucasian females, yet we are serving more diverse communities.

Gossett (2007) led a session at The University of Toledo Spring Workshop entitled *Developing Cultural Competence in Therapeutic Recreation* and cited Dr. Floyd Shoemaker's description of a world that included only 100 people. If the population of the earth was reduced to a village of 100 people, with all the existing human ratios remaining the same, there would be 57 Asians, 21 Europeans, 14 from the Western hemisphere, and eight Africans. Fifty percent of the entire world's wealth would be in the hands of only six people, all of whom would be from the United States. Of the 100 people, 70 would be persons of color, 30 would be white, 30 would be Christian, and 70 would be from other faiths, 70 would not be able to read, 50 would suffer from malnutrition, 80 would live in substandard housing, and only one would have a university education. When the world is considered from such a compressed perspective, the need for cultural competence in TR becomes glaringly apparent (Gossett, 2007). What is now needed in the field of TR is research that details the diverse make-up of the clients that we serve.

The lack of diversity among CTRSs and the extreme diversity that exists among the clients and patients that we serve presents an issue in our field, not only in terms of race and ethnicity, but also in terms of age, disability, religion, and sexual orientation, to name just a few. Sylvester, Voelkl, and Ellis (2001) noted another issue that exists within the field of therapeutic recreation, a profession which advocates the principle of inclusion as it pertains to persons with disabilities, is that we have "not sufficiently incorporated inclusion, or multiculturalism, into its theory and practice" (p. 35).

Thus, there is much to do in terms of training. Concerted efforts are needed in TR to recruit and increase the number of minority students into our TR curricula/profession. It is also important to consider the misconception held by minorities (not just racial and ethnic minorities) and non-minorities that minorities are more culturally competent across the board than they really are. Anderson and Stone (2005) indicated that although minorities may know more about one minority culture, "that does not automatically make them more knowledgeable about all cultures" (p. 71).

It is also important to examine the cultural competency levels of TR practitioners. Stone (2003) indicated that CTRSs self-reported moderate levels of multicultural competencies, particularly in the areas of multicultural skills and counseling relationships, and somewhat lower levels in the areas of multicultural awareness and multicultural knowledge. Blair and Coyle (2005) reported similar findings with CTRSs self-reporting higher levels of multicultural competencies in the area of counseling relationships and lower levels in the area of multicultural awareness. These results lead to the question: "How can CTRSs possess moderate levels of multicultural skills and the ability to develop multicultural counseling relationships when they do not possess at least comparable multicultural awareness and multicultural knowledge?"

What Happens to Clients when TRSs are not Culturally Competent?

The reasons for incorporating cultural competence into pre-service, in-service, and continuing education TR training programs are numerous. The National Center for Cultural Competence (NCCC), housed in Washington, D.C. within Georgetown University's Center for Child and Human Development, provides national leadership and contributes to the body of knowledge on cultural and linguistic competency within systems and organizations. The NCCC's major emphasis is on translating evidence into policy and practice for programs and personnel concerned with the delivery of health and mental health, administration, education, and advocacy (NCCC, 2007a). The Center identified six reasons why cultural competence is important for inclusion in organizational policy. Cultural competence is needed in order to:

- respond to current and projected demographic changes in the U.S.;
- eliminate longstanding disparities in the health status of people of diverse racial, ethnic and cultural backgrounds;
- improve the quality of services and health outcomes;
- meet legislative, regulatory, and accreditation mandates;
- gain a competitive edge in the market place; and,
- decrease the likelihood of liability/malpractice claims (NCCC, 2007b).

The Center's reasons for cultural competence apply to the field of therapeutic recreation. The current and project demographic changes in the U.S. impact our field in the same manner that it is impacting other disciplines. The health status disparities of minorities, as discussed earlier in this chapter, also negatively impact the provision of TR services.

Moreover, the TR definitions provided by both national professional organizations include statements relative to improving health and well-being. In fact, the true essence of TR is to implement the TR process in order to improve functional abilities, health, and overall quality of life. TR providers must understand the beliefs that shape their clients' approach to health and illness, whether the clients are minorities or non-minorities. Knowledge of customs and traditions are crucial to the design of TR interventions. As discussed earlier, our professional organizations and credentialing agencies have produced standards of practice and regulatory and accreditation mandates designed to guide the delivery of culturally competent TR services. Finally, TR programs and organizations potentially run the risk of facing liability claims that their failure to understand and adhere to their clients' beliefs, practices, and behaviors breaches professional standards of care.

So what can or does happen to our clients and patients when we are not culturally competent? Cultural factors are essential to diagnosis, treatment, and care. They shape health-related beliefs, behaviors, and values (Kleinman & Benson, 2006). We must move beyond the "one-size-fits-all" mentality in terms of TR assessment, program design, implementation, and evaluation. If therapeutic recreation specialists appear insensitive to cultural differences or if they ignore cultural influences, they potentially can limit any expectations of success in reaching their pre-established outcomes. If a minority client or patient practices a different religion from the "norm," he/she may have different ways of living his/her life, expressing concerns, or relaying information. For example, many Muslim women choose not to participate in breast cancer screening programs due to spiritual and religious beliefs (Mitchell, Lannin, Mathews, & Swanson, 2002). Some Muslims may tend to be passive in the presence of authority figures and will not make any decisions in isolation of their families (American Psychiatric Association, 2005). Cooke (2004) described yet another healthcare disparity for lesbians and homosexual males who choose not to seek medical care due to their fear of being "the target of homophobia" (p. 27). Culturally competent TR students, practitioners, and educators cannot make negative assumptions about minorities groups based on their cultural differences. Being culturally competent decreases the likelihood of making erroneous assumptions. We must be willing to adjust our attitudes and behaviors to account for our clients' cultural backgrounds and ways of viewing the world. If not, potentially we detract from our clients' unique paths to valued TR outcomes.

Practical Strategies for Enhancing Cultural Competence of TRSs

If we are to become culturally competent as stipulated in our practice standards and codes of ethics, then it is critical for TR practitioners and TR educators to take the responsibility to ensure that we become so (Blair & Coyle, 2005). Sheldon and Dattilo (1997) advocated the use of the following strategies for enhancing cultural competence of TRS: a) working in multicultural settings; b) examining your own biases; c) learning about the community; d) examining your language; e) considering the interaction of families; and, f) learning about individuals and individual differences. The American Therapeutic Recreation Association (2000) also offered the following suggestions for increasing cultural competence: a) attending conferences on the topic; b) seeking out individuals from backgrounds other than your own; c) reading books which are written about a variety of cultures; d) seeking out information from the professional TR organizations; (e) seeking diversity training at work; and f) going to the library to conduct research under the terms: multicultural education, diversity education, health and culture, multicultural counseling, and trans-cultural nursing. Stumbo and Hoss (2007) suggested that TR professionals must consider cultural competency as an equally important skill as any other standard of practice. In fact, Stumbo and Hoss stated that cultural competency must be implemented daily "so that it becomes an automatic response to the populations served" (p. 100). Each of us should evaluate our own individual performance in each of these suggested areas, and if we are not currently adhering to these suggestions, then we should make a concrete plan to do so in order to increase our cultural competence levels.

There is a definite need for TR educators to comprehensively and consistently deliver multicultural information in TR curricula (Blair & Coyle, 2005). Therapeutic recreation educators should carefully consider how to incorporate multicultural education into their TR program. Questions exist as to whether multicultural issues can be appropriately addressed in specific courses or incorporated into the curriculum of many courses. Identifying specific characteristics or experiences that make people more competent with culturally diverse clients warrant investigation in therapeutic recreation. These questions suggest a call for development of a uniform cultural diversity education curricula and accompanying training components for therapeutic recreation students. A logical first step in the curriculum development process is to scrutinize more closely the component of existing course-based cultural diversity training efforts in therapeutic recreation professional preparation programs, both within TR specifically as well as general education courses.

It is our responsibility to offer pre-service opportunities for TR students that will prepare them to provide culturally sensitive services to the clients they will serve. It is equally important for practicing TR professionals to be provided continuing education and in-service opportunities to prepare them to provide culturally sensitive TR services. In essence, culturally competent pre-service education, in-service training, and continuing education opportunities are vital prerequisites and are as equally important as the culturally sensitive services that we provide to our clients/patients. Without one or the other, TRSs cannot have truly culturally sensitive service provision. It is important that TR students as well as practitioners take this issue seriously now rather than later.

Diversity education alone is not enough to meet the challenges of diversity and enhancing cultural competence of TRSs, whether it is pre-service, in-service, or continuing education. It is also important to recruit and commit to hiring members of minority and marginalized groups into the field of TR. The current lack of diversity that exists in the work force of TRSs, in essence, denies TR consumers opportunities for role models and TRSs with whom they can relate. It stands to reason that minority clients or patients will feel more comfortable with TRSs who can understand their cultural background in terms of customs, attitudes, and beliefs as they relate to health and wellness. This does not necessarily mean that individuals from the same background or minority group should be confined to treating clients/patients from their same background or minority group. However, a more diverse workforce would provide us with a unique opportunity to learn from each other and increase our own cultural awareness and professional development.

Remaining Cultural Competence Questions and Concerns in TR

Despite the advances that have been made in TR by professional organizations, accreditation and certification agencies, as well as TR curricula across the country relative to cultural diversity, there are many questions and concerns that still remain. For example, we need more detailed information on the content and length of courses being offered by therapeutic recreation educational institutions and programs. To what extent are courses in history, race relations, sociology, psychology, and other "traditional" courses incorporating content that will prepare TR students to function effectively in an increasingly diverse society and work environment? How are accrediting and certifying bodies assessing the outcomes of existing requirements so that revised requirements may be more effective? How are professional associations ensuring that experienced TR practitioners are including and presenting up-to-date cultural competency topics in their continuing education activities? How are accrediting agencies, professional associations, and educational institutions assessing the impacts of their cultural diversity initiative? There are no easy or readily available answers to these questions. However, we cannot move forward to becoming culturally competent TRSs if we are unwilling to seek out the answers.

Summary

This chapter examined ongoing diversity efforts and remaining issues that exist within TR education and practice. Efforts have been made by credentialing bodies to ensure that TR professionals are culturally competent, such as establishing accreditation and certification standards and guidelines specific to multicultural education and training. Professional associations have also initiated practical strategies to enhance the cultural competence of TR professionals, such as publishing diversity-related materials and resources for use by students, educators, and professionals. While therapeutic recreation professionals are headed in the right direction with regard to cultural competence, the field still needs to make additional progress. The more culturally competent TR providers there are in our agencies and communities, the better the health and human services we can provide and outcomes we can expect for our clients and patients.

Discussion Questions

1. What is our ethical and professional responsibility related to cultural competency in the field of TR? How should we acquire the knowledge and skills necessary to become culturally competent in TR service delivery? What are additional strategies that can be used to increase the cultural competencies of TR professionals and students?
2. Why do you think there are so few minorities in the TR field, including males, racial or ethnic minorities, people with disabilities/illnesses, people from different religious backgrounds and sexual preferences? What can be done to recruit and retain minorities in TR?
3. Check out the non-discrimination policies of your university or agency. What type(s) of "support" exists, if any, for individuals from minority groups that might

be subjected to discriminatory acts, such as those who are poor, gay/lesbian/ transgendered, Muslim (or members of some other religious group)?

4. You are the executive director for your agency. How will you ensure the cultural competence of your staff?

5. In what ways is the lack of cultural competence harmful to clients and TR service delivery? In what ways is cultural competence beneficial in TR?

References

Administration on Aging. (2007). *Statistics on the aging population.* Retrieved December 7, 2006, from http://www.aoa.gov/prof/Statistics/statistics.asp

American Psychiatric Association. (2005). Treatment should consider religious beliefs. *Psychiatric News, 40*(2), 13.

American Therapeutic Recreation Association. (2001). *ATRA Code of Ethics.* Alexandria, VA. Retrieved July 14, 2008, from the American Therapeutic Recreation Association Web site: http://atra-online.com/cms/index.php?option=com_content&task=view&id=19&Ite mid=9

American Therapeutic Recreation Association. (2000). *Diversity and therapeutic recreation: Where to start, what to do.* Alexandria, VA: author.

American Therapeutic Recreation Association. (2008). *Linda Levine Madori single-parent scholarship.* Alexandria, VA. Retrieved July 16, 2008, from http://atra-online.com/ cms/index.php?option=com_content&task=view&id=52&Itemid=29

American Therapeutic Recreation Association. (2007b). *Office of advocacy: Diversity board direction statement.* Alexandria, VA. Retrieved January 10, 2007, from http://www. atra-tr.org/leadershipdiversity.htm

American Therapeutic Recreation Association. (2007a). *Standards for the practice of therapeutic recreation and self-assessment guide.* Alexandria, VA: author.

American Therapeutic Recreation Association. (2006). *Statement on diversity.* Alexandria, VA: American Therapeutic Recreation Association. Retrieved January 10, 2007, from http:// www.atra-tr.org/About%20ATRA/ATRA%20Statement%20on%20Diversity.doc

Anderson, D. M., & Stone, C. F. (2005). Cultural competencies of park and recreation professionals: A case study of North Carolina. *Journal of Park and Recreation Administration, 23*(1), 53-74.

Betancourt, J. R., Green, A. R., & Carrillo, J. E. (2002). *Cultural competence in healthcare: Emerging frameworks and practical approaches.* Retrieved December 12, 2006, from http:// www.vdh.virginia.gov/ohpp/clasact/documents/clasact/general/culturealcompetence.pdf

Blair, D. K., & Coyle, C. (2005). An examination of multicultural competencies of entry-level Certified Therapeutic Recreation Specialists. *Therapeutic Recreation Journal, 39*(2), 139-157.

Cooke, C. A. (2004). Diversity in therapeutic recreation: Why now? *American Journal of Recreation Therapy, 3*(3), 25-29.

Dieser, R. B., & Peregoy, J. J. (1998). Multicultural training in parks and recreation education programs. *Parks and Recreation, 33*(3), 37-44.

Donini-Lenhoff, F. G., & Hedrick, H. L. (2000). Increasing awareness and implementation of cultural competence principles in health professions education. *Journal of Allied Health, 29*(4), 241-245.

Fortier, J. P. (1999). *Multicultural health best practices overview.* Silver Springs, MD: Resources for Cross Cultural Healthcare. Retrieved November 11, 2007, from http://www.diversityrx.org/BEST/1_6.htm

Getz, D., Hironaka-Juteau, J., & Melcher, S. (2005). *Diversity case studies in healthcare.* Alexandria, VA: American Therapeutic Recreation Association.

Gossett, J. (2007). *Developing cultural competence in therapeutic recreation.* Paper presented at the University of Toledo Spring Workshop, Toledo, OH.

Harris-Davis, E., & Haughton, B. (2000). Model for multicultural nutrition counseling competencies. *Journal of the American Dietetic Association, 100*(10), 1178-1185.

Holland, J. (1997). Enhancing multicultural sensitivity through teaching multiculturally in recreation. *Parks and Recreation, 32*(5), 42-50.

Humphrey, H. H. (1967). *All-American tribute to Archbishop Iakovos speech.* Hubert H. Humphrey Quote Page. Chicago, IL. Retrieved December 8, 2006, from http://home.att.net/~howington/hhh.html

Institute for the Future. (2003). *Health and healthcare 2010: The forecast, the challenge.* San Francisco: Jossey-Bass.

Kleinmann, A., & Benson, P. (2006). Culture, moral experience and medicine. *The Mount Sinai Journal of Medicine, 73*(6), 834-839.

Lee, Y. L., & Skalko, T. K. (1996). Multicultural sensitivity: An innovative mind-set in therapeutic recreation practice. *Parks and Recreation, 31*, 24, 26, 28, 30, 32-35.

Mitchell, J., Lannin, D. R., Mathews, H. F., & Swanson, M. S. (2002). Religious beliefs and breast cancer screening. *Journal of Women's Health, 11*(10), 907-915.

National Center for Cultural Competence. (2007a). *Things we do.* Georgetown University Center for Child and Human Development, Washington D.C. Retrieved July 14, 2008, from http://www11.georgetown.edu/research/gucchd/nccc/foundations/need.html

National Center for Cultural Competence. (2007b). *The compelling need for cultural and linguistic competence.* Georgetown University Center for Child and Human Development, Washington D.C. Retrieved July 14, 2008, from http://www11.georgetown.edu/research/gucchd/nccc/foundations/need.html

National Council for Therapeutic Recreation Certification. (2007). *Certification Standards Part V: NCTRC™ National Job Analysis.* National Council for Therapeutic Recreation Certification. New City, NY. Retrieved July 14, 2008, from http://www.nctrc.org/documents/5JobAnalysis_000.pdf

National Recreation and Park Association. (2001). *Vision 2010: A strategic plan for the future.* Retrieved November 11, 2007, from http://www.nrpa.org/content/default.aspx?documentId=492

National Recreation and Park Association. (2003). *National Recreation and Park Association by-laws: Non-discrimination statement.* Retrieved November 11, 2007, from http://www.nrpa.org/content/default.aspx?documentId=1259

National Recreation and Park Association/American Association for Leisure and Recreation, Council on Accreditation. (2004). Standards and evaluative criteria for baccalaureate programs in recreation, park resources and leisure services. National Recreation and Park Association/American Association for Leisure and Recreation, Council on Accreditation. Retrieved November 11, 2007, from http://www.nrpa.org/content/default. aspx?documentId=1010

National Recreation and Park Association. (2006). *NRPA diversity scholarship*. Retrieved November 11, 2007, from http://www.nrpa.org/content/default.aspx?documentId=4325

National Therapeutic Recreation Society. (2001). *National Therapeutic Recreation Society Code of Ethics and Interpretive Guidelines*. Ashburn, VA: National Therapeutic Recreation Society. Retrieved November 11, 2007, from http://www.nrpa.org/content/default. aspx?documentId=867

Peregoy, J. J., & Dieser, R. B. (1997). Multicultural awareness in therapeutic recreation: Hamlet living. *Therapeutic Recreation Journal, 31*(3), 174-188.

Sheldon, K., & Dattilo, J. (1997). Multiculturalism in therapeutic recreation: Terminology clarification and practical suggestions. *Therapeutic Recreation Journal, 31*(3), 146-159.

Smith, L. S. (1998). Concept analysis: Cultural competence. *Journal of Cultural Diversity, 5*(1), 4-10.

Stone, C. F. (2003). Exploring cultural competencies of Certified Therapeutic Recreation Specialists: Implications for education and training. *Therapeutic Recreation Journal, 37*(2), 156-174.

Stone, C. F., & Gladwell, N. J. (2004). An investigation of multicultural awareness and sensitivity of therapeutic recreation educators. *American Journal of Recreation Therapy, 3*(1), 9-19.

Stumbo, N. J., & Hoss, M. K. (2007). Racial and ethnic disparities in healthcare —including therapeutic recreation services: Problems and potential solutions. *Annual in Therapeutic Recreation, 15*, 96-104.

Sylvester, C., Voelkl, J. E., & Ellis, G. D. (2001). *Therapeutic recreation programming: Theory and practice*. State College, PA: Venture Publishing.

United States Census Bureau. (July, 2005). *Disability and American Families: 2000*. Retrieved May 30, 2007 from, http://www.census.gov/prod/2005pubs/censr-23.pdf

United States Census Bureau. (2000). Retrieved November 11, 2007, from http://www. census.gov/statab/www/part1a.html

West, R. E., Kinney, T., & Witman, J. (2008). *Guidelines for competency assessment and curriculum planning for recreational therapy practice* (2nd ed.). Hattiesburg, MS: American Therapeutic Recreation Association.

Zabriskie, R. B. (1998). Accreditation: Are we there yet? Perspectives of a doctoral student. In B. A. Hawkins (Ed.), *Historical perspectives on the development of the NRPA/ AALR Council on Accreditation* (pp. 103-116). Ashburn, VA: National Recreation and Park Association.

CHAPTER 6

International Perspectives of Therapeutic Recreation

Heewon Yang, Ph.D., CTRS™
Southern Illinois University

Marjorie J. Malkin, Ed.D., CTRS™
Southern Illinois University

The TR profession in the U.S. has a relatively long history compared to other countries and may have served as a model for the development of TR elsewhere in the world. In fact, it is an interesting and intriguing task to examine how TR professions in other countries have evolved and developed. While TR in some countries has been developed within the context of their own unique political, economic, and sociocultural situations, TR in other countries seems to have grown somewhat prematurely without recognizing their own sociocultural history and potentials.

The philosophical and practical approaches to therapeutic recreation in one country may be very different from those in other countries. Examining the status, trends, and issues of TR in other countries and finding similarities and dissimilarities in the approaches and practices of TR among different countries can be a challenging exploration. In addition, it may provide an excellent opportunity to investigate ways for international TR professionals to network, collaborate, and learn from each other.

This chapter provides only limited information on the international perspectives in TR. Rather, the authors of this chapter attempt to raise some challenging questions regarding this important issue. The first section discusses the importance of having international and global perspectives of therapeutic recreation. In particular, the concept of globalization of a profession and its importance in global communication and networking and awareness in cultural and philosophical diversity are highlighted. The second section illustrates historical efforts and endeavors some organizations and individuals in the U.S. have made to promote international TR and the development of TR in other countries. The third section presents the current status of therapeutic recreation in countries outside the U.S. (i.e., Australia, Canada, Finland, New Zealand, Japan, and South Korea) and briefly discusses the issues and trends concerning therapeutic recreation in those countries. It should be noted that therapeutic recreation practices and/or movements are not limited to the aforementioned countries. Based on the information about therapeutic recreation in other countries, trends and issues associated with the unique development of therapeutic recreation in other countries are discussed, and lastly, conclusions and future challenges are indicated.

International and Multicultural Perspectives of Therapeutic Recreation

It would be interesting to count how many recreational activities and leisure pursuits are originally from the U.S. Except for some sports, such as basketball and football, most sports, recreation, and leisure activities are either from other cultures or are found in other parts of the world in at least similar forms. Many similar versions of hide-and-seek and simple tag games can be found across town and the world. Currently, the phenomena of cultural diffusion and worldwide exchanges are more evident due to technological advancements and global communication.

Residents of all countries now live in an emerging global society that ranges beyond the local, regional, and even national boundaries. In this global society, therapeutic recreation must also take place in a global community that consists of various people who have various cultural beliefs and cultural heritages. TR is one of the helping professions, and as its basis, TR involves a process of understanding (assessing) people (clients) who have different beliefs, values, functional capabilities, and social backgrounds in today's multicultural society (See chapter 5, Multicultural Diversity and Competence in Therapeutic Recreation).

In a sense, within this context, the process of assessing and understanding our clientele may be somewhat similar to the principles and processes in understanding different people in and from other countries.

It may be true that TR in the U.S. has been playing a critical role and has been a model case for the development of TR in other countries. For some countries, following the concepts and systems of TR in the U.S. (e.g., terminologies, content and process, educational systems, qualification and certification systems, and organizations) may have been the easiest and the most convenient way to develop their TR professions. While some TR professionals in the U.S. may feel proud and satisfied with their achievements and their leadership roles, the TR profession in the U.S. is also encountering many challenges such as an identity crisis, the uncertainty of a future direction, a lack of public awareness, a decreasing number of academic programs, and the shortage of qualified TR faculty in higher education. It is believed that the survival of TR in the U.S. and the future of TR in any nation could be more promising if TR professionals across the world adopt a global and cooperative world-view approach. More specifically, mutual understanding, collaboration, and learning from each other would brighten the future of TR/RT in the world. Also, exchanging and sharing each other's culture and resources may enrich and enhance the quality of TR services and quality of our clients' lives.

In addition, TR professional in the U.S. have an ethical obligation to provide professionals in other countries where TR is now emerging with necessary assistance and resources to promote more successful growth of the profession in these countries. More experienced American TR professionals need to be willing to offer and share their experiences, resources, and know-how with their counterparts in other countries. At the same time, TR professionals in the U.S. should possess a humble attitude to willingly learn from TR in other countries and appreciate different cultural, social, and historical heritages and the uniqueness of other countries.

Efforts and Issues Related to the International Therapeutic Recreation

In order to pursue the mutual learning and development of TR across the world, some efforts have been initiated both by some individuals and organizations in the States. For example, Gerald Hitzhusen played a critical role in establishing the *International Symposium on Therapeutic Recreation* (ISTR), which was based upon the model of the *Midwest Symposium on Therapeutic Recreation*. Both the University of Missouri and Indiana University have a history of collaborated efforts with social service agencies and educational institutions in England. As a result of the relationship and networking, the first ISTR was held in England in 1973. Since the first meeting, ISTR has been held biannually in a different country (i.e., England, Puerto Rico, Canada, U.S., and Canada again) and emphasized the importance of international collaboration in research, program development, sharing ideas and resources, and new technologies to benefit people with disabilities and older adults. Unfortunately, ISTR was discontinued after the terrorist attack on the U.S. on September 11, 2001. ISTR was held six times and, until the year 2001, published six volumes of *Global Therapeutic Recreation*, which was an international journal in TR.

The *Therapeutic Recreation Journal (TRJ)* also contributed to the globalization of TR. In 1981, there was the International Issue of *TRJ*, which was edited by Robb and Hitzhusen. More than two decades later (2007), *TRJ* published a second special issue on global and cultural perspectives on TR, edited by Stumbo and Singleton. However, it should be noted that during the intervening 20-year period, there were also several articles that indirectly dealt with international perspectives of TR such as multicultural issues in TR.

A third major effort toward globalizing communication and knowledge can be found with the International Relations Team (IRT), which is one of the standing committees at the American Therapeutic Recreation Association (ATRA). The mission of the ATRA IRT is to promote ATRA as the premier international recreational therapy association that facilitates the worldwide development of the recreation therapy profession. In addition, the IRT attempts to link local (North America) and international resources to facilitate international development of therapeutic recreation (ATRA, 2007). ATRA IRT supports and coordinates international inquires regarding ATRA and the profession. The team also maintains an international resource network database to promote membership in the Association to international students and professionals.

ATRA IRT hosted the first International Institute session at the 2000 ATRA Annual Conference (Cincinnati, Ohio). This International Institute was coordinated by Austin and a total of four presentations were made specifically about the status of TR in Spain, U.K., and Costa Rica, and Russia. Also eight TR-related (research) studies conducted in other countries (i.e., including South Korea, Spain, India, Japan, etc.) were presented. During the 2006 ATRA Annual Conference (Orlando, Florida), the IRT, coordinated by Malkin and Yang, hosted four mini-sessions on international TR with the current trends and status of TR in Finland, Russia, South Korea, and Taiwan being presented.

These efforts by the IRT were laudable in terms of establishing networks with TR professionals in other countries and providing learning opportunities to view different aspects of TR from different cultural perspectives. The presenters from other countries expressed their interests in future collaboration for the mutual growth and development of TR across the world. However, many potential presenters from other countries expressed and experienced difficulty in attending the conferences due to the expense of attending overseas conferences (i.e., air fare, registration, and lodging), failure to obtain a U.S. visa, and the language barrier. In order to encourage TR professionals to attend conferences in the U.S. and increase the attendance rate of international professionals, more cooperative conference policies regarding international attendees and presenters must be considered and executed. Some strategies may include registration fee waiver or discounts and the use of suitable secondary reinforcers, such as recognition and awards. For foreign speakers who are not English users, interpretation services by other ATRA members may also be provided for more effective presentation and communication. In addition, with the advance of high technology, we may consider conducting computer-based distance conferencing through which international speakers can present and interact with the audience at the conference.

In addition to these organizational efforts mentioned above, there are many other individuals and institutes who made significant contributions to the understanding of the international perspectives of TR. Some of the examples may include, but are not limited to: Dan Ferguson's Romanian study-abroad summer program to work with orphaned children with disabilities and older adults, which is sponsored by Pittsburg State University; Marjorie Malkin's trips to train rehabilitation and substance abuse treatment professionals in Russia and presentation on RT in Costa Rica; Glenda Taylor, Fran Stanat, and Kathy Halberg's work to establish TR in New Zealand; and Bryan McCormick's consultation with rehabilitation and healthcare facilities in Great Britain and a staff training program for people who work in mental institutions in Kosovo; Norma Stumbo's involvement in the development of TR in Australia; and Youngkhill Lee and Heewon Yang's efforts to advocate for TR through seminars and workshops in South Korea for the past several years.

Development of Therapeutic Recreation in Other Countries

Contents and information about TR in other countries have been compiled from several sources, such as accepted manuscripts in the Special Issues on Global and Cultural Perspective on TR in 2007 *Therapeutic Recreation Journal*, the World TR section in *TR Directory*, World TR reports for the International Relations Team at American Therapeutic Recreation Association, and informal verbal and written histories on international TR. In this section, due to the limited space, TR in only six countries is very briefly introduced.

The main purpose of the discussion of therapeutic recreation in these countries is not only to provide the readers with insightful information about therapeutic recreation from a global perspective, but to broaden knowledge about each country's unique philosophical, theoretical, and practical approach to therapeutic recreation. In addition, it will provide the opportunities to explore trends and issues related to international TR.

Australia

In Australia, TR became a formally accepted area of study and a vocational outcome in the late 1970s (Pegg & Darcy, 2007). The terminology used for therapeutic recreation in Australia is Diversional Therapy, and in 1976, the Diversional Therapy Association of Australia was established. In Australia, a broad definition of TR, which is regarded as services that help individuals to promote a healthy lifestyle and higher quality of life through leisure, is widely used. For examples, the Diversional Therapy Association of Australia (DTAA) defines diversional therapy as the facilitation and coordination of recreation and leisure activities for individuals who experience barriers to choosing, deciding, and participating in activities (DTAA, 2007). However, the positive link between leisure and health (i.e., clinical and medical benefits of leisure and recreation activities) has been frequently recognized and documented by many researchers and service providers in Australia (Pegg & Darcy, 2007). Also, with greater accountability for healthcare expenditure and a growing recognition of consumers' rights, Diversional Therapists in Australia are increasingly expected to proactively include research- and outcome-based evidence to survive as a healthcare profession. Currently, there are approximately 2,300 practitioners who are spread across the full gamut of operations in the health and aged care, including rehabilitation, hospitals, community center, residential aged care, palliative care, and mental health. However, the vast majority of the DTAA's members work in aged care.

In 1995, the Diversional Therapy Association of Australia's National Council (DTAANC) was established. Currently, DTAANC implemented a National Course Recognition Process, which ensures that the education of Diversional Therapists reaches at least the minimum level considered essential. The National Minimum Course Standards are related to the three Diversional Therapy Association levels of membership: (a) Level 1 membership (Diversional Therapist), (b) Level 2 membership (Diversional Therapy assistants or recreational activities officers, and (c) Level 3 membership (students at accredited institutes). For more detailed information about those course requirements, please visit DTAANC Web Site (http://www.diversionaltherapy.org.au/p.htm). These actions to establish minimum standards for the diversional therapists are recognized as a purposeful and appropriate step in development of diversional therapy in Australia (Pegg & Darcy, 2007).

Stumbo, who recently retired from the University of Illinois, has worked for the further development of TR in Australia since 2001 and contributed to the growth of TR in Australia in significant ways. She provided continuing education opportunities, such as trainings and workshops, as well as teaching at Australian higher educational settings (i.e., the University of Western Sydney and the University of Queensland).

Canada

The birth of a national TR organization in Canada (the Canadian Therapeutic Recreation Association, CTRA) happened in 1996. In addition, there were and are many active provincial and territorial TR organizations. As of 2007, there are active 12 professional TR provincial associations in Canada. Understanding Canadian federalism may provide helpful hints why the national TR organization was established relatively late compared to the establishment of other provincial and territorial organizations. Canada has two levels of political authorities: the central Canadian Parliament (national government) and ten provincial legislative assemblies (regional governments). Each level is sovereign with respect to certain areas of legislative authority. That is, the political system is divided between these two levels (Wikipedia, 2007). Within the ten provincial areas, different regional and cultural heritages and different policies and regulations associated with health and human services do exist (Vipond, 1991). In other words, healthcare policy in one province may be very different from that of other provinces. Therefore, there may have been no definite needs for the development of a national organization in Canada due to this distinctive multiculturalism within the context of Canadian federalism. However, the Canadian Therapeutic Recreation Association came into existence due to the grassroots support from across the country and a willingness to work together to resolve common issues in TR/RT in Canada. People with different educational, cultural, and health settings recognized the need to create a national organization and worked together to unite TR practitioners across the country (Reddick, 2000).

The philosophy of TR/RT addressed by the CTRA reflects the Leisure Ability Model (Stumbo & Peterson, 2009). Functional intervention, leisure education, and recreation participation opportunities are highlighted as the content of TR and independent leisure, health, and quality of life are identified as its primary purposes. TR professionals in Canada are currently in discussion of developing certification systems. The Certification Task Force was formed in 2002 and continues to work hard to move to a national certification system.

New Zealand

The development of TR/RT in New Zealand is well described in the World TR report from Fran Stanat (2004), at TR/RT Directory Web Site (http://www.recreationtherapy.com) maintained by Charles Dixon. According to the report, Glenda Taylor established a bachelor's degree in TR/RT in 1999 at the Eastern Institute of Technology (EIT). Another bachelor's degree in TR was developed at the Southern Institute of Technology (SIT) in 2001. Interestingly, the establishment of an academic degree (bachelor's) in TR/RT in New Zealand was initiated by American faculty (e.g., Fran Stanat, Kathy Halberg, & Glenda Taylor). In particular, TR in New Zealand was modeled on Carter, Van Andel, and Robb's (1995) theoretical model (Stanat, 2004).

However, the pioneers of TR in New Zealand designed their TR curricula to learn and understand the unique culture and social system in New Zealand. Stanat (2004) stated that it was essential to ensure that TR in New Zealand develops in keeping with the way of life and mores of the people of New Zealand. She further stated that a variety of theoretical and applied sources were analyzed to determine relevant sociodemographic data and sociocultural history and current issues in recreation and other related services. In brief, although TR in New Zealand has been greatly influenced by one of the American theoretical and practice models, it seems to be in the process of integrating its own social and cultural philosophy and systems with the concepts of American TR.

Although the TR programs at EIT and SIT were recently terminated, alumni of these two programs are keen to see TR survive in New Zealand.

Finland

Therapeutic recreation in Finland adopted a unique approach to therapeutic recreation that may be somewhat different from the North American perspectives of TR. According to

Aho (2007), the concept of TR began to emerge when psychiatric hospitals started to use work and activities (work therapy) as a part of care in the mid-1800s. Examples of the work therapy they used are gardening, farming, maintenance work, and transportation. Crafts and other recreational activities were introduced to children's wards in hospitals and people in Finland began to realize the importance of recreational activities in early 1900s. And psychiatric hospitals started to utilize crafts in care and rehabilitation in the 1930s.

Formal higher education for TR specialists emerged in 1947 at HAMK University of Applied Sciences. TR education in Finland is provided only by this institute. Two TR-related major programs are *Pedagogic Crafts and Recreation* and *Therapeutic Crafts and Recreation* (Aho, 2007). While Pedagogic crafts and recreation programs provide the clients with meaningful activities and opportunities for personal growth and development through leisure, Therapeutic Crafts and Recreation aims to assist clients with illnesses and disabilities to promote health, independence, and well-being through the use of leisure. The completion of one of these programs leads to a bachelor's degree in Culture and Arts (Aho). It is interesting that crafts have been a key activity area both in recreation and TR. It is also very interesting that two different approaches toward TR (pedagogic and therapeutic) coexist within one department at HAMK University of Applied Sciences. Culturally and historically, crafts-related activities convey special meanings for Finnish people and additional cultural activities are the predominant activity areas for TR in Finland (Aho).

HAMK University of Applied Sciences is state funded and controlled by the Finnish government. Therefore, their state government functions as a credentialing body, and the minimum qualifications of therapeutic recreation specialist are set by the government regulated curriculum and standard. Thus, any other separate certification system is not necessary for TR professionals in Finland.

Japan

Fukushi recreation is the closest terminology used for TR in Japan. Although the concept of fukushi recreation is similar to that of TR in the U.S., fukushi specifically implies "welfare" instead of the meaning of therapy. And TR in Japan is more closely associated with a welfare system for older adults (Nishino, Chino, & Yoshioka, 2007).

In 1993, the National Recreation Association of Japan initiated a qualification system for fukushi recreation workers. As of 2006, there are over 10,000 qualified fukushi recreation workers in Japan. However, it is often pointed out that the quality of fukushi recreation is not near to the minimum qualification and competence level. Some of the rationales behind this evaluation are lack of recognition of benefits of recreation among the general public, lack of job opportunities for fukushi recreation workers, and lack of education and training opportunities (Nishino, Chino, & Yoshioka, 2007). In addition to these issues, there may be also other historical, societal, and cultural reasons. For a long time, the Japanese have been an agricultural, family-oriented, and collectivistic society that emphasized the duty of children to take care of their old parents. Therefore, public and organized social welfare systems have not been their priorities until recently. Moreover, Japanese people postponed their quality of life issues in favor of improvement in economic affluence since the rapid economic growth in 1960s. Lastly, it is argued that the qualification system for the fukushi recreation worker in Japan was started prematurely without having proper planning and preparation (Nishino, Chino, & Yoshioka, 2007).

It seems that fukushi recreation in Japan is currently facing some challenges primarily both in identity and quality issues. However, it also appears that the current trends in Japanese society, such as the emerging concept of quality of life, health, and well-being, and the need for more solid welfare systems for the dramatically increasing older adult population would potentially promote the growth of fukushi recreation in the near future. Fukushi recreation workers and pioneers of therapeutic recreation in Japan may need to get more actively involved in the revision of the qualification standards and procedures and development of training and continuing education courses for the current and incoming fukushi recreation workers. Moreover, researchers should make a concerted effort to prove and advocate the effectiveness of fukushi recreation to the general public in Japan.

South Korea

In South Korea, some visible therapeutic recreation (chiryo) movements were initiated by individuals with social work backgrounds. In 1993, the *Korean Therapeutic Recreation Association* (KTRA), the first therapeutic recreation professional organization in South Korea, was established. They also use an alternate name for their organization, which is *Korean Digital Therapeutic Recreation Association* (KDTRA). Since KTRA adopted Peterson and Gunn's (1984) Leisure Ability Model, their philosophical and practical approach was mostly influenced by the model emphasizing the importance of recreation participation and an appropriate leisure lifestyle. Since its foundation, KTRA has been doing both community and clinical TR practice in a variety of healthcare and community settings and provides training and education program for potential TR specialists.

In 1995, there was the birth of another professional organization in TR in South Korea. It was the Daehan (Korean) Therapeutic Recreation Association (DTRA), which focus more on treatment and rehabilitation, and it emphasized the importance of TR as a treatment tool. However, due to the lack of awareness of TR and very limited practice and employment opportunities in TR in Korea, it has been very challenging for them to promote and practice TR in healthcare and other allied healthcare settings.

In 2001, certification in TR became available through the Korean Council for Therapeutic Recreation Certification (KCTRC). While KCTRC has a similar organizational system to the National Council for Therapeutic Recreation Certification in the U.S., the minimum standards and qualification requirements for potential TR specialists in Korea are not near the level of the requirements of NCTRC™ in the States.

While a rapid growth of TR in South Korea appears promising, many concerns and difficulties are also arising. In many aspects, the challenges have many similarities with those of the Japanese in terms of their cultural, social, and historical backgrounds. In addition, the somewhat premature administration of a certification system without having proper academic and educational systems may have put TR in South Korea in a perilous situation. The validity of producing certified but not fully prepared TR specialists and the lack of available jobs should be seriously questioned. Strategic and long-term plans for the future of TR in South Korea must be considered.

Summary

The field of therapeutic recreation is faced with changes and challenges. These changes and challenges are not only the problem of TR in the States. Based on studies on TR in other countries, it can be assumed that the profession in these other countries also faces and experiences many similar changes and challenges. However, at the same time, TR in one country grows and reflects its own political, cultural, and social situations and backgrounds. These differences make TR in one country unique from TR in other countries (see Table 6.1).

Awareness of international perspectives and global views of TR has many benefits. In particular, collaboration in research and academic programs and sharing information such as in intervention programs and program ideas, may promote mutual growth and development.

Globalization of TR may be more feasible among countries with similar academic and cultural backgrounds and among countries that use the same language. For example, TR programs in Canada adopted academic curricula that are similar to that of the U.S. and use English. Therefore, future collaboration such as internships, students and scholars exchange program, study abroad programs, common textbooks, and the utilization of the NCTRC™ exam for applicants in both countries can be easily facilitated.

The establishment of international-level conferences or symposia on TR may provide more opportunities for TR professionals around the world to interact and share their knowledge. Existing national-level TR-related conferences may play a more active role in inviting TR professionals from other countries. Of course, organizational sponsorships in terms of financial and social support should be followed to recruit international speakers and attendees. Another possibility in international TR is the establishment of an international organization. For example, the World Leisure Organization is a worldwide, non-governmental association of people and organizations dedicated to discovering and fostering leisure. They facilitate many international affairs related to leisure, such as hosting a world congress, regional conferences and workshops, providing student conference scholarships, and publishing the *World Leisure Journal* and a newsletter. The discussion of possible and economical creation of an international TR organization is beyond the scope of this chapter, but may be a great topic for future discussion.

Another approach to enhance globalization of therapeutic recreation and more effective communication among therapeutic recreation professionals across the world is utilizing the International Classification of Functioning, Disability, and Health (ICF), which has been described in detail in a previous chapter. The development of the ICF may provide healthcare professionals around the world with an opportunity to more effectively communicate and collaborate. Please refer to chapter 4 in the Introduction section of this book for more information.

Lastly, a very complex and challenging philosophical and definitional discussion needs to be conducted. Therapeutic recreation may have different meanings for different people. In addition, in some countries, such as Japan, Korea, and Costa Rica, the terms recreation, leisure, and therapeutic recreation do not really exist. Therapeutic recreation may be a very ethnocentric term, mostly based on North American thinking. Iwasaki, Nishino, Onda, and Bowling (2007) pointed this out in the case of the term leisure in their literature. They

Table 6.1
Therapeutic Recreation in Foreign Countries (As of March 2007)

Country & Terminology	Professional Organizations	Academic Programs or Some Courses	Certification or Similar Qualification Systems
Australia, Diversional Therapy	Diversional Therapy Association of Australia (DTAA, 1976). http://www.diversionaltherapy.org.au/	Academic Programs	National Course Recognition
Canada, Therapeutic Recreation	Canadian Therapeutic Recreation Association (CTRA, 1996) http://www.canadian-tr.org/	Academic Programs	In Process
Finland, Therapeutic Crafts and Recreation	N/A	Academic Program	N/A
Japan, Fukushi (Welfare) Recreation	Under the National Recreation Association of Japan (NRAJ), Web Site not found in English	Academic Programs	Qualified Fukushi Recreation Worker
New Zealand (Therapeutic Recreation)	New Zealand Therapeutic Recreation Association (NZTRA, 2005). http://www.nztr.org/	Academic Programs	N/A
South Korea, Chiryo (Therapeutic) Recreation	Korea Therapeutic Recreation Association (KTRA, 1993). http://ktra.com/ Daehan Therapeutic Recreation Association (DTRA, 2000). http://www.TR/RT4u.co.kr/main/main.htm	Limited Courses at Higher Education, Training courses offered by Professional Organizations	Certification

Note: The countries presented in the table above are not the only countries in which the concept of TR/RT has evolved.

argue that leisure is an ethnocentric term and causes potential misunderstanding between people, especially between Eastern and Western cultures. For instance, for Japanese people and Korean people, there are no exactly matching words for TR. Thus, in Japan, TR was translated into Fukushi (welfare) and in Korea, into Chiryo (treatment). While these translations are close to the meaning of TR in the U.S., it is not possible to have a 100-percent equivalent word both in Japan and Korea.

Iwasaki and his colleagues (2007) suggested an approach to solve this problem. The suggestion was not to use or impose the word leisure in research but rather to let some leisure-like phenomena be described within each cultural context. This may provide many implications for TR because even TR professionals in the U.S. have several different definitions of TR. While we communicate and share our knowledge in TR with other people, we better demonstrate this open-minded attitude toward each other's definitions and theoretical/cultural bases.

Drucker (1993) insisted that the educated people function in terms of global knowledge, not simply grounded in the Western tradition, and the coming society will need people educated to appreciate a wide diversity of cultures and traditions. The educated person must be a citizen of the world, a person of wide-ranging vision, horizon, and information. TR/RT professionals in the U.S. should be willing to work, interact, and collaborate with relevant and similar professionals in the world and to learn from each other.

Discussion Questions

1. What are the potential benefits of international collaboration among TR professionals around the world?
2. Discuss whether the possible establishment of an independent international TR organization would be necessary to better promote the globalization of TR. Would the existing leadership, such as the International Relations Team at ATRA, be able to handle the future international issues? What will be the strengths and weaknesses of each option?
3. What strategies can you suggest to more actively recruit international attendees and presenters from other countries to TR conferences in the U.S.?
4. In your experience, how have varying cultures and diverse clients impacted the profession of TR/RT in the United States? What are some examples of the impact of multicultural issues on practice? How do recent immigration trends affect TR?
5. Discuss the benefits of a universal definition or concept for TR or RT that can be globally used to more effectively communicate. Will definitions and approaches be developed based on the history and culture of each country?
6. In some countries, TR has evolved and developed certification systems without having appropriate academic development and training and sociocultural understanding of TR. What risk factors can you think when TR certification systems develop without appropriate academic supports and sociocultural awareness of TR?
7. If you were part of a group developing TR in a new country, what would your strategic plan look like? Where would you start?

References

Aho, J. (2007). Therapeutic recreation in Finland. *Therapeutic Recreation Journal 41*(2).

American Therapeutic Recreation Association (2007). Welcome to ATRA Global Village. Retrieved on February 28, 2007 from http://www.atra-tr.org/international/index.htm

Carter, M. J., Van Andel, G., & Robb, G. (1995). *Therapeutic recreation: A practical approach* (2nd ed.). Prospect Heights, IL: Waveland Press.

Diversional Therapy Association of Australia. (2007). What is diversional therapy? Retrieved on February 24, 2007 from http://www.diversionaltherapy.org.au/

Drucker, P. (1993). *Post-capitalist society.* New York: Harper-Collins.

Iwasaki, Y., Nishino, H., Onda, T., & Bowling, C. (2007). Leisure research in a global world: Time to reverse the Western domination in leisure research. *Leisure Sciences, 29*, 113-117.

Nishino, H. J., Chino, H., Yoshioka, N. & Gabriella, J. (2007). Therapeutic recreation in modern Japan: Era of challenge and opportunity. *Therapeutic Recreation Journal 41*(2), 119-131.

Pegg, S., & Darcy, S. (2007). Sailing on troubling waters: Diversional therapy in Australia. *Therapeutic Recreation Journal 41* (2), 132-140.

Peterson, C. A., & Gunn, S. L. (1984). *Therapeutic recreation program design: Principles and procedures (2nd ed.).* Englewood Cliffs, NJ: Prentice Hall.

Reddick, P. J. (2000). History of the Canadian Therapeutic Recreation Association. Retrieved on February 24, 2007 from http://www.canadian-tr.org/

Stanat, F. (2004). Therapeutic recreation and rehabilitation services in New Zealand. Retrieved on February 23, 2007 from http://www.recreationtherapy.com/history/newzealand.htm

Stumbo, N. J., & Peterson, C. A. (2009). *Therapeutic recreation program design: Principles and procedures* (5th ed.). San Francisco, CA: Benjamin Cummings.

Vipond, R. (1991). *Liberty and community: Canadian federalism and the future of the constitution.* Albany, NY: State University of New York Press.

Wikipedia (2007). Canadian federalism. Retrieved on February 24, 2007 from http://en.wikipedia.org/wiki/Canadian_federalism

Section II
Education Issues

Section II
Education Issues

CHAPTER 7

Keynote: Perspectives on Therapeutic Recreation Education

Nancy H. Navar, Re.D., CTRS™
University of Wisconsin - La Crosse

Each therapeutic recreation (TR) student is an ambassador for the profession of therapeutic recreation. Most TR students are asked to explain their future profession or course of study. It is wise to have several answers or explanations for such questions. The person who is making polite conversation may be satisfied with a one-sentence response to the question, "What is your major?" Someone else really may be interested in comparing therapeutic recreation to other majors or other professions. If the student has a general understanding and perspective of therapeutic recreation education, a better formulated and appropriate response to such questions is possible.

This chapter briefly looks at the origins of therapeutic recreation education, the relationship between therapeutic recreation and other majors, the components of a quality therapeutic recreation education, and active controversies within the profession as they relate to TR education. With such information, the therapeutic recreation student or professional has a perspective from which to formulate various explanations concerning the education of the therapeutic recreation specialist. Secondly, the informed student or professional can contribute to the improvement of the educational process. Thirdly, students, educators, and practitioners may want to consider the issues presented in this chapter and compare them to their own therapeutic recreation curricula. It is often through reflection and discussion that one finds perspective, recognizes successes, and discovers ways to advance the quality and appropriateness of therapeutic recreation education.

A Short Look Back in Time

The origins of therapeutic recreation education differ from other professions. As an example, the origins of physical therapy or occupational therapy began in medicine

(Quiroga, 1995). Physicians needed help and created curricula to educate professionals who could be of assistance in medical settings. As such, a profession like physical therapy started after the college curriculum in physical therapy was in place.

On the other hand, therapeutic recreation jobs did not begin with formal college curricula in place. After World War I, wounded soldiers needed recreation services while they were hospitalized. Talented yet untrained individuals began to offer such services. Many years later, curricula in therapeutic recreation developed (Fitzgerald, 1948; James, 1997–98; Miller, 1962). In other words, the profession of therapeutic recreation developed from client need, not physician need. Recognizing this provides a source of pride to those in the profession. At the same time, practitioners with and without formal education in therapeutic recreation have practiced side by side. At this point in history, it is more common to find formally educated and certified therapeutic recreation practitioners being hired for new positions. In many cases, such credentials are mandated by licensure and certification requirements.

Placing Therapeutic Recreation Education in Perspective

Professional preparation programs have distinct purposes. On a continuum, professional education lies between technical training and a liberal or discipline-based education (See Figure 7.1). Occupations such as medical technology or nursing assistants, and trades such as cosmetology, carpentry, and computer repair are very technical in nature. Specific skills requiring specific procedures are taught in these fields. At the other end of the continuum are the disciplines such as history, sociology, and philosophy. The main focus of the disciplines is the understanding of theory, concepts, and principles related to that discipline. Little or no emphasis is placed on preparation for a specific type of employment.

Therapeutic recreation is neither a technical trade nor simply a discipline. Therapeutic recreation is a profession; therefore, education for the profession of therapeutic recreation must include both a combination of technical skills as well as theory, concepts, and principles related to a variety of disciplines. The balanced blending of these will vary across curricula.

The question "Is therapeutic recreation a profession?" is quite outdated. The more modern question would be "To what extent has therapeutic recreation been professionalized?" (Wilensky, 1964). The difference between these two questions is not just one of semantics.

Figure 7.1
A Perspective on Therapeutic Recreation Education:
Some Trades, Professions, and Disciplines

Technical Trades	Professions	Disciplines
Nursing Assistant	Therapeutic Recreation	Sociology
Dental Hygiene	Social Work	History
Computer Repair	Nursing	Philosophy
Carpentry	Ministry	Anthropology
Cosmetology	Teaching	Mathematics

Each question represents both a worldview and varying amounts of knowledge of the process of professionalization. From a worldview or belief perspective, reality much more resembles a continuum of events rather than a black-and-white or all-or-nothing perspective. Occupations, including therapeutic recreation, can be found in various stages of professionalization. There is not one specific line of demarcation that turns an occupation into a profession. The level of professionalization achieved by any occupational group is determined by how many elements of professionalization have been achieved and with what degree of effectiveness they have been achieved.

Professionalization involves both structural and attitudinal components or elements. Structural components are determined at the societal level (e.g., existence of university curricula, professional associations, codes of ethics, credentialing, and a body of knowledge) while attitudinal components refer more to the professionalism of the individuals within that occupation (e.g., membership in the professional associations, belief in service to the public, belief in self-regulation, a sense of calling to the field, and a feeling of autonomy) (Snizek, 1972).

Therapeutic recreation education must include teachings about the profession and about the expected behaviors and attitudes of the members of that profession. For example, a curriculum might teach about the professional associations in therapeutic recreation (e.g., ATRA, NTRS). Equally important is acquiring a commitment to becoming active, contributing members in the professional associations.

Therapeutic recreation education helps initiate individuals into their profession. This initiation includes both theory and practice. Like the disciplines, theory, concepts, and principles must underlie what is taught. Like the more technical fields, specific techniques and skills must be taught. The balance and integration of these two approaches is what shapes and defines the professional education of the members of the profession.

Quality Therapeutic Recreation Education: Curriculum Standards

Historically, the National Recreation and Park Association (NRPA) Council on Accreditation (COA) has provided standards for recreation curricula. This group offers a general core accreditation and specific standards for options. Therapeutic recreation has been the most widely used "option" in the COA accreditation program. It is safe to say that for years, many therapeutic recreation curricula have willingly met standards in the attempt to improve curricula. Two changes are occurring with this measure of quality curricula. First, the COA is in the process of revising their accreditation standards. The organization will move from focusing on structures (number of faculty, organization of department and curricula, etc.) and processes (course syllabi, internship experiences, etc.) to outcomes (See Carter and Zabriskie's Chapter 9 for more detail.).

Second, there is much discussion among therapeutic recreation faculty to provide more stringent standards for therapeutic recreation curricula. Concurrently, there is discussion on which overall accreditation group will be a "best fit" for therapeutic recreation curriculum standards. Underlying this effort is a belief that therapeutic recreation needs to be viewed as a profession in its own right, not just as an option within the general field of recreation.

Whether or not COA will continue to host the accreditation for therapeutic recreation will be determined within the next few years. Regardless of the sponsoring accreditation group, therapeutic recreation education must develop more thorough and focused standards for therapeutic recreation education. Outcome standards are or will be mandated at various levels (university accreditation, curriculum accreditation). As TR curricula become more explicit about curricular outcomes, there must be room for differences based on university mission, workforce expectations, and philosophy of therapeutic recreation. The process of developing improved standards for TR curricula is lengthy, yet energies for this task are active and planning is progressing.

Another helpful document for therapeutic recreation education is the publication on curriculum guidelines by the American Therapeutic Recreation Association (West, Kinney, & Witman, 2008). The internship guidelines published by ATRA (Grote & Hasl, 1998) and NTRS (1997) are both helpful documents when developing and identifying quality TR curricula. Many professionals advocate that the NCTRC™ job analysis standards should be the foundation of curriculum design (Monroe & Connolly, 1997-98).

Both ATRA (2000) and NTRS (1995) have developed professional standards of practice whose content should be included in the therapeutic recreation curriculum. While none of these standards actually dictate how to design a therapeutic recreation curriculum, the new graduate is expected to know much more than can be taught in a few therapeutic recreation courses. While most curricula offer three to five courses in therapeutic recreation, some require up to 13 therapeutic recreation courses. The depth and scope of professional preparation varies greatly. What will the minimal curriculum standards be in the next ten years?

Although there is no universally accepted listing of the components of a quality therapeutic recreation education, certain topics continue to surface when educators, practitioners, and students discuss curricula or the reputations of various schools. This next section discusses topics related to the structures, processes, and outcomes of a quality therapeutic recreation education.

Structures Related to a Quality Therapeutic Recreation Education

In addition to curriculum standards just discussed, there are other structures that influence the quality of therapeutic recreation education. The first is the type of university.

Administrative Structure: The mission of the university (e.g., research focus, teaching focus), the home college (e.g., health, physical education, and recreation; education; allied health), and the departmental membership (e.g., Recreation Department, HPER Department, Social Sciences, Leisure Studies) each have different types and degrees of influence on the therapeutic recreation curriculum. Although the administrative structure/ location of the curriculum may have political implications at the local level, more important than the administrative structure is the degree of autonomy over the design of the therapeutic recreation curriculum.

Degree(s): Today there is less of a distinction between a bachelor of science degree and a bachelor of arts degree than in decades past. Similarly, there may not always be a difference between a master of science degree and a master of arts degree. It is important, however, in any profession that there remain a distinction between the content of a bachelor's degree and a master's degree. An individual with a master's degree should be better prepared in specific areas than an individual with a bachelor's degree.

This distinction can be challenged today because so many individuals from other fields seek master's degrees in therapeutic recreation. While someone with a bachelor's degree in psychology may have relevant undergraduate coursework for therapeutic recreation, what about the individual with a bachelor's degree in history or philosophy? Should he be required to take all or most of the undergraduate coursework required of therapeutic recreation undergraduates? What coursework and experiences will prepare master's-level students beyond the bachelor's level while still guaranteeing the acquisition of all the competencies expected of the bachelor's degree graduate?

At the present time, the bachelor's degree is the entry-level degree for the profession. Although this may have many benefits for the individuals seeking education in therapeutic recreation, it is worthy to note that many related professions (e.g., social work, occupational therapy) with whom TRSs will be working do have master's degrees as their entry-level degrees.

Conceptual Structure: There remains variation in the name of the degree awarded to those successfully completing a therapeutic recreation curriculum. Some students graduate with a degree in therapeutic recreation. Others may have a degree in recreation with an emphasis in therapeutic recreation or a degree in recreation therapy. More important than the specific title of the degree is the scope and quality of coursework that has been included in the degree. Yet the variations in titles certainly contribute to the confusion of what qualifies as a solid professional preparation program in therapeutic recreation.

Faculty: The number of faculty and qualifications of faculty affect the therapeutic recreation curriculum. It is not possible for part-time faculty alone to design and manage a quality therapeutic recreation curriculum that is competitive with those schools having several full-time qualified faculty.

Faculty members who have doctorates would be expected to include more scholarship and more depth in the curriculum than those who are prepared at the master's or bachelor's level. Faculty members with degrees and experience in other fields (e.g., adapted physical education) may have different perspectives on professional issues and the scope of practice than would those with degrees and experience in therapeutic recreation. Faculty members with several years of practitioner experience would bring a different perspective to coursework than those who have not worked as a practitioner. Practitioners who teach part-time would bring different contemporary experiences to their teaching than full-time educators. There is no formula for the ideal match of faculty qualifications. Yet, faculty qualifications are a significant and controversial topic throughout the profession.

Related professions (e.g., social work, occupational therapy) would not consider hiring non-credentialed (licensed, certified) faculty. Grandfather clauses aside, no new therapeutic recreation faculty should be hired unless they are Certified Therapeutic Recreation Specialists™ credentialed by the National Council for Therapeutic Recreation Certification™ and licensed if appropriate.

Processes Related to a Quality Therapeutic Recreation Education

Several processes contribute to the quality of therapeutic recreation education. Some of these processes are well established; others are in a fast-changing mode and may be actively different by the time this book reaches press.

Courses: While the number of courses within a curriculum is actually part of the curriculum structure, the sequencing and implementation of these courses can be considered a process. Course sequencing is important. When prerequisites exist for upper-level courses, one can be assured that advanced learning is possible. Without such planned sequencing, courses fail to challenge the more advanced learners. When students transfer into therapeutic recreation during their junior or senior years (a common occurrence), course sequencing becomes quite challenging. Many therapeutic recreation curricula are designed to be completed in two years, after general education coursework is completed.

Courses throughout the curriculum should be clearly linked. For example, a senior seminar student should understand that she is expected to retain the information from her programming and facilitation techniques class when asked to design her senior project. Similarly, if x number of volunteer hours or x number of lab experiences are prerequisite to the assessment and treatment planning class, then the relevance of the class is enhanced. Student interns may be expected to address specific questions that provide direct feedback to particular courses (e.g., What medical terms are you expected to know? or What specific management skills were you expected to have during your internship?).

Scope of Practice: Discussions concerning scope of practice will be influenced both by employers and TR curricula. For example, an employer that values pain management may enlist the TRS on staff to help provide pain management. That professional will have the skills taught within their college curriculum, and those learned after graduation at professional conferences and specialty workshops. The actual curriculum may not be able to provide advanced skills in all pain management techniques appropriate for therapeutic recreation. The curriculum should be influential in providing basic skills (e.g., stress management principles, relaxation techniques) and knowledge of resources for continuing education in the area of pain management.

One problem with narrowing the focus of TR is related to future job flexibility. If a student becomes too narrowly specialized (e.g., focus on physical disabilities) then how skilled will that individual be if the only job available is in mental health or developmental disabilities? One problem with keeping the focus of TR very broad is graduating students without adequate skills (e.g., clinical skills, inclusion skills).

Nurse practitioners who switch job areas (e.g., oncology to pediatrics) go on to gain further education in their new area before beginning practice. Physician assistants (PA) follow a different model when switching professional focus. PAs can move from setting to setting since they obtain training and clinical supervision from an identified M.D. supervisor in each new setting. Which model (nurse practitioner or physician assistant) is most appropriate for TR is yet to be determined. Meanwhile, TR education faces the dilemma of how narrow or how broadly to base coursework and educational experiences.

What does seem to be clear (almost) is that common recreation management courses (e.g., facilities, natural resources management, etc.) are not practical to include in any TR curriculum. The inclusion of such "unnecessary" courses detracts from more relevant TR content (e.g., client assessment, ICF codes, modalities related to pain management or social skill development).

The courses that generate more discussion/controversy are usually those related to foundations of leisure and recreation, recreation leadership and supervision, and recreation administration. While some contend that any administration course has application in therapeutic recreation, others point out that specific clinical administration topics should be addressed within a four-year degree program. This usually requires a separate TR administration course or a place to apply generic administrative skills within a therapeutic recreation context.

The same argument can be made for the acquisition of research skills. Some of these issues might be addressed if most students declared TR as a major when they were freshmen. This is not typically the case. Since most TR curriculum have about four or five semesters to cover all required content, courses must be chosen carefully, sequenced well, and be skillfully taught. This is no small feat.

Therapeutic Recreation vs. Recreation(al) Therapy: Controversy over definitions and scope of therapeutic recreation continues to exist. Some attempt has been made to explain differences in scope of practice by distinguishing between therapeutic recreation and recreation therapy. Some claim that RT focuses on functional improvement, and TR focuses on the leisure experiences. This narrow view completely ignores the original intention of the therapeutic recreation continuum: to bridge the gap between one group focusing on functional improvement and another providing recreation experiences. Although this discussion may appear to be talking about the profession rather than education, this topic has a great influence on the nature of TR/RT education.

Some would say that a name change from TR to RT would focus efforts on functional intervention and leave other purposes (e.g., inclusion, palliative care, prevention) to the general field of recreation or other professions. This is too simplistic for three reasons:

1) Functional improvement and treatment are acceptable terms in healthcare. Other terms (e.g., habilitation) are more common in special education. "Memory care" for individuals with Alzheimer's is not exactly functional improvement, but more appropriately focuses on increasing pleasure or maintaining (not improving) function. "Functional improvement" is much too narrow a term for an entire profession.

2) The APIE process (assessment, planning, implementation, evaluation) is not unique to TR/RT. Many professions use this process. While this process does wonders for accountability and meeting client needs, no profession should base its entire scope of practice on one process. Usually the point being made in this context is that TR doesn't use the process and RT does. This is just plain false. There are many solid TR programs that skillfully use the APIE process. There are many RT programs that continue to remain less than professional and do not use the APIE process. A name change from TR to RT makes no guarantees that APIE will be used or that functions will be improved. A name change from TR to RT at the profession level will further splinter the profession.

3) Public visibility is often cited for a reason to change from TR to RT. What is used for an example here is the widespread use of RT in hospital settings. Granted, it is confusing to the public when both TR and RT are used interchangeably. It seems better, though, to use the terms interchangeably than to pit them as opposites or completely different professions. Feelings are strong on both sides. Living with ambiguity is a hallmark of adulthood. Living with two terms seems much less harmful than the toxic split that would occur by presenting each faction as completely distinct. Additionally, the publicly visible professional credential is Certified Therapeutic Recreation Specialist™. It is fine if a particular agency chooses other terms (e.g., recreation therapist, activity therapist, inclusion specialist, etc.)

as a job title. The overall profession must encompass the entire group. CTRS™ is the legally recognized credential that would be diminished if RT were the only acceptable name for the profession.

Student Selection: The recruitment and admission of students to the therapeutic recreation curricula is increasingly becoming an important issue. Many curricula still have unlimited enrollment, while some curricula have stringent admission criteria. Since grade point is not the only indicator of future professional success, what are the criteria that universities, departments, or programs should be using to select future members of the therapeutic recreation profession?

A more recent development is an undergraduate student wanting to major in therapeutic recreation as a step to a profession that requires a graduate degree (e.g., occupational therapy, physical therapy). There are pros and cons to this issue that are now being discussed.

A frequent occurrence with rehabilitation clients is their new interest in pursuing a career in therapeutic recreation after their rehabilitation. There are many wonderful therapeutic recreation staff members who have disabilities. On the other hand, some disabilities may not lend themselves to being successful in a helping or healthcare profession. Certainly this needs to be evaluated on an individual basis. For example, does this individual with disability x have the ability to become a successful professional? What are the criteria that help faculty advise students into or out of therapeutic recreation as a career path? While one setting requires the ability to lift x number of pounds, another facility may require split second judgment and frequent clinical decisions.

One example of a disabling condition influencing one's performance is an individual with a hearing impairment. This individual was a wonderful professional in a physical rehabilitation setting where most of the programming was one on one. This same individual was not able to perform well in a psychiatric setting, since programming occurred in groups. She could not tell who was talking and therefore was not successful at lip reading. Another example occurred with someone with a traumatic brain injury. He might be a very good fitness professional under the direction of another professional, but did not have the clinical judgment needed to function as a CTRS™. Most of these issues could not be decided upon entry into the TR curriculum. The question is, what is a good advising process to help discover this in an academic setting?

Learning Experiences: All courses are not created equal. There is a vast difference in the type, scope, and depth of learning depending on the types of learning experiences included within the course. While some introductory courses may require students to observe therapeutic recreation programs, more advanced classes may require students to design and evaluate programs. Multiple-choice tests, essay exams, team projects, individual projects, and case reports all measure learning differently. Requiring students to take basic concepts and knowledge to an applied level is very different than simply overlapping topics from course to course.

The students from one school may be energetic and excited about entering their future profession. Students from another school may be graduating simply to "get a job." The learning experiences embedded in the therapeutic recreation curriculum can be influential in either case. Belonging to a professional organization, attending workshops and professional conferences before graduation, or providing an in-service education on the meaning of therapeutic recreation to a local community group often results from the process of being encouraged to get professionally involved while still a student.

Technology certainly can be used to enhance learning. Recent graduates are sometimes shocked to find that their employer may not be as technically up to date as the university was. While some agencies provide laptop computers to patients, others may not have many computers available for staff. Some treatment programs will use the World Wide Web for teaching about leisure resources after discharge; others are limited by parochial attitudes toward the Internet. TR education must graduate technically capable professionals who are able to function with limited or great access to technology.

On the non-technical side, to what extent is there a community of learners within the therapeutic recreation major that joins together in creating rich, contemporary learning experiences? To what extent are educators, practitioners, and students engaged in joint learning that will lead to improved services to clients?

Attitudinal Development: While it is common to expect that therapeutic recreation students are concerned with the whole person and treating individuals with dignity and respect, there are many evolving attitudes that are very much a part of contemporary solid professional practice. "Person-first" language, strong ethical beliefs and practices, cultural competence, and solid social interaction skills are expected of therapeutic recreation students and professionals. Similarly, the belief in lifelong learning is essential. Continuing education is not just a requirement for re-certification; it is a lifeline to maintain competent practice. It is difficult to understand how someone could call themselves a professional and not belong to a professional organization or stay current with evolving practice methods. This area of attitudinal development must be emphasized within the therapeutic recreation curriculum and must be reinforced during the internship experience.

Internship Experiences: Students continuously report that their internship is one of the most significant educational experiences they have. The on-site internship supervisor and the academic internship supervisor can be highly influential in helping the student obtain a quality capstone experience during their internship. While it is common to encourage the development of such traits as initiative or teamwork, it is also important to assist interns with work-related emotional issues, issues of competence, and issues of adjustment, as well as problem-solving and conflict resolution. The process of learning within the internship will vary depending on the maturity, competence, and traits of the individuals involved. The length of one's internship influences the scope and depth of opportunities for learning. A 16-week internship is significantly longer than a 12-week internship, especially when attitudinal learning and issues of competence are emphasized. Some schools are discussing the merits and drawbacks of multiple internships. Availability of agencies, qualified supervisors, and duration of the academic program all contribute to these discussions.

Faculty Roles: In general, therapeutic recreation educators are expected to engage in teaching, scholarship, and service activities. The emphasis or time spent on each of these can influence the nature of the therapeutic recreation curriculum and faculty-student interactions. Faculty members who are active in research, grant writing, professional presentations, and/or service projects bring a rich opportunity to their students who may become collaborators with such efforts. Faculty members who focus more on innovative teaching/learning experiences bring a different energy to their students in and out of the classroom. Each of these scenarios can be variously attractive and beneficial to different types of students. Especially at the graduate level, students should seek a compatible match with the experiences and knowledge available at a particular school.

Practitioner Involvement: Many schools have close working relationships with the local therapeutic recreation practitioners. Pre-internship experiences, advisory committees, guest presenters, joint projects, and collaborative research opportunities can enhance the quality of the therapeutic recreation curriculum and energize practitioners to seek continuous program improvement. Ongoing communication between educators and practitioners can provide opportunities for meaningful input and an increased understanding of the realities within the university and the practice settings.

Becoming a great therapeutic recreation internship supervisor can be an enjoyable process. (See Bloom's Chapter 24). Many practitioners gain satisfaction from the internship process. Some claim that student interns keep them "on their toes" and bring fresh perspectives to the workplace. Working with interns or pre-interns also can bring additional challenges to the supervisor. If the student is not well prepared or still needs much improvement in the areas of professional behaviors and maturity, the supervisor can spend additional time and energy in that educational role. In the long run, the profession advances and the clients benefit when intern supervisors take their responsibilities seriously.

The supervising practitioner accepts the important functions of guiding students to become professionals and redirecting those students who may not be suited to the professional challenges. Providing programmatic, administrative, and clinical supervision to interns is part of the expectation of internship supervisors. Not every skilled therapeutic recreation practitioner needs to become an internship supervisor; however, those who do assume this role have a wonderful opportunity to influence the future of therapeutic recreation service delivery.

Ethical Practices: An important and developing issue in education is the topic of ethics. Both ATRA and NTRS have developed codes of ethics that students need to learn and apply. Within higher education, the topic of ethics often remains theoretical or relegated to the professional issues class.

Woven within each ethical principle is the subtle topic of boundaries. There are professional boundaries, personal boundaries, physical boundaries, value boundaries, conversational boundaries, and so on. A challenge for educators is how to practice boundaries and how to teach about boundaries that are important in therapeutic recreation.

Conflicting or unclear values can make the subject of boundaries appear as if one is negotiating very muddy waters. For example, many human service educators and supervisors teach that the staff-client relationship is an extremely important factor in the client making progress. Concurrently, the faculty teaches that staff and client relationships have limits. How can students find the balance between the limits of an appropriate professional boundary and an effective personal relationship? Certainly class discussions and an emphasis on reflective thinking will enhance the understanding of the complexity of such issues.

It also seems important to avoid overlooking the more traditional, obvious methods of teaching—that of modeling. Can an instructor who has weak boundaries with his students expect to help students learn about proper professional boundaries? Can an instructor who has rigid boundaries with her students expect to help students problem-solve when boundary issues become blurred during an internship? Can an instructor who exhibits these inappropriate boundaries teach students about personal responsibility and the importance of not controlling others? While it is acknowledged that no educator, practitioner, or student will have perfect boundaries 100 percent of the time, it is important to recognize that appropriate relationships are not "just for those other folks." Each individual has a role in discussing and modeling healthy professional and personal boundaries.

What occurs during the educational experience, both in school and throughout one's life, is the process of education. This dynamic component is usually what is remembered by students as they evaluate how well they like learning. Although it is very important to attend to quality educational processes, much energy also needs to be invested in the selection of and identification of outcomes related to therapeutic recreation education.

Outcomes Related to a Quality Therapeutic Recreation Education

What should beginning-level practitioners know as they enter the job market? What should master's-prepared professionals know? What constitutes a quality education at the doctoral level?

Each university is asking faculty to specify outcomes for graduates of each major. This discussion is not an attempt to address that issue from an academic perspective. This discussion, however, does present enough information to demonstrate that the determination of outcomes for therapeutic recreation majors is not as simple a task as one might initially expect.

In a general sense, each student should demonstrate the outcomes stated in the university mission. These statements often refer to outcomes such as being informed citizens, individuals with a solid general education background, or persons with the ability to communicate. The designation of professionally specific outcomes usually is determined at the departmental or curriculum level. Several internal therapeutic recreation documents provide guidance in the determination of outcomes for the therapeutic recreation student (e.g., accreditation standards, certification standards, professional standards of practice, and internship standards). Examples of a few of these are presented in the following paragraphs.

One such document is the NCTRC™ Job Analysis (2007). The therapeutic recreation graduate is expected to have various levels of knowledge in the following areas:

- Professional Roles and Responsibilities (safe environment, CTRS credential, staff development, standards, competence, ethics, quality improvement, committees)
- Assessment (referrals, review, methods, implement, interpret, record)
- Planning Interventions and Programs (use assessment results, individualized plans, approaches, protocols, task and activity analysis, modifications and technology)
- Implementing Interventions and Programs (explain outcomes, individual and group sessions, techniques, safety, observe responses, monitor effectiveness)
- Evaluate Outcomes of the Interventions/Programs (change in functioning, effectiveness of individualized plan, revise plan, determine program termination, effectiveness of modalities and programs)

- Documenting Intervention Services (behavioral observations, risk management, modalities)
- Working with Treatment and Service Teams (Provide TR information, client information, coordination, collaborative services)
- Organizing Programs (supplies and equipment, support services, budget, scheduling)
- Managing TR Services (standards and regulations, needs assessment, written plan of operation, consistency with mission, staff supervision, staff development, internship programs, budgeting, research, quality improvement, reports)
- Public Awareness and Advocacy (networking, participant rights, community education, marketing and public relations)

These guidelines provide each individual with a framework for monitoring minimally expected knowledge of a therapeutic recreation professional (See www.nctrc.org for current standards). Faculty, internship supervisors, and students can each evaluate these knowledge-area outcomes.

Two useful documents to assist in the specification of outcomes are the ATRA Standards of Practice (2000) and the NTRS Standards of Practice for Therapeutic Recreation Services (1995). Knowledge, skills, and abilities in each of the following areas listed in the NTRS standards could be stated in terms of therapeutic recreation curriculum outcomes:

- Scope of TR service (e.g., practicing within one's professional scope of service)
- TR program mission, purpose, goals, and objectives (e.g., ability to formulate relevant goals and translate them into operational procedures)
- Individual treatment/program plan (e.g., appropriate to client needs)
- Documentation (e.g., proper, accountable records)
- Plan of operation (e.g., organized method for implementing services)
- Personnel qualifications (e.g., competence, life-long learning)
- Ethical responsibilities (e.g., ethical actions in difficult situations)
- Evaluation and research (e.g., accountable, contemporary services)

Possibly the most useful document in assisting in the specification of outcomes is *ATRA's Guidelines for Competency Assessment and Curriculum Planning for Recreational Therapy Practice* (West, Kinney, & Witman, 2008). The following content areas are very useful in planning curriculum content and evaluating students' knowledge and abilities in the scope of TR service:

- Foundations of professional practice (e.g., integration of history, service models, philosophy, ethics, credentials, professional conduct, and professional development with therapeutic recreation practice)
- Individualized patient/client assessment (e.g., efficient and effective screening and assessment of individuals)
- Planning treatment/programs (e.g., identification of goals, objectives, strategies, and interventions based on assessment data; development of programs to achieve goals and objectives related to independence in life activities and leisure functioning)
- Implementing treatment/programs (e.g., using evidence-based practice, choosing and applying facilitation techniques)

- Evaluation treatment/programs (e.g., reassessment of individuals; comparing progress to the plan)
- Managing recreational therapy practice (e.g., personnel, fiscal; quality improvement; compliance with standards and regulations; resources; safety and risk management; marketing and public relations; facility and strategic planning; and contractual and legal concerns)
- Support content/competencies (e.g., application of a broad base of liberal arts, science, and health-care knowledge)

The comprehensive assessment of a curriculum involves more than the sum of the classes within the curriculum. The integration of learning, the processes of application and synthesis, communication skills, critical and reflective thinking, and resourcefulness are functions that go beyond any one set of standards and guidelines.

One external set of guidelines is provided by the Pew Health Professions Commission (1995). This commission stated that all health-care professionals (including therapeutic recreation) should have skills in each of the following competency areas (See Figure 7.2.).

This generic list of competencies could be applied to each therapeutic recreation educational program. Not every therapeutic recreation curriculum will address each competency to the same degree. As long as therapeutic recreation curricula are working toward the identification of relevant outcomes, differences among curricula can continue to exist.

What should not exist or be tolerated is therapeutic recreation curricula that maintain the status quo—continuing to do what they did in decades past. Additionally, practitioners must stay within the boundaries of therapeutic recreation's professional scope of practice and not attempt to abandon the core of the profession in order to meet immediate societal pressures (e.g., insurance demands, enrollment management issues, etc.).

Another way of looking at outcomes is packaging or marketing. A student may be skilled in a variety of modalities. Each practitioner must be able to package appropriate modalities for a specific agency or population. For example, claiming to be skilled in aquatics may not be impressive to an employer. Claiming to understand how to use aquatics as a method of pain management might be the selling point. In another example, a student may be well versed with a number of different disabling conditions. An employer may want to hear that the prospective TRS is able to use the ICF (International Classification of Function) codes with persons having Alzheimer's or multiple sclerosis, rather than just hearing that one has experience with aging or a physical disability area.

New trends, such as the ICF codes, have curricular implications. Medical language classes and disability classes can no longer just teach the ICD (International Classification of Disease) vocabulary. Contemporary vocabulary, such as that used in the ICF codes, must be used throughout the therapeutic recreation curriculum (See Chapter 4). Terms such as capacity, performance, activity limitation, and participation restriction need to replace older medical model disease-focused terms (Porter & burlingame, 2007). What will probably happen over the next several years is the uneven acceptance of terms and practices across agencies. During this transition, therapeutic recreation students and practitioners must be able to speak "both languages" as an educational outcome.

Figure 7.2
The Pew Commission's Twenty-One Competencies for the Twenty-First Century

---

1. Embrace a personal ethic of social responsibility and service.
2. Exhibit ethical behavior in all professional activities.
3. Provide evidence-based, clinically competent care.
4. Incorporate the multiple determinants of health in clinical care.
5. Apply knowledge of the new sciences.
6. Demonstrate critical thinking, reflection, and problem-solving skills.
7. Understand the role of primary care.
8. Rigorously practice preventive healthcare.
9. Integrate population-based care and services into practice.
10. Improve access to healthcare for those with unmet health needs.
11. Practice relationship-centered care with individuals and families.
12. Provide culturally sensitive care to a diverse society.
13. Partner with communities in health-care decisions.
14. Use communication and information technology effectively and appropriately.
15. Work in interdisciplinary teams.
16. Ensure care that balances individual, professional, system, and societal needs.
17. Practice leadership.
18. Take responsibility for quality of care and health outcomes at all levels.
19. Contribute to continuous improvement of the health-care system.
20. Advocate for public policy that promotes and protects the health of the public.
21. Continue to learn and help others learn.

Finding the various levels and types of outcomes appropriate to a TR curriculum is a challenging yet exciting task. Although the specific outcomes might remain controversial for a few years, the need to have clearly identified outcomes is no longer controversial.

Recent Developments in Therapeutic Recreation Education

Each national professional organization's (ATRA, NTRS) conferences frequently have sessions that focus on therapeutic recreation education. Both educators and practitioners share ideas and directions for curricular improvements. In May 2005, therapeutic recreation educators and practitioners from both ATRA and NTRS (Joint Taskforce on Higher Education) met at the Therapeutic Recreation Education Conference (TREC, 2005) to discuss the state of the art and future direction of TR education. For three days, discussions occurred on: undergraduate TR education, graduation TR education, recruitment and retention of students, and various topics such as distance education, accreditation, and service delivery.

Ideas were exchanged, proceedings were published, and the tasks of quality improvement for TR education were re-energized and given direction. Work needs to occur in a variety of areas and needs to involve a number of different groups. Each group involved in improving TR education comes with its own focus and traits (e.g., ATRA, NTRS, NCTRC™, students and parents, educators and administrators, clients and families, employers and regulating groups). Each group is composed of individuals with some commonalities and many differences.

When the commonalities are identified, progress can be more efficient (e.g., curricula should include x, y, and z). When the differences are major, then one's worldview greatly influences the speed and direction of progress. For example, if one sees the world as black/white or right/wrong, that person will probably advocate for more narrow academic standards and curricular content (TR is only functional improvement; or TR is only provision of recreation services to persons with disabilities).

If one sees room in a profession for shades of gray, then a wider scope of academic freedom and curriculum content may be embraced. There is room for a continuum of TR services, based on consumer/client needs as well as work context (hospital, camps, etc.). This latter view does not imply that TR can be all things to all people. There still exists a defined scope of practice, yet this scope of practice allows for newer healthcare or human service settings (assisted living, home care, mentoring for inclusion, family education, etc.). To limit TR practice to medical care alone is potentially eliminating TR jobs and certainly defying the healthcare trends of the 21st century (integrative medicine, non-medical settings, cooperative programs).

Therapeutic recreation educators, practitioners, and students all have passion for the profession. It is important to keep that passion open to a variety of possibilities while continuing to improve the TR educational process.

Summary

So many times individuals make conclusions about therapeutic recreation education based on their particular circumstance or setting. It is important to remember that therapeutic recreation education must prepare students for entry positions in the entire profession, not just one setting.

Structures, processes, and outcomes of TR education are becoming more explicit and transparent. Prospective students are becoming more sophisticated as they search for majors that match their abilities and dreams. Through the concerted efforts of attending to the structures, processes, and outcomes of therapeutic recreation education, the profession and society at large will benefit on both individual and collective levels. Quality education can lead to improved practice and improved research. These will, in turn, foster improved contributions to society by students, practitioners, and educators.

Discussion Questions

1. What does it mean that the profession of therapeutic recreation was developed from client need? What are the implications of this?
2. What is a recommended balance of technical skills and theory for inclusion in a professional therapeutic recreation curriculum?

3. Describe your knowledge of the structural components of therapeutic recreation's professionalization process.
4. Describe your behaviors in relation to the attitudinal components of therapeutic recreation's professionalization process.
5. How might the administrative location of the therapeutic recreation curriculum influence the curriculum content?
6. What are the pros and cons of the bachelor's degree being the entry-level degree for the therapeutic recreation profession?
7. Using a professional therapeutic recreation document (e.g., NCTRC™ job analysis, ATRA's curriculum assessment) as the basis for your ideas, discuss the pros and cons of your own therapeutic recreation curriculum.
8. Which courses within your therapeutic recreation curriculum are valued by students after the completion of their internship? Which courses had little relevance to the internship? Which courses contribute to their becoming a quality TR professional? An involved citizen? A responsible individual?
9. Which professional skills should be taught in school? Which can be better acquired after graduation?
10. To what extent can you explain the controversies surrounding TR vs. RT? To what extent do you address the big professional picture vs. the narrower view of a particular agency?
11. What admission criteria/process should be used for selecting new therapeutic recreation students?
12. What opportunities do you create or what groups do you join that demonstrate there is a community of learners among therapeutic recreation students and/or professionals?
13. What attitudes are indicative of a strong professional commitment?
14. What types of attitudes and skills are best taught during the internship?
15. What professional boundaries have you developed? When are these boundaries challenged?
16. What are the major outcomes that you recommend for a therapeutic recreation professional preparation program?

References

American Therapeutic Recreation Association. (2000). *Standards for the practice of therapeutic recreation*. Alexandria, VA: Author.

American Therapeutic Recreation Association. (2005). *Therapeutic recreation education conference manual*. Alexandria, VA: Author.

Carter, M. J., & Folkerth, J. (Eds.). (2007). *Therapeutic recreation education: Challenges and changes*. Ashburn, VA: National Therapeutic Recreation Society

Fitzgerald, G.B. (1948). Education for recreation gives movement professional status. *American Recreation Society Quarterly Bulletin, 2*, 16.

Grote, K., & Hasl, M. (1998). *Guidelines for internships in therapeutic recreation*. Hattiesburg, MS: American Therapeutic Recreation Association.

James, A. (1997–98). Recreation therapy: A history of concern, part I, 1855-1946. *Annual in Therapeutic Recreation, 7,* 83-90.

Miller, N. P. (1962). Professional preparation: New directions in the education of personnel for therapeutic recreation. *Recreation in Treatment Centers, 1,*10.

Monroe, J. E., & Connolly, P. (1997-98). Responsive curriculum development: One approach to comprehensive curriculum design. *Annual in Therapeutic Recreation, 7,* 64-73.

National Council for Therapeutic Recreation Certification™. (2007). *NCTRC™ 1997 job analysis study.* New City, NY: Author.

National Recreation and Park Association. (2000). *Standards and evaluative criteria for recreation, park resources, and leisure services baccalaureate programs.* Alexandria, VA: Author.

National Therapeutic Recreation Society. (1995). *Standards of practice for therapeutic recreation services.* Arlington, VA: National Recreation and Park Association.

National Therapeutic Recreation Society. (1997). *NTRS internship standards and guidelines for therapeutic recreation.* Alexandria, VA: Author.

Pew Health Professions Commission. (1995*). The third report of the Pew health professions commission.* San Francisco: UCSF Center for the Health Professions.

Porter. H. R., & burlingame, j. (2007). *Recreational therapy handbook of practice: ICF-based diagnosis and treatment.* Enumclaw, WA:Idyll Arbor.

Quiroga, V. A. (1995). *Occupational therapy: The first 30 years 1900 to 1930.* Bethesda, MD: American Occupational Therapy Association.

Snizek, W. E. (1972). Hall's professionalization scale: An empirical reassessment. *American Sociological Review 37,* 109-114.

West, R. E., Kinney, T., & Witman, J. (2008). *Guidelines for competency assessment and curriculum planning for recreational therapy practice* (2nd ed.). Hattiesburg, MS: American Therapeutic Recreation Association.

Wilensky, H. L. (1964). The professionalization of everyone? *American Journal of Sociology, 70,* 137-158.

CHAPTER 8

Profile of Undergraduate and Graduate Therapeutic Recreation Curricula

Norma J. Stumbo, Ph.D., CTRS™
Education Associates

Undergraduate education is the bedrock of a profession. It serves as the entry point and springboard for new professionals and shapes the ways in which they practice and work with clients. It is highly related to other professional activities such as personnel credentialing and standards of practice. Each of these is linked in its ability to define the boundaries of the profession. As such, it is vital that they are timely, are improvement-oriented, have a strong degree of consensus within the field, and are linked to the entry-level knowledge base of the profession. When undergraduate education is consistent, of high quality, and up to date with content, processes, and trends, then the profession and its clients are well served.

The purpose of this chapter is to assess the current state of affairs in therapeutic recreation education as evidenced by national studies and to raise issues that this data suggests. The chapter first begins with a brief history of literature on therapeutic recreation education spanning the last 40 years and then moves to presenting data that profiles therapeutic recreation curricula in the United States. As this data is presented, a variety of related issues and questions is raised.

Therapeutic Recreation Education

Therapeutic recreation was first recognized as a "specialty area" during the first national conference on the College Training of Recreation Leaders in 1937 at the University of Minnesota. The Athletic Institute sponsored two conferences in the late 1940s and early 1950s to develop graduate study curricular guidelines (Lindley, 1970). The outcome of a meeting between the American Association for Health, Physical Education, and Recreation and the National Commission on Teacher Education and Professional Standards, as reported by Lindley (1970), was a core curriculum for graduate study in hospital recreation.

During the interim 40 years, scores of articles have discussed a number of important issues related to therapeutic recreation education. Primarily, these writings have discussed the definition of entry-level knowledge, studied the content and status of educational offerings, proposed structures for undergraduate curricula, and addressed therapeutic recreation education in times of crises and challenges. Due to limited space in this chapter, readers are encouraged to locate and read the following references when interested in these four topics further.

- *Definition of entry-level knowledge and its relationship to the professionalization process* (Connolly & Riley, 1995/96; McGhee, 1987; McGhee & Skalko, 2001; National Council for Therapeutic Recreation Certification™ [NCTRC], 2008; Oltman, Norback, & Rosenfeld, 1989; Skalko & Smith, 1989; Stumbo, 1986; Witman & Shank, 1987)
- *Status of college and university offerings* (American Association for Health, Physical Education, and Recreation [AAHPER], 1973; Anderson, Ashton-Shaeffer, & Autry, 2000; Anderson & Leitner, 1978; Anderson & Stewart, 1980; Brasile, 1992; Kelley, Robb, Park, & Halberg, 1976; Kinney, Kinney, & Witman, 2006; Kinney & Witman, 1997; Lindley, 1970; Martin, 1971; Peterson & Connolly, 1981; Smith, 1976; Stein, 1970; Stewart & Anderson, 1990; Stumbo & Carter, 1999a, 1999b; Stumbo, Carter, & Folkerth, 2007; Stumbo, Carter, & Kim, 2006a, 2006b)
- *Proposed structuring of therapeutic recreation curricula* (Brasile, 2006; Kinney, Kinney, & Witman, 2006; Kinney, Witman, Sable, & Kinney, 2001; Monroe & Connolly, 1997/98; West, Kinney, & Witman, 2008)
- *Status of therapeutic recreation curricula on campuses during periods of change and challenge* (Austin & Hamilton, 1992; Compton & Austin, 1994/95)

While there has been growing consensus about the entry-level knowledge base for therapeutic recreation professionals, there is less agreement about how this knowledge base should be packaged and presented to preprofessional students (Brasile, 2006; Kinney, Kinney, & Witman, 2006; Peterson & Connolly, 1981; Skalko & Smith, 1989; Stumbo & Peterson, 1987). It has been noted elsewhere in the literature that systematic efforts in therapeutic recreation curriculum design have been limited and lacking in theoretical and methodological constructs necessary to define a knowledge base and to make sound curricular decisions (Austin, 1980; Brasile, 2006; Stumbo, 1986).

Several authors have expressed concern about the lack of consistency and quality in the delivery of therapeutic recreation content (Navar, 2001; Stumbo, 2001; Zabriskie & McCormick, 2000). This lack of consistent quality and delivery may put therapeutic recreation in dual jeopardy; as a viable program offering within higher education institutions (Austin & Hamilton, 1992; Compton & Austin, 1994/95) and as a viable profession within healthcare and social service arenas (McGhee, 1987; Peterson & Connolly, 1981; Skalko & Smith, 1989; Stumbo & Carter, 1999a, 1999b; Stumbo, Carter, & Kim, 2006a, 2006b).

One conclusion from a review of the above studies is that there is greater consensus on the definition of entry-level knowledge than there is in the "package" (curricula) to deliver it. While the profession generally agrees on what constitutes the boundaries of the field in terms of practice, there is little agreement on curriculum design and content. Kinney, Kinney, and Witman (2006, p. 1) noted:

The product of 'therapeutic recreation education' has been produced like homemade jelly and marketed like Smucker's Jam. Each preparation program seems to have its own recipe for the content and process of educating students for entrance into the profession.

The remainder of this chapter will use data that has stemmed from national therapeutic recreation curriculum studies to explore issues of consistency and packaging. Two sets of data will be used that have sought to provide details about course offerings and their configurations at the undergraduate level (cf., Stumbo & Carter, 1999a, 1999b; Stumbo, Carter, & Kim, 2006a, 2006b). After highlighting the relevant data, related issues will be discussed.

Research Results and Related Issues

This chapter uses data from research studies conducted by Stumbo and Carter (1999a, 1999b) and Stumbo, Carter, and Kim (2006a, 2006b) to examine the state of the art of therapeutic recreation curriculum across the United States. In 1998 (reported in 1999), the sample consisted of 114 institutions, and in 2003 (reported in 2006), 65 schools were included. The data and issues triggered by the data will be presented in the remaining sections. Readers wanting more details about the methodology and the specific data are referred to the original journal articles.

The summary of results is reported by six sections of the original survey: (a) institution and department characteristics; (b) faculty demographics; (c) student demographics; (d) accreditation status; (e) curriculum and course offerings; and (f) internship requirements. Each of these will be discussed individually.

Institution and Department Characteristics

Over 75 percent of the responding institutions in both studies were public. The average size of the colleges/universities was over 11,000 undergraduates and 3,100 graduate students. Therapeutic recreation curricula were housed most often in Colleges or Schools of Education, followed closely by Colleges or Schools of Health, Physical Education, and Recreation, then Social Science or Allied Health. Department titles were almost evenly split between Departments of Recreation and Leisure Studies, and Departments of Health, Physical Education and Recreation (and Dance). Almost three-fourths of the institutions reported that therapeutic recreation was considered an option or sequence, rather than a major or degree. "Recreation therapy" as the degree title showed a gain over "therapeutic recreation" from less than four percent in 1996 to over 13 percent in 2003.

It appears from this data that consensus on titles becomes stronger the closer one gets to the actual degree program. College titles were widely varied, department titles less so, and degree or sequence titles very much less so. "Therapeutic recreation" is the most preferred term for the degree or sequence, typically housed in a department of Recreation/Leisure Studies or HPER(D), within a diversity of college units (although most were Colleges of Education or Health, Physical Education and Recreation (and Dance).

Issues about Institution and Department Characteristics

Most institutions that housed therapeutic recreation curricula were small, public institutions. Consensus on titles grows stronger as one gets closer to the actual degree program. College or school titles varied widely, department titles less so, and sequence or option titles very little.

One issue is the autonomy of therapeutic recreation compared to other allied health professions. The vast majority of curricula were imbedded within larger departments, not having a free-standing major or degree. Few other health professions—for example, nursing, social work, or physical therapy—are sequences or options within a degree program of a different title, in a department with a different name, within such a diversified college or school.

A related issue is the independence of philosophy and mission. It is assumed that majors and departments within a college must have mission statements in alignment with the college or school in which it is housed. In that case, almost half of the therapeutic recreation curricula should be able to align with the "educational" mission within the public school system.

- What are the advantages and disadvantages of therapeutic recreation being offered primarily at smaller, public universities?
- How does the structure of the therapeutic recreation program compare with other allied health programs at your home institution?
- How well does the professional mission of therapeutic recreation align with the mission of the department and college in which it is housed within your home institution? What is the therapeutic recreation program's centrality to the larger university?
- What impact does the administrative structure have on the therapeutic recreation curriculum? What other administrative locations within the university could support the therapeutic recreation curriculum?
- What are the administrative structures of other therapeutic recreation programs within your home state? Why do you think they differ?

Faculty Characteristics

The average number of total recreation and leisure faculty in both studies was about 4.5, with a mode of 3 or 4. Slightly over 74 percent of these individuals were tenured. Most departments employed an average of 4 adjunct or part-time faculty. The average number of therapeutic recreation faculty increased slightly from 1.7 to 1.8, with each study reporting a mode of one and a range from one to five. Use of therapeutic recreation adjuncts increased slightly from 1.8 to 2.0. Most therapeutic recreation faculty was tenured. The ratio of female-to-male therapeutic recreation faculty rose slightly from 58 to 65 percent. Very few members of ethnic minority groups were employed in recreation or therapeutic recreation faculty positions. Nearly 60 percent of therapeutic recreation faculty had earned doctorates. The percentages of individuals with earned doctorates has remained stable; however, the number of faculty holding only bachelor's degrees nearly doubled. Faculty-held ranks for therapeutic recreation educators were almost evenly distributed at instructor/lecturer, assistant professor, associate professor, and full professor levels. NCTRC™ certification (84 vs. 62%), state certification/licensure (17 vs. 9%), state association membership (73 vs.

65%), and national association membership (ATRA: 62 vs. 49%; NTRS: 72 vs. 51 percent) all declined from 1996 to 2003.

Issues Related to Faculty Characteristics

Typically, therapeutic recreation curricula were housed in small departments, averaging three to four faculty members. Usually therapeutic recreation faculty served alone or with one other therapeutic recreation faculty member but were assisted through the hiring of adjuncts. Over half of the therapeutic recreation faculty held doctorates. The percentage of therapeutic recreation faculty holding only bachelors degrees increased from 4 to 6 percent. A declining percentage of therapeutic recreation faculty members were certified or members of state and/or national organizations.

One of the most compelling issues surrounding this data is the vulnerability of therapeutic recreation curricula within their home institutions. When programs are to be cut, university administrators often look for smaller units with few numbers and non-tenured faculty as starting places for budget cuts. Programs that are not central to the mission or success of the university are often vulnerable. Since most of the employing institutions are public, they remain at the near-mercy of state budgets.

- What actions can recreation and therapeutic recreation faculty take to strengthen a program and increase its centrality to a university? What specific actions could your recreation and therapeutic recreation faculty take at your home institution?
- Does the therapeutic recreation program at your institution have enough "critical mass" to make a difference to central administration?
- What are the consequences (good and bad) of having only slightly over half of the therapeutic recreation faculty holding doctorates? Of having individuals with bachelor's degrees teaching at the college level?
- What are the consequences (good and bad) of having adjunct faculty to supplement full-time faculty members? What advantages and disadvantages does it hold for the university? For the curriculum? For the students?
- Should full-time faculty be required by the profession to be certified by NCTRC™? To be a member of professional organizations? What affect does this have on the curriculum or the students? Or the faculty members' interactions with practicing professionals or other faculty?
- In your opinion, what should be the minimum qualifications for teaching faculty at your institution? Think about experience, education, and credentialing requirements.
- In your opinion, what should be the faculty's balance be between teaching, research, and service activities? Think about responsibilities both internal and external to the university.

Student Characteristics

From 1996 to 2003, the average number of undergraduate recreation and leisure majors declined from around 136 to 119 per institution; although the average number of graduate students increased from 22 to 36. The average number of therapeutic recreation majors similarly declined from an average of 51 to 36, with graduate students remaining relatively even at 11 in both studies. The percentage of schools reporting increases in undergraduate therapeutic recreation majors declined from 60 % in 1996 to 8% in 2003.

The demographics of students in the two studies showed that, on average, most therapeutic recreation majors were female (81% in 1996 and 86% in 2003), Caucasian (83% in 1996 and 86% in 2003), and employed full-time (22% in both 1996 and 2003) or part-time (64% in 1996 and 62% in 2003).

Issues Related to Student Characteristics

Enrollments within leisure and recreation programs declined nationally, and this was mirrored by therapeutic recreation enrollments as well, although graduate enrollments remained relatively stable. Most therapeutic recreation majors are female, Caucasian, and employed while attending classes.

- How are recreation and therapeutic recreation students recruited? At the undergraduate level? At the graduate level? Why is therapeutic recreation often labeled a "discovery" major?
- Why are graduate programs in therapeutic recreation found at only half of the universities reporting undergraduate degree programs?
- What patterns are being seen in national demographics? How do the demographics of therapeutic recreation students reflect the general population that they may serve? How will this affect the services provided?
- How closely aligned are the faculty and student demographics of this study's participants? Why do you think this is so? What could or should be done to recruit greater numbers of minority ethnic groups into the profession?
- What factors were occurring during the time of these studies that contributed to the patterns of therapeutic recreation enrollments in higher education?

Accreditation Characteristics

Respondents also were asked for information about status and future with the NRPA accreditation program. A smaller percentage of schools in 2003 (57%) than in 1996 (96%) had their core accredited. The likelihood of the therapeutic recreation option being accredited fell from 35% in 1996 to 30% in 2003. Of those that were accredited, reasons given for maintaining accreditation status included that it: (a) provides indication of quality; (b) supports the mission of improving curriculum across the university; (c) helps recruit potential students; (d) provides a competitive edge over similar departments across the state or region; and (e) supports the mission of improving curriculum across the country. These reasons remained in the same order of support for both studies. Only one school reported not seeking re-accreditation in the future.

Of those that were not currently accredited but planned to seek accreditation within the next five years, fewer (26%) said they would seek accreditation in 2003 than in 1996 (62%). Of those not accredited, the two top reasons were that they could not meet the standards or they could provide quality without accreditation approval.

Issues Related to Accreditation Characteristics

Fewer programs were accredited in the recreation and leisure core as well as therapeutic recreation in 2003 than in 1996. It would appear that therapeutic recreation is the most popular option among those offered by the COA. Almost all of the respondents providing an answer indicated they would seek re-accreditation. Those who had received accreditation equated it with quality and used it as a competitive edge to recruit students as well as promote their program in other ways.

- In your opinion, are programs that are not accredited likely to be of similar quality to those that are accredited? What is the purpose of program accreditation?
- What may be reasons why therapeutic recreation is the most popular option within the NRPA accreditation process?
- When you entered your therapeutic recreation program, were you aware of its accreditation status? When did you become aware of its status? How many therapeutic recreation programs are accredited currently in your state?
- What is the value of being accredited to the recruitment of students? What difference would it make to incoming students? Graduating seniors? Faculty?

Curriculum Characteristics

Each institution was asked about the number of hours required in the therapeutic recreation major. At the "average" institution, graduation requirements decreased from 130 hours in 1996 and 124 hours in 2003. From 1996 to 2003, the average number of general education hours lowered from 50 to 45; the number of supportive coursework hours decreased from 24 to 22, as did general recreation and leisure coursework (from 33 to 31 hours), while therapeutic recreation coursework increased from 19 to 24 hours. The most popular support coursework included psychology/counseling, exercise physiology/anatomy/kinesiology, and health education. The most anticipated changes in therapeutic recreation curriculum included: (a) moving to on-line course offerings (2003), (b) increasing internship requirements (1996 and 2003), (c) adding more therapeutic recreation courses (1996 and 2003), (d) adding more assignments to therapeutic recreation courses (1996 and 2006), and (e) adding more supportive coursework (1996 and 2003).

In both studies, faculty was asked to report the number and titles of required and elective undergraduate therapeutic recreation courses. These courses were analyzed in two ways: (a) by number of required and elective courses; and (b) content of course titles. The first analysis consisted of grouping university and college curriculum according to the number of required and elective courses. Although analysis is made difficult by the diversity of curricula, a few summary statements can be made.

Fewer institutions in 2003 (vs. 1996), even though they claimed to have a degree/sequence in therapeutic recreation, did not meet the NCTRC™ standards in effect at that time for therapeutic recreation coursework—three required therapeutic recreation content courses.

The most common course offered (and always required where offered) in both 1996 and 2003 was Introduction to Therapeutic Recreation. The second most common course in both studies was Principles and Practices of Therapeutic Recreation, especially for those institutions with two, three, six, or seven required courses. In 1996, the third most common course was Program Planning and Design, and in 2003, the third most common class was Leisure Education/Facilitation Techniques.

In 2003, the least frequently mentioned courses were Management of TR, Assessment/Documentation, and Issues. As in 1996, the more courses required by the curricula, the more likely these courses were to be offered and required. The greater the number of required therapeutic recreation courses, the more likely the schools were to have courses (sometimes as many as seven) that focused on disability-related information. There was very little uniformity in course offerings, although those universities offering three, four, and five required courses seemed to be the most parallel.

Issues Resulting from Curriculum Characteristics

Insights about therapeutic recreation echo observations made about the institutions at which they are housed. There is a great degree of variety and variability among and between programs, with little consistency and quality control. Although a significant number of programs reported planning to increase the number of therapeutic recreation courses and increase the stringency of their requirements, some in the sample did not meet minimal therapeutic recreation coursework standards for personnel (NCTRC™) certification in place at the time of the investigations. Most programs required three, four, or five therapeutic courses. These courses typically were Introduction to Therapeutic Recreation, Principles and Practices of Therapeutic Recreation, TR Program Planning, and Leisure Education/ Facilitation Techniques.

- What are the advantages and disadvantages of the high degree of flexibility or inconsistency among therapeutic recreation programs? How and why has this developed within the profession?
- At your institution, what other health-related professions have coursework requirements similar to your therapeutic recreation program?
- What is the relationship between a greater number of courses and a greater competency within graduates, in your opinion?
- What are the likely outcomes for students who graduate from programs who do not meet the minimal requirements for personnel (NCTRC™) certification?
- One therapeutic recreation program had one required TR course and three elective TR courses, while another institution had 11 required TR courses and six elective TR courses. As a consumer or patient of therapeutic recreation services, from which program do you want your therapist to graduate, and why?
- What actions would it take for therapeutic recreation curricula across the country to be more parallel? Why would you want it to be so? Or why not? What organization could or should be responsible for initiating this standardization?

Internship Characteristics

Internship requirements were another area of wide fluctuation between universities. When asked how many formal internships were required of majors, the average response in both 1996 and 2003 was two, with the mode being one. In terms of the number of weeks required for a senior internship, the average was 13 weeks in 1996 and 14 weeks in 2003, with a mode of 10 in 1996 and a mode of 12 in 2003. Similarly, when asked about total hours required within the senior internship, the average in 1996 was 470 and 521 in 2003. The vast majority (94% in 1996 and 98% in 2003) of institutions required the agency supervisor to be NCTRC™ certified, but only 46 to 47 percent, in both 1996 and 2003, required the university supervisor to be nationally certified.

Schools reviewed a variety of qualifications for approving senior internship sites for therapeutic recreation majors. In 2003, more institutions required an approval system (97% vs. 62% in 1996). Of these, 67 percent in both studies required an agency internship manual. Also, 93% in 2003 and 92% in 1996 required the agency supervisor to be certified by NCTRC™. In 2003, 39% required the sponsoring agency to provide proof of adherence to NCTRC™ standards, compared to 35% in 1996.

Issues Related to Internship Characteristics

It appears that for most schools, the NCTRC™ internship standards in effect at the time of the research affected the requirements of the universities. [For example, until December 31, 2002, NCTRC™ internship requirements included 10 weeks and 360 hours. As of 2003, the standards require a minimum 480-hour, 12-week internship.] The respondents' modal responses fell in line with the NCTRC™ standards effective in 1996 and 2003. While the vast majority of institutions required the agency supervisor to be certified, an NCTRC™ requirement, few ensured that the internship experience covered the job analysis areas, an additional NCTRC™ requirement. It would appear that the latter would place students in jeopardy with regard to their future certification.

- What are the typical internship or "clinical" experience requirements of other health-related professions? How do they compare to therapeutic recreation standards?
- What are the advantages and disadvantages of requiring agency supervisors to be NCTRC™ certified? Why would the same requirement not be applicable to university supervisors? Or why should the same requirement be applied?
- How do the NCTRC™ internship standards align with the NRPA/AALR Council on Accreditation internship standards, or those of NTRS and ATRA? Why do the standards differ, and which ones have the greatest impact on therapeutic recreation educational programs?
- How can students be assured of being able to sit for the national NCTRC™ examination when NCTRC™ looks at individual credentials (certification) rather than approving the educational program (accreditation)? What is the difference between certification and accreditation? What are their overall aims?
- How important is the internship to the overall educational experience of students? What are the benefits of multiple internships as the student progresses through coursework?

Summary

The intent of this chapter was to provide data-based information about therapeutic recreation programs across the nation in order to surface issues and questions about their practices, their characteristics, and their uniqueness. Readers have seen that no two institutions are exactly alike in their structure, faculty, or student characteristics. At issue is whether this inconsistency is seen as a high degree of positive flexibility or negative chaos. The remaining chapters in this book focus in more detail on some of these issues, such as accreditation, support courses, internships, and standardization of curricula.

Discussion Questions

1. Compare any three therapeutic recreation programs across the country. What would you want students to know who are entering the programs as freshmen next year?

2. How would you define a quality undergraduate therapeutic recreation program? A master's degree? A doctoral degree? What does a quality education mean? What quality indicators would you look for?

3. Assume you are a new faculty member interviewing for your first therapeutic recreation teaching job. List 12 questions/concerns that you would ask before taking the position, based on the information presented in this chapter.

4. In your opinion, is it more important to learn global skills such as critical thinking and communication, or technical skills such as how to write SOAP notes? Justify your position.

5. What does the student need to know to be a good consumer of therapeutic recreation education? What does the patient/client need to know to be a good consumer of therapeutic recreation services?

References

American Association for Health, Physical Education, and Recreation. (1973). *Guidelines for professional preparation programs for personnel involved in physical education and recreation for the handicapped.* Washington, DC: Author.

Anderson, S. C., Ashton-Shaeffer, C., & Autry, C. E. (2000). Therapeutic recreation education: 1999 survey. *Therapeutic Recreation Journal, 34*(4), 335-347.

Anderson, S. C., & Leitner, M. J. (1978). Course sequencing in recreation curricula. *Therapeutic Recreation Journal, 12*(2), 15-20.

Anderson, S. C., & Stewart, M. W. (1980). Therapeutic recreation education: 1979 survey. *Therapeutic Recreation Journal, 14*(3), 4-10.

Austin, D. R. (Ed.). (1980). *Directions in health, physical education, and recreation: Therapeutic recreation curriculum: Philosophy, strategy, and concepts.* Bloomington, IN: Indiana University School of Health, Physical Education, and Recreation.

Austin, D. R., & Hamilton, E. J. (1992). The future of therapeutic recreation education: In the 1990s and beyond. In G. Hitzhusen, & L. T. Jackson (Eds.), *Expanding horizons in therapeutic recreation XIV* (pp. 77-104). Columbia, MO: Curators University of Missouri.

Brasile, F. (1992). Professional preparation: Reported needs for a profession in transition. *Annual in Therapeutic Recreation, 3*, 58-71.

Brasile, F. M. (2006). Response to concept paper on undergraduate education in therapeutic recreation. In M. J. Carter, & J. E. Folkerth (Eds.), *Therapeutic recreation education: Challenges and changes* (pp. 21-30). Ashburn, VA: National Therapeutic Recreation Society.

Compton, D. M., & Austin, D. R. (1994/95). Perceptions of therapeutic recreation in higher education. *Annual in Therapeutic Recreation, 5*, 57-67.

Connolly, P., & Riley, B. (1995–96). Entry-level job skills: Reinvestigation of the national job analysis of the practice of therapeutic recreation. *Annual in Therapeutic Recreation, 6,* 26-37.

Kelley, J. D., Robb, G. M., Park, W., & Halberg, K. J. (1976). *Therapeutic recreation education: Developing a competency -based entry-level curriculum.* Champaign, IL: University of Illinois.

Kinney, J. S., Kinney, T., & Witman, J. (2006). Concept paper on undergraduate education in therapeutic recreation. In M. J. Carter, & J. E. Folkerth (Eds.), *Therapeutic recreation education: Challenges and changes* (pp. 1-20). Ashburn, VA: National Therapeutic Recreation Society.

Kinney, W. B., Witman, J. P., Sable, J. R., & Kinney, J. S. (2001). Curricular standardization in therapeutic recreation: Professional and university implications. In N. J. Stumbo (Ed.), *Professional issues in therapeutic recreation: On competence and outcomes* (pp. 87-103). Champaign, IL: Sagamore.

Lindley, D. (1970). Relative importance of college courses in therapeutic recreation. *Therapeutic Recreation Journal, 4*(20), 8-12.

Martin, F. W. (1971). Survey of college and university coursework in therapeutic recreation service. *Therapeutic Recreation Journal, 5*(3), 123-129, 140.

McGhee, S. A. (1987). Professional preparation: Matching competency acquisition with appropriate educational experiences. *Therapeutic Recreation Journal, 21*(4), 63-73.

McGhee, S. A., & Skalko, T. K. (2001). A pilot study for the validation of entry-level competencies for therapeutic recreation practice. *Annual In Therapeutic Recreation 10,* 57-71.

Monroe, J. E., & Connolly, P. (1997/98). Responsive curriculum development in therapeutic recreation: One approach to comprehensive curriculum design. *Annual In Therapeutic Recreation, 7,* 64-73.

National Council for Therapeutic Recreation Certification.™ (2008). *2007 Job analysis.* New City, NY: Author.

Navar, N. H. (2001). Keynote: Thoughts on therapeutic recreation education. In N. J. Stumbo (Ed.), *Professional issues in therapeutic recreation on competence and outcomes* (pp. 23-35). Champaign, IL: Sagamore.

Oltman, P. K., Norback, J., & Rosenfeld, M. (1989). A national study of the profession of therapeutic recreation specialist. *Therapeutic Recreation Journal, 23*(2), 48-58.

Peterson, C. A., & Connolly, P. (1981). Professional preparation in therapeutic recreation. *Therapeutic Recreation Journal, 15*(2), 39-45.

Skalko, T. K., & Smith, M. M. (1989). The status of therapeutic recreation in state personnel systems: A national study. *Therapeutic Recreation Journal, 23*(2), 41- 47.

Smith, S. H. (1976). Practitioners' evaluation of college courses, competencies, and functions in therapeutic recreation. *Therapeutic Recreation Journal, 10*(4), 152-156.

Stein, T. A. (1970). Therapeutic recreation education: 1969 survey. *Therapeutic Recreation Journal, 4*(2), 4-7, 25.

Stewart, M. W., & Anderson, S. C. (1990). Therapeutic recreation education: 1989 survey. *Therapeutic Recreation Journal, 24*(3), 9-19.

Stumbo, N.J. (1986). A definition of entry-level knowledge for therapeutic recreation practice. *Therapeutic Recreation Journal, 20*(4), 15-30.

Stumbo, N. J. (2001). A national view of therapeutic recreation curriculum: What does it mean for our future? In N. J. Stumbo (Ed.), *Professional issues in therapeutic recreation on competence and outcomes* (pp. 37-51). Champaign, IL: Sagamore.

Stumbo, N. J., & Carter, M. J. (1999a). National therapeutic recreation curriculum study part A: Accreditation, curriculum, and internship characteristics. *Therapeutic Recreation Journal, 33*(1), 46-60.

Stumbo, N. J., & Carter, M. J. (1999b). National therapeutic recreation curriculum study part A: University, faculty, student, and placement characteristics. *Therapeutic Recreation Journal, 33*(3), 241-250.

Stumbo, N. J., Carter, M. J., & Folkerth, J. E. (2007). Investigation of graduate therapeutic recreation curricula in the United States. *American Journal of Recreation Therapy, 6*(2), 19-31.

Stumbo, N. J., Carter, M. J., & Kim, J. (2006a). 2003 National therapeutic recreation curriculum study part B: University, faculty, student, and placement characteristics. *Therapeutic Recreation Journal, 28*(1), 22-52.

Stumbo, N. J., Carter, M. J., & Kim, J. (2006b). 2003 National therapeutic recreation curriculum study part A: Accreditation, curriculum, and internship characteristics. *Therapeutic Recreation Journal, 28*(1), 53-71.

Stumbo, N. J., & Peterson, C. A. (1987). Therapeutic recreation curricula: Professional preparation and its relationship to the knowledge base. In R. Paulsen, & D. Ferguson (Eds.), *Proceedings of the Fourth Annual Therapeutic Recreation Research Colloquium*, Michigan State University.

West, R. E., Kinney, T., & Witman, J. (2008). *Guidelines for competency assessment and curriculum planning for recreational therapy practice* (2nd ed.). Hattiesburg, MA: American Therapeutic Recreation Association.

Witman, J. R., & Shank, J. W. (1987). Professionalization in therapeutic recreation: State leaders' perceptions of progress, priorities, and strategies. *Therapeutic Recreation Journal, 21*(4), 32-42.

Zabriskie, R. B., & McCormick, B. P. (2000). Accreditation and academic quality: A comparison with healthcare accreditation. *Schole: A Journal of Leisure Studies and Recreation Education, 15*, 31-45.

CHAPTER 9

Accreditation: The Quest for Educational Quality

Marcia Jean Carter
Western Illinois University – Quad Cities

Ramon B. Zabriskie
Brigham Young University

The primary goal of human service professions is the successful provision of the highest quality services possible. In an effort to assure the quality of their services, most professions develop standards and utilize a variety of formal mechanisms to monitor and promote quality. Sometimes these mechanisms are clearly interconnected and dependent upon one another, and other times they are more independent or freestanding. Currently in therapeutic recreation, there are three primary mechanisms that are utilized somewhat independently to help promote and assure quality (see Figure 9.1). In order to enter the profession, individuals seek and maintain credentials that demonstrate their professional competence by voluntarily meeting national certification standards and/or being required to meet professional licensure standards in states with current licensure laws. Practicing professionals are encouraged to provide quality services by voluntarily adhering to American Therapeutic Recreation Association (ATRA) or National Therapeutic Recreation Society (NTRS) standards of practice and codes of ethics. Finally, professional preparation programs and institutions voluntarily demonstrate their quality by meeting the educational standards of institutional and specialized accrediting bodies. Although all three approaches to professional quality are important, assuring quality in the education process is perhaps the most essential as it sets a clear foundation for each of the others whether voluntary, required, or formally connected or not.

Since its inception, the primary purpose of accreditation has been to protect the consumer and to assure quality of the educational experience (Schray, 2006b). It is a form of self-regulation in which institutions and programs come together to develop standards, policies, and procedures for self-examination and judgment by peers (Council for Higher Education Accreditation, CHEA, 2006a). According to CHEA, the national oversight body

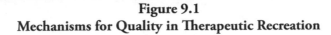

Figure 9.1
Mechanisms for Quality in Therapeutic Recreation

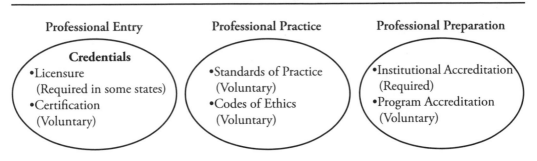

governing accreditation, standards have the intent of (a) advancing academic quality in teaching, learning, research, and service, (b) demonstrating accountability in order to foster continuing public awareness, confidence, and investment, and (c) encouraging, where appropriate, self-scrutiny and planning for change and for needed improvement through assessment of quality, especially student achievement (CHEA, 2006b).

Today, there are two basic forms of accreditation in higher education, institutional accreditation and specialized or programmatic accreditation. Institutional accreditation is a process that examines the quality of postsecondary institutions as a whole. "It provides an external evaluation to confirm that an institution fulfills its mission and goals and is equal in quality to other comparable institutions" (Zabriskie & McCormick, 2000, p. 4). Institutional accreditation is conducted by regional accrediting bodies like the North Central Association of Colleges and Schools that assess, for example, adequacy of financial resources to support the institution's programs. There are more than 6,400 accredited post-secondary institutions across the United States (Schray, 2006a).

Specialized or programmatic accreditation, on the other hand, "focuses on a specific school, department, or professional preparation curriculum that prepares students to enter a given profession" (Zabriskie & McCormick, 2000, p. 4). It utilizes specific standards that address knowledge, skills, and abilities considered important or essential by standards of practice, professional competencies, and/or practitioners in the profession (Peterson, 1980). Presently there over 18,700 specialized accredited programs like those found in the health professions (Schray, 2006a).

Professional or specialized accreditation is based on guided self-evaluation, overseen by non-governmental organizations; relies on peer review; and judges academic unit effectiveness against a set of defined standards (Task Force on Accreditation of Health Professions Education, 1999). The overarching purpose of specialized accreditation is to improve the quality of the educational program and ensure its scope is relevant to professional practice (Wise, 2005). Specialized accreditation is commonplace among the health and human service fields as the assurance of quality is a concern of the public, professions, and institutions in which programs reside. An accreditation program is designed to assist the specialized program to evaluate itself objectively and then for the accrediting body to validate what the professional program has said about itself. The process usually involves five steps: (a) design of a self-study by the program, (b) peer review conducted by faculty, administrators, and public representatives of the accrediting body, (c) site visits by a peer review team composed of members other than those sitting on the accrediting body, (d) recognition actions by the accrediting body, and (e) monitoring and oversight for a designated time period ranging from a few years to ten years (Schray, 2006a).

This chapter considers the historical context of accreditation and the evolution of therapeutic recreation accreditation. The issues surrounding accreditation are examined through the introduction of a model that explores the interrelationships among the entities associated with assuring quality in the delivery of therapeutic recreation services.

Historical Perspective on Accreditation

Alstete (2004) identifies three "generations" of accreditation. The first generation of accreditation addressed admission standards and the role of postsecondary institutions as distinguished from secondary schools (Alstete). This generation saw the role of accreditation as standardizing admission criteria across the nation. Early accreditation efforts were led by regional accreditation bodies like the North Central Association of Colleges and Schools and specialized accreditors in the healthcare field, specifically the American Medical Association (AMA) that focused on quality and existence of common standards in medical schools (Alstete).

Accreditations that emerged around the turn of the century included osteopathy in 1897, medicine in 1904, and nursing in 1916 (Task Force on Accreditation of Health Professions Education, 1999). The Flexner Report prepared by the AMA in conjunction with the Carnegie Foundation in 1910 resulted in the adoption of standards for medical education that saw the consolidation and closure of schools that were out of compliance with the standards. This effort focused on quality, consistency, and improvement in program offerings. The standards and processes used in this effort became the forerunner of present-day specialty criteria and procedures.

During the second generation of accreditation, from the early 1900s to the early 1970s, an attempt was made by national recognition bodies to oversee and standardize regional and specialty accreditation efforts. Six regional accrediting bodies were created between 1885 and 1924 to address relationships between secondary schools and higher education and to strengthen admission criteria. Specialty accreditation also increased with the professionalization and specialization of the healthcare workforce; currently there are more than 50 accreditation programs in the health professions alone (Task Force on Accreditation of Health Professions Education, 1999). Proliferation of regional accrediting bodies and specialty accreditation contributed to a call for coordination of accreditation efforts at the national level. Consequently, commencing in 1949 national oversight entities emerged to recognize accrediting bodies and balance institutional needs with the curricular concerns of regional and specialized accreditation. Today, this oversight body is CHEA, established in 1996, which is basically the accrediting body of accrediting bodies. Concerns of specialized accreditors are the focus of ASPA—Association of Specialized and Professional Accreditors, formed in 1993. National recognition bodies like CHEA require accrediting bodies to undergo review and submit self-studies to retain their status as accrediting agents. During this generation of accreditation, standards of regional and specialized bodies tended to assess inputs like operation of the unit, and structural features like instructional resources of institutions and programs, rather than quality of outcomes like student performance.

The third generation of accreditation, 1970s to present, commenced with the creation of a three-tiered accreditation system. Currently, the three tiers encompass (a) the national recognition bodies like CHEA, (b) regional accrediting bodies like the North Central Association of Colleges and Schools that accredit institutions, and (c) specialty accreditation like the Council on Accreditation (COA) of the National Recreation and Park Association (NRPA) that currently accredits programs, including those offering therapeutic recreation. To achieve accreditation, specialty programs must reside in accredited institutions, and it is desirable for specialty and regional accreditation bodies to achieve recognition by CHEA.

Presently, accreditation entities are concerned with how standards address quality of academic programs while responding to increasing levels of concern from stakeholders. These concerns emanate from the changing environment surrounding higher education like the shift from teaching in traditional classrooms to learning across distances and funding shifts from government to non-government sources. The public is questioning the significance of accreditation as related to its inherent worth and value compared to the increasing costs of earning a degree.

From the second to the current generation of accreditation, the focus has shifted to qualitative measurement of performance, especially student learning outcomes, and the public's call for transparency, consistency, and accountability (Schray, 2006a, 2006b). At present, the focus of assessment is on review of results and qualitative measurements of learner outcomes rather than the input-driven numerical analysis of best practice and structural standards (Alstete, 2004). For example, in therapeutic recreation, the profession is challenged to identify the outcomes desired of effective entry-level practitioners rather than assessing the length of the internship or faculty professional development activities.

History of Accreditation for Therapeutic Recreation

The first therapeutic recreation competencies, 12 at the undergraduate level and five at the graduate level, were listed in 1977 in the accreditation standards of the Council on Accreditation (COA) of the National Recreation and Park Association and the American Association for Leisure and Recreation (NRPA/AALR). They evolved during the second generation of accreditation maturation when the focus was on practice and structural processes. As noted by Zabriskie and McCormick (2000), these standards addressed program inputs and structure rather than learner outcomes. The COA is recognized by CHEA as a specialized accrediting body. Additionally, COA is listed in the AMA Health Professions Career and Education Directory, 2006-2007, as the accrediting agency for the therapeutic recreation specialist occupation (AMA, 2006). A brief review of the evolution of therapeutic recreation accreditation finds the routes of today's standards and processes at the forefront of accreditation efforts in recreation, park resources, and leisure services.

1950s and 1960s—Origin of the Standards

As early as 1953, the Standards and Training Committee of the Hospital Recreation Section of the American Recreation Society made recommendations on professional preparation standards (O'Morrow, 1997). A conference in 1961, Therapeutic Recreation

Curriculum Development Conference, sponsored by the National Recreation Association's Consulting Service on Recreation for the Ill and Handicapped had the intent of (a) identifying competencies needed by a professional in therapeutic recreation, and (b) suggesting a curriculum based on these competencies (Miller, 1962). The six content areas listed as the approval criteria for "Therapeutic Recreation" as a "Professional Emphasis" under "Recreation Program Administration" in the 1975 Standards and Interpretations for Accreditation in Recreation and Parks (NRPA, 1975) were an outgrowth of this conference. MacLean (1963) reported the competencies and a "tentative proposal for therapeutic recreation option at the undergraduate level to meet stated competencies" (p. 27). Criteria in the therapeutic recreation specialization included: (a) ability to adapt recreation activities to the needs of the atypical, and (b) knowledge of anatomy and physiology, disabling conditions, and medical terminology. Recommended coursework included: (a) abnormal psychology, (b) human growth and development, and (c) adapted physical education. Compulsory field experiences in recreation in a medical setting also were proposed (MacLean).

1970s—First Specialization

Therapeutic recreation competencies appeared as the initial undergraduate professional specialization under the "Professional Emphasis" in "Recreation Program Services" in the first revision of the accreditation standards, Standards and Evaluative Criteria Recreation, Leisure Services and Resources Baccalaureate and Masters Degree Programs (NRPA, 1977). Twelve competencies were listed for an undergraduate professional specialization in therapeutic recreation. At the graduate level, five advanced competencies defined the specialization in therapeutic recreation along with three other specializations, recreation program generalist, administration of recreation and park systems, and recreation resources administration. The undergraduate competencies were considered as prerequisites or deficiency areas for the graduate program. Undergraduate competencies introduced included: (a) assessment, (b) documentation, (c) prescription, and, (d) evaluation plans. Hence, the first presentation of the APIE (assessment, planning, implementation and evaluation) process that today remains at the heart of therapeutic recreation practice.

1980s and 1990s—Expansion of the Standards

The standards published (NRPA) in 1981 identified only undergraduate competencies. Baccalaureate degree standards consisted of three components: 1) general education, 2) professional education core, and 3) option standards in four areas, one of which was therapeutic recreation. The previous 12 specialization standards were expanded to 24 option standards. New competencies introduced in these standards included: (a) understanding the role of therapeutic recreation as a component of health-care systems, (b) knowledge of theory and techniques of therapeutic intervention, (c) ability to demonstrate and translate medical record charting techniques, and (d) understanding of a variety of treatment approaches and their implications for therapeutic recreation programming (NRPA).

During the late 1980s and into the 1990s, researchers explored issues related to professional preparation, including the definition of entry-level curricula, curriculum standardization, and the progress toward professionalization as related to professional preparation (Brasile, 1992; McGhee, 1987; Peterson & Connolly, 1981; Skalko & Smith, 1989; Stumbo, 1986; Stumbo & Carter, 1999; Witman & Shank, 1987). Stumbo's (1986) study subjected the existing 24 option standards to experts who concurred that all of the areas were important to entry-level practice. A final outcome of the study was a list of 37 competencies that identified entry-level content areas, incorporating the previous 24 standards to define the therapeutic recreation knowledge base (Stumbo). The COA option standards were revisited. The standards published in 1990 (NRPA) conceptualized the therapeutic recreation option into four foundational standards: 1) anatomy and physiology, 2) medical and psychiatric terminology, 3) abnormal psychology and 4) illness and disability information with 22 additional option standards supported by Stumbo's study. The 1990s standards made reference, for the first time, to competencies in the following areas: (a) healthcare and human service systems, (b) legal aspects of practice, (c) reimbursement, (d) quality assurance, and (e) interdisciplinary approaches (NRPA). Thus, the decade of the 1980s saw the initial reference to healthcare and human service systems complemented by standards that made reference to "treatment" and "medical" competencies. With the publication of the 1990 standards, some began to question the placement of therapeutic recreation accreditation standards under the umbrella of recreation, park resources, and leisure services.

Since 1937, one of the common forums used to generate curricula content has been conferences associated with federally funded grant projects and professional association initiatives. A document published by the American Therapeutic Recreation Association (ATRA) (Kinney & Witman, 1997) grew out of the 1995 ATRA Midyear Issues Forum Curriculum Conference. The competency assessment guide and curriculum planning tool identified seven content areas each with delineated competencies and recommended course titles. This document was updated in 2008 (West, Kinney, & Witman, 2008). Simultaneously, the National Council for Therapeutic Recreation Certification (NCTRC™) published the results of an updated national job analysis that reported a list of job tasks (49) with a revised exam content outline (NCTRC™ 1997). In 1997-1999, a COA taskforce, comprised of representatives from ATRA, NCTRC™, National Therapeutic Recreation Society (NTRS), and COA, conducted a national survey to update the 1990 COA therapeutic recreation option standards. Respondents considered the published statements from the ATRA conference, the NCTRC™ job analysis, and the existing therapeutic recreation option statements. Taskforce recommendations were proposed changes in the 1990 COA standards (NRPA, 2000). Changes to the professional preparation standards required all students to: (a) gain competence in accountability tools like writing outcome-oriented goals, (b) demonstrate understanding of cultural perspectives of service delivery, and (c) demonstrate an awareness of how to comply with regulatory standards. In the therapeutic recreation option standards, the foundational understandings were expanded from four to six with the incorporation of content on (a) pharmacological terminology, (b) holistic health and wellness including disease prevention and promotion, and (c) the self as an instrument. The remainder of the option standards, 22, were consolidated and enhanced with content in the following areas: (a) roles of caregivers, (b) inclusionary practices, (c) therapeutic recreation delivery models, (d) trends in health and human service systems, (e) multiculturalism, (f) standards of practice, (g) discharge and transition processes, (h) evaluative tools with client and program outcomes, and (i) ethical principles in practice and conduct. Figure 9.2 presents a summary of the recreation and therapeutic recreation content in the COA standards from inception to 2013, the date upon which all option standards, including therapeutic recreation, will be phased out.

2000 to 2013—Researching Accreditation Alternatives

Although there were no changes made to therapeutic recreation standards in early 2000, it was a time of great debate in preparation for significant change. Scholars (Zabriskie & McCormick, 2000) noted that the current COA standards focused almost exclusively on structure and process indicators of quality, while trends in quality measurement and accountability demanded a focus on outcomes. Carter and Zabriskie (2006) also concluded that if accreditation was to fulfill the purpose of being a good indicator of educational quality, it was critical for the COA to include outcome-based standards in the accreditation process.

Another highly debated issue closely related to academic accreditation was the concern for consistency in therapeutic recreation curriculum and competencies. Although accreditation is recognized as a primary indicator of quality in higher education, in therapeutic recreation it has also been utilized as a means to identify and verify entry-level professional competencies (Harvey, 2004; Wise, 2005). Furthermore, curriculum studies have consistently reported the need to identify uniform criteria that can be used to define and standardize therapeutic recreation preparation (Brasile, 1992; McGhee & Skalko, 2001; Stumbo & Carter, 1999; Stumbo, Carter, & Kim, 2004; Zabriskie & McCormick, 2000). The content of the COA standards, however, have also been criticized with some scholars (Brasile, 1992; McGhee & Skalko, 2001) suggesting that various content areas are not essential to current practice and there should be a greater healthcare focus.

The COA standards in effect until 2013 reflect the historical development of curricula in recreation, park resources, and leisure services. As a consequence, the professional standards required of all programs seeking accreditation include competencies in (a) conceptual foundations of play, recreation and leisure, (b) professional history and organizations (c) leisure delivery systems, (d) program and event planning, (e) administration and management, and (f) legal aspects of recreation, park resources, and leisure services. As shown in Figure 9.2, therapeutic recreation programs that become accredited address standards of the recreation industry as well as specific option standards in therapeutic recreation. Therefore, some authors have proposed alternative curriculum designs that align preparation with allied health professions (Kinney & Witman, 1997; Monroe & Connolly, 1997/98; Navar, 2001; Powell & Sable, 2001). With questions related to competencies and content, the ability of the COA accreditation process to serve as the mechanism for bringing consistency to therapeutic™ recreation curriculum was also questioned.

Another debate revolved around those institutions that have chosen not to be accredited through the COA. Of the 89 schools accredited by COA as of January, 2008 (NRPA), only 35 had recognized therapeutic recreation options. Furthermore, NCTRC™ Executive Director, Dr. Bob Riley, indicated that sufficient coursework is available for students from approximately 135 programs to be eligible to sit for the Certified Therapeutic Recreation Specialist (CTRS) exam. Thus, with no external monitor of curricular quality for therapeutic recreation programs that are not accredited, many institutions are not held accountable for their therapeutic recreation curricula and may or may not be providing sufficient

---

Figure 9.2
Accreditation Standards of the Council on Accreditation

Date	Recreation Content	Therapeutic Recreation Content
1975	*Professional Education* History; theory; philosophy; community organization; recreation and park services; leadership; programming; services to special groups; administration; prof. lab. experiences; internship	*Professional Emphasis* Anthropology and sociology; anatomy and physiology; physical, mental, emotional disabilities; group dynamics and social psychology; guidance and counseling techniques; medical terms, settings, implication of limitations related to rec. activity
1977	*Professional Education* History; theory; philosophy; community organization; recreation and park services; leadership; programming; services to special groups; administration; prof. lab. experiences; internship	*Professional Specialization* Illness and disability program implications; Treatment/rehab delivery systems; admin. of treatment/rehab settings; facilitation and counseling techniques; needs of clients, activity adaptations; ind./group assess, prescription, eval. plans; treatment/rehab. documentation; admin. of comm. programs for clients; facility accessibility; institution to community service continuum; abnormal growth and development; special education; psychology; sociology; anatomy/physiology/kinesiology; authorized TR practicum
1981	*Professional Education* Rec., park history; rec., leisure theory/philosophy; nat. resources and rec. exp.; leisure delivery systems; legislative process; leisure activities; Assessment techniques; program plan process; Ind/group facilitation; rec. for special pops.; spec. pops. accessibility; facility plan and design; management principles; leisure education; professional issues; concept of rec. profession; research concepts; 300 hr field exp.; advocacy role; ethical/prof. behavior	*Professional Specialization* Anatomy and physiology; etiology of illness and disability; medical and psychiatric terms; self-concepts of disabled persons; societal attitudes towards disabilities; bio-psycho-social limitation of dis.; assistive techniques; healthcare delivery systems; TR in healthcare systems; legal issues in TR; laws, regulations, standards; agency referral procedures; treatment approaches; habilitation, rehab. prevent. concepts; TR continuum of service; TR program planning; client assessment; design individual treatment plan; therapeutic interventions; adaptive devices and equipment; translate medical charts; TR credentialing; TR ethical/prof. behavior; TR as advocate

Figure 9.2
Accreditation Standards of the Council on Accreditation (continued)

Date	Recreation Content	Therapeutic Recreation Content
1990	*Professional Competencies* *Conceptual Foundations* Play, recreation, leisure; history/ significance of PRL; sig. of PRL in life cycle; leisure and natural envir. *Leisure Services Prof.* History of leisure profession; professional issues; profession/organizations; ethical/ professionalism; professional resources *Leisure Delivery Systems* Resources for leisure exp.; diverse leisure systems; leisure for all populations; advocate for all pops. *Program Strategies* Role/content of leisure prog.; organize/ conduct programs; leisure lifestyle/ lifespan; leadership techniques; resources for participants *Assessment, Planning, Evaluation* Prog. participation require.; assessment techniques; planning services, resources; designing leisure services; research; computer / statistical techniques; evaluation principles; evaluate goals/ objectives *Administration/management* Marketing; organizational behavior, accountability; personnel management; operation of resources; financing, budgeting; public relations and promotion; communication tools; computer programs *Legislative and legal aspects* Legal foundations/legislative process; Legal concepts; risk management *Field Experiences* Field experience prior to intern.; 400 hr internship	*TR Option* *Foundational Standards* Human anatomy and physiology; medical and psychiatric terms; abnormal psychology; Characteristics of ill/dis, effect on leisure; *Option Standards* TR theories and concepts; psy/soc/phys/hist. sig. of TR; social attitudes/self-concepts of dis.; TR as advocate; standards of practice; credentialing processes; TR content; healthcare/human service systems/TR; health/human service professionals; Mainstreaming, integration concepts; leisure education content/techniques; activity and task analysis; comp./specific TR programming; ind. / group interventions; assistive/adaptive devices, equipment; assessment techniques; ind. treatment / program plans; management techniques; agency referral processes; documentation and QA; legal tools and processes; legislation, regulation, standards TR Option *Foundational Standards*
2000	Professional Competencies *Conceptual Foundations* Play, recreation, leisure; history/ significance of PRL; tech/econ/	Human anatomy and physiology; medical and psychiatric terms; abnormal psychology;

Figure 9.2
Accreditation Standards of the Council on Accreditation (continued)

Date	Recreation Content	Therapeutic Recreation Content
2000	cultural sig. PRL; sig. of PRL in life cycle; Leisure and natural envir.; environmental ethics *Leisure Services Prof.* History of leisure profession; professional issues; profession/organizations; multiculturalism; ethical / professionalism; prof. competence/resources *Leisure Delivery Systems* Resources for leisure exp.; diverse leisure systems; inclusive practices; advocate for all pops *Program Strategies* Role/content of leisure prog.; outcome goals/objectives; leisure and lifecycle; groups/leadership tech.; resources for participants *Assessment, Planning, Evaluation* Prog. participation require.; assessment techniques; planning services, resources; designing leisure services; research and evaluation; computer/statistical techniques; evaluation principles; evaluate goals/ objectives *Administration/management* Marketing; organizational behavior, accountability; personnel management; operation of resources; financing, budgeting; marketing, public relations/ promotion; communication tools; computer programs *Legislative and legal aspects* Legal foundations/legislative process; legal concepts; regulatory standards; safety, emergency, risk management *Field Experiences* Field experience prior to intern.; 400 hr/10 wk internship in option	Medical and disabling conditions; holistic health and wellness; self as an instrument *Option Standards* Healthcare/TR models/theories/concepts; psy/soc/ phys/hist. sig. of TR; health/human service agencies/TR; social attitudes/self-concepts; TR as an advocate; gov. regulations, SOP, ext. accreditation; credentialing processes; assessment techniques/procedures; healthcare/human service prof./TR; roles of family, client, others in TR process; apply inclusive practices to TR; leisure education content/techniques; TR process/ activity/ task analyses applied; facilitation techniques/ interventions; management; referral, discharge, transition processes; evaluative tools, client/ program outcomes; documentation, QA, improvement in TR; legal and ethical principles; legislation, regulation, standards to TR
2013	Outcomes Standards and Assessment (7.00 series) 1. The academic unit shall have institutionally approved degree	Options no longer exist 8.00 Standards within the 8.00 series will be provided by associations that represent specializations and reflect the

Figure 9.2
Accreditation Standards of the Council on Accreditation (continued)

Date	Recreation Content	Therapeutic Recreation Content
2013	requirements for all programs being considered for accreditation.	specialized knowledge, understanding, and abilities required to achieve minimum competencies in particular professional areas.

2. The academic unit shall maintain an up-to-date assessment plan for the learning outcomes in Section 7.00, along with assessment reports compatible with the respective regional accrediting association's expectations and consistent with institutional expectations.

3. Students graduating from the Program shall demonstrate knowledge of the scope of the profession, professional practice, and the historical, scientific, and philosophical foundations of the relevant recreation, park resources, leisure experiences, or human service industries.

4. Students graduating from the Program shall demonstrate the ability to design, implement, and evaluate recreation, park resources, leisure, and human service offerings facilitating targeted human experiences and that embrace personal and cultural dimensions of diversity.

5. Students graduating from the Program shall be able to demonstrate entry-level knowledge about management/ administration of recreation, park resources, and leisure services.

6. Students graduating from the Program shall demonstrate, through a comprehensive internship of not less than 400 clock hours, the ability to use diverse, structured ways of thinking to solve problems related to different facets of professional practice, engage in advocacy, and stimulate innovation.

educational experiences. Although some claim that preparing students to meet minimum eligibility (sitting) requirements for the NCTRC™ exam is sufficient, Brasile (2006) warned the profession of the pitfalls of using minimum credentialing standards as a benchmark for professional preparation. He explained that a competency based standardized curriculum with a mechanism to hold academic institutions accountable for the education process is essential prior to examining individual students for minimum competencies gained after the education process.

In response to such debate and as the result of an ATRA-NTRS work group that conducted a formal assessment of higher education needs, a Joint Task Force on Higher Education representing the profession was created in June of 2001. Goals of the Task Force included ensuring the continuation and strengthening of therapeutic recreation professional preparation programs and increasing the consistency in preparation of therapeutic recreation professionals. An expected outcome in the Task Force strategic plan was a therapeutic recreation curriculum conference. This meeting, similar to the ATRA meeting held in 1995 that resulted in publication of *Guidelines for Competency Assessment and Curriculum Planning in Therapeutic Recreation: A Tool for Self-Evaluation* (Kinney & Witman, 1997) and led to subsequent recommendations to COA as the standards were revised in 1997-1999, was held in 2005.

To bring focus to the conference, professionals were charged with writing discussion and response papers around which conference sessions were structured. Central themes focused on undergraduate and graduate preparation and accreditation, while ancillary papers addressed retention and recruitment, trends and influences in higher education and healthcare, education in related disciplines, distance education, and a summary report of NCTRC™. Conference attendees concurred with the need to explore accreditation relationships and options. Four accreditation alternatives, previously supported by Brasile (1998), were identified: (a) in concert with COA strengthen the current, operating structure, process and outcome standards, (b) develop an in-house therapeutic recreation accreditation process, (c) align with a CHEA-recognized allied health accrediting body, and (d) develop a specific therapeutic recreation accrediting body and gain CHEA recognition. Each alternative may be viewed as a separate solution or they may be seen as steps in a long-term plan to achieve self-regulation of accreditation for the therapeutic recreation profession. For example, alternative one, revisions in current standards, may lead to monitoring through peer recognition or professional self-reviews and eventually to accreditation by an independent body recognized by CHEA as is found with physical and occupation therapy.

Following the May 2005 Therapeutic Recreation Education Conference (TREC), data analysis teams reviewed the conference papers and narrative notes of conferee discussions with the intent of validating central themes and priorities in higher education preparation. The investigative teams affirmed the need to assess accreditation options. Subsequent rankings by therapeutic recreation educators attending the 2006 ATRA and NTRS national conferences identified "addressing specialized accreditation with COA" as the highest priority on a list of 14 professional preparation concerns.

While therapeutic recreation educators and the professional associations were attempting to address the nature of higher education preparation, two concurrent initiatives with possible impacts on curriculum consensus were underway. The COA convened two strategic planning sessions to address CHEA's focus on outcome measurements and the need to update the current structure and process oriented COA standards. Results of these 2006 sessions were a commitment to rewrite the standards to become outcome focused and an invitation to professional bodies to define their professional specialty criteria to be included in the COA standards. As shown in Figure 9.2, commencing in 2013, the COA will no longer accredit options but rather will rely on associations to present for COA approval professional specialty outcome oriented learner standards. Furthermore, as long as the standards presented in Figure 9.2 (7.00 series) are met and if an association presents and has approved professional specialty standards, for a program having a singular focus such as therapeutic recreation, the professional curriculum and specialization may be one and the same. Simultaneously, NCTRC™ conducted a job analysis study to update the 1997 job tasks and exam content outline information that COA considered as the accreditation standards were revised in 1999. The 2007 Job Analysis results reflected a consistent pattern with the 1997 study: One noted outcome was an observed drop in the reported importance of organization and management tasks with a slight increase in the number of job tasks related to direct client care (NCTRC™, 2007). Thus, the stage was set to assess accreditation alternatives and propose updated outcome-oriented criteria.

Accreditation and Accountability: A Conceptual Model

With the stage set for significant change, it may be useful to re-examine the conceptual role that accreditation can and should play in academic preparation, professional entry, and the overall growth and development of any profession. Accreditation is recognized as the primary measure of quality in higher education and is used as the mechanism that holds academic institutions accountable for providing a comprehensive, consistent, relevant education. Smith (2006) claimed that academic preparation and the accreditation process must be based on "mutually agreed upon standards of practice" (p. 236) so that clear learning outcomes can be established. He also explained that there must be a direct relationship or a complete "feedback loop" (p. 237) between curricula, accreditation, and entry into the field. Brasile (2006) drew similar conclusions while addressing undergraduate curriculum standardization. He argued that the answer to the curriculum standardization dilemma is a curriculum accreditation process that is based on mutually agreed upon "competencies, skills, and experiences" (p. 27) to which all education programs must adhere in order for their graduates to enter the profession through a certification or licensure process. Both authors identified the same essential components necessary for continued growth and improved professional preparation in any profession. These components fit together in an ongoing cycle or feedback loop (see Figure 9.3) that continually improves quality and accountability throughout the professional preparation process.

All professional preparation programs should base curriculum development on current standards of practice, professional competencies, practice regulations, and ethical conduct codes. These are identified through regular job analyses and other interactions with professionals in the field. Professional organizations fulfill an integral role in this process by organizing practitioners and educators and facilitating the development and regular revision of professional practice standards and codes of ethics. Researchers and credentialing bodies also assist in this role by conducting regular studies that identify current competencies needed to provide quality professional services in the field. Professional preparation programs must

Figure 9.3
Quality and Accountability Cycle

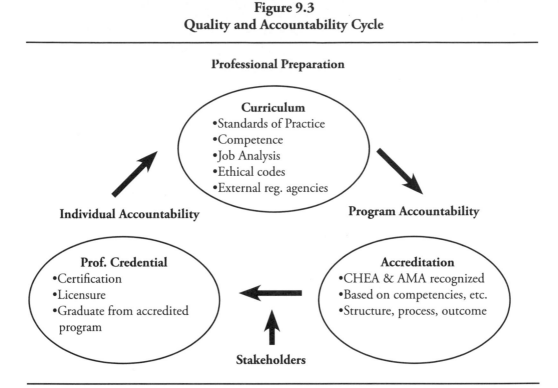

then be held accountable for providing an effective and comprehensive curriculum based on these foundational documents and beliefs.

Specialized or program accreditation is the mechanism that holds academic programs accountable for their curriculum and education process. Accreditation bodies must base their standards and evaluation on the same standards of practice, professional competencies, practice regulations, and ethical conduct codes. Therefore, they must also work closely with practitioners represented by professional organizations and with educators who are developing curricula. Specialized accreditation bodies must also be recognized by oversight bodies such as CHEA in order to maintain the integrity of the accreditation process and assure the use of the most current and effective forms of quality measurement. For example, in therapeutic recreation, the COA had been frequently criticized (Carter & Zabriskie, 2006; Zabriskie & McCormick, 2000) for relying primarily on structure- and process-based standards and not moving toward outcomes, but it was their accountability to CHEA that facilitated the COA's 2006 decision to move to outcome-based measurement. Nevertheless, it is necessary to have an effective accreditation process that utilizes structure, process, and primarily outcome measures based on consistent standards and competencies to hold professional preparation programs accountable for the quality of the education provided. This accreditation process must, then, be linked to entrance into the professional field of practice.

As both Smith (2006) and Brasile (2006) concluded, the accreditation process (or program accountability) must be connected to individual accountability or entrance into the field in order to complete the accountability cycle. Entrance into most professions is typically identified through a credentialing process such as licensure or certification. The credentialing process is the mechanism that holds graduates accountable for knowledge, understanding, and ability related to the same standards and competencies, and typically does so through the completion of practical experiences (e.g., internships, clinical supervision hours), eligibility requirements, and the passing of a competency-based exam.

The primary link to program accountability is generally found in exam eligibility criteria that require applicants to be graduates of accredited professional preparation programs. In other words, a student must first graduate from an accredited program and then can be held accountable by qualifying for and passing a certification and/or licensure exam that indicates successful entry into the field.

Thus, the "full-circle" nature of the quality and accountability cycle enables the accreditation process to hold all universities accountable for consistent quality professional preparation, and allows the professional credentialing process to hold all individuals accountable for meeting minimum competencies. As a result, there are better, more consistently prepared professionals entering a profession. These new practitioners, in turn, are those who will revise and improve future standards of practice and competencies, which in turn will drive curricula and accreditation. The overall process may also be influenced by other stakeholders, such as professional and governmental regulatory bodies that impose standards and expectations on curricula, programs, and individuals. In this manner, the quality and accountability cycle represents an ongoing process that continually and effectively strengthens academic preparation, professional entry, and the overall growth and development of a profession.

Conceptualizing Accreditation Alternatives

The first of the four accreditation alternatives is to strengthen the current COA standards. According to this model, curriculum development and revision should be based on current standards of practice (ATRA, NTRS) and the most current competency evaluation documents (i.e., 2007 NCTRC™ job analysis and West, Kinney, & Witman, 2008). The profession could respond to the COA's 2006 invitation by recommending therapeutic recreation outcome criteria based on the same standards and competencies. Such a move would allow the currently AMA-recognized and CHEA-approved accreditation body to develop a more meaningful, competency-based, outcome-focused accreditation process. And, as Brasile (2006) suggested, with a more "meaningful accreditation process, it should then be very unproblematic for NCTRC™ to change the education-based CTRS™ certification standard to state the student must be a graduate of an accredited recreation therapy program" (p. 28). With this alternative, the quality and accountability cycle would be completed in a timely and fiscally responsive manner, and the COA is already recognized by CHEA and by the AMA as the accreditation body of therapeutic recreation specialists (Donini-Lenhoff, 2008). Also with this approach, professional preparation remains closely aligned with professions in the recreation, park resources, leisure experiences, and human service industry or industries.

Developing an in-house therapeutic recreation accreditation process is the second of four accreditation alternatives. This option could result in an internal review process managed by the profession. This approach, as suggested by Brasile (1998), is a natural outgrowth of the work of a number of authors (West, Kinney, & Witman, 2008; McGhee & Skalko, 2001) and is found among the allied health professions (Commission on Accreditation Approval for Dietetics Education of the American Dietetic Association). This alternative enables the design of a professional preparation program based on current therapeutic recreation standards of practice and competencies. Although it would require substantial financial resources and time, recognition by CHEA and the AMA would be likely goals, and the quality and accountability cycle would also be completed.

The third of four alternatives is to align with an already-CHEA-recognized allied health-accrediting body. The Commission on Accreditation of Allied Health Education Programs (CAAHEP) is the likely entity as the successor to AMA and the largest accreditor that reviews and accredits more than 2,000 educational programs in 21 occupations in the health sciences field (Donini-Lenhoff, 2008). To accomplish this, a committee on accreditation (COA) would be formed to manage the process and make recommendations to the Board of Directors (BOD) of CAAHEP. A committee of interest would also develop the standards, referred to as essentials, for approval with final disposition coming from the BOD. The formation of these two entities requires the profession to devote considerable time, financial resources, and personnel to identify standards and develop an operational structure. Conceptually, this alternative would shift professional preparation to an allied health education curriculum rather than a recreation-based model while benefiting from the CHEA accreditation recognition of CAAHEP. Additionally, the new graduate would have come from an accredited program enabling this criterion to be required by the certifying body and thereby completing the quality and accountability cycle.

The fourth alternative is to develop a specific therapeutic recreation accrediting body and gain CHEA recognition. The outcome is the creation of a nationally recognized accrediting body as found with professions like occupational and physical therapy. Since 2000, approximately one-third of the CAAHEP programs have taken this path in order to gain more visibility and greater perceived autonomy and brand themselves as independent health professions rather than allied health professions (Donini-Lenhoff, 2008). Accrediting bodies of these professions incorporate as private non-profit agents to seek recognition from CHEA. Once recognized by CHEA, the accrediting body operates as an autonomous entity periodically resubmitting self-studies to retain national recognition as a profession or specialty accrediting entity. CHEA ensures accrediting bodies follow due process and have financial resources to sustain the process. Additionally, the body benefits from legal council and advocacy resources of CHEA. Thus, this alternative finds each of the components in the conceptual model focused on therapeutic recreation; the curriculum, accreditation process, and the professional credential. On one hand, this alternative would appear to require even more time and resources than any of the others, yet on the other, outcomes of either or all of the previous options could become resources to facilitate achievement of this alternative and actualize the processes of the quality and accountability model.

Regardless of the accreditation alternative, the timely completion of the quality and accountability cycle is essential. It would lead to better, more consistently prepared

CTRS™'s entering the field, who in turn, would influence future standards of practice and competencies that would drive future therapeutic recreation curricula and accreditation.

Summary

In this chapter, a number of significant factors associated with accreditation were presented. Two basic forms of accreditation in higher education were introduced, and the chapter focused primarily on specialized or programmatic accreditation. A historical perspective of accreditation was summarized, followed by the historical development of specialized accreditation in therapeutic recreation. Considerable detail was given to the current state of accreditation in therapeutic recreation including criticisms of the COA process such as the lack of outcome measurement and questions about content, the limited number of institutions seeking and obtaining accreditation, the lack of a mechanism to promote the need for accreditation, and finally the relationship of accreditation to standardizing curriculum, identifying therapeutic recreation competencies, and professional development. A summary of the 2005 TREC conference presented four accreditation options and identified specialized accreditation as the highest of 14 priorities among therapeutic recreation educators.

Finally, a conceptual model was presented that discussed the relationship of accreditation to academic preparation, professional entry, and the overall growth and development of professions. The Quality and Accountability Model identifies three necessary components that must hold one another accountable to enable an ongoing process that effectively improves the quality of academic preparation, professional entry, level of professional care and service provided in the field, and ultimately the overall growth and development of a profession. The implementation of such a model in therapeutic recreation addresses criticisms and issues related to the current accreditation discussion.

If this model can indeed provide clear direction for therapeutic recreation, the question becomes is the profession willing to follow the necessary steps to activate the cycle and be held accountable? Most significant changes that lead to long-term growth and development of a profession typically require short-term sacrifices in order to progress (i.e., as with the growing pains felt by the profession in the 1980s when NCTRC™ upgraded certification criteria). Whatever the course, the time for action is clearly now. The accreditation stage is set, and the future of therapeutic recreation will depend on the leadership and cooperation of its practitioners, educators, and researchers to take action that clearly links professional preparation to program and individual accountability.

Discussion Questions

1. Compare and contrast the four accreditation options available to therapeutic recreation using Internet resources available from CHEA, CAAHEP, COA and related health professions and the AMA health professions career and education directory. Explain the strengths and weaknesses of each option.
2. Identify the perceptions of students, faculty, professionals, and the public on the significance and relevancy of accreditation standards. Identify how accreditation addresses the issues of curriculum consistency, relevancy, transparency, and accountability.

3. List strengths, criticisms, and issues related to the current accreditation debate in therapeutic recreation. Discuss how each would or would not be addressed through effective implementation of the Quality and Accountability Model.

4. Identify possible steps that would be necessary for the profession to take in order to achieve accreditation option four—an autonomous nationally recognized accreditation process required of all academic programs and used as an eligibility criterion for individual accountability. Discuss possible short-term challenges and growing pains as well as long-term benefits or concerns related to this process for the profession as a whole as well as for any related stakeholders (i.e., accreditation bodies, credentialing bodies, professional organizations, academic institutions, professionals in the field, educators, allied health agencies, third-party reimbursement entities, etc.).

References

Alstete, J. W. (2004). *Accreditation matters achieving academic recognition and renewal.* San Francisco, CA: Wiley Periodicals, Inc.

American Medical Association. (2006). *Health professions career and education directory 34th edition 2006-2007.* Chicago, IL: Author.

Anderson, S. C., Ashton-Shaeffer, C., & Autry, C. E. (2000). Therapeutic recreation education: 1999 survey. *Therapeutic Recreation Journal, 34*(4), 335-347.

Brasile, F. (1992). Professional preparation: Reported needs for a profession in transition. *Annual in Therapeutic Recreation, 3*, 58-71.

Brasile, F. (2006). Response to concept paper on undergraduate education in therapeutic recreation. In M. Carter, & J. Folkerth (Eds.), *Therapeutic recreation education: Challenges and changes* (pp. 21-29). Ashburn, VA: National Therapeutic Recreation Society.

Brasile, F. (1998). The recreation therapy degree program: Trends in education. In F. Brasile, T. K. Skalko, & j. burlingame (Eds.), *Perspectives in recreational therapy* (pp. 367-382). Ravensdale, WA: Idyll Arbor, Inc.

Carter, M. J., & Zabriskie, R. B. (2006). Accreditation in therapeutic recreation. In M. Carter, & J. Folkerth (Eds.), *Therapeutic recreation education: Challenges and changes* (pp. 221-234). Ashburn, VA: National Therapeutic Recreation Society.

Commission on Accreditation of Allied Health Education Programs. (2006). What is CAAHEP? Retrieved December 3, 2006 from http://www.caahep.org

Council for Higher Education Accreditation. (2006a). Fact sheet #5 accrediting organizations in the United States: How do they operate to assure quality? Retrieved December 10, 2006 from http://www.chea.org/pdf/fact_sheet_5_operation.pdf

Council for Higher Education Accreditation. (2006b). *Recognition of accrediting organizations policy and procedures.* Washington, D.C.: Author.

Donini-Lenhoff, F. G. (2008). Coming together, moving apart: A history of the term *Allied Health in education, accreditation, and practice, 37*(1), 45-52.

Harvey, L. (2004). The power of accreditation: Views of academics. *Journal of Higher Education Policy and Management, 26*(2), 207-223.

Kinney, T., & Witman, J. (1997). *Guidelines for competency assessment and curriculum planning in therapeutic recreation: A tool for self-evaluation.* Hattiesburg, MS: ATRA.

MacLean, J. R. (1963). Therapeutic recreation curriculums. *Recreation in Treatment Centers, 2,* 23-29.

McGhee, S. A. (1987). Professional preparation: Matching competency acquisition with appropriate education experience. *Therapeutic Recreation Journal, 21*(4), 63-73.

McGhee S. A., & Skalko, T. K. (2001). A pilot study for the validation of entry-level competencies for therapeutic recreation practice. *Annual in Therapeutic Recreation, 10,* 57-71.

Miller, N. P. (1962). Professional preparation: New directions in the education of personnel for therapeutic recreation. *Recreation in Treatment Centers, 1,* 110-112.

Monroe, J. E., & Connolly, P. (1997/98). Responsive curriculum development in therapeutic recreation: One approach to comprehensive curriculum design. *Annual in Therapeutic Recreation, 7,* 64-73.

National Council for Therapeutic Recreation Certification™. (1997). *1996 NCTRC™ job analysis: Job tasks.* Thiells, NY: Author.

National Council for Therapeutic Recreation Certification™. (2007). *2007 NCTRC™ job analysis report: NCTRC™ report on the international job analysis of Certified Therapeutic Recreation Specialists.* New City, NY: Author

National Recreation and Park Association. (2008). Accredited programs. Retrieved June 3, 2008 from http://www.nrpa.org/content/default.aspx?documentID=826

National Recreation and Park Association. (2008). *Outcomes standards and assessment.* Ashburn, VA: Author.

National Recreation and Park Association. (1975). *Standards and interpretations for accreditation in recreation and parks.* Alexandria, VA: Author.

National Recreation and Park Association. (1977). *Standards and evaluative criteria for recreation, leisure services, and resources curricula baccalaureate and master's degree programs.* Alexandria, VA: Author.

National Recreation and Park Association. (1981). *Standards and evaluative criteria for recreation, park resources, and leisure services baccalaureate programs.* Alexandria, VA: Author.

National Recreation and Park Association. (1990). *Standards and evaluation criteria for baccalaureate programs in recreation, park resources, and leisure services.* Arlington, VA: Author.

National Recreation and Park Association. (2000*). Standards and evaluative criteria for baccalaureate programs in recreation, park resources, and leisure services.* Ashburn, VA: Author.

Navar, N. H. (2001). Keynote: Thoughts on therapeutic recreation education. In N. J. Stumbo (Ed.), *Professional issues in therapeutic recreation on competence and outcomes* (pp. 23-35). Champaign, IL: Sagamore.

O'Morrow, G. S. (1997). Does accreditation of therapeutic recreation programs really make a difference? Pro and con. In D. M. Compton (Ed.), *Issues in therapeutic recreation: Toward a new millennium* (2nd ed.). (pp. 237-254). Champaign, IL: Sagamore Publishing.

Peterson, C. A., & Connolly, P. (1981). Professional preparation in therapeutic recreation. *Therapeutic Recreation Journal, 15*(2), 39-45.

Peterson, D. G. (Ed.). (1980). *A guide to recognized accrediting agencies, 1981-1982*. Washington, DC: Council on Post-secondary Accreditation.

Powell, L., & Sable, J. (2001). Professional preparation of allied health practitioners and special educators using a collaborative transdisciplinary approach. *Schole: A Journal of Leisure Studies and Recreation Education, 16*, 33-48.

Schray, V. (2006a). Assuring quality in higher education: Key issues and questions for changing accreditation in the United States. Retrieved November 5, 2006 from http://www.ed.gov/about/bdscomm/list/hiedfuture/reports/schray.pdf

Schray, V. (2006b). Assuring quality in higher education: Recommendations for improving accreditation. Retrieved November 5, 2006 from http://www.ed.gov/about/bdscomm/list/hiedfuture/reports/schray2.pdf

Skalko, T. K., & Smith, M. M. (1989). The status of therapeutic recreation in state personnel systems: A national study. *Therapeutic Recreation Journal, 23*(2), 41-47.

Smith, S. H. (2006). A response to a concept paper: Accreditation in therapeutic recreation. In M. Carter, & J. Folkerth (Eds.), *Therapeutic recreation education: Challenges and changes* (pp. 235-237). Ashburn, VA: National Therapeutic Recreation Society.

Stumbo, N. J. (1986). A definition of entry-level knowledge for therapeutic recreation practice. *Therapeutic Recreation Journal, 20*(4), 15-30.

Stumbo, N. J., & Carter, M. J. (1999). National therapeutic recreation curriculum study part A: Accreditation, curriculum and internship characteristics. *Therapeutic Recreation Journal, 33*(1), 46-60.

Stumbo, N. J., Carter, M. J., & Kim, J. (2004). 2003 National therapeutic recreation curriculum study part A: Accreditation, curriculum and internship characteristics. *Therapeutic Recreation Journal, 38*(1), 32-52.

Task Force on Accreditation of Health Professions Education. (1999). *Strategies for change and improvement*. San Francisco, CA: Center for the Health Professions [On-line]. Available: http://futurehealth.ucsf.edu/pdf_files/accredit.pdf

West, R. E., Kinney, T., & Witman, J. (Eds.). (2008). *Guidelines for competency assessment and curriculum planning for recreation therapy practice* (2nd ed.). Hattiesburg, MS: ATRA.

Wise, A. E. (2005). Establishing teaching as a profession the essential role of professional accreditation. *Journal of Teacher Education, 56*(4), 318-331.

Witman, J. R., & Shank, J. W. (1987). Professionalization in therapeutic recreation: State leaders' perceptions of progress, priorities, and strategies. *Therapeutic Recreation Journal, 21*(4), 32-42.

Zabriskie, R., & McCormick, B. (2000). Accreditation & academic quality: A comparison with healthcare accreditation. *SCHOLE: A Journal of Leisure Studies and Recreation Education, 15*, 31-46.

CHAPTER 10

Reconciling Different Professional Expectations of Student Internships

Peggy Holmes-Layman, Ph.D., CTRS™
Eastern Illinois University

John Henry Pommier, Ph.D., CTRS™
Eastern Illinois University

The internship in therapeutic recreation is a pivotal learning experience for students, and as such, must be seen as one that needs much thought, planning, and involvement by all the players in the process, including the student, the university supervisor, and the agency/site supervisor. The student on his or her internship is beginning to take on the role of a professional that includes self-responsibility for the guidance and development of her or his career. A successful internship provides the student with the opportunity to integrate class information, field experiences, and accumulated knowledge in a working environment with a qualified practitioner. The student, perhaps for the first time, is actually involved in doing the "job" of a CTRS™. The student greatly benefits from receiving timely feedback and guidance from the agency/site supervisor and the university supervisor. When a student accepts an internship placement at a site, the student also is accepting the policies, rules, and regulations of the agency. Thus, the student is placed in a demanding, yet safeguarded position, representing both the university as its student and the agency as its intern.

It is also important to realize that the benefits extend to individual students, the agency/site supervisor, and the university supervisor. The profession must provide education for those who are entering the profession by those who are practiced. This occurs in work settings where therapeutic recreation services are delivered. Faculty in colleges and universities can convey information that will help students master many aspects of the profession; however, the "real world" always will contain an infinite array of variables that can only be known through experience. Qualified practitioners must offer that opportunity to help students further bridge the gap between theory and practice. For practitioners, who must put in many hours of planning and management to have an intern, the rewards are great. Every person involved benefits from a well-designed and executed internship.

Most universities document specific purposes of the student internship in a course description, a syllabus, or internship manual. These purposes or objectives focus on student competencies, such as applying classroom-acquired theory and skills; learning the varied aspects of service delivery in unique settings; addressing and understanding the range of competencies required to become certified by the National Council for Therapeutic Recreation Certification (NCTRC™); and gaining in-depth practical experiences under the qualified supervision of a Certified Therapeutic Recreation Specialist (CTRS™) with consistent feedback and evaluation. A secondary purpose may be for practitioners to serve the profession and cooperate in the preparation of entry-level professionals.

It is apparent that the student, the university supervisor, and the agency site supervisor have much connection and involvement in the internship process. Where do they get direction for this complex process? Guidance for developing and implementing sound internships is provided by accrediting bodies and the professional organizations of the field of therapeutic recreation. These internship standards and guidelines are presented in the next section.

Internship Standards/Guidelines

At least four organizations are directly involved in defining the therapeutic recreation internship process. The first is the Council on Accreditation (COA) of the National Recreation and Park Association. NRPA's COA accredits recreation and therapeutic recreation college and university curricula. This body appoints representatives who help evaluate the curriculum of recreation, therapeutic recreation, and other related options in a university. They compare the university and its curriculum against a set of standards. If the standards are adequately met, the university curriculum becomes accredited. It is important to note that a university program voluntarily chooses to engage in this review process. These guidelines must be followed if faculty wants its curriculum accredited (see Chapter 9 for a full explanation).

Standard 8:42, specifically mentioning the internship, states the following: "Internship, essentially a full-time continuing experience in a leisure services assignment, of at least 400 clock hours over an extended period of time, not less that 10 weeks (if an option is accredited, the internship should be directly related to such option)" (NRPA, 2000, p. 18). (Current standards may be found at www.nrpa.org).

The credentialing body for therapeutic recreation is the National Council for Therapeutic Recreation Certification (NCTRC™). NCTRC™ is the nationally recognized body established in 1981 that develops the guidelines for certification and certification requirements for therapeutic recreation professionals. They have published guidelines for the internship experience within the *Candidate Bulletin of Information*, describing the minimal elements that must be present for an internship to be considered acceptable (NCTRC™, 1999a). It is important to note that these guidelines are the only guidelines that must be followed if one desires to become certified as a Certified Therapeutic Recreation Specialist (CTRS™). Readers should be reminded that standards periodically change and they should refer to the various organizations' (NCTRC™, NTRS, ATRA, COA) standards that are current at the time of their internship and certification needs. (Current standards may be found at www.nrpa.org).

The third organization that provides direction for the internship is the National Therapeutic Recreation Society (NTRS). NTRS is a professional membership organization serving therapeutic recreation professionals and is a branch of NRPA (a professional organization for the many fields relating to parks and recreation). NTRS (1997) has published standards and guidelines specific to the therapeutic recreation internship experience. They detail recommendations for all aspects of the internship including: purpose and goals; roles and responsibilities of the student, practitioner, and university supervisor; and a section regarding graduate student internships. They also provide a variety of internship-related forms (i.e., internship agreement, internship evaluation, etc.) (NTRS, 1997). (Current standards may be found at www.nrpa.org).

The American Therapeutic Recreation Association (ATRA) is the fourth organization that provides a definition of the student internship. Like NTRS, this professional organization has a publication called *Guidelines for Internships in Therapeutic Recreation*, which describes various recommended aspects. Their guidelines cover basic concerns, such as roles and responsibilities of the student, practitioner, and educator. It also includes an appendix with sample projects, assignments, and protocols. Among other contributions, a unique section is offered on how to market internships (Grote & Hasl, 1998). (Current standards may be found at www.atra-online.org).

Before specific discrepancies and similarities are discussed in depth, general reasons for differences among the professional bodies will be discussed.

Some General Reasons Why Standards Conflict

There is much confusion or differing expert opinions related to the internship experience. These differing opinions extend to something as foundational as the use of terms. Throughout the field, various terms are used to describe the same aspect of the internship experience. For example, the terms "internship experience" and "field placement experience" are used to describe the same situation. The ATRA guidelines recognize this problem and present a glossary for clarification at the beginning of their document (Grote & Hasl, 1998).

It is clear that ensuring a uniform experience for students is nearly impossible when the standards are conflicting. As Stumbo and Carter (1999, p. 59) note, "If there is no standardization of curricula, then it follows that there is little or no standardization of the degree or 'exit skills for graduates.'" As a discipline, therapeutic recreation needs to have all of its students trained according to similar standards for basic competencies, including the competencies learned during the internship experience. Many reasons exist as to why the standards vary.

One of the reasons they vary is that the four organizations differ in terms of their mission and their power. The mission of the NRPA Council on Accreditation is to recognize university and college programs that meet a set of standards for college curricula. Its main purpose is as an accrediting body for specialized university programs. They award accreditation to educational programs and are not in the business of attesting to individual student competence.

Similarly, as a credentialing body, the mission of NCTRC™ is to certify qualified individuals to practice the profession of therapeutic recreation and to develop the most recent and the most relevant guidelines by attending to job analyses collected from representative sample(s) of therapeutic recreation specialists. The data obtained direct NCTRC™ in assessing minimal competencies of individuals. NCTRC™'s power lies in granting the title "CTRS™," and they can deny the right to the title; individuals misrepresenting the title are subject to legal action (NCTRC™, 1999a, p. 20).

The two professional organizations, (ATRA and NTRS), have as their mission the representation of the paid members and their needs, and to advance the therapeutic recreation profession. Membership (of practitioners, students, educators, and other supporting individuals or organizations) is voluntary, and adherence to any of their policies and procedures is a voluntary effort. Their standards and guidelines can exceed minimum levels of competency. Adherence is unenforceable; however, professional organizations have an important role in promoting the highest levels of practice. For further clarification of these issues, the reader is referred to the NCTRC™ newsletter article by Luken (1999).

It is interesting to note that the NCTRC™, the NTRS, and the COA guidelines utilize terms that focus on the agency and university as the primary audience. The ATRA guidelines appear to use terms that address practitioners as the main audience. This can illustrate another reason why the standards are in conflict; it may be due to the different contexts in which those concerned operate (i.e., students, practitioners, educators, accrediting representative, etc.), with each having unique pressures and concerns coloring the interpretation of how an internship can/should be organized. The influence of the different contexts will surface throughout this chapter because they affect the level of standardization possible for internships.

Levels of Agreement Between Organizations

Many of the universities reported adhering to the standards set forth by the COA and the NCTRC™. Sixty-six out of 109 schools were accredited by the COA (Stumbo & Carter, 1999, p. 51-52), and NCTRC™ Certification Standards were one of the top four reasons for curriculum initiation and revision (Stumbo & Carter, 1999, p. 52). With many universities acknowledging the importance of accreditation of programs and certification of professionals, it is sometimes difficult to understand why greater consensus has not been achieved on internship standards. The following discussion consists of dividing the standards into categories that can be described as high, moderate, or low, based on the degree of agreement by ATRA, COA, NCTRC™, and NTRS. Table 10.1 provides a graphic display of these levels of agreement.

High Level of Agreement

Sequence of the internship
Where the internship falls in the curriculum has relative consensus, relatively speaking. The COA has no comment on this aspect, and the ATRA, NCTRC™ and NTRS guidelines are practically in agreement (Table 10.1). According to NCTRC's™ *Field Placement Guidelines*, an acceptable internship takes place after a student completes the majority of

their therapeutic and general recreation courses: "... no less than twelve semester or eighteen quarter units of coursework with six semester and nine quarter units in therapeutic recreation content coursework" (NCTRC™, 1999a, p. 10). As many faculty have seen, students do best when they have finished all TR-related coursework and can make a complete shift to the working world and its demands.

Goal/purpose of the internship

The goal/purpose category is another of the listed guidelines in Table 10.1 that is not in conflict. The guidelines are in general agreement that the purpose of the internship is to experience practical application of coursework, skill development, and competencies related to the practice of therapeutic recreation. This also includes the opportunity to engage in the "TR process." Both ATRA and NCTRC™ give a detailed description of what the TR process is. ATRA's definition of the TR process includes "establishing a therapeutic relationship, individualized assessment, goal setting, and the design of an individual treatment/program plan, implementing therapeutic recreation services with selected interventions, evaluating progress toward the plan, developing a discharge/transition plan, coordinating services, and documenting the outcome of service" (Grote & Hasl, 1998, p. 5). The process as defined can occur in a wide variety of settings. NTRS discusses the purpose and goals in broader terms, though with similar intent, and the COA has no comment. Thus, three of the four show a relatively high level of agreement.

Areas of the Standards Where Agreement is Moderate

These are issues that may be dealt with differently by the various organizations, but it appears that consensus is attainable. Stumbo and Carter (1999) called for "a national movement for consensus on curriculum requirements to be initiated by one of the national membership or credentialing organizations" (p. 59). A national discussion could successfully focus on the following areas of: (a) agency supervision, (b) site requirements, and (c) students' responsibility.

Agency supervision

The COA gives no specific direction to agency/site supervision, and the other three organizations are in moderate agreement. NCTRC™ requires the agency/site to have a full-time (32-hour workweek minimum), actively certified CTRS™ as supervisor (NCTRC™, 1999a, p. 5). Additionally, NCTRC™ requires that an acceptable agency/site practitioner practice the therapeutic recreation process as defined by the knowledge and skill areas (based from NCTRC's™ job analysis study).

NTRS recommends the CTRS™ certification, two years of experience, and the state credential, if appropriate. They also recommend that the supervisor must be a full-time employee and have supervisory policies in place. ATRA states that the site supervisor must be a CTRS™, have two years in the practice of therapeutic recreation, and "six months to one year of employment at the present agency" (Grote & Hasl, 1998, p. 2). In addition, they call for the supervisor to have experience in supervision and related coursework. They recommend a state credential if the site is in a state where state credentialing exists. ATRA has the most involved recommendation, requiring the practitioner to have courses or experience

Table 10.1
Current Internship Standards for Therapeutic Recreation

Current Standards	COA	NCTRC™	ATRA	NTRS	Degree of Agreement
Sequence of Intership	No comment	Can occur after 12 semester or 18 quarter units with at least 6 semester and 9 quarter units in TR content	After 120 hrs. of fieldwork or 3 academic credits; all TR classes & most other classes	After required academic courses	High
Length of Internship	400 clock hrs., not less than 10 weeks (for Gen. Rec. and TR)	480 hrs.; 12 consecutive weeks (effective Dec. 31, 2002)	15 weeks, 600 hrs.	15 weeks, at least 35 hrs./week; 525 hrs.	Low
Purpose/ Goals	No comment	Experimental learning of TR service as defined by NCTRC™ Job Analysis	Apply knowledge; develop skills develop & expand competencies; learn/do TR process	Practical experience; apply theory/skills; develop TR competency; opportunity to augment or improve TR service	High
Agency/Site Supervisor	No comment	FT (min 32 hrs./wk.), on site; CTRS™	CTRS™; 2 yrs. in TR; 1 yr. at agency; state credential; supervisory experience or courses in supervision	FT CTRS™; 2 yrs. in TR; state credential; plus supervisory policies	Moderate
University Supervisor	No comment	"Faculty"	CTRS™; has role to select good site for student; list various tasks including providing latest TR info to agency	CTRS™; state credential; role includes various tasks including contact, advising, evaluation	Low
Student Responsibilities	No comment	Get copy of supervisor CTRS™ documents; follow NCTRC™ booklet/ CTRS™ certification documents	Variety of tasks including using ATRA's competency assessment; portfolio development; establish goals	Follow school manual	Moderate

Table 10.1 (continued)
Current Internship Standards for Therapeutic Recreation

Current Standards	COA	NCTRC™	ATRA	NTRS	Degree of Agreement
Agency Manual	No comment	None; state "if no manual, student ask site/school how experience will be structured"	Detailed listing of what content should be	Guidelines given in appendix for content	Low
University Manual	No comment	(Same as for agency manual above)	College should develop manual; guidelines given	Guidelines given in appendix for content; as well as content for course description	Low
Site Requirements	No Comment	Site should follow TR practice/process as outlined in Job Analysis; intern program should be well established at site	Gives detail in language geared to practitioner as opposed to agency	Site comply with NTRS intern standards, NTRS Standards of Practice; NTRS Guidelines for Administration, ADA & other regulations; meet voluntary standards such as JCAHO; have TR policy manual, WPO and intern plan; TR service should be comprehensive & interdisciplinary; TR service shall facilitate leisure lifestyle through Tx, LE, & Rec Parr.; have specified areas for program; private work area for student & supervisor	Moderate
Affiliation Agreement Contracts	No comment	Should be shared responsibility between university and agency	Should be affiliation agreement	University should develop agreement; example given in appendix; also example given of letter of agreement	Low
Agency Application Guidelines	No comment	No comment	No comment	Sample given in appendix	Low

Table 10.1 (continued)
Current Internship Standards for Therapeutic Recreation

Current Standards	COA	NCTRC™	ATRA	NTRS	Degree of Agreement
Screening of Agencies	No comment	No comment	Presented as task for practitioners to do; suggested tips given	No comment	Low
Documents to Refer to	No comment	Application booklet; field placement guidelines	University and agency follow Guidelines for Competency, Assess & Curriculum Planning; ATRA Standards, ATRA Code of Ethics, NCTRC™ Job Analysis	NTRS documents, Guidelines, university manual, agency manual	Low
Evaluation and Grading	No comment	Shared responsibility between university & agency; expectations stated as university responsible for academic work; agency covers site responsibilities; internship must be reflected on transcript as receiving academic credit; grade developed from agency and university information	Suggest midterm and final evaluations developed & done by site supervisor; lists university supervisor responsibilities	Appendix provides guidelines to evaluate all aspects; all involved student, practitioner, educator	Low
Intern Sites Charging Fee- or Providing Student Responsibilities	No comment	No comment	States charging as a possibility; info on this plus benefits should be included in school's database of intern sites and in info about the agency program	States benefits to student should be explained on forms	Low

in supervision, albeit the organizations do not differ significantly in their recommendations. It is interesting to note that Stumbo and Carter's (1999) study found that 94% of universities required an agency supervisor to be certified by NCTRC™, leaving 6% of the universities offering therapeutic recreation internship experiences under the supervision of individuals not considered qualified by NCTRC™ standards. Students experiencing the latter situation would be ineligible to sit for the NCTRC™ exam and to later become certified themselves.

ATRA, NTRS, and NCTRC™ address how supervision occurs when several layers exist in the organization. A common example of this situation is when there is a person whose job is to coordinate volunteers or interns, but who is not a CTRS™ themselves. This internship/volunteer coordinator may be supervising the CTRS™, and thus technically supervising any of the TR interns. The language concerning this in the documents is more clarifying in its impact than in generating much disagreement.

In considering the site supervisor and his or her qualifications, two additional differences are worth presenting. Both of these differences have a major ethical impact. The first issue is the motivation of a CTRS™ in assuming the responsibility of supervising a student intern. There is the broad reasoning that a professional helps educate the future professionals of the field. That is certainly true, yet practitioners may be more likely to take a student intern and supervise him/her well if additional motivations exist. Supervising an intern correctly is a very involved task. Projects such as preparing and updating a manual for the site (NTRS and ATRA suggestions) and marketing one's program (an ATRA suggestion) take time, energy, and resources. How can a practitioner justify this effort against competing responsibilities? ATRA suggests universities provide incentives for practitioners to take on their student interns. Grote and Hasl (1998) listed ideas such as honorariums, guest lecture invitations, free textbooks, free tuition, or an appointment to advisory committee(s). None of the three other organizations (COA, NCTRC™, or NTRS) address this concern.

The second issue is practitioners charging students for the experience of completing an internship at a site. ATRA's guidelines singularly mention that some agencies require a fee from the student for the internship experience. This appears to be a relatively new practice, but those who promote it have argued it forcefully. Since a student intern needs the time and energy of the CTRS™, why shouldn't the student pay for the experience? In some situations where this occurs, part or all of the money goes to the agency and to funding for staff development. Ethically it is a sticking point. When a student enters a degree program, all aspects of what comprises that program are presented, with associated tuition and fees. Any costs related to course or program completion are specified beforehand (i.e., university catalog, course description, syllabus). Does the one paying for their internship have a greater guarantee that the experience will be superior? What are the associated liabilities?

Site Requirements

Site requirements are another area of moderate agreement. The COA has no direction for this concern. ATRA's guidelines emphasize practitioner preparation as opposed to agency/site preparation. ATRA provides practitioners with direction related to internship preparation including referrals to ATRA's *Guidelines for Competency Assessment* (West, Kinney & Witman, 2008), *ATRA Standards of Practice* (1993), and other publications. ATRA's *Guidelines* also include a well-written section identifying reasonable, weekly tasks expected of a student intern and appendices including protocol samples and competency checklists.

The NTRS document recommends that the site comply with NTRS internship standards of practice (1997), NTRS guidelines for administration of TR (1990), other pertinent local, state, and federal regulations plus any additional agency regulatory standards (i.e., JCAHO or CARF).

NTRS suggests that potential sites have a TR policy manual, a written plan of operation, and an intern itinerary. In addition, the TR service should be comprehensive, interdisciplinary, and facilitate a leisure lifestyle through functional intervention, leisure education, and recreation participation (Stumbo & Peterson, 2009). They further suggest program activity spaces and private work areas for the student and the site supervisor. The direction given to agencies for site requirements from NCTRC™ include following the TR process and practices as outlined in the Job Analysis and having the intern program well established at the agency.

The three organizations (ATRA, NCTRC™, and NTRS) differ in their recommendations in terms of their level of detail and inclusions/exclusions of certain topics related to site requirements. For example, NTRS guidelines state that an appropriate agency would meet regulatory standards (i.e., JCAHO, CARF, etc.); ATRA does not address this in their guidelines, yet they would likely advocate them in practice. Consensus could be obtained easily so that all three (ATRA, NCTRC™, and NTRS) organizations reflect equivalent policies. In addition, the TR service should be comprehensive, interdisciplinary, and facilitate a leisure lifestyle through functional intervention, leisure education, and recreation participation (Stumbo & Peterson, 2009).

Student Responsibility

Recommendations for the range of student responsibilities are another area where moderate agreement exists. The COA does not address this concern. The ATRA *Guidelines* list a variety of tasks for the student, including utilizing ATRA's competency checklist. They provide several suggestions about students having a portfolio and establishing goals for themselves. NTRS asks the student to refer to and follow the university manual as a guideline for his or her internship; however, under the student responsibility section, no mention occurs about the student following the agency manual. (In other sections of NTRS's guidelines, the development of an agency manual is discussed.) NCTRC™ recommends getting copies of various documents. They, of course, require adherence to the NCTRC™ standards, which include information about the Job Analysis. The student should select a site that currently employs a full-time CTRS™. Again, with this issue (student responsibility), the three organizations (ATRA, NCTRC™, and NTRS) have similar intentions. It would appear that discussion between the three groups could yield consensus.

Areas of the Standards Where Consensus is Low

Length of the Internship

The length of an internship has been and will continue to be debated among the four organizations with little consensus likely in the near future. The COA for all recreation curricula (general and specialization areas) requires a 400-clock-hour experience, covering no less than 10 weeks. ATRA recommends a 15-week, 600-hour experience. NTRS suggests

15 weeks, 525 hours for at least 35 hours/week. NCTRC™ is increasing the length of the internship experience because they recorded a significant rise in scores on the NCTRC™ exam related to increased length of internship (NCTRC™, 1999a). Their 1997-1998 study revealed nearly 75 percent of the field placements met or exceeded 12 weeks (NCTRC™, 1999b). Stumbo and Carter's study (1999) reported that the average length of a student internship was 12.60 weeks, ranging from 10 to 32 weeks with a mode of 10. NCTRC's™ study (1999b) reported an average of 12.51 weeks, ranging from eight to 16 weeks. Recommendations from NTRS and ATRA's data obtained from recent national studies helped propel NCTRC's™ minimum week duration (10 weeks) to a higher standard (12 weeks) (Luken, 1999).

The reasons for the difference across universities may be due in part to term structures. Universities that operate on the quarter system typically have 10-week terms; therefore, constraints are imposed on the department. On the other hand, programs operating under a 16-week term (semester) frequently offer longer internship experiences and are unlikely to reduce their length. TR internships also may be affected by wider department and university policies relating to student experiences of this nature, thus making it difficult for program requirement changes at the lower program level. For example, in order for a program to meet NCTRC's™ requirement of a 12-week internship, a creative approach will be needed so that the 12-week requirement can be met in a 10-week system and be recorded appropriately on the transcript.

University Supervisor

Another issue concerns the university supervisor or faculty member. The COA provides no guidance in this area. The ATRA guidelines suggest the university supervisor hold professional NCTRC™ certification and take a large role in selecting a site for the student. ATRA lists other recommended tasks to be done by the university supervisor before, during, and after the internship. The NTRS guidelines recommend the university supervisor have the CTRS™ certification and the state credential, if appropriate. They also suggest a variety of tasks, though the task list is not as detailed as ATRA's list. NCTRC™ refers to the university supervisor as "faculty" and does not expand on additional qualifications.

The COA and NCTRC™ have not listed any qualifications for the university supervisor. In Stumbo and Carter's study (1999), only 47 percent of the responding universities required the university supervisor of therapeutic recreation interns to be NCTRC™ certified. The comparable NCTRC™ study did not appear to have university supervisor qualifications as a variable in their study (cf. NCTRC™, 1999b). Supervising students takes many different forms at universities depending on a variety of situations. For example, many interns complete their internships over the summer session. At some schools, the summer responsibilities may be rotated between all faculty members, some of whom may not have the NCTRC™ certification. Additionally, NCTRC™ certification is a practitioner certification, not one designed for educators. Educators must meet other qualifications related to teaching, research, and service that do not necessarily meet qualifications related to the practice of therapeutic recreation. For example, most universities require faculty to hold advanced degrees.

Agency Manual

A third area of concern in the standards relates to agency/site manual requirements. COA standards do not address this. ATRA provides a detailed guide as to what a practitioner should include in an agency manual. NTRS provides a less detailed listing of possible content for an agency manual. NCTRC™ addresses it indirectly, stating that if there is no manual, the student should ask the site and the university to explain what is expected. Problems may occur when both agency/sites and universities: (a) have manuals with conflicting requirements and/or (b) the amount of expectations in both manuals add up to more work than is reasonable for a student to complete during a 35-to-40-hour week practical experience. The university supervisor and the site supervisor must have excellent communication to ensure that the student is not overburdened with unreasonable expectations. National guidelines for agency internship manuals will need to be broad since each agency is unique (i.e., population served, funding practices, organizational structure, etc.)

University Manual

Another area is the development of a university manual for the experience. Most educational programs develop their own, and several are available for purchase. The COA does not have recommendations for the university manual. ATRA recommends the university have a manual and provides guidelines for it. NTRS recommends that universities have a manual and a course description, and they provide guidelines for both. NCTRC™ implies that a manual should exist (refer to comments under the Agency Manual section).

"Frequently, practitioners and educators offer assignments based on NCTRC™, though the scope of content areas covered by the assignments is random and incomplete as opposed to being a consistent and comprehensive reflection of the NCTRC™ job analysis" (Pommier, 2000, p. 5). Pommier (2000) recommends one manual, based on the NCTRC™ job analysis, to be used by agencies and universities.

Affiliation Agreements Contracts

A fourth area of concern is "guidelines for agreement" related to the internship. The COA has no recommendation. ATRA guidelines, under tasks to be completed by the university supervisor, refer to signing an affiliation agreement. Under tasks to be completed by the practitioner, they list the development of a plan that includes an affiliation agreement between the "academic curriculum and the agency and any required agreement between the agency and the student" (Grote & Hasl, 1998, p. 14). The NTRS guidelines state that the university should develop an agreement, and the guidelines provide samples in the appendices of both an agreement form and of a letter of agreement. As with other issues, NCTRC™ gives broad direction, stating the agreement is a shared responsibility between the university and the agency. The discrepancy lies not in the establishment of an affiliation agreement or contract. Rather, disagreement exists about the entity responsible for initiating or developing the agreement.

Evaluation and Grading

The four organizations vary in their recommendations concerning grading and evaluation of outcomes. The COA does not address this. NCTRC's™ comments refer to these tasks as a shared responsibility, with the university being responsible for academic work and the agency being responsible for site activities. NCTRC™ requires that the experience appear on the student's transcript as receiving academic credit. ATRA guidelines list a few aspects that relate to evaluation and grading under university supervisor tasks and suggest that midterm and final evaluations be developed and done by the site supervisor. NTRS's approach is to provide direction in the appendices of the standards and guidelines, encouraging all involved (practitioner, student, and educator) to evaluate all components of the experience.

Evaluations often are used to provide valuable direction for student interns and agency and university supervisors. The feedback obtained from the evaluations should be instrumental in helping the student develop sound professional practice. Agency supervisors are encouraged to supplement university-developed evaluations; however, comprehensively developed evaluations by the educator typically diminish the need for supplements. There also should be many types of evaluations (i.e., student intern performance, agency, university supervisor, etc.) that represent various formats (Likert, narrative, etc.) so that a comprehensive representation of the internship experience results.

University Screening of Agencies Marketing Their Programs

COA, NCTRC™, and ATRA do not address the idea of screening agencies for student referral by a university program. NTRS does give some direction in the appendices for agency application for student interns from a university program.

Students need an internship where the most comprehensive demonstration of the therapeutic recreation process occurs. The therapeutic recreation process (i.e., "assessment, intervention planning, implementation of services, evaluation of plan, documentation, collaborating with treatment teams, organizing and managing services, outreach, public relations, and professional development" [NCTRC™, 1999a, p. 18]) is often recognized as an important skill set that differentiates therapeutic recreation from other recreation disciplines. Yet according to Stumbo and Carter (1999), only 35% of the universities in their study required an approval form showing adherence to NCTRC™ standards (p. 57). Making the assumption that all current CTRS™'s practice a sound therapeutic recreation process, thus allowing students to complete internships with any CTRS™, would be a mistake by the university supervisor. Educators should request that practitioners complete an application for student interns, which focuses on staff credentials, the practitioner's ability to practice the therapeutic recreation process and information as to how the student will be exposed to the NCTRC™-identified knowledge and skill areas.

Having agencies market their programs to potential student interns is a relatively new idea for most practitioners. ATRA's internship publication provides a unique and in-depth presentation of this aspect. COA, NCTRC™, and NTRS do not address this topic.

Miscellaneous

Three other areas have minimal agreement primarily because they are not addressed by each of the four groups. These include agency application, documents used, and intern sites charging a fee for interns. Only ATRA specifically addresses an agency application and the possibility of internship sites charging a fee. Not surprisingly, each organization (except COA, which makes no reference) references its own documents for further internship information and details.

How Are Universities Following Standards?

The fact that the internship is an academic experience must be highlighted. NCTRC™ requires that a potential CTRS™ candidate provide a transcript, which clearly indicates that academic credit was granted for the internship experience (NCTRC™, 1999a). Responsibilities associated with the internship experience should be conscientiously applied by the educator and the academic unit and not shifted to the agency by default. Thus, it is imperative for universities and educators to give a high priority to their role in preparing a student to become an entry-level professional. Simply offering an internship manual, providing a university supervisor, and assisting with site selection(s), among other responsibilities, is not enough. Therapeutic recreation educators need to be more responsible for ensuring the internship manual, internship supervisor, site selections, etc. are based upon standards that are driven to strengthen the students' competencies and the profession as a whole.

Two attempts have been recently made to research how universities and educators are currently following standards. Stumbo and Carter (1999) presented the results of their therapeutic recreation curriculum study, which detailed the status of 114 universities according to several characteristics, including internship requirements. Related to internships, they reported information on how many internships were required, number of weeks required, total hours required, site supervisor professional status, university supervisor professional status, whether site-screening methods were used, plus a variety of other data. Some of the data from their study, which are similar to the standards and guidelines of the four organizations, are detailed in Table 10.2. The results of the study prompted the authors to recommend "that a national movement for consensus on curriculum design and internship requirements be initiated" (Stumbo & Carter, 1999, p. 59).

Another recent effort at examining the range of internship requirements occurring at universities was completed by NCTRC™ and reported in NCTRC™ *Educators Link* in fall, 1999. This study gathered information from 78 universities on variables similar to and unique from the Stumbo and Carter study. Table 10.2 also reflects the results from this study. Only those results are displayed that relate to the internship.

All aspects of curriculum and student preparation traditionally have been a concern for the field. There seems to be a consensus as to what competencies an entry-level practitioner needs to possess (Connolly & Riley, 1995-96; Stumbo & Carter, 1999; Stumbo, 1986), yet the academic preparations (i.e., curriculum design, content, sequence, etc.) are grossly erratic (Carter & Folkerth, 1997; Stumbo & Carter, 1999).

Summary

There are a variety of concerns regarding the internship experience. This chapter has examined the current standards promoted by four organizations (COA, NCTRC™, ATRA, and NTRS) and differences related to them. There are many more issues that are involved. Several concerns were highlighted in Stumbo and Carter's study (1999) (e.g., students' costs involved with internship supervision, faculty supervision details, students taking coursework during internship, etc.) and the NCTRC's™ study (e.g., nature of assignments, liability insurance, who determines site selection, etc.). The internship is a universe of its own. If standardization is to exist in the internship experience, therapeutic recreation professionals must start with the basic differences discussed in this chapter.

Discussion Questions

- What are the consequences (to students, agencies, and universities) of having NCTRC™ increase the number of internship weeks and hours as of December 31, 2002?
- What are the advantages and disadvantages to receiving specialized program accreditation for therapeutic recreation?

Table 10.2
Curriculum Study Comparisons

Curriculum Studies	Stumbo and Carter's (1999) Study (n=114)			NCTRC™'s (1999b) Study (n=78)	
	Percent	Average	Range	Percent	Average
# weeks required	—	10	10-32	—	12.51
# of hours required	—	469.63	90-640 hrs	—	471.09
Agency supervisor NCTRC™-Certified	93.86	—	—	84.6	—
University supervisor to be NCTRC™-certified	47.37	—	—	—	—
Agency must have intern manual	66.97	—	—	96.2	—
Grading is Pass/Fail	33.33	—	—	—	No data directly dealing with grading, through several variables detailing evaluation and assignments were reported
Grading includes A/B/C/D/F	64.91	—	—	—	

- For what reasons do CTRS™'s assume responsibility of supervising a student intern?
- Develop a list of pros and cons regarding a student paying an agency/site for an internship experience. Does paying for an internship experience increase chances that the experience will be superior? What are the associated liabilities?
- What are the benefits of having the university supervisor certified by NCTRC™ (for student, practitioners, and the profession)?

References

American Therapeutic Recreation Association. (2000). *Standards for practice of therapeutic recreation.* Alexandria, VA: Author.

Carter, M. J., & Folkerth, J. E. (1997). Credentialing and its impact on higher education. In D. Compton (Ed*.), Issues in therapeutic recreation: Toward a new millennium* (2nd ed.). (pp. 255-274). Champaign, IL: Sagamore.

Connolly, P., & Riley, B. (1995-96). Entry-level job skills: Reinvestigation of the national job analysis of the practice of therapeutic recreation. *Annual in Therapeutic Recreation, 6,* 26-37.

Grote, K., & Hasl, M. (1998). *Guidelines for internships in therapeutic recreation.* Hattiesburg, MS: American Therapeutic Recreation Association.

Luken, K. (1999). The role of professional associations and certifying organizations: Who does what? *NCTRC™ Newsletter,* (1), 1.

National Recreation and Park Association. (2000). Standards and evaluative criteria for baccalaureate programs in recreation, park resources and leisure services. Arlington, VA: Author [available on-line at www.nrpa.org]

National Council for Therapeutic Recreation Certification. (1999a). *Candidate bulletin of information.* New City, NY: Author.

National Council for Therapeutic Recreation Certification. (Fall, 1999b). Results of the 1998 survey of curricula and field placement requirements. *NCTRC™ Educator's Link.* New City, NY: Author.

National Therapeutic Recreation Society. (1997). *Internship standards and guidelines for therapeutic recreation.* Arlington, VA: National Recreation and Park Association.

Peterson, C. A., & Stumbo, N. J. (2000). *Therapeutic recreation program design: Principles and procedures* (3rd ed.). Boston, MA: Allyn and Bacon.

Pommier, J. (2000). *Therapeutic recreation internship manual: Certification based.* Ravensdale, WA: Idyll Arbor.

Stumbo, N. J. (1986). A definition of entry-level knowledge for therapeutic recreation practice. *Therapeutic Recreation Journal, 20*(4), 15-30.

Stumbo, N. J., & Carter, M. J. (1999). National therapeutic recreation curriculum study part A: Accreditation, curriculum and internship characteristics. *Therapeutic Recreation Journal, 33*(1), 46-60.

Stumbo, N. J., & Peterson, C. A. (2009) *Therapeutic recreation program design: Principles and procedures* (5th ed.). San Francisco: Benjamin Cummings.

West, R. E., Kinney, T., & Witman, J. (2008). *Guidelines for competency assessment and curriculum planning for recreational therapy practice* (2nd ed.). Hattiesburg, MS: American Therapeutic Recreation Association.

CHAPTER 11

Perspective: The Value of Support Courses and Fieldwork in the Therapeutic Recreation Curricula

Jean E. Folkerth, Re.D., CTRS™

What impact do support courses have on a curriculum? How can they change the focus of a curriculum? What is the difference between fieldwork, practicum, and internship? What do they contribute to a student's knowledge? How do accreditation and certification address support courses? Practicum experiences beyond internship? According to Kinney, Kinney and Witman (2006), "Significant variation exists in regard to the types of practicum and internships required, the level of proficiency required in supportive coursework, and the ways in which outcomes are measured" (p. 1). This chapter will provide the reader with some understanding of the importance of support course work and fieldwork placements (not to be confused with the internship) in therapeutic recreation curricula.

Current Curricular Influences and Practices

Currently, there are two credentialing organizations that have an impact on therapeutic recreation curricula: the Council on Accreditation (COA) of the National Recreation and Park Association (NRPA) and the National Council for Therapeutic Recreation Certification (NCTRC™). Although the two bodies have significantly different foci, and accreditation is generally thought to have the most impact on curricula, it is the National Council for Therapeutic Recreation Certification that seems to have the greater influence on therapeutic recreation curricula. To understand this impact it is important to look briefly at the organizations and their standards or requirements.

Council on Accreditation

The Council on Accreditation (COA) is the accrediting body for higher education in the parks and recreation field. The Council on Accreditation of the National Recreation and

Park Association establishes the competencies and standards that a program/department must meet in order to be accredited. The Council itself is made up of educators, practitioners, and administrators appointed by the sponsoring agencies.

There are two major parts to the accreditation standards—Part A: Organization and Operations Standards, and Part B: Baccalaureate Degree Standards. According to the COA (2004b), Part A focuses on "non-curricular aspects of the academic program" (p. 13). It is concerned with Unit Characteristics; Mission; Philosophy, Goals and Planning; Administration, Faculty, Students, and Instructional Resources. An example of a standard that could be found in this part is:

> 4.05 There shall be at least three full-time-equivalent faculty members of the academic unit serving the undergraduate curriculum. Two of these faculty shall be full-time, and must hold a minimum of one degree, baccalaureate or above, with a major in recreation, park resources, or leisure services. In addition to the foregoing, there shall be another full-time faculty member for each option with a degree in recreation, park resources, or leisure services and with credentials appropriate to the respective option (COA, 2004b, p. 2).

Part B, the Baccalaureate Degree Standards, focuses on Foundation Understandings, Professional Competencies, and then the "opportunity for the academic unit to offer options which are accredited" (COA, 2004b, p. 15). Foundation Understandings requests that the program/department explain the institution's general education program and how the program/department fulfills those requirements. The standards found in Professional Competencies are comprehensive. These competencies relate to the following areas: conceptual foundations; profession; delivery systems; program and event planning; administration/management; legal aspects; and field experiences. An example of a competency found in the area of Conceptual Foundations is:

8.05 Understanding of environmental ethics and its relationship to leisure behavior (COA, 2004b, p. 8).

Accreditation standards also address practical experiences. It requires that students have both a fieldwork experience of 100 hours *and* an internship of no less than 400 hours. If the TR option is accredited only the internship must be done through a site providing a therapeutic recreation program. The fieldwork experience can be completed anywhere.

To attain professional accreditation, a program/department must demonstrate that it can meet the competencies of Part A, and in Part B it must meet the competencies in both Foundation Understandings and Professional Competencies. A department with different emphases may elect to have both professional accreditation and an "option" accredited. There are four possible options that a program/department can have accredited; therapeutic recreation is one of those options. To be accredited as an option, there are five general standards that all options must meet directly related to personnel, goals of the option, and library resources. For a program to receive accreditation in therapeutic recreation, currently an additional 28 standards, six of which fall under the 7.00 series, which pertains to foundations or support competencies, must be met. It is these six competencies that give direction to "support coursework." The six competencies are:

7D.01   Understanding of human anatomy and physiology

7D.02   Understanding of and ability to use basic medical, psychiatric, and pharmacological terminology

7D.03   Understanding of abnormal psychology

7D.04   Understanding of medical and disabling conditions, disorders and impairments that affect an individual's physical, cognitive, emotional, and social functioning across the lifespan

7D.05   Understanding of wholistic health and wellness including disease prevention and health promotion

7D.06   Understanding of the use of self as an instrument in therapeutic relationships and the ability to establish such relationships (COA, 2004b, p. 20).

Additionally, there are currently 22 standards that apply directly to therapeutic recreation. An example of a competency for the therapeutic recreation option is:

9D.14   Understanding of and ability to apply the therapeutic recreation programming process, including activity and task analyses, to design individual and group programs and/or treatment plans in various settings (COA, 2004b, p. 21-22).

Thus, if a program/department were to seek professional accreditation with an option in therapeutic recreation, it must demonstrate how it has met standards regarding department administration, faculty, and students; standards for the professional core; and other standards for the therapeutic recreation option including the "support standards" and while not requiring the student to complete a field experience in therapeutic recreation, the student must complete an internship in therapeutic recreation as stated in the standard.

National Council for Therapeutic Recreation Certification

Although the National Council for Therapeutic Recreation Certification (NCTRC™) is the certifying body for therapeutic recreation professionals as individuals, it has a profound effect on curricula. According to Brasile (2006) "…NCTRC has, up until now, had the largest impact on what is currently being taught in our undergraduate and graduate curriculums" (p. 25). Stumbo and Carter (1999) and Stumbo, Carter and Kim (2004) concur and found that the NCTRC™ certification standards were the primary reason that departments/programs revised their therapeutic recreation curricula. The reasoning is that in order for therapeutic recreation graduates to be certified they must demonstrate through coursework that they are prepared to take the national certification exam. According to NCTRC's™ *Candidate Bulletin* (2007), a candidate for certification using the "Academic Path Requirements" must display on his or her academic transcript a "major in therapeutic recreation or a major in recreation with an option in therapeutic recreation" (p. 6).

Because there is no standardized curriculum (see Chapter 12) for therapeutic recreation, NCTRC™ (2007) has defined a "major in therapeutic recreation" or a "major in recreation with an option in therapeutic recreation" as including:

• A minimum of 12 semester or 18 quarter credit hours in therapeutic recreation content. A minimum of four courses in therapeutic recreation is required in therapeutic recreation content. Each course must be a minimum of three hours; and

• Supportive courses to include a total of 18 semester units or 27 quarter hours of support coursework with a minimum of: (i) three semester hours or three quarter hours coursework in the content area of anatomy and physiology; (ii) three semester hours or three quarter hours coursework in the content area of abnormal psychology; and (iii) three semester hours or three quarter hours coursework in the content area of human growth and development. The remaining semester hours or quarter hours must be fulfilled in the content area of "human services" as defined by NCTRC™; AND

• A minimum 480-hour, twelve (12) consecutive-week field placement experience in therapeutic recreation services that uses the therapeutic recreation process as defined by the current NCTRC™ Job Analysis Study under the supervision of an on-site field placement supervisor who is NCTRC™-CTRS™-certified and meets the standards for field placement supervision. An acceptable field placement experience is one which is completed after the majority of required therapeutic recreation and general recreation coursework is completed as verified on the official transcript and the required fieldwork verification form (2007, p. 6).

These definitions have become the standards by which many therapeutic recreation curricula establish coursework and implement internship requirements (see Chapter 10). Please see www.nctrc.org for current NCTRC™ standards.

Therapeutic Recreation/Recreation Coursework

In 1981 when the original NCTRC™ standards were established, there was a "co-emphasis" on therapeutic recreation and recreation courses. The original standard required three courses in therapeutic recreation and three courses in recreation (1987, p. 3). This was appropriate since it was not known how therapeutic recreation was practiced. However, in 1989 when NCTRC™ conducted their first job analysis (Oltman, Norback, & Rosenfeld, 1989), it was determined that when practicing, therapeutic recreation professionals required little knowledge of the material covered in traditional recreation coursework and more knowledge in therapeutic recreation coursework. Thus, the standard was changed to reflect this finding (Connolly, personal communication, January 28, 2000).

According to a recent study, the majority of universities with therapeutic recreation majors require "between 3 to 10 content courses with an average of 4.47 courses" (Riley & Connolly, 2006, p. 195). Note that when the data for this study was collected, only three therapeutic recreation courses were needed for certification. It should also be noted that "no significant differences in NCTRC exam performance were identified" dependent upon the number of courses required (Riley & Connolly, 2006, p. 196).

Supportive Coursework

To complete the major, NCTRC™ also requires supportive courses. "NCTRC recognizes the important role of coursework outside the fields of therapeutic recreation and general recreation as contributing to the knowledge base for practice in therapeutic recreation" (NCTRC, 2007, p. 12). NCTRC™ currently requires a course in anatomy and physiology, abnormal psychology, and human growth and development (see www.nctrc.org for the most current standards). The program faculty or the student with faculty assistance determines the other nine hours, although the courses must have a human service focus. The majority of support courses recommended by therapeutic recreation programs seem to be centered on the introductory level human service courses, i.e., General Psychology and Introduction to Sociology (Riley & Connolly, 2006, p. 200-201). These support courses were the most frequently used followed by a variety of human service support courses.

It is important to realize that, for the most part, therapeutic recreation curricula are being driven by requirements for certification, and, in other words, a majority of curricula are providing the minimum number of courses necessary for a person to meet the sitting requirements for certification. What is unknown is whether the student is ready for the field placement after taking the required coursework. Does it matter whether the student has taken three courses in therapeutic recreation and three courses in recreation, or is the student more prepared having taken six courses in therapeutic recreation? Is it the responsibility of the field placement site to prepare students to pass the national exam, or is it the responsibility of the field placement site to assist the student in applying the knowledge learned to actual practice? Up to this point, it can be said that curricula are at least meeting the structural requirements for certification. However, it must be questioned whether all curricula are actually preparing students for practice in hospitals with patients who are severely injured or seriously ill. (Note that this shift from a structure-and-process orientation to that of an outcomes orientation is similar to that noted in healthcare. (Note Navar's Chapter 7.)

According to the American Therapeutic Recreation Association (ATRA) *Curriculum Guidelines Support Requirements* (West, Kinney, & Witman, 2008), there are specific courses that should be taken for support coursework beyond the requirements of NCTRC™. It recommends that students also take courses in Educational/Cognitive psychology, Healthcare Organization/Delivery, Kinesiology, Legal Aspects of Healthcare, Pharmacology, and courses on medical and disabling conditions.

Many therapeutic recreation programs are using support coursework to create emphasis areas within the major. According to Doug Boleyn, a practitioner who works in rehabilitation, a student who wants to work in that setting needs to have taken: Exercise Physiology, Functional Anatomy, Neuroscience for Rehabilitation, Kinesiology, and Assistive Technology (Boleyn, personal communication, February 21, 2007). Students interested in working in geriatrics can take coursework in death and dying, physical activity and aging, and many other gerontology related classes.

If the therapeutic recreation program has accepted the philosophy that therapeutic recreation is a profession and does not require the students to take recreation courses, it is possible that at some time down the road recreation coursework can become human service support coursework. This will then enable a student to be able to provide inclusive recreation in community programs. It will become a focus just like other focus areas.

Other potential support courses can add depth and breadth to a student's special skill area or modality. For example, a student who is gifted in art could take classes in adaptive methods in art, art education for the special child, or therapeutic art for adult populations. Persons interested in aquatics can take all different courses in aquatic rehabilitation, etc. By taking courses in these areas, a student will learn to utilize a special skill to work with a variety of populations. Too many students have not taken the courses outside of the professional coursework that will support their future practice. This lack of emphasis or inclusion of modality coursework could be because of the decision of NCTRC™ to consider these courses "skill" or "activity" courses because most were one-hour classes and to not count these courses toward certification. Once again, departments focused on what was needed for certification and not on what was needed for practice. There must be recognition that a program that is providing students with the skills needed for practice may need additional courses for certification.

As previously defined by NCTRC™, supportive course work must support the practice of therapeutic recreation. It is through supportive course work that students can gain knowledge related to seriously ill or severely injured patients and healthcare practices. Support courses can provide information that enables a student to successfully transition into a career.

The overlooked potential of support courses is to create mechanisms for students to transfer knowledge while the course is occurring. Normally, knowledge gained in courses such as abnormal psychology and anatomy/physiology might be randomly incorporated in concurrent classes, not incorporated until a later date, or not incorporated until internship. The mismatch of timing can result in a missed opportunity to operationalize and contextualize the knowledge into therapeutic recreation theory and practice (S. Ross, personal communication, March 9, 2007).

Clientele

According to the NCTRC™ (1997) Job Analysis Study, 45% of practice occurs in the hospital setting (p. 2). In this day of healthcare reform, if the person is not seriously injured or ill, the person is not in the hospital. This implies that a therapeutic recreation specialist is expected to be able to work with seriously injured or ill persons. Thus, much of practice is with very sick people, whether mentally ill, physically injured from a traumatic occurrence such as a cardiovascular accident, seriously ill from cancer, or physically and cognitively impacted from Alzheimer's disease. Entry-level professionals need to be prepared to work with these groups of clientele. Through supportive coursework, a better understanding of the needs of seriously ill persons can be provided.

Most curricula provide a rudimentary understanding of persons with disabilities. A "Recreation for Persons with Disabilities" or an "Introduction to Therapeutic Recreation" course is required by most curricula. These courses provide a basic understanding of the cognitive, physical, social, emotional, and environmental needs of persons with disabilities; however, there is often more breadth than depth. Support courses have the built-in opportunity to provide therapeutic recreation students with a more in-depth understanding of disability or illness.

Courses in psychology, sociology, and gerontology can provide much needed information regarding the cognitive and emotional needs of people. Introductory courses in these areas are currently required by most curricula. However, it is the higher level courses that can provide more insight and understanding into the behavior and thought processes of people who have mental diseases or cognitive/behavioral disorders. Requiring or encouraging students to take courses such as social psychology, psychology of aging, theories of personality, juvenile delinquency, and the aging process, can only enhance the future professional's ability to provide appropriate treatment programs while on internship or working.

At this time, it is not appropriate to encourage students to "specialize" in a specific area or with a specific population, because it is unknown with what population they will be working. So along with courses in the social sciences, students should be taking courses beyond anatomy and physiology. They need to have an understanding of what the body does in motion. An understanding of kinesiology, biomechanics, and physiology of exercise/activity are excellent courses for helping students gain this knowledge. Support courses that assist students in gaining more information about the working of the human body physically, cognitively, socially, and emotionally can only enhance students' ability to practice more effectively.

Healthcare Practices

An understanding of the healthcare environment is important. When reviewing other health science curricula, such as occupational therapy and physical therapy, it has been observed that only therapeutic recreation students are not required to take courses on healthcare. It is as if therapeutic recreation is not involved in the healthcare arena when, in fact, according to NCTRC™ it is the largest environment in which therapeutic recreation professionals work (1997, p. 2).

Healthcare environments are totally different than leisure services environments. If possible, students need to be introduced to healthcare environments through interdisciplinary courses with other healthcare professions, such as occupational therapy and physical therapy. These courses offer the opportunity for students to work in teams, as they will in their practice. It allows professors to develop tasks that require communication between all students, giving them a respect and understanding of the professions that may carry over into practice. There are practices and concepts in healthcare that are best provided through support courses.

All therapeutic recreation students should have a solid understanding in medical terminology; however, in Riley and Connolly's (2006) study of students who applied for certification between the years of 2000 and 2003, only 33% took a course in Medical Terminology (p. 201). An understanding of pharmaceutical drugs, their side effects, and potential impact on clients would be another excellent support course; only 4.6% of the applicants in this study took such a course (p. 201). Social work and communication departments often offer courses in group dynamics and interpersonal relations. Philosophy departments offer courses in heathcare ethics that can provide a better understanding of the dilemmas faced in healthcare situations and assist the student in working through such situations.

Fieldwork and Practical Experiences

Another often neglected area is fieldwork or practical experiences that occur *before* the internship, which can also be seen as support coursework. According to COA, all students must participate in a 100-hour experience prior to the internship. However, those hours are not directed necessarily toward an option, and many take place in a recreation setting. Brasile (2006) sees "fieldwork as the most important component of our professional preparation program. There should be no fewer than three full-time fieldwork opportunities as part of our educational process" (p. 25). Kinney, Kinney, and Witman (2006) concur, stating

"Experiential opportunities need to be integrated throughout course work so that students develop critical thinking skills as well as build skills and abilities required of TR specialists" (p. 7).

Many programs realizing the importance of these practical experiences are building in requirements for students to experience a variety of populations through both credit and non-credit experiences. It seems important that if a program believes a student needs to have experiences with a variety of populations, it takes the time to make the experiences "directed." Encouraging a student to volunteer with a variety of populations in different settings does not seem to be enough.

Very often, students come into the TR program with preconceived notions about certain populations that only experience with those populations can confirm or refute. Also, most graduates do not have the opportunity to choose their population and setting after graduation. The more experience that each student has with different populations, the better prepared the student will be for the future.

Some programs are able to offer one-credit-hour courses with specific learning activities, such as developing case studies, assessing clients, leading treatment-oriented activities, and developing activity protocols, etc. Other programs are not able to offer credit for experiences but consider them extremely valuable. San Jose State University requires a competency-based field learning experience of 450 hours in which the students work in each population/type of setting and complete reading assignments, review regulatory procedure binders and documents, case studies, observe assessments/ documentation, investigate various diagnosis, co-lead groups, complete a work project, interview the administrator, do guided journaling, and have guided debriefing with the practitioners (Ross, personal communication, March 10, 2007). Experiences such as these can add to classroom learning and help the student be more prepared for their internship and their future. It eliminates the onus of one experience (internship) prior to a job.

Summary

Supportive courses have not been given the respect or attention they deserve. For so long, the profession has been overlooking these necessary courses. Support courses can provide depth and breadth to a curriculum that may feel locked in to specific combinations of therapeutic recreation/recreation courses. It is through supportive coursework that students can become more knowledgeable about the clientele with whom they will be working. In fieldwork, students can improve their clinical knowledge and practice. It is through support courses and fieldwork that one can ensure that students have the knowledge base to practice with a better understanding of the needs of clientele and the environment. Carefully selected support coursework and fieldwork experiences can provide essential knowledge and skills that, when combined with therapeutic recreation coursework, will ensure that entry-level therapeutic recreation specialists are prepared to take their place beside other health-care professionals.

Discussion Questions

1. Using the Internet, collect three different college curricula in therapeutic recreation and bring them to class. With the other students, compare and contrast the curricula noting the diversity of courses and lack of similar courses. What are the different support courses?

2. Complete the ATRA self-assessment guide. How well prepared do you feel for practice? Using your college catalog, what courses could assist your preparation for field experience and a job?

3. Look around your area for potential sites where you could do some fieldwork. What kinds of experiences would be helpful? What have you learned in the classroom that you would like some hands-on experience with before internship? With your instructor, design a plan of study for a fieldwork class.

References

Brasile, F. (2006). Response to concept paper on undergraduate education in therapeutic recreation. In M. J. Carter, & J. E. Folkerth (Eds.), *Therapeutic recreation education: Challenges and changes.* (pp. 21-29). Ashburn, VA: National Recreation and Park Association.

Kinney, J. Kinney, T., & Witman, J. (2006). Concept paper on undergraduate education in therapeutic recreation. In M. J. Carter, & J. E. Folkerth (Eds.), *Therapeutic recreation education: Challenges and changes.* (pp. 1 - 20). Ashburn, VA: National Recreation and Park Association.

National Council for Therapeutic Recreation Certification. (2007). Information for the Certified Therapeutic Recreation Specialist. Certification standards Part I: Information for New Applicants Retrieved March 8, 2007, from National Council for Therapeutic Recreation Certification Web site: http://nctrc.org/documents/1NewAp012007CB.pdf

National Council for Therapeutic Recreation Certification. (1997). Certification Standards Part V: NCTRC National Job Analysis Retrieved March 8, 2007, from National Council for Therapeutic Recreation Web site: http://nctrc.org/documents/5JobAnalysis062005CB.pdf

National Recreation and Park Association Council on Accreditation. (2004a). Procedural guidelines for the accreditation process for baccalaureate programs in recreation, park resources and leisure services. Retrieved March 8, 2007 from the National Recreation and Park Association Web site: http://www.nrpa.org/content/default.aspx?documentId=1012

National Recreation and Park Association Council on Accreditation. (2004b). Standards and evaluative criteria for recreation, park resources, and leisure services baccalaureate programs. Retrieved March 8, 2007 from the National Recreation and Park Association Web site: http://www.nrpa.org/content/default.aspx?documentId=1010

Oltman, P. K., Norback, J., & Rosenfeld, M. (1989). A national study of the profession of therapeutic recreation specialist. *Therapeutic Recreation Journal, 23*(2), 48-58.

Riley, B., & Connolly, P. (2006). NCTRC summary report: Current status of professional preparation in therapeutic recreation. In M. J. Carter, & J. E. Folkerth (Eds.), *Therapeutic recreation education: Challenges and changes.* (pp. 187 - 219). Ashburn, VA: National Recreation and Park Association.

Stumbo, N. J., & Carter, M. J. (1999). National therapeutic recreation curriculum study part A: Accreditation, curriculum, and internship characteristics. *Therapeutic Recreation Journal, 33*(1), 46-60.

Stumbo, N. J., Carter, M. J., & Kim, J. (2004) 2003 national therapeutic recreation study part A: Accreditation, curriculum and internship characteristics. *Therapeutic Recreation Journal, 38*(1), 53 – 71.

West, R. E., Kinney, T., & Witman, J. (2008) *Guidelines for competency assessment and curriculum planning for recreational therapy practice* (2nd ed.) Hattiesburg, MS: American Therapeutic Recreation Association.

CHAPTER 12

Perspective: Curricular Standardization in Therapeutic Recreation: Professional and University Implications

Jeffrey P. Witman, Ed.D., CTRS™
York College of Pennsylvania

Walter B. (Terry) Kinney, Ph.D., CTRS™
University of North Carolina, Wilmington

Janet R. Sable, Ed.D., CTRS™
University of New Hampshire

Judy S. Kinney, Ph.D., CTRS™
University of North Carolina, Wilmington

The parameters of therapeutic recreation curricula are relatively finite. That is to say, there are only so many semester hours (or courses) that a curriculum can require its students to take. Therefore, those instructors who develop college and university curricula have a responsibility to utilize the limited number of available courses so that they can best prepare students for entry into the profession of therapeutic recreation.

Given this finite nature, one could assume that therapeutic recreation curricula would look relatively similar. In fact, however, there is little similarity. Research conducted by Connolly and Riley (1995-96) found very little commonality across curricula of those graduates sitting for the NCTRC™ national exam. Stumbo and Carter (1999a) and Stumbo, Carter, and Kim (2004a) examined therapeutic recreation curricula across the country and recommended that a national movement for consensus on curriculum design and internship requirements be initiated by one of the national professional or credentialing organizations. The authors voiced concern, if not alarm, at the lack of uniformity across curricula. They stated, "If there is no standardization of curricula, then it follows that there is no or little standardization of the degree or 'exit skills' for graduates" (p. 59). Practitioners in therapeutic recreation have also expressed a need for standardized curricula content/process and for standardized internship expectations/requirements (Witman & Saville, 2006).

Given the fact that in the early 1980s predictions were made that curricula would be standardized by the year 2000 (Hitzhusen, 1983), one could ask, why hasn't it happened? During this time, curricula in medicine and allied health have gained rigor and become more standardized (Pierce & Peyton, 1998). Within therapeutic recreation, however, continued philosophical debate and the diversity of schools and programs offering curricula have worked against standardization. Arguments for greater standardization have been met with counter arguments for academic freedom and diversity, and some have voiced the hope that the distinctiveness of the field can best be realized by not bowing to healthcare trends that encourage standardization (Mobily, 1996). Proponents of more standardized curricula have argued that consumers, employers, and payers have limited assurance of the professional competence of new graduates under the current diverse array of professional preparation programs in the field (West, 1995). Recently the notion has been advanced that the real issue is standardization of accreditation requirements for curricula, not standardization of curricula design (Brasile, 2006).

The intent of this chapter is to provide a framework for review and discussion of professional preparation in therapeutic recreation. The advantages and disadvantages of greater standardization in curricula will be presented with a review of generic competencies that guide curriculum planning. A theoretical curriculum provides an option and a framework for discussion regarding curricular standardization.

Historical Framework

There is a history of research efforts to determine the competencies upon which TR curricula should be based. In the 1970s, the University of Illinois published a report, *Therapeutic Recreation Education: Developing a Competency-Based Entry-Level Curriculum* (Kelley, Robb, Park, & Halberg, 1976). Soon after, Temple University produced *Theory and Design of Competency-Based Education in Therapeutic Recreation* (Jordan, Dayton, & Brill, 1977). These early research studies provided the foundation for the therapeutic recreation specialization accredited by the NRPA/AALR Council on Accreditation (COA). These research studies became the models for many of the curricula that developed in the 1980s. At the same time, research on specialty areas were undertaken, as evidenced in the work of Indiana University's Project INSPIRE (Austin & Powell, 1981), which identified competencies professionals needed to work with individuals with disabilities in the community.

The research on competency for entry-level TR practitioners continued in the 1980s. A research study by Peterson and Connolly (1981) led to the identification of 12 content areas and 81 competency statements. Revision of accreditation standards for an option in therapeutic recreation expanded in 1981 from 12 to 24 statements (NRPA, 1981). In 1986, Stumbo investigated the knowledge base required by entry-level practitioners to deliver service and recommended 37 entry-level content areas. The results of Stumbo's study (1986) were incorporated into the revision of the therapeutic recreation option in 1990 (NRPA, 1990) resulting in four foundation and 22 option statements in therapeutic recreation.

In an effort to update these standards, a 19-member work group that included representatives of the NRPA/AALR Council on Accreditation, the National Therapeutic Recreation Society, and the American Therapeutic Recreation Association studied the standards for accreditation as they related to therapeutic recreation. They reviewed the *Guidelines for Competency Assessment and Curriculum Planning: A Tool for Self-Evaluation* (Kinney & Witman, 1997), the *Standards and Evaluative Criteria for Baccalaureate Programs in Recreation, Park Resources, and Leisure Services* (NRPA, 1990), the *1997 Job Analysis* (NCTRC™, 1997), and the *National Certification Exam Content Outline* (NCTRC™, 1997). After a review by a random sample of currently certified CTRSs™, college/university educators involved with accreditation, and accreditation visitors, comments and revisions were presented to the COA Board. These revisions then were reviewed and accepted by the COA Board in 1999. The intent of these revisions was to assure that accreditation standards reflect contemporary practice. The current COA standards (2004) continue to include an option in therapeutic recreation. However, when the new COA standards are implemented, the designation of options will not be available.

Another major influence on the academic preparation of TR professionals has been through the NCTRC™ *National Job Analysis Project for Therapeutic Recreation Specialists* (Oltman, Norback, & Rosenfeld, 1989). The purpose of this national study was to define entry-level, competent practice of professional therapeutic recreation personnel. The study provided a description of the job responsibilities of a therapeutic recreation specialist and the 96 knowledge areas necessary for competent performance. The knowledge areas identified in this study provided the basis for the content of the initial national certification exam in 1990. NCTRC™ conducted subsequent *Job Analysis Studies* (1997, 2006) to ensure that the national certification exam continues to be linked to the practice of therapeutic recreation. Although the job analysis and the knowledge areas do not dictate curriculum, it is in the interest of colleges and universities to prepare students who can successfully pass the certifying exam.

Research studies and certification requirements are not the only influences on curriculum design. Members of the profession, often by way of their professional organizations, have responsibility for defining the profession and the roles and responsibilities for which the education programs prepare their graduates. This influence might best be represented in publications that directly address professional preparation. Both NTRS and ATRA have published internship guidelines that impact the quality of the field experience component of TR professional preparation. NTRS's *Internship Standards and Guidelines for Therapeutic Recreation* (1997) and the *ATRA Guidelines for Internships in Therapeutic Recreation* (Grote & Hasl, 1998) provide clear direction for the structure of the student internship experience. Beyond internship guidelines, professional organizations share the commitment to quality professional preparation. In 1995, ATRA held a curriculum conference in conjunction with their Mid-year Issues Forum to discuss curricular issues related to undergraduate education in therapeutic recreation. At the conference, 60 educators and practitioners met in small groups to discuss critical issues related to undergraduate education. This resulted in the 1997 publication of *ATRA's Guidelines for Competency Assessment and Curriculum Planning in Therapeutic Recreation: A Tool for Self-Evaluation*. In the introduction to these guidelines, it is stated that the primary foundation for guaranteeing a sound future for the discipline rests in ensuring the quality of academic education (Kinney & Witman, 1997). The seven content areas in the *Self-Evaluation* include: (a) foundations of professional practice, (b) individual patient/client assessment, (c) planning and development of treatment/program plans, (d) implementation of the treatment/program plan, (e) evaluation of patient/client functioning and interventions/programs, (f) organizing and managing TR services, and (g) support competencies (Kinney & Witman, 1997). This document has been updated and expanded in *Guidelines for Competency Assessment and Curriculum Planning for Recreational Therapy Practice* (West, Kinney, & Witman, 2008).

In 2001, the Alliance for Therapeutic Recreation (joint venture of the American Therapeutic Recreation Association and the National Therapeutic Recreation Society) established a Joint Taskforce on Higher Education. A focal point of this effort was the Therapeutic Recreation Education Conference (TREC) held in 2005. The objectives of TREC were to identify concerns of therapeutic recreation education, gather input to provide direction for the future of therapeutic recreation education, develop proceedings that describe the state of the art of therapeutic recreation education and provide guidance for the improvement and continuance of therapeutic recreation education programs. These proceedings, *Therapeutic Recreation Education: Challenges and Changes* (Carter & Folkerth, 2006), provide a grounded perspective of current professional preparation in therapeutic recreation and needs for the future. The summative Taskforce report identified 15 possibilities for subsequent action. These actions were prioritized by educators attending the ATRA and NTRS annual meetings in 2006. As Table 12.1 indicates, several of the top priorities established relate to standardization. These include "standardization of competency-based TR education" and development of an "undergraduate competency list." The important question of who or what entity will take responsibility for working on these priorities has not been answered.

Support for Standardization

Therapeutic recreation is accountable to consumers and employers to ensure that graduates of a curriculum in TR have an understanding of the knowledge base and skills to be effective as contemporary practitioners. Members of the profession, in concert with other constituency groups, are responsible for defining the profession and the roles and responsibilities for which the education programs prepare graduates. Practitioners must be prepared to participate in today's healthcare environment by providing direct services, consultation, education, research, and advocacy to individuals and groups by contributing to improved healthcare delivery. The dynamic nature of health and human service delivery systems requires professional education that is rigorous yet responsive to change.

The professional literature of the past decades is replete with calls for a standardization of academic curricula. Numerous studies have articulated the need for a standardized curricula to ensure that all TR graduates have an understanding of the knowledge base and professional competencies needed for practice (Anderson, Ashton-Shaeffer, & Autry, 2000; Brasile, 1992, 1998; Kinney & Witman, 1997; Monroe & Connolly, 1997–98; Skalko & Smith, 1989; Stumbo & Carter, 1999a, 1999b; Stumbo, Carter, & Kim, 2004a, 2004b; West, 1993). These researchers and professional leaders have called for curriculum design and content to ensure that professional competencies are consistently developed across

Table 12.1
Higher Education Taskforce Future Tasks For the TR Profession

Item	Rank of Educators (N = 42)	
	ATRA (n = 22)	NTRS (n = 20)
Distinct Accreditation	1	1
(Specialization option with COA)		
Standardization of competency-based TR education	2	4
Undergraduate competency list	3	3
Initiatives to enhance recruitment/retention	4	2
Materials/methods for marketing TR ed. programs	5	5
Materials to train internship site supervisors	6	8
Repository for undergraduate syllabi	7	11
Interdisciplinary course materials/experiences	8	13
Core competencies for TR graduate education	9	6
Identification of external funding resources	10	7
Repository for graduate syllabi	11	14
Avenue of communication for grad. programs	12	10
Network identifying grad. faculty expertise	13	12
Graduate research funding sources	14	9

Notes:
- top five are the same for both groups
- correlation between groups is high, significant, and positive (p = +.76)
- educators who attended both meetings were counted only with ATRA

TR curricula. Such standardization would ensure employers and consumers of therapeutic recreation services that TR graduates shared a common competence reflective of "best practices" in the field.

Academic environments need to provide students with a climate that fosters intellectual challenge and inquiry while also supporting excellence in professional practice. The ever-growing body of knowledge and skills required within the profession necessitates that future professionals have an ability to apply knowledge in order to function competently within the ever-changing and evolving world of practice. Examples of such knowledge specific to therapeutic recreation are the recommendations for contemporary curricula offered by Keogh Hoss, Powell, and Sable (2006):
- increase emphasis on chronic disease needs;
- strengthen knowledge and skills relevant to an aging population;
- integrate core interdisciplinary competencies (Pew) into TR curricula, accreditation standards, and certification process;
- seek out learning opportunities that promote development of interdisciplinary, collaborative skill sets;

- teach competency/strategies needed to demonstrate cost effectiveness of TR;
- understand the broad spectrum of applications of the International Classification of Functioning Disability and Health and the relevance of these applications to TR;
- adopt TR competencies for support content and TR content that are consistent with TR continuum of service/scope of practice; and
- prepare students for new and emerging community based health service models (i.e, outpatient, home healthcare, free-standing programs, and health promotion programs). (p. 120)

The curricula must incorporate a combination of didactic, clinical, and research learning experiences that are reflective of contemporary TR practice. Students must be culturally competent, aware of multiple styles of learning, diverse social concepts, values, and ethical behaviors that enable them to fulfill their responsibilities to society.

TR practitioners must understand the connection to the larger community and society in which they live. Social responsibilities and ethical behavior that will help them determine and define their responsibility to society and the profession are integral components of the academic environment. Equally important is the development of critical inquiry and decision making reflected in clinical reasoning, clinical judgment, and reflective practice.

As previously indicated, the establishment of academic accreditation, personnel credentialing through a national certification examination, professional organizations, professional codes of ethics, and professional standards of practice all contribute to defining the profession of therapeutic recreation (Brasile, 1998; Stumbo & Carter, 1999a, 1999b). These professional activities all guide and influence curricula design. These influences, however, do not dictate what a college or university program of study entails. In general, the certification standards of therapeutic recreation have not dictated curriculum design, as is the case in other disciplines such as Speech and Language Pathology and Occupational Therapy.

Constraints on Standardization

The basic rationale opposing standardization of TR curricula is that TR education needs to be eclectic. Richter and Kaschalk (1996) contended that success in the field requires a well-rounded generalist rather than a narrow specialist. The generalist can better respond to the needs of diverse settings and populations. Several major factors have contributed to the continued variance among curricula. The therapeutic recreation vs. recreation therapy debate continues to impact curricula in TR (Monroe & Connolly, 1997-98). A major point of contention is whether the field is a component of recreation or of allied health.

Therapeutic recreation as a specialization within the recreation profession is evidenced in the accreditation standards of the discipline and the continued status of most therapeutic recreation curricula as options within recreation departments. Recreational therapy advocates, in contrast, have stated that continued affiliation with recreation will widen the gap between the needs of healthcare providers and the abilities of the recreational therapist to meet those needs (Rhodes, 1998). They have proposed and developed curricula separate from traditional recreation and park programs. Included in these efforts are independent therapeutic recreation programs housed in more healthcare-oriented schools and colleges, such as health studies, nursing, or allied health.

As noted by the National Council for Therapeutic Recreation Certification (NCTRC™, 1999), there is no significant relationship between where the academic program is housed and scores on the certification exam. Perhaps, however, there may be differences in perceptions consumers, colleagues, and employers have of the competence of TR practitioners based on academic background.

Resource differences also impede standardization. Opportunities for TR students to volunteer or work at agencies that have TR programs vary depending on the location of the college or university. The number of faculty members and their backgrounds vary. Some TR faculty have limited or no experience in the field. Others have no recent experience. The type of support courses available to students varies greatly by school, as does the level of available technology. Similarly, the academic background of faculty evidences significant variations. Faculty degrees range from bachelor's through doctorates, and areas of study vary (Stumbo & Carter, 1999b). Students, too, are different. Some begin programs as freshmen; others transfer into programs after some years in other disciplines. Additionally, TR attracts some non-traditional students whose age and experience are significantly different than other undergraduates. Adding to the confounding mix of differences are geographic factors. Some states, for example, have a significant job market in community-based programs (e.g., the special recreation districts in Illinois) which may require a different mix of competencies. Perhaps of greatest impact is the lack of symmetry among internship requirements. Length, content, and supervision are varied. NCTRC™ (1999) reports a relationship between longer time spent in internships and greater passing rates on the certification exam. They also report much variance among schools on the amount of coursework devoted to various job knowledge areas (Riley & Connolly, 2006).

Differences in the practice of therapeutic recreation make standardization problematic. The tremendous range of settings, populations, expectations, and modalities/techniques found in the field are not easily reduced to a common body of knowledge or a common protocol for obtaining it. Similarly, internship experiences at these varied settings lack uniformity. In contrast, the field of occupational therapy has developed a standardized assessment for all clinical affiliations.

Standardization Efforts in Related Fields

TR is not unique in its efforts to develop a standard curriculum while providing latitude that allows response to change, specialization, and innovation. In certain professions, such as physical therapy and speech-language pathology, accreditation is linked to the credentialing process (licensure, certification). For example, in physical therapy, graduation from an accredited program is a requirement for licensure, and all states require licensure for practice. Institutions seeking to initiate or maintain a physical therapy education program, therefore, also seek accreditation because they wish to have their graduates become eligible for licensure (Commission on Accreditation of Physical Therapy Education [CAPTE], 1998). In therapeutic recreation, there is no required link between graduation from an accredited program and qualifying to sit for the national exam offered by NCTRC™ for the title of "Certified Therapeutic Recreation Specialist™." Due to the current structure of

NRPA/American Association for Physical Activity and Recreation (APAR) accreditation, it is not predetermined that a graduate from an accredited program has completed TR certification sitting requirements. A student could graduate from an accredited program with a generalist accreditation but not have the necessary coursework completed for TR certification. Given the current structure of the NRPA/AAPAR accreditation process, linkage between certification and accreditation does not seem eminent.

Audiology and speech-language pathology uses its accreditation process to evaluate programs in light of their own training models and goals and judges the degree to which a program has achieved those goals and objectives. Their Council on Academic Accreditation (CAA) does not explicitly prescribe a program's educational goals or the processes by which they should be reached; rather it judges the degree to which a program achieves outcomes and goals that are consistent with its stated training model and guiding principles. Standards related to curriculum design assess if the program provides appropriate and sufficient curricular offerings to support the mission, goals, and objectives established by the program's faculty. The curriculum standards rely heavily on the American Speech-Language-Hearing Association's (ASHA, 1998) standards for the Certificates of Clinical Competence to guide the curriculum design. Academic requirements for certification are divided into basic science and professional coursework categories. Certification standards identify the number of credit hours required and the emphasis areas of selected courses.

All coursework and graduate clinical practica required in the professional area for which certification is sought must be completed at an institution whose program is accredited by the Council on Academic Accreditation in Audiology and Speech-Language Pathology (CAA). Curriculum design is guided by the certification standards with the accreditation process supporting those guidelines (ASHA, 1998).

In occupational therapy (OT), accreditation is viewed as the major influence in driving standardization of professional competency. A three-year revision of accreditation standards conducted by a subcommittee of the Accreditation Council for Occupational Therapy Education (ACOTE) entailed extensive input from both practitioners and educators, intertwining professional practice with education. These accreditation standards (ACOTE, 1998) are viewed as the minimal level, and each academic program is free to go beyond the required standard to develop expertise, specialization, or innovation in their curricula. Accreditation standards are less prescriptive than in physical therapy or nursing. Some OT programs may have a more medical model, while other academic programs reflect a health and human service model. This encourages the fit between the program and the particular institution's mission and culture. OT programs must meet the professional standards for OT education, but there is latitude for the program to establish objectives that are in keeping with the mission and resources of the institution. The certification exam—reflecting practice competency—influences and impacts curricula, but the more direct influence is the accreditation process. Similar to audiology and speech-language pathology, to become an occupational therapist, students are required to graduate from an ACOTE-accredited program before they are permitted to sit for their national certification exam. As of 2004, master's degrees became the entry-level degree for practice in OT (Murray & Coyle, 2006).

The professional initiatives related to revision of accreditation standards and the research associated with occupational therapy's Practice Analysis Study mirrors the process of therapeutic recreation's professional activities. The issue may, in fact, not be standardization of professional education, but a demand for more quality in therapeutic recreation's professional education programs. If these programs were comprehensive and of high quality, the issue of standardization might be less compelling. If, as in athletic training, for example, certification testing included simulations and actual practice, a clearer link between preparation and outcomes in practice could be established.

Murray and Coyle (2006) identified several issues important for therapeutic recreation professionals to consider based on their comprehensive review of education trends in other health and human service professions (e.g., nursing, OT, PT, social work). These include:

- having a clear sense of identity was consistently viewed as important by all disciplines;
- each discipline clearly identified the aging population as an opportunity for new/ expanded service delivery;
- the need for and understanding of research was identified as a concern;
- many disciplines had their own accreditation standards;
- clearly evident in each discipline was the growing awareness of the interdependency between practitioners and the academy;
- technology was embraced by all the disciplines as a new venue for enhancing instruction;
- modeling professional identity and behaviors relevant to competent practice was emphasized;
- critical thinking and effective writing were critical skills identified for effective practice; and
- adaptability and responsiveness to market trends was apparent in many disciplines' educational programs (pp. 156-160).

The authors suggest a variety of responses for therapeutic recreation specific to the concerns above. Collaboration with other disciplines at schools and among therapeutic recreation educators at various schools is recommended. These approaches also would have much utility in regard to students' acquisition of facilitation skills for modalities and techniques used in practice. Most modalities and techniques are utilized by multiple disciplines sometimes in co-leadership/co-treatment formats with professionals from other disciplines. Collaboration across disciplines to sponsor training programs (e.g., Arthritis Association exercise program) and classes (e.g., movement experiences for children) can be cost-effective. They can also serve to build understanding and rapport among disciplines. Cooperation among therapeutic educators at various schools as well as with local practitioners can serve to ameliorate one of the salient complaints practitioners have expressed about educators. The complaint is that "they focus too much on populations and modalities that were part of their personal experience" (Witman & Saville, 2006, p. 280). The solution may well be distance education and local networking opportunities which allow students to gain a more comprehensive perspective regarding practice. Regional and national cooperation among therapeutic recreation educators could enhance the quality and consistency of instruction in these important skills.

The Bases of Competence: A Beginning for Formulating Standardization

Skills for lifelong learning and employability provide a core of competence from which students can adjust to changing job markets and responsibilities. As respected corporate trainers, Wilson and Wilson (1998) asserted, "Deeply prepared people create their own weather." The vagaries of healthcare and human service systems, like unpredictable weather, have caught many people by surprise. They have been well prepared for the practice of therapeutic recreation as it was, rather than as it is now or will be in the future. Evers, Rush, and Bendrow (1998) identified and validated a core of skills that allow individuals to adapt and flourish in changing conditions. They include: (a) managing self, (b) communicating, (c) managing people and tasks, and (d) mobilizing innovation and change.

Managing self is defined as "constantly developing practices and internalizing routines for maximizing one's ability to deal with the uncertainty of an ever-changing environment" (Evers et al., 1998, p. 57). TR curricula, which foster student responsibility—learning how to learn and how to solve problems—impart important skills.

Communicating is defined as "interacting effectively with a variety of individuals and groups to facilitate the gathering, integrating, and conveying of information (e.g., verbal, written, visual) in many forms" (Evers et al., 1998, p. 78). TR practitioners have many levels of customers—clients, co-workers, administrators, other agencies, and so forth. Additionally, the range of clients served by TR programs is broad. Exposure to and interaction with many types of prospective clients is important as well as in-depth engagement with several client groups.

Managing people and tasks is completing responsibilities by "planning, organizing, coordinating, and guiding both resources and people" (Evers et al., 1998, p. 98). Clinical reasoning and thinking like practitioners is an aspect of this skill area with particular relevance to TR professional development. Neistadt (1996) detailed a continuum of clinical reasoning behaviors from novice to expert and a sequence of teaching strategies toward acquiring them.

Mobilizing innovation and change is defined as "conceptualizing as well as setting in motion ways of initiating and managing change that involve significant departures from the current mode" (Evers et al., 1998, p. 118). Relevant to TR is the move away from traditional organization by departments to organization by service lines or programs within many healthcare organizations. Practitioners in such systems should be able to work effectively as team members in organized settings that emphasize high-quality, cost-effective integrated services. Skills beyond individual disciplines are needed (Shires & Tappan, 1992).

Fostering these four skill areas in the college curriculum should guide curriculum development in TR and can be accomplished in a variety of ways. The following examples emphasize the notion that the "process" of curricula can be as important as "content:"

- Career development planning—Individuals create a matrix that compares courses and experiences they have had and what competencies they address. A similar matrix is devised for lifelong learning and employability skills.
- Skill portfolios—Just as the artist's portfolio provides a display of his work, so too, can a portfolio that includes examples of a student's competence in various skill areas.

- Interdisciplinary courses and programs—Exposure to working with individuals in other disciplines and forming teams that transcend traditional boundaries can be provided through cooperative projects with other disciplines.
- Experiential learning—Sections of all classes can involve practice of skills. On a basic level, job shadowing and visits to work settings can be implemented. Additionally, service learning projects can serve the dual purpose of enhancing student skills while at the same time meeting community needs.

Perhaps the greatest accomplishment of professional preparation programs is the development of a commitment by students to lifelong or lifespan learning. Change is the central reality of lifespan learning. Therapeutic recreation constantly changes, and while the rubrics of the work may remain the same (professionals still assess, plan, implement, and evaluate), the ways in which they are done and the context in which they are done are ever different.

The Pew Health Commission's Competencies for 2005 (Finocchio, 1994) included two areas with particular relevance to the fluidity of healthcare provision. First, prospective practitioners need to "accommodate expanded accountability." The relevance of formal preparation programs to patient outcomes needs to be established and monitored. Academic programs and internship sites need to be judged not just on how many graduates pass the certification exam or procure jobs in the field but also on how those graduates impact their patients/clients. Secondly, the commitment to "continue to learn" needs to be fostered along with the skills necessary to access and utilize new information. The effectiveness of students who have memorized a fixed body of knowledge of the field will diminish, while students skilled in the process of problem-solving and committed to doing something (not just to valuing and talking) about their learning needs will be positioned to adapt and to flourish as systems change.

As readiness to practice is assessed (e.g., by schools, by NCTRC™, by prospective employers), measures of competence to continue learning need to be included. During the period of induction into the profession, mentors and materials need to be available that assist with the translation of knowledge into skills and abilities. Similarly, continuing education programs need to develop mechanisms which provide assistance to participants in applying information gained at programs. Learning during practice is often stimulated through the need to address problems, concerns, and crises. The decision-making that these situations create can be a catalyst for seeking learning opportunities. Questions like "What can I do with this group, client, or dilemma?" generate a variety of needs for information and support. While curricula cannot possibly provide answers to all prospective problems associated with practice, they can produce individuals "educated" to think, network, and problem solve when confronted with new situations or ethical dilemmas.

Another area of concern are practice duties and responsibilities beyond the traditional scope of therapeutic recreation practice. A recent study of the "other related duties" of therapeutic recreation and activity professionals (Witman & Rakos, 2008) revealed that, on average, more than 20% of professionals' time at work is devoted to such duties. Examples include assisting consumers with Activities of Daily Living (ADL's), serving on committees, helping with agency-wide events, conducting non-recreation education/

treatment programs, and performing a variety of administrative, safety and general duties. Developing competency in some of the more common of these responsibilities should, perhaps, be considered, as a component of curricula.

Career change also needs to be a curriculum concern. Preparation in TR should allow students to qualify for subsequent involvement in a broad spectrum of graduate and specialty education. Furthermore, it should provide a sound base of generic skills to those who take on broader responsibilities with service systems and/or transition into related fields. Ideally, preparation in TR will transcend simply passing the certification exam and will prepare professionals, thinkers, researchers, communicators, and leaders—valued members of communities and society. Finally, the format of curricula needs to be responsive (specific and consistent enough) to those who move into TR from other fields.

Conceptualizing Curricular Standardization

What might a standardized curriculum look like? In order for individuals to engage in the standardization debate, they must have more than a philosophical stance; they must also have a concept of what the curriculum might look like, and on the basis of that conceptualization formulate a set of advantages and disadvantages.

The following conceptualization model incorporates standardization of TR curricula while allowing some degree of curricular flexibility. This conceptualization model includes three tiers: (a) critical courses, (b) recommended courses, and (c) specialty courses. The first tier includes critical coursework that includes required courses in TR, fieldwork/internship, and externally required courses. The second tier is a set of recommended courses in TR and external courses. The third tier includes an area of specialization in TR. This tier would make each TR program unique to that college or university. The tier system allows curricula to expand course options as their resources allow. Tier 1 should be the central focus. To the extent that resources permit, curricula could provide courses in tier 2 as a set of recommended courses where flexibility is more evident. Tier 3 would include specialty areas that would make each curriculum unique to that setting or university.

The first tier requires seven TR courses plus fieldwork, internship, and three outside required courses; the second tier includes a total of two TR courses and two recommended outside courses; and the third tier could have between one to three TR courses depending on the specialization of the program. It is recognized that this recommendation may be unrealistic considering the findings by Stumbo and Carter (1999a, 1999b) and Stumbo, Carter, and Kim (2206a, 2006b) that indicated some TR programs do not even meet the required number of courses for NCTRC™ certification and that the most common number of TR courses is between three and five. The question becomes whether the therapeutic recreation industry wants to maintain the status quo or move to a new level in order to better prepare graduates to provide services and be competitive in the healthcare arena. It should be noted that this conceptualization model requires an average of 10 TR content courses, which appears to be well below what is required for students in related disciplines.

The courses in the conceptualization model reflect the knowledge areas identified by NCTRC™, as well as NRPA accreditation standards and the competencies outlined in *Guidelines for Competency Assessment and Curriculum Planning for Recreational Therapy*

Practice (West, Kinney, & Witman, 2008). They also reflect the National Healthcare Skills Standards (U.S. Department of Labor and Education, 1996).

Tier 1: Critical Courses

A. TR Required Courses
1. Foundations of TR. This would be the introductory course and cover such topics as history, concepts, theories, models, philosophy, life-long learning, and professional organizations.
2. Clinical Practice. This course would cover assessments; treatment plans; TR settings documentation; clinical supervision; therapeutic relationships; physical, emotional, social, and behavioral functioning; interviewing; type, frequency, intensity, and duration of interventions; clinical reasoning, etc.
3. Program Planning/Design in TR. This course would cover theories of programming, implementing the treatment plan, communication skills, group dynamics, leadership styles, group and activity protocols, activity and task analysis, and problem-solving skills.
4. Disabling Conditions. This course would cover a minimum of the four major disability groups with whom TR specialists work including physical disabilities, mental health, developmental disabilities, and aging.
5. Modalities and Facilitation Techniques in TR. This course would address individual facilitation techniques that can be utilized in TR (e.g., reality orientation, group therapy, etc.) and selected therapeutic modalities (activities).
6. Administration (Organization and Management). This course would cover the organization and delivery of healthcare services; recruitment, orientation, supervision, and performance evaluations; life-long learning; finance/budgeting; health-care accreditation standards; state and local regulations; public relations/ marketing; risk management; quality improvement; managing resources; legal liabilities/issues on infection control; managing change; and networking.
7. Research and Evaluation. This course would address the research process, statistical analyses, types of research, the scientific method, program evaluation, and outcome and efficacy studies. A major focus would be contributing to/utilizing evidence-based practice. If taught in a general recreation core, it should still include content relative to clinical trials and epidemiological methods.

B. TR Required Fieldwork/Internship
All students would be required to complete volunteer hours plus at least two practica during their course of study. Additional contact through course structure would require students to make observations and complete service-learning assignments and class projects.
1. Volunteer/Service Learning Hours. Exposure to recipients of therapeutic recreation services and practitioners should be a required element in all therapeutic recreation curricula, particularly in the introductory major courses. Ideally, these experiences should reflect course content and allow the student to begin to bridge the gap

between classroom learning and applied techniques.

2. Fieldwork. Fieldwork (junior/initial internship) would require students to complete a minimum of 120 clock-hours in a therapeutic recreation setting.

3. Internship. The internship (senior internship) requirements should be a minimum of 600 clock-hours of experience under the supervision of a certified therapeutic recreation specialist and meet all the requirements of NCTRC™. The university supervisor should also be NCTRC™ certified.

C. External Required Courses

All TR majors would be required to take these three courses to meet the requirements of NCTRC™ for certification standards:

1. Anatomy and Physiology
2. Human Growth and Development
3. Abnormal Psychology

Tier 2: Recommended Courses

Students are required to take at least two of the following courses

A. TR Recommended Courses

1. Leisure Education/Counseling. This course would cover philosophy of leisure education and counseling, theoretical and practice models, leisure assessment tools, social competence skills, counseling skills, clinical interviews, leisure education programs and resources, and leisure counseling protocols.

2. Issues and Trends in TR. This course would address the current trends and issues that affect TR. The nature and content of the course would change as new issues and trends are identified as having an impact on the TR discipline.

3. Computer Technology in TR. This would not only be an introductory course on how to use various computer programs but would identify and teach those current expectations and technology skills required for entry-level therapists.

4. Specific Disability Courses. This would include such courses as TR and Mental Health, TR and Physical Disabilities, and TR and Older Adults, etc. These courses would enable the specific disabling condition and potential TR interventions to be studied in depth by students.

5. Senior Seminar. This seminar-style course would maximize and facilitate the learning process by requiring students to review the literature on the concepts, principles, and practices of TR with persons who have illnesses and disabilities. Emphasis would be on placing their TR education in context and developing the skills and knowledge to become a contributing professional.

B. External Recommended Courses
1. Medical Terminology
2. Interdisciplinary Approaches to Treatment

Tier 3: Specialty Courses

Specialty areas would make TR programs unique to that particular school, geographic location, or faculty interests. Each program would have one or more specialty areas that would enhance the overall educational program of their students. Some examples are: Outdoor and/or Adventure Programming, Community/Inclusive Recreation for Special Populations, Use of Technology and Adaptive Equipment in TR, TR and the Schools; Aquatics; Adapted Sports and Games.

Summary

Standardization of TR education programs has been a long-standing debate within the TR discipline. Many of those calling for standardization thought that standardized TR curricula would be in place by the end of the last century. This did not happen. Monroe and Connolly (1997-98) identified three components to this debate including philosophical issues of TR services, healthcare reform, and curricular reform in higher education. They suggested that it is more important to focus on the content of the curriculum than to be concerned with the location/department where the TR program resides. When considering standardizing TR curricula, the ideal model also should allow a certain amount of flexibility to enable TR programs to create areas of specialty. This could include developing a specialty area that coincides with geographic settings conducive to certain types of TR programming (e.g., outdoor recreation) or areas of interest of the faculty within the program.

As the discipline struggles with the issue of standardization, the ever-changing evolution of healthcare in the U.S., as well as curricular reform/standardization in other allied health disciplines, compels the TR discipline to consider taking the final step to standardization. Many have urged the discipline to standardize the TR curriculum (Austin & Hamilton, 1992; Brasile, 1998; Kinney & Witman, 1997; Monroe & Connolly, 1997-98; Skalko & Smith, 1989; Stumbo & Carter, 1999a, 1999b; Stumbo, Carter, & Kim, 2004a, 2004b), and compelling arguments exist to implement standardization to meet the challenges that confront the discipline.

However, the number of courses that would be required to bring TR curricula closer to other allied health disciplines would place considerable stressors on university resources. Perhaps the relationship between therapeutic recreation and other components of the recreation and leisure services umbrella needs rethinking. For example, should universities require that new faculty be NCTRC™ certified and be able to teach in the TR curriculum even if hired for other specialty areas, e.g., outdoor recreation or general recreation? Similarly, the number of TR courses proposed in the conceptual model would create a logistical problem for those programs that desire NRPA/AAPAR accreditation. The number of competencies that are required of all students by that accreditation provides severe limitations on the number of TR requirements that can be expected. One must ask, is it more important for a TR student to have competence in park planning or in TR assessment and documentation? Clearly, pursuing standardization would present a major challenge for small programs. With many schools now providing only the minimum four (as of December 2007) TR courses required to sit for the NCTRC™ examination, there would be major resistance to a requirement to increase the number of TR courses.

Defenders of the status quo could argue that modules or sections of courses could be developed that touch on all of the important competency areas in TR. They could also suggest that some competencies (e.g., modality leadership) could be developed apart from academic requirements. Furthermore, they could argue that some excellent professionals have been produced through the current system. None of the arguments, however, negate the nagging questions, "Do we really believe there is so little substance to the discipline that it can be covered in a total of four courses?" and "Do we want to strive for minimum competence or maximum competence?"

With so many potential barriers confronting the issue of standardization, it is logical to wonder if it will ever happen. The enormous investment that programs have in preventing standardization from happening and, thus, facing the resource question, makes it seriously questionable. In all likelihood, standardization will only occur if individuals, university faculty, and leaders in professional organizations are willing to rethink the relationship of TR to the other specialty areas in recreation and leisure. That will probably not occur unless there is increased pressure from the healthcare industry to turn out more competent practitioners. Will therapeutic recreation programs be able to respond adequately and in time? Judged by the actions of the profession in the seven years since the first edition of this text was published, the answer would be no. Concerns and pronouncements have not been transformed into actions.

Discussion Questions

1. Divide into two groups in class. Debate the pros and cons of a standardized curriculum. Each group should address the issue of whether standardization benefits students, consumers, and employers. If in support of standardization, what is the method for reaching this goal? If opposed, what are the ways to insure mastery of entry-level "exit skills"?

2. Imagine that you have been appointed to chair a joint ATRA/NTRS Task Force charged with improving the quality of professional preparation in TR. As the head of this task force, outline (following the TR process of assessment, planning, implementation, and evaluation) your approach to the task. Include your personal list of five keys to more effective curricula in TR.

3. Review the "Tasks for the Profession" identified in Table 12.1. Which three do you feel are most important to the future of the TR profession? Outline a plan of action toward achieving them.

4. Review the list below of "other related duties" that therapeutic recreation personnel report that they are sometimes involved with. State your opinion, with each duty, of whether or not you feel it is appropriate for TR professionals to be performing the particular task. Also identify which, if any, you feel should be concerns for TR education and how they could be included in course and fieldwork experiences.
   Other Related Duties:
   a.   Assisting clients with activities of daily living
   b.   Serving on an agency safety committee

c.   Coordinating an agency promotional event
d.   Leading the daily goals group for clients
e.   Recruiting volunteers for the agency
f.   Performing routine maintenance on vehicles and equipment
g.   Generating an agency newsletter
h.   Leading teambuilding activities for agency personnel
i.   Speaking to community groups about the purpose/programs of your agency
j.   Writing grants to support agency initiatives

References

Accreditation Council for Occupational Therapy Education. (1998). *Standards for an accredited educational program for the occupational therapist.* Bethesda, MD: American Occupational Therapy Association.

American Speech-Language-Hearing Association. (1998). *Accreditation handbook.* Rockville, MD: Author.

Anderson, S. C., Ashton-Schaeffer, C., & Autry, C. E. (2000). TR education: 1999 survey. *Therapeutic Recreation Journal, 34* (4), 335-347.

Austin, D., & Hamilton, E. (1992). The future of therapeutic recreation education: In the 1990s and beyond. In G. Hitzhusen, & L. T. Jackson (Eds.), *Expanding horizons in therapeutic recreation* (pp. 77-104). Columbia, MO: Curators University of Missouri.

Austin, D. A., & Powell, L. G. (1981). Competencies needed by community recreators to serve special populations. *Directions in Health, Physical Education and Recreation, Monograph Series No. 1,* 33-35.

Brasile, F. (1992). Professional preparation: Reported needs for a profession in transition. *Annual in Therapeutic Recreation, 3,* 58-71.

Brasile, F. (1998). The recreational therapy degree program: Trends in education. In F. Brasile, T., Skalko & j. burlingame (Eds.), *Perspectives in recreational therapy: Issues of a dynamic profession* (pp. 367-382). Ravensdale, WA: Idyll Arbor.

Brasile, F. (2006) Response to concept paper on undergraduate education in therapeutic recreation. In M. Carter, & J. Folkerth (Eds.), *Therapeutic recreation education: Challenges and changes* (pp. 21-29) Ashburn, VA: National Recreation and Park Association.

Carter, M. J., & Folkerth, J. E. (Eds.). (2006). *Therapeutic recreation education: Challenges and changes.* Ashburn, VA: National Recreation and Park Association.

Commission on Accreditation in Physical Therapy Education. (1998). *Evaluative criteria for accreditation of education programs for the preparation of physical therapists.* Alexandria, VA: American Physical Therapy Association.

Connolly, P., & Riley, B. (1995-96). Entry-level job skills: Reinvestigation of the national job analysis of the practice of therapeutic recreation. *Annual in Therapeutic Recreation, 6,* 26-37.

Evers, F. T., Rush, J. C., & Bendrow, L. (1998). *The bases of competence: Skills for lifelong learning and employability.* San Francisco, CA: Jossey-Bass Publishers.

Finocchio, L.J. (1994). Looking into the future of allied health: Recommendations of the Pew Health Professions Commission. *Journal of Allied Health, 31*(1), 29-33.

Grote, K. A., & Hasl, M. A. (1998). *Guidelines for internships in therapeutic recreation.* Hattiesburg, MS: American Therapeutic Recreation Association.

Hitzhusen, J. (1983). Therapeutic recreation-2000. In G. A. Gillespie (Ed.), *Leisure 2000, scenarios for the future* (pp. 136-156). Columbia, MO: University of Missouri.

Jordan, J. J., Dayton, W. P., & Brill, K. H. (1977). *Theory and design of competency-based education in therapeutic recreation.* Philadelphia, PA: Department of Recreation and Leisure Studies, Temple University.

Kelley, J., Robb, G. M., Park, W., & Halberg, K. J. (1976). *Therapeutic recreation education: Developing a competency-based entry-level curriculum.* Champaign, IL: Office of Recreation and Park Resources—Department of Leisure Studies, University of Illinois.

Keogh Hoss, M.A., Powell, L., & Sable, J. (2006) Healthcare trends: Implications for therapeutic recreation. In M. Carter, & J. Folkerth (Eds.), *Therapeutic recreation education: Challenges and changes* (pp. 107-122) Ashburn, VA: National Recreation and Park Association.

Murray, S. B., & Coyle, C. P. (2006). Education and training trends of related disciplines: Learning from others. In M. Carter, & J. Folkerth (Eds.), *Therapeutic recreation education: Challenges and changes* (pp. 129-164). Ashburn, VA: National Recreation and Park Association.

Mobily, K. E. (1996). Therapeutic recreation philosophy re-visited: A question of what leisure is good for. In C. Sylvester (Ed.), *Philosophy of therapeutic recreation: Ideas and issues, volume II* (pp. 57-70). Ashburn, VA: National Recreation and Park Association.

Monroe, J., & Connolly, P. (1997–98). Responsive curriculum development in therapeutic recreation: One approach to comprehensive curriculum design. *Annual in Therapeutic Recreation, 7,* 64-73.

National Council for Therapeutic Recreation Certification. (1997). *NCTRC™ job analysis study.* New City, NY: Author.

National Council for Therapeutic Recreation Certification. (1999). Sound bytes vs. reality bytes. *NCTRC™ Newsletter,* Spring, 4.

National Recreation and Park Association. (1981). *Standards and evaluative criteria for recreation, park resources, and leisure services baccalaureate programs.* Alexandria, VA: Author.

National Recreation and Park Association. (1990). *Standards and evaluative criteria for recreation, park resources, and leisure services baccalaureate programs.* Arlington, VA: Author.

National Therapeutic Recreation Society. (1997). *NTRS internship standards and guidelines for therapeutic recreation.* Ashburn, VA: Author.

Neistadt, M. E. (1996). Teaching strategies for the development of clinical reasoning. *American Journal of Occupational Therapy, 50,* 676-684.

Oltman, P. K., Norback, J., & Rosenfeld, M. (1989). A national study of the profession of therapeutic recreation specialist. *Therapeutic Recreation Journal, 23*(2), 48-58.

Peterson, C. A., & Connolly, P. (1981). Professional preparation in therapeutic recreation. *Therapeutic Recreation Journal, 15*(2), 39-45.

Pierce, D., & Peyton, C. (1998). A historical cross-disciplinary perspective on the professional doctorate in occupational therapy. *American Journal of Occupational Therapy, 53,* 64-71.

Rhodes, M. (1998). Mentorship: Transitioning from student to practitioner. In F. Brasile, T. K. Skalko, & j. burlingame (Eds.), *Perspectives in recreational therapy: Issues of a dynamic profession* (pp. 417-431). Ravensdale, WA: Idyll Arbor, Inc.

Richter, K. J., & Kaschalk, S. M. (1996). The future of therapeutic recreation: An existential outcome. In C. Sylvester (Ed.), *Philosophy of therapeutic recreation: Ideas and issues, volume II* (pp. 86-91). Ashburn, VA: National Recreation and Park Association.

Riley, B., & Connolly, P. (2006). NCTRC summary report: Current status of professional preparation in therapeutic recreation. In M. Carter, & J. Folkerth (Eds.), *Therapeutic recreation education: Challenges and changes* (pp. 187-219). Ashburn, VA: National Recreation and Park Association.

Shires, B., & Tappan, T. (1992). The clinical nurse specialist as brief psychotherapist. *Perspectives in Psychiatric Care, 28*(4), 15-18.

Skalko, T. K., & Smith, M. M. (1989). The status of therapeutic recreation in state personnel systems: A national study. *Therapeutic Recreation Journal, 23*(2), 41-47.

Stumbo, N. J. (1986). A definition of entry-level knowledge for therapeutic recreation practice. *Therapeutic Recreation Journal, 20*(4), 15-30.

Stumbo, N. J., & Carter, M. J. (1999a). National therapeutic recreation curriculum study part A: Accreditation, curriculum, and internship characteristics. *Therapeutic Recreation Journal, 33*(l), 46-60.

Stumbo, N. J., & Carter, M. J. (1999b). National therapeutic recreation curriculum study part B: University, faculty, student, and placement characteristics. *Therapeutic Recreation Journal, 33*(3), 241-250.

Stumbo, N. J., Carter, M. J., & Kim, J. (2004a). 2003 national therapeutic recreation study part A: Accreditation, curriculum and internship characteristics. *Therapeutic Recreation Journal 38*(1), 32-52.

Stumbo, N. J., Carter, M. J., & Kim, J. (2004b). 2003 national therapeutic recreation survey part B: University, faculty, student and placement characteristics. *Therapeutic Recreation Journal, 38*(1), 53-71.

U.S. Departments of Labor and Education. (1996). Part III: National healthcare skill standards. In National Health-Care Skill Standards Project. San Francisco, CA: WestEd.

West, R. E. (1995, March). *Entry-level competencies: What managers expect.* Paper presented at the 1995 ATRA Professional Issues Mid-Year Forum, Minneapolis, MN.

West, R. (1993, September). *Practice competencies for recreational therapists: Are we keeping pace with allied health disciplines?* Paper presented at the annual conference of the American Therapeutic Recreation Association, Towson, MD.

West, R. E., Kinney, T., & Witman, J. (Eds.). (2008). *Guidelines for competency assessment and curriculum planning for recreational therapy practice* (2nd ed.). Hattiesburg, MS: American Therapeutic Recreation Association.

Wilson, L., & Wilson, H. (1998). Play to win!: Choosing growth over fear in work and life. Austin, TX: Bard Press, Inc.

Witman, J. P., & Rakos, K. S. (2008). Determining the "other related duties" of therapeutic recreation and activity professionals: A pilot study. *American Journal of Recreation Therapy, 7*(2), 29-33.

Witman, J. P., & Saville, J. F. (2006). Practitioners' perspectives on the strengths and weaknesses of TR education. In M. Carter, & J. Folkerth (Eds.), *Therapeutic recreation education: Challenges and changes* (pp. 280-282) Ashburn, VA: National Recreation and Park Association.

Section III
Practice Issues

Section III
Practice Issues

CHAPTER 13

Keynote: Therapeutic Recreation Practice: Art, Science, or Magic?

Sharon Nichols, CTRS™
Genesis Healthcare Corporation

The practice of therapeutic recreation has assumed many forms along its evolutionary journey. Various texts chronicling the profession's roots (Austin & Crawford, 2000; Carter, Van Andel, & Robb, 2003; Kraus & Shank, 1992) traced the evolution back to early civilization. They speak to the application of play and recreation as a healing poultice applied to the ill or injured. More recently, James (1998) underscored the influence that Florence Nightingale had in applying the use of the arts, music, humor, pets, writing, and conversation in facilitating the recovery of ill, injured, and dying soldiers. In reviewing the profession's history, it is safe to conclude there has long been a foundation that supports recreation's capacity to contribute positively to one's health and quality of life.

What continues to be more perplexing to ponder is under what realm does the practice of therapeutic recreation really belong? Does the practice of therapeutic recreation fall within a framework of art? Does the practice of therapeutic recreation exist as a science? Or does the practice of therapeutic recreation equate to the practice of magic?

Therapeutic Recreation Practice as Art (All Recreation is Therapeutic)

"Art," as defined by the *American Heritage Dictionary* (1994), is "human effort to imitate, supplement, alter, or counteract the work of nature." In reflecting back over time, as well as looking to the present, it is possible to pinpoint the practice of therapeutic recreation as art. The practitioner seeks to supplement, alter, or counteract the effects that an illness or injury has upon the person. The therapeutic recreation practitioner introduces various media to tap into and supplement the body's capacity for healing and for health. The practitioner encourages the individual to be autonomous and to seek experiences that are meaningful and improve one's sense of self. The effect of that encouragement in the context of illness, injury, or impairment is that the person's condition improves in some way. This view of therapeutic recreation practice has been long standing. It centers on the aesthetics of the environment and the value of self-expression and creativity in causing one to feel good. In addition, this perspective of therapeutic recreation does not necessarily adhere to any particular rules other than arranging interventions in a way that effects a sense of quality or goodness. As with art, the participant interprets the value of the arrangement. It equates to the notion of art for art's sake or as recreation as a means unto itself.

Therapeutic Recreation Practice as Science
(Therapeutic Recreation as the Means to Outcomes or Ends)

The evolution of therapeutic recreation practice as science is a more recent phenomenon. It is due to a number of internal and external influences. Again, consider the *American Heritage Dictionary* (1994) definition of science: "The observation, identification, description, experimental investigation, and theoretical explanation of phenomena." It is through research that phenomena and theories are tested and explained. The scientific investigation of the practice of therapeutic recreation took shape in the 1950s (Carter, Van Andel, & Robb, 2003). It was also during the 1950s that formal training programs for practitioners began to emerge. The profession began its journey in trying to understand which interventions were effective and what skills practitioners needed in order to be effective with clients. The therapeutic recreation profession began its analysis into cause and effect relationships and began to develop a perspective on the importance of constancy of purpose and consistency of approach.

Evidence of this perspective surfaced internally with the development of professional organizations and with the proliferation of education and training programs to prepare practitioners. A body of knowledge was evolving shaped by theoretical questioning of a definition of therapeutic recreation and observation and investigation of the practice of therapeutic recreation.

One can track therapeutic recreation's practice as a science by reviewing the content of professional journals such as the *Therapeutic Recreation Journal* published by the NTRS, the *Annual in Therapeutic Recreation* published by the ATRA, and the *American Journal of Recreational Therapy,* published by Prime National Publishing Corporation. The profession also developed standards to guide the practice (ATRA, 2003; NTRS, 2002). In addition, the profession implemented guidelines for professional preparation programs through an accreditation process (cf. NRPA, 2004). Two milestones are significant to the notion of therapeutic recreation practice as science. The first was the establishment of an autonomous credentialing program for practitioners (NCTRC™) based upon a scientific analysis of therapeutic recreation job functions and the knowledge needed to perform those functions. The second was the 1991 National Consensus Conference on the Benefits of Therapeutic Recreation in Rehabilitation (cf. Coyle, Kinney, Riley, & Shank, 1998).

The National Council for Therapeutic Recreation Certification™ was born out of early efforts to establish a system for professional self-regulation. Through extensive research and analysis, NCTRC™ determined that the prerequisites to practice consisted of formal preparation along with an internship under the supervision of a qualified person, and that minimum job knowledge could be tested through a standardized examination. The certification standards became the first real measure of consistency of practice knowledge.

The 1991 National Consensus Conference on the Benefits of Therapeutic Recreation in Rehabilitation resulted from a grant to Temple University from the National Institute of Disability Rehabilitation Research (NIDRR). NIDRR set as a research priority to study the efficacy of therapeutic recreation in rehabilitation (Malkin, Coyle, & Carruthers, 1998). The Temple Project sought to consolidate the research in therapeutic recreation and culminated with the 1991 Consensus Conference. The Conference brought together researchers and practitioners in an effort to come to agreement on consistent, uniform treatment outcomes associated with the practice of therapeutic recreation with particular population groups. The results of this project not only helped to foster consistency of approach but also helped establish the future research agenda for the profession.

Externally, during this same evolutionary period, the profession felt the impact of the environments in which it practiced. Most therapeutic recreation practice had occurred and continues to occur in healthcare environments. Healthcare also felt the movement toward standardization and accreditation as evidenced by the development of the Joint Commission on Accreditation of Healthcare Organizations (JCAHO) and the Rehabilitation Accreditation Commission (CARF). In addition, organizations faced greater regulatory accountability if they received support through the Medicare and Medicaid programs regulated by the Healthcare Financing Administration (HCFA), now known as the Centers for Medicare/Medicaid Services (CMS). Concerns centered on the quality and appropriateness of care delivered by healthcare entities. Also, during this period, the costs for providing care skyrocketed, and the insurance industry imposed restrictions concerning access to healthcare.

Another component to this external environment surfaced with the evolution of technology and consumers' access to information. Not only were people living longer and surviving with catastrophic illness and injuries, but consumers were also better informed as to their options for care. With the demands of this external environment comes a greater emphasis on the accountability and efficacy of practice. The profession continues to face these external challenges. The practice of therapeutic recreation exists in the scientific arena because of these factors.

More recently, there has been substantial effort within the profession to develop evidenced-based protocols or practice guidelines. The first such set of guidelines was published by ATRA in 2003. *The Dementia Practice Guideline for Recreational Therapy* was the first in a series that provided credence for the need to establish practice protocols that were clearly linked to a theoretical framework that had scientific evidence to support the efficacy of the treatment approaches. The next set of practice guidelines that will soon be released by ATRA are guidelines for the management and treatment of pain. ATRA has other clinical teams that are working on practice guidelines for the treatment of obesity and guidelines for the treatment of stroke or other neurological events. It is clear that the profession is evolving into an arena that has a much stronger scientific base.

It will be important to monitor practice trends that can provide strong indications as to the direction that research and scientific inquiry must go in order to respond to the changing healthcare trends and the implication of those trends on the efficacy of treatment that may be needed. One must note here that there will be a tremendous need to link the practice of therapeutic recreation to worldwide health initiatives such as the World Health Organization's (2002) International Classification of Functioning, Disability, and Health (ICF). This classification system is the first movement away from the classification of illness and disease and is moving toward classification of health and health-related domains and how the individual is impacted, not only by internal body functions and structures, but also activity participation, performance, and functioning in relation to social perspective. Additionally, this system considers the impact that environment has on promoting or limiting one's abilities and capabilities. There will be significant study generated that will look at health and health promotion and therapeutic recreation's impact on promoting and sustaining the health and well-being of individuals across all settings and across all population groups.

Given this framework of moving toward health and health promotion, what is the scientific inquiry that will need to be investigated? Will we need to study the impact of environment in contributing to excess disability, or will we seek to explore how modification of environment can further promote independence?

Therapeutic Practice as Magic
(The Holistic or Spiritual Perspective of Therapeutic Recreation)

This final perspective of therapeutic recreation practice may be considered to be slightly "new age"—or is it? The *American Heritage Dictionary's* (1994) definition of magic is: "Possessing distinctive qualities that produce unaccountable or baffling effects."

Some practitioners have mastered the craft more by doing than by having a foundation rooted in either art or science. They do not rely on understanding how or why it works; they simply know that they get results through the power of charisma, charm, and perhaps the persuasiveness of their personalities.

As has been noted by such prominent authorities as Deepak Chopra, MD, Bernie Seigal, MD, Andrew Weil, MD, and Herbert Benson, MD, the power of the mind to restore health has been underrated. Although there may be a mysterious quality about these nonstandard therapeutic recreation techniques, there is something to be said in support of these qualities connected to healing.

Eastern civilizations have tapped into these qualities for thousand of years, and it is becoming accepted as legitimate practice in Western civilization, as evidenced by the acceptance of acupuncture, chiropractic, and naturopathic medicine, etc. Is it such an inconceivable notion, then, that therapeutic recreation practice can benefit from a greater understanding of the mind-body connection? Perhaps it is not.

There is a far greater awareness in today's world with regard to alternative or complementary approaches to health and well-being. There has been attention given to the use of certain energy-based modalities, such as yoga or Reiki or guided imagery and autogenics. Unfortunately, despite the fact that some of these techniques have been used for centuries, there is still limited scientific evidence to support the efficacy of these techniques. So until there is stronger support, some of the claims for the value of these techniques in practice fall closer toward these being "magical elements." There is greater attention given to the mind-body-spirit connection in today's world and greater consideration of a divine energy that influences us all, but we are still baffled in trying to understand how it works.

Consider Dorothy in the Land of Oz. The good witch, Glinda, reminded her that she always was able to return home. She told her to click her heels together and believe, and in moments she would be home. The concept of believing that one has the power to make something happen still prevails. How many times have practitioners said to clients, "If you believe that you can, you can"? We can prepare people and provide them with training/ education and modifications, but does that ensure that they will be successful participants in life? Not necessarily. We know that attitude (the mind and behaviors) plays a substantial role in recovery. The question then becomes have we as practitioners affected the person by design, or was it really just magic that caused the person to change?

Summary

The discussion set forth in this commentary is meant to stimulate thought and, more likely, question or debate. The remaining chapters of this text's practice section delve more deeply into an examination of therapeutic recreation practice. The authors look at the framework of practice through a review of therapeutic recreation models and through explanations of reimbursement and legislative and regulatory issues. Others explore the content of practice by looking at issues in client assessment, ethics, protocols, and service provision. The reader is left with a challenge to consider whether therapeutic recreation practice is art, science, or magic.

Discussion Questions

1. Provide further evidence and examples of the practice of therapeutic recreation as art, science, or magic. Cite any literature that indicates that particular service settings (e.g., rehabilitation, mental health, long-term care, etc.) are more likely to employ one practice perspective more consistently than others.
2. What other professions (e.g., music therapy, psychology) have similar perspectives of their practice as being art, science, or magic? Provide evidence to support the similarities between other professions and therapeutic recreation as art, science, or magic.
3. Provide an outline indicating the pros and cons of adherence to each of the practice perspectives.

References

The American Heritage Concise Dictionary, Third Edition (electronic version). (1994). Boston, MA: Houghton Mifflin Company.

American Journal of Recreational Therapy. Weston, MA: Prime National Publishing Corporation.

American Therapeutic Recreation. Annual in Therapeutic Recreation. *ATRA's Research Journal*. Alexandria, VA: American Therapeutic Recreation Association.

American Therapeutic Recreation Association. (2000). *Standards for the practice of therapeutic recreation and self-assessment guide*. Alexandria, VA: American Therapeutic Recreation Association.

Austin, D. R., & Crawford, M. E. (2000). *Therapeutic recreation: An introduction* (3rd ed.). Needham Heights, MA: Allyn & Bacon.

Buettner, L., & Fitzsimmons, S. (2003). *Dementia practice guideline for recreational therapy: Treatment of disturbing behaviors.* Alexandria, VA: American Therapeutic Recreation Association.

Carter, M. J., Van Andel, G. E., & Robb, G. M. (2003). *Therapeutic recreation: A practical approach* (3rd. ed.). Prospect Heights, IL: Waveland Press.

Coyle, C. P., Kinney, W. B., Riley, B., & Shank, J. W. (1998). *Benefits of therapeutic recreation: A consensus view.* Ravensdale, WA: Idyll Arbor.

Kraus, R., & Shank, J. (1992). *Therapeutic recreation service: Principles and practices* (4th ed.). Dubuque, IA: Wm. C. Brown, Publishers.

James, A. (1998). The conceptual development of recreational therapy. In F. M. Brasile, T. K. Skalko, & j. burlingame (Eds.), *Perspectives in recreational therapy: Issues of a dynamic profession.* Ravensdale, WA: Idyll Arbor.

Malkin, M. J., Coyle, C. P., & Carruthers, C. (1998). Efficacy research in recreational therapy. In F. M. Brasile, T. K. Skalko, & j. burlingame (Eds.), *Perspectives in recreational therapy: Issues of a dynamic profession.* Ravensdale, WA: Idyll Arbor.

National Recreation and Park Association. (2004). *Standards and evaluative criteria for recreation, park resources, and leisure service programs.* Alexandria, VA: Council on Accreditation.

National Therapeutic Recreation Society. (2002). *Standards of practice for a continuum of care in therapeutic recreation.* Ashburn, VA: National Recreation and Park Association.

World Health Organization. (2002). *International classification of functioning, disability, and health.* Geneva, Switzerland: author.

CHAPTER 14

Therapeutic Recreation Practice Models

Jo-Ellen Ross, Ph.D., CTRS™

Candace Ashton-Shaeffer, Ph.D., LRT/CTRS™
University of North Carolina Wilmington

Recreation therapists frequently are confronted with the need to explain therapeutic recreation services and practice to peers from other professions, clients and their significant others, administrators, managers, and payers. The following questions frequently need to be answered: What is therapeutic recreation? What are the anticipated outcomes of therapeutic recreation services? What strategies or interventions are utilized to bring about these outcomes? What is the profession's scope of practice? What are the key components of practice? What is unique about therapeutic recreation? How does therapeutic recreation fit into healthcare and human service delivery systems?

In today's fast-paced society, it is critical to the survival of a profession that it can effectively and efficiently explain its practice. Therapeutic recreation practice models, by providing a schematic representation of therapeutic recreation services, serve as a tool to facilitate communication and assist with accountability and program development. It is these very models that should define how the practice of therapeutic recreation is implemented. Choosing a practice model means choosing a philosophical orientation as well as a theory (or theories) and the delivery methods of practice. This has a large impact on therapeutic recreation practice in each facility as well as on the profession as a whole.

Therapeutic recreation practice models should be built on philosophy and theory and provide the framework for the delivery of therapeutic recreation services. Beyond communicating to others, therapeutic recreation practice models also should guide recreation therapists in designing, implementing, and evaluating their programs and services. Additionally, practice models should provide a foundation for research, public policy, and further development of the profession.

It is important to recognize that there are two types of practice models used in therapeutic recreation: content models and process models. Content models identify the "what" or substance of therapeutic recreation services. In contrast, process models identify the "how" or means; that is, the procedures and tasks for designing therapeutic recreation services.

Although it would be potentially simpler if a single practice model represented therapeutic recreation, this is not the case. Therapeutic recreation takes place in a wide variety of settings; serves a variety of clientele, including individuals of different ages, backgrounds, diagnoses, and functioning abilities; and utilizes a variety of assessments and interventions. It is not homogeneous. Therapeutic recreation historically and currently is not represented by a single professional organization, a single philosophy, a single definition, a single set of practice standards, or a single code of ethics. This plurality extends also to practice models. Given the reality of multiple therapeutic recreation practice models, the challenge for each recreation therapist is to evaluate the different models and select the most appropriate model on which to base services and program. As Voelkl, Carruthers, and Hawkins (1997) stated, "The choice of a practice model is a very important decision. It will guide the outcomes toward which the professional will strive and everything that is done in practice to achieve those outcomes" (p. 210-211).

This chapter will review the development of therapeutic recreation practice models, examine the most common practice models currently existing in therapeutic recreation, and explore challenges for the future of therapeutic recreation practice models. The following therapeutic recreation practice models will be examined in depth: (a) Health Protection/ Health Promotion Model (Austin, 1991, 1996, 1998, 1999, 2004, 2009), (b) Leisure Ability Model (Peterson & Stumbo, 2000; Stumbo & Peterson, 1998, 2004, 2009), (c) Leisure and Well-Being Model (LWM) (Carruthers & Hood, 2007; Hood & Carruthers, 2007), (d) Leisure-Spiritual Coping Model (Heintzman, 2008), (e) Optimizing Lifelong Health through Therapeutic Recreation (OLH-TR) (Wilhite, Keller, & Caldwell, 1999), (f) Self-Determination and Enjoyment Enhancement: A Psychologically Based Service Delivery Model for Therapeutic Recreation (Dattilo, Kleiber, & Williams, 1998), (g) Therapeutic Recreation Accountability Model (TRAM) (Stumbo, 1996; Stumbo & Peterson, 2004, 2009), and (h) Therapeutic Recreation Service Delivery Model (TR Service Delivery Model) and Therapeutic Recreation Outcome Model (TR Outcome Model) (Carter, Van Andel, & Robb, 1995, 2003; Van Andel, 1998). The review of each model, however, is abbreviated, and readers are encouraged to go to the primary sources for full explanation and discussion.

Toward An Understanding Of Therapeutic Recreation Practice Models

Recreation and Leisure

Practice models are developed from beliefs and theories and represent a particular way to look at a profession's definition(s), philosophy(ies), and practice(s). Therapeutic recreation has a long, rich history of debating definitions, terminology, focus, and philosophy. Central to all models of therapeutic recreation, however, are the concepts of leisure and recreation.

Leisure is defined as an experience characterized primarily by perceived freedom and secondarily by intrinsic motivation (Kelly, 1996; Mannell & Kleiber, 1997; Neulinger,

---

[1]Abbreviations are used for some models and not for others based on the preference (i.e., previous writings) of the model's author(s).

1981). A variety of personal meanings are found through leisure including enjoyment, self-development, self-expression, relaxation, and social interaction (Dattilo & Kleiber, 1993; Kelly, 1996; Kelly & Godbey, 1992; Mannell & Kleiber, 1997). Leisure, therefore, takes on different forms and meanings for different people, and even different forms and meanings for the same person at different times. Although recreation is often equated with leisure (e.g., Driver, Brown, & Peterson, 1991; Kelly, 1996; Kelly & Godbey, 1992), it tends to be more focused on activity that is organized, restorative, and beneficial to society (Kelly, 1996; Kelly & Godbey,1992).

How therapeutic recreation practice models utilize the concept(s) of leisure and/or recreation varies. Some models consider leisure and/or recreation as a means; that is, a tool to produce some other outcome, such as improved health and well-being or decreased depression. Other models view leisure and/or recreation as an end; that is, the outcome or product that therapeutic recreation services aim to produce. Still other models regard leisure and/or recreation as both a means and an end; that is, both a tool and a product of therapeutic recreation services. Additionally, each model may use the terms leisure and recreation differently.

To understand the models, it is critical that one comprehend the difference between an end and a means. According to Mobily (1985a):

> An end is anything that is valuable in its own right and done for its own sake. It is not immediately aimed toward anything else, although it may be related to other ends and at times may even become a means to another end. Nonetheless, as a discrete concept, an end is good for its own sake.

> Conversely, a means is anything that contributes to the attainment of an end. It receives its value in proportion to its utility for yielding an end. A means, therefore, is subordinate to an end and has no value unless directed toward one. (p. 9)

Historically, the central debate within the therapeutic recreation profession has been the issue of leisure as a means vs. leisure as an end (Halberg & Howe-Murphy, 1985; Lee, 1987; Mobily, 1985a, 1985b; Mobily, Hunnicutt, & Weissinger, 1987; Peterson, 1989; Sylvester, 1985, 1987, 1996a, 1996b; Sylvester et al., 1987). Peterson (1989) summarized the dilemma as follows:

> The leisure [end] orientation implies that the ultimate outcome or guiding set of beliefs is related to leisure behavior, and the orientation draws on the existing body of knowledge related to leisure as its source and foundation. The therapy [means] orientation, on the other hand, indicates change or improvement of functional behaviors as the desired end, and draws from a medical, psychiatric, psychological, and human development body of knowledge. (p. 28)

Since the 1990s, the move in therapeutic recreation practice has been toward a combination of nonfunctional (e.g., health and well-being) and functional outcomes with leisure and recreation as the means. The practice models, however, have tended toward nonfunctional outcomes; that is, health and well-being. The non-functional outcomes tend to draw heavily from theories of leisure and social psychology.

Healthcare and Human Services

Therapeutic recreation practice models must complement and be able to co-exist within the context of the larger health and human service delivery systems in which therapeutic recreation services are delivered. Currently, therapeutic recreation services are delivered primarily within the healthcare arena (Bureau of Labor Statistics, U.S. Department of Labor, 2007; Riley & Connolly, 2007). The predominant service delivery paradigm of healthcare is the medical model, although that is gradually changing as a result of managed care and deinstitutionalization (Pew Health Professions Commission, 1995), and recent paradigm shifts by the World Health Organization (WHO), 2002). At the same time, it must be remembered that therapeutic recreation services take place in a wide variety of settings and environments and serve a broad range of clients (Riley & Connolly). Therapeutic recreation, therefore, also is delivered under nonmedical models such as the Psychosocial Model of Disability, the rehabilitation model, and wellness models such as the Six Dimensional Wellness Model (National Wellness Institute, n.d.).

Therapeutic recreation practice models also need to be congruent with public policy, such as those set forth by the World Health Organization, the United States Department of Health and Human Services (2000) in Healthy People 2010, the Centers for Medicare and Medicaid Services (CMS), and Center for Disease Control and Prevention's Health Protection Goals, the United States Department of Justice, and the United States Department of Education; and in such laws as the Americans With Disabilities Act (ADA) and the Individuals with Disabilities Education Improvement Act, 2004 (IDEIA). Additionally, therapeutic recreation practice models need to reflect the professional organizations that represent therapeutic recreation (e.g., American Therapeutic Recreation Association, National Therapeutic Recreation Society). Therapeutic recreation practice models also need to co-exist with the standards of accrediting bodies (e.g., CARF, The Joint Commission) and state regulations for facilities in which therapeutic recreation is delivered. Finally, practice models need to take into consideration societal trends, such as increased longevity for persons with illnesses and disabilities, inclusion, diversity, and advances in technology.

Limitation of Models

Before proceeding, it is important to acknowledge the limitations of practice models. All schematic models are two-dimensional and static in nature, whereas practice is multifaceted and dynamic (Peterson & Stumbo, 2000; Stumbo & Peterson, 2004). Models can neither encompass the full breadth of practice nor demonstrate the interactions and overlapping of components that often take place in the real world. Models are only diagrams with key words and symbols that provide a visual overview of practice. It is important to keep this in perspective when reviewing each model and deciding on which therapeutic recreation practice model to use.

---

[2]Healthy People 2020 currently is in draft form and was out for public comment between November 2006 and January 2007.

Development Of Therapeutic Recreation Practice Models

The first practice models for therapeutic recreation, developed in the late 1960s and early 1970s, were continuums and leisure-oriented (Ball, 1970; Frye & Peters, 1972). These models laid the foundation for future practice models. In 1978, Gunn and Peterson introduced the Therapeutic Recreation Service Model, which was later renamed the Leisure Ability Model (Peterson & Gunn, 1984). This model has been slightly revised twice since 1978 and continues to be widely used in practice 30 years later (cf., Gunn & Peterson, 1978; Peterson & Gunn, 1984; Stumbo & Peterson, 1998, 2004, 2009). It has influenced the development of most of the succeeding models.

In the late 1970s and early 1980s, there was a push to unify therapeutic recreation in both philosophy and practice. During that time, three philosophical views were identified that can be summed up as (a) therapeutic recreation as recreation, (b) therapeutic recreation as treatment (therapy), and (c) therapeutic recreation as both recreation and treatment (Meyer, 1981). Eventually, four philosophical statements were put forth, which included the three above plus a fourth that identified therapeutic recreation as treatment, education, and recreation (Reynolds & O'Morrow, 1985). In 1982, the Leisure Ability Philosophy, which represented the latter philosophical statement and is exemplified by the Leisure Ability Model, was adopted by NTRS (Reynolds & O'Morrow).

In the mid-to-late 1980s, recreation therapists began to question the congruency between the purpose of therapeutic recreation services as "the development, maintenance, and expression of an appropriate leisure lifestyle" (Peterson & Gunn, 1984, p. 4) and healthcare trends (Shank & Kinney, 1987). The overriding issue continued to be "whether therapeutic recreation is or should be therapy-oriented [means] or leisure-oriented [outcome]" (Peterson, 1989, p. 27).

In the 1990s, as the profession continued to evolve, new models for the practice of therapeutic recreation began to emerge in part due to the changing nature and challenges of healthcare and third-party payers. The Health Protection/Health Promotion Model, presented by Austin in 1991, was the first challenge to the Leisure Ability Model.

As the 1990s drew to an end, there appeared to be an acceptance of the diversity of therapeutic recreation. Numerous models were being developed and discussed, seemingly without the need to accept one model to represent the entire profession. The majority of models tended toward health and wellness as the ultimate outcome. All proposed models, however, incorporated aspects of leisure and leisure theory to some degree. Additionally, all models seemed to embrace the basic therapeutic recreation process: assessment, planning, implementation, and evaluation (APIE). This was evident in the writings of the models' authors (cf., Austin, 1998; burlingame, 1998; Dattilo, Kleiber, & Williams, 1998; Russoniello, 1994; Stumbo, 1996; Stumbo & Peterson, 1998; Van Andel, 1998; Widmer & Ellis, 1998; Wilhite, Keller, & Caldwell, 1999).

Since the start of the 21st century, there appears to be a decreased focus on therapeutic recreation models. A review of the major therapeutic recreation journals revealed only two new models being published (Carruthers & Hood, 2007; Heintzman, 2008; Hood & Carruthers, 2007), limited discussion about the models (c.f., Dieser, 2002, 2003; Dieser & Peregoy, 1999), and only a scant amount of research or practice discussion related to models (c.f., Boothman & Savell, 2004; Crawford, Livingston, & Swango, 2004; Stumbo & Hess, 2001; Wilhite, Keller, Hodges, & Caldwell, 2004).

Evaluating Practice Models

Before a practice model can be deemed valid and utilized effectively, it must be evaluated. How does one evaluate the different therapeutic recreation models? Guba and Lincoln (1981) indicated that evaluation "involves both describing and judging or valuing" (p. 39). They identified two forms of valuing—intrinsic or merit, and extrinsic or worth. Merit is inherent in an object, whereas worth is determined against external requirements. Further, merit is relatively stable while worth changes as the context changes.

Merit—Intrinsic Value

A model's merit is based on the model's conceptualization and development and only changes with revisions in the model itself. Models strong in merit may or may not have much worth. In the next major section, nine therapeutic recreation practice models will be examined and evaluated for merit based on the following variables: (a) theoretical underpinnings, (b) graphic depiction, (c) clarity of terms and concepts, and (d) direction for practice and research.

Worth—Extrinsic Value

To evaluate the worth of a model, the model needs to be examined in terms of relevance to the context in which the model must operate; that is, evaluation of how the model relates to healthcare and human services, including public policy, and society on a broad basis as well as in terms of the specific setting in which therapeutic recreation services are being implemented. For the purpose of this chapter, the worth of each model will be evaluated against the general backdrop of healthcare and human services and societal influences. As each recreation therapist must choose the best model for his or her specific setting and practice, the ultimate worth of any model is left to the discretion of the user. The worth of each model will be discussed within the discussion of each model in the next major section under the subheading "relevance."

Healthcare and Human Service Context

The predominant force impacting much of therapeutic recreation today is the changing face of healthcare. According to the Pew Health Professions Commission (1995), there has been a gradual shift away from the medical model and its focus on illness, cures, and the separation of mind and body. The evolving paradigm is one that is moving toward holistic health that combines mind and body and focuses on wellness and prevention of illness rather than remediation. The definition of health no longer is equated with absence of illness, disease, or sickness. In fact, today someone with a chronic physical illness or disability may be considered healthy. Optimal wellness has become more of a goal than absence of disease or illness.

The World Health Organization (WHO) since 1948 has employed the following definition of health: "Health is a state of complete physical, mental, and social well-being and not merely the absence of disease or infirmity" (WHO, 1984). Most recently, WHO adopted the International Classification of Functioning, Disability, and Health (ICF) to complement the International Classification of Disease – 10th edition (ICD – 10) (WHO,

2002, p. 3). "In short, the ICD-10 is mainly used to classify causes of death, but ICF classifies health" (WHO, p. 3). ICF is based on a biopsychosocial model of disability that builds on the medical and social models of disabilities. One key component of the model is its ecological perspective. Within ICF "disability and functioning are viewed as outcomes of interactions between *health conditions* (diseases, disorders and injuries) and *contextual factors* [e.g., environmental factors, internal personal factors]" (p. 10). Furthermore, ICF "acknowledges that every human being can experience a decrement in health and thereby experience some disability. This is not something that happens to only a minority of humanity. ICF thus 'mainstreams' the experience of disability and recognizes it as a universal human experience" (p. 3). Consequently, disability becomes just one dimension of a person. And, as noted by Porter and burlingame (2006), the ICF:

> represents a major shift in healthcare. It looks at health, not from the perspective of disease, disorder, or injury, but from the perspective of how a person's health fits in with the rest of his or her life, the kinds of things the person does, and the environment the person lives in. (p. 1)

Coupled with this shift, attention has been given to cost containment via managed care. There has been a significant reduction in hospital stays as hospitals focus on rapid stabilization and patient discharge and an increase of healthcare services within the home and community settings. The focus of treatment has shifted from process to outcome and cost effectiveness. In this context, therapeutic recreation practice models that embrace health and wellness as ultimate outcomes yet include functional outcomes would appear to have much worth.

The United States government via Healthy People 2010 (U.S. Department of Health and Human Services, 2000) identified the following two goals for the nation's health agenda: (a) "increase quality and years of healthy life" (p. 2) and (b) "eliminate health disparities" (p. 2). These goals are more inclusive than the evolving holistic model of healthcare discussed above. Specifically, expanding on the first goal, Healthy People 2010 states:

> Quality of life reflects a general sense of happiness and satisfaction with our lives and environment. General quality of life encompasses all aspects of life, including health, recreation, culture, rights, values, beliefs, and aspirations, and the conditions that support a life containing these elements. (p. 10)

Additionally, the Centers for Disease Control and Prevention (CDC) has identified four overarching Health Protection Goals: (1) Healthy people in every stage of life, (2) Healthy people in healthy places, (3) People prepared for emerging health threats, and (4) Healthy people in a healthy world (CDC, n.d.). Each goal has starter objectives, and within these starter objectives are references to leisure. For example, Overarching Goal #2 – Starter Objective 13 states, "Increase the numbers of children who live, learn, and play in social and physical environments that are accessible, that support health, safety, and development, and that promote healthy behaviors" (CDC, 2006, p. 8) and Starter Objective 33 states, "Increase the numbers of older adults and the elderly who live, work, and play in social and physical environments that are accessible, that support their health, safety, and quality of life, and that promote healthy behaviors" (CDC, 2006, p. 11). As one reads through the different objectives, it becomes apparent that therapeutic recreation services can influence the outcome of these objectives. As such, it can be concluded that leisure and health are both important outcomes for therapeutic recreation services, and therefore, models that address both would have much worth.

Finally, the Pew Health Professions Commission (1995) has advocated for a decrease in specialization and an increase in collaboration among professionals as well as encouraged transdiciplinary models of service. In this context, the therapeutic recreation models that broadly define the scope of therapeutic recreation practice and its uniqueness may likely have the most worth.

Societal Context

Society also has undergone numerous changes in the last three decades, partly due to technology. People are now living longer, and many health conditions previously considered terminal are now considered chronic conditions. Individuals previously considered "helpless" or "handicapped" due to disabilities are now active, contributing members of society. Technology has facilitated the adaptation of the environment to the person rather than the person always needing to adapt to the environment. Additionally, technology has enabled persons with disabilities to engage in a wider variety of activities. Disability literature and related public policy and social network literature support the concept of interdependence over independence (Condeluci, 1995; Developmental Disabilities Assistance and Bill of Rights Act Amendments of 1996). Quality of life and wellness are being recognized as important (CDC, 2006; Developmental Disabilities Assistance and Bill of Rights Act Amendments of 1996; U.S. Department of Health and Human Services, 2000). In this context, models that utilize leisure as an intermediate or end outcome, as well as models that have health and wellness outcomes would appear to have much worth.

Finally, the United States has become an increasingly multicultural society (Roberts, 1993; U.S. Census Bureau, 2007). Public policy (e.g., Americans with Disabilities Act of 1990; Civil Rights Act of 1991; Developmental Disabilities Assistance and Bill of Rights Act Amendments of 1996; Individuals with Disabilities Education Improvement Act of 2004) promotes inclusion of persons with disabilities and other minority groups of individuals within society. Additionally, the United States is fast becoming a society where the majority of the population consists of minority cultures (Roberts). Subsequently, models that are multiculturally sensitive or have cross-culture application would appear to have much worth.

The worth of a model can vacillate and will vary in different contexts and times. With the evolving nature of health and human services and society, as well as the increasing variety of settings for the delivery of therapeutic recreation services, it is essential not to make a hasty decision on a model's worth. It is important to note that the Leisure Ability Model (Gunn & Peterson, 1978; Peterson & Gunn, 1984; Peterson & Stumbo, 2000; Stumbo & Peterson, 1998, 2004, 2009), the Health Protection/Health Promotion Model (Austin, 1991, 1996, 1998, 1999, 2004, 2009), and the Therapeutic Recreation Service Delivery Model (TR Service Delivery Model) and the Therapeutic Recreation Outcome Model (TR Outcome Model) (Carter, Van Andel, & Robb, 1995, 2003; Van Andel, 1998) have been in existence for a number of years and have enjoyed use in practice. The Self-Determination and Enjoyment Enhancement: A Psychologically Based Service Delivery Model for Therapeutic Recreation (Dattilo, Kleiber, & Williams, 1998), the Optimizing Lifelong Health through Therapeutic Recreation (OLH-TR) (Wilhite, Keller, & Caldwell, 1999), and the Therapeutic Recreation Accountability Model (TRAM) (Stumbo, 1996; Stumbo & Peterson, 2004) emerged in the late 1990s. The Leisure and Well-Being Model (LWM) (Carruthers & Hood, 2007; Hood & Carruthers, 2007) and the Leisure-Spiritual Coping Model (Heintzman, 2008) are the newest models in print.

Therapeutic Recreation Practice Models

In the following section, each therapeutic recreation practice model identified above will be briefly reviewed and critiqued according to its merit and worth. Seven of the practice models are content models. These models are presented based on their purported outcome(s); that is leisure, health, and well-being, or functional improvement. Two of the models are primarily process models and are presented with the content models that each was developed to support. As previously stated, the review of each model is abridged and readers are encouraged to go to the original sources for full explanation and discussion. It should be noted that the Therapeutic Recreation Accountability Model (TRAM), the Leisure and Well-Being Model, and the Leisure-Spiritual Coping Model have not been publically critiqued prior to this publication.

Leisure Outcome Models

Only one pure leisure outcome model currently exists, the Leisure Ability Model. The Therapeutic Recreation Accountability Model, a process model, however, will also be discussed in this section, as it was developed by Stumbo in 1996 to complement the Leisure Ability Model (personal communications, July 2008).

Leisure Ability Model

The first model examined is the Leisure Ability Model, originally introduced as the Therapeutic Recreation Service Model (Gunn & Peterson, 1978). This model has been in use the longest of all the therapeutic recreation practice models. According to Stumbo and Peterson (2009), "the overall anticipated outcome of therapeutic recreation service delivery [as defined by the Leisure Ability Model] is a satisfying leisure lifestyle—the independent functioning of the client in leisure experiences and activities of his or her choice" (p. 33). "When the individual can independently and successfully engage in leisure of his or her own choice, the individual has the chance to receive the psychological, physical, and social benefits, as well as the more global benefits of improved health, wellness, and quality of life" (p. 29). Consequently, "the ultimate outcome of therapeutic recreation services is the improved ability of the individual to engage in a successful, appropriate, and meaningful independent leisure lifestyle that, in turn, leads to improved health, quality of life, and well-being" (p.29). Thus, the development of a satisfying and appropriate leisure lifestyle is the focal point of the model.

The Leisure Ability Model is based on three assumptions (Stumbo & Peterson, 2009): first, that "every human being needs, wants, and deserves leisure" (p. 28); second, "that many, if not most individuals, experience barriers to full and satisfying leisure" (p. 29); and third, "that many individuals with disabilities and/or illnesses may experience more frequent, severe, or lasting barriers" (p. 29) to leisure compared with their cohorts without disabilities simply due to the presence of the disability or illness, "their reactions and/or perceptions about their disability and/or illness, or the environment in which they live and work" (p. 29). Therefore, they may need the assistance of "a therapeutic recreation specialist to eliminate, reduce, overcome, or compensate for their leisure barriers" (p. 29).

The Leisure Ability Model conceptualizes therapeutic recreation practice as a continuum that consists of three major components: functional intervention, leisure education, and recreation participation (Peterson & Stumbo, 2000; Stumbo & Peterson, 2004, 2009). See Figure 14.1 for a graphic depiction of the Leisure Ability Model. Functional intervention (formerly called treatment and therapy) addresses physical, cognitive, affective, and social functioning that interferes with but is necessary for leisure involvement.

Leisure education focuses on the acquisition of knowledge and skills to make informed choices for leisure participation (Peterson & Stumbo, 2000; Stumbo & Peterson, 2004, 2009). The four subcomponents of leisure education are: (a) leisure awareness, (b) social interaction skills, (c) leisure activity skills, and (d) leisure resources. Leisure awareness is further divided into knowledge of leisure, self-awareness in relation to leisure, leisure and play attitudes, and related participatory and decision-making skills. Social interaction skills in the newest version of the model consist of communication, relationship-building, and self-presentation skills. Leisure activity skills include traditional and nontraditional leisure skills. Leisure resources consist of activity opportunities, personal resources, family and home resources, community resources, and state and national resources.

Recreation participation is the third component of the model. The purpose of a recreation participation program "is to provide opportunities for fun, enjoyment, and self-expression within an organized delivery system" (Peterson & Stumbo, 2009, p. 62). According to Stumbo and Peterson, recreation participation services can serve at least six roles, depending on the needs of clients and settings: "(a) practice and application of skills, (b) inclusion into community services, (c) normalization of institutional routines, (d) focus on 'well' aspects, (e) expression of a leisure lifestyle, and (f) diversion or palliative care" (p. 66). Recreation participation programs are provided with the "assumption that the participant has the activity skills and participatory ability necessary for satisfying or enjoyable involvement" (p. 64). Recreation participation focuses on the broader outcomes of decision-making and personal responsibility for leisure.

Theoretically, as the client moves along the continuum from functional intervention to recreation participation and begins to master the skills relevant for participation in satisfying and enjoyable leisure experiences, his or her freedom increases and the therapeutic recreation specialist's control decreases. It is important to note, however, that the client can enter the continuum at any point, and movement within the model does not have to be linear (Peterson & Stumbo, 2000; Stumbo & Peterson, 2000, 2004, 2009). Functional intervention programs are prescriptive by design and controlled by the therapeutic recreation specialist, thus giving the client little opportunity for freedom of choice. This is in contrast to recreation participation programs that are facilitated by the therapeutic recreation specialist but participated in voluntarily and independently by the client (Stumbo & Peterson).

Merit and Worth of the Leisure Ability Model

The Leisure Ability Model, with its recent revisions (Peterson & Stumbo, 2000; Stumbo & Peterson, 1998, 2004, 2009), demonstrates a high degree of merit. Mobily (1999) concurs and stated that the model's "focus on leisure results in a considerable degree of succinctness and, more importantly, lends an 'internal consistency' to the relationship among service components that is unmatched by the other models" (p. 180). Its worth varies by setting.

Theory. Although a version of the Leisure Ability Model has existed in the literature since 1978 (Gunn & Peterson), its theoretical basis was first identified in 1998 (Stumbo & Peterson). The model is tied strongly to leisure behavior theory and research. Peterson and Stumbo (Peterson & Stumbo, 2000; Stumbo & Peterson, 1998, 2004, 2009) identified the relevant research basis and theoretical underpinnings of the model as being learned helplessness, mastery or self-determination, intrinsic motivation, internal locus of control and causal attribution, and flow.

Bullock (1998) and Yaffe (1998), however, felt that the theoretical basis, although improved, remains insufficient. Bullock advocated for the inclusion of theoretical constructs from the disability literature, most notably interdependence, and a decreased focus on learned helplessness. He also questioned the inclusion of flow as described by Csikszentmihalyi, feeling that it is rarely obtainable and not a necessity for leisure. It should be noted, however, that flow is frequently cited as a component of leisure in the leisure behavior literature. Finally, Yaffe suggested that Aristotle's ethics and Maslow's Hierarchy of Needs be incorporated into the model's theoretical basis.

Graphic depiction. The Leisure Ability Model's graphic depiction (see Figure 14.1) is clear, concise, and comprehensive. The model in general, as well as its graphic representation, serves to communicate to recreation therapists and other professionals, managers, and consumers the purpose, goals, means, uniqueness, and scope of practice of therapeutic recreation services.

Clarity of terms and concepts. With the newest version of the Leisure Ability Model (Peterson & Stumbo, 2000; Stumbo & Peterson, 2004, 2009), the difficulty with the terms treatment and social skills have been resolved. Now the three major components and all of the subcomponents are concise, distinct, and parallel.

Direction for practice and research. A strength of the Leisure Ability Model for practice and research is that it uses the systems approach for the development of specific programs within the different service components (Peterson & Gunn, 1984; Peterson & Stumbo, 2000; Stumbo & Peterson, 2004, 2009). According to Peterson and Stumbo (2000), the benefits of using a systems approach is that "each program focuses on just one of the major categories of service or an aspect of [client] need within a major category" (p. 27), thus enabling "programs to be designed, implemented, and evaluated with a high degree of accountability" (p. 28). In addition, "system design assumes that there is a well-defined, goal-oriented *purpose* to the activity or program being provided" (Stumbo & Peterson, 2009, p. 85). Functional intervention and leisure education strategies are designed with a singular emphasis to facilitate predetermined, observable, and measurable client outcomes. These are imperative to determining quality of care and efficacy of service. Additionally, the model provides enough information to implement therapeutic recreation services in accordance with the assessment, planning, implementation, and evaluation (APIE) process of therapeutic recreation.

Figure 14.1
Leisure Ability Model (Stumbo & Peterson, 2009, p. 34)

Less control by the specialist

Leisure Lifestyle

ROLE OF SPECIALIST

DEGREE OF CONTROL

Opportunity for participation provided by specialist for client — Leader Facilitator Supervisor

Responsibility shared between specialist and client — Instructor Advisor Counselor

Intervention mostly controlled by specialist — Therapist

NATURE OF INTERVENTION (Role of specialists)

Recreation Participation

Leisure Education

Functional Intervention

(Need of the client)
PURPOSE OF INTERVENTION

More control by the specialist

Improve functional ability	Acquire leisure knowledge and skills	Engage in organized participation opportunities
Necessary antecedent to leisure involvement	Acquisition of leisure-related knowledge and skills	Acquired leisure ability participated in voluntarily

DEGREE OF FREEDOM
IN PARTICIPATION

OBLIGATORY
BEHAVIOR
Constrained
Prescriptive
Dependent
Extrinsically
rewarded

LEISURE
BEHAVIOR
Independent
Self-regulated
Intrinsically
rewarded

BEHAVIOR OF THE CLIENT

From: Therapeutic recreation program design: Principles and procedures *(5th ed.) (2009). Stumbo, N. J., &*
Peterson, C. A. © Reprinted by permission of Pearson Education Inc.

Relevance

The Leisure Ability Model is relevant to the many contexts and settings within which therapeutic recreation is practiced and to the clients it serves. According to Stumbo and Peterson (1998), "The content of the Leisure Ability Model is not specific to any one population or client group, nor is it confined to any specific service or delivery setting" (p. 93). Programs within the Leisure Ability Model are designed based on "distinct client needs" and "the nature of the setting and its mandate for service" (Stumbo & Peterson, 2009, p. 69). Peterson and Stumbo (Peterson & Stumbo, 2000; Stumbo & Peterson, 2004, 2009) provided numerous examples of how the model can be implemented within a wide variety of settings, including inpatient and community-based. They also showed how the model is used for group-oriented and one-on-one programming. Mobily (1999), however, pointed out that the model's strong leisure orientation is not in concert with the focus of current healthcare "which places a premium on functional outcomes" (p. 181).

The model identifies any person "with physical, mental, social, or emotional conditions that limits leisure functioning" (Stumbo & Peterson, 2009, p. 30) as a potential client of therapeutic recreation and develops services based on identified client needs related to leisure involvement. "Clients are assessed individually and appropriately placed within programs that relate to their unique problems, areas for development, or needs for improvement" (Peterson & Stumbo, 2000, p. 27). A recurring criticism of the model, however, is that it was developed on the leisure behavior of adults without disabilities (Peterson & Gunn, 1984; Stumbo & Peterson, 1998) which not only makes extrapolation of the construct of leisure behavior difficult to adults with disabilities, but also to children, individuals from diverse ethnic and cultural backgrounds, and people with different lifestyles with or without disabilities (Mobily, 1999).

Summary

The Leisure Ability Model is leisure oriented. That is, leisure is the end product or outcome toward which services are directed and evaluated. The model has a minimal therapy role for the recreation therapist; more of the emphasis is on the recreation therapist as educator and facilitator. Conceptually, the Leisure Ability Model demonstrates a high degree of merit and worth. There are still concerns regarding its theoretical framework and its relevance to settings where only functional outcomes, rather than leisure, are the foci. Yet, the model does incorporate functional outcomes within the functional intervention and leisure education components. Consequently, functional outcomes could potentially be viewed as the intermediate outcomes for the ultimate outcome of leisure. Like all therapeutic recreation practice models, the Leisure Ability Model still needs to be tested through sound research methods to determine its true merit and worth.

Therapeutic Recreation Accountability Model (TRAM)

The Therapeutic Recreation Accountability Model (TRAM) (Stumbo, 1996; Stumbo & Peterson, 2004, 2009) is a process model rather than a content model. As such, the TRAM does not specify content of therapeutic recreation services but rather provides direction for designing the accountability and documentation tasks in the delivery of therapeutic recreation services (Stumbo & Peterson). Its intent is to aid the recreation therapist to "conceptualize the connections between different tasks in the delivery of services to clients" (p. 95) and understand "the relationship between program input factors (such as activity analysis and assessment) and output factors (such as program outcomes and client outcomes)" (p. 97). TRAM is most frequently presented in conjunction with the Leisure Ability Model, and according to Stumbo (personal communications, July 2008), TRAM was created to complement the Leisure Ability Model. At the same time, however, Stumbo (1996) indicated that TRAM could be utilized with any therapeutic recreation content model.

The TRAM was developed in response to third-party reimbursement and external accreditation agencies' mandate to produce and document client outcomes. It was created to "be used to comprehensively conceptualize and create accountable therapeutic recreation programs that produce reliable and valued client outcomes" (Stumbo & Hess, 2001, p. 45). Its goal is to assist recreation therapists in understanding "the interactive nature of documentation and decision points involved in the delivery, implementation, and evaluation" of programs (Stumbo, p. 251). By identifying the parts and steps of comprehensive program planning in therapeutic recreation, the model attempts to strengthen the design and development of therapeutic recreation services. Stumbo also indicated that the TRAM expands on Carter, Van Andel, and Robb's (1998) TR Service Delivery and Outcome Models.

The TRAM is based on systems theory, which underlines the "interdependent and interactional nature of relationships that exist among all components of a system" (Losardo & Notari-Syverson, 2001) including inputs, processes, and outputs. The intent of the TRAM is to provide the foundation for and guide the design and development of all therapeutic recreation service delivery components (i.e., APIE) as an integrated system for the purpose of producing relevant, important, and attainable client outcomes. It was designed to be used for comprehensive program planning in any setting with any population.

The TRAM is a linear model with 11 interactive components and feedback loops (see Figure 14.2). The first component is Comprehensive and Specific Program Design[3], which involves developing the master implementation and evaluation plan for the therapeutic recreation department, unit, or agency. This is done through analysis of those macro factors that influence service delivery, such as the community, agency mission, types/diagnoses/functioning abilities of clients served, professional service models, and standards of the profession and external accrediting and licensing bodies. One important aspect of comprehensive program design is determining which programs/interventions to provide. Once this phase is completed, the second step[4] in the TRAM, Activity Analysis, Selection, and Modification is implemented (Stumbo & Peterson, 2004, 2009). "Activity analysis is the process used to systematically review specific activities [which will occur in specific programs/interventions] to determine whether they have the potential to help clients achieve

---

[3]In the original version of the TRAM (Stumbo, 1996), this component was named Comprehensive Program Design.

[4]In the original version of the TRAM (Stumbo, 1996), Activity Analysis, Selection, and Modification occurred after Protocol Development and Assessment Planning. Stumbo provides no justification for the change.

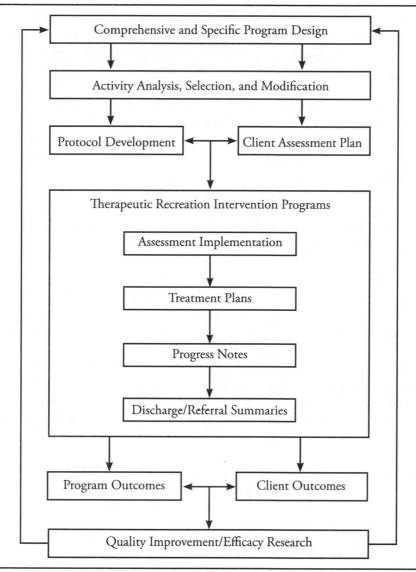

Figure 14.2
Therapeutic Recreation Accountability Model (TRAM)
(Stumbo & Peterson, 2009, p. 96)

*From:*Therapeutic recreation program design: Principles and procedures *(5th ed.) (2009). Stumbo, N. J., & Peterson, C. A.© Reprinted by permission of Pearson Education Inc.*

targeted outcomes" (Stumbo & Peterson, 2009, p. 98) and to assist the recreation therapist in making appropriate modifications to those activities if needed (Stumbo & Peterson, 2009).

The third and fourth components in the TRAM, Protocol Development and Client Assessment Plan, seem to occur simultaneously. According to the TRAM, diagnostic and/ or treatment protocols are then developed for standardization of intervention programs.

Assessment planning involves developing procedures for determining clients' strengths, weaknesses, and limitations so individualized treatment planning can occur and clients can be placed in appropriate programs and intervention that will facilitate predetermined outcomes. "Client assessment, conducted in a systematic and meaningful manner, is a major foundation for providing outcome-based services" (Stumbo & Peterson, 2009, p. 99).

Once protocols have been developed and assessment procedures are in place, the next four components of the TRAM are implemented: Assessment Implementation, Treatment Plans, Progress Notes, and Discharge/Referral Summaries. These four components are actually client documentation tasks, although they are identified under the umbrella of "Therapeutic Recreation Intervention Programs." The purpose of these tasks is to focus on the "expected or planned behavioral change (outcomes) within the client as a result of receiving appropriate and quality services" (Stumbo & Peterson, 2009, p. 100).

The next two steps in the TRAM are evaluation components for determining program and client outcomes—Program Outcomes (Program Evaluation/Program Outcomes) and Client Outcomes (Client Evaluation/Client Outcomes). Program evaluation is the systematic and logical process of determining "the quality, effectiveness, and/or outcomes of a program" and "closely follows the plans for program implementation" (Stumbo & Peterson, 2009, p. 100). In contrast, but closely related to program evaluation, is the evaluation of client outcomes; that is, determining if the clients' goals (changes in functioning or behavior), as identified in their treatment plans, have been accomplished as a result of the intervention. An important aspect of client outcome evaluation is choosing appropriate outcome measures and documenting change.

The final component of the TRAM is Quality Improvement/Efficacy Research—both of which are meant to provide meaningful data to document and improve client services and care. Quality improvement is a method of evaluating therapeutic recreation programs at the comprehensive program level. Efficacy research aims at documenting the effectiveness of services to a particular group or groups of clients. Both quality improvement and efficacy research connect directly back to and influence Comprehensive and Specific Program Design and Therapeutic Recreation Intervention Programs to complete the model.

Merit and Worth of the Therapeutic Recreation Accountability Model

The TRAM demonstrates both merit and worth. It is able to stand alone but is only completely applicable when utilized in conjunction with a therapeutic recreation content model (e.g., Leisure Ability Model, OHL-TR model). The interesting part is that the TRAM must be in operation before the selection of a model. Within the first component of the TRAM, the recreation therapist should review existing therapeutic recreation models and select an appropriate one on which to build the comprehensive program.

Theory. Stumbo and Peterson (Stumbo, 1996; Stumbo & Peterson, 2004, 2009) provide excellent rationale for the development of the model (accountability) but need to do a better job of discussing how systems theory guides both the development and use of the model. Additionally, they do not relate the model to other constructs such as the medical model.

Graphic depiction. The graphic depiction of the model (see Figure 14.2) is reasonable and adheres to systems theory. It would be more meaningful, however, if sub-components were embedded into the Comprehensive and Specific Program Design component as was done in Therapeutic Recreation Intervention Programs component. Also, it would help to use bold for all major components and non-bold for sub-components. Additionally, the following changes should be made to more accurately reflect the activities and appropriate sequences of service delivery and documentation:

- Specific Program Design needs to be a separate component and not subsumed under Comprehensive and Specific Program Design, because therapeutic recreation client services are based on the programs delivered to clients, and without detailed development of those programs, especially intervention programs, client outcomes cannot be documented.
- The TRAM component titled "Therapeutic Recreation Intervention Programs" should be changed to "Intervention Programs and Client Documentation." When writing about this component of the model, Stumbo and Peterson (2009) use the latter terms (see p. 99), which are more representative of the actual tasks and purpose of the component.
- A component titled "Intervention Program Implementation" should be inserted between "Treatment Plan" and "Progress Notes." Progress notes cannot be written unless an intervention has been implemented. This seems to be a glaring omission in the model.

Clarity of terms and concepts. Terms and concepts are inconsistent in the level of clarity. The bulleted items above need to be considered within the clarity of terms and concepts. Also, as mentioned above, the term "Therapeutic Recreation Intervention Programs" as put forth by Stumbo and Peterson (2004, 2009) is at times identified as "Intervention Programs and Client Documentation" as noted above. It would be helpful if terms such as client documentation and program documentation, program outcomes and client outcomes, and diagnostic protocols and treatment protocols were more clearly delineated.

Direction for practice and research. The TRAM model is particularly useful in traditional medical settings where all parts of the model would be applicable. For many community-based settings and long-term care settings, some of the parts do not fit (e.g., protocols). The model assists the recreation therapist in selecting and implementing the chosen content model in a meaningful way and creating a foundation on which to build congruent service components that will support accountability and outcomes research. Further, the model takes the recreation therapist beyond just APIE in terms of designing and developing a systematic program. The model provides the steps to take in creating and ensuring a meaningful therapeutic recreation program so that assessment instruments are not just selected based on ease or liking and interventions are not selected that do not match the program purpose and assessment. Yet, the model does not provide enough direction for the recreation therapist to know how to make the connection between content models and the TRAM, the process model. Additionally, the model neglects mention of the selection of an appropriate content model during the comprehensive program planning phase. Further, it omits any direction for interdisciplinary collaboration that is part of the norm today in most treatment facilities where interdisciplinary care plans are often required and even interdisciplinary assessment forms exist.

In terms of research, the model provides the researcher with a foundation on which to build outcome, evidence-based, and efficacy research. More importantly, the model might strengthen therapeutic recreation programs so as to provide a foundation for much-needed applied research, including outcome and evidence-based research. Hopefully, this then would promote more practitioner-researcher collaboration.

The TRAM is one of the few models in therapeutic recreation upon which a research study has been conducted. Stumbo and Hess (2001) implemented a small and very limited study to determine which factors of the TRAM influenced the ability of therapeutic recreation departments to produce client outcomes. While their methods were weak because they only looked at perceived clients' outcomes, they concluded that although there was inconsistent adherence to, and lack of clarity about, the TRAM's components, more predictable client outcomes were produced when the TRAM was followed. Based on their findings, they offered numerous useful recommendations for education, practice, and research.

Relevance. Stumbo and Peterson (1998, 2004, 2009) build a strong case for the relevance of the model in terms of health and human services in light of current pressures for accountability and outcomes. They, however, do not address many of the realities of health and humans services that recreation therapists face within the work setting. For instance, the population in any given setting is becoming more diverse in multiple ways. Additionally, a few of the parts of the model—protocols for example—are not used in all settings. Also, in many inpatient rehabilitation hospitals, state regulations now call for the provision of recreation for patients as part of the therapeutic recreation program (e.g., New Jersey Department of Health and Senior Services, 2005). It would be useful for recreation therapists, therefore, if the model provided a connection with this piece of therapeutic recreation programming.

Summary

The TRAM is the only therapeutic recreation model that is a stand-alone process model, although typically it has been paired with the Leisure Ability Model. In addition, it is the only pure process model. It remains to be seen how well it will guide other therapeutic recreation content models. In essence, all content model developers have called for a systematic approach to the delivery of services and acknowledged the APIE process. The TRAM has the potential to move therapeutic recreation services to the point where outcome and efficacy and effective research will be easy to conduct. For now, the authors need to clarify some of the model's terms, concepts, and "stages;" incorporate within the model the review of and selection and use of content models to build programs; provide a better discussion of systems theory; and explore how to operationalize it in different settings against the current forces in health and human services (e.g., interdisciplinary collaboration, diversity of clients within single setting, and movement away from medical model).

Health and Wellness Outcomes Models

Four models specifically identify health and/or wellness as the outcome. These models are (a) Health Protection/Health Promotion Model (Austin, 1991, 1996, 1998, 1999, 2004, 2009), (b) Therapeutic Recreation Outcome Model (Carter, Van Andel, & Robb, 1995, 2003; Van Andel, 1998), (c) Optimizing Lifelong Health through Therapeutic Recreation (Wilhite, Keller, & Caldwell, 1999), and (d) Leisure and Well-Being Model (Carruthers & Hood, 2007; Hood & Carruthers, 2007). The Therapeutic Recreation Outcome Model is partnered with a partial process model, the Therapeutic Recreation Service Delivery Model (Carter, Van Andel, & Robb, 1995, 2003; Van Andel, 1998). Consequently, the two models will be discussed together. A fifth model, the Leisure-Spiritual Coping Model (Heintzman, 2008) will also be discussed in this section as spirituality is considered an element of health and wellness (Heintzman). Within all five of these content models, leisure is a means to health and well-being. For four of the models, the Health Protection/Health Promotion Model, Optimizing Lifelong Health through Therapeutic Recreation, the Leisure and Well-Being Model, and the Leisure-Spiritual Coping Model, the experience of leisure is pivotal; that is, leisure is the path to overall health and wellness. Within these models, the primary focus is on the development of the skills, resources, attitudes, knowledge, and/or experiences that enable clients to experience leisure. In the Therapeutic Recreation Outcome Model, leisure is less central but important if one is to reach the full goal of the model.

Health Protection/Health Promotion Model [HP/HP Model]

The first health and wellness outcomes model examined is the Health Protection/Health Promotion Model, which was first introduced by Austin in 1991 and was recently revisited by Austin in 2009. This model is different from the Leisure Ability Model in that health and wellness are the outcomes or goals of therapeutic recreation services, and recreation and leisure are means of reaching the goals of health and wellness.

According to Austin (2009), "the basic goal of therapeutic recreation, under the Health Protection/Health Promotion Model, is for clients to achieve the highest level of health" (p. 161). Specifically, "the purpose of therapeutic recreation is identified as enabling the client to recover following a threat to health (health protection) and to achieve optimal health (health promotion)" (p. 172). According to Austin, therapeutic recreation uses three means to help people overcome barriers to health and enable them to grow toward their highest levels of health and wellness: (a) prescriptive activity, (b) recreation, and (c) leisure. This model is founded on humanistic concepts, high-level wellness, stabilization and actualization tendencies, and health. As such, it ties therapeutic recreation closely with healthcare providers (Austin, 1998, 2004, 2009).

The Health Protection/Health Promotion Model is based on two assumptions. First, the humanistic perspective identifies "that human beings have an innate or inherent drive for health and wellness that can be nurtured by nonjudgmental, caring professionals" (Austin, 1998, p. 112). Second, "people have a stabilizing tendency that comes into effect when there is a threat to health and an actualization tendency that motivates growth-enhancing behaviors leading to health promotion" (p. 112). This implies that the natural tendency of all human beings is to move constantly toward health protection and health promotion.

The Health Protection/Health Promotion Model represents a continuum of health that ranges from poor health/illness to overall well-being/optimal health (Austin, 1999). Prescriptive activities, recreation, and leisure are the components of the model that are used at various points along the continuum to assist clients in overcoming barriers to health and experiencing optimal levels of health and wellness. See Figure 14.3 for a graphic depiction of the Health Protection/Health Promotion Model.

Prescriptive activities are used when clients are in poor health as a means to engage them in activity so that they may begin to "gain control over the situation and to overcome

---

Figure 14.3
Health Protection/Health Promotion Model (Austin, 2009, p.173)

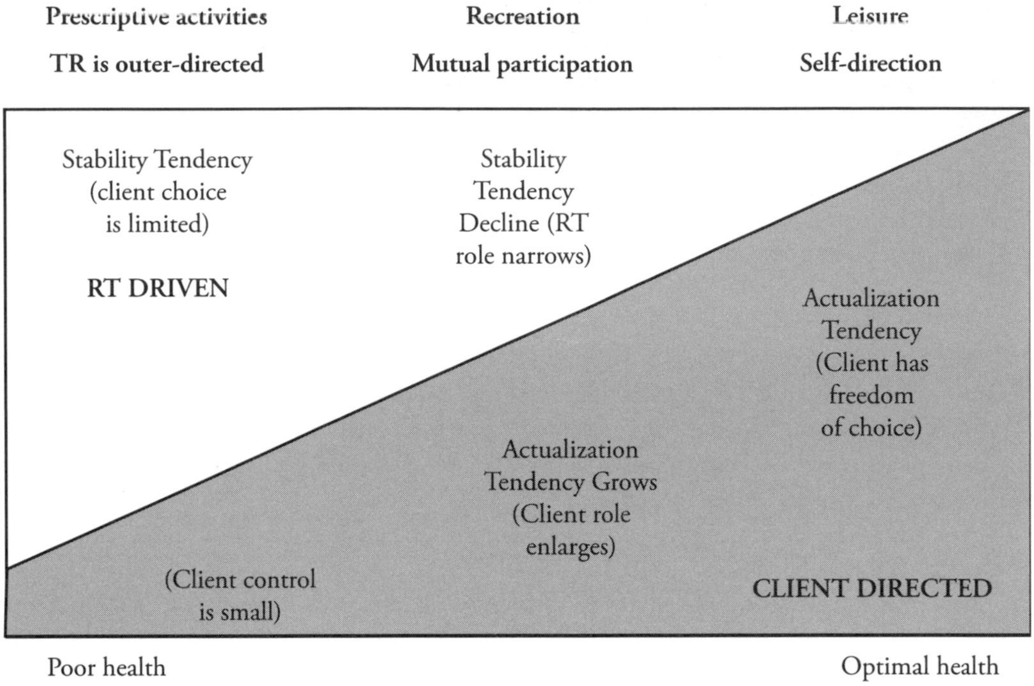

Prescriptive activities	Recreation	Leisure
TR is outer-directed	Mutual participation	Self-direction

Stability Tendency (client choice is limited)

Stability Tendency Decline (RT role narrows)

RT DRIVEN

Actualization Tendency (Client has freedom of choice)

Actualization Tendency Grows (Client role enlarges)

(Client control is small)

CLIENT DIRECTED

Poor health   Optimal health

From: Austin, D. R. (1998). The Health Protection/Health Promotion Model. Therapeutic Recreation Journal, 32, 109-117, figure p. 113. Reprinted with permission.

---

feelings of helplessness and depression" (Austin, 2009, p. 174). Recreation intervention is used for its restorative properties for the "mind, body, and spirit" as clients transition from poor health to optimal health to enable them to "regain their equilibrium so they may once again resume their quest for actualization" (Austin, 2009, p. 175). Leisure, then, provides the avenue for optimal health. Clients can start at any place in the continuum and might even be receiving services at different parts of the continuum concurrently (Austin, 2009).

By using prescriptive activities to "energize" clients in poor health to gain control over their situation and restore their health, the therapeutic recreation specialist provides the necessary structure and support to encourage them to become active. As clients begin to experience feelings of mastery and self-efficacy, they become motivated to pursue therapeutic outcomes and form a partnership with the therapeutic recreation specialist. Together, they choose and participate in recreation activities that are restorative and have the potential to reduce their symptoms and optimize their health. Finally and ideally, clients then progress to optimum levels of health and wellness where they engage in self-directed leisure pursuits (Austin, 1998, 2004, 2009). Such pursuits should lead to feelings of self-efficacy, empowerment, excitement, and enjoyment. As clients move through the health continuum to optimal health, their control and freedom to choose activities increases, and the therapeutic recreation specialist's role and control decreases. Austin (2009) identified the potential clients for therapeutic recreation services as "all individuals who wish to achieve a higher level of health and wellness . . . whether or not they are categorized as 'ill or disabled'" (p. 179).

Merit and Worth of the Health Protection/Health Promotion Model

Relevant to both merit and worth, the HP/HP Model's weaknesses exceeds its strengths. These are articulated by Lee (1998), Mobily (1999), and Ross (1998) as summarized below, as well as by the authors of this chapter.

Theory. Austin (1998, 2004, 2009) believed his model's strength was its strong theoretical foundations of humanism, wellness, actualization, and health. Numerous scholars (e.g., Lee, 1998; Mobily, 1999; Ross, 1998), however, disagreed. Mobily (1999) strongly questioned the model's assumption that "all human beings have an inherent drive for health and wellness" (Austin, 1998, p. 111-112) and explained how this is in conflict with current theories of psychology and human behavior that reject the existence of built-in drives. Lee (1998) asserted that adopting the humanistic perspective of health places too much responsibility on the client for both ill health as well as for changing to achieve optimal health while ignoring society as an influencing force. Finally, Ross (1998) suggested that leisure theory, and theory related to motivation and existentialism needed to be incorporated into the model, especially since leisure is one of the model's major components. In Austin's 2009 text, leisure theory remained undeveloped and at times appeared to contain misconceptions related to recreation versus leisure. Theory related to motivation continued to be scant and in terms of existentialism was nonexistent.

Graphic depiction. The model's graphic depiction (see Figure 14.3) is simplistic but incomplete and not clear-cut. The components and the role of the therapist and the client are appropriately placed on the continuum in relation to each other, leisure theory, and wellness. The model's "picture," however, neither shows movement nor does it clearly articulate the ultimate goal or indicate the transition from health promotion to health protection. Additionally, Mobily (1999) pointed out that the diagonal line relates to two relationships (i.e., therapist-client and stabilization tendency-actualization tendency) that do not share a causal relationship.

In 2009, Austin modified the model slightly but did not address any of the above weaknesses. Austin (2009) also did not acknowledge any changes in the graphic picture of the model in 2009 from 1996. In 2009, Austin changed "TRS directed" to "RT Driven" under Perspective Activities and "TRS" to "RT" under Recreation. This would be indicative of current terminology in the field, which is leaning toward the use of the term Recreation/ Recreational Therapist rather than Therapeutic Recreation Specialist. Austin (2009) also omitted "in unfavorable environment" under Poor Health and "in favorable environment" under Optimal Health. These two changes are evident in the graphic, but the former remains in use in Austin's writings. By omitting the use of environment in the graphic, Austin visually eliminated the idea of an ecological perspective.

Clarity of terms and concepts. This is a major weakness of the model. According to Lee (1998) "the terminology used in the model confounded the concepts among prescriptive activity, recreation, and leisure. . . . There is little difference in meaning between prescriptive activity and recreation" (p. 121). Ross (1998) pointed out that it is "unclear if Austin intended the component names to be simply titles or also tasks, content, or outcomes of the particular component" (p. 126). Although Austin (2004, 2009) later attempted to provide more clarity among the model's three components, there remains ambiguity. For example, Austin's definition and description of recreation are more aligned with the traditional definition of leisure as he defines the "true recreational experience" as "to have clients enjoy their recreational pursuit so much they are not simply engaging in them in order to gain some goal or outcome but, instead, because the activities have become *ends in themselves* [italics added]" (Austin, 2009, p. 176). Additionally, Austin (2009) relates the concept of flow to recreation when typically flow is equated with leisure rather than recreation. This leads to confusion between the Recreation component of the model and the Leisure component.

Direction for practice and research. On face value, the model appears to define the scope of practice for therapeutic recreation. On further examination, however, problems become evident. Mobily (1999) pointed out that by defining the client as "anyone who wishes to improve his or her level of health" (Austin, 1998, p. 115), the boundaries between therapeutic recreation and other services that promote health (e.g., physical education, health education) become unclear. Additionally, Lee (1998) and Ross (1998) both concluded that the terms and components lack clarity to direct practice and research. For example, Austin does not operationalize the term "prescriptive activities." Mobily felt there was a need for a clearer description of the recreation services, and Lee pointed out that there is little difference in Austin's definitions of prescriptive activities and recreation.

Lee (1998) also was concerned about the model's concept of holistic health and felt that it needed to be operationalized more for practical application to therapeutic recreation practice and research. He stated, "In short, the holistic concept of health is difficult, if not impossible, to be observed, measured, and tested" (p. 120). Ross (1998) concurred, stating the model lacks operational definitions of health protection and health promotion and does not specify techniques or content. While Austin (2009) made attempts to address these concerns, further explanation is warranted.

Relevance. The Health Protection/Health Promotion Model is an "attempt to bring therapeutic recreation closer to the current and future healthcare market" (Lee, 1998, p. 119). Austin concurred in 2009 when he stated that the HP/HP Model "is more in keeping with the purpose of healthcare agencies—to restore, maintain, and promote health" (p. 180). The model, however, does not include functional outcomes, which are a major concern in healthcare today. Austin (1998) admitted that the model "does not apply in agencies that do not have health as their major goal" (p. 116). As pointed out by Lee, this model then leaves out many of the social service agencies that target poverty, juvenile delinquency, education, substance abuse, and incarceration and that "are a significant part of our heritage" (p. 119). Although Austin (1999, 2004, 2009) speaks frequently of the APIE process for therapeutic recreation, he does not provide enough direction to implement this model accordingly. Consequently, this limits its use in efficacy research.

Summary

The Health Protection/Health Promotion Model is health-oriented. That is, its outcome is optimal health, and recreation and leisure are part of the means toward this outcome. The model has a significant therapy role for the recreation therapist. Both the merit and worth of the Health Protection/Health Promotion Model are questionable, as pointed out by numerous authors. The model's strength is its endeavor to align therapeutic recreation with current trends in healthcare. Yet, it seems to be somewhat incomplete and ambiguous, especially with regard to its graphic representation, its clarity of terms, and its direction for practice. Questions are raised regarding the assumptions that underlie its theory, and it fails to identify the functional outcomes of therapeutic recreation services.

Therapeutic Recreation Service Delivery Model (TR Service Delivery Model) and Therapeutic Recreation Outcome Model (TR Outcome Model)

The next models examined are actually a pair of models: the Therapeutic Recreation Service Delivery Model (TR Service Delivery Model) and the Therapeutic Recreation Outcome Model (TR Outcome Model). These models were first introduced by Carter, Van Andel, and Robb in 1995. Although the two models are separate, the TR Outcome Model was designed as an extension of the TR Service Delivery Model (Van Andel, 1998). Taken together, the models purport that "the purpose of therapeutic recreation is the maintenance or improvement of the health status, quality of life, and/or functional capacities of clients through the use of specially designed recreation or experiential activities and processes" (Carter, Van Andel, & Robb, 1995, p. 19). The models' ultimate outcome, however, is quality of life, whereas improvement of health status and functional capacities are viewed as intermediate outcomes (Van Andel, 1998).

The TR Outcome and TR Service Delivery Models are based on the assumption that leisure as a means and an end can coexist (Van Andel, 1998). This is accomplished by combining theory grounded in developmental social psychology and existentialism with Neulinger's work that distinguishes leisure from non-leisure experiences based on one's state of mind. In essence, Van Andel's models provide the option for the therapeutic recreation intervention to be designed as leisure or non-leisure, as well as experienced by the client as leisure or non-leisure. The former depends on the agency's orientation, whereas the latter depends on the client's skills and perception. In either situation, positive outcomes can be achieved. Leisure, however, will only be experienced if the client perceives the intervention as leisure. Van Andel (1998) intended for the models to be flexible and able to be implemented in any therapeutic recreation setting; the recreation therapist and the agency dictate the focus of practice. Van Andel indicated that the potential clients of therapeutic recreation services would be individuals with disabilities or illnesses.

TR Outcome Model

According to the TR Outcome Model, the goal of therapeutic recreation is to assist the client in achieving the highest possible level of health and well-being through leisure and non-leisure experiences (Van Andel, 1998, p. 187). The model consists of three primary components: (a) functional capacities/potential, (b) health status/wellness, and (c) quality of life. See Figure 14.4 for a graphic depiction of the TR Outcome Model. Leisure function

---

Figure 14.4
Therapeutic Recreation Outcome Model (Van Andel, 1998, p. 187)

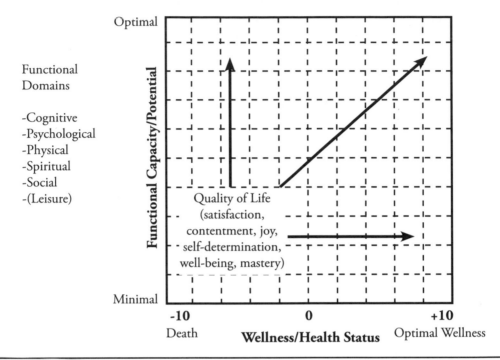

Functional
Domains

-Cognitive
-Psychological
-Physical
-Spiritual
-Social
-(Leisure)

From: Van Andel, G. E. (1998). Therapeutic Recreation Outcome Model. Therapeutic Recreation Journal, 32, 180-193, figure p. 187. Reprinted with permission.

---

is considered a functional domain along with cognitive, psychological, physical, spiritual, and social domains. According to Van Andel (1998), "leisure function represents a complex interaction of all the domains working together" (p. 187). This model purports that quality of life—identified as feelings of satisfaction, contentment, joy, self-determination, well-being, and mastery—is interrelated to functional capacities and wellness. Therefore, the purpose of therapeutic recreation is to facilitate outcomes related to functional capacity, health and wellness, and quality of life.

TR Service Delivery Model

The goal of therapeutic recreation, according to the TR Service Delivery Model, is to "empower the client to achieve her or his desired goals and optimally experience a sense of fulfillment, satisfaction, mastery, and well-being" (Van Andel, 1998, p. 181). The model is made up of three components: (a) scope of therapeutic recreation services, (b) nature of services, and (c) nature of therapeutic recreation specialist/client interaction. This model functions as a hybrid content-process model as it defines the scope of practice and identifies the means of delivering services. See Figure 14.5 for a graphic depiction of the TR Service Delivery Model.

Figure 14.5
Therapeutic Recreation Service Delivery Model (Van Andel, 1998, p. 181)

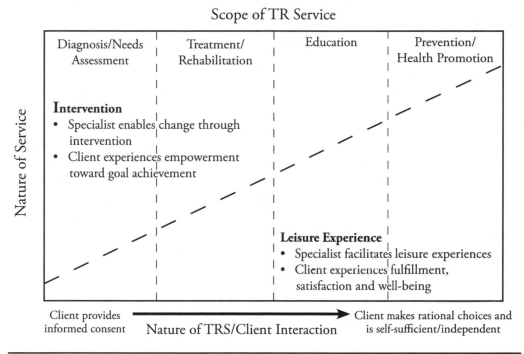

From: Van Andel, G. E. (1998). *Therapeutic Recreation Service Delivery Model.* Therapeutic Recreation Journal, *32, 180-193, figure p. 181. Reprinted with permission.*

The scope of the therapeutic recreation services component includes diagnosis/needs assessment, treatment/rehabilitation, client education, and prevention/health promotion (Van Andel, 1998). Diagnosis/needs assessment involves using assessment techniques to determine clients' abilities, strengths, and limitations. Treatment/rehabilitation involves restoring or stabilizing clients' health or functional abilities. "Educational strategies are used to develop the attitudes, values, and skills needed to function more effectively in society, to improve overall health, and/or to achieve a higher quality of life" (Van Andel, p. 182). Van Andel identified modalities such as assertiveness training, leisure education, and social skills training as examples of educational strategies. Prevention/health-promotion activities, in contrast to educational strategies, are those, such as stress management or exercise programs, that protect or promote healthy lifestyles (Van Andel). Once an assessment has been completed, a client may enter the continuum at any place and be at more than one place at the same time, which is similar to both the Leisure Ability and Health Protection/Health Promotion Models. Unlike the Leisure Ability Model, however, the TR Service Delivery Model is designed so that services and programs are not mutually exclusive; that is, a given program, although organized according to its primary goals, may achieve treatment/rehabilitation, education, and/or prevention/health promotion goals (Carter, Van Andel, & Robb, 1995, 2003).

The nature-of-services component distinguishes between planned interventions that are goal-oriented and leisure experiences recognizing that "the nature of experiences may vary from individual to individual or even for the same individual over time" (Van Andel, 1998, p. 182). The diagnosis/needs assessment and treatment/rehabilitation services are intended to produce functional outcomes, whereas education and prevention/health promotion services are more likely to facilitate leisure experiences as well as both functional and existential outcomes. According to the TR Service Delivery Model, the nature of therapeutic recreation services is dynamic and flexible depending on the clients served, their individual strengths and needs, and the mission and philosophy of the agency serving the clients.

The third component of the TR Service Delivery Model, nature of the therapeutic recreation specialist/client intervention, is based on the "professional's inherent respect for every person as a unique human being, and the recognition of the right to leisure experiences and the client's ability to make informed choices regarding his or her care" (Van Andel, 1998, p. 183). This component attempts to delineate the roles of the recreation therapist and the client. "The therapeutic recreation specialist is charged with assisting the client in making an informed decision regarding his or her care . . . choosing valid and reliable assessment tools . . . and selecting appropriate intervention strategies to assist the clients in achieving their . . . goals" (Van Andel, p. 183).

Merit and Worth of the TR Outcome Model and the TR Service Delivery Model

The TR Outcome Models and TR Service Delivery are two interrelated, but separate, models that when used in tandem have merit and worth. The strength of the models is in their combination. To fully comprehend therapeutic recreation practice according to these models, they must be viewed together.

Theory. The model's underlying theoretical basis is tied primarily to the leisure theory of Neulinger, and theory that relates to developmental contributions of leisure to functional outcomes (Van Andel, 1998). Coyle (1998) acknowledged that the use of Neulinger's theory to reconcile the means/end controversy within the TR Service Delivery Model is a unique strength of the model. She, however, also stressed that theory related to helping relationships and client change are missing and should be incorporated into this model as well as all of the other therapeutic recreation practice models.

Graphic depiction. Mobily (1999) pointed out that the graphic depiction of the TR Service Delivery Model (see Figure 14.5), like the Health Protection/ Health Promotion Model, places two variables (i.e., nature of TRS/client intervention and nature of service: intervention/leisure experience) in the same space, yet the variables do not have a causal relationship. Additionally, Mobily questioned the implication by the graphic depiction of the TR Outcome Model (see Figure 14.4) that quality of life, wellness, and function capacity are predictable from one another. Others, however, believed that showing the interrelationship between these concepts as well as the relationship between leisure experience and intervention are the strengths of the models and assists in communicating the uniqueness of therapeutic recreation (Parker & Carmack, 1998).

Clarity of terms and concepts. Coyle (1998) addressed this as an area of concern within the TR Outcome Model. She pointed out that on viewing the model, it appears that health status and wellness are equivalent or synonymous when such is not the case; they are distinct and different constructs. Mobily (1999) felt that another problem related to clarity of terms in the TR Outcome Model concerned the interrelatedness of the outcomes. He, along with Parker and Carmack (1998), believed that one outcome could not be used to predict another outcome, but they could be viewed as, and thus described as, interrelated. Coyle (1998) also felt that the distinction between function and form of service in the TR Service Delivery Model was not articulated clearly.

Direction for practice and research. The models taken together provide direction for practice, including the APIE process, and research. Coyle (1998) cautioned, that the broadness of the models diminished the uniqueness of the profession and advocated that both models be used together. Yet, these models would potentially fit better with the Pew Health Professions Commission's global recommendations. Parker and Carmack (1998) pointed out that the models' continuum and flexibility allowed for framing therapeutic recreation services as a process rather than as a setting. The TR Outcome Model, specifically, provides a useful framework for documenting and researching the efficacy of therapeutic recreation services (Coyle, 1998; Parker & Carmack, 1998). Coyle (1998) suggested that the models be used to research motivation of clients for rehabilitation. She, however, also warned that "an obstacle to using the TR Outcome Model is the lack of consistent, reliable, and valid measures for the proposed outcomes" (Coyle, p. 200). This seems to be a universal limitation in each of the models of therapeutic recreation and is compounded by the wide range of ages, abilities, and diagnoses of individuals who receive therapeutic recreation services.

Relevance. The models taken together seem to represent or at least be applicable to current practices in therapeutic recreation in a wide variety of healthcare and human service settings. Coyle (1998) stated that functional outcomes, quality of life, and health promotion are issues embraced not only by the field of therapeutic recreation but by such groups as the Agency for Health-Care Policy and Research, the National Center for Medical Rehabilitation, and the Institute of Medicine. Coyle concluded by stating that "Van Andel's models provide the discipline [of therapeutic recreation] with a contemporary focus and future-oriented focus for service delivery (i.e., prevention/health promotion) and research" (p. 210).

Summary

The TR Outcome and TR Service Delivery Models are meant to be used together, and as a pair are considered to be strong in both merit and worth. These models are based on a strong theoretical foundation that connects the developmental contributions of leisure to functional outcomes, provides solid direction for both practice and research in therapeutic recreation, and is relevant to many, if not most, practice settings. Additionally, the models are unique because the two were developed as a unit to address both content and process of practice. The graphic depiction and terms, however, need to be developed further and operationalized more clearly.

Optimizing Lifelong Health through Therapeutic Recreation (OLH-TR)

The fifth content model examined is the Optimizing Lifelong Health through Therapeutic Recreation (OLH-TR) model developed by Wilhite, Keller, and Caldwell (1999). According to the authors, the purpose of therapeutic recreation based on this model is to assist clients "to achieve and maintain leisure lifestyles that will enhance their health and well-being across the life course" (Wilhite et al., p. 98). The recreation therapist's role is "to facilitate the adoption of healthy leisure lifestyles that prevent or minimize the impact of disabling or dysfunctional conditions, or secondary consequences for persons who already experience a chronic or disabling condition, while promoting optimal health and well-being" (Wilhite et al., p. 101-102) through education and facilitation strategies. The model is based on the assumption that "engagement in a healthy leisure lifestyle reduces the probability of pathology or secondary consequences of disability across the life course," (p. 101) and "a healthy leisure lifestyle includes a flexibility that enables individuals to make continuous accommodations to internal and external changes" throughout the life course (p. 102).

Wilhite et al. (1999) base their model on three concepts: (a) health enhancement, (b) reform in health and human services, and (c) the life-course perspective. Health enhancement refers to those behaviors "individuals may use to prevent health risks, maintain or promote health, and facilitate functional independence" (Wilhite et al., p. 99) and includes individual- and societal-level interventions. The reform in health and human services they refer to is basically shortened lengths of stay in acute in-patient facilities due to managed care practices and an increased focus on client self-reliance. Thus, they contend therapeutic recreation should expand its health enhancement role in post-acute and community-based services. Finally, they take a life-course perspective in their model that contends that individuals continue to grow and develop over the life course and "reinvent themselves again and again in response to changing needs, resources, health status, and environment" (Wilhite et al., p. 100). This life course perspective is grounded on the work of Baltes' and Baltes' (1990) developmental theory of human aging and adaptation, which is based on the concept of selective optimization with compensation.

The OLH-TR model has four basic elements; selecting, optimizing, compensating, and evaluating. These elements are the primary activities that therapeutic recreation clients utilize in cooperation with the recreation therapists. Selecting involves assisting clients in setting goals that focus on their capabilities, skills, and motivations related to their functional domains (i.e., cognitive, physical, social, emotional) and match their environmental demands "that support their efforts to achieve, maintain, or regain leisure lifestyles that optimize health" (Wilhite et al., 1999, p. 103). Optimizing is the process of using educational strategies to assist clients in "actively and selectively engaging in activities" (Wilhite et al., p. 103) that focus on maximizing their personal and environmental resources and meet their leisure goals. Compensating involves assisting clients in using psychological (e.g., coping skills) or social (e.g., friends) efforts, and/or assistive technology to compensate for loss of ability or skill. "Compensating can include substituting one activity for another or making adaptations so the activity can be accomplished" (Wilhite et al., p. 103). Finally, evaluating is the process of making decisions regarding the costs or inputs (e.g., time, energy, money) and benefits or outputs of selecting, optimizing, and compensating. Wilhite et al. indicate that the four elements work together according to basic systems theory (i.e., input, process, output, and evaluation).

The authors specify that recreation therapists employ the APIE process and utilize educational and facilitative strategies. The recreation therapist uses educational techniques to help the client acquire awareness, knowledge, and skills related to using leisure to lessen health risks and promote health. The recreation therapist also facilitates opportunities for the client to apply what they learned and experience leisure. Additionally, the recreation therapist advocates for the client. Finally, the recreation therapist enables the client to value interdependency and "learn (a) that interdependent leisure functioning (i.e., with optimal support from TRSs and other care providers, family, friends) might be ideal and (b) that interacting cooperatively with others in a self-determined manner enables goal attainment" (Wilhite et al., 1999, p. 104).

Another aspect of the OLH-TR is its non-linear approach (see Figure 14.6). In fact, the model is intended to show continual motion. First, as therapeutic recreation clients repeatedly "reinvent" themselves based on changes in condition and situations, they move through the process of selecting, optimizing, compensating, and evaluating their leisure throughout their lives. Second, according to Wilhite et al. (1999), the model is nonlinear because the recreation therapist "helps clients achieve a balance between dependence (with maximum support) and independence" (p. 104) and individuals need to be able to move

Figure 14.6
OLH-TR Model (Wilhite, Keller, & Caldwell, 1999, p. 102)

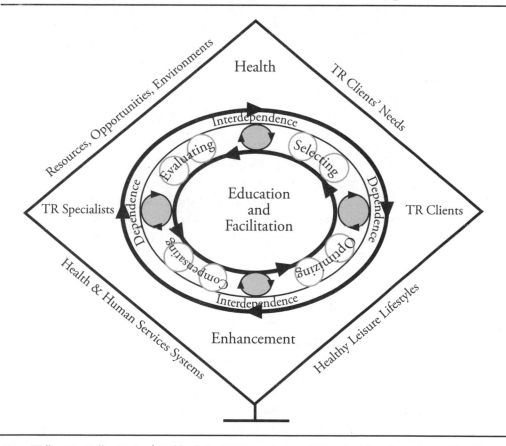

From: Wilhite, B., Keller, M. J., & Caldwell, L. (1999). Optimizing lifelong health and well-being: A health-enhancing model of therapeutic recreation. Therapeutic Recreation Journal, 33, 98-108, figure p. 102. Reprinted with permission.

between the two in order to achieve lifelong optimal health and well-being. The model's diamond shape represents the notion of moving back and forth from dependence and independence—when one gets out of balance the diamond shifts to the left or right side indicating that too much of either may be unhealthy—balance seems to be represented by the notion of interdependence. The nonlinear movement of the model is also illustrated in the model by inner concentric circles. What appears as the middle circle containing four small spheres represents the four elements of the model constituting clients' actions, and according to the authors should be conceptualized as ball bearings. The inner circle represents the actions taken by the recreation therapist, while the outer circle represents "the achievement of interdependency" (Wilhite et al., p. 104). The inner circle moves counterclockwise, and the outer moves clockwise as the client and recreation therapist interact.

Merit and Worth of the Optimizing Lifelong Health through Therapeutic Recreation Model

The OLH-TR Model has the potential for merit, but currently there are a few problems relating theories and outcomes. With its focus on health enhancement through leisure experiences and its value of interdependence while maintaining self-determination and empowerment, the model has much worth given the paradigm shifts in today's health and human service arenas.

Theory. The authors claim the model is based on "a life-course perspective which merges health enhancement and self-care approaches" (Wilhite et al., 1999, p. 99). Freysinger (1999), however, argues that it does not have a life-course perspective due to the lack of relating the model directly to age, the aging process, or some aspect of it. In their material, Wilhite et al. omit any discussion of self-care approaches or definition of health while presenting a limited discussion of leisure. They claim the model is "grounded in Baltes' and Baltes' (1990) developmental theory of human aging/adaptation" (Wilhite et al., p. 101), which is a current well-developed theory that explains the process of successful aging. Freysinger (1999) and Binkley (1999) each questioned the use of this theory. In addition to the issue raised above, Freysinger commented that Baltes' and Baltes' theory of selective optimization with compensation (SOC) was meant to be a process rather than consisting of distinct elements (Freysinger, p. 114). Binkley stated that "caution must always be exercised when borrowing theories from outside disciplines in order to ensure that their application remains true to the original intent" (p.119).

Wilhite et al. (1999) briefly examine disability theory in relationship to life course and Baltes' and Baltes' concept of SOC and make assumptions that successful adaptation to aging is similar to successful adaptation to disability or illness. With the growth in disabilities studies, research related to aging with a disability, and the new paradigms, this could be better developed. It appears that Wilhite et al. are making the assumption that successful aging over the life course could also be reflective of successful adaptation to disability or illness. They fail, however, to identify what constitutes successful adaptation to disability or illness or how this would evolve as one ages. Additionally, Freysinger (1999) argues that "we need to rethink our notions of health and aging and include resistance and argumentativeness, instead of adaptation and accommodation, as indicators of health and optimal well-being" (p. 112). The strength here, however, is that Wilhite and her colleagues acknowledge that individuals with disabilities and illnesses develop and grow over their life course. This is an important concept not to be missed, as society still tends to hold some individuals with disabilities at the age of onset or what might appear on the surface as their cognitive, emotional, social, or physical age.

Finally, the authors relate the model to systems theory without giving a full explanation of systems theory. Additionally, they limit their discussion of systems theory in the model to the four basic elements (i.e., selecting, optimizing, compensating, and evaluating). At one time, they identify evaluating as the forth element, and at another time, they identify the evaluating element as the feedback loop; yet in systems theory, feedback should happen at every stage. They indicate that the model is dynamic and fluid, which corresponds with systems theory.

Graphic depiction. Given the non-linear dynamic nature of the model (see Figure 14.6), it is very difficult to depict two-dimensionally. The authors have done a reasonable job in doing so. However, there are a few problems in the graphic depiction. On first viewing the figure and knowing the model is tied to system theory, one can identify the major components of systems theory. Input appears, although not explicitly identified by Wilhite et al., to be the items on the outside of the diamond; that is, Health & Human Services Systems; Resources, Opportunities, Environments; TR [therapeutic recreation] Clients' Needs; and Healthy Leisure Lifestyles. It is questionable, though, if Healthy Leisure Lifestyles is really the input rather than leisure experiences, as healthy leisure lifestyles evolve from the engagement in healthy leisure. Given that the authors do not discuss in depth the items on the outside of the diamond, one does not know their thoughts. Process appears to be the items in the concentric circles. Process is indicated by use of moving circles and implies somewhat of a feedback loop, but there is none among all the components. The outcome is Health Enhancement, which is represented in the largest font and bolded. In conclusion, the graphic depiction of the model is initially a bit hard to grasp, which may be in part due to the fact that we are accustomed to continuum models. Another aspect of the model's graphic that shows movement is the pedestal upon which the model sits. This shows how the individual can be out of balance due to too much dependence or independence. The figure, however, does seem to fit the model but could use further development.

Clarity of terms and concepts. The terms and concepts (e.g., health, healthy leisure lifestyle) used throughout the presentation of the model (Wilhite et al., 1999) are not defined in a usable manner. Freysinger (1999) identifies this as one of her three major concerns with the model. It should be noted that Wilhite and her colleagues directly admit this weakness in their discussion of the need for further development of the model.

Direction for practice and research. In spite of the model's shortcomings as noted above, the OLH-TR model does provide direction for both practice and research. In their presentation of the model, Wilhite et al. (1999) provide excellent examples of how the model would work in practice, yet they do not clearly indicate the strategies to use. Freysinger (1999), however, points out that without clarity of terms and concepts, it is hard to identify appropriate clients for services, what the specific goals of therapeutic recreation would be and when clients had achieved the goals, the specific tasks of the recreation therapist, and how to implement therapeutic recreation services. Without the examples provided by the model's authors, the recreation therapist would not know how to utilize education and facilitation to enable clients to achieve desired outcomes along the process. Additionally, without a discussion of leisure and disability across the life span, the recreation therapist is lacking direction. Further, the OLH-TR model does not provide sufficient direction for using the APIE process, which limits the model's merit and worth.

To the authors' credit, they have sought to test some of the model's assumptions (cf., Wilhite, Keller, Hodges, & Caldwell, 2004). Wilhite and her colleagues used the model to investigate how individuals living with multiple sclerosis "enhance[d] their development and optimize[d] their health and well-being" (p. 185). Although not solely focused on leisure as a health enhancer, their study supported the use of selective optimization with compensation as a way to achieve optimal health and lent support for use of the OLH-TR model in practice. Overall, the model provides significant direction for research, yet without clear definitions of terms and concepts it is not apparent if they were truly examining what was intended.

Relevance. The OLH-TR model's true strength is in its relevance to society at the start of the 21st century. It is congruent with public policy and initiatives and the changing paradigms of disability and health and human services, including "health enhancement, health promotion, habilitation, rehabilitation, and palliative care" (Wilhite et. al., 1999, p. 104). Further, it has the potential to move therapeutic recreation services beyond inpatient acute facilities into other domains of health and human services and serve all populations. The authors have used the term health services rather than healthcare, thereby opening the door for the provision of therapeutic recreation services within health services not traditionally linked with healthcare (e.g., parks and recreation departments, YMCAs). As with any model, certain models will fit different populations and settings better than others. For example, this model would fit exceptionally well with therapeutic recreation in assisted living.

In terms of relevance, the major weakness of this model is its Western culture orientation. As Freysinger (1999) points out, the model "focus[es] on the individual and individual changes" (p. 112). The OLH-TR model, however, is more multicultural than the other models with its strong value of interdependence rather than independence. While the model acknowledges the influence of the environment on one's leisure lifestyle and health and identifies one role for the recreation therapist as an advocate, it does not move toward the ecological perspective. It remains bound to changes being made within or by the individual rather than changes in the environment. If the authors modified the model to incorporate the ecological perspective, it would be a major contribution to the field and make the model more meaningful in the disability culture.

Summary

Within the OLH-TR model, leisure is the means and optimal health and well-being is the end. The model is enticing as it moves the field beyond the medical model and independent leisure functioning and incorporates health prevention and promotion. It, however, appears to have more worth than merit. In addition to addressing the weaknesses cited above, the model would benefit therapeutic recreation clients if it were modified to incorporate an ecological perspective as well as to encompass more multicultural (non-Western) viewpoints. In conclusion, Freysinger (1999) stated in her critique of the model that it is "somewhat useful in its current state and as having the potential to be very useful. The model provides a starting point but needs development" (p. 111). Binkley (1999) and the authors of this chapter concur.

Leisure and Well-Being Model (LWM)

The Leisure and Well-Being Model (LWM) was developed by Carruthers and Hood (2007; Hood & Carruthers, 2007) at the start of the 21st century. The LWM is based on positive psychology and leisure behavior, especially the works of Seligman and Csikszentmihalyi. Rather than focusing solely on clients' problems or diseases and disorders, the model calls for the development of clients' already-existing strengths and facilitation of the positive aspects of life rather than simply remediation of problem areas. The model's ultimate outcome for the client is well-being; that is, "a state of successful, satisfying, and productive engagement with one's life and the realization of one's full physical, cognitive, and social-emotional potential" (Hood & Carruthers, p. 301). According to Hood and Carruthers, "the two mechanisms through which to develop well-being articulated in this model are (a) to increase the value of leisure in building resources, creating positive emotions, and cultivating one's potential, and (b) to provide psycho-educational interventions that facilitate resource development" (p. 300). Leisure is prominent in both these mechanisms, and thus identified as an important means to well-being and considered a crucial intermediate outcome (Carruthers & Hood). Carruthers and Hood, however, are quick to point out that well-being is dependent on the *quality* of the leisure experience rather than just engaging in any leisure experience or recreation activity. Thus, leisure is defined as "those experiences that are pleasant in expectation, experience, or recollection; intrinsically motivated; optional in nature; autonomous; and engaging . . . thus [leisure] includes play and recreation activities as well as other less structured meaningful engagements" (p. 300).

The LWM is a systems-based model (see Figure 14.7) consisting of two major components: Developing Resources and Enhancing Leisure Experience. The Developing Resources component consists of five overlapping and interconnected sub-components: (a) psychological resources, (b) social resources, (c) cognitive resources, (d) physical resources, and (e) environmental resources. The first four sub-components are resources within the individual, whereas the fifth sub-component, environmental resources, are resources outside the individual. See Figure 14.8 for a listing of resources within each sub-component. According to Hood and Carruthers (2007), "not all of these resources would be addressed for any one client group; it is up to the professional expertise of the TR practitioner to identify which resources align most closely with the goals and aspirations of the clients served. However, this compilation of resources represents those resources that are most appropriate for TR service and are amenable to change" (p. 310). Hood and Carruthers also note there are other resources that might contribute to well-being that they did not identify within their model. Regardless of the resources addressed, leisure is often the key means to the development of these resources (Hood & Carruthers).

The Enhancing Leisure Experience component also consists of five sub-components: (a) savoring leisure ("paying attention to the positive aspects of, and emotions associated with, leisure involvement and purposefully seeking leisure experiences that give rise to positive emotions" [pp. 310-311]), (b) authentic leisure ("purposive selection of leisure involvement

Figure 14.7
The Leisure and Well-Being Model (LWM)
(Hood & Carruthers, 2007, p. 301)

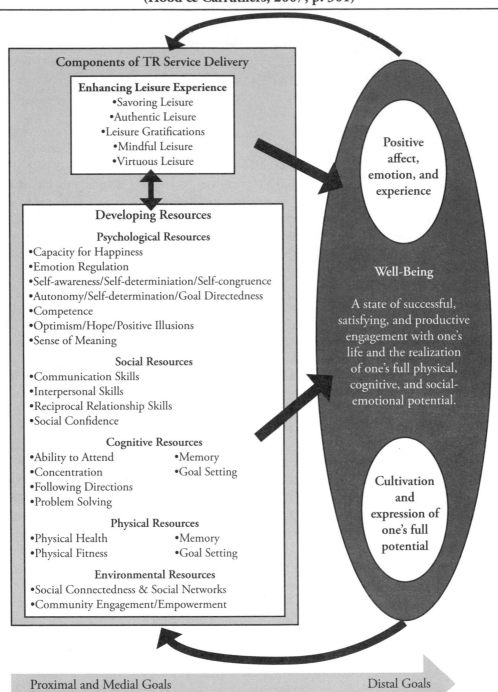

From: Hood, C. D., & Carruthers, C. (2007). Enhancing leisure experiences and developing resources: The Leisure and Well-Being Model, Part II. Therapeutic Recreation Journal, 1, 298-325, figure p. 301. Reprinted with permission.

that is reflective of essential aspects of the self" [p. 312]), (c) leisure gratifications ("leisure experiences that are optimally challenging and engaging, and that lead to sustained personal effort and commitment to the experience" [p. 314]), (d) mindful leisure (leisure experience that facilitates nonjudgemental full engagement and conscious awareness of one's unfolding present experiences with a simultaneous disengagement from concerns about daily life, the past, or the future" [p. 315]), and (e) virtuous leisure ("capacity to engage in leisure experiences that develop and/or mobilize personal strengths, capacities, interests, and abilities in the service of something larger than oneself" [p. 316]). These sub-components are utilized "to cultivate and enhance leisure experiences as an avenue through which to support well-being" (Hood & Carruthers, p. 310).

The role of the recreation therapist within the LWM is to (a) "focus attention on clients' strengths so that they may be further developed and used by clients to improve their own lives" (Hood & Carruthers, 2007, p. 299), (b) "help clients construct a life of ongoing personal development and contribution to the world" (Hood & Carruthers, p. 300), and (c) develop a collaborative relationship with clients "in which the therapist encourages hope and inspires change, validates clients' experiences, and supports clients to mobilize their assets and capacities towards the desired end" (Carruthers & Hood, 2007, p. 282). To enable the client to achieve well-being, the recreation therapist uses the following "tools:" leisure, psycho-educational intervention, therapeutic relationship, and advocacy (Hood & Carruthers).

Merit and Worth of the Leisure and Well-Being Model

The LWM appears to have both a high degree of merit and worth, although worth will vary by setting and population. The model is fairly well substantiated by theory, but it needs to be revisited for consistency and further direct for practice. It is on the cutting edge in terms of worth and provides a positive twist to therapeutic recreation treatment by focusing and building on the positive strengths of clients.

Theory. The model is built on a strong foundation that arises from leisure behavior and positive psychology theory and research. Each of the components and sub-components is linked directly to either leisure behavior or positive psychology or both. Further, the model relates to the most current concepts and theories within the fields of leisure, psychology, disability, and well-being. The authors, however, fall short in their discussion of disability studies literature.

Graphic depiction. The authors present two graphic illustrations of their model (Hood & Carruthers, 2007) plus a graphic representing the foundation of the model (Carruthers & Hood, 2007). The first graphic (see Figure 14.7) provides an overview of the model and the second graphic (see Figure 14.8) depicts the interrelationship among the Developing Resources component's sub-components and well-being. This model tends to continue the more recent trend in therapeutic recreation models in being a non-continuum, systems model.

The overview graphic (see Figure 14.9) depicts appropriately the two major components interacting with each other as well as each leading to the ultimate outcome of well-being and is congruent with systems approach. It has feedback loops from the ultimate outcome to the two major components, and all components interact with one another. The two

Figure 14.8
The Resource Development Framework for the LWM
(Hood & Carruthers, 2007, p. 302)

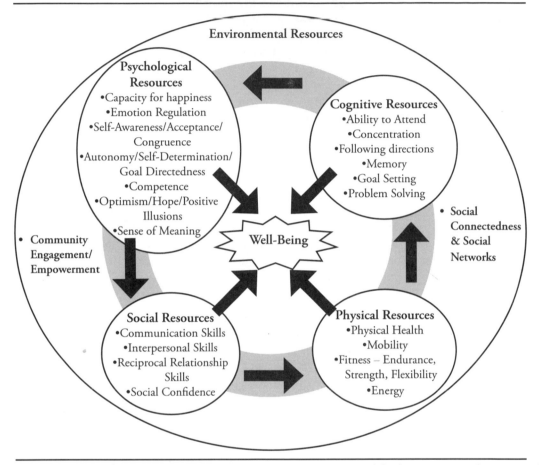

From: Hood, C. D., & Carruthers, C. (2007). Enhancing leisure experiences and developing resources: The Leisure and Well-Being Model, Part II. Therapeutic Recreation Journal, 1, 298-325, figure p. 302. Reprinted with permission.

major components are designated the "Components of TR Services Delivery," which helps in defining the focus of interventions. At the bottom of the overall graphic is an arrow going from the components to the overall outcome. Within the arrow, the components are considered proximal and medial goals, and the ultimate outcome of well-being is considered distal goals. The bottom arrow is helpful in conceptualizing the model, but the text lacks discussion of medial goals. Also, in today's healthcare climate with its focus on outcomes, it would have been useful if the authors carried over the label of "distal goals or long-term outcomes" from the foundations model rather than just using "distal goals." Finally, the graphic does not depict the roles of the client or the therapist.

The graphic related to the Developing Resource component (see Figure 14.8) is incorrectly labeled as "The Resource Development Framework" (Hood & Carruthers, p.

Figure 14.9
The Foundation Graphic for the LWM
(Carruthers & Hood, 2007, p. 279)

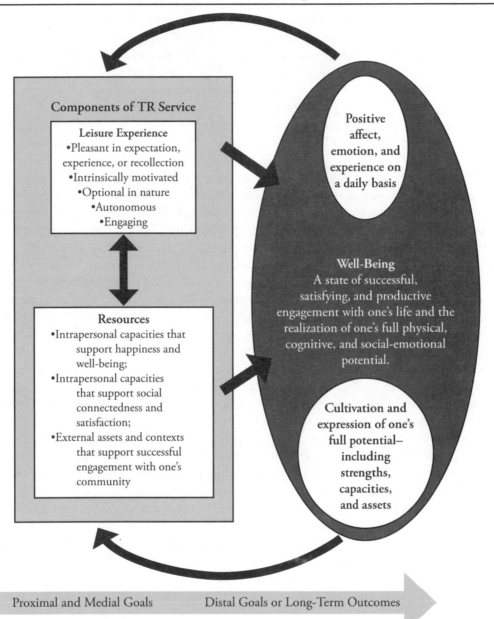

From: Carruthers, C., & Hood, C. D. (2007). Building a life of meaning through therapeutic recreation: The Leisure and Well-Being Model Part I. Therapeutic Recreation Journal, 1, 276-297, figure p. 279. Reprinted with permission.

302) when it should be titled "The Developing Resources Framework" *or* "The Framework for Developing Resources," so as to be consistent with the terms of the model. Further, the resources identified within the five sub-components of the Developing Resource component in both graphics are not always parallel to each other or with the authors' writings. The third graphic related to the LWM is the foundations graphic (Carruthers & Hood, 2007) (see Figure 14.9), which is meant to be viewed first and is presented prior to the practice model graphics. This is unique to this model and adds to an understanding of the three major components of the model; that is, leisure experience, resources, and well-being. This graphic, as well as the overview graphic, indicated distal goals when the ultimate outcome appears to be well-being, a multidimensional single goal/outcome.

Overall, the illustrations are simple and direct, include indication of flow and general identification of process, and adhere to systems approach. The model illustrations need to be revised so as to (a) be consistent in wording among the three and with the authors' writings and (b) include the role of and relationship between the recreation therapist and client.

Clarity of terms and concepts. The three major terms utilized are (a) Enhancing Leisure Experience, (b) Developing Resources, and (c) Well-Being. Each of these terms is reflective of the theory and concepts on which they are based. The sub-components and related terms, however, are not always used consistently throughout the writings and diagrams (see discussion above under graphic depiction). In addition, Hood and Carruthers (2007) use the words "energy" and "vitality" as if they are different, when in essence these two words are synonymous. Within Psychological Resources, they identify Emotion Regulation as one resource but also refer to it as "emotional expression and regulation" (p.303). The section discussing Social Resources under Developing Resources begins by addressing social connectedness, which is part of the sub-component under Environmental Resources but never makes the connection between Social Resources and Environmental Resources/Social Connectedness & Social Networks. In essence, the authors need to review their writings and graphics to be sure they are consistent.

Additionally, two elements seem to be missing from the model. First, one would expect that external leisure opportunities might be included within the environmental resources as a third element, particularly since Hood and Carruthers indicate that environmental resources "include access to social, educational, career, and leisure opportunities and supports" (p. 308), and that meaningful leisure opportunities are not restricted to community or social settings. Second, the Developing Resources component does not contain an element for developing leisure activity skills. Although developing leisure activity skills may be the means toward the other resources, it may also be a resource in its own right for some clients to cultivate in order to enhance their leisure experience.

Direction for practice and research. The LWM has great potential for practice but needs to be further developed to provide sufficient direction for practice and the APIE process. The roles, tasks, and responsibilities of the client and the recreation therapist are not well delineated particularly if the model is to be utilized with clients with significant cognitive deficits and of all ages. Additionally, there is no direction for the therapist to know where to begin with a client. The authors elaborate on the different components and elements of the model in a way that provides a basis for building therapeutic recreation interventions. Additionally, they offer some guidance for the selection of intervention techniques and strategies and occasionally identify a few specific interventions to employment. More direction, however, is still needed in terms of facilitation techniques and overall design of the intervention to successfully implement this model, particularly with different populations. Further, the model provides a basis on which to develop assessment and evaluation instruments and short-term and long-term goals. Once more direction is provided for practice, the model should facilitate research as it has a solid theoretical foundation.

Relevance. Carruthers and Hood (2007; Hood & Carruthers, 2007) intend for the model to be applicable in all settings and with all populations. Given the recent surge in positive psychology, the WHO's definition of health and its ICF, Healthy People 2010 and the Center for Disease Control and Prevention's Health Protection Goals, and the new paradigm on disability (National Council on Disability, 1998), the model appears to have the potential to take therapeutic recreation into the 21st century while linking it with its past. The critical issue is how the recreation therapist communicates the model so that therapeutic recreation does not lose its meaning in clinical settings that demand active treatment and compliance with Centers for Medicare & Medicaid Services (CMS) regulations and various accrediting bodies nor be delegated to the sidelines in school settings under IDEIA. Further, and unfortunately, within today's healthcare climate, the recreation therapist may not be able to provide the client with the individualized attention the model appears to demand so that the client may reach the defined outcomes.

Hood and Carruthers (2007) intend for the model to be applicable in all settings and with all populations. Given the heavy reliance of the LWM on cognitive processes, it may be difficult to utilize it with individuals with significant cognitive deficits and the very young who have not yet developed the necessary cognitive skills to enact this model. This problem may be eliminated if the developers provide more explicit direction for implementation of the model.

Summary

Within the LWM, leisure is the predominant means and well-being is the end. Conceptually, it demonstrates a high degree of merit and worth. The model appears to bring therapeutic recreation into the 21st century by strengthening the value of leisure as the strong hold of therapeutic recreation and expanding the realm of therapeutic recreation. Yet, it requires the therapeutic recreation profession to rethink its niche, return to its roots, and identify the uniqueness of therapeutic recreation within the realm of leisure thereby distinguishing it from other allied health providers. Further, this model supports the notion that there is no one leisure activity or group of activities that will promote well-being for all individuals and continues therapeutic recreation's longtime focus on client/person-centered services. For this model to actually be implemented, it will require sophistication on the part of the recreation therapist in terms of (a) communication of how therapeutic recreation fits into treatment and (b) the design and implementation of interventions. Finally, this model has the potential to (a) take therapeutic recreation to the forefront in many treatment settings, (b) strengthen the relationship between the recreation therapist and the client, and (c) facilitate well-being among clients with limited functional abilities.

Leisure-Spiritual Coping Model

The Leisure-Spiritual Coping Model (Heintzman, 2008) is the newest therapeutic recreation model to be published. According to Heintzman, it is grounded on theoretical and empirical findings that spirituality can play an important role in recovery for people with mental illness (Pargament, 1997), and that recreation and social activities have been identified as spiritual activities (e.g., Bellamy et al., 2007; Van Andel, 1998). Van Andel (1988) felt that spirituality was important to one's health status, quality of life, and functional ability—thus reflecting a holistic understanding of both health and therapeutic recreation. Shank and Coyle (2002) also identified spirituality as a dimension of health and wellness and an area for therapeutic recreation to address. Researchers such as Gosselink and Myllykangas; Heintzman and Mannell, Iwasaki and colleagues; MacKay, Mactavish, Ristock and Bartlett; and Schmidt and Little (as cited in Heintzman) have focused on empirically exploring the relationship between leisure and spirituality as a contributor to coping with stress. Heintzman and Mannell theorize that leisure is a coping strategy because it fosters self-determination and enhances social support, empowerment, palliative coping, and mood; and that these coping strategies "may be associated with, and enhanced by, the spiritual dimension of life" (p. 57). Spirituality is defined as "the feelings, thoughts, experiences, and behaviors that arise from a search for the sacred" (Larson, Swyers, & McCullough, 1998, p. 21, as cited in Heintzman, p. 58).

The purpose of leisure, according to the Leisure-Spiritual Coping Model, is well-being—with spirituality being an integral component of wellness. According to Heintzman (2008), the Leisure-Spiritual Coping Model can be used by both recreation therapists and leisure service providers "as they work with people experiencing stress due to a variety of personal stressors" to enable persons "to cope with, adapt to, and transcend life challenges," "promote mental health," and "enhance their quality of life" (p. 58)—that is, experience wellness. Thus, leisure and spirituality work together to mediate the effects of stress.

Heintzman (2008) describes the Leisure-Spiritual Coping Model as "process-oriented, transactional, dynamic, and relational" (p. 67), which seems to be a just portrayal. He based the model on Folkman's (1997) transactional model of stress and coping and Gall's (Gall et al., 2005) spiritual framework of coping. According to Folkman, spirituality is multidimensional, and at any given time it may function on many levels of stress and coping. Heintzman uses most of the components of Gall's spiritual framework of coping. These components include (a) spiritual appraisals (e.g., attribution), (b) person factors (e.g., religious orientation, worldviews, hope), (c) leisure-spiritual coping behaviors (e.g., prayer, grounding, contemplative leisure, leisure as time and space), (d) leisure-spiritual connections (resources) (e.g., connections with nature, others, etc.), and (e) leisure-spiritual meaning making (e.g., life purpose, personal growth).

According to the Leisure-Spiritual Coping Model (see Figure 14.10), when someone experiences a stressor (e.g., a chronic or terminal illness, a disabling condition, poverty, death of a loved one, etc.), they often first appraise the situation within the context of spiritual causes (e.g., God, the devil, fate); thus, spiritual appraisal is the first component of the model. There are two types of appraisal: (a) primary—the extent the event negatively affects one's relationship with God or other sacred aspects of one's life; and (b) secondary—the assessment that spiritual coping strategies may be helpful in dealing with the stressor.

Both of these types of appraisals determine the types of leisure-spiritual coping behaviors the individual chooses to employ. According to Heintzman, this component of the model is used for assessing the client's attributions by adding spiritual appraisal questions to the therapeutic recreation assessment.

The second component of the model is referred to as person factors, which "function as a contextual framework that guides a person in her or his interpretation, understanding, and response to stressful experiences" (Heintzman, 2008, p. 67). These include the person's religious denomination and doctrine, as these often affect how a person copes with stress, and according to Iwasaki (2007) (as cited in Heintzman, p. 62), religious doctrine is one of the six domains of quality of life. Heintzman advocates for incorporating individuals' religious beliefs into the therapeutic recreation process for some groups. He also includes religious orientation—extrinsic and intrinsic—in this component. Extrinsic religious orientations are based on comfort, safety, and guilt, anxiety, or external pressure—not a result of faith. Intrinsic religious orientations are characterized by "a selfless motivation to pursue purpose and meaning in life for its own sake and an internal understanding of transcendence" (Heintzman, p. 61). Heintzman feels that therapeutic recreation programs should "encourage movement from an extrinsic to an intrinsic religious orientation" (p. 61).

The next three components of the model—leisure-spiritual coping behavior, leisure-spiritual connections (resources), and leisure-spiritual meaning making—are where leisure experiences enter the model and affect wellness. According to Gall and his colleagues, spiritual coping behaviors include "organizational religious practices, private religious or spiritual practices, and nontraditional spiritual practices" (Gall et al, 2005, p. 93 as cited in Heintzman, 2008, p. 61). Heintzman notes that leisure may be a context for developing organizational and private religious resources and that nontraditional spiritual practices include leisure activities with a spiritual dimension. Other aspects of leisure-spiritual coping behaviors include sacrilization (i.e., being sensitive to the sacred) (e.g., meditation, relaxation) and grounding (i.e., diversion) (e.g., jogging, gardening, tai chi), contemplative leisure (i.e., having a receptive mental and spiritual attitude—being open and being aware), leisure as time and space for renewal (e.g., holidays, Sabbath keeping), and being away (i.e., getting away from the everyday environment). Leisure-spiritual connections or resources act as mediating factors to stress and include connections with nature, others, and the transcendent other (e.g., God). Leisure-spiritual meaning-making is the idea of using leisure experiences to discover meaning in a stressful situation and using leisure as a way to express spirituality. Leisure-spiritual coping behaviors, connection, and meaning making, along with spiritual appraisals "are assumed to function as mediating factors in the stress coping process" (Heintzman, p. 67).

Merit and Worth of the Leisure-Spiritual Coping Model

The Leisure-Spiritual Coping Model (Heintzman, 2008) seems to hold some degree of merit based on its conceptualization and development. Its merit is strongest in its theoretical underpinnings and its graphics. However, in regard to its clarity of terms and concepts and its application to practice, its merit is rather weak. Overall, with today's concerns with stress and wellness, and the popularity of nontraditional/alternative medicine, the model tends to have some degree of worth.

Theory. The theoretical foundation of the Leisure-Spiritual Coping Model is one of its strongest areas, as it is solidly grounded on principles that integrate stress, coping, spirituality, leisure, and health and wellness. Based on Gall's (2005, as cited in Heintzman, 2008) conceptual framework of spirituality, coping and health; Folkman's (1997) model of stress and coping; and numerous research linking leisure with spirituality and coping; and beliefs about the role of spirituality in quality of life and therapeutic recreation (Van Andel, 1998), Heintzman makes a strong case for developing a model connecting leisure and spirituality. However, an area neglected in the theoretical constructs is that of disability. While Heintzman connects mental illness and spiritual and leisure activities based on the

Figure 14.10
The Leisure-Spiritual Coping Model
(Heintzman, 2008, p. 59)

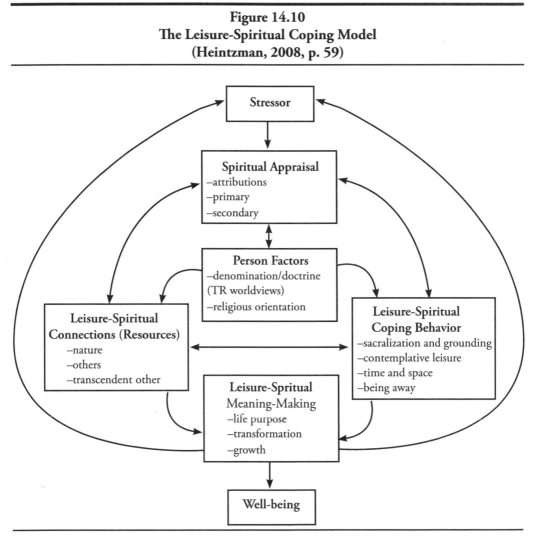

From: Heintzman, P. (2008). Leisure-spiritual coping: A model for therapeutic recreation and leisure services. Therapeutic Recreation Journal, 1, 56-73, figure p. 59. Reprinted with permission.

works of Bellamy and colleagues (Bellamy et al., 2007, as cited in Heintzman), disability literature in general is missing. Perhaps this is an area where more research is needed.

Graphic depiction. The model's graph (see Figure 14.10) is relatively clear and easy to understand. It is evident that the impetus for using the model is based on a stressor, and the outcome of the model is well-being. It does not, however, define therapeutic recreation's scope of practice or uniqueness. The components are clearly identified, and some explanation is given under each component. The directionality or motion of the model seems appropriate; however, there is one area, as discussed below, that needs explanation.

The model clearly identifies the stressor as the impetus for implementing the model. It is clear and logical that the first steps in the process would involve a spiritual appraisal of the stress or making causal attributions, which are influenced by one's religious orientation and/ or doctrine (person factors). The connections between the appraisals and person factors with the behavioral components (leisure-spiritual connections, coping behaviors, and meaning making) to well-being are also clear, and the recursive nature is logical and dynamic. However, Heintzman provides no explanation for the arrows connecting leisure-spiritual meaning-making back to the stressor. The leisure-spiritual meaning-making component is the only leisure-related component that leads back to the stressor, which doesn't fit with the conceptualization of the model. It seems as if the arrow is misplaced and the directional flow should go from well-being back to the stressor because new life stressors are always reappearing. This needs to be further developed, explained, or amended.

Clarity of terms and concepts. Numerous terms and concepts used throughout the model are relatively new to practitioners. For example, "primary" and "secondary spiritual appraisals," "person factors," and "sacralization" are new to the therapeutic recreation literature. Because of this, special attention needs to be given when defining and explaining them. The case study provided by Heintzman attempts to do this. One term in particular that is used both in the graphic depiction and in the text but never defined is "TR worldview" as a person factor. Because of this omission, it almost seems as if this concept was added as an afterthought to make the model fit into the practice of therapeutic recreation. This is a weakness of the model and reduces its merit.

Direction for practice and research. While Heintzman provides a thoughtful and insightful case study based on his personal experience with cancer that illustrates the components of the model, it does not explain how the model could be used in programming. Heintzman admits this by stating, "the case study does not involve a therapeutic recreation service, a therapeutic recreation specialist, or a leisure service practitioner," but "illustrates the components" of the model (2008, p. 68). The only place in the description of the model where Heintzman offers an example of how the model could be used in practice is when he describes the spiritual appraisal component. He suggests including questions related to an individual's spiritual appraisal into the assessment process. However, he does not provide specific examples of useful questions. While he doesn't propose this, questions regarding an individual's religious denomination or doctrine could also be included in the assessment and often are included.

A second suggestion made by Heintzman (2008) regarding the use of the Leisure-Spiritual Coping Model in the practice of therapeutic recreation is for programs "to encourage movement from an extrinsic [religion "for the person's own sake to gain personal benefits" (p. 61) or to provide comfort and safety, or religion "as a result of guilt, anxiety, or external pressure" (p. 61)] to an intrinsic religious orientation" (p. 61), yet he offers no suggestions about how to do this. One might also question whether this is in the scope of therapeutic recreation practice, and are recreation therapists trained to do this? If not, it calls into question the ethics of such practice by recreation therapists.

Heintzman (2008) provides the reader with a case study illustrating how the model was useful to him during an extremely stressful time in his life. The case study affords insight to how different recreational activities and leisure experiences can be utilized for developing a spiritual connection. Heintzman, however, admits the case study does not involve the use of professional services by a recreation therapist, thus bringing into question the model's applicability to the APIE process and the role of the recreation therapist. This aspect of the model needs to be developed further.

The Leisure-Spiritual Coping Model does provide a framework for research. As noted by Heintzman (2008), the model is based on and integrates theory and research. The leisure-spiritual connection, however, needs to be investigated further and the various pathways tested.

Relevance. A major strength of the Leisure-Spiritual Coping Model is that it seems applicable to a wide range of diverse religious and spiritual beliefs and practices, as well as ethnicities and cultures. However, a major weakness of the model is its limited relevance to a wide range of therapeutic recreation practice. Over 20 years ago, Howe-Murphy and Murphy (1987) advocated for a spiritual paradigm for therapeutic recreation practice that included the "development of personal consciousness, leading to a lifestyle of wellness, and which incorporates the elements of mind, body, spirit" (p. 47). Almost ten years later, Van Andel (1998) identified the spiritual function as one of the six functional capacities that should be addressed by therapeutic recreation. Yet, little has been done to systematically address this issue.

This lack of attention to the spiritual aspect of life may be attributed to the secular nature of healthcare in the United States and the personal nature of spirituality. While Heintzman (2008) frequently points out the difference between religion and spirituality and illustrates how the model can be used with traditional and non-traditional practices, the model is still very much grounded in the idea of religious orientation, denomination, and/or doctrine. These person factors provide "the contextual framework for understanding and responding to . . . stress" (Heintzman, p. 68).

Another reason spiritual functioning may have been neglected in practice is that most healthcare today is focused on functional rather than existential outcomes. While one may argue that the ultimate outcome of the Leisure-Spiritual Coping Model is wellness, the process is very existential and difficult to measure. There are, however, a number of therapeutic recreation service arenas that do value and facilitate non-functional outcomes such as spirituality and well-being. These include settings that serve individuals with terminal illnesses or conditions, such as long-term care, hospice, and oncology. Another practical consideration related to therapeutic recreation practice that may make this model difficult to implement is the breadth of religious practices the recreation therapist may need to be knowledgeable of to successfully implement this model. In addition, there may be the chance that the therapist's personal spiritual or religious beliefs may be in direct conflict with his or her client's. While therapists may always encounter beliefs, values, and behaviors in their clients that are an antithesis to their own, because of the very personal and entrenched nature of religious beliefs that directly impact one's world view, these may be more difficult to reconcile. Finally, if the recreation therapist is not personally spiritual or grounded in a religious doctrine, he or she may find this model extremely difficult to comprehend or even value.

Summary

While the Leisure-Spiritual Coping Model is unique and has some degree of merit, its potential worth is applicable to very limited and specific settings for specific clients. It may hold a high degree of worth in settings where (a) holistic and nontraditional practices are valued and utilized, (b) settings that are religious-based, or (c) for cultural or ethnic groups where spirituality is a foundation of their belief system.

Heintzman (2008) points out that many leisure activities and experiences can by their nature be spiritual and facilitate coping with stress (i.e., contemplative; connect one with nature, others, and/or a transcendent other; palliative, grounding, transformational). However, these are very difficult outcomes for which to program. Like leisure, spirituality is an individual and dynamic experience. While one may feel connected to "God" on one hiking trip, he might not experience that same feeling on the next—it may be a successful coping strategy one time and not the next. Thus, from a therapeutic recreation practice perspective, this model's worth is definitely determined by the user.

Functional Improvement Outcomes Model

Only one model, the Self-Determination and Enjoyment Enhancement: A Psychologically Based Service Delivery Model (Dattilo, Kleiber, & Williams, 1998), indicates functional improvement as its ultimate outcome. Functional improvement or a similar concept is contained within a number of the other models but never as the terminal outcome.

Self-Determination and Enjoyment Enhancement: *A Psychologically Based Service Delivery Model for Therapeutic Recreation*

The last model to be examined is the Self-Determination and Enjoyment Enhancement: A Psychologically Based Service Delivery Model for Therapeutic Recreation, developed by Dattilo, Kleiber, and Williams (1998). This model identifies the purpose of therapeutic recreation as supporting participants in achieving the goals of self-determination and enjoyment and, ultimately, functional improvement (p. 259). The model is based on the assumption that self-determination and enjoyment can lead to functional improvement and personal growth, thus making the model unique in that existential outcomes are said to lead to functional outcomes rather than the reverse. The model's philosophical underpinnings are grounded in Csikszentmihalyi's notion of optimal experience and Deci's theories of self-determination and intrinsic motivation.

This model evolved from Dattilo and Kleiber's work in 1993 that attempted to explain the relationship between self-determination and enjoyment in relationship to therapeutic recreation. The Self-Determination and Enjoyment Enhancement: A Psychologically Based Service Delivery Model for Therapeutic Recreation consists of six outcomes referred to as components: (a) self-determination, (b) intrinsic motivation, (c) perception of manageable

Figure 14.11
Self-Determination and Enjoyment Enhancement: A Psychologically Based Service Delivery Model for Therapeutic Recreation
(Datillo, Kleiber, & Williams, 1998, p. 260)

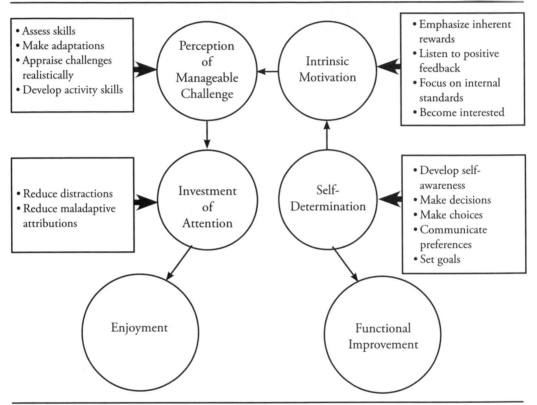

From: Dattilo, J., Kleiber, D., & Williams, R. (1998). Self-determination and enjoyment enhancement: A psychologically based service delivery model for therapeutic recreation. Therapeutic Recreation Journal, 32, 258-271, figure p. 260. Reprinted with permission.

challenge, (d) investment of attention, (e) enjoyment, and (f) functional improvement. See Figure 14.11 for a graphic depiction of this model. This model is a closed-systems model rather than a continuum model. That is, each component of the model interacts with and is interdependent upon the other components of the model, and all the components must be operational for the model to work; the model cannot be implemented without one of the components. As noted by Dattilo et al. (1998), the model is intended to be used holistically, because changes to one component of the model are likely to influence changes in another (p. 266).

The self-determination component of the model is defined as "acting as a primary causal agent in one's life and making choices and decisions free from external influence or interference" (Dattilo et al., 1998, p. 260). Dattilo and his colleagues contend that when individuals are able to be in control of their free time, they are more likely to experience enjoyment. The intrinsic-motivation component is seen as a means to, as well as a result of, self-determination. According to Dattilo et al., intrinsically motivated activities are energizing, exciting, challenging, and even relaxing and are associated most often with recreation and leisure experiences. The component of perception of manageable change is related to the notion of flow and implies an awareness of the challenge being presented and the perception of ability to meet the challenge. Successful experiences are necessary in order to perceive that challenging experiences can be managed. The investment-of-attention component involves "concentration, effort, and a sense of control. These outcomes are obtained when goals are clear, feedback is relevant, and challenge and skills are in balance" (Dattilo et al., p. 261). According to Dattilo et al., the enjoyment component is a result of investing one's attention (the investment-of-attention component) in actions that are intrinsically motivating (the intrinsic-motivation component). As the authors pointed out, enjoyment is more than just fun, it entails psychological involvement (e.g., investment of attention, perception of manageable challenge) that results in positive feelings. The final component of the model is functional improvement. Dattilo et al. readily admit that the causal relationship between enjoyment and functional improvement is not extensively documented. They, however, identify research that suggests the following relationship: when an individual is intrinsically motivated to engage in an activity that provides him or her with challenge, freedom, and enjoyment, involvement will increase and functional improvements should follow.

Dattilo et al. (1998) described strategies for facilitating the psychological outcomes identified above. These strategies are listed within the boxes in Figure 14.11. They inferred that potential clients for this model would be persons with illnesses and disabilities.

Merit and Worth of the Self-Determination and Enjoyment Enhancement: A Psychologically Based Service Delivery Model for Therapeutic Recreation

The Self-Determination and Enjoyment Enhancement: A Psychologically Based Service Delivery Model for Therapeutic Recreation as a closed system appears to have potential merit as the theories and outcomes are interrelated and fit with systems theories. With its focus on functional improvement and leisure-related outcomes (i.e., intrinsic motivation, enjoyment, and self-determination), the model has much worth in today's health and human service arenas.

Theory. The model has a strong theoretical basis for the most part. The prominence of self-determination as it relates to leisure is a theme throughout much of the leisure literature (e.g., Coleman & Iso-Ahola, 1993; Mannell & Kleiber, 1997). The main criticism of the model seems to revolve around the functional-improvement component; both its prominence and its relationship to enjoyment (Caldwell, 1998; Mobily, 1999; Murray, 1998). Murray (1998) suggested that the model's theoretical underpinnings be expanded to include the ecological perspective to take into account the client's environment. Dattilo et al. (1998) also acknowledged this need. Caldwell (1998) questioned the validity that many of the theoretical links between components purported by the model. Mobily (1999), however, concluded that the model is "unusually sound in its integration of theory and practice" (p. 186).

Graphic depiction. The outcomes of services are clearly identifiable in the model's graphic representation as are the facilitation strategies for achieving the outcomes (see Figure 14.11).

The graphic depiction provides direction for the delivery of therapeutic recreation services. The components are clear. Caldwell (1998), however, felt that the model should include an emotional component. Another potential problem with the diagram of the model is that there is no clear entry point. The facilitation strategy box in the upper left-hand corner includes skill assessment related to perception of manageable change, leading one to assume that this may be the entry point into the system.

Clarity of terms and concepts. The titles of the components are clearly identified. The material in the boxes, however, is less than clear due to the inability of the reader to decipher whether the material in the boxes is meant to be processes, outcomes, or a combination of both. With the addition of the functional-improvement component, the model's title does not accurately describe it, and its title is too long to be very useful. Perhaps the model should be renamed "Functional Improvement, Self-Determination, and Enjoyment Enhancement: A Service Delivery Model for Therapeutic Recreation" or something else and given an acronym.

Direction for practice and research. Dattilo et al. (1998) pointed out that there may be ambiguity between the components that may be problematic for implementing the model in practice as well as researching the efficacy of the model. The scope of therapeutic recreation practice, as directed by this model, might become unclear and might not distinguish therapeutic recreation from other treatment modalities due to the strong presence of the enjoyment-enhancement and functional-improvement components (Caldwell, 1998, p. 288). Additionally, due to the lack of clarity, the model does not lend itself to be easily implemented in accordance with the APIE process. Dattilo and his colleagues also felt the model was not yet ready for research.

Relevance. Dattilo et al. (1998) identified that a weakness of their model was that it focused on the micro-system of the individual. They suggested that by adding an ecological perspective to the model it might be relevant to a wider range of settings and populations. Caldwell (1998) also questioned the relevance of the model related to context, type of disability, and developmental stage; stating, "For example, the need or desire for control differs across the lifespan" (p. 284). This model, by focusing on self-determination, enjoyment, and functional improvement, enables the recreation therapist to focus on both leisure and functional outcomes and thereby be congruent with health and human service providers' emphasis.

Summary

Self-Determination and Enjoyment Enhancement: A Psychologically Based Service Delivery Model for Therapeutic Recreation is one of the newer practice models. With its ultimate outcome being functional improvement and enjoyment being the intermediate outcome, this model is unique in its reversal of the more common sequence of outcomes; that is, functional outcomes yielding to a non-functional/enjoyment outcome. Additionally, with the interaction between the components of enjoyment and functional improvement, the model is also partially leisure as a means model.

The model's strong grounding in psychological theory is its strength and is where most of its merit is found. Its graphic depiction, terms, and direction for practice and research need to be clarified and developed further. As its authors noted, it is focused at the individual level, which limits its relevance to many settings and populations. Finally, it would be useful if the authors shortened the model's name or at least presented an acronym for it.

Summary and Challenges for the Future

Each of the eight models reviewed here show great promise in directing the practice and research of therapeutic recreation. The field has certainly come a long way in both theory and practice in the last 40-plus years, yet it faces numerous challenges in articulating and validating its services in order to continue developing and being a viable part of healthcare and social services.

Selecting the appropriate practice model is one of the first steps toward providing quality therapeutic recreation services. The next challenge is to operationalize the practice model; that is, to translate the practice model into the design and delivery of meaningful services that produce specified and valued outcomes. Most therapeutic recreation practice models to date provide only the framework for the development of therapeutic recreation services, thus they are content models. As such, they do not delineate the process for determining, implementing, and evaluating services and programs. Thus, practice models need to be further developed to include content and process or complementary process models. The TR Service Delivery Model (Van Andel, 1998), by including diagnosis/needs assessment as part of the scope of service component begins to address process. Currently, however, only the Leisure Ability Model by means of the Therapeutic Recreation Accountability Model (TRAM) addresses this issue (Peterson & Stumbo, 2000; Stumbo, 1996, Stumbo & Peterson, 2004, 2009). As process models are developed or current practice models are expanded into more comprehensive models that include content and process, research needs to be undertaken to confirm the validity of the models in practice.

As new models are developed and old ones revised, an emphasis on efficient and effective client-centered services, client satisfaction and dignity, and multiculturalism must be kept in the forefront. In conjunction with these issues, clients must be considered part of an ecological system that includes their caregivers and significant others, their home and community, and society at large. Only three models, the Optimizing Lifelong Health through Therapeutic Recreation (OLH-TH) model, the Self-Determination and Enjoyment Enhancement: A Psychologically Based Service Delivery Model for Therapeutic Recreation, and the Leisure and Well-Being Model (LWM), mention the environment. The OLH-TH model acknowledges the environment as a contributing factor to quality of life but only in terms of matching the client, based on his or her functioning, with the appropriate environment to achieve the desired outcome (Wilhite et al., 1999). The Self-Determination and Enjoyment Enhancement: A Psychologically Based Service Delivery Model for Therapeutic Recreation discusses modifying the environment as part of the intervention but only until the client gains the skills necessary to enable the individual to manipulate the environment for his or her benefit (Dattilo et al., 1998). The LWM discusses the components and influences of environmental resources in relation to well-being and alludes to facilitating client connectedness and empowerment via environmental resource modification and development. The ecological perspective, which focuses on the interaction between the client and the environment (Howe-Murphy & Charboneau, 1987), should be revisited and incorporated directly into the models as appropriate. Further, this addition would facilitate the delivery of therapeutic recreation services in an increasingly culturally diverse society.

In the late 1990s, professionals in the field of therapeutic recreation began to discuss the issue of functional outcomes vs. existential outcomes (cf. Murray, 1998; Richter & Kashchalk, 1996). Functional outcomes focus on observable behavior change, whereas existential outcomes focus on the meanings of experiences to life and life satisfaction. Traditionally, healthcare and human services have addressed only functional outcomes. Within the last decade, however, the federal government has begun to include improved quality of life and life satisfaction as healthcare and human service goals (U.S. Department of Health and Human Services, 2000). Accreditation organizations (i.e., The Joint Commission and CARF) have also been moving beyond evaluation of medical care and improvement to including focus on quality of life. Given the existential nature of leisure and the relationship of leisure to quality of life and life satisfaction, it might now be time to place more emphasis on existential outcomes. The most recent model to emerge, the Leisure and Well-Being Service Model, seems to be the only one to address this issue.

For models of therapeutic recreation to take on significance, efficacy and outcome research, development and testing of assessment instruments, and program evaluation need to be tied to the models. Since 2000, articles related to research of interventions, outcomes, and assessments have rarely identified the therapeutic recreation model that provided the foundation upon which their work was operationalized. In reviewing the *Therapeutic Recreation Journal*, the *Annual in Therapeutic Recreation*, and the *American Journal of Recreation Therapy*, only five articles identified the therapeutic recreation model on which the work was based (cf., Baldwin, Hutchinson, & Magnuson, 2004; Boothman & Savell, 2004; Crawford, Livingston, & Swango, 2004; Reel & Kleiber, 2008; Stumbo & Hess, 2001; Wilhite, Keller, Hodges, & Caldwell, 2004). None of these, however, actually tested the validity of a model.

In conclusion, for the profession to remain relevant in the ever-demanding health and human service arenas, it is critical that practitioners, researchers, educators, and students utilize models in their daily work. For this to happen, it is important that model developers clearly define terms and concepts for operational purposes and provide materials to assist researchers and practitioners in utilizing the models. It is also important that students are exposed to more than just a survey of models. They need to be shown how models can be operationalized in practice and be challenged to evaluate, apply, and discuss the various models against different settings, population, and issues. Models of practice have the potential to significantly advance the field of therapeutic recreation but only if they are well conceptualized, tested, utilized, and continuously re-evaluated.

Discussion Questions

1. Why are practice models important?
2. What is meant by leisure-oriented models and by health-oriented models?
3. Which practice models are leisure-oriented and which are health-oriented?
4. What is the difference between a content model and a process model?

5. Identify the similarities and differences among the different practice models (e.g., clients, settings, outcomes, services provided).
6. Discuss the pros and cons of having one practice model vs. multiple practice models for therapeutic recreation.

References

Americans with Disabilities Act of 1990, Pub. L. No. 101-136, U.S.C. (1994, suppl 4).

Austin, D. R. (1991). Introduction and overview. In D. R. Austin, & M. E. Crawford (Eds.), *Therapeutic recreation: An introduction* (pp. 1-29). Englewood Cliffs, NJ: Prentice-Hall.

Austin, D. R. (1996). Introduction and overview. In D. R. Austin, & M. E. Crawford (Eds.), *Therapeutic recreation: An introduction* (2nd ed.) (pp. 1-21).Needham Heights, MA: Allyn & Bacon,

Austin, D. R. (1998). The Health Protection/Health Promotion Model. *Therapeutic Recreation Journal, 32*, 109-117.

Austin, D. R. (1999). *Therapeutic recreation: Processes and techniques* (4th ed.). Champaign, IL: Sagamore.

Austin, D. R. (2004). *Therapeutic recreation: Processes and techniques* (5th ed.). Champaign, IL: Sagamore.

Austin, D. R. (2009). *Therapeutic recreation: Processes and techniques* (6th ed.). Champaign, IL: Sagamore.

Baldwin, C. K., Hutchinson, S. L., & Magnuson, D. R. (2004). Program theory: A framework for theory-driven programming and evaluation. *Therapeutic Recreation Journal, 38*, 16-31.

Ball, E. L. (1970). The meaning of therapeutic recreation. *Therapeutic Recreation Journal, 4*(1), 17-18.

Baltes, P. B., & Baltes, M. M. (1990). Selective optimization with compensation. In P.B. Baltes, & M. M Baltes (Eds.). (pp.1-34) *Successful aging: Perspectives from the behavioral sciences.* New York: Cambridge University.

Bellamy, C. D., Jarrett, N. C., Mowbray, O., Mac Farlane, P., Mowbray, C. T., & Holter, M. C. (2007). Relevance of spirituality for people with mental illness attending consumer-centered services. *Psychiatric Rehabilitation Journal, 30*(4), 287-294.

Binkley, A. L. (1999). OLH-TR Model critique: A practitioner's view. *Therapeutic Recreation Journal, 33*, 116-121.

Bureau of Labor Statistics, U.S. Department of Labor. (2007). *Occupational Outlook Handbook, 2006-07 Edition*, Recreational Therapists. Retrieved March 01, 2007, http://www.bls.gov/oco/ocos082.htm.

Boothman, S., & Savell, K. (2004). Development, reliability and validity of the Measurable Assessment in Recreation for Resident-Centered Care (MARRCC). *Therapeutic Recreation Journal, 38*, 382-393.

Bullock, C. C. (1998). The Leisure Ability Model: Implications for the researcher. *Therapeutic Recreation Journal, 32*, 97-102.

burlingame, j. (1998). Clinical practice models. In F. Brasile, T. K. Skalko, & j. burlingame (Eds.), *Perspectives in recreational therapy: Issues of a dynamic profession* (pp. 83-106). Ravensdale, WA: Idyll Arbor.

Caldwell, L. L. (1998). In response to Dattilo, Kleiber, & Williams' "Self-determination and Enjoyment Enhancement: A psychologically based service delivery model for therapeutic recreation." *Therapeutic Recreation Journal, 32*, 283-289.

Carruthers, C., & Hood, C. D. (2007). Building a life of meaning through therapeutic recreation: The Leisure and Well-Being Model, Part 1. *Therapeutic Recreation Journal, 1*, 276-297.

Carter, M. J., Van Andel, G. E., & Robb, G. M. (1998). *Therapeutic recreation: A practical approach* (3rd ed.). Prospects Heights, IL: Waveland.

Centers for Disease Control and Prevention. (n.d.) *CDC's Health Protection Goals.* Retrieved March 01, 2007, http://www.cdc.gov/osi/goals/goals.html.

Centers for Disease Control and Prevention. (2006). *CDC Achieving Greater Health Impact Goals for the 21st Century.* Retrieved March 01, 2007 from http://www.cdc.gov/osi/goals/AllStarterObjectives921.pdf.

Civil Rights Act of 1991, Pub. L. No. 102-166, U.S.C. (1994, suppl 4).

Coleman, D., & Iso-Ahola, S. E. (1993). Leisure and health: The role of social support and self-determination. *Journal of Leisure Research, 25*, 111-128.

Condeluci, A. (1995). *Interdependency: The route to community.* Boca Raton, FL: St. Lucie.

Coyle, C. P. (1998). Integrating service delivery and outcomes: A practice model for the future? *Therapeutic Recreation Journal, 32*, 194-201.

Crawford, M. E., Livingston, C., & Swango, A. (2004). Developing age-appropriate playground skills in children with developmental disabilities: An application of the model for movement confidence combined with precision teaching methodology. *Annual in Therapeutic Recreation, 13*, 38-51.

Dattilo, J., & Kleiber, D. (1993). Psychological perspectives for therapeutic recreation research: The psychology of enjoyment. In M. J. Malkin, & C. Z. Howe (Eds.), *Research in therapeutic recreation: Concepts and methods* (pp. 57-76). State College, PA: Venture.

Dattilo, J., Kleiber, D., & Williams, R. (1998). Self-determination and enjoyment enhancement: A psychologically based service delivery model for therapeutic recreation. *Therapeutic Recreation Journal, 32*, 258-271.

Developmental Disabilities Assistance and Bill of Rights Act Amendments of 1996, Pub. L. No. 104-183, U.S.C. (1996).

Dieser, R. B. (2002). A cross-cultural critique of newer therapeutic recreation practice models: The self-determination and enjoyment enhancement model, Aristotelian good life model, and the optimizing lifelong health through therapeutic recreation model. *Therapeutic Recreation Journal, 36,* 84-96.

Dieser, R. B. (2003). Understanding cross-ethnic interactions when using therapeutic recreation practice models. *Therapeutic Recreation Journal, 37*, 175-189.

Dieser, R. B., & Peregoy, J. J. (1999). A multicultural critique of three therapeutic recreation service models. *Annual in Therapeutic Recreation, 8,* 56-69.

Driver, B. L., Brown, P. J., & Peterson, G. L. (1991). Research on leisure benefits: An introduction to this volume. In B. L. Driver, P. J. Brown, & G. L. Peterson (Eds.), *Benefits of leisure* (pp. 3-11). State College, PA: Venture.

Folkman, S. (1997). Positive psychology and states of coping with severe stress. *Journal for the Scientific Study of Religion, 33*, 362-375.

Freysinger, V. (1999). A critique of the "Optimizing Lifelong Health through Therapeutic Recreation" (OLH-TR) Model. *Therapeutic Recreation Journal, 33*, 109-115.

Frye, V., & Peters, M. (1972). *Therapeutic recreation: Its theory, philosophy, and practice.* Harrisburg, PA: Stackpole.

Gall, T. L., Charbonneau, C., Clarke, N. H., Grant, K., Joseph, A., & Shouldice, L. (2005). Understanding the nature and role of spirituality in relation to coping and health: A conceptual framework. *Canadian Psychology/Psychologie canadienne, 34*(2), 88-104.

Guba, E. G., & Lincoln, Y. S. (1981). *Effective evaluation: Improving the usefulness of evaluation results through responsive and naturalistic approaches.* San Francisco: Jossey-Bass.

Gunn, S. L., & Peterson, C. A. (1978). *Therapeutic recreation program design: Principles and practices.* Englewood Cliffs, NJ: Prentice-Hall.

Halberg, K. J., & Howe-Murphy, R. (1985). The dilemma of an unresolved philosophy in therapeutic recreation. *Therapeutic Recreation Journal, 19*(3), 7-16.

Heintzman, P. (2008). Leisure-spiritual coping: A model for therapeutic recreation and leisure services. *Therapeutic Recreation Journal, 42* (1), 56-73.

Hood, C. D., & Carruthers, C. (2007). Enhancing leisure experiences and developing resources: The Leisure and Well-Being Model, Part II. *Therapeutic Recreation Journal, 41*(4), 298-325.

Howe-Murphy, R., & Charboneau, B. G. (1987). *Therapeutic recreation intervention: An ecological perspective.* Englewood Cliffs, NJ: Prentice-Hall.

Howe-Murphy, R. & Murphy, J. (1987). An exploration of the New Age consciousness paradigm in therapeutic recreation. In C. Sylvester, J. Hemingway, R., Howe-Murphy, K. Mobily, & P. Shank (Eds.), *Philosophy of therapeutic recreation: Ideas and issues* (pp. 41-54). Arlington, VA: National Recreation and Park Association.

Individuals with Disabilities Education Improvement Act of 2004, Pub. L. No. 108-446, U.S.C. (2004).

Kelly, J. R. (1996). *Leisure* (3rd ed.). Needham Heights, MA: Allyn & Bacon.

Kelly, J. R., & Godbey, G. (1992). *The sociology of leisure.* State College, PA: Venture.

Lee, L. L. (1987). A panic attack in therapeutic recreation over being considered therapeutic. *Therapeutic Recreation Journal, 32*, 118-123.

Lee, Y. (1998). Critique of Austin's Health Protection and Health Promotion Model. *Therapeutic Recreation Journal, 32*, 118-123.

Losardo, A., & Notari-Syverson, A. (2001). Alternative approaches to assessing young children. Retrieved March 04, 2007, from http://textbooks.brookespublishing.com/losardo/chapter1/keyterms.htm.

National Council for Therapeutic Recreation Certification. (n.d.). *"CTRS Profile"* Retrieved March 01, 2007, http://nctrc.org/documents/NCTRCProfileBroch_001.pdf.

National Council on Disability. (1998). Reorienting disability research. Retrieved March 02, 2007, from http://www.ncd.gov/newsroom/publications/1998/reorienting.htm.

National Wellness Institute. (n.d.). *Six Dimensional Wellness Model.* Retrieved March 01, 2007, http://www.nationalwellness.org/index.php?id=391&id_tier=381.

Mannell, R. C., & Kleiber, D. A. (1997). *A social psychology of leisure.* State College, PA: Venture.

Meyer, L. E. (1981). Three philosophical positions of therapeutic recreation and their implication for professionalization and NTRS/NRPA. *Therapeutic Recreation Journal, 15*(2), 7-16.

Mobily, K. E. (1985a). A philosophical analysis of therapeutic recreation: What does it mean to say, "We can be therapeutic?" Part I. *Therapeutic Recreation Journal, 19*(1), 14-26.

Mobily, K. E. (1985b). A philosophical analysis of therapeutic recreation: What does it mean to say, "We can be therapeutic?" Part II. *Therapeutic Recreation Journal, 19*(2), 14-26.

Mobily, K. E. (1999). New horizons in models of practice in therapeutic recreation. *Therapeutic Recreation Journal, 33*, 174-192.

Mobily, K. E., Hunnicutt, B., & Weissinger, E. (1987). The means/ends controversy: A framework for understanding the value potential of TR. *Therapeutic Recreation Journal, 21*, 7-13.

Murray, S. B. (1998). A critique of the Self-Determination and Enjoyment Enhancement Model. *Therapeutic Recreation Journal, 32*, 272-282.

Neulinger, J. (1981). *To leisure: An introduction*. Boston: Allyn and Bacon.

New Jersey Department of Health and Senior Services. (2005). N.J.A.C. title 8 chapter 43H: Licensing standards for rehabilitation hospitals.

Pargament, K. I. (1997). *The psychology of religion and coping*. New York: The Guildford Press.

Parker, V. B., & Carmack, R. W. (1998). A critique of Van Andel's TR Service Delivery and TR Outcome Models. *Therapeutic Recreation Journal, 32*, 202-206.

Peterson, C. A. (1989). The dilemma of philosophy. In D. Compton (Ed.), *Issues in therapeutic recreation: A profession in transition* (pp. 21-34). Champaign, IL: Sagamore.

Peterson, C. A., & Gunn, S. L. (1984). *Therapeutic recreation program design: Principles and procedures* (2nd ed.). Englewood Cliffs, NJ: Prentice-Hall.

Peterson, C. A., & Stumbo, N. J. (2000). *Therapeutic recreation program design: Principles and procedures* (3rd ed.). Needham Heights, MA: Allyn & Bacon.

Pew Health Professions Commission. (1995). *Critical challenges: Revitalizing the health professions for the twenty-first century.* San Francisco: University of California - San Francisco Center for the Health Professions.

Porter, H. R., & burlingame, j. (2006). *Recreational therapy handbook of practice: ICF-based diagnosis and treatment.* Ravensdale, WA: Idyll Arbor.

Reel, H. A., & Kleiber, D. A. (2008). Promoting positive aging through the therapeutic use of animals: Theoretical underpinnings and practical possibilities. *Annual in Therapeutic Recreation,18*, 142-152.

Reynolds, R. P., & O'Morrow, G. S. (1985). *Problems, issues, and concepts in therapeutic recreation.* Englewood Cliffs, NJ: Prentice-Hall.

Richter, K., & Kashchaulk, S. M. (1996). The future of therapeutic recreation: An existential outcome. In C. Sylvester (Ed.), *Philosophy of therapeutic recreation: Ideas and issues, Volume II* (pp. 86-91). Ashburn, VA: National Therapeutic Recreation Society/National Recreation and Park Association.

Riley, B., & Connolly, P. (2007). A profile of certified therapeutic recreation specialist practitioners. *Therapeutic Recreation Journal, 41* (1), 29-46.

Roberts, S. (1993). *Who we are: A portrait of America based on the latest U.S. census.* N.Y.: Times Books/Random House.

Ross, J. (1998). Critique of Austin's Health Protection/Health Promotion Model. *Therapeutic Recreation Journal, 32*, 124-129.

Russoniello, C. V. (1994). Recreational therapy: A medical model. In D. Compton, & S. E. Iso-Ahola (Eds.), *Leisure and mental health* (pp. 247-258). Park City, UT: Family Development Resources.

Shank, J., & Coyle, C. (2002). *Therapeutic recreation in health promotion and rehabilitation.* State College, PA: Venture.

Shank, J., & Kinney, T. (1987). On the neglect of clinical practice. In C. Sylvester, J. Hemingway, R. Howe-Murphy, K. Mobily, & P. Shank (Eds.), *Philosophy of therapeutic recreation: Ideas and issues, Volume I* (pp. 65-75). Alexandria, VA: National Recreation and Park Association.

Stumbo, N. J. (1996). A proposed accountability model for therapeutic recreation services. *Therapeutic Recreation Journal, 30,* 246-259.

Stumbo, N. J., & Hess, M. E. (2001). The status of client outcomes in selected programs as measured by adherence to the therapeutic recreation accountability mode. *Annual in Therapeutic Recreation, 10,* 45-56.

Stumbo, N. J., & Peterson, C. A. (1998). The Leisure Ability Model. *Therapeutic Recreation Journal, 32,* 82-95.

Stumbo, N. J., & Peterson, C. A. (2004). *Therapeutic recreation program design: Principles and procedures* (4th ed.). New York: Pearson Benjamin Cummings.

Stumbo, N. J., & Peterson, C. A. (2009). *Therapeutic recreation program design: Principles and procedures* (5th ed.). San Francisco: Pearson Benjamin Cummings.

Sylvester, C. (1985). Freedom, leisure, and therapeutic recreation: A philosophical view. *Therapeutic Recreation Journal, 19*(1), 6-13.

Sylvester, C. (1987). Therapeutic recreation and the end of leisure. In C. Sylvester, J. L. Hemingway, R. Howe-Murphy, K. Mobily, & P. A. Shank (Eds.), *Philosophy of therapeutic recreation: Ideas and issues, Volume I* (pp. 92-105). Alexandria, VA: National Recreation and Park Association.

Sylvester, C. (1996a). Instrumental rationality and therapeutic recreation: Revisiting the issue of means and ends. In C. Sylvester (Ed.), *Philosophy of therapeutic recreation: Ideas and issues, Volume II* (pp. 92-105). Alexandria, VA: National Recreation and Park Association.

Sylvester, C. (Ed.). (1996b). *Philosophy of therapeutic recreation: Ideas and issues, Volume II.* Alexandria, VA: National Recreation and Park Association.

Sylvester, C., Hemingway, J. L., Howe-Murphy, R., Mobily, K., & Shank, P. A. (Eds.). (1987). *Philosophy of therapeutic recreation: Ideas and issues, Volume I.* Alexandria, VA: National Recreation and Park Association.

United States Census Bureau. (2007). State and City Quick Facts. Retrieved March 01,2007, from http://quickfacts.census.gov/qfd/states/00000.html .

United States Department of Labor. (1998). *Occupational Outlook Handbook, 1998-99 Edition.* Chicago: Bureau of Labor Statistics.

United States Department of Health and Human Services. (2000). *Healthy People 2010: Understanding and improving health.* Washington, D.C.: Author.

Van Andel, G. E. (1998). TR Service Delivery and TR Outcome Models. *Therapeutic Recreation Journal, 32,* 180-193.

Voelkl, J., Carruthers, C., & Hawkins, B. (1997). Special series on therapeutic recreation practice models: Guest editors' introductory comments. *Therapeutic Recreation Journal, 31,* 210-212.

Widmer, M. A., & Ellis, G. D. (1998). The Aristotelian Good Life Model: Integration of values into therapeutic recreation service. *Therapeutic Recreation Journal, 32,* 290-302.

Wilhite, B., Keller, M. J., & Caldwell, L. (1999). Optimizing lifelong health and well-being: A health-enhancing model of therapeutic recreation. *Therapeutic Recreation Journal, 33,* 98-108.

Wilhite, B., Keller, J., Hodges, J., & Caldwell, L. (2004). Enhancing human development and optimizing health and well-being in persons with multiple sclerosis. *Therapeutic Recreation Journal, 38,* 167-187.

World Health Organization. (1984). Preamble to the Constitution of the World Health Organization as adopted by the International Health Conference, New York, 19 June - 22 July 1946; signed on 22 July 1946 by the representatives of 61 States (Official Records of the World Health Organization, no. 2, p. 100) and entered into force on 7 April 1948. Geneva, Switzerland: author.

World Health Organization. (2002). *Towards a common language for functioning, disability and health: ICF.* Geneva, Switzerland: author. Retrieved March 06, 2007, http://www.who.int/about/en/.

Yaffe, R. M. (1998). The Leisure Ability Model: A response from a service perspective. *Therapeutic Recreation Journal, 32,* 82-96.

CHAPTER 15

Integrating Evidence into Recreational Therapy Practice: An Important Focus for the Profession

Ray E. West, MS, LRT, CTRS™
Management and Consultation Services

Much has been written in the healthcare literature and the literature of various health and allied health professions, including therapeutic recreation, about evidence-based medicine, evidence-based care, and evidence-based practice, since the concept was introduced in the early 1990s. Haynes (2002) credits the origination of the term to clinical epidemiologists in 1991. The notion of basing healthcare and practice on empirical evidence fits well with current healthcare trends to reduce risks and harm to patients, to reduce unnecessary costs, and to consistently provide outcomes that are valued by key stakeholders such as patients or consumers, payers, employers, regulatory agencies and policy makers.

The recent increase in healthcare expenditures is expected to bring additional interest to the need to better manage the costs of healthcare. According to the National Center for Health Statistics (2007), national healthcare expenditures have risen to $2 trillion in 2005, a 7% increase over 2004. Healthcare expenditures in 2005 represented 16% of the gross domestic product (GDP), a larger share of the nation's GDP than any major industrialized country in the world (p. 375). One of the current trends in healthcare expenditures expected to be of concern to many in public policy positions is the increasing number of uninsured, including children and young adults, and the growing percentage of the middle class who are without health insurance. In Health, U.S. 2007 (National Center for Health Statistics, 2007), it is reported that the number of uninsured individuals, under the age of 65, has grown from 29.8 million persons in 1984 to 43.9 million persons in 2006 (p. 404). It is also reported in Health, U.S. 2007 that about 22.6 percent of those under the age of 65, uninsured for all or part of 2006, did not receive needed healthcare because of cost (p. 299). In response to these alarming healthcare trends, it should be expected that financing healthcare costs and controlling the rate of growth of health expenditures will receive renewed and increased attention by policy makers. As a result of the attention on healthcare costs, an increased focus on eliminating unnecessary costs of healthcare should also be expected in the near future.

The interest in reducing or containing healthcare expenditures will draw more attention to evidence-based care that consistently achieves valued outcomes. Evidence-based care can reduce variations in care and unnecessary costs, an important consideration in challenging financial times. Healthcare disciplines use evidence-based care to demonstrate they consistently achieve necessary outcomes that are valued by stakeholders. Evidence-based care becomes a means to demonstrate that healthcare disciplines are necessary and effective and should be supported, even during times that are financially challenging. This chapter will review aspects of the changing healthcare paradigm and will provide information about evidence-based practice including definitions of evidence-based practice, a description of the importance of evidence-based practice, the use of evidence as a basis for practice, steps to finding evidence, and ways to integrate evidence into recreational therapy practice. This chapter will also describe issues and concerns about integrating evidence into recreational therapy practice. For the purpose of this chapter, the term recreational therapy is defined as treatment services and interventions that are provided in clinical settings and are designed to restore, remediate, or rehabilitate patients in order to improve functioning and independence in life activities.

The Changing Healthcare Paradigm

Healthcare is continually evolving, but in the past eight years the rate and amount of changes in healthcare have dramatically accelerated. In 1999, the Institute of Medicine (IOM), a private non-profit organization that provides advice about health policy under a congressional charter granted to the National Academy of Sciences, issued the report titled *To Err is Human: Building a Safer Health System*, that reported as many as 44,000 people and possibly as many as 98,000 people die in hospitals each year from preventable medical errors (IOM, 1999, p. 1). The IOM report also identified that total cost of the errors amounted to between $17 billion and $29 billion per year, taking into account additional care necessitated by the errors, lost income and productivity, and disability. This report generated a rapid and significant public and private national response that resulted in an increased focus on safety, risk management, cost-effective care, and evidence-based healthcare that continues today. Watson (2000, p. 3-7) described aspects of the changing paradigm in healthcare that has been experienced in response to the increased need to demonstrate cost-effective care including:

- A move away from doing everything, sometimes anything, for our patients, regardless of outcomes, to a focus on providing services of proven value by those with specific expertise;
- The new focus of healthcare service delivery is equitable and appropriate allocation of resources to people who have the potential to achieve worthwhile outcomes; and

- The goal of national, state, and local service delivery initiatives is to offer more cost-effective services by providing the right service to the right person at the right time in the right setting. (Watson, 2000)

Several different drivers of the change in the healthcare paradigm were also discussed by Watson (2000), including:

1. Consumers are still interested in high-quality care, but are also more concerned about the amount of money spent.
2. Payers are more sophisticated and more concerned buyers of healthcare.
3. There is substantial evidence of the variability, in services provided to address a health problem, as well as quality of care, cost of care, and outcomes.
4. Policy makers are, once again, interested in reform to at least slow the growth, if not reduce, the national expenditures for healthcare, because expenditures have increased without measurable improvement in general health and well-being.
5. In response to growing pressure for fiscal accountability and the need to manage expenses to produce positive operating margins, healthcare administrators and practitioners must be more focused on effectiveness and efficiency of services provided. (Watson, 2000, p. 3-7)

In the best of financial times, this changing paradigm requires healthcare disciplines, including recreational therapy, to demonstrate evidence that their services contribute to valued outcomes achieved as an aspect of cost-effective service. In challenging financial times and in response to the IOM report, the pressure for accountability has increased significantly. Demonstrating cost-effective, evidence-based outcomes is necessary to maintain the resources needed to provide effective care and to survive as a service or discipline in healthcare settings.

To address the concern for cost-effective healthcare, the Institute of Medicine (IOM) proposed recommendations to redesign healthcare in a 2001 report titled *Crossing the Quality Chasm: A New Health System for the 21st Century*. In this report the IOM (2001) recommended that the healthcare system should better meet patients' core healthcare needs and be:

- Safe: avoiding injuries to patients from the care that is intended to help them.
- Effective: providing services based on scientific knowledge to all who could benefit and refraining from providing services to those not likely to benefit.
- Patient-centered: providing care that is respectful of and responsive to individual patient preferences, needs, values, and ensuring that patient values guide all clinical decisions.
- Timely: reducing waits and sometimes harmful delays for both those who receive and those who give care.
- Efficient: avoiding waste, including waste of equipment, supplies, ideas, and energy.
- Equitable: providing care that does not vary in quality because of personal characteristics such as gender, ethnicity, geographic location, and socioeconomic status. (IOM, 2001, p. 3)

The IOM report, *Crossing the Quality Chasm* (2001), recommended evidence-based decision making as one of the ten rules of redesign: "Decision making is evidence-based. Patients should receive care based upon the best scientific knowledge. Care should not vary illogically from clinician to clinician or place to place" (p. 4).

The emphasis on making decisions based upon evidence that care provided to patients should be based upon the best scientific knowledge and that variance in care should be reduced underscores the primary focus of evidence-based practice and the reasons for the change in the paradigm for healthcare. In describing the new paradigm for healthcare, Watson (2000) wrote:

> The new healthcare environment and our professional ethics demand that we be able to predict, on average or within a certain range, the outcome of treatment before it begins; achieve that outcome on or before the predicted date; provide the highest possible, most sustainable level of functional improvement at the lowest cost; and offer satisfaction to our customers. (p. 3)

Given this scenario, a logical question for the discipline is how can recreational therapists consistently and predictably reach valued patient outcomes? An answer to this question is that recreational therapists are more likely to consistently and predictably achieve outcomes valued by stakeholders by demonstrating consistent, relevant competencies and by practicing consistent, evidence-based care. Evidence-based medicine has been described by Sackett, Rosenberg, Gray, Haynes, and Richardson (1996) as:

> Evidence-based medicine is the conscientious, explicit, and judicious use of current best evidence in making decisions about the care of individual patients. The practice of evidence-based medicine means integrating individual clinical expertise with the best available external clinical evidence from systematic research. (p. 71)

Haynes (2002) noted that there are many variations of the term evidence-based medicine, but the objectives of the various terms remain the same (p. 2). Two definitions of evidence-based practice (EBP) are provided to delineate emphasis and focus for recreational therapists. In the first, McKibbon (1998) defined evidence-based practice as:

> Evidence-based practice (EBP) is an approach to healthcare wherein health professionals use the best evidence possible, i.e., the most appropriate information available, to make clinical decisions for individual patients. EBP values, enhances, and builds on clinical expertise, knowledge of disease mechanisms, and pathophysiology. It involves complex and conscientious decision-making based not only on the available evidence but also on patient characteristics, situations, and preferences. It recognizes that healthcare is individualized and ever changing and involves uncertainties and probabilities. Ultimately, EBP is the formalization of the care process that the best clinicians have practiced for generations. (p. 396)

West (2006) defined EBP to include professional standards of practice and practice delivered in accordance with clinical practice guidelines:

> Evidence-based recreational therapy practice is based upon the judicious use of the current best evidence to make effective clinical decisions about the treatment of patients to reach outcomes valued by stakeholders. Evidence-based practice is consistent with professional standards of practice. Evidence-based practice encompasses both individualized treatment plans and treatment delivered by the use of clinical practice guidelines or clinical pathways. (p. 3)

McKibbon emphasized that EBP builds upon the clinical expertise, including knowledge of disease mechanisms and pathophysiology competencies that is developed by physicians in their training and practice. McKibbon also described that the best evidence is integrated with clinical expertise and patient characteristics, situations, and preferences. West added that evidence-based recreational therapy practice is consistent with professional standards of practice and encompasses both individualized assessment and treatment, and treatment delivered by the application of clinical guidelines and pathways. Both definitions clarify and enhance the traditional definition of evidence-based medicine. The extensive literature on evidence-based medicine, care, and practice describes many definitions and variations of the traditional definition. Stumbo (2003a), in *Client Outcomes in Therapeutic Recreation Services*, cited a number of healthcare authors and identified other synonymous terms for evidence-based practice including: empirically validated treatment, empirically supported treatment, empirically evaluated treatment, empirical practice, research-based practice, research utilization, evidence-based treatment, and evidence-based healthcare (p. 26).

While many terms have been used to define clinical practice based upon the best evidence available, the trend toward EBP has been with us since the early 1990s and is expected to continue to be a trend in healthcare until some of the variations in healthcare services that result in unnecessary costs and risk of harm or actual harm to consumers are significantly reduced.

Importance of Evidence-based Practice

The idea that practice should be based upon evidence in order to achieve valued patient outcomes has gained significant support over the years. Haynes (2002), a healthcare author, described that EBM is linked to quality healthcare:

> A fundamental assumption of EBM is that practitioners whose practice is based upon an understanding of evidence from applied healthcare research will provide superior patient care compared with practitioners who rely on understanding of basic mechanisms and their own clinical experience. (p. 2)

A number of authors, including those of therapeutic recreation literature, have noted the importance of evidence-based practice. In the popular text *Therapeutic Recreation Program Design: Principles and Procedures*, Stumbo and Peterson (2009) identified evidence-based practice as one of two trends affecting therapeutic recreation program design, the second trend being theory-based programming (p. 110). Russoniello (2003) credited the systematic development of evidence-based practice as an effective way to ensure success at achieving patient outcomes (p. 113). Lee and McCormick (2001, 2002) discussed the value of empirical practice and research (e.g., evidence) as a basis for practice.

Another approach to understanding the importance of evidence-based practice is to consider the alternatives to EBP. Because recreational therapists are not trained in pathophysiology and do not develop extensive knowledge of disease mechanisms, if the care or treatment interventions provided by recreational therapists are not based upon evidence, what is the basis or rationale for providing the care or using the interventions used to treat patients? Is it the customary practice or a current trend? Is it the opinion of colleagues or the desire of practitioners to use a particular intervention? Evidence must drive practice decisions to provide safe and effective care and treatment to consistently reach outcomes valued by stakeholders. With the focus on outcomes within the financially strained healthcare system, evidence-based practice has become the routine method of practice for many healthcare disciplines. Consistent, evidence-based practice is the best means for recreational therapists to demonstrate contributions to valued outcomes and cost-effective healthcare. More stakeholders need to understand the value and benefits of recreational therapy if the discipline is to be supported in challenging financial times. Consistent and competent practice incorporating the principles of EBP provides the best opportunity for recreational therapists to gain the understanding and support of stakeholders.

Use of Evidence as the Basis for Practice

Patrick (2001) described the need for evidence-based therapeutic recreation in the statement "TR finds itself seeking legitimacy in a culture that is embracing an evidence-based model; thus it is thrust into a somewhat uncomfortable role of providing evidence of efficacy for all of its treatments" (p. 401). Patrick (2001) proposed that clinical evaluation, often conducted as an aspect of quality improvement activities and clinical research, is a means to demonstrate evidence of the effectiveness of therapeutic recreation (p. 406). Watson (2000) described the types of evaluations and research that may be used in clinical practice to demonstrate the value of a clinical service including clinical evaluations, program evaluations, and economic evaluations (pp. 10-12). Clinical evaluations determine the effects of interventions and include efficacy evaluations to determine the benefits of the intervention expected when conducted in highly controlled or ideal situations with highly skilled staff and effectiveness evaluations to determine the benefits of the intervention expected when conducted with average skilled staff in ordinary circumstances (Watson, 2000, p. 10). Program evaluations assess the structure, process, and outcome for a service or intervention (Watson, 2000, p. 10). Economic evaluations are necessary to evaluate costs and outcomes of different service options to determine relative value of the service options (Watson, 2000, p. 12).

If the premise is accepted that evidence-based recreational therapy practice is a way to consistently and predictably achieve valued patient outcomes and ensure greater understanding and support for the provision of services, then the challenge becomes how

and where should recreational therapists begin to demonstrate evidence-based practice? Stumbo (2003a) cited the writing of Belsey and Snell (2001) and identified the four actions of healthcare personnel who demonstrate evidence-based practice:
1. Production of evidence through research and scientific review;
2. Production and dissemination of evidence-based clinical guidelines;
3. Implementation of evidence-based, cost-effective practice through education and management of change; and
4. Evaluation of compliance with agreed practice guidance and patient outcomes; this process is called clinical audit. (p. 26)

West (2006) offered several recommendations for demonstrating evidence-based recreational therapy practice, including:
- Recreational therapists must demonstrate an increased focus on patient safety and risk management and must demonstrate that they help patients and do not put patients at risk, or worse yet, cause harm.
- Recreational therapists must provide well-designed interventions that are structured to consistently and predictably achieve worthwhile outcomes supported by evidence-based care literature.
- Recreational therapists must demonstrate they are competent and skilled providers of interventions that treat patient needs and problems associated with a particular illness or medical condition as documented in evidence-based care literature.
- Recreational therapists must evaluate services and interventions, often through quality-management activities, to demonstrate that interventions and services are effective in meeting specific health needs of defined patient populations.
- Recreational therapists must demonstrate the relative value (an analysis of costs of the intervention provided versus outcomes) and cost-effectiveness of the outcomes achieved so policy makers can make informed decisions about which services and interventions to provide. (p. 4-5)

These recommendations expanded and delineated various ways recreational therapists could integrate evidence-based practice into routine work responsibilities. The actions to demonstrate EBP, as described by Stumbo, should be collectively implemented by recreational therapists, educators, and those who conduct evaluation and research to determine the effectiveness of recreational therapy services. This collective approach could change the paradigm of how therapists are prepared for practice.

Perhaps Stumbo (2003a) provided the best statement in support of evidence-based practice "through evidence-based service delivery, each practitioner should feel confident that she or he is providing the best possible care that is known to produce the most desirable, intended, and meaningful outcomes" (p. 26). In a client-centered helping profession, can we have any other central focus, other than consistently producing the most meaningful outcomes for our patients?

Steps to Finding Evidence for Practice

EBP requires that evidence is a foundation for effective clinical decision making. The process of EPB involves integrating evidence about clinical effectiveness with knowledge about a patient's circumstances and preferences to influence decisions about patient care. Decisions are made by incorporating the clinician's expertise and clinical judgment with the evidence and knowledge about the patient. EBP starts with finding the evidence that will be used in clinical decisions. Stumbo (2003a) cited Sackett (1997) and Straus and Sackett (1998) and identified the five steps to connect research evidence and practice.
1. Formulate a clear clinical question from a patient's problem.
2. Search databases for relevant clinical evidence.
3. Appraise the evidence.
4. Implement and use findings in practice.
5. Evaluate the impact of change in practice. (p. 31-36)

Stumbo (2003a) cited Belsey and Snell (2001) and Straus and Sackett (1998) and identified the four components of a focused clinical question that must be the basis of formulating a clear, clinical question from a patient's problem:
1. the patient or problem being addressed,
2. the intervention being considered (i.e., cause, prognostic factor, or treatment),
3. another intervention for comparison when relevant, and
4. the clinical outcomes of interest (p. 31).

In Step 1, using the four components of a clear clinical question, an example of a clinical question might be "Will a 20-year-old patient with anorexia nervosa benefit more from a progressive muscle relaxation and imagery intervention or from a biofeedback intervention to reduce anxiety associated with eating?" In Step 2, the evidence to assist in answering the clinical question would be searched for and located. Evidence might include research literature, diagnostic or treatment protocols, standards, quality improvement data, medical record documentation audit data, clinical evaluation data, program evaluation data, or data from various evaluations of cost effectiveness according to predetermined rules for evaluating and accepting the elements selected as evidence (Stumbo, 2003a, p. 33-34). Stumbo (2003a) and Lee and McCormick (2001) identified resources for finding evidence including online research and evidence-based sites and databases (See Stumbo, 2003a, p. 33-34; Lee & McCormick, 2001, p. 179-180 for evidence-based care research sites and databases). In Step 3, the strength of evidence is evaluated. Stumbo (2003a) cited Belsey and Snell (2001) and Lee and McCormick (2002), who identified the following five-level scheme to classify the strength of research evidence (p. 35-36).

- Level I (Highest): Strong evidence from at least one systematic review of multiple well-designed, randomized controlled trials;
- Level II: Strong evidence from at least one properly designed, randomized controlled trial of appropriate size;
- Level III: Evidence from well-designed trials such as nonrandomized trials, cohort studies, time series, or matched-case controlled studies;

- Level IV: Evidence from well-designed, nonexperimental studies from more than one center or research group; and
- Level V (Weakest): Opinions of respected authorities based on clinical evidence, descriptive studies, or reports of expert committees.

Stumbo (2003a) referenced Belsey and Snell (2001) and identified that when using this evaluation scheme, questions to be answered include: "Are the results of the review valid? What are the results? Will the results help me locally?" (p. 35). In Step 4, the results of the search for evidence are used to answer the relevant clinical question raised initially and to determine the best treatment to provide, taking into account the relevance and applicability of the evidence to the case and situation that was the basis of the clinical question. In this step, the clinician integrates the evidence with knowledge of the patient's circumstances and preferences and uses clinical judgment to make decisions about the best treatment to provide. Stumbo identified Step 5 as the evaluation of the impact of the change in practice (p. 36). The evaluation would involve formative evaluation, such as progress evaluated during the process of providing treatment, and summative evaluation such as patient outcomes that result from the treatment provided. In this stage, the primary question to be answered is: "Did the process and outcome work effectively in answering the patient treatment question that was the basis of the evidence-review?"

This section presented a very simplified review of the basic steps to searching for evidence and a five-level scheme for determining the strength of the evidence found to provide a general understanding of the process involved in determining evidence to be used in clinical practice. For a more thorough understanding of the basics of searching for evidence upon which to base practice, the following chapters are recommended reading: *The Importance of Evidence-Based Practice in Therapeutic Recreation* (Stumbo, 2003a, p. 25-48) and *Toward Evidence-Based Therapeutic Recreation Practice* (Lee & McCormick, 2002, p. 165-183). Assistance and training should be sought from medical librarians, who are an excellent resource for learning how to conduct searches for evidence-based care.

Implementing Evidence-Based Recreational Therapy Practice

Lee and McCormick (2002) provided a model for evidence-based practice that integrates concepts of evidence-based practice with the stages of direct practice or treatment: assess, plan, implement, and evaluate (p. 171-174). In this model, Lee and McCormick provided examples of how practitioners might integrate empirical practice and evidence-based practice into the routine functions of recreational therapy practice. An adapted version of the model is provided in Figure 15.1. In this adapted model of practice (see Figure 15.1) the central focus is competent, evidence-based, and client-centered practice. The idea of client-centered practice is well described in therapeutic recreation literature. The model in Figure 15.1 introduces the idea that competent practice should include an evidence-based as well as a client-centered approach to service provision including assessment, treatment planning, treatment implementation, and evaluation of treatment and outcomes. In regard to defining competent practice, the *ATRA Guidelines for Competency Assessment and Curriculum Planning for Recreational Therapy Practice* provide a detailed description of the knowledge, skills, and abilities necessary for effective practice and also provide self-assessment guides to assist in

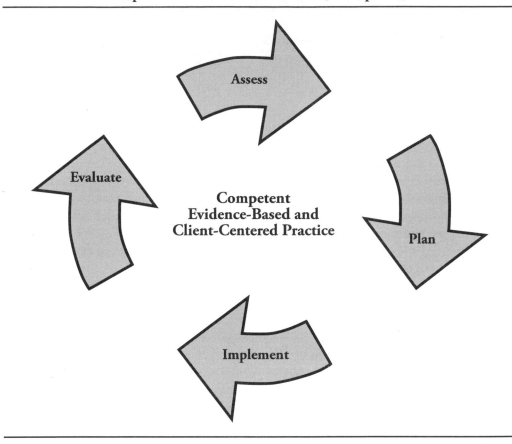

Figure 15.1
Model for Evidence-Based and Client-Centered Practice
Adapted from Lee and McCormick (2002, p. 172)

determining the degree of compliance one has with the recommended competencies. Also, other chapters in this text discuss the issues of academic preparation and competencies. The following description of the routine functions of recreational therapy practice includes examples related to the definition of EBP offered by West (2006) and incorporates suggestions offered by Lee and McCormick.

Assess

The American Therapeutic Recreation Association's (ATRA) *Standards for the Practice of Therapeutic Recreation* (SOP) were based upon a review of relevant literature, including standards of regulatory agencies, and developed through a consensus-building process using a modified Delphi approach (ATRA, 2000, p. 1-2). As a result, the SOP represents a type of preliminary evidence to guide practice. Adherence with professional standards of practice requires that agency structures, such as policies and procedures, be developed to guide practice so that it is performed in accordance with the standards and criteria in order to achieve patient outcomes. A way to incorporate evidence into the assessment process is to define and structure, by agency policies and procedures, a systematic and consistently performed assessment process that is completed in compliance with standards of practice requirements (ATRA, p. 9). Evidence should be used by the recreational therapist to increase understanding of the illness/disabling condition and factors relevant to treatment including etiology, diagnosis, symptoms and signs, course and progression, treatment needs, treatment, prognosis, activity limitations, and restrictions to participation. Lee and McCormick (2002) described the need to use valid and reliable assessment measures to collect baseline data for the purpose of identifying priorities for intervention and to compare the baseline level of functioning with the level of functioning after the intervention to assess the level of improvement, or outcome, achieved (p. 172). As the definition of evidence-based practice described, patient interests, preferences, and priorities for improved functioning are determined in the assessment to be used in planning the interventions to achieve the desired outcomes. Evidence-based practice must be incorporated into the assessment process if it is to be effective in guiding the planning, implementation, and evaluation of interventions used to reach patient outcomes.

Plan

According to the ATRA SOP, the process for planning treatment interventions is defined in agency policy and procedures and performed consistently in compliance with the standards and criteria of the SOP (ATRA, 2000, p. 11). The SOP requires that functional outcome goals are effectively written to connect assessed needs to planned interventions and to the planned outcomes. Lee and McCormick (2002) recommended that research and empirical evidence be used to identify the options and content for interventions to be used to address an assessed patient need and to assure that the intervention selected has a reasonable potential to reach the planned outcomes (p. 173). Evidence is incorporated with patient preferences and the clinical experience, and judgment of the recreational therapist is used to prioritize the most relevant needs to treat and the most effective interventions to use to reach the best outcomes. If the interventions selected incorporate client interests and preferences, patients may be more motivated to engage in the interventions and may be interested in continuing to use the interventions after active treatment. Incorporating evidence with patient interests and preferences as the basis to determine the interventions used to address needs may also enhance the likelihood that valued outcomes will be achieved.

Implement

The SOP structure criteria (ATRA, 2000) require that the process of providing treatment and interventions is defined in policy and procedures, and consistently performed in compliance with the content of the standards and criteria (p. 13). The structure criteria require that the type, frequency, duration, and intensity of the interventions needed to achieve the expected outcomes are selected and documented and are appropriate to the individual's diagnosis, age, and cultural and socioeconomic factors (p. 13). The implication is that therapists use evidence to not only select and plan the interventions to address assessed patient needs, but to also apply the interventions, using appropriate strategies, facilitation, and leadership techniques, in the manner most likely to enhance the effectiveness of the interventions and to achieve the outcomes desired. Lee and McCormick (2002) also recommended that evidence be used to determine the most effective manner of providing patient feedback to enhance imparting efficacy beliefs (p. 173). Patient efficacy beliefs can have a significant influence on the outcomes achieved and the likelihood that patients will continue to use the interventions to address assessed needs, potentially reducing the need for additional interventions.

Evaluate

In the final phase of the treatment process, Lee and McCormick (2002) recommended that practice and outcomes are evaluated to determine whether the services and interventions provided were effective in meeting the assessed patient needs (p. 173). Patrick (2001) also identified the need for effective evaluation often done as an aspect of quality improvement activities. The ATRA SOP (ATRA, 2000) structure standard and criteria for reassessment and evaluation require that procedures for reassessment and evaluation are documented in policies and procedures (p. 15). SOP criteria require that routine, systematic, and established methods for evaluation are included in the policies and procedures (p. 15). Formative and summative evaluation of the individualized treatment plan should be conducted. Lee and McCormick stated, "Practitioners can demonstrate effectiveness by systematically tracking whether the service provided achieved its intended results" (p. 173). Evaluation of the treatment plan and process can include the following factors: (a) whether functional outcome goals are achieved, (b) whether interventions are effective in addressing assessed patient needs and achieve goals of treatment, and (c) whether client outcomes (such as satisfaction, improved functioning, reduction of symptoms, etc.) are achieved.

Evaluation produces evidence of effectiveness. Evaluation also will identify opportunities for improving practice and interventions that will increase the predictability and consistency of valued outcomes achieved. Evaluation also will determine opportunities to reduce variations in practice that impede the achievement of valued outcomes. Finally, effective evaluation will identify opportunities for clinical and empirical research.

Integrating evidence into practice requires that evidence be used in each phase of the treatment process. Adherence to professional standards of practice provides a guide for the therapist of the structures and processes to use in practice, with an evidence-based approach to providing care and services, and will increase the likelihood that valued patient outcomes are achieved.

Issues and Concerns Associated with Evidence-Based Practice

No discussion about evidence-based practice is complete without a review of concerns associated with evidence-based practice. As compelling as the support for evidence-based practice is, some healthcare practitioners still have concerns about, or have difficulty using, an evidence-based approach to practice in their respective disciplines. The literature about evidence-based practice identifies concerns of healthcare disciplines that result from the pressures to increase evidence-based practice. This section will review issues and concerns about evidence-based practice and will present methods to address concerns and to increase the use of evidence in practice. Specific attention will be given to how to identify evidence and initiate the use of evidence in practice, in the academic preparation of new practitioners and in continuing education of those currently in practice.

Stumbo (2003a) identified the following problems and concerns associated with evidence-based practice that are documented in healthcare literature:

- Potential erosion of the autonomy of clinical practice while possibly increasing risk to the practitioner who does not adhere to established evidence-based norms for treatment.
- Empirical evidence to guide effective practice is limited by the quality and quantity of the research base, and better practice must be delivered while more convincing and relevant evidence is produced.
- Developing effective evidence-based clinical guidelines is time consuming, and the cost benefit of guidelines is uncertain.
- Implementation of evidence-based, cost-effective practice requires education, evidence-based evaluation and research skills, and a change in the paradigm for practice. (p. 36-41)

As unnecessary variations in recreational therapy practice are reduced by the use of evidence-based practice, the concerns identified by Stumbo may become more significant for the profession. Currently these concerns may be somewhat less significant until the profession demonstrates more consistent, evidence-based practice. Perhaps the greater concern at this time is how to integrate more evidence into practice.

Healthcare literature also addresses ways to address or resolve concerns about using an evidence-based approach to practice. Lee and McCormick (2002) identified the following actions as a means to increase evidence-based practice:

- Evidence-based practice requires a collaborative relationship between researchers and practitioners who must work together to produce the best clinical questions and the best evidence that is relevant for adoption in practice.
- Continuing education content should be based upon the best evidence to influence practice and should include opportunities to develop practice-oriented research training to enhance the skills needed to find and interpret evidence-based research.
- The academic curriculum that prepares new therapists needs to become evidence-based. This will necessitate using evidence in teaching practice skills and techniques as well as increasing the evaluation and research skills of those who will become therapists. (p. 178-180)

Widmer (2001) and Bedini (2001) identified the need to establish a greater depth and breadth of research to support outcomes as well as effectiveness and efficacy of services provided. Clearly evidence-based practice requires close collaboration between researchers and therapists to identify appropriate clinical questions to be researched for evidence. Evidence-based care research needs to have a high priority on the research agenda for recreational therapy. Efficacy and effectiveness research that documents the value and benefits of recreational therapy practice needs to be produced in much greater volumes. Until more evidence is available about specific interventions used by recreational therapists, evidence of the benefits of interventions used by allied disciplines and also used by recreational therapists should be studied to determine the related value for recreational therapy practice.

Stumbo (2003b, 2003c) contributed two very well-written articles to professional literature that described how to conduct systematic reviews and how to appraise systematic reviews for evidence-based practice. Stumbo cited Shannon (2002) and defined the term systematic review (p. 30):

> Systematic reviews can help clinical decision makers with the sheer volume of research literature. These reviews analyze and summarize the results of many research trials that assess the effects of healthcare to provide new information that may not be apparent or useful from small or individual studies. When combined with clinical expertise and patient values, this information can be used for clinical decision making.

Identifying Evidence to Improve Practice

The use of systematic reviews is a reasonable starting point to determine what evidence currently exists to improve practice. Systematic reviews can be used as a technique to assess the evidence about problems and needs routinely identified for the illnesses and disabling conditions most frequently treated by recreational therapists. Systematic reviews also can be used to assess the evidence for the interventions most frequently used by recreational therapists to treat assessed patient problems and needs. The results of systematic reviews can provide a focus for the professional research agenda and prioritize which controlled studies are most important. Systematic reviews also provide the information necessary for the development of clinical guidelines and pathways. A starting point for the systematic reviews could be the typical outcomes or benefits of therapeutic recreation interventions used to address specific patient needs and problems as reported by Coyle, Kinney, Riley, and Shank (1991). Evidence from systematic reviews can immediately be used by practitioners, educators, and researchers as a basis to improve evidence-based practice. For example, evidence should influence which patient needs and problems are selected for treatment as well as the interventions that are selected to treat the particular need or problem. Using evidence in this manner reduces variations in care and treatment provided and increases the likelihood that valued patient outcomes are achieved, which is a goal sought by all respected healthcare professions. As was discussed earlier, the use of methods to appraise the value or strength of the evidence is necessary before using the evidence in practice. Some consider that even the use of weak or preliminary evidence is better than no evidence, and when used judiciously by competent, experienced professionals, it can be useful in making clinical decisions and can provide direction for evaluation and research.

Use of Evidence in Continuing Education

Continuing education, including publications, workshops, and conferences, is another aspect of professional functioning that would benefit from an increased focus on evidence-based practice. Lee and McCormick (2002) recommended that continuing education should be evidence-based. Publications used for continuing education are usually based upon reviews of related literature, some of which are evidence-based care literature. Publishing systematic reviews of evidence in journals and on association web sites and focusing more content in professional journals on evidence-based practice would make evidence more readily available to practitioners and educators. Those sponsoring conferences and workshops, as a form of continuing education, have an opportunity and a responsibility to incorporate more evidence into the presentations to establish an evidence-based and outcomes focus to some of the presentations. To increase the awareness of evidence for practice, more presentations are needed on the relationship between assessed patient needs and evidence-based care interventions that can be used to achieve valued patient outcomes. Conference presentations and workshops could also devote additional content to developing evidence-based care research skills, as Lee and McCormick (2002) recommended. The use of evidence-based care case studies is another means to incorporate preliminary evidence about outcomes achieved as a result of interventions provided in practice. Evidence-based case studies use evidence to connect assessed needs with functional outcome goals and interventions provided to achieve valued patient outcomes. Evidence-based case studies can provide an initial evaluation of the effectiveness of the services and interventions provided and can be used as a means to encourage more evidence-based care presentations at conferences and more evidence-based care research. Recreational therapists should seek training in the basics of evidence-based practice, writing functional outcome goals, and developing evidence-based case studies to improve the consistency and predictability of achieving valued patient outcomes.

Toward Evidence-Based Academic Preparation

Lee and McCormick (2002) recommended that curricula prepare new therapists by integrating evidence-based care into the skills for practice that are being taught (p. 180). O'Neil and The Pew Health Professions Commission (1998) recommended in the publication *Re-creating Health Professional Practice for a New Century* that all professional groups establish competency in evidence-based care.

Competency 3: Provide evidence-based, clinically competent care.
- Health professionals are obligated to provide clinically competent care, driven by the latest knowledge from the biological, behavioral, discipline-specific, and health management sciences. This challenge grows with the rapid expansion of new knowledge and the growing complexity of the health system, but it can be made manageable through awareness and use of information technologies like computerized decision-support. Health professionals must be able to evaluate a variety of sources on care-related evidence, including current research findings and clinical practice guidelines, and apply them appropriately to the management and treatment of disease. Any application must be measured against its ability to provide empirical evidence of contributing to enhancing outcomes or making more efficient use of scarce resources.
- Design and implement a curriculum that reflects up-to-date knowledge from the biological and behavioral sciences, the practice of the discipline, and the health management sciences.
- Incorporate research findings and clinical practice guidelines in the curriculum as sources of information for providing evidence-based care.

- Supervise, mentor, and evaluate students' acquisition of the identified clinical competencies (knowledge, skills, values) that are essential for contemporary practice. (p. 30)

As is described in several chapters in this text (see chapters in Section II: Education Issues), much needs to be done to improve the consistency of academic preparation and competency of new therapists. Integrating competency in evidence-based practice into curricula may be a challenge for some academic programs but one that is necessary to meet the current demands for evidence-based practice in healthcare settings. Teaching basic evaluation and evidence-based research skills is necessary, but incorporating the use of research evidence into the teaching of all aspects of practice skills including assessment, planning, implementation, evaluation, and management of practice must also be a high priority if students (future therapists) are to develop the necessary competency for practice recommended by the Pew Health Professions Commission.

Summary

Evidence-based practice has been described in healthcare literature since the early 1990s and is becoming more prevalent in the literature of allied health professions, including recreational therapy. The value and benefit of evidence-based care in reducing unnecessary variations in care, contributing to reductions of unnecessary costs, and improving the quality of care is well described in the literature. Those who influence policy have consistently recommended that healthcare and allied health disciplines include more use of evidence in practice. As a result, healthcare and allied health disciplines have developed more knowledge and skills in using evidence in practice.

Demonstrating consistent, relevant practice competencies and practicing evidence-based care can be perceived as a significant challenge for recreational therapists. While this might be true, the questions about effectiveness of interventions and benefits of recreational therapy in treating patients with various illnesses and medical conditions can only be answered by consistent evidence of valued outcomes achieved. As advocated by Lee and McCormick (2002), therapists, educators, and researchers need to increase collaboration to improve the amount and effectiveness of evidence-based recreational therapy practice. Universities, credentialing organizations, and professional associations that prepare practitioners, assess entry-level competency, and provide support for the profession, also need to adopt more practice-centered and evidence-based thinking to enhance their contributions to professional practice. Competent, evidence-based recreational therapy practice is the best way to enable the discipline to thrive in the very competitive healthcare work environment. Proponents of evidence-based practice argue that the paradigm for educating therapists for practice and the focus of maintaining life-long professional competency in healthcare settings must change to become significantly more evidence-based. In healthcare settings the patient is the focus of the care provided and outcomes are increasingly used to measure effectiveness and value. It is time for the discipline of recreational therapy to refocus the practice paradigm to be more evidence-based to complement the client-centered focus. Given the growing challenges for accountability in healthcare settings, those interested in the discipline of recreational therapy are encouraged to consider the question: If not evidence-based care, what means should be employed to demonstrate that recreational therapy is a necessary and effective treatment service that should be provided in healthcare settings?

Discussion Questions

1. What evidence currently exists to support the value and benefits of recreational therapy in healthcare settings? Identify the evidence and the evidence-based care resources used to support your conclusion about the benefits and value of recreational therapy.
2. How can professional associations increase the evidence that supports recreational therapy practice? Identify specific actions that are currently provided by professional associations and new actions that should be taken to increase the evidence that supports recreational therapy practice.
3. How can the National Council for Therapeutic Recreation Certification (NCTRC™) contribute to the effort to increase evidence-based recreational therapy practice? Identify current efforts of NCTRC™ that support evidence-based practice and new efforts you recommend that NCTRC™ take to increase evidence-based recreational therapy practice.
4. How can the competencies required for evidence-based recreational therapy practice be consistently developed by university academic programs? What specific steps should be taken by universities to increase the competencies and the consistency of preparation for evidence-based practice and to reduce variations in practice and outcomes?
5. How will you increase your competency to practice evidence-based recreational therapy? Develop a personal development plan that identifies specific competencies to be obtained for evidence-based practice, the date you will demonstrate the competency, the method you will use to obtain the competency, and the method you will use to assess the level of competency achieved.
6. Select a healthcare profession and search their literature. How are they prepared for evidence-based practice? Are they ahead or behind us in application of evidence-based practice?

References

American Therapeutic Recreation Association. (2000). *Standards for the practice of therapeutic recreation & self-assessment guide.* Arlington, VA: Author.

Belsey, J., & Snell, T. (2001). What is evidence-based medicine? Retrieved November 9, 2002, from http://www.evidence-based-medicine.co.uk.

Bedini, L. A. (2001). Status of therapeutic recreation research. In N.J. Stumbo (Ed.), *Professional issues in therapeutic recreation: On competence and outcomes.* (pp. 335-348). Champaign, IL: Sagamore.

Coyle, C. P., Kinney, W. B., & Shank, J. W. (1991). A summary of benefits common to therapeutic recreation. In C. P. Coyle, W. B. Kinney, B. Riley, & J. W. Shank (Eds.), *Benefits of therapeutic recreation: A consensus view* (pp. 353-385). Philadelphia, PA: Temple University Press.

Haynes, R. B. (2002, March 6). What kind of evidence is it that evidence-based medicine advocates want healthcare providers and consumers to pay attention to? BMC Health Services Research. 2. Retrieved August 17, 2006 from http://www.biomedcentral.com/1472- 6963/2/3

The Institute of Medicine. (1999). Report Brief. To err is human: Building a safer health system. The Institute of Medicine of the National Academies. Washington, D.C. Retrieved April 16, 2007 from: http://www.iom.edu

The Institute of Medicine (2001). Report Brief Crossing the Quality Chasm: A New Health System for the 21st Century. The Institute of Medicine of the National Academies. Washington, D.C. Retrieved August 17, 2006 from: http://www.iom.edu

Lee, Y., & McCormick, B. P. (2001). Research into practice: Building knowledge through empirical practice. In N. J. Stumbo (Ed.), *Professional issues in therapeutic recreation: On competence and outcomes.* (pp. 383-389). Champaign, IL: Sagamore.

Lee, Y., & McCormick, B. P. (2002). Toward evidence-based therapeutic recreation practice. In D. R. Austin, J. Dattilo, & B. P. McCormick (Eds.), *Conceptual foundations for therapeutic recreation* (pp. 165-183). State College, PA: Venture.

McKibbon, K. A. (1998). Evidence-based practice, *Bulletin of the Medical Library Association. 86*(3), 396-401.

National Center for Health Statistics. (2007). Health, United States, 2007 with chartbook on trends in the health of Americans (DHHS Publication No.2007-1232). Washington, D.C.: U.S. Government Printing Office.

O'Neil, E. H., & the Pew Health Professions Commission. (1998). *Recreating health professional practice for a new century.* San Francisco: Pew Health Professions Commission.

Patrick, G. (2001). Clinical research: Methods and mandates. In N. J. Stumbo (Ed.), *Professional issues in therapeutic recreation: On competence and outcomes.* (pp. 401-418). Champaign, IL: Sagamore.

Russoniello, C. V . (2003). The efficacy of therapeutic recreation: Back to the future. In N. J. Stumbo (Ed.), *Client outcomes in therapeutic recreation services* (pp. 111-126). State College, PA:Venture.

Sackett, D. L., Rosenberg. W. M., Gray, J. A., Haynes, R. B., & Richardson, W. S. (1996). *Evidence-based medicine: What it is and what it isn't.* [Electronic Version]. *British Medical Journal, 312,* 71-72.

Sackett, D. L. (1997). Evidence-based medicine. *Seminars in Perinatology, 21*(1), 3-5.

Sackett, D. L., & Straus, S. E. (1998). Finding and applying evidence during clinical rounds: The evidence cart. *Journal of the American Medical Association, 280*(15), 1336-1338.

Straus, S. E., & Sackett, D. L. (1998). Using research findings in clinical practice. *British Medical Journal, 317,* 339-342.

Stumbo, N. J. (2003a). The importance of evidence-based practice. In N. J. Stumbo (Ed.), *Client outcomes in therapeutic recreation services* (pp. 25-48). State College, PA: Venture.

Stumbo, N. J. (2003b). Systematic reviews part I: How to conduct systematic reviews for evidence-based practice. *Annual in Therapeutic Recreation, 12, 29-44.*

Stumbo, N. J. (2003c). Systematic reviews part II: How to appraise systematic reviews for evidence-based practice. *Annual in Therapeutic Recreation, 12,* 45-56.

Stumbo, N. J., & Peterson, C. A. (2009). *Therapeutic recreation program design: Principles and procedures* (5ᵗʰ ed.). San Francisco: Benjamin Cummings.

Watson, D. E. (2000). *Evaluating costs and outcomes: Demonstrating the value of rehabilitation services.* Bethesda, MD: The American Occupational Therapy Association, Inc.

West, R. E. (2006, September/October) Demonstrating evidence-based recreational therapy practice. *ATRA Newsletter, 22,* 3-5.

Widmer, M. A. (2001). Methods for outcome research in therapeutic recreation. In N. J. Stumbo (Ed.), *Professional issues in therapeutic recreation: On competence and outcomes.* (pp. 365-381). Champaign, IL: Sagamore.

CHAPTER 16

Clinical Practice Guidelines: A Decision-Making Tool for Best Practice?

Nancy E. Richeson, Ph.D., CTRS™
University of Southern Maine

Suzanne Fitzsimmons, MS, ARNP-BC
University of North Carolina–Greensboro

Linda Buettner, Ph.D., CTRS™
University of North Carolina–Greensboro

Everyone of us has all we need…
In our yellow submarine.
– Paul McCartney

A new paradigm for the practice of recreational therapy is emerging. It is a de-emphasis on intuition, individual opinion, tradition, folklore, customs, and the reliance on "the way it was always done." In their place is the use of evidence-based practice guidelines to assist in clinical decision making. Evidence-based practice guidelines are published by first conducting extensive literature searches to find the most up-to-date research on a specific problem, and then these studies are evaluated to determine the strength of the clinical research literature. Finally, an expert consensus team makes recommendations for the profession based on this information. The next step in the guideline process is educating others to use the information and the process outlined. This is most commonly accomplished through professional continuing education and through recreational therapy degree programs that educate future therapists in the practice of evidence-based care. This education process includes how to read the research summarized in the practice guideline and how to apply it to a specific client or a specific situation. In addition, a commitment to lifelong learning is necessary to remain abreast of new research and evidence as it is updated every few years. This chapter will examine the issues of evidence-based practice, the barriers within and outside the profession, and some suggestions on how the profession can move toward this best-practice approach.

What is Evidence-based Practice?

Evidence-based practice includes an orderly identification and synthesis of scientific theories and scientific evidence that leads to the development of evidenced-based practice guidelines. A team of experts generally works together to examine research on a specific problem, locates the latest information, and grades it to identify the strength of each study (see Chapter 15). Evidence-based practice is the process of integrating individual clinical expertise with the profession's guidelines to make clinical decisions. Clinical decisions are made based on summarized research in the guideline that shows what works, with consideration to the particular client's strengths, weaknesses, likes, and dislikes. "The evidenced-based concept is highly favored by power holders in government and healthcare organizations because of its capability to (a) advance quality of care and services recreational therapists provide, (b) have fewer variations in recreational therapy practice, (c) provide cost savings that flow from appropriate and timely recreation therapy intervention use, and (d) improve health outcomes in general" (Buettner & Fitzsimmons, 2003, p. ii). The therapist who uses the combination of clinically relevant research, patient preferences, and clinical expertise ensures individualized and effective client care. See Table 16.1.

What are Evidenced-based Guidelines?

A standard definition of clinical practice guidelines (CPGs) is a manual of systematic statements developed to assist practitioners on selecting appropriate healthcare for specific situations (Field & Lohr, 1992). These guidelines summarize and evaluate the strength of the evidence related to a particular healthcare problem and make practice recommendations (Titler, 2002). Guidelines identify the questions and possible options related to best practice outcomes. Often guidelines will contain specific protocols for implementing best practice. Protocols are more specific than guidelines as they contain comprehensive information outlining the steps to implement a specific intervention.

The Agency for Healthcare Research and Quality (AHRQ), a part of the United States Department of Health and Human Services, is a federal agency whose mission is

---

Table 16.1
Purpose of Evidenced-Based Practice Guidelines

- Identify care based on the best available scientific evidence and expert consensus.
- Justify and highlight the need for continuing education.
- Promote cost-effective use of resources.
- Ensure quality control.
- Justify actions in cases of audits or lawsuits.
- Identify gaps in knowledge and research.
- Reduce the occurrence of ineffective interventions.
- Provide a direction for future research.

"improving the quality, safety, efficiency, and effectiveness of healthcare for all Americans" (AHRQ, 2005, p. 1). The AHRQ supports health services research that will improve the quality of healthcare and promote evidence-based decision making. This agency maintains The National Guideline Clearinghouse™ (NGC), a comprehensive database of evidence-based clinical practice guidelines and related documents. The NGC's (2007a) mission is "to provide physicians, nurses, and other health professionals, healthcare providers, health plans, integrated delivery systems, purchasers, and others an accessible mechanism for obtaining objective, detailed information on clinical practice guidelines and to further their dissemination, implementation, and use" (NGC, http://www.guideline.gov/about/about. aspx). This searchable database contains the guideline summaries and contact information for the specific guidelines. Guidelines may be submitted by a variety of different organizations, including societies and other developers of practice guidelines. The NGC currently has 1945 guideline summaries available on its website with an additional 200-plus guidelines in the process of being reviewed. For a document to be considered by NGC (2007b) as an evidenced-based guideline, it must meet all following criteria:

> The guideline must contain systematically developed recommendations, strategies, or other information to assist healthcare decision making in specific clinical circumstances; the guideline must have been produced under the auspices of a relevant professional organization (e.g., medical specialty society, government agency, healthcare organization, or health plan); the guideline development process must have included a verifiable, systematic literature search and review of existing evidence published in peer-reviewed journals; and the guideline must be current and the most recent version (i.e., developed, reviewed, or revised within the last five years).

Evidence-based practice is important across all healthcare disciplines. In fact, PubMed (U.S. National Institutes of Health, 2006) indexes 42 currently published healthcare journals featuring evidence-based medicine. Thousands of articles have been published in health and medical journals on the topic of evidence-based practice since the concept was introduced in the early 1990s. In these health and medical journals, there has been an explosion of information (M. K. Hartung, personal communication, May 15, 2006). Over the last decade, rapid advances have occurred in information technology, medical record keeping, and dissemination of health information. According to Hartung (personal communication, May 15, 2006) in 1997, over 100 million people were using the Internet worldwide, a number that increased to more than one billion by 2005. With so much specialized information about health problems and interventions that may help, it is daunting for practitioners in the recreational therapy field to sift through and make sense of it. Practice guidelines are written in a concise way to help practitioners digest the most current research and theories on specific topics so to better apply them to their everyday practice.

Using evidence-based practice guidelines is initially about asking the right questions and finding what practice guidelines are available for clients with a specific problem or condition. The next step in the process is reading and appraising the research summaries in the guideline and reviewing the expert recommendations. Finally the information from the practice guideline is used as a basis for clinical decision making. An evidence-based recreational therapy practice uses the strength of research as evidenced in the practice guideline, together with clinical knowledge and reasoning, and the values of a client to make decisions about interventions that are effective for a specific client or group of clients. Thus, recreational therapy interventions are not solely driven by research studies, but also by the clinical recommendations of experts in the field and the wishes of the patient and family when determining optimal interventions and approaches.

There are currently two published guidelines specific to recreational therapy. The first, and the only one in the NCG database, is *Wheelchair Biking for the Treatment of Depression*. This was written by Suzanne Fitzsimmons, MS, ARNP, and Linda Buettner, Ph.D., CTRS, and was published by The University of Iowa Gerontological Nursing Interventions Research Center, Research Dissemination Core (Fitzsimmons, 2001). The second is the Dementia *Practice Guidelines for Recreation Therapy: Treatment of Disturbing Behaviors* (Buettner & Fitzsimmons, 2003).

Issues within the Profession

Intervention Research

Issue one: few intervention studies are published in our profession. Many therapists develop and implement interventions that have, or seem to have, a positive impact on clients. Some of these interventions may already have supportive research evidence, while others may just be presumed to be effective. In order to move the profession of recreational therapy forward, interventions need to be written in a comprehensive, standardized protocol format. The protocol must then be tested and the findings published in a peer-reviewed journal to further validate the recreational therapy intervention for a specific problem area or population.

Funding

Issue two: clinical funding lines have not been fully developed. Without funding, there is limited research available to develop evidence-based guidelines. However, slowly the field is recognizing this deficit and working toward improvement. One example would be the preparation of doctorally prepared professional with clinical research agendas. Unlike other healthcare professions, little funding is allocated specifically to build the skills of new investigators in recreational therapy, and few postgraduate opportunities exist to advance clinical research. Once a new researcher has completed pilot work or a small study for a graduate degree, he or she needs mentoring to continue to the next level of funding. At the next level of research, the investigator should include graduate students in the process to teach others how to continue the research. There are numerous reasons for this gap in research funding and the dearth of clinical lines of study. The lack of awareness of the recreational therapy profession by governmental and other agencies has left our profession out of many requests for funding proposals (RFPs).

Other funding issues are specific to the practicing recreational therapist. The practitioner working in the field may have some excellent programs but is unaware of, or not capable of writing research proposals to test these interventions without the assistance from research faculty at a university. Research funding for a specific disease or condition, for example

Alzheimer's Disease, means the recreational therapist will be competing against nursing, psychology, social work, and a host of other professions for these dollars. In a Catch-22 situation, the funding generally goes to researchers who have a history of funding for a specific research area, making it difficult for the practicing recreational therapist to get the initial funding to establish a funding history. An additional barrier is the low number of doctorally prepared recreational therapists who currently engage in efficacy research or work with practitioners in the field. Many organizations that fund research require the principal investigator to have a doctorate and to be affiliated with an academic institution. Typically, funding priority goes to universities that have the personnel and resources to perform research. A research bridge is needed between practicing recreational therapists and university-based personnel to obtain funding and create important lines of clinical research for the profession.

Who is Doing Clinical Recreational Therapy Research?

Issue three: research evidence from other disciplines may drive our clinical practice guidelines. Although recreational therapists practice at a certified level, recreational therapy as a profession is a relative beginner in the field of evidence-based practice (Stumbo, 2003). It is a much younger profession than medicine, nursing, and other rehabilitation therapies. Added to this is the problem that so many non-professionals in the health and leisure field are doing "recreation" work. There are limited numbers of recent intervention studies in the recreational therapy literature, and many more are needed. Currently other professions, including nursing, psychology, social work, occupational therapy, and others provide the majority of the evidence for recreational therapy. Some authors (American Medical Association, 1997; DeAngelis, 2006; Schlosser, 2004) argue that evidence from other fields of practice such as social work, nursing home care, animal-assisted therapy, exercise science, special education, nursing, and speech therapy, can be applied across practices. Increasingly, recreational therapy interventions are becoming involved in multidisciplinary randomized controlled trials (Gumley et al., 2006; Henggeler et al., 1997). Both of these studies are in mental health settings and are taking place in Europe. Recreation therapy is not a certified program in these settings, but the interventions are seen as valuable. Some feel it is unfortunate that research dollars for recreational therapy are not going to healthcare professionals trained in the therapeutic recreation process, and other professions are getting credit for recreational therapy interventions.

The *Dementia Practice Guidelines for Recreation Therapy*, developed by Buettner and Fitzsimmons (2003), listed over 30 pages of references, but less than 20% of these references came from recreational therapy research. The American Therapeutic Recreation Association's (ATRA) clinical practice guideline team is currently preparing evidence for use in recreational therapy in the treatment of pain, obesity, and stroke. Due to the lack of research in recreational therapy, these practice guidelines have had to rely on evidence from other fields to make clinical recommendations. The practice of developing evidence-based guidelines without recreational therapy evidence brings forth many concerns about its validity. If more clinical evidence for recreational therapy were available for use in practice guidelines, healthcare administrators and governmental agencies would further validate the need for the profession.

Training in Recreational Therapy Practice

Issue four: training faculty, students, and recreational therapists to implement practice guidelines. This might begin by training faculty on clinical guidelines, in addition to developing undergraduate curriculums that support the need for students to understand the science of recreational therapy practice. Additionally, building graduate programs that produce expert clinicians with practice-based research skills and doctorate programs that teach translational research will fundamentally improve clinical practice.

To enhance clinical practice and ensure continuing education recreational therapists would benefit by supporting the certification process and seeking credentialing through the National Council for Therapeutic Recreation (NCTRC™). Furthermore, reading professional journals, joining national professional organizations, and seeking continuing education units from qualified professionals who implement clinical guidelines in their practice would demonstrate the usability of clinical guidelines. Using clinical practice guidelines can assist the recreational therapist in making clinical decisions based on research, thus enhancing the quality of care for the clients served.

Translating Evidence into Practice

Issue five: translating evidence into practice. According to Titler (2002), translating evidence into practice is "the process of finding the best empirical evidence about a particular healthcare phenomena, evaluating the evidence, implementing the evidence in a day-to-day care process, and evaluating the effectiveness of the evidence-based practice for improving patient outcomes" (p. 6). Therefore, more research is needed to understand what interventions work under what circumstances and with what populations of people. This issue is not new; most healthcare professions struggle with making decisions about how to translate evidence into practice. Therefore, partnerships between our professional organizations, recreational therapists, and universities are essential to move evidenced-based practice and the development of practice guidelines forward.

> *You may say I'm a dreamer*
> *But I'm not the only one*
> *I hope someday you'll join us*
> *And the [RT] world will be as one.*
> John Lennon

Building a Vision

Building a vision for 21st century healthcare environments is very important for the recreational therapy profession. It is time to provide what is essential for good practice and our roles on the interdisciplinary healthcare team. That means recreational therapy must have efficacy research, research-based continuing education training that includes competency testing, opportunities to gain advanced skills in a supportive training environment, teams to collect effectiveness measures and revisions of clinical practice guidelines based on these data, and research that is meaningful for clinical practice built into every recreational therapy curriculum.

Imagine finding articles reporting recreational therapy efficacy research that answer real-world practice questions. What recreational therapy interventions would be most efficacious for men recovering from a stroke? What is the ideal group size for teens with developmental disabilities taking part in community integration? What is the best time of day to offer exercise to individuals with dementia? Which relaxation techniques are most efficacious for outpatient substance abuse clients? The profession should be moving toward research to support our basic premises for service provision, the practice decisions we make in terms of duration of therapy, the procedures we use during interventions to ensure and maintain improvements, and we would only use valid and reliable tools to measure these ideas interventions.

Imagine continuing education sessions at regional conferences for recreational therapists that teach the theory behind what we do and the best practices for each specialty area based on research evidence across disciplines. It would truly be continuing education to advance our profession if we had training sessions that helped us understand our role in the treatment plan, along with what each profession on the team offered. Conference and workshop presenters would be selected to present evidence from field-based research, providing real-world case studies, and opportunities to gain the skills needed to try the techniques. Surgeons learn from other expert surgeons, first observing an operation, and then practicing the surgical techniques while supervised by experts. Finally, these surgeons use the newly learned evidence-based techniques in their own practices. It is time that recreational therapists attending continuing education sessions receive competency testing to ensure their understanding and ability to apply the practice guideline information in their own practice settings.

Imagine practicing recreational therapists implementing practice guidelines and evaluating the impact of them on their clients. Each recreational therapist trained to use practice guidelines would report on the effectiveness of the process and new techniques and discoveries made in the field as part of recertification or renewal. Guidelines would be updated and improved as these data from the field evolved and were analyzed.

Imagine every undergraduate student taking a class in the use of research in recreational therapy practice. Research classes would provide real-world problems that recreational therapists experience, and students would learn to work in teams to discover the best evidence and complete projects that would impact on the profession (for example, the problem of delirium in older adults who are hospitalized). What could hospital-based recreational therapists do to prevent this condition? What type of treatment plan could the hospital-based recreational therapist implement? Future professionals would delve into the literature and discover the answers under the tutelage of a professor and practitioner. Once this process is implemented, future clinical decisions would be based on research instead of intuition.

Imagine practice-based research networks in our national organization. Specialty area researchers should work hand in hand within each treatment area to teach, to assist, to upgrade skills of therapists, and help build our professional base of efficacy research. Different recreational therapists at different levels of responsibility within evidence-based organizations will require different skills. Not everyone has to complete clinical trials of recreational therapy interventions, but everyone needs to understand how to read efficacy studies and practice guidelines and weigh different types of evidence. It must be a minimum requirement that all practitioners understand the principles of evidence-based practice, implement evidence-based policies in their facilities, and have a critical attitude to their own practice and toward evidence others present. Without these skills and attitudes, recreational therapists will find it difficult to provide "best practice" and will remain underutilized and stagnant in the rapidly advancing healthcare world. Educators, the staff of our national organizations, and those in positions of leadership within these organizations will require appraisal skills that come with higher training, and with those skills they must promote efficacy research through every professional avenue available.

Table 16.2
Scenario: Evidence-Based Practice in Action

Julie CTRS, a consulting recreation therapist at Cypress Cove, was asked to work to improve care and provide therapy for residents with dementia and behavioral problems. Julie used the *Dementia Practice Guidelines for Recreational Therapy* developed by Buettner and Fitzsimmons (2003) to establish her process and procedures. Based on these guidelines, she ruled out delirium, and then completed her assessment on Mr. Smith. She found that beyond the dementia symptoms, Mr. Smith had moderate depression that was not treated. This older man would lie on the unit couch all day long, refusing general activities, and in the evening he routinely became aggressive with staff and other residents. He had 10 nightly incident reports in 14 days because of these behaviors. Julie implemented a midafternoon wheelchair biking program based on evidence that this intervention helps with depression in persons with dementia. Mr. Smith was encouraged to spend time outdoors talking to Julie and other residents after each ride. After two weeks of treatment, Julie CTRS completed a chart review and found that Mr. Smith had only four incident reports. Discussion question: What would be the next step in Mr. Smith's care plan?

Reference: Conversation with Julie Munnings, CTRS, Cypress Cove, Fort Myers, FL on February 17, 2007

Discussion Questions

1. Do you support the development of clinical-based practice guidelines and protocols for practice, or do you see these as limiting recreational therapy practice? What are the advantages or disadvantages of each side? Discuss this in class with other students.
2. Review a variety of continuing education opportunities offered through your local, state, and national recreational therapy professional organizations. Next, read the program descriptions of the educational offerings and note which sessions offer the skills needed to understand and implement evidence into practice. What did you find?
5. What can you do as a student and emerging professional to remedy the lack of evidence that supports the profession of recreational therapy?
6. What type of vision should our profession embrace in the 21st century?

7. Why would we need to begin by funding small pilot efficacy studies in each of the specialty practice areas?
8. If pilot projects show promise, what should the profession do next?
9. Why should these efforts be coordinated?
10. You have just become the president of a national professional organization. Where would evidenced-based practice be as a priority for your presidency?

References

Agency for Healthcare Research and Quality. (2005). *At a glance: Agency for healthcare research and quality.* Department of Health and Human Services. AHRQ Pub No. 06-P003-1.

American Medical Association. (1997). *Users Guides to Evidence-based Medicine.* (1997 May 21; 277(19): 1552-1557) and (1997 Jun 11; 277(22): 1802-1806) (Published erratum in 1997 Oct 1; 278(13): 1064).

Buettner, L., & Fitzsimmons, S. (2003). *Dementia practice guideline for recreational therapy: Treatment of disturbing behaviors.* Alexandria, VA: American Therapeutic Recreation Association.

DeAngelis, T. (2005). Shaping evidence-based practice. *Monitor on Psychology, 36*(3), 26-32.

Field, M. J., & Lohr, K. N. (1992). *Guidelines for clinical practice: From development to use.* Washington DC: Institute of Medicine, National Academy Press.

Fitzsimmons, S. (2001). Easy rider wheelchair biking. A nursing-recreation therapy clinical trial for the treatment of depression. *Journal of Gerontological Nursing, 27*(5), 14-23.

Gumley, A., Karatzias, A., Power, K., Reilly, J., McNay, L., & O'Grady, M. (2006). Early intervention for relapse in schizophrenia: Impact of cognitive behavioral therapy on negative beliefs about psychosis and self-esteem. *British Journal of Clinical Psychology, 45*(2), 247-60.

Henggeler, S. W., Rowland, M. D, Pickrel, S. G., Miller, S. L., Cunningham, P. B., Santos, A. B., et al. (1997). Investigating family-based alternatives to institution-based mental health services for youth: Lessons learned from the pilot study of a randomized field trial. *Journal of Clinical Child & Adolescent Psychology, 26*(3), 226-233.

The National Guideline Clearinghouse. (2007a). About the national guideline clearinghouse. Retrieved April 9, 2007, from http://www.guideline.gov/about/about.aspx.

The National Guideline Clearinghouse. (2007b). Inclusion criteria. Retrieved April 9, 2007, from http://www.guideline.gov/about/inclusion.aspx.

Titler, M. G. (2002). *Toolkit for promoting evidence-based practice.* Iowa City, IA: The University of Iowa Hospitals and Clinics, Department of Nursing Services and Patient Care Research.

Schlosser, R. W. (2004). Evidence-based practice in AAC: 10 points to consider. *The ASHA Leader,* June 22, (6-7), 10-11.

Stumbo, N. (2003). Systematic reviews part I: How to conduct systematic review for evidence-based practice. *Annual in Therapeutic Recreation, 12,* 29-44.

U.S. National Institutes of Health. (2006). PubMed Central. U.S. National Library of Medicine's digital archive of life sciences journal literature. Available from: http://www.ncbi.nlm.nih.gov/entrez/query.fcgi?db=PMC.

CHAPTER 17

Issues and Concerns in Therapeutic Recreation Assessment

Norma J. Stumbo, Ph.D., CTRS™
Education Associates

In 1980, Witt, Connolly, and Compton called for an increased sophistication in therapeutic recreation assessment while acknowledging its importance. "It seems improbable that any professional in the field would deny the importance of assessment within therapeutic recreation services. On the other hand, there appears to be some confusion over the purpose, approach, and use of the assessment process in our services" (Witt, Connolly, & Compton, 1980, p. 5). While some progress has been made over the last 30 years, much still remains to be done.

The purpose of this chapter is to explore some of the assessment concerns and issues that are likely to occur when providing therapeutic recreation intervention. These concerns and issues affect the quality of daily practice of therapeutic recreation specialists. To set the stage for this discussion, a case will be made for closely examining the relationship between client assessment and program design and implementation. This includes a serious review of both assessment planning and assessment implementation concerns. Assessment decision points, such as selecting, administering, interpreting, and utilizing client assessment information, provide the structure for this discussion.

Connection Between Client Assessment and Program Delivery

Client assessment is "the systematic process of gathering and analyzing selected information about an individual client and using the results for placement into a program(s) that is designed to reduce or eliminate the individual's problems or deficits with his or her leisure, and that enhances the individual's ability to independently function in leisure pursuits" (Stumbo & Peterson, 2009, p. 251).

Assessment is the initial step in establishing a meaningful baseline of the client's leisure-related interests, abilities, knowledge level, and/or attitudes. These baseline results provide the essential information for placing clients into the "right" intervention programs and also provide the foundation for later determining the outcomes of therapeutic recreation intervention (Stumbo, 1996, 2001, 2002a; Stumbo & Peterson, 2009). Horvat and Kalakian (1996, p. 9) stated "assessment is the critical link in the testing process that renders worthwhile the time spent gathering data. Assessment also provides the basis for what instruction should follow."

Client assessment and program design and delivery are linked strongly in those programs that are considered intervention. Perschbacher (1995, p. 1), in discussing the need for accurate and timely assessments in long-term care, stated: "Resident assessments are the first step in understanding individuals. Assessments viewed as mere paperwork miss the point at which the activity program can make real differences in individual lives."

Intervention programs are intended to bring about some behavioral change in the client as a direct result of participation and involvement. The focus of intervention programs is on producing client outcomes; that is, some specific, predictable, measurable change in the client's behavior, skills, attitudes, and/or knowledge (Stumbo & Peterson, 2009). On the other hand, diversional (non-intervention) or purely recreational programs, are designed and delivered with the intent of providing fun and entertainment for participants. Client assessment is crucial to intervention programs and cursory to diversional or non-intervention programs. An important task for therapeutic recreation specialists is to determine the overall intent of their programs and the assessments used to place clients into programs. According to Lee, McCormick, and Perkins (2000, p. 66):

> The [therapeutic recreation specialist] should be able to identify individual clients' needs, and at the same time see the broad perspective of what outcome the [specialist] can offer individuals. [A therapeutic recreation specialist] focuses on specific functional strengths and weaknesses that have particular relevance to the outcome(s) being assessed. Furthermore, by understanding the social, emotional, physical, mental, spiritual, and recreational needs of the client in relation to outcome opportunities, [the therapeutic recreation specialist] can facilitate the design of plans that will maximize outcomes.

As therapeutic recreation services move further toward intervention and away from diversion, the need for systematic and meaningful assessments increases. The connection between client assessment, intervention, and client outcomes is a strong one and has been noted throughout the therapeutic recreation literature (Carter, Van Andel, & Robb, 2003; Dunn, Sneegas, & Carruthers, 1991; Lee, McCormick, & Perkins, 2000; Navar, 1991; Olsson, 1992; Riley, 1991; Robertson & Long, 2008; Shank & Coyle, 2002; Sheehan, 1992; Stumbo, 2002a; Stumbo & Peterson, 2009; Sylvester, Voelkl, & Ellis, 2001). Shank and Kinney (1991) noted that client outcomes are observable changes in the client's status as a direct result of the specialist's interventions and interactions. Riley (1991) discussed these as "measurable changes" and stated "the causal relationship between the process of care (intervention) and the outcomes of care (change in patient behavior) is crucial" (p. 59).

Both of these thoughts about the connection between intervention and outcomes assume that a valid and reliable baseline of information is gathered in order to later "prove" the change in behavior or status. That is, the client assessment collects the baseline information on the needs, strengths, limitations, and current status of the client. This information provides the framework from which systematic intervention programs are designed, provided, and prescribed for individual clients. An "end-of-services" summary (perhaps the assessment readministered as a post-test) may provide the evaluative data to determine whether the appropriate client outcomes have been achieved at the conclusion of the intervention or the client's length of stay. This evaluative measurement allows for conclusions about the achievement of client outcomes to be made. "An outcome evaluation is a systematic process of monitoring the efficacy of the treatment provided. The intent of the evaluation is to provide specific feedback on client performance and outcomes as they relate to the intervention" (Lee, McCormick, & Perkins, 2000, p. 68). Thus, the alliance between the assessment, the intervention, and the measurement of outcomes is of paramount importance.

Therapeutic Recreation Accountability Model

Although the Therapeutic Recreation Accountability Model (TRAM) has been discussed elsewhere in the therapeutic recreation literature (Stumbo, 1996, 1997; Stumbo & Peterson, 2009), it is reviewed briefly here so that the multiple connections can be emphasized between programs, assessments, and client outcomes mentioned above. Essentially the TRAM (see Figure 17.1) attempts to graphically provide an explanation of the whole of therapeutic recreation intervention programming. It is of great importance to note that the content and style of programs offered (as determined through program design and activity analysis) match the needs and characteristics of clients (as determined through client assessment). Although other steps are involved, it is the connection between these two and the foundation that they provide that increase the likelihood that the programs will be delivered as intervention and will produce measurable client outcomes.

Note that client and program outcomes, quality improvement, and efficacy research efforts all provide feedback information for the improvement of the entire program delivery system. In other words, every component of the therapeutic recreation program delivery system is interrelated and provides feedback and direction for the improvement of other components and the entire system. Therapeutic recreation specialists who understand and utilize these relationships are most likely to provide the highest quality therapeutic recreation programs.

Decisions About Client Placement Into Programs

A major factor in establishing validity and reliability is the alignment between the content of the programs offered and the content of the assessment (Stumbo & Peterson, 2009). The importance of this match cannot be overstated. When the match exists, the potential for intervention is maximized; when the match does not exist, the potential for

Figure 17.1
Therapeutic Recreation Accountability Model (Stumbo, 1996)

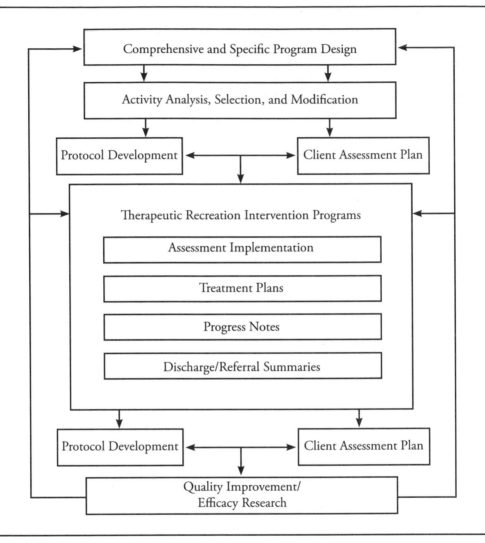

diversion is maximized. For example, if the therapeutic recreation program content includes physical functional abilities, leisure attitudes, social skills, and leisure awareness, then the assessment content for clients being assessed for that program should include physical functional abilities, leisure attitudes, social skills, and leisure awareness.

The alignment between the content of the client assessment and the therapeutic recreation program is similar to the way in which Navar (1991) used the term "appropriateness." Navar stated that the appropriateness of therapeutic recreation services hinged on whether the specialist is "providing the right patient with the right service [at] the right time in the right setting at the right intensity and for the right duration" (p. 5). The right client cannot be placed into the right program unless the assessment contains the right information (valid) and is refined to the point that placement is accurate (reliable). (A full discussion of the measurement concepts of validity and reliability will not be presented here because this is found elsewhere in the therapeutic recreation literature. See specifically Dunn, 1983, 1984, 1987, 1989; Horvat & Kalakian, 1996; Howe, 1984, 1989; Sneegas, 1989; Stumbo, 1991, 1992a, 1992b, 1993–94, 1994–95, 2002a, 2002b; Stumbo & Peterson, 2009).

Figure 17.2 helps to explain the relationship between program placement and client needs. The four quadrants represent accurate and poor decisions, whether the client needed the therapeutic recreation programs, and whether the therapeutic recreation programs were provided to the client. Quadrants I and IV indicate correct decisions—the match between the client needs (from assessment results) and their placement into programs is correct. Clients who need programs receive services, while clients without need do not. In Quadrant II, the assessment results indicate needed program involvement that is not realized—an incorrect decision. The end result is that clients involved with erroneous Quadrant II decisions do not receive the necessary services. Quadrant III also indicates faulty matches or decisions. In these cases, clients receive services that do not match their needs. Programs provided in Quadrant III are likely to be diversional in that clients without need are involved in programs. Whether this is due to agency mandates, high staff/client ratios, client diversity, or other reasons, the specialist often resorts to diversional programming. Translated, this means that programming is intended to "keep clients busy." Intervention is less likely in situations where clients with widely varying characteristics and needs are placed into one program.

Clearly, Quadrant I contains the "right" programs in which the "right" clients are placed. As such, it has the greatest likelihood to be intervention, that is, produce measurable,

---

Figure 17.2
Relationship between Client Placement into Programs and Client Needs
(Stumbo, 1997)

	Client Placed Into Program	Client Not Placed Into Program
Client Needs Program	*I. Correct Decision* Client receives necessary services - Likely to be intervention	*II. Incorrect Decision* Client does not receive necessary services - no unnecessary program involvement
Client Does Not Need Program	*III. Incorrect Decision* Client receives unnecessary services - not likely to be intervention	*IV. Correct Decision* Client does not receive services - program involvement not necessary

predetermined client outcomes. Clients with needs are placed into a program or activity specifically designed and implemented to meet those targeted needs. It requires the mix of an appropriate assessment procedure that is able to produce valid and reliable assessment results and appropriate programs that are designed based on common client needs. This match is essential for correct client placement decisions to be made as well as for intervention to be provided and outcomes to be measured.

Although the concepts above are relatively simple to understand, they become difficult to put into practice when programs are not designed to produce specific outcomes and client assessments are not designed to align specifically with those programs. Only with these basic but necessary building blocks to achieving predictable and meaningful client outcomes will accountability for therapeutic recreation programs become a reality.

Issues in Implementing the Assessment Process

In the previous section, the direct relationship between therapeutic recreation intervention programming and client assessment was illustrated. This section will focus on the factors that influence the assessment process, from knowing what to assess to documenting for client outcomes. The two models utilized by Stumbo and Peterson (2009) [the Therapeutic Recreation Assessment Plan Model (p. 269) and the Therapeutic Recreation Assessment Implementation Model (p. 283)] to illustrate the entire client assessment process will be simplified into five topics for discussion: (a) assessment resources and specialist expertise, (b) measuring desired characteristics or behaviors, (c) implementing assessments correctly, (d) scoring and analyzing assessments correctly, and (e) documenting for client outcomes. This framework will be used, not to address necessarily how this process works, but to show the issues that must be considered while implementing it.

Assessment Resources and Specialist Expertise

In order to perform assessment duties in a high-quality manner, the profession must have adequate resources, and the professional must have adequate expertise. Both of these areas are concerns for client assessment in therapeutic recreation. Not only is there a limited number of client assessments, there is a clear lack of appropriate and standardized assessments and available information about them. Therefore, it is not surprising that therapeutic recreation specialists often enter their jobs with less than adequate competence and continue to experience difficulties in the client assessment process throughout their careers. This section will discuss four issues: (a) lack of an adequate number of therapeutic recreation assessments, (b) lack of high-quality therapeutic recreation assessments, (c) lack of assessment resources, and (d) specialist competence.

Lack of An Adequate Number of Assessments

For a profession as large and diverse as therapeutic recreation, there are few quality instruments commercially available for use. There simply are not enough instruments to meet the demands of the diverse programming of therapeutic recreation professionals. There are not enough commercial instruments that have the content to reflect the content of programs offered within therapeutic recreation services—meaning that most of the instruments available are not valid for the programs with which specialists would like to use them.

So what's a therapist to do? First, the specialist might buy instruments that are not appropriate (valid, reliable, or usable) for the purpose for which she or he would like to use them. The specialist then encounters the problem of not being able to make proper programming placement decisions, resulting in incorrect Quadrants II and III decisions. This happens frequently when the specialist buys a popular assessment as the "magic bullet" and discovers that it provides no more useful results than any previous instrument the therapist had used.

Second, the specialist may "borrow" an assessment from a related field, such as adapted physical education. This may seem fairly attractive, and some therapeutic recreation textbooks advocate this approach. However, if the content of the assessment does not match the content of the therapeutic recreation program, the results will likely lead to random program placement, again resulting in faulty program-placement decisions and lack of client outcomes. The same scenario is repeated: An assessment is selected and used, but the results do not help place the right clients into the right program, and the specialist is left with faulty Quadrant II and III decisions once again.

Third, the specialist may develop an assessment specifically for use within his or her agency. Unless the therapeutic recreation specialist is quite familiar with and complies with accepted assessment development and validation methodologies, this option can be problematic (Dunn, 1984; Kinney, 1980; Stumbo, 1991, 2002a; Stumbo & Peterson, 2009; Touchstone, 1975). To counteract these pitfalls, the specialist needs to develop considerable expertise in assessment, including competence in ensuring a reasonable degree of validity and reliability of the results. Stumbo's (2002a) book and Dunn's (1987) article are beginning points for increasing competence in assessment development.

Lack of High-Quality Therapeutic Recreation Assessments

There are two difficulties. One is that some assessments have not been validated in an appropriate manner. This may include those that use faulty validation techniques, and it may include those that have never been tested for the purpose of client assessment.

Both commercial and agency-specific assessments can have validation problems. "The available assessment instruments that are nonagency-specific are still sketchy, still evolutionary, and still conceptually cloudy" (Howe, 1989, pp. 217-218). For example, one assessment publisher reported inter-rater reliability results on a four-point observation scale to within one point either way. So if one rater scored the client a 2 on some specific behavior, the other rater got counted for the same score if he or she had rated the same behavior a 1, or 2, or 3. Not surprisingly, raters averaged a 91% agreement using this method! In cases like this, the buyer needs to be aware that just because something is in print, it is not necessarily true or good or usable. Caveat emptor!

Another problem is the use of measurement instruments for client assessment when they were not built or validated as client assessment instruments. For example, some instruments on the market were developed for research purposes to describe leisure attitudes, motivations, and satisfaction within a certain research population. They may have excellent statistics reflecting that purpose and for those populations for which they were intended. But to assume those statistics mean anything for client assessment is absolutely erroneous.

For example, even though the National Council for Therapeutic Recreation Certification™'s test might be excellent, would it be appropriate for physical therapist licensure? Of course not. A test in and of itself does not have goodness for all purposes; an assessment tool or procedure is only as good as the statistics dictate for that specific purpose and for that specific population. Again, this clearly is a case where specialists must become educated consumers before buying products that have no value for their programs or clients.

A third problem exists with activity-interest inventories. "The tension between the applied and theoretical dimensions of the assessment process continues, especially with the continual proliferation of agency-specific assessment devices that are little more than interest inventories but are incorrectly used and touted for purposes way beyond those of such inventories" (Howe, 1989, pp. 217-218).

The specific problems with activity-interest inventories and similar instruments have been outlined elsewhere in the literature (Stumbo, 1992b, 1993-94, 2002a; Stumbo & Peterson, 2009), and these problems remain in practice today. Stumbo (1991) stated that since activity-interest inventories and other similar tools contain a relatively narrow activity definition of services, they miss the mark in helping to understand the broader leisure behavior and functional independence focus of most therapeutic recreation programs. As such, they may provide little help in understanding client behavior. "A frustrating outcome of this misguided use of assessment as measurement is the realization that the results derived from an irrelevant assessment instrument are of little informative value in providing program direction and may totally misdirect program decisions" (Witt, Connolly, & Compton, 1980, p. 6). In other words, without adequate standardization and validation of client assessment tools, improper program placement decisions (Quadrants II and III) will be made.

Lack of Assessment Resources

Another area for concern with therapeutic recreation assessment is the difficulty that most specialists have in locating information about available and usable assessments. Keeping abreast of current information about assessments and related issues is essential, although largely a difficult and fragmented enterprise.

It will take everyone working together to reverse the current situation. Specialists need to assume responsibility to expend (sometimes great) effort to locate, read, and understand the published assessment literature. Authors need to continue to write and publish quality articles and books on assessment that are of high value to practice. Professional organizations and publishers need to continue to create avenues to provide easy access to the newest information. Educators need to ensure that the latest techniques and tools are an integral part of therapeutic recreation curricula. Only as each group continues to take responsibility for its part of the information chain will better and more timely assessment information be widely available to all who desire it.

Specialist Expertise

Sneegas (1989), among others, identified the need for specialists to be better trained in assessment, research methods, and leisure behavior, and called for better communication between investigators and practitioners to conduct needed research on client assessments (p. 233). This requires a give and take between specialists and researchers and between programming knowledge and measurement expertise. A balance is necessary for competence and for working relationships to be successful.

Horvat and Kalakian (1996) identified several qualifications for professionals conducting assessments. Among these are:

- knowledge of measurement principles, including validity, reliability, and objectivity;
- knowledge of potentials and limitations of test interpretations;
- competence in the administration and interpretation of specific tests;
- competence in assessment validation procedures; and
- knowledge of procedures to avoid undue discrimination, such as age, gender, or cultural biases.

These generic assessment competencies are complemented by those more specific to therapeutic recreation as identified by the National Council for Therapeutic Recreation Certification's *2007 Job Analysis* (NCTRC™, 2007) and West, Kinney, and Witman's (2008) *Guidelines for Competency Assessment and Curriculum Planning for Recreational Therapy Practice*. Both of these documents outline the assessment processes and contents with which therapeutic recreation specialists must be familiar.

These competencies require that education about assessments become a life-long process for the specialist, who needs to continue to learn about improving client-assessment procedures throughout his or her career. Howe (1989, p. 219), in summarizing her book chapter on assessment, stated:

> But, what [this chapter] cannot give is the thorough and complete education needed to use assessment instruments or procedures well, mindful of both their strengths and their weaknesses. That training requires either formal degree work or continuing professional education. It takes time and study to gain the insight and skills to validate instruments, let alone to practice one's skills at assessment design, quantitative and qualitative data collection and analysis, and the interpretation and application of results. So, in that sense, any assessment is only as good as the TRS [Therapeutic Recreation Specialist] conducting it.

Measuring Desired Characteristics or Behaviors

An additional problem for the field of therapeutic recreation is that leisure behavior and independent functioning (two intended outcomes of therapeutic recreation programming) are such a challenge to define and then measure.

Complexities of Measurement

Citing work completed by Dunn (1984), Howe (1984), and Stumbo and Thompson (1986), Sneegas (1989, p. 226) noted that "there are few instruments designed to obtain assessment information related to leisure behavior which demonstrate adequate reliability, validity, and practical utility." Leisure behavior and functional independence are complex entities and their measurement is fraught with measurement dangers.

. . .the measurement of leisure behavior in individuals with disabilities and in special populations is not as simple as it might appear on the surface. The current state of the art for assessing leisure behavior is relatively undeveloped because obtaining valid and reliable measures of the leisure behavior of anyone (not even considering any additional problems presented by disability) is a complex process. (Sneegas, 1989, p. 224)

For instance, Sneegas (1989) discussed problems with how leisure is defined (time, activity, or state of mind), and therefore, measured through assessments. Sneegas (1989) warned against simplistic or univariate studies, and those that lack richness or contextual/qualitative information. In addition, this contribution to the literature examined some of these difficulties in light of assessing individuals with disabilities and special needs. For example, Katsinas (1992) made the case that most therapeutic recreation assessment tools are not refined enough to measure low levels of functioning or regressed behavior, and are not sensitive enough to measure small increments of behavioral change. Howe (1989, p. 217) noted that most therapeutic recreation assessments lacked the ability to measure richness and complexity of the individual client.

The lack of ability to measure the complexities of human behavior—especially for individuals with disabilities, illnesses, and/or special needs—is a major concern for therapeutic recreation assessment. The field needs more and better research describing and measuring the leisure behavior of clients. This, in turn, will improve the ability to standardize and validate tools to measure baseline and subsequent information.

Students and specialists alike must make the commitment to learn as much as possible about intervention programming, measurement qualities, and client assessment as they coalesce on one of the most powerful decision points in the therapeutic recreation intervention process—that of describing an adequate baseline of client behavior. As knowledge and use of assessments improve, so too will the quality of intervention programs and the success of therapeutic recreation within the healthcare arena.

Implementing Assessments Correctly

Assessment Planning

Assessment planning (Stumbo & Peterson, 2009, p. 269) includes (a) analysis of the environment, (b) defining parameters of the assessment, (c) selecting or developing assessments, (d) establishing assessment protocols, and (e) training staff and interns on the assessment protocols. These five steps establish the foundation for knowing what to assess and establishing the proper procedure to ensure the assessment will collect the best possible results. These first steps often are overlooked or taken for granted, which sometimes results in an assessment procedure that does not align with the agency's mission and overall targeted client outcomes.

Analysis of the Environment

While in the planning stage, specialists should take time to gather information about the agency's view on assessment. "For example, several agencies might serve individuals with substance abuse problems. However, they may differ greatly in whether they primarily deliver inpatient, outpatient, or day treatment programs; whether their intent is detoxification, individual counseling, or group peer counseling; or whether they are accredited by the Joint Commission. . . . The agency's characteristics will impact greatly the assessment chosen by the therapeutic recreation specialist and other disciplines" (Stumbo & Peterson, 2009, p. 270). Likewise the client characteristics (e.g., demographics such as gender, age, recidivism, home environment, etc.) and program characteristics (e.g., targeted client outcomes, program content, professional standards, etc.) affect the assessment plan.

Defining the Parameters

In addition, the function, content, and implementation strategy also become issues. Client assessment generally serves four functions: (a) screening; (b) identifying the problem(s); (c) narrowing the problem(s); and (d) re-assessing or monitoring progress. *Screening* serves as a generalized sorting function and may be given to all clients upon admission (Horvat & Kalakian, 1996). For example, an assessment that is used as a screening device may have a dozen basic questions to determine whether or not an individual is appropriate for therapeutic recreation services, i.e., does the person need social skills training? Yes or no? *Identifying the problem(s)* requires more in-depth questioning that aids in program placement and may be given to those individuals who were identified as needing further assessment from the screening device. For example, an assessment may help identify problems that can be worked on during therapeutic recreation services, (i.e., what kinds of social skills does the person lack? interpersonal conversational skills? body space/proximity issues? hygiene? and so forth).

Assessments involved with *narrowing the problem(s)* provide the most in-depth information and can be most useful for providing direction for working with clients on an individualized basis, i.e., what kinds of interpersonal skills does the person lack? eye contact? initiating conversations? maintaining conversations? terminating conversations? and the like. These assessments have the most utility in programs where clients participate for a considerable amount of time (adequate to work on in-depth problems) and where specific outcomes are targeted.

Assessments can also serve the purpose of *evaluating or monitoring client progression or regression*. If the assessment is of high quality and provides both valid and reliable results, then there is no better device to re-assess a client to determine if outcomes have been achieved (Perschbacher, 1995; Stumbo, 2002a, 2002b).

As mentioned previously, the content of the assessment must coincide with the content of the program.

> While assessment clearly provides the foundation for individual program planning, its relationship to the program's conceptual foundation is as critical. The theory or philosophy that drives the program should be reflected in the assessment procedures. If the program seeks to build a client's repertoire of leisure skills in certain areas then an appropriate skill or activity-oriented inventory is needed. If the intent of the program is to increase the client's perceived competence or effectiveness in leisure, an instrument which measures levels of learned helplessness . . . or perceived leisure competence . . . may be needed. (Stumbo & Rickards, 1986, p. 3)

Each chosen implementation strategy (e.g., interviews, observations, self-administered questionnaires, and records reviews) also has implications because its purpose, methods, and outcomes differ fairly significantly from the other strategies. The decision of which data-collection technique to use should be made with care.

Selecting or Purchasing Assessments

Regardless of whether the assessment tool or procedure is developed for a specific agency by the therapeutic recreation staff or purchased from a commercial vendor, the same basic measurement requirements apply. According to Dunn (1983, p. 63):

> . . . it should be expected that assessments used in therapeutic recreation:
> • fulfill their intended purpose;
> • have the ability to gather specified information;
> • gather that information accurately;
> • utilize an appropriate method;
> • are appropriate for clients; and
> • are appropriate for the agency and the situation.

Specialists must consider both the purpose and content, as well as other factors, before selecting or developing an assessment procedure. If a commercially available assessment can be located that meets the purpose and content needed in the assessment, then purchase is logical. However, this is relatively rare in that therapeutic recreation programs are based on unique factors such as community resources, agency mission, client characteristics, department resources, and the like (Stumbo, 2002a; Stumbo & Peterson, 2009) and are not uniform across the country or, in fact, any state. Many professionals, then, must rely on developing assessments to meet their departments' needs.

The major concern, regardless of whether the assessment is purchased or developed, is that professionals often fail to consider the purpose or function of the assessment and the necessity to match the content of the assessment with the content of the program. This match requires that the professional use comprehensive program design to create programs and that these areas be translated into assessment content. Failure to consider the link between program placement and assessment data results in poor decisions in Quadrant II and Quadrant III. This means that the link between the assessment results and the placement into programs is likely to be faulty and lack validity. If this link is not established, the content of the assessment will tend to be haphazard and not lead to appropriate program placement decisions. This, obviously, is a major concern in therapeutic recreation assessment and program delivery.

Establishing and Following Protocols

In this step, the specialist is responsible for preparing to administer a client assessment. All assessments, whether commercially sold or self-developed, should be accompanied by adequate documentation that includes information on the development of the tool as well as standardized procedures for its use, analysis, and interpretation. For example, documentation should include the conceptual development of the tool, the validity and reliability statistics of validation studies and pilot tests, and resources needed to perform all steps of the assessment. Additionally, documentation should include standardized procedures for training (both staff and interns), preparing the assessment environment (including supplies), and administering, scoring, and interpreting the procedure. Dunn (1987, 1989) provides excellent guidelines for using or creating the necessary documentation to accompany assessments.

The major concern of this step is that both commercially available and self-developed assessments rarely have adequate accompanying documentation. The lack of this documentation decreases the opportunities for standardized (and hopefully valid and reliable) procedures across staff and units. This means that results will be interpreted and reported based on the fluctuating perceptions of individual staff members. The lack of uniform implementation of assessments, even within a single department, reduces the likelihood of correct and consistent placement decisions. For example, when personal interviews with clients are used as the primary data-gathering technique, the specialist "becomes" the instrument. Any fluctuation in environment, body language, use of probes, length of interview, and the like can produce results that are more affected by the specialist than by the client. Therefore, the results may not be valid for that client, and subsequent program placement may be in error. This lack of precision weakens the assessment process and increases the likelihood of incorrect program placement decisions—another important concern for the profession.

Training Staff/Interns on the Assessment Protocol

The most typical training that a new therapist or student intern receives on the assessment tool or procedure involves watching an experienced specialist conduct two to three assessments and then independently administering assessments on his or her own. Shadow training typically is inadequate to teach the new employee or intern about the validation and development of the tool or the procedures with which the tool was validated. What are the procedures for a person unable to communicate? What are the standardized probes to the interview questions? How are uncooperative clients handled? What happens if the client becomes too fatigued to continue? What if the therapist detects that the answers being given are not truthful? All these situations and more should be documented and handled in the same manner by each therapist and intern. Protocols should include the frequency of inter-therapist checks to make sure each therapist is administering the assessment to all clients in exactly the same way. The accuracy and dependability of the assessment results are influenced greatly by the thoroughness and detail included in the protocol. The ability to be confident in the assessment results are a direct factor of these details.

Administering Assessments

In this step, the specialist implements the procedures that were outlined and reviewed in the last stage. Assessments in therapeutic recreation tend to be of four kinds: (a) interviews (with clients and/or their families) (see Ferguson, 1983); (b) observations (see Stumbo, 1983); (c) self-administered surveys; and (d) records reviews. Each type collects unique information and has its own advantages and disadvantages. Types may be used in combination to strengthen the validity of the results. Stumbo and Peterson (2009) discussed the relative advantages and disadvantages of each type of information-gathering assessment technique.

The primary concern with administration is that because there is no documented protocol, it is often inconsistent between departments (no two departments administer the assessment in the identical way), between specialists (no two specialists administer the assessment in the identical way) and within specialists (each specialist is not consistent from one administration to the next). These inconsistencies greatly affect the outcome of the assessment, thus affecting the placement of clients into programs. Again, incorrect decisions may be made, jeopardizing the likelihood that clients will receive needed treatment and will achieve the desired or intended outcomes. Adequate and uniform documentation, training, and guidelines assist in alleviating this weakness.

An additional concern is the differing abilities of clients on singular or multiple units. Since administration needs to be consistent, when client abilities differ greatly (some clients with lack of reading abilities, some with cognitive disabilities, some with visual or hearing impairments, etc.), then the assessment(s) must be designed to meet these varying needs and must be administered as consistently as possible when these conditions are present.

As Stumbo and Peterson (2009) reminded us: "Assessments need to be administered consistently to the fullest extent possible. That means that each assessment technique needs a specific protocol that is consistent across: (1) departments (if programs are similar), (2) specialists, (3) administrations by an individual specialist, (4) clients, and (5) assessment environments. Deviations from these consistencies lower the confidence that can be placed in the results and program placement decisions" (Stumbo & Peterson, 2009, pp. 288-289).

Scoring and Interpreting Assessments Correctly

Following the established protocol for scoring the assessment, the therapeutic recreation specialist, in this step, summarizes the assessment results in a clear and concise manner. This summary (often referred to as data reduction) condenses quantitative (numbers) and/or qualitative (words) data into an understandable and cohesive picture of the client. This summary communicates the results of the assessment and provides the basis for development of a treatment plan.

Like previous steps, the major concern here is one of dependability and consistency. The overwhelming majority of therapeutic recreation assessments lacks adequate protocols for reliable and efficient scoring. In fact, because they rely on purely qualitative or open-ended data, many are difficult to score due to the lack of an agreed-upon, congruent method of gathering and synthesizing information. For example, asking, "How do you spend your leisure time?" as an open-ended question with no established categories for marking an answer, is likely to result in a diversity of answers that are difficult to categorize after the fact.

This diversity of answers and difficulty in categorization lead to one of the most problematic areas in assessment for therapeutic recreation specialists. Because standardized scoring procedures are all but nonexistent (especially for agency-specific assessments), the specialist often is forced to rely on personal judgment for summarizing the results. Without protocols, the interpretation of results can be influenced by forces such as mood, need to fill programs, personal preference, and the like. In these cases, the specialist collects assessment data (perhaps largely because of external or agency mandates), but then is left without any systematic procedure to score the results. The therapist then has no choice but to place clients into programs based on personal preferences or the need to fill certain programs—or worse yet, places every client into every program.

> One frustration, if the previous . . . steps have been done incorrectly or incompletely, is that the therapeutic recreation specialist may have little valuable or unique information to report. When prior assessment steps have not followed a logical, consistent, and justifiable sequence the information provided by therapeutic recreation specialist may not differ greatly from other disciplines or may not contribute to the client's goals or treatment plan." (Stumbo & Peterson, 2009, p. 291)

Documenting for Client Outcomes

The goal of the final step is to make objective, consistent, and correct decisions for placing clients into therapeutic recreation programs. Program placements should be based on the results of the assessment process (not personal whims or agency pressures), so that scoring, interpretation, and program placement are highly interrelated. If the results were obtained through a valid and reliable process, the interpretation of the results and placement decisions become easier and are more likely to be valid and reliable. If data reduction is problematic, then interpretation of the data similarly will be problematic.

Take the following example: If two clients have similar scores or results on the assessment and they are placed in similar programs, as indicated as necessary from the assessment, then these "right" individuals are likely to be receiving the "right" service. On the other hand, if two clients have similar scores or results on the assessment, and they are placed in dissimilar programs, then the process is probably not producing valid or reliable results and is resulting in faulty interpretation and placement decisions. This results in either clients not receiving necessary services (Quadrant II) or clients receiving unnecessary services (Quadrant III).

Documenting the Placement/Treatment Plan in the Client Record

While the format of client records often are decided at the agency level, the content that professionals enter into the record usually is decided by the department's staff, in consultation with other disciplines. The content to be reported from the results of the assessment is determined by the content of the programs, and in turn, the content of the assessment.

One of the frustrations, if the previous steps have been done incorrectly or incompletely, is that the specialist has little valuable or unique information to report. When prior assessment steps have not followed a logical, consistent, and justifiable sequence or if programs are not based in a systematic analysis of client needs, the information provided by the therapeutic recreation specialist might not differ greatly from other disciplines or might not contribute to the client's goals.

For example, a therapeutic recreation specialist may be providing valuable intervention programs with the content of: (a) leisure awareness; (b) social interaction skills; (c) leisure resources; and (d) community reintegration skills. These are well-designed, outcome-oriented intervention programs that were developed based on an analysis of client needs and that appear to be successful and complement the treatment programs of the other disciplines. However, her assessment content includes: (a) personal history; (b) past leisure interests; and (c) future leisure interests. How well does the content of the assessment match the content of the program? How will the assessment results be used to place clients into programs? What connection can be made between the assessment "scores" and the placement into programs? How will the "right" clients be placed systematically into the "right" programs? How will she know in which Quadrant her placement decisions are?

The answer is that client placement into the correct programs is unlikely and the specialist will have little of value to report in the client record or to the treatment team. As a beginning, the specialist needs the assessment content to reflect the program content of: (a) leisure awareness; (b) social interaction skills; (c) leisure resources; and (d) community reintegration skills. Unless the program-to-assessment connection is made clear, other information may have little value and may be regarded poorly by other members of the treatment team.

Re-Assessing as Necessary to Show Progression or Regression

Documenting client outcomes relies on the ability of the specialist to measure change in the client's knowledge, attitudes, and/or skills. It was noted previously that one of the many difficulties with therapeutic recreation client assessment is that the results of assessment tools often lack validity and reliability, and are imprecise. This compounds, then, the difficulty in being able to document client changes. However, when the assessment results are obtained by using a protocol that yields valid and reliable data, the opportunity to measure client change is enhanced.

If the chosen assessment tool produces results that are valid and reliable, then no better tool exists to determine the progression or regression of a particular client. The specialist conducts the assessment, implements the intervention program, and administers the assessment again to measure client outcomes. This does mean that the original assessment must have the precision (reliability) to determine sometimes small increments of movement. For example, if it is determined from the original assessment that a client lacks social interaction skills (and, therefore, the client is placed into a social skills program), the assessment must measure these skills with enough accuracy to determine if change has been made during or at the completion of the program. If the assessment provides rough or crude estimates of ability, then reassessment will be difficult, if not impossible. If this is the case, the specialist will have an extremely difficult time proving that the client achieved the intended outcomes of the therapeutic recreation program.

Of course, this last phase is made more difficult by the fact that specialists often start the entire assessment process with weak, vague, or misdirected instruments. This brings to mind the computer phrase of "GIGO" or "garbage in, garbage out." One cannot end at the correct destination if the map is faulty.

Every step in the assessment process is intricately linked. Poor analysis of client need or selection of a weak commercial tool are examples of faulty starting points that have significant impact on the remainder of the assessment process. The entire process requires a considerable amount of specialist expertise, competence, and effort to ensure that better decisions are made regarding each client's treatment. Without proper assessment, even the best intervention programs will have little meaning in the lives of clients.

The Challenge

Therapeutic recreation assessment will advance rapidly and issues will be minimized greatly only when each student and specialist meets the challenge of improving the future state of the art in assessment. To meet this end, the reader is challenged to answer the following questions:

- What specific actions will you take to improve your personal knowledge of validity, reliability, and usability as measurement characteristics that affect the quality of therapeutic recreation assessments? What articles, chapters, or books will you read?
- What specific actions will you take to better understand the crucial link between program design and client assessment in therapeutic recreation assessment? How can you use the two models (Figures 17.1 and 17.2) discussed in this chapter?
- What specific actions will you take to improve your ability to implement assessments through observations, interviews, self-administered surveys, or record reviews? Will this include practice sessions under peer review?
- What specific actions will you take to remain informed about new developments and literature concerning therapeutic recreation assessments? Does this plan include reading periodicals, journals, and books? Attending conferences and workshops? Developing assessments through research and cooperative partnerships?
- What specific actions will you take to become a better consumer of the therapeutic recreation literature? By what standards will you judge the "goodness" of published therapeutic recreation assessments?

Summary

The intent of this chapter is to provide a starting point for discussion about the improvement of therapeutic recreation assessment. The challenges outlined, including issues about selecting and implementing assessments; specialist expertise; and instrument validity, standardization, and availability, point to the continued need to improve the current state of the art of therapeutic recreation assessment. This will happen only when each student and professional in the field meets the challenge of improving his or her own knowledge, skills, and understanding of assessment and its crucial link to intervention programming. How will you respond to the challenge?

Discussion Questions

1. What is the relationship between program design, activity analysis, and client assessment? Review several of your therapeutic recreation textbooks as references to provide the answer.
2. What do you think is the primary reason client assessment is still an issue for the therapeutic recreation profession? What would it take to overcome this problem?
3. Locate several published therapeutic recreation client assessments. Review their documentation on validation procedures, implementation protocols, and scoring

procedures. For what types of programs, if any, would you recommend the purchase of these tools? For what types of programs would the assessment content match the program content? If you do not recommend purchase, what other options would the therapeutic recreation specialist have for client assessment?

4. Locate any one published therapeutic recreation client assessment. Write a draft protocol for administering, scoring, interpreting, and documenting the results of the assessment. Ask two peers to review your draft protocol.

5. Locate several non-published, agency-specific therapeutic recreation client assessments. What do you project the therapeutic recreation program's content to be? What can you tell about the programs from the assessment? Do they match? How can the assessment be improved?

References

Carter, M. J., Van Andel, G. E., & Robb, G. M. (2003). *Therapeutic recreation: A practical approach* (3rd ed.). Prospect Heights, IL: Waveland Press.

Compton, D. M. (Ed). (1997). *Issues in therapeutic recreation: Toward the new millennium.* (2nd ed.). Champaign, IL: Sagamore.

Dunn, J. K. (1983). Improving client assessment procedures in therapeutic recreation programming. In G. L. Hitzhusen (Ed.), *Expanding horizons in therapeutic recreation X* (pp. 61-84). Columbia, MO: University of Missouri.

Dunn, J. (1984). Assessment. In C. A. Peterson, & S. L. Gunn, *Therapeutic recreation program design: Principles and procedures* (2nd ed.) (pp. 267-320). Englewood Cliffs, NJ: Prentice-Hall, Inc.

Dunn, J. K. (1987). Establishing reliability and validity of evaluation instruments. *Journal of Park and Recreation Administration, 5*(4), 61-70.

Dunn, J. K. (1989). Guidelines for using published assessment procedures. *Therapeutic Recreation Journal, 23*(2), 59-69.

Dunn, J. K., Sneegas, J., & Carruthers, C. A. (1991). Outcome measures: Monitoring patient progress. In B. Riley (Ed.), *Quality management: Applications for therapeutic recreation* (pp. 107-116). State College, PA: Venture.

Ferguson, D. (1983). Assessment interviewing techniques: A useful tool in developing individual program plans. *Therapeutic Recreation Journal, 17*(2), 16-22.

Horvat, M., & Kalakian, L. (1996). *Assessment in adapted physical education and therapeutic recreation* (2nd ed.). Madison, WI: Brown & Benchmark.

Howe, C. (1984). Leisure assessment instrumentation in therapeutic recreation. *Therapeutic Recreation Journal, 18*(2), 14-24.

Howe, C. Z. (1989). Assessment instruments in therapeutic recreation: To what extent do they work? In D. Compton (Ed.), *Issues in therapeutic recreation: A profession in transition.* (pp. 205-221). Champaign, IL: Sagamore.

Katsinas, R. P. (1992). Social skills assessment for long-term care residents who have cognitive and multiple impairments. In G. Hitzhusen, & L.T. Jackson (Eds.), *Expanding horizons in therapeutic recreation XIV* (pp. 193-224). Columbia, MO: University of Missouri.

Kinney, W. B. (1980). Clinical assessment in mental health settings. *Therapeutic Recreation Journal, 14*(4), 39-45.

Kloseck, M., Crilly, R. G., Ellis, G. D., & Lammers, E. (1996). Leisure Competence Measure: Development and reliability testing of a scale to measure functional outcomes in therapeutic recreation. *Therapeutic Recreation Journal, 30*(1), 13-26.

Lee, Y., McCormick, B., & Perkins, S. (2000). Outcome engineer? Therapeutic recreation practice in the third millennium. *Parks and Recreation, 35*(5), 64-68.

National Council for Therapeutic Recreation Certification. (2008). *2007 Job Analysis.* New City, NY: Author.

Navar, N. (1991). Advancing therapeutic recreation through quality assurance: A perspective on the changing nature of quality in therapeutic recreation. In B. Riley (Ed.), *Quality management: Applications for therapeutic recreation* (pp. 3- 20). State College, PA: Venture.

Olsson, R. H. Jr. (1992). Assessment and progress note writing: Skills needed for treatment documentation. In G. Hitzhusen, & L. T. Jackson (Eds.), *Expanding horizons in therapeutic recreation XIV* (pp. 167-176). Columbia, MO: University of Missouri.

Perschbacher, R. (1995). *Assessment: The cornerstone of activity programs.* State College, PA: Venture.

Riley, B. (1991). Quality assessment: The use of outcome indicators. In B. Riley (Ed.), *Quality management: Applications for therapeutic recreation* (pp. 53-68). State College, PA: Venture.

Robertson, T., & Long, T. (Eds.) (2008). *Foundations of therapeutic recreation: Perceptions, philosophies, and practices for the 21ˢᵗ century.* Champaign, IL: Human Kinetics.

Shank, J., & Coyle, C. (2002). *Therapeutic recreation in health promotion and rehabilitation.* State College, PA: Venture.

Shank, J. W., & Kinney, W. B. (1991). Monitoring and measuring outcomes in therapeutic recreation. In B. Riley (Ed.), *Quality management: Applications for therapeutic recreation* (pp. 69-82). State College, PA: Venture.

Sheehan, T. (1992). Outcome measurement in therapeutic recreation. In G. Hitzhusen, & L. T. Jackson (Eds.), *Expanding horizons in therapeutic-recreation XIV* (pp. 177-192). Columbia, MO: University of Missouri.

Sneegas, J. J. (1989). Can we really measure leisure behavior of special populations and individuals with disabilities? In D. Compton (Ed.), *Issues in therapeutic recreation: A profession in transition* (pp. 223-236). Champaign, IL: Sagamore.

Stumbo, N. (1983). Systematic observation as a research tool for assessing client behavior. *Therapeutic Recreation Journal, 17*(4), 53-63.

Stumbo, N. J. (1991). Selected assessment resources: A review of instruments and references. *Annual in Therapeutic Recreation, 2*(2), 8-24.

Stumbo, N. J. (1992a). *Leisure education II: More activities and resources.* State College, PA: Venture.

Stumbo, N. J. (1992b). Re-thinking activity inventories. *Illinois Parks and Recreation Magazine, 23*(2) 17-21.

Stumbo, N. J. (1993–94). The use of activity interest inventories in therapeutic recreation assessment. *Annual in Therapeutic Recreation, 4*, 11-20.

Stumbo, N. J. (1994-95). Assessment of social skills for therapeutic recreation intervention. *Annual in Therapeutic Recreation, 5*, 68-82.

Stumbo, N. J. (1996). A proposed accountability model for therapeutic recreation services. *Therapeutic Recreation Journal, 30*(4), 246-259.

Stumbo, N. J. (1997). Issues and concerns in therapeutic recreation assessment. In D. M. Compton (Ed.), *Issues in therapeutic recreation: Toward the new millennium* (2nd ed.), (pp. 347-372). Champaign, IL: Sagamore.

Stumbo, N. J. (2001). Revisited: Issues and concerns in therapeutic recreation assessment. In N. J. Stumbo (Ed.), *Professional issues in therapeutic recreation: On competence and outcomes* (pp. 215-236). Champaign, IL: Sagamore.

Stumbo, N. J. (2002a). *Client assessment in therapeutic recreation services.* State College, PA: Venture.

Stumbo, N. J. (2002b). (Ed.). *Leisure education: A manual of activities and resources* (2nd ed.). State College, PA: Venture.

Stumbo, N. J., & Peterson, C. A. (2009). *Therapeutic recreation program design: Principles and procedures* (5th ed.). San Francisco: Benjamin Cummings.

Stumbo, N. J., & Rickards, W. H. (1986). Selecting assessment instruments: Theory into practice. *Journal of Expanding Horizons in Therapeutic Recreation, 1*(1), 1-6.

Stumbo, N. J., & Thompson, S. R. (Eds.). (1986). *Leisure education: A manual of activities and resources.* State College, PA: Venture.

Sylvester, C., Voelkl, J. E., & Ellis, G. D. (2001). *Therapeutic recreation programming: Theory and practice.* State College, PA: Venture.

Touchstone, W. A. (1975). The status of client evaluation in psychiatric settings. *Therapeutic Recreation Journal, 14*(6), 166-172.

West, R., Kinney, T., & Witman, J. (2008). *Guidelines for competency assessment and curriculum planning for recreational therapy practice.* Hattiesburg, MS: American Therapeutic Recreation Association.

Witt, P., Connolly, P., & Compton, D. (1980). Assessment: A plea for sophistication. *Therapeutic Recreation Journal, 14*(4), 3-8.

CHAPTER 18

Ethics and the CTRS™

Sharon Nichols, CTRS ™
Genesis Healthcare Corporation

Mary Ann Keogh Hoss, Ph.D., CTRS, FACHE, FDRT
Eastern Washington University

It is no wonder that the discussion of ethics and the integration of ethics in therapeutic recreation practice is such a conundrum. There are so many factors in life and in our practice environment that influence one's ethics and our understanding of how we ought to behave in various situations where there is no right answer that is clearly evident. How ought I behave? Would my profession support my behavior? Is my behavior consistent with that of other practitioners? The prevailing question that emerges is why explore ethics and professional conduct? The resounding answer is that it is "the right thing to do!"

There are numerous forces that shape our view of ethics such as our family values, our education, our government and judicial systems, our religious beliefs, our cultural heritage, our peers both personal and professional, business values and corporate culture, and our own personal experiences.

In 2000, the Veterans Administration Center for National Ethics proposed a model (see Figure 18.1) that provided a framework for looking at ethics in healthcare from an integrative perspective. The model considers internal and external forces that press upon healthcare organizations. The outcome of those forces ought to result in a comprehensive view of ethics within organizations. The VA Model clearly demonstrates that a discussion of ethics in professional practice is not a simple one.

In our current healthcare environment, there have been tremendous focus and resources that are placed upon healthcare fraud and abuse as well as business fraud and abuse. In today's world, no one is exempt from the magnifying glass. In a *Washington Post* story (Lee, 2008) highlighting the results of a study conducted by the Ethics Resource Center (retrieved January 30, 2008), "almost one-quarter of public sector employees identify their work environments as conducive to misconduct—places where there is strong pressure to

---

Figure 18.1
Forces that Shape Ethical Healthcare Practices

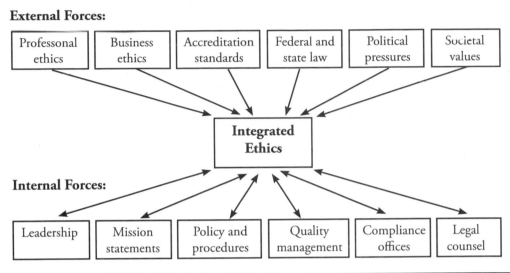

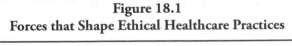

VA Center for National Ethics, 2000.

---

compromise standards, where situations invite wrongdoing, and/or employees' personal values conflict with the values espoused at work." Is the public sector the next Enron arena?

In April 1999, just before the fall of Enron, Ken Lay, CEO of Enron said, "there is little doubt in my mind, indeed no doubt, that a strong, independent, and knowledgeable board can make a significant difference in the performance of any company. ... The responsibility of our board ... is to ensure legal and ethical conduct by the company and everyone in the company." Enron was only one small domino in a series of events that brought us to the place where we are today.

HIPAA

In 1996, the president signed into law the Health Insurance Portability and Accountability Act (HIPAA). One of the outcomes of this act was the creation of the Healthcare Fraud and Abuse Control Program, which fell under the joint direction of the U.S. Attorney General and the Secretary of the Department of Health and Human Services acting through the Department's Inspector General. This program is designed to coordinate federal, state, and local law enforcement programs as it relates to healthcare fraud and abuse. HIPAA allowed for new criminal and civil enforcement tools and resources that resulted in an expansion and intensification in the fight against healthcare fraud and abuse. Since the inception of this program, the government has been able to see a tremendous return on their investment in this program.

In FY 2005, the government won or negotiated approximately $1.47 billion in judgments and settlements. The Medicare Trust Fund received nearly $1.55 billion during this period as a result of these efforts (August 2006). Since its inception in 1997, there has been $8.85 billion turned over to the Medicare Trust Fund.

In FY 2005, GlaxoSmithKline paid the U.S. $140 million to settle allegations of fraudulent drug pricing and marketing. AdvancePCS paid the U.S. $138.5 million to resolve allegations that AdvancePCS received kickbacks from drug manufacturers in exchange for marketing their drugs.

HealthSouth Corporation paid the U.S. $32 million to settle allegations of fraud against Medicare and other federally insured heath programs. The University of Alabama in Birmingham and two other entities will pay the U.S. $3.39 million to settle allegations that the violated the False Claims Act (FCA) in claims submitted in connection with the school's health science research program.

United Healthcare Insurance Company agreed to pay the U.S. $3.5 million to settle allegations that the insurance company had defrauded the Medicare program.

These are merely a series of recent events that serve to emphasize the extent of scrutiny now imposed upon our practice environment. The healthcare fraud initiatives protect our nation's healthcare system by directly impacting the current operating budget of the Medicare system through the prevention of cheating hundreds of millions of dollars from taxpayers and by using well-publicized, high-impact cases as a deterrent for future crimes by those who previously believed their activities would go unnoticed.

Sarbanes-Oxley Act of 2002

One of the repercussions of the Enron scandal was the passage of the Sarbanes–Oxley Act of 2002. This law requires attestations by CEOs and CFOs of all publicly traded companies that all financial certifications are accurate. It further requires that companies set up strict conflict of interest rules. It protects whistleblowers. It promotes reporting mechanisms that skip chain of command.

Quite obviously, there exists an environment in healthcare today where recreation therapy practitioners must be mindful and diligent regarding the risks that they face when it comes to professional and ethical conduct.

Some of the apparent risks that currently exist are billing for items or services that were not provided, providing medically unnecessary services, substandard quality of care to nursing home residents, submitting false claims or false cost reports, and being in violation of the scope of practice of state licensure laws.

Fortunately, as a profession, we have consistently explored the nature of professional conduct and ethics. We do have yardsticks with which we can measure ourselves. ATRA and NTRS have Standards of Practice and Codes of Ethics. We have a framework for ethical decision making. It is imperative that these tools be ever present in our collective conscience. We must maintain the integrity of our practice by being ever mindful of these resources.

Ethical issues can be the most stressful experience on the job for the therapist. For some, ethics is a complicated word that provides little direction and much confusion. According to Encarta (retrieved January 9, 2007), ethics (Greek *ethika,* from ethos, "character," "custom") is defined as principles or standards of human conduct, sometimes called morals and by extension, the study of such principles. Ethics is a branch of philosophy that studies human conduct, character, and values. Ethics is also called moral philosophy. Ethics as moral philosophy studies human actions in respect to their being right or wrong.

History

The beginning of the ethical definitions used today in healthcare generated in the fifth century B.C. in the School of Hippocrates with the Hippocratic Oath: "I will use treatment to help the sick according to my ability and judgment, but never with a view to injury or wrongdoing" (Glannon, 2005, p. 1). This served as the basis of the central Latin principle of medical practice: *Primum non nocere*: "First, do no harm" (Glannon, 2005, p. 1). These concepts have followed the healthcare professions for hundreds and hundreds of years.

An English physician, Thomas Percival in 1803, expanded the concept to include a broader social ethic of medicine as the professional responsibility of the physician. These concepts were incorporated into the American Medical Association's first Code of Medical Ethics in 1849. The 1946 revision of the code included nonmaleficence (no harm), beneficence (benefiting), as well as the doctor's responsibility to the medical profession and the society at large (Glannon, 2005). The code one lived by and practiced was much simpler and straightforward. Gene Autry's Cowboy Code, written in 1939, illustrates these basic concepts.

1. The Cowboy must never shoot first, hit a smaller man, or take unfair advantage.
2. He must never go back on his word or a trust confided in him.
3. He must always tell the truth.
4. He must be gentle with children, the elderly, and animals.
5. He must not advocate or possess racially or religiously intolerant ideas.
6. He must help people in distress.
7. He must be a good worker.
8. He must keep himself clean in thought, speech, action, and personal habits.
9. He must respect women, parents, and his nation's laws.
10. The Cowboy is a patriot.

Up until World War II, the physician was the authority. With the knowledge of human experimentation under the Nazi government, a gradual shift in decision-making authority occurred from the physician to the patient. The concept of autonomy, the patient-based principle of having the capacity and right to self-determination became married to the Hippocratic concepts of nonmaleficence and beneficence. Implications of significant ethical issues have been experienced as advances in medical technology have occurred, starting with kidney dialysis and respirators in the 1960s (Glannon, 2005). One can only guess at the issues that will present themselves during the twenty-first century with the rapid medical and technological advances.

According to MacIntyre (1998), historians of morals "suggest that although what is held to be right or good is not always the same, roughly the same concepts of right and good are universal" (p. 1). MacIntyre goes on to say that "In fact, of course, moral concepts change as social life changes"(p. 1). These changes promote many of the demands experienced by therapists.

Today

Discussions regarding ethics are difficult for many reasons. For those in healthcare, the discussion is not only difficult, it is also demanding and at times heart-wrenching.

Paul and Elder (2006) view the basis of ethics as clear: "Human behavior has consequences for the welfare of others. We are capable of acting toward others in such a way as to increase or decrease the quality of their lives. We are capable of helping or harming" (p. 4).

Ethics has several meanings. The dictionary defines ethics as the discipline dealing with what is good and bad and with moral duty and obligation and the principles of conduct governing an individual or a group. The therapist encounters both of these definitions through the organization one works for based on the philosophy defined through the mission, vision, and values of the organization for the care and services provided. The principles of conduct are experienced both through the organization one works for and the credentialing and professional membership organizations to which a therapist belongs.

For therapists, ethics are experienced at a personal level, a professional level, and an organizational level. An ethical dilemma occurs when a decision/action must be made/ taken that has two or more competing courses of action that are based on different value sets, moral frameworks, or varying or inconsistent organizational philosophy. In order for a decision to be made, a thoughtful process must be engaged in to explore the best path or course of action. The decision itself should be considered the "best" possible under the circumstances, because if there were a "right" answer, the professional would be duty bound by his/her professional and/or organizational code of ethics to execute it.

In order to assist the therapist in arriving at the best possible decision, *Finding the Path: Ethics in Action* (1998) proposes the following Decision-Making Model (Figure 18.2).

The decision-making model identifies in step four that the therapist consider the laws that pertain to the situation. Darr (2005) states the following:

> The relationship between law and ethics is dynamic. ... Law may be defined as a system of principles and rules of human conduct prescribed or recognized by a supreme authority. This definition includes criminal and civil law. In contrast, ethics is the study of standards of moral judgment and conduct. For individuals, this is the personal ethic. For a professional, it is the guiding system or code of ethics. (p. 5). ... For professionals, ethics is much more than obeying the law. The law is but the minimum standard of morality established by society to guide interactions among individuals and between them and government. ... Professionals are bound by the law but have a higher calling, one that includes numerous positive duties to patients and society and to one another. (p. 7)

Henderson in 1982 described the relationship between law and ethics as a matrix of possible outcomes with four quadrants. The quadrants are legal and ethical, unethical and legal, unethical and illegal, and ethical and illegal. Decisions made are rated and fall into one of the four quadrants. According to Darr (2005), "There is ample evidence of ethical and legal problems in the world of business. Despite occurring less often and having less impact on the economy and society, there have been enough ethical and legal misadventures in the health services management field to know that it faces important challenges" (p. 11).

Figure 18.2
The Decision-Making Model Ethical Situations in Professional Practice/Business

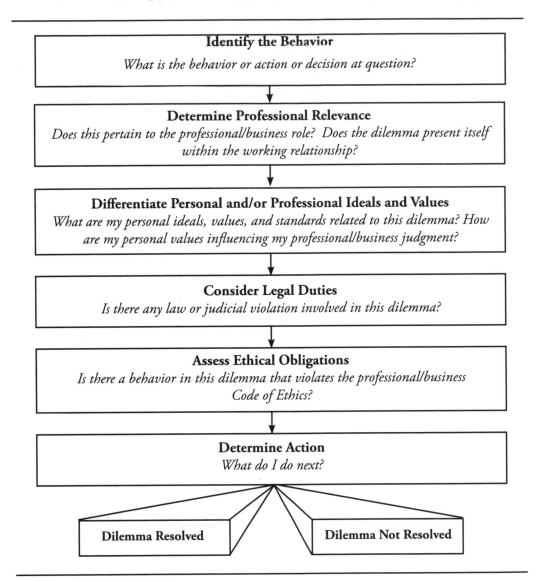

Adaptation permitted by the American Therapeutic Recreation Association. Finding the Path: Ethics in Action. *1998.*

Discussion Questions

1. Review the NTRS and ATRA *Codes of Ethics*. How are they alike? How do they differ?
2. Look on the Internet for recent data on HIPAA. What effect is it having on healthcare?
3. Create a healthcare scenario that involves an ethical dilemma. Bring it to class, and with other students, use Figure 18.2 to go through an ethical decision-making process.

References

American Therapeutic Recreation Association. (1998). *Finding the path: Ethics in action.* Hattiesburg, MS: Author.

Autry, G. (1939). Gene Autry's Cowboy Code. Retrieved January 9, 2007 from http;//www.geneautry.com

Darr, K. (2005). *Ethics in health services management* (4th ed.). Baltimore, MD: Health Professions Press.

Glannon, W. (2005). *Biomedical ethics.* New York: Oxford University Press, Inc

Henderson, V.E. (1982). The ethical side of enterprise. *MIT Sloan Management Review, 23,* 37-43.

Lee, C. (2008). Study Finds Government Ethics Lapses. Retrieved January 30, 2008 from Washington Post on the World Wide Web: http://www.washingtonpost.com

MacIntyre, A. (1998). *A short history of ethics.* Notre   Dame, IN: University of Notre Dame Press.

 Microsoft. (1996). Ethics. Encarta. Retrieved January 9, 2007, from Encarta on the World Wide Web: http://www.encarta.msn.com

Paul, R., & Elder, L. (2006). *The thinker's guide to understanding the foundations of ethical reasoning* (2nd ed.). Dillon Beach, CA: Foundation for Critical Thinking.

United States Department of Health and Human Services and The Department of Justice, Healthcare Fraud and Abuse Control Program. Annual Report for FY 2005. August 2006. Retrieved January 30, 2008 from Office of the Inspector General on the World Wide Web: http://oig.hhs.gov

United States Department of Veteran's Affairs, National Center for Ethics in Healthcare. 2000. World Wide Web: http://www.ethics.va.gov

Reimbursement: Surviving Prospective Payment as a Recreational Therapy Practitioner

G.T. Thompson, CTRS™, M.Ed., NHA
Susquehanna Health

Challenges of Healthcare

The reasons that motivate a person to enter a caring profession such as recreational therapy are numerous. No list of these potential motivators, however, probably includes a fondness for cost analysis, price setting, productivity monitoring, and financial management! Unfortunately, these are some of the very skills that will drive the survival and future success of this healthcare profession. Without competencies associated with sound financial management, recreational therapy practitioners will struggle in the ever-changing healthcare environment.

Providers of healthcare have come under increasing challenges and pressures related to the financing of their services. Since the advent of the Medicare Acute Hospital Diagnostic Related Groups (DRG) payment system as part of Public Law 98-21 Social Security Act Amendments in the early 1980s (Lohr & Marquis, 1984), healthcare has seen a steady decrease in funding. Recreational therapists had just established a toehold in the retrospective fee-for-service reimbursement world when the rules began to change. The implementation of prospective capitates reimbursement has increased the complexity of recovering the costs of healthcare treatment services. As healthcare practitioners, recreational therapists must be competent in the financial management and accountability of their treatment services. As healthcare dollars become more precious, the demand for validation of treatment effectiveness and efficiency has followed. Recreational therapists who master these critical competencies will be successful even in the most difficult reimbursement environment.

Windows of Opportunity

As a healthcare professional, it is easy to become anxious as new changes are announced in the payment and regulations of healthcare. Frequently, any change is viewed as bad. We have come to expect that any required changes will only detract from patient access and quality of care. While the changes in healthcare reimbursement have largely brought negative consequences to the provider community, some positive opportunities exist. Healthcare consumers requiring recreational therapy services have been denied access under archaic 1960s language in Section 1861 of Title XVIII of the Social Security Act. When initially drafted, the federal Social Security Act specifically listed those rehabilitation services that had evolved as recognized treatment services. At the time of this legislation, this did not include recreational therapy. The attempt at global healthcare reform during the 1990s missed an opportunity for increased access by simply updating this outdated language. Since 1983, incremental changes in Medicare payment systems have created some windows of opportunity for recreational therapists. From the implementation of DRGs, comprehensive rehab TEFRA payment (American Rehabilitation Association, 1994), partial hospitalization component billing (Woodridge et al., 1993), and the impact of the 1997 Balanced Budget Act, core aspects of prospective payment have opened access of recreational therapy treatment to more Medicare beneficiaries.

A move away from a provider-based, specific coverage to an outcome-driven, bundling-of-service coverage allows for recognition of recreational therapy and other effective services. This market-driven change replaces a prescriptive approach that involved choosing from an antiquated list of treatment options. Bundling of services recognizes the value of applying the most cost-effective mix of treatments and procedures. Providers have been given the flexibility to exercise medical judgment in delivering the most appropriate combination of services according the individual needs of the patient. Medical and rehabilitation services must demonstrate effectiveness and efficiency to be viable under these changes.

Specific identification and coding revisions have created opportunities for recreational therapy. These changes include comprehensive rehab TEFRA system inclusion of recreational therapy in the three-hour screening criteria and partial hospitalization's incremental billing activity code. Additionally, the skilled nursing prospective payment system (HCFA's RAI Version 2.0 Manual, 1995) definitions, the reporting of recreational therapy data, and the inclusion of therapeutic recreation on the Rehab Prospective Payment System (PPS) Minimum Data Set Post Acute Version 1 therapy menu and even the change of therapeutic recreation to section t of the Minimum Data Set version 2.0 have all been very positive changes for this profession.

In measuring the value of recreational therapy, focus has been almost solely on the benefits delivered to patients. While this emphasis is not misplaced, recreational therapists must begin to broaden their measurement to include cost. Enhanced value of effective services being delivered at reasonable costs positions recreational therapy well for the future. Recreational therapy costs have been traditionally significantly lower than alternative therapy services. The primary cost components of any service is labor, resources, and technology. While the lower average salaries have been one of the profession's most frequent complaints, under a capitated reimbursement system, this becomes a significant marketing advantage. The durable and nondurable resources utilized in the delivery of recreational therapy resources typically are nominal in cost. Finally, as a high-touch, low-tech caring profession, recreational therapists do not routinely rely on expensive technology for facilitating effective outcomes.

Balanced Budget Act of 1997

The signing of the Balanced Budget Act (Public Law 105-33) by former President Clinton in August 1997 had significant impact on both healthcare consumers and providers. The 1997 BBA has been very successful in fulfilling its primary objective—to reduce the spending of healthcare dollars. Almost every initiative within the 1997 BBA mandated reduced federal healthcare dollars and tied payment rates to costs since its inception. The 1997 BBA is credited with surpassing the budgeted savings and contributing toward the 1999 federal budget surplus.

The 1997 BBA mandated the development of prospective payment system changes in skilled nursing, outpatient hospital, home health, and comprehensive rehabilitation. The practical impact of PPS on healthcare has been significant.

Hospital Inpatient
- A penalty now exists for a transfer too quickly, where hospitals previously had incentive to transfer patients as soon as possible.
- There are fewer incentives for skilled nursing facilities to accept high-acuity patients resulting in discharge disposition problems.
- Reducing the length of stay is no longer a consistent answer to a positive financial picture.
- Hospitals must focus on reducing the cost of delivering outcomes.
- The processes for smooth and timely transfer to a skilled nursing facility or home with referrals must be streamlined.

Hospital Outpatient
- Outpatient rehab is now paid based on the Medicare physician fee schedule.
- The Medicare physician fee schedule payment rates have continually been under review and in many instances reduced.
- Outpatient services will remain a growth and revenue opportunity area.
- Efficient delivery of services will remain important.
- Treatment procedures that are easily coordinated and require fewer resources will be highly valued.

Home Health
- Reimbursement will be based on national averages versus agency specific costs.
- High-cost services will be disadvantaged.
- Home health, where previously a profit center, will more likely be unprofitable or will break even.
- There will be stricter limits on per-beneficiary services.
- Agencies will need to maintain a larger base of patients to be financially successful.

Skilled Nursing
- Hospital-based units experienced a reduction in revenue compared to pre-PPS.
- Residents with high-acuity needs are no longer profitable for facilities.
- Profitability is difficult for skilled-nursing facilities.
- Hospitals are no longer transferring some low-acuity patients due to the transfer penalty.
- Hospitals are looking to transfer patients who are high-resource users.

Comprehensive Rehabilitation
- The next generation of Inpatient Rehab Facility (IRF) PPS was implemented, starting April 1, 2001.
- A classification system assigns patients in IRFs into case-mix groups (CMGs).
- Assignment is based on rehabilitation impairment categories (RICs), functional status, and age.
- Payments under the IRF PPS are made on a per-discharge basis.
- Joint replacement patients have difficulty qualifying for admission without accompanying co-morbidities including age, high body mass index, and bilateral replacements.
- Inpatient rehab facilities need to refocus on neurological cases.
- With the loss of qualifying orthopedic admissions satisfying the CMS criteria for at least 75% admission form qualifying diagnoses will be a challenge for most facilities.

Overview of Prospective Payment

What is Prospective Payment?

Prospective payment is a payment system for medical/rehabilitation services at a predetermined price. The rate of payment is calculated prior to service delivery. Prospective payment can be based on a statistically determined price or historical costs. Most base costs are then adjusted to reduce the rate of cost and control cost growth. A review of the recent prospective payment systems identifies five basic elements. These elements of prospective payment are outlined below:

1. It is a price-based system.
2. Rates (prices) are set in advance.
3. The price is inclusive of all services provided.
4. No additional payment or settlement will occur.
5. The current year's actual costs do not impact the price established.

Why PPS?

Prospective payment is based on four underlying principles. Although each prospective payment system may appear distinctly, each is designed to assure the following:

Cost Containment—without a doubt this was the primary motivating principle under the 1997 BBA. PPS has had a significant impact on the delivery of healthcare services. Since the implementation of PPS, the majority of hospitals must now closely manage both revenue and costs in their hospital-based operations.

Quality—even the earliest forms of prospective payment have included safeguards for assuring quality of the services delivered to Medicare beneficiaries. Audits and surveys constitute just two methods utilized for this purpose.

Access—Assuring that Medicare beneficiaries have access to healthcare services is also important. The stretching of limited healthcare dollars has to do with maintaining access to medically necessary treatment services.

Beneficiary Centered—PPS is to maintain a beneficiary-centered focus. Classification systems are developed for payment based on specific resident needs. The 2006 skilled nursing MDS classification system update expanded from 44 to 53 resource-utilization groups. Residents are assigned daily to a specific group based on the individual need as reflected by their resource use.

Price-Based Versus Cost-Based Payment

Healthcare organizations have experienced a transition from being in the driver's seat for establishing a price for services rendered, to reimbursement of the costs required to provide the service and back to a price-based form of reimbursement. The primary distinction between then and now with pricing is control. Previously, the seller or healthcare provider had complete control. Slowly this position has eroded to the point today where the buyer arbitrarily sets this price. The pendulum has swung so far to buyer pricing that the financial ruination of many providers is very possible. A reasonable prediction of the future would call for a more balanced price determination negotiated between provider and payer.

Per-Diem Versus Per-Episode Payment

Prospective payment comes in two different designs. Hospital and rehabilitation PPS has traditionally been paid under a per-episode system. This system is based on an episode of care such as discharge, admission, or diagnosis. Skilled nursing PPS has traditionally been paid under a per-diem payment system. The per-diem system of payment is designed on the costs of delivering each day's services. This system requires more resources for frequent data collection and analysis, although it is considered more effective in reflecting day-to-day service costs.

Required Definitions

Reimbursement	Recovering the costs of resources used in delivering treatment services.
Coverage	Identification and inclusion as a treatment service within the terms of a managed care contract/plan.
Prospective Payment	Payment for medical rehabilitation treatment services at a predetermined price, calculated prior to service delivery.
Retrospective Payment	Payment for medical/rehabilitation treatment services at a cost submitted after service delivery.
Routine Service	Services routinely required by all patients. Routine services are predictable and manageable.

| *Ancillary* | Services specific to patient need. Services differ in scope, |
| *Service* | intensity, and duration for each patient. |

Evolution of Payment and Coverage

Fee for Service

Definition/Background

To draw an example from a favorite leisure interest, fee for service is ordering off the menu. When dining out, we make informed decisions in our choice of food selection. We select the items we want knowing what the cost will be and under what terms we will pay that fee. Healthcare payment has roots in fee for service. Many healthcare services were delivered under a bartering system of fee for service. Some of our older adults today still recall the exchange of home-delivered medical services for livestock or dry goods. Hospitals and healthcare providers were in a boom time under this payment system. The provider controlled prices, which led to the significant growth of the healthcare industry. Fee for service continues to exist, although with less frequency. The growth of managed care has replaced this original payment system out of necessity to control costs to payers and consumers. Ironically, the limitation in choice imposed by most managed care options creates a need for fee for service to allow access to treatment services desired but not covered under the terms of a managed care contract.

Implications for Recreational Therapy

When someone requires and receives medically necessary and appropriate recreational therapy treatment services, the resource cost of providing these services must be paid for. If a recreational therapy service manager fails to have the necessary processes in place to capture this reimbursement, then this opportunity is lost. With the financial difficulties faced by healthcare organizations within today's reimbursement environment, the recovery of every possible reimbursement dollar is a significant event. The effectiveness and efficiency of the RT treatment must be validated. There must be a reasonable expectation that the service will improve the patient's condition. Precedents exist for payment of recreational therapy services under fee for services throughout the nation. A fee-for-service's cost-based charge system offers an excellent tool for tracking costs and productivity. Implementation and management of a fee-for-service system requires energy and leadership by the service manager. Medicare compliance issues and accountability require vigilance on the part of the recreational therapy manager.

Examples of Recreational Therapy Payment

Recreational therapy has received successful fee-for-service reimbursement beginning at least in the mid-1980s. Examples of successful fees for service can be found throughout the country. Despite this success, great discrepancy does occur in many geographic locations for specific recreational therapy services. This discrepancy is driven largely by a lack of knowledge, misinterpretation of regulations, or resistance to change. Recreational therapy providers have demonstrated successful fee-for-service reimbursement with private pay;

government payers, i.e., vocational rehabilitation, Medicaid, or worker's compensation; and most traditional third-party indemnity insurance.

Discounted Fee for Service

Definition /Background

Discounted fee for service is obtained through negotiation within the price-setting process. Discounts are negotiated between the healthcare provider and payer. Discounting resulted as a first measure in controlling the growth of healthcare costs. Payers were at the mercy of the payment rates set solely by healthcare providers. Payers began to negotiate discounts using leverage such as identification as a participating healthcare provider and some assurance of increased business. Discounting might face Medicare compliance issues. Before discounting, healthcare providers must determine they are in compliance with all state and federal regulations. Discounting of less than the established rates for Medicare might be in violation of regulations.

Implications for Recreational Therapy

To provide discounts on established fees, a service must first have a fee-for-service system in place. As previously discussed, the recreational therapy service must have the processes in place to capture reimbursement. These processes include the basis to establishing procedure specific fees and mechanisms for patient/payer billing. Recreational therapy procedures are well positioned under this model of reimbursement. As a service with traditionally low direct costs, recreational therapy treatment procedures may be more easily discounted while maintaining a reasonable net margin. Some recreational therapy treatments utilize a group structure to facilitate specific outcomes. This format provides an opportunity to allocate costs across multiple patients. Treatment delivered in groups should be largely limited to those where the reasonable expectation of improving the patient's condition is facilitated from the group treatment design.

Examples of Recreational Therapy Payment

One example of the application of discounting in recreational therapy included the provision of outpatient aquatic therapy. A local school district was interested in obtaining outpatient aquatic therapy. Within the school district's geographic location, this service was available from the recreational therapists at an area rehabilitation center. The school was reluctant to pursue this service based on the individual inpatient pool therapy fee. The school was able to commit to a specific volume and duration of treatment sessions. Based on the treatment volumes, the recreational therapy aquatic therapy fee was negotiated to a mutually acceptable level. Considerations in this process included:
- Number of patients
- Duration of treatment
- Frequency of treatment
- School personnel assistance with pre- and post-pool functions
- Presence in pool of school personnel

Per Diem

Definition/Background

Under fee for service, healthcare providers were quick to learn that to raise reimbursement only required adding additional billable procedures. The need to control healthcare costs resulted in the implementation of per-diem reimbursement. Per-diem reimbursement provides one daily charge for the costs of all the services required and rendered. If fee for service is reflective of ordering from the menu, then per diem is buying from the buffet.

Implications for Recreational Therapy

Under per-diem reimbursement, there is an increased emphasis on interdisciplinary treatment. Team collaboration skills are vital to the success of practitioners in this arena. Rehabilitation professionals, including the recreational therapist, must coordinate within the interdisciplinary treatment plan while avoiding inappropriate duplication. Rehabilitation is delivered utilizing the most cost-effective mix of treatment services. The strategy for success is clear. Services are valued that can achieve results at a reasonable cost and/or quickly. Specific services do need to be identified and negotiated for inclusion as a covered service. Under per-diem reimbursement, educating for recognition of recreational therapy as a qualified covered service is a key job task for the service manager.

Examples of Recreational Therapy Payment

Recreational therapy is delivered in some settings that are predominantly reimbursed on a per-diem system. Licensed skilled nursing settings are driven by Medicare and Medicaid per-diem reimbursement.

Capitated Per Diem

Definition/Background

Healthcare providers once again found strategies to extend revenues under the per-diem method of reimbursement. If payment is limited to an amount per day, then logically to increase overall revenue requires increasing the number of days. Capitated per diem maintains a daily charge for services provided with a limitation in the number of days covered.

Implications for Recreational Therapy

Under capitated per-diem reimbursement, services will be valued that can facilitate quicker results and transition the patient to the next level of care. Under the constraints of limited treatment days, treatment services will lose value that produce slow results despite the costs.

Examples of Recreational Therapy Payment

Medicare partial hospitalization coverage is just one example of recreational therapy coverage under these conditions. With the 1993 implementation of component billing, recreational therapy, meeting strict active treatment definitions, was recognized and coded as "Activity Therapy." This setting is reimbursed based on a daily price. Coverage is limited to a specified number of days. Long-term care is a classic example of capitated per diem. A Medicare beneficiary is entitled to only 100 skilled nursing facility days of Medicare coverage. Beneficiaries must meet specific criteria to be eligible for this coverage. In both settings, if the facility chooses to employ a recreational therapist to treat Medicare beneficiaries, then the costs of those services are assumed under the per diem amount the facility receives.

Prospective Payment Level of Care

Definition/Background

Prospective payment level of care is a predetermined amount of payment calculated on historical or statistical costs. The first significant use of this payment system was in acute-care hospitals with Diagnostic Related Groups (DRGs). This method of healthcare payment expanded on the concept of per diem. It extended a set of payments to an entire episode of care (i.e., an acute care hospital stay or a comprehensive rehabilitation discharge). Prospective payment requires classifying patients into groupings for payment. In acute care, diagnostic groups were established. In Inpatient Rehabilitation, each facility was formerly assigned a rate based on the historical cost required for treating and discharging patients. The most recent prospective payment reform in Inpatient Rehabilitation classifies patients according to rehabilitation impairment categories (RICs), functional status, and age.

Implications for Recreational Therapy

The prospective payment level of care provided an opportunity for the growth of recreational therapy service access to consumers. As part of the bundle of comprehensive rehabilitation services, recreational therapy is now a primary rehabilitation service. Within this method of healthcare payment, services are valued that can reduce costs and length of stay. Recent PPS changes for acute-care hospitalization have established penalties for transferring patients too soon. Despite this change, incentive remains to value services that can deliver the needed outcomes at lower cost. Recognition of recreational therapy as a qualified and covered service is key under this form of reimbursement. Many times, regulatory language holds the definition of what services are included in the bundle of qualified treatment services. Proactively influencing these regulations is absolutely critical to allow consumers access to medically necessary and appropriate recreational therapy services.

Examples of Recreational Therapy Payment

Recreational therapy services delivered in comprehensive DRG-exempt rehabilitation settings are covered under the prospective payment level of care method. The new Inpatient Rehab Facility prospective payment rates were designed including the costs of recreational therapy. This was stated as "Under the prospective payment system (PPS) for IRF's the costs of recreational therapy services are included in the "base payment rate" in September 2005 correspondence from Herb Kuhn, CMS Director of the Center for Medicare Management to former United States Senator Rick Santorum. Under the public policy leadership of the American Therapeutic Recreation Association, the profession has received specific recognition as a qualified service to satisfy the three-hour screening criteria for comprehensive rehabilitation. Recreational therapy is a primary rehabilitation service that can be instrumental in assuring effective rehabilitation outcomes while lowering direct costs. The Recreational therapists employed to treat Medicare beneficiaries in the acute-care setting are also covered under the prospective payment level of care. This setting is paid based on the statistical cost calculated for each diagnostic group (DRG rate).

Prospective Payment for Continuum of Care

Definition/Background

Prospective payment for continuum of care represents the next generation of payment in healthcare. Healthcare services are delivered under a larger system or network. As a healthcare consumer, patients will be going to one agency or organization for what can be described as cradle-to-grave services. Healthcare practitioners have all witnessed the beginning of this phenomenon. Healthcare organizations are combining efforts through mergers, acquisitions, and alliances. These moves position providers for the future by eliminating duplicated service costs and by assuring service through the healthcare continuum. These mega-organizations will provide some assurance that all consumers' healthcare needs will be met for the fee provided.

Implications for Recreational Therapy

Under this concept of reimbursement, the same rules apply as discussed for the previous forms of payment. This type of service delivery would include some unique opportunities. A recreational therapy service in this organization would have opportunity to diversify as the system offered care ranging from prevention to skilled nursing, home care, or hospice. The recreational therapy manager will need to be keenly aware of and able to articulate the implications of all payment systems. Diversifying recreational therapy services will occur through the assertive advocacy of the service in the organization's strategic planning process.

Examples of Recreational Therapy Payment

As this form of reimbursement is just now shaping up, examples of recreational therapy successes must be left to the assertive, creative, business-smart recreational therapy managers who first encounter these opportunities.

PPS Application and Recreational Therapy Across the Spectrum of Care

Acute Care Hospital Inpatient

Recreational therapy can be covered in the acute care hospital settings for Medicare beneficiaries. The reimbursement is under the per-episode DRG payment. This payment is based on the statistical cost assigned to the diagnostic group. Reducing cost is a primary strategy for positioning a treatment service for success. Recent changes have limited the benefits in many rehab-related DRGs to decreasing lengths of stay.

Inpatient Rehabilitation Facility (IRF)

Recreational therapy is covered in Inpatient Rehab under the Centers for Medicare and Medicaid Services (CMS) per-episode system of payment. This system was developed with input of a Technical Expert/Panel that includes representation by the American

Therapeutic Recreation Association. A classification system is used to assign patients in IRFs into case-mix groups (CMGs). The IRF PPS uses Federal prospective payment rates using rehabilitation impairment categories (RICs), functional status, and age. The IRF PPS uses federal prospective payment rates using rehabilitation impairment categories. Payments under the IRF PPS are made on a per-discharge basis.

Partial Hospitalization

Recreational therapy was formerly covered in the partial hospitalization setting. The 1993 component billing policy for psychiatric partial hospitalization programs clarified the mechanism for recreational therapy coverage. Recreational therapy is one of several "Activity Therapy" services that was able to be billed under HCPCS code Q0082. Payment is made on a per-diem basis. The most recent changes to Medicare Partial Hospitalization coverage has restrained many partial programs in the scope of services that are offered.

Outpatient

Recreational therapy is not covered for outpatient Medicare at this time. This primarily is based on the outdated language of the Social Security Act that does not identify recreational therapy specifically. The regulation language does include coverage of hospital inpatient services provided in an outpatient setting. Under this premise, one could interpret recreational therapy as being covered. Limited successful coverage has been documented to date.

Skilled Nursing Facilities/Units

Recreational therapy is certainly covered in the skilled nursing arena under the Medicare Part A coverage. Skilled nursing Part A is paid on a per-diem prospective-payment system. Long-term care regulations require that services must be provided that are medically necessary and appropriate. Additionally, skilled nursing facilities must contract for services if a qualified provider is not on staff. Medicare Part B benefits do not cover recreational therapy because of the same restrictions discussed above in "Outpatient."

Strategies for Success

What can a recreational therapy manager do to succeed in maximizing the coverage of his or her department's treatment services? Based on today's healthcare environment, six specific strategies will go a long way toward successful recognition and coverage. Assuring active treatment, obtaining specific physician orders, making a clear distinction between recreational therapy and activities, skill in cost analysis and accountability, appropriate staffing based on volume productivity, and compliance with regulatory mandates would assure a bright future for a recreational therapy service.

Assure Active Treatment

Recreational therapy services or therapeutic recreation treatment must consistently satisfy the definition of active treatment. Treatment must: (a) be furnished under an individualized plan of treatment or diagnosis, (b) have a reasonable expectation to improve the patient's condition (c) be for diagnostic purposes, (d) be supervised periodically, and (e) be evaluated by a physician. Therapeutic recreation services that do not satisfy the definition of active treatment, although therapeutic, cannot be represented as active treatment (therapy).

Specific Physician Orders

Physician orders remain the key indicator of medical necessity. Today's healthcare environment requires a high degree of accountability. Physician orders must provide more direction than "recreational therapy consult." Physicians' initial or clarification orders should include an indication of the scope of service to be provided, the intensity of the service, and the duration of the treatment intervention.

Clear Distinction between Recreational Therapy and Activity Services

With the growing presence of rehabilitation within the long-term care industry, the need for recreational therapy treatment services has experienced significant growth. These recreational therapy treatments are in addition to the mandated activity services. In smaller operations, many individuals have the responsibility for delivering both services. It is very important that the recreational therapy manager clearly distinguish between the recreational therapy and activity services. Opportunity should be exercised to define this distinction through policies and procedures, performance improvement indicators, and budget cost centers.

Cost Analysis and Accountability

Cost accountability is a key competence for all healthcare managers. The recreational therapy service manager must be knowledgeable about the costs and revenues related to their treatment service. Knowing the cost of delivering a treatment service is necessary in demonstrating cost-effectiveness. Where managers were once responsible for their annual cost/expenses, they must now have an accurate accounting of the cost for each 15-minute unit and, preferably, each treatment minute.

Staffing and Productivity

In today's healthcare environment, managing staffing costs through productivity is critical. Like all businesses, personnel costs are the primary expense within a recreational therapy service. Productivity measures provide a mechanism for assuring the appropriate level of staffing according to treatment volumes. Productivity measures are a ratio of staff hours to treatment volumes delivered. These usually are expressed as a percentage of the staff scheduled hours.

This measure does vary from organization to organization. Factors such as organization mission, patient acuity, and complexity can all influence the targeted productivity rate.

Compliance with Regulatory Mandates

Regulatory standards provide the foundation for an effective recreational therapy service. Compliance with the Centers for Medicare and Medicaid Services (CMS) (formerly Healthcare Finance Administration) regulations provide a framework for managing any healthcare operation and avoiding criminal penalties. The Joint Commission for the Accreditation of Healthcare Organizations (JCAHO) and Rehabilitation Accreditation Commission (CARF) accreditation regulations contribute to the design of an effective recreational therapy treatment service. A recreational therapy manager must be aware of any applicable state or local health regulations that could impact his or her service.

Related Professional Practice Issues

Several professional practice issues are currently under review that could have a significant impact on the practice of recreational therapy. These issues include the coding of treatment services, outcome efficiency, outcome effectiveness, state-qualified provider recognition, the development of Medicare Local Coverage Determinations (LCD), and the Recreational Therapy Medicare Project.

Coding Issues

As healthcare payment systems become more complex, the coding of healthcare procedures has made claim submission and payment more manageable. Without the assignment of a proper code, no healthcare practitioner will receive payment despite the effectiveness of their outcomes. The current procedural terminology published by the American Medical Association is an industry standard. Currently, recreational therapy procedures are coded using codes from the Physical Medicine and Rehabilitation chapter. Many of these codes are defined in functional task terminology consistent with the nature of recreational therapy interventions and outcomes. These codes are not limited to any one discipline. The American Therapeutic Recreation Association continues to address coding issues.

Efficiency of Practice and Treatment Outcomes

Recreational therapy managers must become skilled at the financial management of their treatment service. They must know the actual direct and projected indirect cost of treatment units and minutes. With this information, practitioners can communicate the cost by which their outcomes are delivered. This knowledge also provides the baseline by which resources can be managed to reduce cost and increase the competitiveness of recreational therapy in the market place.

Outcome Effectiveness Accountability

The integration of valid scientifically based research methods and outcomes into recreational therapy practice is very important. Therapeutic recreation no longer relies on instinct or casual observation that its treatment services are effective. Recreational therapy professionals must integrate research data into their treatment intervention protocols (see chapter 16) for rationale in procedure design and application. Treatment intervention must also be designed to allow evaluation of outcomes in a manner that provides valid outcome data consistent with research design (see chapters 25-29).

State Recognition of the Certified Therapeutic Recreation Specialist™ as a Qualified Healthcare Provider

The recognition of the CTRS™ as a qualified healthcare professional is a key practice issue. The primary benefit of any credentialing plan (licensure, certification, or registration) is the protection of consumers from harm. This benefit serves the consumers of recreational therapy through the identification of qualified providers. The issue of who is a qualified healthcare provider in a state holds significant impact on the providers as well. Having the Certified Therapeutic Recreation Specialist™ recognized as a qualified healthcare professional is critical, as healthcare policy is delegated to the state legislatures. Designation as a qualified provider allows consumers access to the services of the qualified recreational therapist. Both government and commercial health plans have used the state-qualified provider recognition to determine provider eligibility.

Local Coverage Determinations or LCDs are policy directives developed by local Medicare Fiscal Intermediaries that impact coverage and access to treatment interventions and services.

Panels of physicians are retained by Medicare Fiscal Intermediaries to develop local determinations on coverage decisions. These LCDs, while subject to broad guidelines from CMS, have significant latitude in publishing local determination that impact access and coverage of services including recreational therapy. The growth of this type of policy directive reinforces the importance of recreational therapy professionals supporting the public policy advocacy work of the recreational therapy profession through their state chapters and national organization.

The Recreational Therapy Medicare Project was launched in 2004 as a result of Medicare beneficiaries often being denied access to medically necessary and appropriate recreational therapy services. Much of this was the result of inconsistent and often-inaccurate interpretation of regulations by contracted Medicare Fiscal Intermediaries. To assure that Medicare beneficiaries have access to recreational therapy required regulatory action. Only through regulatory and statutory changes can recreational therapy be recognized in all inpatient healthcare settings. Initial efforts were focused on advocacy and education with the Center for Medicare and Medicaid Services. Remedies were sought to secure consistent recognition of recreational therapy in the Inpatient Psychiatric, Inpatient Rehabilitation, and Skilled Nursing Settings. Under the direction of the American Therapeutic Recreation Association, the first phase of the project included establishing and continuing a dialogue with CMS to seek policy change at this level. While some progress in CMS acknowledgment of recreational therapy cost inclusion in PPS rate setting was realized in this effort the broader goals were not obtained. Actually during the course of Phase I, CMS removed previous recognition of recreational therapy from the Inpatient Psychiatric setting. Phase II of the project is currently concluding. This has involved the education of and enlistment of support of members of the United States House of Representatives and United States Senate regarding the R.T. Medicare Project. Phase II has realized significant success with 48 house members and 21 senators signing on to respective "Dear Colleague" letters sent to CMS urging their support of recreational therapy.

Phase II was highlighted by two of the most significant public policy events in the history of the recreational therapy profession. The 2004 and 2007 ATRA Mid Year Conferences each included visits with federal elected officials on Capitol Hill in Washington D.C. by hundreds of recreational therapy professionals. These events were instrumental in fulfilling the objectives of education and advocacy resulting in the support of federal lawmakers. Phase III has been initiated at the time of this writing. This final phase involves the development of specific legislative language that mandates the required regulatory change by CMS.

Sponsors and co-sponsors in the United States Congress are currently being secured to allow this legislative process to go forward.

Ten Steps to Recreational Therapy Coverage and Reimbursement

As a primer for recreational therapy professionals, there are 10 concrete steps that explore expanded coverage and reimbursement opportunities within their services. While these are by no means inclusive of the barriers practitioners experience in this process, they do reflect a logical order of steps in considering expanded revenue opportunity.

1. *Develop Competency*
   The successful coverage or reimbursement of any recreational therapy practice begins with the individual provider(s). A qualified recreational therapist must be prepared with the competencies for the patient population and setting where he or she practices.

2. *Determine Payment Processes*
   Seeking reimbursement does not include reinventing the wheel. Work with your fiscal services to determine the different payers who cover patients referred to your facility. Research those payers to gain knowledge of their coverage specific to recreational therapy. Initiate a comprehensive advocacy program that includes education of your outcomes and costs.

3. *Assure Efficient/Effective Outcomes*
   Have the documentation in place to show your treatment interventions and outcomes are efficient in cost for the outcomes that are delivered.

4. *Establish Procedure Terminology*
   Select procedural terminology for your interventions that reflects the outcomes for which the customers are looking. The *CPT Manual* published by the American Medical Association provides an excellent reference within the Physical Medicine and Rehabilitation chapter.

5. *Obtain Charge Projections*
   Determine what a prudent charge would be for each of your treatment interventions. These can be set using a cost analysis of the resources required to deliver one unit (15 minutes) of each intervention. These rates should be compared with other recreational therapy procedure rates in the area to determine competitiveness.

6. *Gain Administrative Support*
   Administrative support is critical to maximizing coverage and reimbursement. Although there exists significant opportunity for capturing additional revenue, this requires the cooperation of clinical, administrative, and fiscal services.

7. *Complete a Retrospective Review*

Review your patient cases from the past six months. Calculate the number of 15-minute units delivered for each intervention. Apply the projected procedure rates to the total units in each procedure category. Work with your fiscal services to determine the different payers who covered these patients during their stay and what their percentage of payment was.

8. *Complete a Selected Concurrent Pilot Study*

With administrative support, select a specific case or cases to conduct a concurrent study of actual reimbursement. The patient case selected should be a referred recreational therapy patient. To maximize your success, you should begin with a payer who has a prior history of recreational therapy treatment in your market region. Provide your treatment services, as referred. Submit recreational therapy charges with the hospital bill for all ancillary services. Monitor the payment reconciliation. This can take several months until payment is actually received by your agency. Prior to therapy, it is prudent to make an agreement not to pass unpaid charges onto the patient during these initial pilot studies.

9. *Develop a Marketing Plan*

With your cost-effectiveness assured and your billing system designed, you can operationalize your reimbursement system through a proper marketing plan. The target audiences in this market plan would be payers including the traditional indemnity insurance and managed-care entities. Effective advocacy material on outcomes and cost efficiency are available through the American Therapeutic Recreation Association (see www.atra-online.org).

10. *Closely Monitor Effectiveness*

Once established, a coverage and reimbursement system must be monitored and maintained. Change is constant in the world of healthcare services and payment. As a recreational therapy manager, you must assure your services are delivering the outcomes the consumer needs. You have to comply with all regulatory and legal requirements and a fiscal responsibility to recover the cost of the healthcare resources utilized.

Discussion Questions

1. What are the implications for the recreational therapy practitioner as a majority of healthcare payments become based on prospective payment systems?
2. While the language of the Social Security Act provided access to many healthcare services for older adults, in what way did this language limit access to medically appropriate recreational therapy services?
3. Explain the difference between per-diem forms of reimbursement and per-episode forms. In what settings would you most likely encounter each of these systems?
4. What differences exist between the implications for recreational therapy services in a fee-for-service versus prospective payment level of care?

5. Discuss the application of prospective payment within at least three different settings where recreational therapy is delivered.
6. Describe what you can do as a recreational therapy manager or practitioner to maximize the recognition and payment of your treatment service.
7. Discuss the implications for at least one professional practice issue that is critical to the advancement of the recreational therapy profession.
8. Given the information in this text, what are the primary barriers to establishing systems for recovering the cost of recreational therapy resources used in delivering effective treatment services? What strategies exist for overcoming these barriers?
9. Describe the purpose of the Recreational Therapy Medicare Project. What are the three phases of this project?

References

American Rehabilitation Association. (1994). *Tech brief: Application of the three-hour rule to recreational therapy.* Washington, DC: Author.

Healthcare Finance Administration. (September 1995). HCFA's RAI Version 2.0 Manual. Chapter 3: MDS Items T, 3-167.

Lohr, K. N., & M. S. Marquis, Medicare and Medicaid: Past, present and future, The Rand Corporation, N-2088-HHS/RC, May 1984.

Woodridge, K., Wagner, D., & Thompson, G. (1993). Reimbursement for partial hospitalization. *American Therapeutic Recreation Newsletter.* Alexandria, VA.

CHAPTER 20

Legislative and Regulatory Issues in Therapeutic Recreation

John W. Shank
Temple University

It is expected that a professionalizing occupation establishes the ability to seek and maintain legal support for its services. Houle (1980) included legal support as a distinct characteristic of a profession. He suggested that the worthiness of the profession is deemed by the legal structures that can ensure its continuation by providing support for training these professionals, and by providing monies to support the services the profession provides to the public. Indeed, Thom Skalko (1998), former American Therapeutic Recreation Association (ATRA) president, fervently contended that the most salient endeavors of the therapeutic recreation profession are those that influence public policy and healthcare regulation.

Given its size and resources, the therapeutic recreation (TR) profession has an impressive track record in influencing public laws. However, its advocacy action needs to establish and maintain continuity and consistency. The ability to increase legal support and to influence public policy will prove to be one of the most crucial issues determining the advancement of the profession. Compton reports, "It appears that if the TR profession is to survive in the future, it must become more politically astute" (Compton, 1997, p. 74). The purpose of this chapter is to provide an overview of the TR profession's involvement in the legislative arena and to accentuate the critical factors challenging our future success in this area. The chapter is intentionally detailed so as to preserve an historical record of legislative activities and to reflect the socio-political context in which the discipline is emerging and continually defining itself.

A 40-Year History

The legislative advocacy action of the TR profession has occurred in a relatively short span of 40 years, following the 1966 creation of the National Recreation and Park

Association (NRPA) and its branch, the National Therapeutic Recreation Society (NTRS) to the present. The early history of legislative advocacy reflected the Association's immediate commitment to governmental relations and corresponded with the nation's interest in social policy that would advance the conditions of all persons. The profession's record of legislative advocacy was also influenced by the founding of the American Therapeutic Recreation Association (ATRA) in 1984 and the corresponding responses to legislative and regulatory issues associated with healthcare reform.

The legislative involvement of NTRS began in 1970 when its president, John Nesbitt, declared legislative advocacy to be a priority for the NTRS. He arranged for the executive director for the National Rehabilitation Association to provide direction to the board of NTRS on procedures and strategies for becoming involved in governmental affairs. In 1971, NRPA hired the former legislative counsel for Common Cause, a consumer rights lobbying group. For the next three years, the NRPA Public Affairs staff of six governmental specialists drew significant attention to recreation in Washington. The NTRS enjoyed the exclusive efforts of one of these staff members who worked closely with David Park, the executive secretary of NTRS, and branch president Bill Hillman on matters pertaining to individuals with disabilities.

This was a critical time in the history of legislation for individuals with disabilities. The *Rehabilitation Act of 1973*, considered to be the "civil rights law for disabled persons," contained the original and important references to recreation as an integral part of comprehensive rehabilitation. It was also during the time when legislation was being introduced by Senator Ted Kennedy on education for individuals with disabilities. Physical education and recreation professionals officially formed the National Consortium on Physical Education and Recreation for the Handicapped (NCPERH) in 1975 and focused its energies on the *Education for All Handicapped Children Act* (PL 94-142). This consortium worked closely with the NRPA and the American Alliance for Health, Physical Education, Recreation and Dance (AAHPERD) to successfully lobby for federal regulations that defined recreation as a "related service" in the education of handicapped children. However, by 1975, economic difficulties of the NRPA peaked, resulting in a major reduction of staff, including those in public affairs. From this point on, all legislative action directed by the NTRS would be coordinated through voluntary action.

This began with Park and continued with several other professional members who have voluntarily coordinated TR legislative action since 1983. Although the NRPA again has a full complement of public affairs staff and devotes a portion of its time to legislative and regulatory matters of concern to TR, the NTRS continues to depend heavily on voluntary membership action for the coordination and conduct of the branch's governmental affairs. To the extent possible, the program director of the NTRS branch, who is a full-time staff member of the NRPA, collaborates with the voluntary head of the NTRS legislative committee to coordinate member education and action.

Likewise, the ATRA, founded in 1984, is also heavily dependent on membership action coordinated by a Public Policy Team leader appointed by the Association president. However, by 1993, the ATRA Board of Directors concluded that legislative action was an absolute priority of the Association and deserved significant financial support. ATRA contracted with a law firm that provided two attorneys who possessed deep understanding of rehabilitation and familiarity with the myriad advocacy groups located in Washington, as well as the political process. This has proven to be so worthwhile that ATRA can be expected to maintain legislative counsel as a top financial priority for the organization.

In summary then, the apparently impressive array of Washington-based resources for TR legislative advocacy, initially spearheaded by NTRS, lasted for a very brief period during the early years of the profession. Even with the ongoing guidance of legislative counsel to ATRA, the profession as a whole must continue to depend on reliable and responsive member action emerging from the grassroots. Indeed, this voluntary legislative advocacy has been significant.

An Overview of Legislative Advocacy

The past 40 years have seen increasing evidence of legal support for the provision of TR services and the training of its providers in a number of laws and their associated regulations (Park, 1980). Support can be found for recreation as a form of treatment, rehabilitation, education, and community service for individuals who are ill, have disabilities, or are otherwise are in need of specialized support and service. Certain laws, however, have been the consistent target of TR legislative action, including those pertaining to rehabilitation, education, and nursing home reform.

Rehabilitation

The original view that rehabilitation pertained only to vocational preparation and training underwent a major conceptual shift with the *Rehabilitation Act of 1973* (PL 93-112). The federal government would then embrace the notion of "comprehensive rehabilitation," which includes those services that prepared individuals for the fullest possible participation in life, including living independently in the community. This expanded view enabled Congress to be more receptive to considering the role of recreation in rehabilitation and independent living, which has been a longstanding focus of TR legislative advocacy action.

Based on persuasive testimony from NTRS on the importance of recreation to comprehensive rehabilitation, the U.S. Senate amended the law in 1978 to include a new authorization for special recreation demonstration projects (Title III, Section 316), intended to increase the mobility and socialization of disabled persons through such activities as camping, sports, and the arts. When the Act was reauthorized in 1986 (PL 99-506), testimony was offered by Diana Richardson, a TR professor who had personal experience with the role of recreation in her rehabilitation process. Once again, compelling testimony helped amend this law in ways that extended and expanded the role of recreation in independent living and community integration, and identified TR personnel as bonafide rehabilitation personnel eligible for rehabilitation training monies. The Congress, by its actions, recognized recreation and therapeutic recreation as more than a specific category of activities and as a means toward desirable goals in the overall rehabilitation process. These significant advances were largely due to persuasive oral testimony, solid written testimony, and many letters from professionals in the field during the creation and enactment of these amendments.

Education

Federal legislation affecting education has also received thorough attention from the therapeutic recreation profession, beginning with the *Education for All Handicapped Children Act* (PL 94-142). This 1975 law mandated a free and appropriate education for all children with disabilities, provided in the least restrictive learning environment possible. The TR profession staged an impressively convincing argument to the Congress, contending that recreation was a vital service to a child's learning and a necessary support to all other education. It is important to note, however, that this major accomplishment was actively supported by friends of the special recreation movement, such as Harold Russell, the former chairman of the President's Committee on Employment of the Handicapped. He carried the banner of recreation in his testimony to congressional committees when the regulations were being drafted for PL 94-142.

The law was crafted so that recreation would appear as a content area "related" to special education. Thus, if a child's evaluation indicated a need, the individualized education plan would include either an assessment of leisure functioning, therapeutic recreation, leisure education, or recreation programs in the school or the community.

The entire professional recreation community—NRPA/NTRS, the AAHPERD, and the NCPERH (now known as the National Consortium for Physical Education and Recreation for Individuals with Disabilities (NCPERID)—worked together to press Congress to recognize the importance of recreation in the complete preparation of handicapped children. After witnessing an unprecedented level of coordination and cooperation among these major professional organizations in influencing the role of recreation in this law, NCPERH President John Nesbitt said, "Recreation is organized; recreation is committed; recreation is ready to move forward with PL 94-142" (1977, p. 54).

Unfortunately, early analyses (Bullock, 1986; Coyne, 1981; Stanley, 1985) indicated that recreation was rarely included in an IEP, but was more likely to be found as an after-school extracurricular program. As a result of lobbying efforts by the TR profession, the 1986 amendments to this law (PL 99-457) included therapeutic recreation services as a relevant transition service to assist students with disabilities to move from school to adult life. In 1991, this law was retitled *Individuals with Disabilities Education Act* (IDEA, PL 101-476). The law continues to imply a relevant role for recreation in the education for students who have disabilities. The 1991 amendments reflect an even greater emphasis on education's role in preparing the student for life after school ends and an emphasis on full inclusion. However, evidence of well-established and fully accepted TR services in public schools remains limited (Bedini, Bullock, & Driscoll, 1991; Mische, Coyle, & Ashton-Schaffer, 2001).

Stanley (1987) suggested that the lack of TR in schools was due to the failure of the profession to work with state and local education authorities to ensure application of the law's provisions. Hope was raised for changing this situation during a 1995 national summit on TR and public education. This summit produced a set of strategies and a commitment for annual meetings, but these subsequent meetings have not happened. While there are approximately 30 recreation therapists involved with schools, recreation continues to be included rarely in a child's education plan. There are some impressive exceptions (Kavanaugh, 2006), yet the presence of TR in education seems far short of the profession's goals. Reasons for this include teachers and administrators being unfamiliar with the benefits of recreation in special education and their assumption that recreation needs are met through physical education (Bullock & Johnson, 1998) and the failure of state education administrators to track TR specialists in their Comprehensive System of Personnel Development (CSPD). The 2001 publication, *Therapeutic Recreation in Public Education: An IDEA for the Future* (Mische, Coyle, & Ashton-Schaeffer), serves as a blueprint to guide TR practitioners to bring TR to public education as Congress intended in IDEA. Additionally, a well-written position paper, as recommended by Sable, Powell, and Aldrich (1994) coupled with solid evidence of program outcomes would help the discipline argue for the continued and perhaps expanded inclusion of TR in public education. The School Systems Treatment Network maintained by ATRA provides a forum for members committed to this issue to strategize greater presence of TR in education.

Long-Term Care

Nursing home reform is another area of legislation and regulation that has received extensive and intensive input from the TR discipline. Under the tenacious leadership of Karin Vecchione, ATRA, NTRS, and the National Association of Activity Professionals (NAAP) urged TR and activity professionals to fight reform proposals contained in the 1987 Omnibus Budget Reconciliation Act (PL 100-203). These OBRA regulations weakened the requirements for nursing home activities programs and the staff members who organize and deliver them. While these advocacy efforts were unsuccessful in blocking regulatory changes, the lobbying activities actually earned the TR discipline important recognition and respect. Volunteer representatives of ATRA have routinely influenced regulations governing nursing homes and interpretive guidelines for surveyors. Because of such persistent lobbying efforts, the HCFA added a new section in 1998 (Section T) for recording recreation therapy within the Minimum Data Set (MDS), thereby helping to distinguish recreation therapy services from diversionary activities programs. More recently, ATRA's lobbying efforts have resulted in recreation therapy being located in Section P of the MDS along with the other rehabilitative therapies.

Accessibility

The Americans with Disabilities Act (PL 101-336), passed in 1990, is one of the most significant pieces of legislation to impact access to recreation opportunities for individuals with disabilities. Although this law does not contain specific provisions for TR practice or personnel training, both the NRPA/NTRS and ATRA submitted testimony urging Congress to pass this landmark legislation that prohibits disability discrimination in employment, government services, public accommodations, telecommunications, and certain other services, like insurance.

The Legislative Process

One cannot be critical of or completely objective about the legislative action of the TR profession without appreciating the complexities of legislative and regulatory processes. This appreciation requires an understanding of the three most fundamental processes related to introducing, passing, and implementing laws in America's system of government—authorization, appropriation, and regulation.

Authorization

Authorization is the law under which a program is established or continued (as in reauthorization) for a stated number of years. An authorization bill contains statutory language that specifies the aim and conduct of the program and, unless open-ended, puts a ceiling on monies that can be used to finance it. An authorization bill gives authority to a federal agency to use federal funds for purposes specified in the Act, although it does not mean that the monies will actually be spent for the program. Authorization typically lasts for a brief time, perhaps five years, and then must be reauthorized by Congress. This is a time for TR legislative action.

For example, whenever laws such as the Rehabilitation Act or IDEA have been up for reauthorization, House and Senate committees hold hearings. Over the years, the TR profession has presented oral and written testimony, including recommendations for changes in the statutory language. At times the profession has been successful. It persuaded Congress to alter statutory language to the Rehabilitation Act so that programs involving more than traditional recreational activities, such as leisure education, could be funded. At other times, the profession has not been successful in effecting changes, such as the case with ATRA's lobbying efforts to have recreation therapy included as an early intervention service when IDEA was reauthorized in 2004 and retitled *Individuals with Disabilities Education Improvement Act* (PL 108-446).

Appropriation

Appropriation is the means by which authorized programs are actually funded by Congress for the particular fiscal year. An appropriations bill is introduced, but it might not necessarily include funding levels consistent with the total permissible under the bill authorizing the program. An appropriations bill originates in the House and is followed by one in the Senate. If there are any differences between the two—and there usually are—the two appropriations committees come together in conference and work out a compromise to be taken back to their respective houses for passage.

Appropriations for the Rehabilitation Act have been an ongoing focus of TR legislative advocacy action. Each year special recreation programs, authorized by the Rehabilitation Act, are in jeopardy of not receiving funds in the fiscal year budget because the Administration and many in Congress question the appropriateness of the federal government funding recreation programs. Therefore, a case must be made to members in both the House and the Senate legitimizing the appropriation of monies for discretionary programs, such as recreation. Fortunately, TR lobbying efforts over the years have been successful in persuading the Congress to override the Administration's recommendation for zero funds for special recreation demonstration projects. Testimony highlighting actual impact proved useful to the Senate because of evidence that nearly 75% of these programs continue to serve disabled persons long after the "seed" monies provided by the federal government are expended (Thomas, 2003).

Regulation

Finally, regulation is the organization, rules, and procedures used by a federal agency to distribute funding for and monitor the conduct of programs authorized by specific legislation. Regulations govern access to federal monies. They usually describe the purpose of the program, identify the types of activities that are eligible for support, set forth the process for selecting funding priorities, and describe the various weighted criteria for successfully obtaining federal funds.

Proposed regulatory changes are announced in the *Federal Register,* and the public is invited to offer comment. For example, each time the Rehabilitation Act is reauthorized, the Department of Education's Rehabilitation Services Administration (RSA) is responsible for promulgating new regulations that reflect the statutory changes contained in any amendments. The agency also publishes its responses to any public comment received regarding rule changes. For example, in the late 1980s, the National Institute on Disability and Rehabilitation Research (NIDRR) sought input on setting research funding priorities, as announced in the *Federal Register.* Comments were submitted to the NIDRR supporting proposed research priorities on recreation as a component of community integration programs for individuals with mental retardation and on the efficacy of therapeutic recreation as a treatment modality. The NIDRR responded to this input by including these topics among the funding priorities for 1988, and it funded a three-year research project on TR and rehabilitation. That project, awarded to Temple University, included a 1991 national conference which led to a valued publication, *Benefits of Therapeutic Recreation: A Consensus View.*

Reviewing these three processes is important for illustrating two of the most important points in understanding legislative action. First, the legislative and regulatory process contains these three distinct yet interrelated processes. Even if the TR profession is successful in lobbying for including and maintaining TR in the language of the law, monies may not be appropriated for the conduct of TR services, and a federal agency, representing the Administration, may not necessarily administer the program in ways consistent with the intentions of Congress.

The second point is that legislative advocacy is a constant, seemingly never-ending task! No one else is going to assume the responsibility for ensuring that the laws are implemented to provide for the recreational needs of all persons (therapy or otherwise), nor will anyone else take the lead in ensuring that there is compliance with the law and its regulations.

Regulating practice

Monitoring and providing input at the regulatory level has been the most significant focus for the profession in recent years. This is evident in the ATRA *Recreational Therapy Medicare Project*, initiated in 1984. For many years, the TR profession has had to be vigilant in its advocacy action regarding coverage for its services by the CMS. Despite regulatory language implying that recreational therapy is a covered Medicare service in skilled nursing, in-patient rehabilitation, and in-patient psychiatric facilities, Medicare beneficiaries are often denied these services due to inconsistent and inaccurate interpretation of the regulations by fiscal intermediaries. ATRA initiated this grassroots campaign to raise awareness of these inconsistencies, educate lawmakers about potential denial of valuable and effective care, and to get CMS to clarify unequivocally its coverage regulations.

The typical response to ATRA by the CMS has been to issue letters stating that its regulation does not preclude recreational therapy coverage, which in its opinion ought to be sufficient guidance for intermediaries. For ATRA, these responses were actually inconsistent with actual regulatory language and insufficient for administrators who needed explicit assurance that they were making correct coverage decisions. Therefore, the *Recreational Therapy Medicare Project* has aimed for legislators to direct CMS to be more forthcoming. During 2005 and 2006, members of both the U.S. House of Representatives and the Senate issued "sign-on" letters to CMS (i.e., a letter signed by multiple members of the House and Senate) asking for corrective action. Of course, given the enormous cost for healthcare coverage in this country, the Administration is concerned about escalating Medicare costs. However, ATRA members have argued that this corrective action does not represent increased cost; it merely represents access for Medicare beneficiaries to the full range of allowable services that may be medically necessary and appropriate. The sign-on letters had been the first step in leveraging legislative influence on the CMS. Finally, in the autumn of 2007, Representatives Taucher (D-CA) and English (R-PA) introduced H.R. 4248, *Ensuring Medicare Access to Recreational Therapy Act of 2007,* containing explicit statutory language directing CMS to conclusive action. From that point forward, it has been up to members of ATRA to lobby their congressional representatives to sign on to this bill.

The significance of this initiative for the profession is because of the unprecedented level of commitment from TR professionals. Indeed, the campaign has required a grassroots effort from individual members and ATRA Chapter Affiliates to communicate with their legislators. It has also depended on financial contributions from members to support the $250,000 projected cost of this initiative. ATRA has done what it can to engage its membership in this campaign and to provide the tools needed to press legislators into action. It has sponsored Mid-Year Professional Issues Forums in Washington D.C., during which members meet with their legislators on this and other issues. It has also provided guidelines for corresponding with legislators in person and in writing. With the guidance of its legal counsel and through the tireless efforts of volunteer member leadership, ATRA took a major step forward in 2007 in influencing significant regulatory changes for the profession and the persons its members serve.

Again, the point of this short review is to stress the interactive nature of the authorization, appropriation, and regulation processes, and to illustrate the need for consistent, organized, and vigilant lobbying efforts. Whatever the issue, it is important to realize that TR legislative advocacy is primarily dependent on members who volunteer their time to coordinate advocacy action, and the time and effort taken by TR professionals to respond to action alerts. The obvious question is one of resources. What are the resources for the lobbying efforts of therapeutic recreation? What are the dominating concerns that will guide this action? With this chapter's preceding information as a backdrop, the remainder will identify and explore some of the most critical issues that have shaped and will continue to influence the profession's involvement in legislative and regulatory action.

Getting the Work Done: Resources For Legislative Action

The legislative and regulatory issues relevant to TR are wide-ranging—education, rehabilitation, long-term care, independent living, health and wellness, and access to the mainstream of community living for persons with disabilities. These issues impact the discipline's opportunity to practice, train new professionals, and conduct research, as well as determine whether recreation and recreation therapy will be included in comprehensive healthcare, education, and community life. In short, the territory is vast and, as stated earlier, the need for informed, consistent, and productive advocacy action is enormous. What then are the resources of the TR discipline to get the job done?

As a branch of NRPA, the NTRS receives support from the Association's Division of Public Affairs. Issues concerning NTRS are addressed along with all other equally important legislative and regulatory matters affecting parks and recreation, such as the Land and Water Conservation Fund. Historically, issues pertaining to individuals with disabilities have been viewed as "TR" concerns and must compete with broader recreation matters for NRPA resources. Since 2001, NRPA has embraced broader public health issues, such as obesity and "active living," which have implications for all citizens. It has addressed broad issues concerning persons with disabilities, including testimony to rulemaking by the Department of Justice on revised guidelines to the ADA, and rulemaking by the U.S. Access Board on accessibility to outdoor recreation environments for persons with disabilities. The NRPA has publicly supported the U.S. Surgeon General's *Call to Action to Improve the Health of Persons with Disabilities* (U.S. Public Health Service, 2005). Consistent with its mission, NRPA is less likely to have traditional healthcare issues as priorities. NRPA also has to balance competing branch demands for public affairs resources. NTRS receives support and guidance from NRPA staff, but it has had to rely very heavily on an appointed member-volunteers to work closely with the NTRS branch manager to coordinate advocacy action.

Since its inception in 1984, ATRA has devoted significant attention to legislative matters that directly impact TR services in healthcare and rehabilitation. Recognizing the limits of volunteer action alone and the need for expert guidance, ATRA retained legislative counsel for guidance. Attorney Peter Thomas has been extremely effective in keeping the Association informed of the issues and has been pivotal in helping the membership access their legislators. The ATRA's Public Policy Team has developed a very useful public policy link on the main website that provides members with current and archived "action alerts" related to various legislative and regulatory issues. There are separate links for federal and state issues, and there are sample letters and other "tips" members can use with their legislators. These on-line resources have been instrumental to member action with the Medicare initiative.

It is unlikely, however, that either ATRA or NTRS will amass the resources other professions have. For example, the occupational therapy association has three full-time government affairs specialists and contracted attorneys to address their legislative concerns. In a relative sense, then, the TR discipline has accomplished quite a lot and is fortunate that its volunteer legislative leadership works diligently to keep members informed and involved.

Essentials for Legislative and Regulatory Action

Given its resources and wide-ranging agenda, the TR profession must reaffirm its commitment to be politically astute and active in legislative advocacy. Several fundamental approaches to this work will be essential for building on past successes and responding to the competing interests and issues in the future.

Building and maintaining coalitions

When it comes to influencing public policy, truly, there is strength in numbers. Also, being "wired" to Capitol Hill through a network of contacts is critical to success. During the 1970s and early 1980s, recreation and therapeutic recreation causes received crucial lobbying support from important organizations such as the Kennedy Foundation, The President's Committee on Employment of the Handicapped, and the National Easter Seals Society. Therapeutic recreation has also benefited from government insiders for information, insight, and guidance. Bill Hillman, a past president of NTRS, had been a recreation and physical education technical advocate within the Department of Education, Office of Special Education and Rehabilitation Services, and Andrea Farbman, a past NTRS legislative action committee chairperson, served as the Public Affairs Director for the National Council on Disability. ATRA's current chief legislative counsel, Peter Thomas, has served on former President Clinton's Commission on Patient Rights and chaired a subcommittee on disability issues. His background and stature in Washington are a valuable part of his guidance to ATRA members concerned with the changing landscape of healthcare regulation.

For more than 20 years, NTRS and ATRA have tried to maintain involvement in some of the most important and powerful coalitions in Washington, D.C. These have included the National Rehabilitation Caucus, The Coalition for Citizens with Disabilities, The National Coalition for Nursing Home Reform, the National Association for Pupil Services Organization, and the Alliance for Disability Sport and Recreation. In 2006, ATRA joined the large and diverse Nursing Home Quality Campaign to improve quality of care and quality of life in America's nursing homes. These coalitions represent consumer, provider, and other advocacy groups in their shared interest to influence public policy affecting individuals with disabilities. Participation in these coalitions affords access to information and representation on issues of mutual concern. It is also a critical opportunity to advocate for therapeutic recreation and to garner support for the profession's special interests. Having a seat at the table provides an opportunity to present the profession's positions on the issues. Yet, the appearances of separate TR organizations to consumer and provider groups provoke questions about the difference between the groups and concern about the need for more than one professional organization.

Shortly after the founding of ATRA in 1984, the importance of speaking with a unified TR voice became abundantly clear. The Rehabilitation Act and the Education for Handicapped Act were both due for reauthorization in 1986. In anticipation of a critical lobbying year, then-NTRS President David Compton convened a meeting in Dallas to discuss strategy. He assembled representatives from NTRS, ATRA, the NCPERH, AAHPERD, and congressional staff members assigned to the Senate Subcommittee on the Handicapped. It was clear that only through a unified presence would those organizations associated with recreation and therapeutic recreation make an impact on this reauthorization process. As a result of this meeting, a Legislative Coalition for Therapeutic Recreation was formed, representing NTRS, ATRA, and the NCPERH.

The legislative coalition for therapeutic recreation issued numerous alerts to members in all three organizations and, in a coordinated and collaborative fashion, drafted and submitted testimony to House and Senate committees. Speaking with one unified voice, the TR profession successfully influenced changes in these significant pieces of legislation and demonstrated that combining the lobbying resources of the organizations and issuing joint statements would result in greater receptivity on Capitol Hill. The TR Legislative Coalition maintained itself through the Clinton administration's effort to reform healthcare but was disbanded once ATRA secured its own legislative counsel.

While the benefits of this coalition were obvious, it was not problem free. It is politically naive to think that forming and operating a coalition is simply a matter of desire and earnestness. Operating as a coalition requires a willingness to share resources and to keep the channels of communication open. The political realities of professional organizations, like competition for dues-paying members and equitable use of limited resources in lobbying efforts, will inevitably complicate the work. Is it possible that one organization will unfairly benefit from the hard work and perhaps greater financial contributions of the other organization? This is certainly the case with the Medicare project, which is driven by ATRA, but it will likely benefit members of NTRS as well.

There is also the issue of representation. That is, if comments at one of the national coalition meetings, or the oral or written testimony of the Legislative Coalition for TR presented to a congressional body, are not cleared by all organizations involved, there is the risk of misrepresenting one of the organization's views on an issue. This had been a thorny problem for NRPA when the TR Legislative Coalition was active. The NRPA maintained a policy that only NRPA staff members are to represent the Association at national coalition meetings. Since NTRS is only a branch of the NRPA, it is a concern to NRPA that the actions of the NTRS are consistent with the views of the NRPA. Taken a step further, if NTRS is a part of a legislative coalition with ATRA and the ATRA representative to the Coalition meets with a Congressional staff person as a representative of the coalition, this person is, in effect, representing NRPA. In part to avoid such confusion, both organizations have essentially taken their own action on matters of mutual concern. Nevertheless, the question remains; who speaks for TR professionals and for the profession?

The formation and maintenance of coalitions are influenced by the salience of the forming issue; the priorities and long-term agenda of the participating organizations affect the extent to which the organizations are willing to coalesce and also tend to influence the direction of the coalition's activities (Roberts-DeGennaro, 1986). Certainly, the forming issue of the Legislative Coalition for TR was clear—to influence the reauthorization of education and rehabilitation laws as they pertained to recreation and physical education. However, other issues may emerge and challenge the basis of coalescing.

While several organizations share a commitment to advancing the role of recreation in the lives of people with disabilities, each has an agenda that reflects its own priorities. For instance, the NCPERID has a majority membership of physical education professionals. Its legislative and regulatory agenda is primarily centered on the role of adapted physical education and recreation in public education. The NRPA's efforts on the Special Recreation authorization (Section 316 special demonstration projects) and the prevention of juvenile crime stand to reason; the continued funding of these projects has had major impact on developing and expanding community-based recreation for people with disabilities and at-risk youth. However, ATRA's emphasis on issues related to recreation therapy as a specialized healthcare service can be in conflict with the primary mission of NRPA—improving health and quality of life through parks and recreation. In contrast, ATRA has been most active in monitoring regulatory changes impacting recreation therapy while also doing what it can to advocate for recreation opportunities for individuals with disabilities. Thus, while the Legislative Coalition for TR lasted 10 years, NTRS and ATRA do not have a consistently unified and coordinated approach to the advocacy action. Given the vastness of the issues, is it even reasonable to think such a coordinated effort is possible?

Determining a Legislative Agenda

The political action of TR professionals has been characterized largely by reactive measures; that is, trying to respond to legislative and regulatory matters as they arise. There has never been a thorough explication of a long-term legislative agenda for the TR profession and endorsed by both professional organizations. Yet, one must ask whether such a unified perspective is necessary or even possible, or whether the NTRS and ATRA are too different philosophically and in their organizational priorities to articulate a common legislative agenda. As indicated earlier, there are many impediments to operating as a "coalition," but it may be time for these two organizations to figure out how they can use their respective resources to complement each other's agenda. Certainly the agenda is broad enough, and the challenges of influencing social policy warrant serious consideration.

In 1998, the board of directors of the NTRS and ATRA created the Alliance for Therapeutic Recreation with an explicit commitment to communicating and collaborating on significant issues of the profession that transcend organizational boundaries (*NTRS Report*, 1999). Perhaps it is time for both organizations to explore the benefits and liabilities of establishing a joint task force on legislative and regulatory action within a scope of social policy that impacts the role of play, recreation, and leisure in the health promotion, rehabilitation, and life quality of citizens with chronic illnesses and disabilities.

The first challenge would be to cooperatively produce a series of white papers on healthcare (including health promotion and wellness), rehabilitation, education, aging and geriatric care, active living, and livable communities. These position papers would guide the actions of the profession and would be very useful educational materials for state and federal agencies and policy makers. More importantly, the papers would represent a single, unified voice of the TR profession. These papers might also respond to Sylvester's (1995) criticism that the lobbying documents of the profession lacked critical thinking and reflected more concern with professional self-interests than with serving the public good. Indeed, legislative advocacy, or any other form of advocacy, is more than "playing the political (lobbying) game;" it is a genuine reflection of professional values, beliefs, and ethics, through the use of the theoretical and practical body of knowledge.

Training Members to be Advocates and "Hill Invaders"

The most predictably successful grassroots action has come in those instances where job security has been in question. Although this is to be expected, a deeper commitment to influencing social policy will determine the character and morality of the profession. During the past few years, both ATRA and NTRS have heeded the political imperative urged by Compton (1997) to create a membership skilled in the art and science of politically shaping public policy. Each year, the NRPA/NTRS mid-year meeting is held in Washington, D.C., so members can be assisted in visiting their legislators on Capitol Hill. ATRA has also had many very successful Mid-Year Forums in Washington, D.C., which have included day-long legislative workshops, organized visits to legislators, and receptions for members of Congress and their staff. One particular reception included the U.S. women's wheelchair basketball team silver medal winners at the 1992 Olympics in Barcelona. The team's presence underscored the importance of recreation and competitive sport in the health and well-being of individuals with disabilities. Overall, these training programs have paid off significantly. In his 1999 report to the ATRA membership, Peter

Thomas attributed unprecedented awareness and understanding of TR among legislators to these annual legislative summits. The lobbying momentum is evident in the growing attendance each year at these mid-year forums and the success ATRA members have had in carrying to the Hill their message of Medicare reform. Of course, long-term success depends on all TR professionals to embrace their duty to advocate. Fortunately, ATRA's use of Internet technology has provided members with support and guidance for their advocacy even when they cannot invade Capitol Hill in person.

State Action

Training is crucial if professionals are going to be politically active at the state level as well. In fact, state level action may actually be more critical than action at the federal level. Throughout the 1990s, Congress steadily maneuvered to shift the balance of influence and control from the federal government to the states. A great deal of federal legislation and regulation is applied at the state level, where state agencies implement the law. This includes educational, rehabilitation, and developmental disabilities services, all of which are mandated by federal legislation and contain federally determined regulations, but are implemented at a state level. For example, each state must develop a state plan for developmental disabilities services, and the states have the prerogative to identify certain services that they want to include and for which they will obtain federal funds. Likewise, each state office of vocational rehabilitation determines its service priorities, which may include recreation. It is up to professionals at the state level to educate these agencies and to advocate for state-level attention to the recreational needs of its constituents. Thus, it is the state agencies with which TR professionals should be interacting to set state priorities for services based on state-run need assessments.

There have been some notable examples of state-level preparation. In 1994, the state of Colorado introduced a new initiative called "advocates for therapeutic recreation," a state training program intended to train TR professionals to be legislative advocates. It is a model for other statewide training. When the 1997 Balanced Budget Act authorized states to have greater control over managing Medicaid services, ATRA formed a State Initiatives Committee. This network of representative from more than 20 states shared information and strategies for advocating for TR services with state legislators, health regulatory agencies, and case managers of private health insurance carriers. Professionals in many states held successful "Days on the Hill" and applied what had been learned from similar action in Washington, D.C. (Griffin, 1999).

Even one professional (or just a few) who is/are vigilant and committed can make an enormous difference. In 1994, the attentiveness of G.T. Thompson helped to reveal that the Pennsylvania State Health Services Plan, mandated by the 1992 amendments to the state's Health-Care Facilities Act, did not include TR among clinical health services identified as being necessary to serve the needs of citizens of Pennsylvania. He alerted TR professionals statewide and coordinated a flurry of letters from practitioners. Consequently, TR services must now be tracked in terms of its availability and affordability, and its provision must be addressed in certificate-of-need applications when health facilities are built or expanded.

Similarly, in 1999, a handful of professionals from New Jersey challenged the state licensure regulations for rehabilitation hospitals and submitted recommendations pertinent to recreation therapy. While the outcome is not known at this time, having the opportunity to meet face to face with the Governor of New Jersey and the Department of Health and Senior Services undoubtedly advanced the visibility and credibility of the profession. Based on this experience, one gratified member of the group wrote, "A passion for what you do, a commitment to make a difference, a phone call, a brief letter, or e-mail is all it takes to make a world of difference!"(Sears, 1999, p. 6).

State Regulation of TR Practice

Two thousand six was an important year for regulating recreation therapy practice. First, the state of North Carolina renewed and extended regulatory controls of recreation(al) therapists. The existing Practice Act was extended to a licensure act. The State of New Hampshire also succeeded in having a licensure act introduced and passed in its legislature. These states joined with Utah in legal, governmental regulation of recreation therapy practice. Two other states, (Washington and California), maintain a registration program, while several other states are in the early stages of seeking licensure to regulate TR practice. It is apparent, therefore, that legal recognition of TR practice, including licensure, practice acts, and registration, although limited, is a growing focus of state-level lobbying efforts of TR professionals.

Obtaining legal recognition for the practice of recreation therapy has been a priority of the Alliance for Therapeutic Recreation, mentioned earlier. In 2002, ATRA and NTRS joined with NCTRC to form the States Recognition Project, to help guide the efforts of recreation therapists at the state level to seek licensure. Ultimately, the NCTRC produced a document (Shank & Riley, 2006) that has been disseminated to state TR affiliate chapters and organizations. The document provides general guidelines for pursuing practice regulation, including a defined scope of practice for recreation therapy and common terminology and definitions that can aid in the uniformity of these initiatives. As is the case with all current licensure acts, this document promotes the use of the CTRS credential as a basis for establishing eligibility for licensure.

The primary reason for regulating practice is the protection of the public from harm, and so the overriding question is whether there is sufficient evidence to indicate that unregulated practice of recreation therapy could result in harm. It is incumbent on those who seek licensure to establish that healthcare and human service professionals who are charged with providing recreation as a form of therapy or intervention could harm consumers of these services if the service providers were not trained properly or did not follow the established professional standards of practice and codes of ethical conduct. Typically, there are few records of such negligence or harm, yet the decision of governmental bodies to regulate practice is based on their duty to protect the public from harm. Thus, the desire for recognition and respect as a healthcare and human service professional is not enough to warrant being licensed. Does it really make any difference what one's background is or how one delivers a service called recreation therapy? How could the public be harmed? The argument for regulating practice through a governmental entity (i.e., licensing board) must be compelling. "The process of seeking legal regulation requires that professional leaders provide direct evidence of public harm that has or could result from the unregulated practice of recreation therapy. This is typically provided in the form of "case review" and/or assessment of available qualified service providers and is usually germane to the state or province in which the regulation is being sought" (Shank & Riley, 2006, p. 5).

Beyond Passionate Appeals

As a discipline, the lack of hard data on the nature, scope, and efficacy of therapeutic recreation services hampers the profession. TR's advocacy efforts have involved passionate appeals to an intuitive appreciation of recreation's importance in a person's life, especially when one's life circumstances are inadequate. It is rare to find a policy maker opposed to recreation, although they might see it as much less important than many other things. Influencing licensure acts or social policy will require data on facts, particularly as they emerge from research. The profession has been at a disadvantage when it has been asked by legislators, congressional sub-committees, and agencies like CMS to produce evidence of cost effectiveness and demonstrated outcomes. More than 10 years ago, ATRA produced the document *Recreational Therapy: A Summary of Health Outcomes* (ATRA, 1994) and began a national effort to gather data on cost-utilization of recreation therapy. Clearly, the TR profession will be expected to continuously produce findings from outcome-oriented evaluation and research. Without it, TR will not garner the support of federal and state legislative mandates.

Summary

The role of legislative advocacy is an important determinant of the success of therapeutic recreation as a legitimate and contributing healthcare and human service profession. This success will be measured not only by what can be accomplished for the profession directly, but by what can be accomplished on behalf of children and adults who need special assistance in accessing recreational opportunities and whose lives can be improved through recreation as a clinical, rehabilitative, educational, and community service. The legislative and regulatory imperatives for these outcomes are clear; it is up to the entire TR profession to respond to its moral and professional obligations to be active in promoting and protecting play, recreation, and leisure in treating illnesses, preventing health-related problems, preparing students with disabilities to live life fully in their communities of choice, and in general, raising the quality of life for all. What will be required is a reaffirmation that these issues are worth the fight.

Discussion Questions

1. What would be the particular benefits and limitations if the therapeutic recreation profession aligned its lobbying efforts with a) allied health, b) public recreation, or c) special education groups?
2. Select three major services a professional organization ought to provide its members, and compare and contrast legislative advocacy with these three services. How important is legislative advocacy?
3. Construct a position paper on TR and any of the following issues: nursing home reform, "active living," special education, or comprehensive rehabilitation. Prepare this position paper for a state or federal agency that sets policy or administers these particular services.

4. Review the memberships of the House and Senate committees on Health and Human Services, Education, and Justice, and determine which of your legislators holds important membership. Send her or him a copy of your position paper.
5. Identify three state agencies responsible for providing or regulating healthcare and human services, and assemble a packet of information suitable for informing each agency of the role and function of therapeutic recreation.
6. Prepare a visitation itinerary for your state and federal legislators. Include in this plan the specification of TR programs that can serve as models and the particular learning experiences you will offer these legislative representatives.
7. Examine the lobbying materials developed and used by ATRA and NTRS over the past five years. Identify similarities and differences in their public policy agendas, and develop a rationale for unifying their lobbying efforts or keeping them separate and distinct.
8. Review the materials on the ATRA website that help guide your interaction with a legislator. Arrange a visit to Capitol Hill and write a reaction to this visit for your local organizational newsletter.
9. Examine the legislative lobbying efforts that led up to and immediately followed the introduction of H.R. 4248. What is the current status of CMS regulations regarding recreational therapy? For what reasons would you conclude that this has been a significant event in the maturing of this profession's legislative and regulatory action?
10. What can you do to contribute to the advocacy efforts needed by this profession in the legislative and regulatory arenas?

References

American Therapeutic Recreation Association. (1994). *Recreational therapy: A summary of health outcomes*. Hattiesburg, MS: Author.

Bedini, L., Bullock, C., & Driscoll, L. (1991). From schools to community: Achieving independence and community integration through leisure education. *Palaestra*, Fall, 38-43.

Bokee, M. (1994). Fiscal years 1982 through 1994 adapted physical education and therapeutic recreation program analysis: Division of Personnel Preparation. Unpublished paper, Washington, D.C.: U.S. Department of Education, Office of Special Education Programs.

Bullock, C. (1986). Recreation as a related service. Unpublished paper submitted to the U.S. House Select Education Committee, U.S. House of Representatives.

Bullock, C., & Johnson, D. (1998). Recreational therapy and special education. In F. Brasile, T. Skalko, & j. burlingame (Eds.), *Perspectives in recreational therapy* (pp. 107- 124). Ravensdale, WA: Idyll Arbor.

Compton, D. (1997). Political imperatives for therapeutic recreation. In D. Compton (Ed.), *Issues in therapeutic recreation: Toward a new millennium* (pp. 53-76). Champaign, IL: Sagamore.

Coyne, P. (1981). The status of recreation as a related service in PL 94-142. *Therapeutic Recreation Journal, 15*(3), 4-15.

Griffin, P. (1999). States are taking the initiative. *ATRA Newsletter, 15*(5), 6.

Houle, C. (1980). *Continuing learning in the professions.* San Francisco: Jossey Bass.

Kavanaugh, T. (2006). The role of recreational therapy in the Las Cruces public schools – Part II. *ATRA Newsletter, 22*(4), 12-13.

Mische, L., Coyle, C., Ashton-Schaeffer, C. (2001). *Therapeutic Recreation in special education: An IDEA for the future.* Arlington VA: American Therapeutic Recreation Association.

Nesbitt, J. (1977). Professional advocacy at the national level in physical education and recreation for handicapped children: 1976-77 report to the president from the president of the NCPERH. Unpublished report.

Nesbitt, J. (1986). Guide to U.S. government special recreation resources. *Special Recreation Digest, 3*(2), 27-56.

National Therapeutic Recreation Society. (1999). Alliance for therapeutic recreation. *NTRS Report,* 24(3), 5.

Park, D. (1980). *Legislation affecting park services and recreation for handicapped individuals.* Washington, D.C.: Hawkins and Associates.

Roberts-DeGennaro, M. (1986). Building coalitions for political advocacy. *Social Work,* July-August, 308-311.

Sable, J., Powell, L., & Aldrich, L. (1994). Transdisciplinary principles in the provision of therapeutic recreation services in inclusionary school settings. *Annual in Therapeutic Recreation, 4,* 69-81.

Sears, D. (1999). Fighting the chance to color outside the lines. *ATRA Newsletter,* July-August, 6.

Shank, J. (1997). Engaging the legislative process. In D. Compton, (Ed.), *Issues in therapeutic recreation: Toward a new millennium* (pp.77-102). Champaign, IL: Sagamore.

Shank, J., & Riley, B. (2006). NCTRC position paper on the legal regulation of the practice of recreation therapy. New City, NY: National Council on Therapeutic Recreation Certification. Unpublished paper.

Skalko, T. (1998). Future of the profession. In F. Brasile, T. Skalko, & j. burlingame (Eds.), *Perspectives in recreational therapy* (pp. 499-515). Ravensdale, WA: Idyll Arbor,

Stanley, J. (1985). Recreation in PL 94-142: Won the battle and lost the war? Unpublished paper presented at the National Recreation and Park Association National Congress, Dallas, TX.

Stanley, J. (1987). Recreation in the education of handicapped students. Unpublished report. Trenton, NJ: New Jersey Department of Community Affairs.

Sylvester, C. (1995). Critical theory, therapeutic recreation, and healthcare reform: An instructive example of critical thinking. *Annual in Therapeutic Recreation, 5,* 94-109.

Thomas, P. (2003). ATRA governmental relations update. Unpublished paper.

CHAPTER 21

Certification and Licensure: Recognition and Oversight of the Profession

Peg Connolly, Ph.D., LRT/CTRS™
Western Carolina University

Therapeutic recreation or recreational therapy has had a form of professional registration since the 1950s. The original plan, developed and administered by the Commission for the Accreditation of Hospital Recreation (CAHR), was first initiated to register Hospital Recreation Workers in 1959 (Carter & Folkerth, 1989; Connolly, 1998b). That program was then incorporated into the National Therapeutic Recreation Society's (NTRS) Voluntary Registration Program for Therapeutic Recreation from 1967 to 1981 (Carter, 1981). In 1981, the National Council for Therapeutic Recreation Certification™ (NCTRC™) was established as an independent national organization for the certification of therapeutic recreation personnel (Carter, 1981; Carter & Folkerth, 1989; Connolly, 1998b). Under the leadership of NCTRC[1], the certification program for therapeutic recreation became refined and gained national recognition through accreditation by the National Commission for Certification Accreditation of the National Organization for Competency Assurance (Connolly, 1998b). The NCTRC™ credential Certified Therapeutic Recreation Specialist™and its acronym CTRS™ are now the benchmark for qualification as a therapeutic recreation professional.

Licensure has not been as well accepted within the profession. Two states obtained licensure in the 1970s—Utah and Georgia. North Carolina originally received state recognition in the form of a state certification or title-protection in the mid-1980s. In 2005, North Carolina was successful in passing a licensure law for recreational therapists in the state and, in 2006, New Hampshire gained passage of a licensure act for recreational therapists.

Certification and licensure are forms of oversight for a profession (Dower, O'Neil, & Hough, 2001). These voluntary and governmental programs are forms of regulation that

---

[1]NCTRC Certification Standards are periodically revised, and the reader is encouraged to visit www.nctrc.org for current information on the NCTRC Certification Standards.

exist to protect the consumer of therapeutic recreation services. While the profession's certification program is well established and respected, licensure is not as well recognized throughout the country. In order to understand the status of certification and licensure in therapeutic recreation, it is important to understand these regulatory processes in general and how they are defined and operated in related professions. To the individual professional, obtaining certification and licensure is often considered a form of recognition of professional accomplishment or competence. There is somewhat of a dichotomy between the purpose of these regulatory functions to society and their meaning to professionals. The public expects protection and assurance of who the qualified professionals are, while the professional expects recognition. Protection and recognition can, at times, be at odds through the mechanisms of regulation.

Regardless of the level of acceptance of credentialing in therapeutic recreation, there are many questions about their purpose and meaning both within and outside the profession. What is the purpose of certification and licensure to the field of therapeutic recreation? How credible is our certification process within healthcare and human services, and how does it relate to certification in other fields? Is there a new trend toward more state initiatives to obtain licensure throughout the U.S., or is licensure not desired by our professionals or not attainable in the current political climate? What other forces in society are impacting the regulation of professionals? What needs to happen in the future to continue credible certification and licensure activities in the profession? The purpose of this chapter is to provide an overview of trends and issues in certification and licensure in therapeutic recreation today and for the future.

This chapter will address the importance of a job/practice analysis in the oversight and regulation of a profession, the state of certification in the profession of therapeutic recreation and the nature of certification in other professions, the current status of licensure of recreational therapy in the U.S., and issues and trends that will impact certification and licensure now and in the future. It is important that the profession understand the critical importance of certification and licensure as a form of oversight and self-regulation of the quality of therapeutic recreation professionals.

Job/Practice Analysis of a Profession

The major basis for any certification or licensure program is a job/practice analysis or role delineation study. The first National Job Analysis for therapeutic recreation was conducted in 1987 (Oltman, Norback, & Rosenfeld, 1989). Stumbo (1989) indicated that the 1987 job/practice analysis was the first time that a nationally based study was conducted on entry-level competence for the profession. A job/practice analysis determines the minimal knowledge, skills, and abilities that are generally accepted for practice in a profession. It is imperative to the profession that this national study be updated periodically to reflect any changes in practice in the field, and NCTRC has recently completed its third national job analysis study for the profession (NCTRC, 2007b). The 2007 NCTRC Job Analysis emphasized the critical importance of direct client services and the significance of the therapeutic recreation process including assessment, planning, implementation, and evaluation within the job of the therapeutic recreation practitioner (NCTRC, 2007b). In the 2007 study, slight changes were documented in job tasks, increasing the number from

54 to 58. Thus, the role delineation of the practice of therapeutic recreation, based on three national studies involving the input and consensus of thousands of therapeutic recreation professionals, has remained fairly consistent in the delineation of job tasks considered essential for entry-level practice for the last 20 years.

Perhaps the greatest change to the National Job Analysis of Therapeutic Recreation within the 2007 study was the creation of a new format for knowledge areas and the proposed categorization of therapeutic recreation exam content into four main domains. The four domains of knowledge and their respective weighting recommended for test specifications for the certification exam are: foundational knowledge (33.3%), practice of TR/RT (46.7%), organization of TR/RT (13.3%), and advancement of the profession (6.7%) (NCTRC, 2007b).

The National Job Analysis for the profession is the basis for establishing certifying standards and the examination content for the national certification exam (Connolly & Riley, 1996; NCTRC, 2007b; NOCA, 2004). Without a national job/practice analysis study, it is questionable if a valid and reliable national exam for the profession can be developed. Without a valid and reliable national exam that can be relied on by certification and licensure programs, there is a question of the credibility of these programs for a profession. The role delineation study of a profession is a benchmark for the profession to further establish and refine the knowledge, skills, and abilities essential to practice in the field. Without NCTRC's stewardship role in assuring that the National Job Analysis for Therapeutic Recreation is maintained and updated periodically, it would be difficult for the Council to defend the quality of its national credentialing program. Furthermore, all states with licensure in the profession currently require passage of the NCTRC exam in order for individual recreational therapy practitioners to be licensed in the respective states. These states would not designate the NCTRC exam unless there were evidence of a quality and current job/practice analysis as the basis of the national exam. Nor could these states incur the costs of conducting a national job/practice analysis for the profession individually. Therefore, the most critical component of credentialing in the profession is the availability of a valid and reliable role delineation study that documents the minimum knowledge, skills, and abilities for practice in the field.

While the major purpose of the National Job Analysis may be to serve as the foundation for the national standardized certification exam, its influence reaches further. The job tasks documented in the study are often used in education and practice to guide the development of skills and evaluation of performance in jobs and internships. The knowledge areas of the Job Analysis are often used to guide curricular decisions on the development of coursework in academic programs and to guide the content of continuing professional education. The importance of the job/practice analysis of a recognized profession cannot be underestimated, and without an organization such as NCTRC, which accepts responsibility for maintenance and review of this important research, it is questionable if the profession would be as established and recognized as it is today.

Certification of Therapeutic Recreation Personnel

Certification, as a phenomenon, has grown significantly in the past 20 years, and the National Organization for Competency Assurance (NOCA) boasts over 300 certification agency members who certify close to four million individuals (Knapp & Knapp, 2002). NOCA is a membership organization that establishes quality standards for credentialing through research, conference, publications, and other services (NOCA, 2007). NOCA is recognized as the national authority for certification promoting competency assessment for practitioners in all occupations. The National Commission for Certifying Agencies (NCCA) is the accreditation body of NOCA through which credentialing organizations may be accredited if they demonstrate compliance with NOCA/NCCA standards. The certification program for therapeutic recreation has been a part of this explosion of certified individuals in the U.S. NCTRC has followed the NOCA/NCCA standards for certification organizations since it was incorporated as an independent credentialing organization for therapeutic recreation. NCTRC was nationally accredited as a recognized certifying agency by NCCA in 1993 (NCTRC, 2007a). As such, NCTRC has a nationally recognized certification program for therapeutic recreation personnel.

Certification, as provided by NCTRC, is a voluntary process offered by a non-governmental agency, whereby qualified individuals are recognized as meeting established standards of minimum knowledge and skills for practice in a professional area (Browning, Bugbee, & Mullins, 1996; Connolly, 1998a; Knapp & Knapp, 2002; Schoon & Smith, 2000). Since NCTRC follows nationally established standards for certification programs, it parallels, in substance and quality, other health and human service certification programs that also meet national credentialing standards.

What are the general components of a nationally accepted certification program? According to NOCA (2004), "NCCA Standards address the structure and governance of the certifying agency, the characteristics of the certification program, the information required to be available to applicants, certificants, and the public, and the recertification initiatives of the certifying agency" (p. 1). Browning et al. (1996) indicated that a certification organization has a responsibility to certificants and certification applicants, employers, and the public. Certification programs accredited under NCCA typically include policies and procedures governing such things as eligibility and applicant requirements, standards for certification and recertification, a valid and reliable exam based on a valid and reliable job/practice analysis of the occupation, appeals or due process and disciplinary procedures, fiscal and administrative autonomy in certification matters, and a governing board composed of members of the profession as well as public members who do not practice nor receive fees/payment from the discipline being certified (Browning et al., 1996; NOCA, 2004).

The NCTRC certification program has been revised and improved since its inception based on the standards of NOCA/NCCA. The certification of therapeutic recreation professionals is quite different from the earlier registration and certification programs of CAHR and NTRS. But is the NCTRC certification program comparable to other healthcare and human service occupations?

Certification Relates to Competence beyond the Minimum

For most occupations in healthcare, state licensure is required to practice. In this situation, a "license" to practice determines minimum competence and certification that is used to recognized advanced and/or specialty competence. According to Greiner and Knebel

(2003), "certification is a voluntary process that is meant to confer recognition of clinical excellence" (p. 108). Grossman (1998) indicated that certification recognizes advanced education or training beyond basic competence for entry. Since the field of therapeutic recreation does not have licensure laws in the majority of states that would regulate entry-level job competence, certification in therapeutic recreation under the authority of NCTRC recognizes minimum competence rather than advanced or specialty competence. This places our certification program at an opposite pole of most other health and medical certification programs. There is often confusion that NCTRC certification is in some way an "advanced" recognition mechanism like other national certification programs, when in fact, the opposite is true. NCTRC certification recognizes the minimum education, experience, and knowledge for practice in recreational therapy (NCTRC, 2007a). It does not examine advanced credentials for practice as do the majority of other national certification plans for other professions. Therapeutic recreation certification exists at a minimum recognition level because there is largely an absence of entry-level recognition or regulation of therapeutic recreation in most states via licensure or other means. Whether right or wrong that NCTRC standards focus on the "minimum" level, it is the only national voluntary regulation plan available for the profession.

The disadvantage of certification focused on minimal competence is that veteran professionals whose knowledge base and expertise has gone beyond minimum expectations for competence in the field have no avenue in therapeutic recreation for identifying their advanced knowledge and skill. Additionally, the field has not challenged itself to develop advanced credentialing mechanisms in any significant way. Even with recertification required by NCTRC, the recertification standards do not place demands on CTRSs to advance their knowledge and skill in any systematic manner but only to maintain minimum entry-level knowledge in therapeutic recreation. Some may argue that demonstrating continuing competence for recertification in therapeutic recreation will naturally result in advanced knowledge and skill with veteran professionals. However, without an oversight authority to measure or test this assumption, there is no proof that professionals are in fact advancing in the competence required for practice in therapeutic recreation.

Licensure in Therapeutic Recreation

Licensure, historically, was initiated because it was "believed to protect consumers from incompetents, charlatans, and quacks" (Young, 1987, p. 15). However, Young (1987) reported that more often licensing laws were initiated and promoted by professionals to protect their own interests rather than those of the public. Atkinson (2000) defined a license as:

A property right bestowed on an applicant by a regulatory board based on statutorily set criteria designed to assess and determine minimum competence to safely practice the particular profession. (It is assumed that one must possess such a license to lawfully practice the profession.). (p. 126)

Licensure, for most health and human professions, is determined on a state-by-state basis and is the most restrictive form of regulation of a profession. Licensure restricts the right to practice in a professional area, not only the title used by practitioners. As Shimberg (2000) indicated, "governmentally sanctioned credentialing is called licensure and is based on the legal concept of the police power of the state" (p. 145).

Some key elements of licensing a profession include public protection, accountability, delineation of a professional practice act, examination or competency assessment, regulatory boards, legal principles such as due process, and disciplinary action (Atkinson, 2000). Public protection needs to be considered in the initiation of licensing laws and in their enforcement. In most states, the profession will need to prove how the consumers in the state would be harmed if the profession were not regulated. Public members participate on regulatory boards in most state licensing programs, which include the public interest in the enforcement of licensing laws. Accountability in licensing laws often refers to the requirement that any new licensing law be submitted to a regulatory review of the economic need for the regulation prior to passage and, in some states, the periodic review of licensing laws to determine the need for continuation once passed. These are often referred to as sunrise and sunset laws (Connolly, 1998a).

In order for a profession to secure licensing, it must delineate its scope of professional practice, including practice areas and areas where practice is not allowed because it is beyond the scope of the licensed professional's authority. Usually, states will look for a job/practice act or role delineation study to determine its scope of practice. The state of North Carolina also incorporated the American Therapeutic Recreation Association (ATRA) Standards for the Practice of Therapeutic Recreation (ATRA, 2000) as a requirement of the practice act for licensing recreational therapists in that state.

Establishment of regulatory boards allows professional involvement and control in self-regulation. The regulatory boards often will have the political appointment of one or more public members, which incorporates the public interest in the regulation of the profession. The regulatory board is responsible for monitoring the application of the law, including recommending rules for the implementation of the law, appeals of licensing decisions to incorporate due process principles, and disciplinary monitoring and action to assure that impaired professionals have their license to practice removed when necessary to protect the public.

The first state to obtain licensure in therapeutic recreation was Utah in 1974. The next year brought passage of a licensing law in Georgia for activity therapy with coverage of the therapeutic recreation profession. However, the Georgia law was not renewed after an audit of the law was conducted in 1990 and it was determined that the law was no longer necessary to protect the public. No new state laws were initiated until 1986, when North Carolina passed a law regulating the profession through certification. States may enact a certification law to regulate a profession by restricting the use of the title for the profession to only those who meet the regulatory requirements stipulated under the law. In 2005, North Carolina House Bill 613 was passed to update the regulation of recreational therapy in North Carolina by instituting licensure. The next state to enact a licensure law was New Hampshire in 2006. The licensing laws for Utah, North Carolina, and New Hampshire all refer to the regulation of recreational therapists, although Utah and New Hampshire use a licensing designation that includes the term "therapeutic recreation" as the official designation. North Carolina uses the designation "licensed recreational therapist."

Why was there such a time gap between the mid-1970s licensing laws for Utah and Georgia and the passage of two new licensing laws in 2005 and 2006? During the 1970s, regulatory reform acts were passed in most states to review the economic impact of laws and acts prior to passage. Sunrise and sunset state laws sought to conduct a regulatory review of any new or existing professional credentialing legislation at the state level to assure that such laws were necessary to protect the public from harm and that no other means of regulating the profession exist (Connolly, 1998a). There is a cost to administering licensure laws to protect the public, and these costs are borne not only by licensing fees but by state funds as well. In an effort to protect the state from unnecessary costs, only those professions had licensing laws passed that were deemed critical for the state to regulate in order to protect the public from harm.

Another issue limiting a robust trend of initiating licensure of therapeutic recreation in more states during the 1970s and 1980s was the state of development of the profession. NCTRC was not founded until 1981. The first national job analysis study was not completed until 1987, and the first standardized national exam for therapeutic recreation was not implemented until 1990. Therefore, if a state were to consider licensure of therapeutic recreation at that time, it did so without the resources of a recognized national role delineation study for the profession or a standardized national exam. Further, since state licensure is said to exist to protect the public, the profession seeking licensure had to show evidence of potential harm that might be caused to the public if nonlicensed professionals were allowed to practice. Very little investigation of disciplinary matters in therapeutic recreation had been conducted prior to NCTRC's work in this area during the 1990s.

It seems that states are more willing to consider regulation of a profession when they do not have to incur the costs of a role delineation study nor the establishment of testing procedures for a profession. Since the NCTRC certification program includes a standardized national certification exam of minimum entry-level knowledge, it may be feasible for states to now pass laws and designate the NCTRC exam as the entry-testing requirement for state licensure. This is how the laws in Utah, North Carolina, and New Hampshire are structured. Further, NCTRC (2007c) recently published a position paper on the legal regulation of the practice of recreational therapy where the Council indicates a willingness to work with professionals in states to establish licensure or other forms of state regulation. NCTRC's position is:

> National organizations sponsoring professional credentialing programs and governmental regulatory bodies share a common goal: protection of the public from unqualified and incompetent providers. To this end, the purpose of this position paper is to document NCTRC's unequivocal support for the legal regulation of the practice of recreation therapy within the United States and Canada. NCTRC stands ready to assist and support professional organizations who are attempting to secure legal recognition of recreation therapy within their respective states and provinces. The establishment of a collaborative relationship between NCTRC and professional organizations seeking legal recognition will ensure that the legislative process proceeds in a timely and cost-effective manner. Working cooperatively with NCTRC and utilizing authorized NCTRC proprietary materials will also ensure

that the network of legislative regulation pertaining to recreation therapy practice throughout the United States and Canada remains portable and accessible to all qualified CTRSs™. (p. 7)

This NCTRC position paper provides significant resources to any state considering the licensure of therapeutic recreation, including use of the NCTRC National Job Analysis and exam with permission from NCTRC. The question is, with an increased interest in licensure of the profession and with NCTRC's position of support, will more states enact legislation to govern the practice of recreational therapy? The answer to this question is still unknown.

Issues and Trends Affecting Certification and Licensure

There are several issues that seem to linger in the profession. One relates to the definition and title of the occupation. The official title is recreational therapy (Code: 076.124-014) according to the Dictionary of Occupational Titles (DOT) of the U.S. Government (Department of Labor, 2006). In the 1960s, the term "therapeutic recreation" was coined as a common term to bridge a wide spectrum of services in the profession from inpatient hospital care to community-based services for people with disabilities. Along with this newly coined term for a profession officially entitled "Recreational Therapy" by the DOT, the National Therapeutic Recreation Society was formed as the national organization that sought to bring together those from a clinical practice perspective (i.e., recreational therapy) together with those from the community service perspective dedicated to the provision of recreation services to people with illnesses and disabilities (i.e., therapeutic recreation) under one umbrella organization. It was assumed an umbrella organization would keep the field together and increase numbers of those aligned with a national organization. Historically, this never happened in the profession, as the number of individuals holding membership in any professional organization representing therapeutic recreation has consistently been small when compared to the numbers of professionals holding the CTRS credential in the field (Riley & Connolly, in press).

However, something did happen based on the umbrella definition of therapeutic recreation that shaped and directed the field in a way that pulls it from the focus of its historical and current position as a profession in healthcare services. Educational programs became housed within parks and recreation curricula as a specialty or emphasis of parks and recreation rather than in allied healthcare as a focus of health treatment and healing. This dichotomy of philosophy and practice has created problems for the field and its ability to advance in the healthcare market. Rather than direct our practice and research to the needs of the provided service or mission of the agencies that provide jobs and the authority to practice, the profession continues to struggle with its definition, philosophy, and educational structure. This issue will continue to present a challenge to certification and licensure activities in the field.

Another issue that repeatedly emerges for the profession is the issue of practice setting. Some would say that the profession of therapeutic recreation will move into community service arenas as the primary job setting. While these indications have been discussed in the field for the past 30 years, the predominant employment settings remain in healthcare.

Riley and Connolly (in press) reported that about 16% of CTRSs reported working in community settings, while over 70% work in hospitals, skilled nursing facilities, and other health-oriented settings. The importance of certification and licensure to a professional in therapeutic recreation is more significant in healthcare settings, where holding such credentials is expected in all professions practicing in healthcare services. In a recent study by the Robert Wood Johnson Foundation (2006), recreational therapists are considered frontline healthcare workers. There is a concern that the frontline healthcare workforce is increasing dramatically yet, as the Robert Wood Johns Foundation (2006) indicated, "We know little about whom these workers are and what employment needs they face" (p. 1). While most frontline healthcare professions are experiencing dramatic growth, recreational therapy is projected to have only 7% growth in the near future, and it is indicated that little is known about this occupation. It is interesting to note from this study that salaries appear to be higher for those healthcare occupations that are licensed than for those that are not.

Certainly, one of the motivations for seeking licensure is to secure reimbursement for services. According to Dower et al. (2003), "for many emerging professions, securing regulation (especially licensure) in all the states has become a goal because of the associated benefits—such as reimbursement from federal programs or insurers—that often come with licensure" (p. 12). With so few states licensing recreational therapists, it is difficult to determine if licensure will convey such benefits to the field of therapeutic recreation. Reimbursement of recreational therapy services is considered one of the major reasons for seeking licensure and, subsequently, securing a more favored position among other licensed healthcare professionals. Therefore, reimbursement of services must be considered in the future status of the profession, and many insurers will not consider an occupation that is not regulated by the states. Why do insurers rely so heavily on reimbursing licensed healthcare professionals? One explanation is that with state regulation, such as licensure, comes oversight of a profession, especially in disciplinary monitoring and sanctions (e.g., removal of a license to practice) for negligent or harmful practice. One of the key issues for the profession has long been the desire to be recognized as highly as other healthcare providers such as occupational and physical therapists, who are reimbursed for their professional services in healthcare. Since recreational therapy is primarily a healthcare service, the desire for obtaining reimbursement for services may, in fact, drive the profession toward obtaining licensure in more states across the country.

At the same time that therapeutic recreation continues to emerge as a healthcare profession, great demands are being placed for reform of healthcare services and the professions who provide such services. The cost of healthcare led to a movement to control professional regulation in the 1970s as healthcare reform began to evolve (Connolly, 1998a). Healthcare reform remains a critical issue today because of the cost and demands for quality healthcare in the U.S. The Institute of Medicine indicated that any healthcare reform must include a reform of health professions, especially their education and regulation (Greiner & Knebel, 2003). Five core competencies were recommended for all health professions in this hallmark study (Greiner & Knebel, 2003) including: providing patient-centered care, working within interdisciplinary teams, employing evidence-based practice, applying quality improvement, and utilizing informatics.

The Institute of Medicine does not limit its dialogue to the education of the health professions but extends the need to provide oversight of these core competencies via certification and licensure. Certification and licensure, according to the Institute of Medicine study, are challenged to include measurement of the five core competencies in their exams and in the requirements for maintenance of licensure and certification. Licensing and certification authorities are additionally challenged to require all renewing professionals "to demonstrate periodically their ability to deliver patient care—as defined by the five competencies—through direct measures of technical competence, patient assessment, evaluation of patient outcomes, and other evidence-based assessment methods" (Greiner & Knebel, 2003, p. 9).

The implications of these five core competencies for health professions to the field of therapeutic recreation are dramatic. Not only would our educational programs have to be revised to accommodate these competencies, but our certification and licensing programs would need to incorporate competent patient care practice as recertification and re-licensing requirements. This would create a dramatic shift in our certification and licensing programs to not only adhere to direct practice as the dominant area of job skills and knowledge, but to also require all credentialed professionals to engage in therapeutic recreation practice as a condition of recertification and renewal of the CTRS credential and, where applicable, state licenses.

Summary

Given that therapeutic recreation is predominantly a healthcare occupation, and that great changes are on the horizon to improve healthcare services, there are many challenges facing certification and licensure in the future. Whether or not the profession seeks greater governmental regulation through licensure, it is apparent that the desire to prove that therapeutic recreation services are worthy of reimbursement may drive the field to obtain governmental regulation through state licensure. Regardless of whether governmental regulation becomes a reality, it is clear that the profession must examine current certification practices and consider recertification requirements to demonstrate practice competence as a mandated requirement for all.

While there is an established and recognized national certification program in the profession of therapeutic recreation, there has not been an organized or extensive movement to establish governmental regulation of the profession through state licensure. Only a few states have enacted licensure laws for recreational therapy. Some of the issues that hold the profession back from establishing itself firmly in the healthcare arena are philosophical. Using the umbrella term "therapeutic recreation," the profession has attempted to bring together the diverse needs of those working in the community leisure service arena and those who work in healthcare. While those who work in healthcare to deliver recreational therapy services far outnumber those working in the community sector, the dominant focus of educational programs preparing professionals for the field remains in the parks, recreation, and leisure arena rather than in the health professions. Further, certification and licensure may not be as highly demanded in community sector jobs as they are in the healthcare arena. Deciding what our focus is in service delivery and providing a unified direction from education to certification and licensure to recognize the field as a member of the healthcare community is essential to future growth and development of the field.

Discussion Questions

1. Consider how the use of the umbrella term "therapeutic recreation" helps the field either advance its mission in providing a quality national certification program or how it may limit such establishment. What are the pros and cons of attempting to maintain such a broad and diverse title in the profession? How does this broad and diverse focus of the profession limit the development of a sound and recognized national certification program?

2. Should the field establish a national agenda to obtain licensure in all 50 states? If so, why? If not, why not?

3. What is the relationship of professional education in therapeutic recreation to the programs of national certification and licensure of the profession? Is there a need for reform of therapeutic recreation education to improve the qualifications of professionals? Is it desirable to incorporate the five core competencies recommended by the Institute of Medicine as required competencies within therapeutic recreation education programs? Why or why not?

4. Why is reimbursement of therapeutic recreation services so important to the field? Will establishment of licensing laws in all 50 states lead to automatic reimbursement of therapeutic recreation services in healthcare since insurers usually rely on state licensing laws to determine which health professionals are reimbursed? If so, why? If not, what else does the profession need to improve in order to gain reimbursement of services?

5. You live in a state that does not currently license recreational therapists. You are a member of your professional society in that state, and you have volunteered to serve on a committee to investigate the possibility of seeking a licensure law in your state for recreational therapists. Where would you begin? Create a strategic plan of the steps you would take to investigate the feasibility of initiating a project to obtain licensure in your state.

References

Atkinson, D. J. (2000). Legal issues in licensure policy. In C. G. Schoon, & I. L. Smith, (Eds.). *The licensure and certification mission: Legal, social and political foundations*, (pp. 124-144). New York: Professional Examination Service.

American Therapeutic Recreation Association (2000). *Standards for the practice of therapeutic recreation, revised.* Alexandria, VA: Author.

Browning, A. H., Bugbee, A. C., & Mullins, M. A. (Eds.). (1996). *Certification: A NOCA handbook.* Washington, D.C.: National Organization for Competency Assurance.

Carter, M. J. (1981). Registration of therapeutic recreators: Standards from 1956 to present. *Therapeutic Recreation Journal, 15*(2), 17-22.

Carter, M. J., & Folkerth, J. F. (1989). The evolution of the National Council for Therapeutic Recreation Certification. In D. M. Compton (Ed.), *Issues in therapeutic recreation: A profession in transition* (pp. 505-510). Champaign, IL: Sagamore.

Connolly, P. (1998a). Healthcare credentialing. In F. Brasile, T. K. Skalko, & j. burlingame, (Eds.), *Perspectives in recreational therapy: Issues of a dynamic profession* (pp. 403-417). Ravensdale, WA: Idyll Arbor, Inc.

Connolly, P. (1998b). NCTRC certification. In F. Brasile, T. K. Skalko, & j. burlingame, (Eds.), *Perspectives in recreational therapy: Issues of a dynamic profession* (pp. 383-402). Ravensdale, WA: Idyll Arbor, Inc.

Connolly, P., & Riley, R. (1996). Entry-level job skills: Reinvestigation of the National Job Analysis of the practice of therapeutic recreation. *Annual in Therapeutic Recreation, 6,* 26-37.

Department of Labor. (2006). Dictionary of Occupational Titles. Retrieved April 7, 2007, from http://www.occupationalinfo.org/onet/32317.html.

Dower, C., O'Neil, E. H., & Hough, H. J. (2001). *Profiling the professions: A model for evaluating emerging health professions.* San Francisco, CA: Center for the Health Professions, University of California, San Francisco.

Greiner, A. C., & Knebel, E. (Eds.). (2003). *Health professions education: A bridge to quality.* Washington, D.C.: National Academies Press.

Grossman, J. (1998). Continuing competence in the health professions. *American Journal of Occupational Therapy, 52*(9), 709-715.

Knapp, L. G., & Knapp, J. E. (2002*). The business of certification: A comprehensive guide to developing a successful program.* Washington, D.C.: American Society of Association Executives.

National Council for Therapeutic Recreation Certification. (2007a). Overview of NCTRC. Retrieved April 1, 2007, from http://nctrc.org/aboutnctrc.htm.

National Council for Therapeutic Recreation Certification. (2007b). 2007 NCTRC job analysis report: NCTRC report of the international job analysis of certified therapeutic recreation specialists. New City, NY: Author.

National Council for Therapeutic Recreation Certification. (2007c). NCTRC position paper on the legal regulation of the practice of recreational therapy. New City, NY: Author. Retrieved April 7, 2007, from http://nctrc.org/documents/NCTRCLegalRecognitionPape r.doc.

National Organization for Competency Assurance. (2004). Standards for the Accreditation of Certification Programs. Washington, D.C.: Author.

National Organization for Competency Assurance. (2007). About us. Retrieved May 22, 2007, from http://www.noca.org/about/about.htm.

Oltman, P. K., Norback, J., & Rosenfeld, M. (1989). A national study of the profession of therapeutic recreation specialists. *Therapeutic Recreation Journal, 23*(2), 48-58.

Riley, B., & Connolly, P. (in press). A profile of certified therapeutic recreation specialist practitioners. *Therapeutic Recreation Journal.*

Robert Wood Johnson Foundation. (2006). Workers who care: A graphical profile of the frontline health and healthcare workforce. Princeton, NJ: Robert Wood Johnson Foundation. Retrieved April 7, 2007, from http://www.rwjf.org/files/publications/other/ workers_who_care.pdf?gsa=1.

Schoon, C. G., & Smith, I. L. (Eds.). (2000). *The licensure and certification mission: Legal, social, and political foundations.* New York: Professional Examination Service.

Shimberg, B. (2000). The role that licensure plays in society. In C. G. Schoon, & I. L. Smith, (Eds.), *The licensure and certification mission: Legal, social and political foundations,* (pp. 145-163). New York: Professional Examination Service.

Stumbo, N. J. (1990). Licensure in therapeutic recreation: Issues and current status. *Illinois Parks and Recreation, 21*(1), 10-14.

Stumbo, N. J. (1989). Credentialing in therapeutic recreation: Issues in ensuring the minimal competence of professionals. In D. M. Compton (Ed.), *Issues in therapeutic recreation: A profession in transition* (pp. 67-86). Champaign, IL: Sagamore.

Stumbo, N. J. (1986). A guide to certification in therapeutic recreation. *Illinois Parks and Recreation, 17*(6), 19-22.

Young, S. D. (1987). *The rule of experts: Occupational licensing in America.* Washington, D.C.: CATA Institute.

CHAPTER 22

Walking The Tightrope, Juggling, and Slow Dancing: Metaphors for Building Effective Therapeutic Relationships

Susan L. Hutchinson, Ph.D.
Dalhousie University

Walking a tightrope, juggling, and slow dancing may all be considered enjoyable leisure activities. These activities can also be considered metaphors for the processes associated with building and maintaining therapeutic relationships with clients in therapeutic recreation (TR) settings. The purpose of this chapter is to explore the challenges and dilemmas associated with establishing effective therapeutic alliances.

Before reading further, it is helpful to frame your reading by reflecting on the following questions:

- What knowledge, skills, awareness, and abilities should TR practitioners possess in order to build relationships with clients (and their families/care providers) that will be effective in facilitating change through the TR process?
- What do you see as key to building and maintaining a healthy therapeutic relationship with clients?

Like all expert practitioners, your own experiences and beliefs are important guides for how you think about establishing and maintaining effective therapeutic relationships.

Many students seem to quickly grasp the ways they need to think about designing a comprehensive program plan and writing goals and objectives. They understand how to creatively develop specific programs that will accomplish a department's mission *and* meet the needs of clients. They have a strong understanding of the presenting needs and problems of client groups, but also an equally strong conviction about the need to focus on enhancing client abilities and strengths. They firmly believe in the power of leisure and recreation to do this. Yet, the nature of the relationship with a potential client—and their role in structuring and cultivating this relationship—is much more elusive. Even experienced practitioners often struggle to define the kind of relationships they should try to build with clients as part of facilitating an effective therapeutic process. My students often use the term "friend" to name the kind of relationship they imagine they would ideally want to have with a client, perhaps without fully thinking through all of what is implied in what it means to "be a friend."

This chapter draws on research and thinking that evolved from an ethnographic case study conducted in a rehabilitation setting (see Hutchinson, 2000; Hutchinson, LeBlanc, & Booth, 2002, 2007) for more details about the study). Although many basic principles of effective helping are consistent across different disciplines and practice settings, for the most part, the ideas presented here are framed within the context of building therapeutic alliances with clients who possess the cognitive (e.g., memory, problem-solving) and communicative abilities to actively participate in setting the course for their participation in a TR change process.

Walking the Tightrope While Juggling: Metaphors for Relationship Dilemmas in Therapeutic Recreation

As noted earlier, many students initially use the term "being a friend" to characterize the nature of their ideal relationship with a potential client. As we explore more fully what it means to be a friend, it is clear that a nonjudgmental attitude and genuine caring *do* contribute in meaningful ways to both friendships and therapeutic relationships. However, the students also come to see that other things like *reciprocity* (i.e., equality, mutuality) in sharing confidences and personal problems may be essential to being a good friend, but they are inappropriate in a therapeutic relationship.

Before looking at the issues associated with relationship dilemmas in TR, it is useful to begin by identifying what makes a good therapeutic alliance. Carter, Van Andel, and Robb (2003) provided a comprehensive overview of what it means to be a "helper." They noted that an effective therapeutic relationship becomes the "means by which a helper assists a client in mobilizing his or her resources" (p. 72). From this perspective, the TR practitioner is an instrument or tool in the therapeutic process; as such, Carter et al. emphasized that the therapists' "interpersonal skills contribute to client impact and outcomes" (p. 73). Carter et al. identified a constellation of skills, self-awareness, and knowledge necessary to be an expert helper, including: (a) being self-aware of one's own motives/needs for being a helper; (b) awareness of one's cultural/personal values and biases; (c) a commitment to honesty, genuineness, ethical integrity, competence, and personal responsibility (e.g., holding one's self and others accountable for actions); (d) the need for effective helpers to communicate positive regard, warmth, caring, empathy, and acceptance; and (e) communication competence and client empowerment (see also Brammer & MacDonald, 2003; Egan, 2002; Hutchins & Vaught, 1997; Okun, 2002) for more detailed information about helping relationships). Carter et al. noted that the therapeutic process and relationship "is dependent on many variables, including personality, emotional health, competence, and motivation of the helper and the client; type of intervention; attitudes; and congruence or harmony with the values and norms of diverse populations" (p. 73). They also highlighted the challenges and dilemmas of being an effective helper, such as the clients' over-identification with the therapist or the therapist's own motivations and behaviors that are affected by self-esteem, status, and intimacy needs.

How do TR practitioners walk the tightrope between being an effective educator, facilitator, expert, and "cheerleader" (all important and necessary roles in TR) and finding one's self in an unhealthy relationship with a client? This dilemma is not a new one in therapeutic recreation. Several other writers have noted the ethical dilemmas posed when TR specialists are uncertain about how to create and maintain a healthy balance in relationships with clients, (e.g., Jacobson & James, 2001).

In the last edition of the *Professional Issues* volume, Jacobson and James (2001) described previous research by James (1999) in which 60% of the ethical problems identified by therapeutic recreation specialists involved improper therapist-client relationships. They elaborated the challenges of the multiple roles a therapist assumes, and the confusion this creates if not clearly communicated and carefully managed:

> In what other profession could one teach a client anger-management strategies, engage him in a volleyball game, interview his wife regarding their leisure patterns, communicate the client's problems with impulse control to the treatment team, and take the client fishing, all in the same week? Whom does the client relate to: the social director, the instructor, the fishing buddy, the potential date, or the therapist? (p. 241)

Jacobson and James noted that there are many danger signals warning that the TR specialist may be falling off the tightrope, including: (a) the therapist's over-identification with the client, (b) the need to be needed and appreciated by clients, (c) spending an inordinate amount of time with one client, including off-duty time, (d) keeping secrets the client has shared, or (e) withholding information from the rest of the treatment team. They suggested that not only do these behaviors violate ethical practice guidelines of the TR profession, but they can lead to the potential for exploitation and manipulation on the part of either the client or therapist and to the delay or denying of the client's right to, and need for, independence. In other words, these practices can undermine the therapeutic relationship and the potential for meaningful change in the therapeutic process.

Can you imagine trying to juggle while walking a tightrope? This image captures the challenges of trying to juggle the need to quickly build rapport and an open, caring relationship with a client, while also trying to communicate the purpose of TR and the role of a TR specialist in clear terms. Juggling continues as the TR practitioner walks the tightrope between initially assessing needs, interests, and abilities while also assuaging fears or confusion and negotiating possible treatment goals. This occurs in the context of juggling relationships with other clients and their families, as well as with other staff, volunteers, allied professionals, and managers. In turn, relationship building occurs while juggling a multitude of other work demands, like attending team meetings, tracking down resources, completing documentation, cleaning up and maintaining physical spaces, and all that is involved in planning and implementing programs. Finally, of course, all this juggling and tight-rope walking takes place in an uncertain and changing healthcare or social services environment, and in the context of practitioners' own personal life demands and challenges. As one senior student commented, "We think we will (or should) be able to separate ourselves or 'leave our baggage at the door,' but in reality we do not" (Jessica Ross, personal communication). From these perspectives, it is truly amazing that practitioners can even take one step along the tightrope without falling off!

Slow Dancing: A Metaphor for Building Effective Therapeutic Relationships

In her memoir following her rehabilitation from a stroke, Bonnie Klein (1996) provided a compelling image of the slow dance that stroke survivors (and other people living with physical limitations) and care providers do when they try to successfully negotiate transfers (e.g., from sitting in wheelchair to toilet). Slow dancing can also be a metaphor for the flow of actions and interactions that occur between clients and therapists as they tentatively negotiate some shared understanding of their respective roles in the TR process, of the goals to which they will each work (individually and together), and of the nature (content and form) of their work together.

Dilemmas arise when trying to balance the expectation to follow a systematic assessment protocol and engage in processes of relationship building and assessment that may often unfold in a more chaotic and unstructured way. Part of the dilemma is that therapists are trying to accomplish multiple goals at the same time. At the same time that they are trying to build rapport and gain trust (i.e., all the requisite tasks of relationship building), they are also trying to understand the meaning of leisure in their clients' lives in the past, as well as their present fears and hopes for the future. In addition to building a therapeutic relationship and gaining awareness of their client, the TR specialist must also try to help his/her client see that working on leisure-related needs or goals *is* a worthwhile investment of their limited energy and time. I coined the term "talking a problem into being" (Hutchinson, 2000) to describe the tentative and often difficult task of goal-setting with clients in some therapeutic settings.

While the idea of "talking a problem into being" might seem manipulative and perhaps self-serving, it is clear that most clients do not come into a rehabilitation setting with leisure as an identified problem or need. As a result, they are often not prepared to address leisure-related issues, even though they may identify leisure-related needs or concerns in the screening/assessment process. Talking a problem into being implies helping clients to identify a problem/need in a way that makes sense within their worldview (e.g., of themselves in the present and future, as well as their values and beliefs). This requires more than just assessment or goal setting; it becomes the slow dance that must occur in the midst of trying to build a therapeutic relationship.

Negotiation of a future therapeutic relationship often rests on how the screening/assessment process evolves. Much of this depends, in turn, on how the purpose of TR and the meanings of leisure are initially communicated to the client and his/her family. How does the therapist describe TR? How does she explain her role? Does the therapist focus on past leisure/activity participation in initial descriptions of TR? Conversely, should the therapist focus on the future, linking his description of TR to a client's goals and view of him or herself in the future? Does the therapist begin by identifying barriers to returning to past activity participation or by emphasizing the potential benefits of leisure-related activities for addressing rehabilitation goals?

Dilemmas also emerge in the decision about what assessment tools to use in the assessment process. While standardized assessment tools may provide reliable and valid results, what do they also communicate to potential clients? For one client I observed in the rehabilitation hospital, the Leisure Diagnostic Battery was so alienating that he refused all subsequent involvement in TR (Hutchinson, 2000). His idea of recreation was incompatible with this formal assessment tool. Alternatively, while informal assessment processes may allow, as one therapist said, "the flexibility of going where people are in terms of their leisure interests and needs" and provide a chance to "test the waters," the question arises as to whether these processes adhere to requirements for standardization that are the hallmark of good assessments (Stumbo & Peterson, 2009).

The therapists who participated in the study of TR practice in rehabilitation (Hutchinson, 2000; Hutchinson et al., 2002) explained that within the context of the initial screening, for example, they would often have to give people the option of "buying in" to the TR process or not. From these therapists' perspectives, the key to effectively carrying out assessments was their ability to monitor, "how he is *really* feeling or thinking about things he says will be 'fine' or 'no problem'." In a similar fashion, suggestions of possible TR-related goals and interventions were based on the therapists' assessments of people's responses to their initial questions about free time or recreation. "If the person answers about what they *do*, then I focus the planning and discussions on activity skill development, not leisure awareness, values, etc." One of the therapists described this process as "trying to get a sense of their expectations. How tied are they to their activities, or are activities a vehicle for socializing with friends?" The therapists explained that if they could find *one* thing that individuals were willing to give a try, they would use some form of activity participation as a way to further explore issues that they could then address in future education or other interventions.

The metaphor of a slow dance seems to fit with the ways the therapists I observed in the rehabilitation setting described their work. A slow dance begins with tentatively exploring how to move together. Questions that we might ask when beginning to learn how to dance with a new partner (e.g., "what music do we dance to?; where do we put our feet?") parallel questions the therapist must ask him or herself in deciding how to help clients identify not only leisure-related needs but the importance of working on them through TR. Clearly, how therapists talk about their role *and* leisure will have a significant influence on the content and course of the subsequent therapy process. In fact, the therapeutic process and relationship is subject to ongoing negotiation; what issues to address, next steps in the therapy process, even continued participation are negotiated on an ongoing basis throughout the therapy process. The dilemma is how can this slow dance occur in the context of the increasing requirements for standardized procedures for practice?

Relationship Building in the TR Process

Walking a tightrope, juggling, and slow dancing all require a level of improvisation, of tuning into and responding to the unique cues of the situation and the setting. These activities are also metaphors for the improvisational nature of the processes that contribute to an effective therapeutic alliance. Clearly, building an effective therapeutic relationship in TR requires more than being empathetic, caring, and genuine (i.e., the characteristics of a good friend). It requires clearly understanding and being able to communicate their purpose as TR professionals in ways that make sense to clients, given their life context and current situation. It also means framing actions and interactions in ways that help clients clearly see the benefits of, and experience meaning from, their participation in TR.

From my observations in the rehabilitation setting, it was clear that when the therapists were able to align their interactions and interventions with the understandings and perceptions of clients, they were able to negotiate a successful therapeutic relationship over time. Figure 22.1 represents what happens when the therapists are able to define, negotiate, and frame their work with clients in ways that are congruent with a client's worldview. The dashed circle represents the shared understanding and therapeutic alliance that exists when (a) the therapist understands and attends to the client's worldview, including his/her views of TR, leisure, and rehabilitation, and when (b) the client understands and agrees to the purpose of TR and the role of the therapist in the therapeutic process. In these situations, not only is the therapeutic relationship strengthened, but a shared understanding between the therapist and client ensures there is a greater possibility of the TR process resulting in positive change.

Alternatively, when therapists and clients hold dissimilar views or when the therapist is not able to fully understand the client's worldview, this can lead to tensions or points of disjuncture. In situations where therapists and clients hold divergent views of what they are there to do, it is more difficult to maintain a therapeutic alliance and sustain clients' participation in the TR process. Figure 22.2 represents this situation.

Developing Relationship-Building Skills

I have come to believe that effective clinical practice is embedded within the relationship that exists between a client and therapist; without both it would be extremely difficult to

---

Figure 22.1
Shared understanding in the therapeutic process

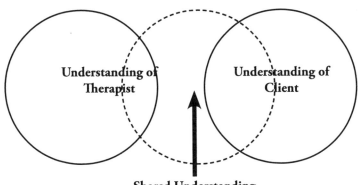

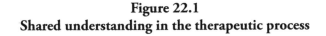

Shared Understanding
Therapist aligns talk-interventions to be congruent with
client's self-understanding and perceptions of TR

Figure 22.2
Divergent understanding in the therapeutic process

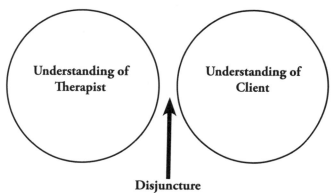

Disjuncture
Therapist is unable to align talk/interventions to be congruent with
client's self-understandings and perceptions of TR

effect change. How then can a student or practitioner develop skills to make decisions about building and maintaining effective therapeutic relationships?

First, it seems students and practitioners need opportunities for *self-reflection*. As students or practitioners, the first step is to take time to understand yourself and, as Carter et al. (2003) recommended, your role as a TR practitioner as an instrument or tool in the TR process. Do you have a clear and accurate (i.e., being honest with yourself) understanding of: (a) your own beliefs and philosophies of what it means to be a professional, a helper, a therapist?; (b) how your professional training or membership in a professional association has influenced how you understand and operationalize your role as a TR specialist?; (c) how your own needs, desires, motivations, and experiences influence your interactions and actions with clients?; and (d) how your other life roles/responsibilities affect your practice?

Likewise, an effective therapeutic relationship is grounded in having a clear and accurate picture of the setting within which practice is embedded (e.g., the institutional policies and procedures, the "culture" of the setting, the TR department mission and goals, disciplinary boundaries) and a strong (evidence-based) understanding of the needs and abilities of the client group you are mandated to serve. Stumbo and Peterson (2009) wrote about the steps in gaining this knowledge and information as part of the broad assessment process involved in designing an effective comprehensive program plan for TR services. Together, self-understanding as well as understanding of the setting and client group form the foundation for an effective therapeutic alliance with clients in TR settings.

Second, students and practitioners need ongoing opportunities to *reflect on their practice*; this includes reflecting not only on what they did but how they thought about what they did. As educators or internship supervisors, what can we do to foster reflection on practice? Schön (1987) has written about educating the reflective practitioner, and his ideas are outlined in more depth in Hutchinson et al. (2002). In almost all practical and written assignments, our goal should be to encourage students to become increasingly reflective about how they can take what they have learned, practiced, or observed and apply it to the way they think about their work with clients. Encouraging students to reflect on what they learned and how this learning can be applied to their current and future practice is akin to the kind of transfer or processing of experiences we want our clients to engage in during or after participation in TR interventions (Hutchinson & Dattilo, 2001). How can we do this? Alongside most content or skills-focused assignments, students can be encouraged to think about and share (either through a reflective journal or dyad/group discussion) what they learned from the process of doing the assignment and how they can take what they have learned and apply it to some future situation. For example, student presentations to class members can become a vehicle for reflecting on self-presentation skills if they are encouraged to reflect critically on their performance. Likewise, a practical project involving opportunities to facilitate more than a single session or to repeat an assignment can also support a sequence of trial (and error), reflection, and re-trying and further reflection. Even shadowing experiences with more experienced practitioners or observing fellow students provide rich opportunities for critical reflection.

As managers or leaders within professional organizations, creating opportunities for practitioners and interns to reflect on their clinical practice becomes critical to supporting the development of skills. In a practice setting, beyond meeting to review administrative issues or to discuss client-related treatment goals, it is important to facilitate opportunities for practitioners and interns to share, discuss, and reflect on the various ways they might approach a challenging client-related situation. In team meetings devoted to reflecting on clinical practice, Mattingly (1991) would use videotapes to enable occupational therapists to describe the "story" of their interactions with a client. In so doing, the clinical reasoning used by the therapist would become more visible to him or herself and others as well. Within professional TR organizations, opportunities to reflect on and share can occur in multiple ways, from a problem/answer discussion board to creating a forum for sharing and learning from others through case-study presentations at local or regional meetings or conferences.

Summary

As suggested previously, while walking a tightrope, juggling, and slow dancing may all be enjoyable leisure activities, they can also be considered metaphors for the processes associated with building and maintaining therapeutic relationships with clients in TR settings. Developing effective therapeutic relationships begins with getting to know one's self and the client groups and setting in which one works, and is fostered through ongoing opportunities to reflect on what one has learned. Building effective therapeutic relationships is not only an inherent part of walking a tightrope to negotiate a shared understanding of TR with clients, but it is essential to effecting change through the TR process. Enjoy the dance and share with others along the way!

Discussion Questions

1. How would you describe the ideal therapeutic relationship between a TR specialist and client?
2. How, and in what ways, does this relationship shift/evolve throughout the TR process?
3. What are the different roles you might assume with clients through the TR process?
4. What are key strategies to building and maintaining a healthy therapeutic relationship with clients?
5. What are key strategies to avoiding some of the pitfalls and dangers of unhealthy therapeutic relationships?
6. What do you do if you see that you—or the relationship—has fallen off the "tightrope" (i.e., to repair an unhealthy therapeutic relationship)?

References

Brammer, L. M., & MacDonald, G. (2003). *The helping relationship: Process and skills* (8th ed.). Boston, MA: Allyn & Bacon.

Carter, M. J., Van Andel, G. E., & Robb, G. M. (2003). *Therapeutic recreation: A practical approach*. Prospect Heights, IL: Waveland Press.

Egan, G. (2002). *The skilled helper: A problem-management and opportunity-development approach to helping* (6th ed.). Pacific Grove, CA: Brooks/Cole.

Higgs, J., & Jones, M. (1995). *Clinical reasoning in the health professions*. Oxford: Butterworth-Heinemann.

Hutchins, D. E., & Vaught, C. C. (1997). *Helping relationships and strategies* (3rd ed.). Pacific Grove, CA: Brooks/Cole.

Hutchinson, S. L. (2000). *Discourse and the construction of meaning in the context of therapeutic recreation*. Unpublished doctoral dissertation. University of Georgia, Athens, GA.

Hutchinson, S. L., & Dattilo, J. (2001). Processing: Possibilities for therapeutic recreation. *Therapeutic Recreation Journal, 35*(1), 43-56.

Hutchinson, S. L., LeBlanc, A., & Booth, R. (2007). More than "just having fun": Reconsidering the role of enjoyment in therapeutic recreation practice. *Therapeutic Recreation Journal, 40*(4), 220-240.

Hutchinson, S. L., LeBlanc, A., & Booth, R. (2002). "Perpetual problem solving:" An ethnographic study of clinical reasoning in a therapeutic recreation setting, *Therapeutic Recreation Journal, 36*(1), 18-34.

Isaacs, S. L., & Schroeder, S. A. (2004). Class-the ignored determinant of the nation's health. *New England Journal of Medicine, 351*, 1137-1142.

Jacobson, J. M., & James, A. (2001). Ethics: Doing right. In N. J. Stumbo (Ed.), *Professional issues in therapeutic recreation: On outcomes and competence* (pp. 237-248). Champaign, IL: Sagamore.

James, A. (1999, January/February). Ethical dilemmas. *ATRA Newsletter, 5,* 8.

Kennedy, K., Moran, L., & Upcraft M. L. (2001). Assessing cost effectiveness. In Schuh, J. H., & Upcraft, M. L. (2001). *Assessment practice in student affairs: An applications manual.* San Francisco: Jossey-Bass.

Klein, B. (1996). *Slow dance: A story of stroke, love, and disability.* Toronto, ON: Knopf Canada.

Mattingly, C. (1991). The narrative nature of clinical reasoning. *American Journal of Occupational Therapy, 45,* 998-1005.

Okun, B. F. (2002). *Effective helping: Interviewing and counseling techniques* (6th ed.). Pacific Grove, CA: Brooks/Cole-Thomson Learning.

Schön, D. A. (1987). *Educating the reflective practitioner.* San Francisco, CA: Jossey-Bass.

Stumbo, N. J., & Peterson, C. A. (2009). *Therapeutic recreation program design: Principles and procedures* (5th ed.). San Francisco, CA: Benjamin Cummings.

CHAPTER 23

Higher Education And Healthcare: Parallel Issues Of Quality, Cost, And Access

Norma J. Stumbo, Ph.D., CTRS™
Education Associates

Mary Ann Keogh Hoss, Ph.D., CTRS™**, FACHE, FDRT**
Eastern Washington University

As institutions concerned with providing the best services at a reasonable price for the individuals they serve, both universities and healthcare organizations share common concerns of quality, cost, and access. A large volume of literature in both higher education and healthcare has centered on these issues. The intent of this chapter is to synthesize this literature in order to explore many analogous issues pertaining to these two massive institutions within the U.S. Specifically, this chapter targets these institutions' focus on defining and measuring value, skyrocketing internal costs coupled with reduced governmental [taxpayer] funding, and their evolving demographics and service disparities. Educators and healthcare practitioners will find that their institutions share consistently similar concerns and language in their quest for the best possible service delivery to their constituents. The discussion covers demographics, quality, cost, and access.

Demographics

Higher Education Institutions' Demographics

Cleary (2001) reported that in the U.S., more than 4,000 public and private institutions spend more than $190 billion on educating 14 million students each year. The National Center on Education Statistics (NCES, 2007) reported that in 2005 some 17.5 million individuals were enrolled in higher education institutions in the United States. NCES also estimated that 20.4 million students will be enrolled by 2016. Ruppert (2003) estimated that this is without eight million students who will not have adequate access to higher education in the next decade. Meanwhile, currently $52 billion of institutional spending originates from state taxpayers, who continue to demand that their monies are being judiciously allocated (Cleary).

> American colleges and universities continue to be challenged by the need to increase access to higher education, to improve the quality of student learning, and to contain or reduce the rising costs of instruction. . . . If the quality of the curriculum inhibits students from successfully completing courses and programs, promises of increased access become hollow. . . . Historically, either improving quality or increasing access has meant increasing costs. Reducing costs, in turn, has meant cutting quality, access, or both. In order to sustain higher education's vitality while serving a growing and increasingly diverse student body, it must find a way to resolve this familiar—and seemingly intractable—trade-off between cost and quality. (Twigg, 2003, p. 22)

Colleges and universities in the U.S. face a triple challenge—that of making higher education more accessible, more affordable, and more effective (van Dusen, 2000), while simultaneously encountering shifting policies, politics, and demands. Due to a steady erosion of state and federal monies to higher education since 1965, a large share of these lost dollars has been replaced by increased tuition and fees costs. At the same time, there also has been a growing disparity between high- and low-income families, meaning many students are paying a greater percentage of their own education, which now costs more due to technology and higher administrative costs. Whether these increased costs represent greater quality is often called into question, as is the best method for measuring institutional quality (e.g., ACT/SAT scores of incoming students? Reputation of faculty? Graduation or employment rates of students?) "In truth, if issues of quality were not so complex and contentious, issues of access and cost would be much less difficult to resolve satisfactorily"

Table 23.1
Number of U.S. Higher Education Institutions in 2005-2006 (NCES, 2007)

Public 4-year institutions	656
Private 4-year institutions, not-for-profit	1,584
Private 4-year institutions, for-profit	414
Public 2-year institutions	1,161
Private 2-year institutions, not-for-profit	223
Private 2-year institutions, for-profit	829
Total	6,441

Table 23.2
Enrollments in U.S. Higher Education Institutions in Selected Years
from 1976 to 2005 (NCES, 2007)

	1976	1980	1990	2000	2002	2003	2004	2005
Total	100.0	100.0	100.0	100.0	100.0	100.0	100.0	100.0
White	82.6	81.4	77.6	68.3	67.1	66.7	66.1	65.7
Total Minority	15.4	16.1	19.6	28.2	29.4	29.8	30.4	30.9
Black	9.4	9.2	9.0	11.3	11.9	12.2	12.5	12.7
Hispanic	3.5	3.9	5.7	9.5	10.0	10.1	10.5	10.8
Asian or Pacific Islander	1.8	2.4	4.1	6.4	6.5	6.4	6.4	6.5
American Indian/ Alaskan Native	0.7	0.7	0.7	1.0	1.0	1.0	1.0	1.0
Nonresident Alien	2.0	2.5	2.8	3.5	3.6	3.5	3.4	3.3

(van Dusen, 2000, p. 60). Tables 23.1 and 23.2 outline U.S. higher education demographics with regard to number of institutions as well as number of enrollments.

Healthcare Institutions' Demographics

The American Hospital Association's (AHA, 2005a) *Hospital Statistics 2006 Edition* shows 5,759 registered hospitals in the U.S. Rural hospitals represent 2,003 institutions, with 2,916 urban hospitals. These institutions represent a total number of staffed beds at 955,768, with almost 37 million total patient admissions in 2004 (AHA, 2005a). The total expenses for 2004 were almost $545 billion. These hospitals as well as the rest of the healthcare continuum face the same triple threat that the colleges and universities wrestle with regarding cost, quality, and access.

Hospitals are considered the cornerstone of the U.S. healthcare system (AHA, 2005c). Table 23.3 shows the number and kinds of healthcare institutions in America. Although costs for healthcare have steadily been on the rise, the financial status of hospitals has been in a decline since the passing of the Balanced Budget Act of 1997. "In 2003, nearly one-third of hospitals lost money overall" according to the AHA (2005c, p. 1). Kovner and Knickman (2005) noted, within the American healthcare system, "the quality of care is uneven . . . the most expensive care is often fragmented or insufficient, and may not restore the patient to health or adequate functioning" (p. 4). Quality and cost often are at odds in healthcare as they are in higher education. Accessibility is the third major issue for healthcare with estimates as high as one in every five Americans not having access to quality healthcare (LeBow, 2002).

Table 23.3
Number of U.S. Healthcare Institutions (AHA, 2005a)

Not-for-profit	2,967
For-profit	835
Government	1,356
Psychiatric	466
Long-term Care	112
Units of Institutions	23
Total	**5,759**

The intent of this article is to explore more deeply and to draw parallels between three prominent issues—quality, cost, and access—for both higher education and healthcare in the U.S. These issues will be the focus of the reminder of this article.

Definitions and Measurement of Quality

Higher Education Institutions

According to Cleary (2001), quality is a subjective construct and is thus influenced by unique perspectives and is open to various interpretations by different stakeholder groups. Pressures for increasingly stringent accreditation requirements, stronger competition for students, limited financial resources, and greater demands by employers are combining to force universities to be more accountability driven and to use performance indicators to assess quality. In a positive sense, performance indicators can help institutions identify problems, develop solutions to those problems, make improvements in programs, policies, and services, as well as celebrate areas of excellence (Alstete, 1995). However, the National Opinion Research Center (1997) explained that institutional quality, since it is often compared in light of institutional goals that vary within or across institutions, is difficult to define or measure. Two additional reasons cited for this difficulty were lack of publicly available information (especially compared to hospitals) and that there is no one "best" college for all students.

Cleary classified quality measures into input, process, output, and outcome indicators (NB: Most other authors equate output with outcomes) and noted "there are really no 'all-purpose' measures for assessing institutional quality across all institutions" (2001, p. 22). In his study of various stakeholders at a community college, all groups rated outcome indicators (e.g., pass rates on licensure/certification exams) as the highest priority for measuring institutional quality. He added "those within higher education, producers and consumers alike, have the collective responsibility for the provision, protection, and promotion of institutional quality in all of its forms, facets, and functions" (p. 24).

Berg (2005) explained that proprietary universities that focus on business models equate quality with outcomes, and therefore are forcing nonprofit universities to re-examine their philosophies and practices related to quality measurement. Additional pressures to measure outcomes are coming from the public at large (Goral, 2005). However, Hartman (1999) countered that studies attempting to tie directly educational inputs or processes to outcomes are inherently flawed or simplistic and results have been "inconsistent and inconclusive" (p. 390).

Four systems of measuring quality within higher education will be examined: (a) rankings, (b) accreditation, (c) benchmarking, and (d) economic modeling. Each of these four will be reviewed briefly as they are used within higher education.

Among the many sources of college and university ranking systems, one of the most popular is the *U.S. News and World Report's America's Best Colleges* (Cleary, 2001; Klein & Hamilton, 1998; Vedder, 2004; Young, 2003). This system divides institutions into four categories of national universities, national liberal arts colleges, regional universities, and regional liberal arts colleges, which are then divided into four geographic areas, North, South, Midwest, and West. The *U.S. News* college rankings are based on several key measures of academic quality and are divided into seven broad categories: (a) peer assessment; (b) graduation and retention rate; (c) faculty resources (e.g., class size); (d) student selectivity (e.g., average admission test scores of incoming students); (e) financial resources; (f) alumni giving; and, only for national universities and liberal arts colleges, (g) graduation rate performance. The indicators include both input measures, which reflect the quality of students, faculty, and other resources used in education, and outcome measures, which capture the results of the education an individual receives. A weighted, category-based formula then is used to determine an institution's score (Young, 2003). The National Opinion Research Center (1997) considered that seven variables were input, four were process, four were output variables, and one was a global measure.

Some detractors of the ranking system are concerned that they have nothing to do with measuring the quality of the so-called "black box of higher education" but rather measure the "artifact of endowment. . .[that] tells U.S. what selectivity does, and selectivity is in large measure a function of the richness of the school" (Goral, 2005, p. 2). Vedder (2004) agreed that the *U.S. News and World Report* rankings are partially based on the amount spent on inputs (such as faculty resources) so that the more a school spends, the higher the ranking. With regard to law schools, Klein and Hamilton (1998) noted that the differences in rankings actually come down to two scores, student selectivity and academic reputation, making all other scores superfluous. In an additional twist, the Career College Association, a lobbying group for proprietary universities, is asking Congress to mandate all institutions to annually publish "institutional report cards" that address how well the institution retains and graduates students, as well as prepares them for life beyond their school years (Burd, 2003).

The second, more traditional quality evaluation system is accreditation (Flower, 1998). She also remarked that while traditional accreditation processes examine the credentials and experience of faculty, the availability of resources, the depth and breadth of course offerings, and other academic "assets," there is some movement toward student outcomes as the preferred method of judging quality. She warned that two byproducts are likely to occur due to this changed emphasis. First, the university's responsibility for creating a "place for discovery, synthesis, reflection, and evaluation of knowledge" (p. 28) would be lost. Second, students would be judged on factual knowledge, leading faculty to "teach to the test" (p.

28), much like the consequences of the No Child Left Behind scheme in elementary and secondary education. Hartman (1999) noted that in such a scheme, education inputs, such as student/teacher ratio or class size, teacher education level, experience of the teacher, teacher salary, and expenditure per student, are compared with student outcomes, typically student scores on standardized tests to measure student achievement.

The Society for College and University Planning (SCUP, 2008) noted that much of Europe is currently involved in an effort to develop a set of student learning outcomes (qualification frameworks) that can be measured by degree completion, essentially answering the question, "What should be expected of a student at the time of degree completion?" SCUP also commented that the United States "may have no choice but to judge U.S. institutions on how well their students meet these quality standards" (p. 11) if additional countries outside Europe adopt this framework.

A third exercise that many institutional managers invoke on the faculty and staff is performance benchmarking. Alstete (1995) cited Spendolini in defining benchmarking as "a continuous, systematic process for evaluating the products, services, and work processes of organizations that are recognized as representing best practices for the purpose of organizational improvement" (p. 8). Schuh (2003) discussed three forms of benchmarking undertaken at colleges and universities: (a) internal benchmarking (compares costs between units within an institution or division); (b) competitive benchmarking (compares costs with competitors); and (c) functional or generic benchmarking (compares costs with like organizations). Alstete (1995) added generic benchmarking (looking at the "best of the best" regardless of industry).

Shuh proposed that programs, units, or services within colleges and universities be evaluated for quality, the efficiency/effectiveness, and what the absence of the unit would mean to the students and the campus. "Having the data . . . that directly support the conclusion that various units contribute to the persistence and graduation rates moves units from peripheral status at an institution to one of centrality" (2003, p. 93). Next he suggested that alternatives be considered: "1. Should the unit be eliminated? 2. Could the unit be provided for less money? 3. Could the unit be downsized? 4. Could the unit be outsourced? 5. Can the unit be funded differently?" (p. 94). Certainly a current challenge for higher education institutions in the U.S. is "how to keep providing value under conditions of constant change. . . . The evolution of institutions, like individual development, requires a balancing of continuity and change in response to a changing environment" (Berg, Csikszentmihalyi, & Nakamura, 2003, p. 40).

A fourth, but less-used quality-evaluation method is predictive modeling. Martin (2003) posited an economic modeling equation that is based on the assumption that the public—including parents and prospective students—base their judgment of institutional quality on the success of its alumni and from the quality of students who attend the institution. He noted that in order to be judged a quality institution, students with high native abilities must be attracted and admitted, they must be exposed to as many opportunities as possible while enrolled, and they must be well placed in a career track after graduation. He further noted that the institution's ability to fulfill these goals is constrained by its current financial resources (including alumni donations) and enrollment demand. Enrollment demand is of course based on prospective students' perception of institutional quality.

Healthcare Institutions

Defining and measuring quality is an ongoing challenge in healthcare. The quality initiative was initially imposed upon hospitals in the late 1970s and early 1980s to ensure quality assurance. The concepts employed were based on tried and true practices in business, as it was felt that healthcare was growing similar to business and would benefit from these practices (Scholtes, 1988). Quality efforts were seen as an additional burden taking away from the essential services provided by the hospital staff. Often these initiatives were not seen as a part of the heart and soul of the operation but something that had been forced onto the hospital as an additional regulation imposed by federal and state government and accrediting bodies (LeBow, 2002). Although healthcare institutions were mandated to participate and comply, hospitals were allowed to develop their own versions for creating and implementing the quality initiative. This allowed much variation in both education of the workers and implementation of the process, yielding yet even greater confusion and inconsistencies (Zuckerman & Coiles, 2004). Some administrators felt implementation was going to be their facility's salvation, while others barely gave lip service to quality. Through an education process consisting of trial and error and documentation of exceptional results, today the concepts of quality are typically incorporated into a healthcare organization's core mission, vision, and/or value. Truly great systems are committed to quality as a way of life (Zuckerman & Coiles, 2004). Major inconsistencies still, however, remain within the healthcare system (Institute of Medicine [IOM], 2000).

This is demonstrated by the Institute of Medicine (2000) in the first of a series of reports on the Quality of Healthcare in America project. The report, *To Err Is Human: Building A Safer Health System,* addressed patient safety as a serious issue affecting the quality of healthcare. "The decentralized and fragmented nature of the healthcare delivery system (some would call 'nonsystem') also contributes to the unsafe conditions for patients, and serves as an impediment to efforts to improve safety" (IOM, 2000, p. 3). This report estimated that between 44,000 and 98,000 Americans die each year as a result of medical errors in hospitals (IOM, 2000).

The four systems of measuring quality in higher education (rankings, accreditation, benchmarking, and economic modeling) also are used in healthcare. Rankings are used for hospitals, and like the one for education, the annual *U.S. News and World Reports' Best Hospitals* are very popular. In 2005, 176 medical centers were identified, with 16 earning honor-roll status, a mark of distinction. The report focuses on selecting the right hospital for the individual's need in 17 specialties. Some of the factors used in choosing the medical centers included mortality ratio, reputation sampling of board-certified physicians from the American Medical Association's masterfile, and reputational specialties. In some specialties, reputation is the only standard for ranking. These specialties are ophthalmology, pediatrics, psychiatry, rehabilitation, and rheumatology (*Best Hospitals,* 2005).

Accreditation and certifications processes through the Joint Commission on Accreditation of Healthcare Organizations (JCAHO), the Rehabilitation Accreditation Commission (CARF), and the Centers for Medicare and Medicaid Services (CMS) as well as state departments of health ensure that minimum standards of care are met. Loss of accreditation or certification may mean a loss of federal or insurance funding, such as decertification from CMS causing a loss of Medicare dollars. Some argue that these processes do not enhance patient care and add to the costs of the provision of services for the hospitals, creating a paperwork nightmare (Lamm, 2003).

Benchmarking, defined as seeking comparative data from other institutions to identify the best possible performance, is a practice that all hospitals engage in to some degree (Griffith & White, 2002). As one example, CMS has a new initiative assessing payment adequacy and is moving toward value-based purchasing, requiring hospitals to report their performance on various indicators. More and more benchmarking will be occurring in all aspects of healthcare delivery as various economic models are proposed for healthcare (Medicare Payment Advisory Commission [MedPAC], 2005). Dominance of one model over another to date has not been proven (MedPAC, 2005).

Wakefield and Wakefield (2005) discussed four different stakeholders' perspectives on healthcare quality. They noted: the providers' focus is on technical quality, the patients' focus is on touch quality, and the payers' focus is on technical and touch quality, as is that of the policy makers. Such differing perspectives demonstrate that quality focus and function have not as yet reached consensus in healthcare settings.

Higher education and healthcare institutions are both increasingly being accountability driven, often from external constituents and forces. Both consumers and payers are mandating quality initiatives, such as national rankings, external accreditation, internal and external benchmarking, and economic modeling, in both educational and healthcare systems. Quality will remain a key impetus for both higher education and healthcare in the foreseeable future.

Cost

Higher Education Institutions

Higher education is in a phase of both expansion and diversification. According to Johnstone, Arora, and Experton (1998) five forces are responsible: (a) the expansion of primary and secondary education is creating a strong demand for tertiary education; (b) the rate of growth in the proportion of college-aged individuals who choose higher education is increasing as the labor market places greater demands on the workforce (with higher education becoming an entry-level necessity) and as urbanization continues; (c) higher education is diversifying to meet the growing demands of the modern and complex world; (d) governments are creating standards, and in some cases, incentives to universities to ensure equal access for students; and (e) students are increasing the amount of time they spend in higher education.

At the same time, Johnstone et al. (1998) stated that higher education is in fiscal crisis due to: (a) higher demand than can be met by current higher education capacity; (b) tendency of higher education unit costs to rise faster than unit costs in overall economy (due to technology and rapid changes in fields in the greatest need or demand); (c) increasing scarcity of public revenue due to growing and competing costs such as for public infrastructure, public education, healthcare, and policing costs; and (d) political attitudes becoming disenchanted with the "public sector" and the subsequent move to a market (or private) economy. These resulted in a cost move from "the public" to "the user," producing a "more reasonable alignment of those who pay with those who benefit" (Johnstone et al., 1998, p. 5).

van Dusen (2000) noted a semantic difference between cost and price. Price is the amount of money it takes to acquire something, while cost is the purchase price plus all other expenses related to owning, operating, or maintaining it. One of higher education's main concerns is setting the purchase price of an education at a level that not only covers the costs but also makes it attractive to the purchaser(s).

In the 20 years prior to 2004, Vedder (2004) found that real per-student spending rose 70%, while Flower (1998) reported a gain of 35% for public institutions and 55% for private schools (after factoring in inflation) between 1987 and 1996. Vedder (2004) reported that within all these large funding gains, only 21 cents per dollar since 1976 had gone toward instruction.

Lee and Clery (2004), among others, underscore that public higher education is becoming state-supported rather than state-funded. State support for higher education in constant dollars has declined over the last 30 years. Gamage and Mininberg (2003) explained that as economic demands on different levels of government were expanding, dollars appropriated to universities were shrinking. *The Chronicle in Higher Education* reported that in the 2004-2005 academic year, states were slashing appropriations for public colleges, putting little new money toward student aid and raising tuition and fees. State support dropped by 2.1% from 2003-2004 to 2004-2005 ("The Almanac," 2004). However, Ewell (2004) countered that state allocations to higher education grew more than 60% in inflation-adjusted dollars between 1993 and 2003. He emphasized that institutions needed more money over this period because they cost more, not by and large that the states gave less.

Losco (2005) stated that in 2002, the National Center for Public Policy and Higher Education issued a report that showed while state support increased by 13% from 1982 to 1998, tuition and fees increased by 107% over the same period. Flower (1998) noted that a college education is still a largely "subsidized" enterprise, as each student pays far less than the cost of his or her education. Funding now is approximately one-third state supported, one-third supported by students, and one-third institutionally supported in the form of endowments, philanthropy, grants, and other entrepreneurial activities (Gamage & Mininberg, 2003).

As financing education has shifted to the individual students, more students are working, competing for limited scholarships, borrowing money, and taking an average of 6.5 years to graduate (Gamage & Mininberg, 2003). NCES (2007) reported that in the 2005-2006 academic year, the average annual tuition at four-year institutions was $17,447 ($12,108 at public and $27,317 at private).

NCES (2007) noted that 63% of all undergraduate students enrolled in 2003-04 received some kind of financial aid. About half of the students received grants, and about one-third took out loans. Grants averaged $4,000, yet loans averaged $5,800. SCUP (2008) found that students who borrowed as much as they could rose from 57% in 1997 to 73% in 2007.

Losco (2005) also noted that while tax-credit programs provide welcomed relief to middle-class families, many low-income families and students earn too little to benefit from tax reduction. For example, in the 1990s, there was an increase in the percentage of students in the highest income quartile who received institutional aid, from 12 to 18%, with middle income students going from 17 to 23% (Losco, 2005). Flower (1998) reported that while more students are getting financial aid, the amount received per student has lowered.

Losco explained that part of this was due to a transfer from many needs-based financial programs to more merit-based programs. Ewell (2004) found that students in the lowest income quintile in 1976-1977 required just over 40% of their annual income to attend a four-year public college, yet now need 70% of their annual income to do the same. The highest income quintile of students used about 6% in 1976-1977 and 7.5% in 2003. Massa (2005) noted another set of curious trends: scholarship aid to students from families making $40,000 or less increased 22% from 1995 to 2000, but students from families making $100,000 or more, aid rose by 145% during the same period. Massa stated "the commitment to access is taking a back seat to leveraging dollars to ensure enrollments and net revenue" (p. 1), and "higher education jeopardizes its future by increasingly discounting price to those well able to afford tuition and to benefit from a quality experience" (p. 1). This may well be related to the previous discussion of quality in which universities often are judged by what cohorts of students they attract, rather than other performance indicators.

Twigg (2003) noted that nationwide just 25 large-enrollment introductory courses (usually in general education) generate about half of all community college enrollments and about a third of all university enrollments. While these courses are crucial to degree completion, typical failure rates are 15% at research universities, 30 to 40% at comprehensive institutions, and 50 to 60% at community colleges. These course failures contribute heavily to drop-out rates between first and second year for many attendees. In a similar vein, Manzo (2004) reported that although 40% of community college students expect to complete a baccalaureate degree, only 25 actually transfer to a four-year program, and of those students, fewer than 40% attain bachelor's degree. Manzo attributes this to lack of coordination and communication between two-year and four-year sectors.

Berg (2005) noted that by the end of the 1990s, 42% of undergraduate and 59% of graduate students attended part-time; and of those, the largest segment was women 35 years and above. Flower (1998) reported part-time students required more student services than their full-time counterparts in relation to the number of credit hours they take. Codhoe and Helms (2005) remarked that the longer a student stays at an institution, the higher the cost of losing that student becomes.

Three major financial reforms have emerged in the last ten to 20 years: (a) supplementation of public or governmental revenues with non-governmental revenues (e.g., higher tuition, student grants and loans, entrepreneurial activity by faculty, greater push for endowments and philanthropy); (b) reform of public sector financing (e.g. lump-sum budgets that the institutional management allocates); and (c) restructuring (Johnstone et al., 1998). In regard to restructuring, Johnstone et al. further noted that

> Radical change or restructuring of an institution of higher education means either fewer and/or different faculty, professional staff, and support workers. This means lay-offs, forced early retirements, or major retraining and reassignment, as in: the closure of inefficient or ineffective institutions; the merger of quality institutions that merely lack a critical mass of operations to make them cost-effective; and the radical alteration of the mission and production function of an institution—which means radically altering who the faculty are, how they behave, the way they are organized, and the way they work and are compensated. . . . Yet, while public universities resist radical change, they are not immune to the loss of large amounts

of public revenues occasioned by the forces listed above. In fact, the very short-term robustness of the university—its seeming ability to "make do" with larger and larger classes, or part-time, low-paid lecturers, or without replacing laboratory equipment or replenishing the library, or by admitting more fee-paying students, or by diverting faculty energies to entrepreneurial activities—may be its worst enemy in the competition for increasingly scarce public revenues. These short-term 'fixes' sometimes allow the government or ministry to cut funds to the public institutions without coming to grips with the need to close down inefficient campuses, or lay off faculty no longer relevant to the needs of the students, the economy, or for that matter of the university (Johnstone et al., 1998, p. 23-24).

Schuh (2003) cited Kennedy, Moran, and Upcraft (2001, in identifying three vital questions to ask in assessing the effectiveness of expenditures on college campuses:
1. How does the service or program contribute to the institution's mission?
2. In what direction is the institution headed?
3. What are the institution's budget policies?

Many institutional management teams, especially in austere budget times, ask these or similar questions to determine the centrality of each unit, program, department, or college to the mission of the university. "Centrality, meaning that the unit contributes to the heart of the institution's mission, is crucial. The more peripheral a unit becomes, the greater its chances of being perceived as unimportant and a potential target for budget reduction or elimination" (Schuh, 2003, p. 87).

Healthcare Institutions

Healthcare has been "pummeled by pressures to reduce costs, improve quality, assume economic risk and broker affiliations" (Zuckerman, 1998, p. 7). Healthcare spending equaled spending on education at 6% each in the federal budget in 1965. In 2000, healthcare spending as part of the federal budget equaled the combined spending on education, defense, prisons, farm subsidies, food stamps, and foreign aid (Lamm, 2003). This rapid escalation of healthcare spending is expected to reach 15% of the GNP in 2005 with no upper limit in sight. Lamm added, "Economists worry that we are unbalancing our economy and that it's not wise national policy to spend one dollar out of every seven of our gross domestic product (GDP) on healthcare" (Lamm, 2003, p. ix).

The cost of healthcare in the United States has increased 102% over the past two decades, according to Magee (2005). "Healthcare is a complex set of services, and thus it is not surprising that the way we pay for healthcare is so complicated" (Kovner & Knickman, 2005, p. 47). They attribute much of the complication to the complexities of health insurance. Each health insurance plan has a variety of benefits, exclusions, and conditions that relate directly to payment of services provided. Health insurance plans may vary greatly. A consumer may not understand what is included in his or her plan. All of these variables add to the complexity of health insurance and payment.

With more than 45 million Americans lacking health insurance coverage, hospitals provided nearly $25 billion of uncompensated care in 2003 (AHA, 2005c). Hospitals and other healthcare providers, however, remained a prime target for policy-makers looking for ways to cut the federal deficit, projected at $308 billion in 2005 (AHA, 2005c, p. 1). Even as the U.S. healthcare system as a whole continues to experience soaring costs, the quality of care remains uneven, hospitals are losing money, and the demand for services is increasing. The financial foundation for healthcare is shaky at best (AHA, 2005b).

Higher education and healthcare are experiencing unprecedented increases in the costs of service delivery. In part due to consumers' elevated and often lofty expectations, both types of settings are scrambling to deliver increasingly complex services while holding down or at least stemming the tide of rising costs. While both kinds of service providers face the fact that the demand for services continues to grow while finances continue to shrink, they are forced to diversify and search for alternative funding sources outside of their former revenue streams as well as eliminate units that are not revenue-enhancing.

Access

Higher Education Institutions

In October 1997, the Office of Management and Budget (OMB) announced the revised standards for federal data on race and ethnicity. The minimum categories for race are now:

- American Indian or Alaska Native,
- Asian,
- Black or African American,
- Native Hawaiian or Other Pacific Islander,
- White, and
- Some other race.

Instead of allowing a multiracial category as was originally suggested in public and congressional hearings, the OMB adopted the Interagency Committee's recommendation to allow respondents to select one or more races when they self-identify. There are also two minimum categories for ethnicity: Hispanic or Latino and Not Hispanic or Latino. Hispanics and Latinos may be of any race (U.S. Census Bureau [USCB], 2005).

The U.S. population as of September 4, 2008, was estimated to be 305,060,500 individuals. The population is growing more diverse with each passing year and this will continue for some time. The USCB reported that all minority groups combined increased 88% between 1980 and 2000, while the white, non-Hispanic population grew by only 7.9% during the same 20-year period. Younger age groups contained higher percentages of minority individuals than did older age groups; for example, in 2000, only 16% of those over 65 were considered to be in a minority population, while over 39% of those under 25 years of age were (Hobbs & Stoops, 2002). These changing population statistics affect higher education access and enrollments.

Within the nearly 16 million individuals attending higher education institutions in 2004-2005, approximately 1 million are Asian, almost 2 million are black, and over 1.5 million are Hispanic. Non-white students make up approximately 29% of college students in the U.S., representing a 10% increase over their respective numbers in the general population. Almost 18% of people in the U.S. speak a language other than English in their homes. Almost 570,000 (or 3.5%) college students are counted as foreign students. Women represent 56.3% of college attendees (*The Almanac*, 2004).

According to the U.S. Department of Education, from 1990 to 2000, black undergraduate enrollment rose 18%, while white enrollment declined by 10%. Additionally, Hispanic enrollment jumped 45%, Asian enrollment increased 40%, and American Indian participation grew 39% ("A Welcome Increase," 2003). The same article cited the American Council on Education's document that minorities accounted for virtually all of the enrollment growth nationally over that past 20 years, as their numbers increased to more than 4.3 million, a 122% increase since the early 1980s. In addition, minorities outpaced whites in the growth rate of academic degrees completed.

However, Gomstyn, in a 2003 article in *The Chronicle of Higher Education*, reported on a Education Commission of the States report that said while college enrollment is expected to increase by 13% over the next 12 years, there are projections of stagnant or falling rates of college participation, especially for Hispanics. The report noted that the U.S., once in first place for college participation by its citizenry, is now ranked as 13th among developed nations (Ruppert, 2003).

Berg (2005), Losco (2005), and SCUP (2008) noted that traditional postsecondary education has become less affordable and accessible, especially to low-income students, since both public and private institutions have increased tuition levels at rates higher than the consumer price index. Berg also noted that as the present trend of rising costs, high demand for higher education, and lessened state and federal funding continues, a disproportionately high percentage of poor and non-white students will be denied a college education. The National Association of Student Financial Aid Administrators reported that blacks are more likely to receive financial aid than whites, while the individual amount of aid is lower for blacks than whites ("A Welcome Increase," 2003).

Perhaps in response to those statistics, they also reported that blacks are more likely to attend less expensive community colleges than they do four-year institutions ("A Welcome Increase," 2003). Berg revealed that for-profit institutions serve 16% of all African American students, 14% of Hispanic, and 4% of Native American students, due to targeted marketing efforts, lower costs, convenient scheduling, and "applied" approach to coursework. Renner (2003), in a rousing article about racial equity and higher education, noted that although historically black colleges and universities constitute only 3% of all U.S. institutions, they educate 14% of the nation's black students. Of the 30 institutions with the highest absolute numbers of black students, 23 are two-year institutions, and only three are research universities (Temple, Wayne State, and University of Maryland). Twenty-seven of these institutions are near or in large urban areas. Renner reported that Hispanic students experience similar statistics. Of the 30 colleges and universities that have the largest absolute numbers of Hispanic students, 17 offer two-year degrees, and only one (University of New Mexico) is a research university. Nineteen are in or near large urban cities. In contrast, of the 30 institutions enrolling the largest absolute numbers of white students, only one is a two-year school, 26 are research universities, and only six are located in or near a large urban area. Renner also noted that these latter 30 institutions enrolled only 5% blacks and 5% Hispanics, even though the states in which they were housed had large minority populations. Renner strongly admonishes higher education for the failure of affirmative action admissions policies:

We should stop using "diversity" as the primary line of justification for selective admissions. It is a weak argument that has little practical validity. Minorities who make it to a "white" college or university already know how to function in a white world. Further, the main value of "diversity" is for white students to learn from minorities. This uses blacks and Hispanics for white ends. It should hardly be surprising that blacks on our campuses often prefer to associate with other blacks and that, in practical terms, physical proximity fails to foster social and education diversity. (Renner, 2003, p. 41)

Blackshire-Belay (1998) noted that black faculty make up nearly 5% of the nation's higher education faculty, and about half of those individuals teach at historically black institutions. Burgan (1998) emphasized that "we need to find collective, public ways to support our minority colleagues and students, because without that support they may wonder whether we want them on campus at all" (p. 72). "Diversity is critical to higher education . . . increased access that leads to increased campus and classroom diversity will allow higher education to fulfill its mission of preparing students for active civic engagement and participation in a diverse workforce" (Mortenson, Carter, & Olivas, 1998, p. 43).

Ruppert (2003) and Palfreyman (2004) expressed concern over these disparities, as a lack of education means a lack of income over a lifetime. Ruppert noted that persons with a baccalaureate degree earn 40% more, the equivalent of $900,000 over a lifetime, compared to individuals with a high school diploma.

International students demonstrate unique needs while attending higher education institutions. Pardue and Haas (2003) studied Israeli nursing students who were enrolled in a U.S.-based RN to BSN program. In this program, Israeli nurses completed the final intensive semester with a short-term residency program at the University of New England in Portland, Maine. The authors described some of the adjustments that needed to be made by the teaching faculty. They explained that language, culture, and educational expectations were major factors in planning cross-cultural education; for example, faculty needed to develop rapid and accurate assessment of the students' ability to read, understand, orally participate in, and write in English. Technical language (e.g., medical terminology) often proved difficult to translate. Culturally they noted that this particular cultural group was accustomed to "collective" learning rather than the more competitive American model. In addition, the students (like most international students) encountered adjustments in language, living space, culture, and distance from family and friends. Such student adjustments included first-time experiences using English language computer keyboards. Pertinent faculty adjustments included extensive planning and preparation, reorganizing course materials, employing writing support specialists, and frequently assessing and realigning course materials and student learning. A "taxing delivery modality for instructors" is how Pardue and Haas characterized the experience at the same time calling it "instructive and beneficial" for both students and faculty.

Healthcare Institutions

Like education, the future of healthcare will be determined by demographics. According to Isaacs and Schroeder (2004), "Race and class are both independently associated with health status, although it is often difficult to disentangle the individual effects of the two factors"(p. 1137). "It is clear that prejudice and discrimination, the hallmarks of racism, impact the health of minorities in America, but it is becoming increasingly obvious that low socioeconomic status, which is often a byproduct of racial discrimination, also has a significant impact on health"(Magee, 2005 p. 90). A shift is occurring because of the "aging baby boomers, the increasing ethnic and racial diversity, the growing disparity between the richest and the poorest households, and the burden of disease" (Institute for the Future, 2003, p. 17).

Access to healthcare in today's environment is of major concern. Ethnic and minority healthcare disparities became recognized as a national problem in the 1980s and 1990s. It became clear that racial and ethnic Americans were experiencing considerable disparities in the incidence, prevalence, mortality, burden of diseases, and adverse health outcomes compared to white Americans (Copeland, 2005).

In 2000, the U.S. Congress passed P.L. 106-525, creating the National Center on Minority Health and Health Disparities (NCMHD) to serve as a catalyst for planning and managing minority health and health disparities research (IOM, 2005) as well as P.L. 106-129 mandating the Agency for Healthcare Research and Quality (AHRQ) to produce an annual report to monitor prominent racial and socioeconomic factors related to healthcare disparities (Moy, Dayton, & Clancy, 2005). The AHRQ's first report, issued in 2003, provided the comprehensive national baseline data concerning access to and quality of healthcare among racial, ethnic, and socioeconomic groups (AHRQ, 2003). The second report, issued in 2004, evaluates the nation's progress toward amelioration of these disparities (AHRQ, 2004). Three key themes were highlighted in the 2004 report, including: (a) disparities are pervasive, (b) improvement is possible, and (c) gaps in information exist, especially for specific conditions and populations (AHRQ, 2004).

Two of the most prominent healthcare disparities highlighted in the 2004 report included (a) Blacks, Asians, American Indians, and Alaskan Natives, and Hispanics received lower quality care and had reduced access to healthcare than whites, and (b) individuals who were poor received lower quality care and had reduced access to healthcare than higher income individuals. Although they noted several areas of improvement in the last five years prior to the report, they also expressed a need for more and better data to track healthcare trends (AHRQ, 2004).

The above healthcare discrepancies noted on a national level have many implications for communities and individuals. Many individuals of racial, ethnic, or socioeconomic groups do not have health insurance and are not able to access health services until their health situation is dire which, in turn, usually means that the cost of care will be much higher (Eichner & Vladeck, 2005). According to Williams (2001), "access problems can lead to poorer health status, delays in obtaining care, and episodic or fragmented care" (p. 35). He continued, "It is not only important to assure access, but also to control access in such a way that resources are rationally allocated and carefully utilized in the provision of care" (p. 35). Copeland (2005), among other authors, noted that inequity and barriers to access of adequate healthcare are "multivariate, complex, and rooted in an inequitable healthcare system" (p. 265). Among the many contributing factors are increased risk of disability and disease resulting from occupational exposure; biologic, socioeconomic, ethnic, and family factors; cultural values and education; social relationships between majority and minority population groups; autonomous institutions within ethnic minority group populations;

culturally insensitive healthcare systems; geographic concerns; limited cultural competence of providers; stereotypical thinking, prejudice, and biased decision making among providers; and problems with literacy and the limited English proficiency of some client groups (Baicker, Chandra, & Skinner, 2005; Copeland, 2005; Nerenz, 2005). Access may become a serious issue for all U.S. citizens, except the most wealthy, as workforce shortages are anticipated to severely limit the quality of and access to American healthcare (Frist, 2005).

Higher education and healthcare face similar issues on access. Nonwhite ethnic and racial groups as well as older individuals and those with low incomes have difficulty accessing higher education and health services. There is some data to support that some white individuals also are experiencing greater degrees of lower quality and restricted access. Both systems must strive to keep access to services and institutions open and become more creative in removing or overcoming barriers currently faced by many consumers attempting to enter into these systems.

Implications for Therapeutic Recreation Specialists

This chapter has covered a great deal of information concerning quality, cost, and access in higher education and healthcare and has noted many similarities between these two settings. Therapeutic recreation specialists should consider a number of points when using this information. Chief among these considerations are:

1. The number and types of both higher education and healthcare institutions, as well as enrollments/admission are increasing dramatically, with no respite in sight. Institutions are increasing the diversity of their delivery styles (e.g., online and distance education and telehealth) that will, in turn, increase the complexity of therapeutic recreation services. Therapeutic recreation professionals must acquire and maintain their competence of various delivery systems used by these two types of institutions in order to remain viable to their organizations. Professionals also need to acknowledge that the diversity of students/clients is expanding to include increasing numbers of individuals from varied racial and ethnic groups as well as growing numbers of people who are foreign born and prefer to speak a language other than English. At a minimum, therapeutic recreation educators and practitioners must ensure their cultural awareness, sensitivity, and competence. Ensuring quality service to various constituents using a multitude of service delivery methods will add another layer of complexity to therapeutic recreation practice.

2. The focus in the recent past and in the foreseeable near future will be on service outcomes. Regardless of whether rankings, accreditation, benchmarking, or economic modeling is used, the focus of measuring quality will be on how the individual consumer has changed (hopefully improved) through the provision of specific, targeted educational and health services. Therapeutic recreation educators and practitioners need to gain understanding of and proficiency in methods of quality measurement, especially those used by their particular institution. This, of course, requires a foundational understanding of the relationship between goals, program delivery, and service outcomes. In addition, therapeutic recreation specialists are cautioned to ensure that quality measurement and improvement are integral within their daily service and evaluation activities and not seen as a

separate entity to be undertaken immediately prior to a quality review. Highly valuing and embracing continuous quality and performance improvement will best serve therapeutic recreation professionals.

3. Higher education and healthcare institutions will need to do everything within their powers to contain costs, as costs continue to spiral upward at astronomical rates. This implies that therapeutic recreation specialists must document high-quality services based on client need, resulting in proven outcomes at the lowest cost possible. Therapeutic recreation specialists must remain accountable, cost-efficient, and central to the mission of their organization.

4. Access to and quality of services is uneven at best in both higher education and in healthcare. This is true of many allied health services, and it remains true for therapeutic recreation services as well. Therapeutic recreation practitioners and educators need to conduct the necessary research to determine where needless or unintentional disparities exist in their own services and, if found, then take steps to eliminate those discrepancies. In addition, awareness and use of clinical practice guidelines and standards of practice are essential to improve the reliability and uniformity of service delivery wherever possible.

5. Therapeutic recreation professionals also need to keep informed of the quality, cost, and access concerns effecting higher education and healthcare. These issues will loom even larger in the near future for professionals in both arenas. This may be accomplished through a variety of activities such as performing and reading literature reviews, attending workshops and conferences, and subscribing to listservs or newsletters from national higher education and healthcare groups concerned about these issues. Therapeutic recreation professionals must be committed to continuing their competence in these areas or else suffer the staff and service reductions likely to occur to those who remain uninformed and uninvolved.

Therapeutic recreation educators and specialists who are concerned about quality, cost, and access of their services will be well served by considering these five points. This article is but one step in becoming more aware of the issues and how they apply to therapeutic recreation education and practice.

Summary

Both universities and healthcare organizations grapple with triple challenges—that of making services more accessible, more affordable, and more effective, while simultaneously encountering shifting policies, politics, and demands. Institutions concerned with providing the best services for the individuals they serve often battle balancing costs and quality. A large body of literature supports this struggle in both higher education and healthcare. The intent of this chapter is to synthesize this literature in order to explore myriad parallel issues within these two behemoth systems within the U.S. Specifically, this chapter targets these institutions' focus on defining and measuring value, balancing skyrocketing internal costs coupled with reduced governmental (taxpayer) funding, and their evolving demographics and service disparities. Educators and healthcare practitioners will find that their institutions share similar concerns and language in their quest for the best possible service delivery to their constituents while considering both cost and quality. Both educators and healthcare practitioners will profit from acknowledgment that comparable concerns impact their work in both settings and that they have much to learn from one another. Five implications for therapeutic recreation educators and practitioners relevant to quality, cost, and access were highlighted.

Discussion Questions

1. How do the changing demographics of the U.S. affect provision of therapeutic recreation education? Therapeutic recreation practice? Does the diversity of the therapeutic recreation workforce reflect the diversity of the population demographics?

2. If you were a university president or on the state board of higher education, how would you want quality to be measured? What "evidence" would you seek to demonstrate quality? If you were a chief executive officer of a large hospital, how would you want quality to be measured? What "evidence" would you seek to demonstrate quality? What are the advantages and disadvantages of the methods you chose?

3. If you were a university president or on the state board of higher education, how would you increase revenue when state support is lessening? Where would you decrease costs? If you were a chief executive officer of a large hospital or hospital corporation, how would you increase revenue? Where would you decrease costs? What are the advantages and disadvantages of the methods you chose?

4. In what ways do the changing demographics of the American population affect higher education? What new strategies will institutions, faculty, and staff need to employ to accommodate this growing diversity? In what ways do the changing demographics of the American population affect healthcare? What new strategies will healthcare facilities, professionals, and staff need to employ to accommodate this growing diversity?

5. Beyond cost, quality, and access, what other trends and issues are important to higher education and healthcare?

References

Alstete, J. W. (1995). Benchmarking in higher education: Adapting best practices to improve quality. *ASHE-ERIC Higher Education Reports #5*, 1-112.

American Council on Education. (ACE). (2005). *An agenda for excellence: Creating flexibility in tenure-track faculty careers.* Washington, D.C.: Author.

Agency for Healthcare Research and Quality. (2003). *National healthcare disparities report.* Retrieved November 15, 2005, from: http://www.ahrq.gov/qual/measurix.htm

Agency for Healthcare Research and Quality. (2004). *National healthcare disparities report.* Retrieved November 15, 2005, from: http://www.ahrq.gov/qual/measurix.htm

"The Almanac." (2004). *The Chronicle of Higher Education, 51*(1), 28.

American Hospital Association (AHA). (2005a). Fast facts on U.S. hospitals from *AHA Hospital Statistics*. Retrieved November 9, 2005, from: http://www.aha.org/aha/resource_center/fastfacts/fast_facts_U.S._hospitals.html

American Hospital Association. (2005b). *The fragile state of hospital finances*. Retrieved November 1, 2005, from: http://www.aha.org/aha/resourcecenter.html

American Hospital Association. (2005c). *Taking the pulse: The state of America's hospitals*. Retrieved November 1, 2005 from http://www.aha.org/aha/resource center.html

"A Welcome Increase." (2003). *Black Issues in Higher Education, 20*(18), 36-37.

Baicker, K., Chandra, A., & Skinner, J. S. (2005). Geographic variation in healthcare and the problem of measuring racial disparities. *Perspectives in Biology and Medicine, 48*(1), S42-S53.

Berg, G. A. (2005). Reform higher education with capitalism? *Change, 37*(3), 28-34.

Berg, G. A., Csikszentmihalyi, M., & Nakamura, J. (2003). Mission possible? *Change, 35*(5), 40-47.

"*Best Hospitals 2005.*" (2005). Retrieved November 15, 2005, from: http://www.usnews.com/usnews/health/best-hospitals/methodology.htm

Blackshire-Belay, C. A. (1998). Under attack: The status of minority faculty members of the academy. *Academe, 84*(4), 30-36.

Burd, S. (2003). Will Congress require colleges to grade themselves? *The Chronicle of Higher Education, 49*(3), A27.

Burgan, M. (1998). Access: A matter of justice. *Academe, 84*(4), 72.

Cleary, T. S. (2001). Indicators of quality. *Planning for Higher Education, 29*(3), 19-28.

Codhoe, H. M., & Helms, M. M. (2005). A retention assessment process. *Planning for Higher Education, 33*(3), 31-42.

Copeland, V. C. (2005). African Americans: Disparities in healthcare access and utilization. *Health & Social Work, 30*(3), 265-270.

Eichner, J., & Vladeck, B. C. (2005). Medicare as a catalyst for reducing health disparities. *Health Affairs, 24*(2), 365-375.

Ewell, P. T. (2004). Money matters: The real reason why money matters is that our current way of obtaining it is fast making higher education unaffordable. *Change, 36*(4), 4-5.

Flower, R. (1998). Cost and quality of higher education. *Education Digest, 63*(2), 23-29.

Frist, W. H. (2005). Overcoming disparities in U.S. healthcare. *Health Affairs, 24*(2), 445-451.

Gamage, D. T., & Mininberg, E. (2003). The Australian and American higher education: Key issues of the first decade of the 21st century. *Higher Education, 45*, 183-202.

Griffith, J. R., & White, K. R. (2002). *The well-managed healthcare organization* (5th ed.). Chicago: Health Administration Press.

Gomstyn, A. (2003). U.S. faces a college-access crisis, education-policy group warns. *The Chronicle of Higher Education, 50*(7), A35.

Goral, T. (2005). Higher education at risk: A new documentary and companion book examine the state of post-secondary education in America. *University Business, 8*(6), 43-45.

Hartman, W. T. (1999). Education funding disparities: What do the dollars buy? *Journal of Education Finance, 24*(3), 389-408.

Hobbs, F., & Stoops, N. (2002). *Demographic trends in the 20th century: Census 2000 special reports.* Washington, D.C.: U.S. Census Bureau.

Institute for the Future. (2003). *Health and healthcare 2010: The forecast, the challenge.* San Francisco: Jossey-Bass.

Institute of Medicine. (2000). *To err is human: Building a safer health system.* Washington, D.C.: National Academy of Sciences.

Institute of Medicine. (2005). *Review and assessment of the national institute of health's strategic research plan to reduce and ultimately eliminate health disparities.* Retrieved November 15, 2005, from: http://www.iom.edu/project.asp?id=22356

Isaacs, S. L., & Schroeder, S. A. (2004). Class—the ignored determinant of the nation's health. *New England Journal of Medicine, 351,* 1137-1142.

Johnstone, D. B., Arora, A., & Experton, W. (1998). *The financing and management of higher education: A status report on worldwide reforms.* Retrieved January 18, 2005, from: http://www.esib.org/commodification/documents/financing_education_wb.pdf

Klein, S. P., & Hamilton, L. (1998). The validity of the *U.S. News and World Report* ranking of ABA law schools. Retrieved October 20, 2005, from: http://www.aals.org/validity.html

Kovner, A. R., & Knickman, J. R. (2005). *Jonas and Kovner's health delivery in the United States* (8th ed.). New York: Springer.

Lamm, R. D. (2003). *The brave new world of healthcare.* Golden, CO: Fulcrum.

LeBow, B. (2002). *Healthcare meltdown.* Boise, ID: JRI Press.

Lee, J., & Clery, S. (2004). Key trends in higher education. *American Academic, 1*(1), 21-36.

Losco, J. A. (2005). Ensuring the nation's future: Preserving the promise of higher education. *Academe, 91*(1), 62-66.

Magee, M. (2005). *Health politics: Power, populism and health.* Bronxville, NY: Spencer.

Manzo, K. K. (2004). Report: Transfer barriers loom large for two-year students. *Black Issues in Higher Education, 21*(15), 6, 8.

Martin, R. E. (2003). Pricing and enrollment planning. *Planning for Higher Education, 31*(4), 29-37.

Massa, R. J. (2005). The perils of price competition: Discounting the price of college to influence student enrollment is a risky business. *University Business, 8*(6), 88.

McGinnis, J. M., Williams-Russo, P., & Knickman, J. R. (2002). The case for more active policy to health promotion. *Health Affairs 21*(2):78-93.

Medicare Payment Advisory Commission (MedPAC). (March 2005). *Report to Congress: Medicare payment policy.* Washington, D.C. Retrieved November 15, 2005, from: www.medpac.gov

Mortensen, T. G., Carter, D. J., & Olivas, M. A. (1998). A conversation about access and diversity. *Academe, 84*(4), 41-44.

Moy, E., Dayton, E., & Clancy, C. M. (2005). Compiling the evidence: The national healthcare disparities reports. *Health Affairs, 24*(2), 376-387.

National Center on Educational Statistics. (2007). Fast facts. Retrieved September 4, 2008, from: http://nces.ed.gov/fastfacts/display.asp?id=98

National Opinion Research Center. (1997). *A review of the methodology for the U.S. News and World Report's ranking of undergraduate colleges and universities.* Retrieved October 20, 2005, from: www.washingtonmonthly.com/features/2000/norc.html

Nerenz, D. R. (2005). Healthcare organizations' use of race/ethnicity data to address quality disparities. *Health Affairs, 24*(2), 409-416.

Palfreyman, D. (2004). The economics of higher education: Affordability & access; Costing, pricing & accountability. Retrieved October 18, 2005, from: www.oxcheps.new.ox.ac.uk

Pardue, K. T., & Haas, B. (2003). Curriculum considerations for enhancing baccalaureate learning for international students. *The Journal of Continuing Education in Nursing, 34*(2), 72-22.

Renner, K. E. (2003). Racial equity and higher education. *Academe, 89*(1), 38-43.

Ruppert, S. S. (2003). *Closing the college participation gap: A national summary.* Denver: Education Commission of the States.

Schuh, J. H. (2003). Selected accountability and assessment issues. *New Directions for Student Services, 103,* 87-94.

Scholtes, P. R. (1988). *The team handbook: How to use teams to improve quality.* Madison, WI: Joiner Associates.

Society for College and University Planning. (2008). *Trends in higher education.* Ann Arbor, MI: Author.

Twigg, C. A. (2003). Improving quality and reducing cost. *Change, 35*(4), 22-29.

U.S. Census Bureau. (2005). *Factfinder.* Retrieved November 16, 2005, from: http://www.factfinder.census.gov

van Dusen, G. C. (2000). Digital dilemma: Issues of access, cost, and quality in media-enhanced and distance education. *ASHE-ERIC Higher Education Reports, 27*(5), 1-120.

Vedder, R. (2004). A fortune in tuition: Why does college cost so darn much? *National Review, 56*(19), 38-40.

Wakefield, D. S., & Wakefield, B. J. (2005). The complexity of healthcare quality. In A. R. Kovner, & J. R. Knickman (Eds.), *Jonas & Kovner's Healthcare delivery in the United States* (pp. 538-585). New York: Springer.

Williams, S. J. (2001). *Essentials of health services.* Albany, NY: Delmar.

Young, J. R. (2003). In response to critics: "U.S. News" changes its formula for ranking colleges. *The Chronicle of Higher Education, 19*(15), A28.

Zuckerman, A. M. (1998). *Health strategic planning: Approaches for the 21st Century.* Chicago: Health Administration Press.

Zuckerman, A. M., & Coiles, R. C. (2004). *Competing on excellence.* Chicago: Health Administration Press.

CHAPTER 24

Perspective: Facilitating the Transition from Student to Professional Through Internship

Charles W. Bloom MS, CTRS™
Oak Forest Hospital

Internship is the final academic requirement for students prior to becoming therapeutic recreation professionals. It marks the last "leg" of a four-year journey of instruction and practical experience. Internships are often the most anxiously anticipated part of academic preparation for many reasons. In the opinion of this author, internships are the most significant indication of what a student has learned and how he/she will be able to apply this knowledge in his/her chosen profession. It has been the privilege of this author to have prepared several students through the professional practice of internship during a career spanning nearly 20 years.

Supervising interns provides a professional the opportunity and responsibility of taking a student to the next level of his/her professional development. An internship is the "game time" equivalent within this process. It is in this stage that students are required to apply concepts, theories, and principles of therapeutic recreation in a practical, structured, and supervised environment. It is an arena that allows mistakes, hones skills, and develops a multitude of professional skills and characteristics.

The intent of this chapter is to provide professional insight based on experiences with students. Chapter content will examine several major areas: (a) the importance of internship, (b) the primary roles of educators, practitioners, and students (key points of each will also be identified), (c) the transition from student to professional, using job analysis "tasks" and "required knowledge areas" and "knowledge areas," and (d) insight from years of practice.

Common Characteristics of Internship Supervisors

Intern supervisors must be fairly unique in their professional make-up. In order to assist in the development of other professionals, one must be confident in his/her own philosophies, judgments, and viewpoints. Successful internship supervisors must demonstrate a great deal of passion toward the field of TR. Supervision of students can be very rewarding, yet at times it can be equally as challenging. One must be willing to answer and sometimes reanswer student questions. Patience and tolerance are a must. In order for students to improve in areas, they must be given the opportunity to fail. We tend to learn more from experiences that begin less than perfect. "Providing programmatic, administrative, and clinical supervision to interns is part of the expectation of internship supervisors"(Navar, 2001, p. 30).

Supervisors are oftentimes required to take time away from their own duties in order to provide support and assistance. Achieving the balance of pushing toward achievement or backing off until skills are perfected is a beneficial trait for the internship supervisor to possess. It is also the opinion of the author that practitioners who are able to supervise students effectively have also made and continue to make contributions to the field above and beyond daily professional practice. These contributions include such things as: serving on national and/or state boards, being active in local and national TR organizations (e.g. NTRS, ATRA), and involvement in legislation related to healthcare topics as well as TR and supervising student interns.

Common Characteristics of Students

In the last semester prior to graduation, students are ready for the final requirement, the internship or professional practice. Students usually welcome this with a combination of nervousness, anxiety, and enthusiasm. Hopefully, by this time, students are at least confident that therapeutic recreation is their career of choice. There are some exceptions, however, and a well-structured and well-supervised internship experience may point this out.

Because students are accustomed to the structure of the university, practical experience for a duration of 12 or more weeks might prove challenging. Students are familiar with and appear comfortable with methods of teaching in higher education. However, when learning and retaining information for the purpose of a "grade," students may be unaware that classroom content is to become the foundation on which their professional knowledge will be based. Even leadership and practicum experiences tend to be looked at more as credit-earning milestones rather than skill-building experiences that will continue to be enhanced as their academic career progresses.

Educators, practitioners, and internship supervisors are well aware that coursework information is not processed by the student in the context that will be applied during the internship experience and professional career. It is oftentimes necessary for intern supervisors to facilitate the connection between content learned and how it is applied.

Students have a tendency to be overconfident at times. Grades in school do not guarantee a student's ability to successfully apply coursework material in a practical setting. Students also may have a variety of experiences from which they draw confidence. The intent is not to suppress knowledge gained from experience but to make sure that students are willing keep their minds open when learning professional application skills in a new environment. We can refer to this as "emptying your cup."

Emptying Your Cup

Oftentimes students are very willing to share their experiences with supervisors and other professionals. Sometimes students may be consumed by what they have done and by what they feel they know. At times, it becomes difficult to teach the application of knowledge or offer constructive criticism that will facilitate improvement. An exuberant young karate student wished to study with the greatest sensei in the land. He was finally invited to meet with this sensei. At tea the sensei asked the prospective student, "Why do you wish to train with me?" The student then began to verbalize in great detail his accomplishments and successes as a karate student. While he listened, the sensei began to pour tea for the student. He continued pouring until the student's cup overflowed. For the first time the student paused from talking. Bewildered he asked the sensei why he continued pouring after the cup was full. The sensei calmly replied, "Your cup of knowledge is so full, there is no room for any more." The sensei explained that in order to gain knowledge you must be willing to "empty your cup." This is also true for student interns. It is necessary to make room for the new knowledge that can be gained through an internship experience. Additionally, knowledge is usable at an optimal level when it can be applied in daily practice.

Extending Your Line

During the internship experience, students also learn other professional skills such as multitasking, interpersonal communication, organization, and prioritizing assignments. A good repertoire of professional skills will serve a student well. Mastering leadership, for example, is different in real settings as opposed to classroom simulations. Similarly, implementing treatment plans for real clients requires and addresses professional skills not met in classroom scenarios. A good student as well as a good practitioner learns to extend his/her "line" when needed.

A frustrated martial arts student went to his instructor and proceeded to tell him how his opponent was able to dominate him in competition. The student became fixated on how to defeat his opponent by minimizing the effectiveness of his opponent's abilities. The instructor calmly voiced his rebuttal to the student. "You will never be able to decrease the skills that someone else knows." With this he drew a line in the sand. "The only way to become more proficient than your opponent is to increase your own skills," he said, as he drew a longer line next to first line. "To be successful, you must extend your line."

This illustration rings very true as it relates to professional development. We must be willing and dedicated to extending our own professional lines. Students extend their lines through study in the classroom and during professional practice. Practitioners extend their line through continuing education and practicing TR in a professional manner.

The Role of Educators

The role of the educator is a critical one. Although this chapter focuses mainly on the internship experience, it would be incomplete without recognizing the contributions made by educators. Theirs is the responsibility of laying the foundation for professional practice. All primary skills in leadership, planning, documentation, evaluations, etc., are developed through classroom instruction. Over the years, it has become very important for universities to design curriculums that will address the tasks and knowledge areas in the NCTRC™ Job Analysis. It is the opinion of this author that standardization of TR curriculums would be appropriate. Steps are being made in the field to improve this. There is still some division of thought regarding this topic. Teaching content information in such a way so that its practical application is better understood must be challenging. Standardized curriculums would ensure that all students are prepared with knowledge in the same areas of content. It would also require the same level of emphasis on critical content areas (Stumbo & Carter, 1999). For example, standardized curriculums would ensure that the amount of time and emphasis placed on a topic such as assessment or documentation would be more consistent.

Key Points for Educators, Internship Supervisors, and Students

Before addressing specific ways to facilitate the transition from student to professional, it seems appropriate to examine "key points" that (a) make the connection between educational experiences and internships experiences, (b) connect the practical application of academic knowledge with practical experience, and (c) examine the relationship between student interns and internship supervisors.

Key Points for Educators
- Upon completion of TR coursework, TR students frequently express difficulty with writing program plans and performance measures.
- Students often express that it is much easier to write goals and treatment plans in the context of a scenario or case study than in reality.
- Students should be encouraged to increase competency in a variety of leisure skill areas. (i.e., sports, outdoors, fitness, art, etc.) It appears to have become a trend, whereas students have limited exposure in a variety of these skill areas.
- Students appear to have limited knowledge and/or exposure to facilitation techniques such as leisure education, stress management, and cognitive retraining, as detailed in Dattilo, (2000).
- Students are not always able to transfer knowledge into application. Increased hands-on contact with clients in structured settings would be optimal.
- Facilitate experiences in the classroom that assist in the development of professional behaviors. Students at times have difficulty adapting a "college" frame of mind into a professional work setting. These include: professional behaviors, professional language, dress, appearance, etc.

The key points listed above reflect the opinions of the author and are based on experiences with students. No inferences to any specific instructor or university are intended.

Key Points for Internship Supervisors

- Agencies accepting interns should approach acquisition of an internship similar to the acquisition of an employee.
- Student expectations as well as materials on the agency should be provided in writing and well before the beginning of the internship.
- Interviews should be conducted similar to those for acquiring paid positions.
- Students should be required to present a resume, cover letter, and references.
- Internship supervisors should provide an agency, department, or unit orientation as applicable. The orientation should be long enough to provide essential information yet short enough as to not just fill time.
- Students should be provided a detailed calendar of placement assignments, days off, and work schedules.
- Internship supervisors should set guidelines and expectations on a day-to-day or week-by-week basis. Communicate information with students as often as required.
- Internship supervisors should schedule weekly meetings with students. Select an available date that accommodates both schedules. Make every effort to keep these appointments.
- Internship supervisors should allow students the chance to observe but engage in actual experience as appropriate.
- Internship supervisors are reminded to keep in mind the role of the internship. It is to prepare TR professionals. Limit assistive roles. Refrain from "jumping in" when students are in charge of leadership.
- Students are not volunteer observers. Assign professional roles as soon as it is deemed appropriate.
- Students are not there to do menial tasks that therapists do not wish to do, but should be required to do whatever tasks therapists must do.
- Internship supervisors should introduce student interns to as many "key players" as necessary. This includes consumers, clients, and patients, as well as administrators and other therapists.
- Internship supervisors should facilitate, encourage, and reinforce responsibilities as a TR professional.
- Internship supervisors are encouraged to balance coursework review with new information and application.
- Internship supervisors should remember that hands-on experience with explanation is often more effective than mere verbal instruction.
- Internship supervisors should encourage the awareness and usage of available resources.
- Internship supervisors should demand a professional level of decorum in the workplace.
- Internship supervisors should gradually promote the transition from dependence to autonomy in the performance of TR roles.
- Internship supervisors should gradually encourage students to problem solve situations, i.e., "put out fires." Sometimes practitioners make this look too easy.
- In community-based settings, emphasize involvement, participation, skill development, and leisure experience.

- In clinical settings, emphasize behavioral outcomes in physical, cognitive, social, and emotional domains.
- Internship supervisors should demand perfection in documentation skills. "If it is not in writing accurately, then it did not happen."
- Internship supervisors should reinforce the approach of TR as a process. TR service delivery requires a systematic approach. All components are connected.
- Internship supervisors should promote the development and reinforcement of interpersonal communication skills, such as empathy, active listening, and overall relationship skills with clients.
- Internship supervisors should provide students with the opportunity to express needs and process experiences briefly but on a daily basis.
- Internship supervisors should provide immediate, accurate, and constructive feedback for student tasks.
- Internship supervisors should consider student strengths, weaknesses, and set a pace of professional development that is challenging yet not impossible to manage.

The above list of key points is by no means a definitive list for supervisors of student interns. These techniques and suggestions, however, have proved to be successful with this author.

Key Points for Students

- Although learning should be considered a lifelong process, the internship is the last milestone in preparation for the student's chosen career.
- Students should be as selective in choosing an internship site as the sites are in selecting interns.
- Students should take responsibility in finding details about the agency in which they will do their internships.
- Students need to realize that it is their responsibility to make sure that the agency they select is in compliance with NCTRC™ standards.
- Students are encouraged to ask questions. This particularly holds true when related to patient/client safety.
- Students are encouraged to find things out for themselves whenever possible.
- Students should take responsibility in transitioning from the mind-set of a student to that of a professional.
- Students should appreciate that a great deal of time and effort is being spent on their professional development.
- Students should make professional contributions whenever they can. They should leave their "mark" as interns the agency would want to hire.
- Students should recognize and understand the role of the internship supervisor.
- Students need to remember it is sometimes difficult to hear constructive criticism. Learn to use it as a means to improve.
- Students must be willing to give 100% effort into their internships; anything less is somewhat obvious.
- Students shouldn't strive for success in their internships for an "A." They should strive to become professionals who are assets to the field of TR.

- Students should realize that success as a TR professional requires a sound personal philosophy. This may take several years to develop.
- Students are reminded to pay attention to details in all aspects of TR programming. Murphy's Law is prevalent in TR practice.
- Students should observe the professional relationship between practitioners and the people they serve. Pattern yourself after the positive things you observe.

Job Task Analysis

In 2008, NCTRC™ updated the Job Analysis Study, which outlined tasks and required knowledge areas for the purpose of the certification exam. It seems only practical that these outlined tasks and required knowledge areas be used as a framework of concepts used to assist in the preparation of student interns.

The Job Tasks and Knowledge Areas of the Job Analysis both contain headings that are useful to the therapeutic recreation intern, to ensure that he or she is getting a well-rounded experience and meeting the expectations of the field.

The headings for the Job Tasks include:
- Professional Roles and Responsibilities (9 areas)
- Assessment (6 areas)
- Planning Interventions and/or Programs (6 areas)
- Implementing Interventions and/or Programs (6 areas)
- Evaluating Outcomes of the Interventions and/or Programs (5 areas)
- Documenting Intervention Services (3 areas)
- Working with Treatment and/or Service Teams (4 areas)
- Organizing Programs (4 areas)
- Managing TR/RT Services (11 areas)
- Public Awareness and advocacy (4 areas)

The headings for the Knowledge areas include:
- Foundational Knowledge (19 areas)
- Practice of Therapeutic Recreation/Recreation Therapy (29 areas)
- Organization of Therapeutic Recreation/Recreation Therapy Service (13 areas)
- Advancement of the Profession (12 areas)

According to NCTRC™ (2008), the list of Job Tasks represent the "current tasks performed by the Certified Therapeutic Recreation Specialist. These job tasks represent the therapeutic recreation process. The knowledge base for therapeutic recreation practice forms the basis of the NCTRC exam content and is used to evaluate pre-service and continuing education for therapeutic recreation" (p. 3). Students, professionals, and educators should visit the NCTRC web site [www.nctrc.org] frequently to ensure they are following the latest standards.

In supervising students, this chapter's author has found the following therapeutic recreation texts to be the most useful in helping students prepare for the internship, for the certification examination, and then their first professional position:

- Carter, M. J., & O'Morrow, G. S. (2006). *Effective management for therapeutic service.* State College, PA: Venture Publishing.
- Dattilo, J. D. (2000). *Facilitation techniques in therapeutic recreation.* State College, PA: Venture.
- Mannell, R. C., & Kleiber, D. (1997). Leisure behavior over the life span. In *A social psychology of leisure* (pp. 243-268). State College: Venture. This chapter provides an overview of development through the lifespan as it relates to leisure.
- Melcher, S. (1999). *Introduction to writing goals and objectives.* State College, PA: Venture.
- Stumbo, N.J. (2002). *Client assessment in therapeutic recreation service.* State College, PA: Venture.
- Stumbo, N. J., & Peterson, C. A. (2009). *Therapeutic recreation program design* (5th ed.). San Francisco: Benjamin Cummings.
- Mobily, K. E., & MacNeil, R. D. (2002). *Therapeutic recreation: The nature of disabilities.* State College, PA: Venture.

A number of web sites are also very useful for finding the latest information about the field:
- NTRS at http://www.nrpa.org/content/default.aspx?documentId=530
- ATRA at www.atra-online.org
- NCTRC at www.nctrc.org
- JCAHO at www.jcaho.org
- CARF at www.carf.org

Research journals are also important. The three main therapeutic recreation journals are:
- *Therapeutic Recreation Journal*
- *ATRA Annual in Therapeutic Recreation*
- *American Journal of Recreation Therapy*

Other journals, such as *Spinal Cord, Exceptional Children,* and *Behavior Modification* are available on-line through a number of sources like www.findarticles.com and www.scholar.google.com, as well library databases. Additional specialty resources can also be located at organizations' web site. Examples include The Spinal Cord Injury Association and the National Head Injury Foundation.

Evaluating the Internship

Evaluation is defined as the systematic and logical process of gathering and analyzing selected information in order to make decisions about the quality, effectiveness, and/or outcomes of a program, function, or service (Stumbo & Peterson, 2009). In this case, the quality of the internship is being evaluated. What the student has accomplished will determine his or her level of professional preparation.

All universities and agencies have developed and utilize evaluation instruments. Honestly, some are better than others. The best methods of evaluation are those that use the Job Task Content Areas (or at least a majority of them) as areas to be evaluated. A Likert Scale is usually used to rate the level of competency. The more information that can be provided for the student here, the better. The author feels that it is imperative to provide detailed comments related to performance areas. Citing specific examples or specifying particular skills is a productive way to accomplish this. Comment sections also give a more comprehensive overview of student performance. Practitioners need to keep in mind that it is difficult to evaluate levels of competency without data to substantiate the evaluation. It is also important to not leave discussion of progress, improvement, etc. until the end of the internship. Surprises do not go over well in final evaluation meetings.

Students should question areas that may require explanation. If a professional relationship has been established, this process usually goes fairly smoothly. Students must realize that learning of areas that may require improvement is not as negative as it may seem. Remember "Extending your line"?

It is the opinion of the author that becoming a fair evaluator of student interns is a very important role of the internship supervisor. In addition to levels of competency, effort and improvement should also factor into the equation. Grades are not given, they are earned. Devise good methods of evaluation at your agency/university, and use them. Look at validity and reliability. Don't be afraid to tweak such methods of evaluation.

Summary
More Insights from the Field

Some of the most rewarding experiences for this author have been the numerous phone calls, E-mails, etc., from former interns stating that they have landed a job in the field of TR. On one hand, preparing students is a difficult job. As we have examined, there are many aspects involved in preparing professionals. The application process can only be as meaningful as the base of knowledge. On the other hand, the internship supervisor is required to be the "bridge" that connects the two.

The following conclusions have been drawn by this author:

- Need for standardized curriculums (Stumbo & Carter, 1999). This would ensure that all accredited TR programs are teaching the same TR content.
- NCTRC™ standards should be introduced to students early in their academic careers. Why prepare students in a manner that will make it difficult for them to become certified? (NCTRC™, 2008).
- Curriculums must account for "activity skill" areas, (i.e., sports, art, music, etc., in order to maximize a strong repertoire of skills).
- A strong background from supportive coursework (see Folkerth in this book) is essential for clinical settings.
- All students should be required to do a "clinical" portion of internship. This is the best way to learn job tasks and apply basic knowledge areas. If they can be applied clinically, they can be applied anywhere.

- Find innovative, creative ways to teach or reinforce goal and objective writing. (Melcher's workbook is recommended). Quiz students on condition, behavior, and criteria frequently.
- TR is an outcome-based field. Behavioral change is evidence that outcomes have been met. Activities are the "vehicles" used to arrive an outcome.
- Internship is the last experience before becoming a professional, and the author hopes it has become evident that it is a most important one.
- Therapeutic recreation standards of practice are guidelines used to assist the practitioner in carrying out TR service delivery in a prudent, conscientious manner. It is the responsibility of each professional to know these guidelines.
- Ethics are also important guidelines for TR practitioners to follow. They are the rules of professional conduct that one must adhere to in order to serve people with disabilities with integrity and respect.
- Another book recommended to me by several professional colleagues is Internships in Recreation and Leisure Services (Seagle & Smith, 2002). It contains information that may assist a student in finding a meaningful internship in the field of therapeutic recreation. It prioritizes student interests as well as student needs in selecting a career direction. It also includes formats and content areas for a cover letter and resume. Tips on interviewing are also explained.

Life's a Dance

Life's a dance you learn as you go.
Sometimes you lead. Sometimes you follow.
Don't worry 'bout what you don't know.
Life's a dance you learn as you go.

John Michael Montgomery

Discussion Questions

1. Professionals: Look back at your internship. What aspects of it made you the professional you are today?
2. Students: When you think of internship, what aspects of it do you feel are most conducive to your professional development? What type of skills do you plan on learning? How prepared will you be for your internship?
3. What is your personal philosophy of recreation, leisure, play, and TR? How will you convey your philosophy to clients and other professionals in daily practice?
4. Besides coursework, what can students do while still in school to prepare themselves for internship?
5. What types of things do you feel universities (TR curriculums) could do to improve the preparation of students?
6. Discuss the professional content areas outlined in the job analysis? Are any of these less or more important than others? Why or why not?

7. How will you market yourself for internship? What are important qualities of a potential intern?
8. Professionals and educators: What types of qualifications should students possess to be considered quality candidates for internship placement?
9. As educators, practitioners, or students, if you were to add to this chapter, what types of information would you include?
10. What issues has this chapter raised related to internships and professional practice?

References

American Therapeutic Recreation Association. (1997). *Standards for the practice of therapeutic recreation.*

Carter, M. J., & O'Morrow, G. S. (2006). *Effective management for therapeutic service.* State College, PA: Venture.

Dattilo, J. D. (2000). *Facilitation techniques in therapeutic recreation.* State College, PA: Venture.

Hyams, J. (1979). *Emptying your cup: Zen in the martial arts.* New York: Bantam Books.

Kinney, J. S., Kinney, W. B., Sable, J. R., & Wittman, J. P. (2001). Curricular standardization in therapeutic recreation: Professional and university implications. In Stumbo, N. J. (Ed.), *Professional issues in therapeutic recreation: On competence and outcomes* (pp 87-104). Champaign, IL: Sagamore.

Mannell, R. C., & Kleiber, D. A. (1997). Leisure behavior over the lifespan. *In a social psychology of leisure* (pp. 243-268). State College, PA: Venture.

Melcher, S. (1999). *Introduction to writing goals and objectives:, A manual for recreation therapy students and entry-level professionals.* State College, PA: Venture.

Mobily, K. E., & MacNeil, R. D. (2002). *Therapeutic recreation: The nature of disabilities.* State College, PA: Venture.

National Council for Therapeutic Recreation Certification. (1997). *NCTRC™ 1997 Job Analysis Study.* New City, NY: Author.

National Council for Therapeutic Recreation Certification. (1997). *NCTRC™ 1997 Standards.* New City, NY: Author.

National Therapeutic Recreation Society. (2000). *Standards of Practice for Therapeutic Recreation Services.* Arlington, VA: National Recreation and Park Association.

Navar, N. H. (2001). Keynote thoughts on therapeutic recreation education. In Stumbo, N. S. (Ed.), *Professional issues in therapeutic recreation: On competence and outcomes* (p. 30). Champaign, IL: Sagamore.

Peterson, C. A., & Stumbo, N.J., (2004). *Therapeutic recreation program design: principles and procedures.* Boston, MA: Allyn and Bacon.

Seagle, E. E., & Smith, R. W. (2002). *Internships in recreation and leisure services.* State College, PA: Venture.

Stumbo, N. J., & Carter, M. J. (1999). National therapeutic recreation curriculum study part A: Accreditation, curriculum, and internship characteristics. *Therapeutic Recreation Journal, 33*(1), 46-60.

Stumbo, N.J. (2002). *Client assessment in therapeutic recreation service.* State College, PA: Venture.

Section IV
Research Issues

Section IV
Research Issues

CHAPTER 25

Keynote: Status of Therapeutic Recreation Research

Leandra A. Bedini, Ph.D., CTRS™, LRT
The University of North Carolina at Greensboro

There is something I don't know that I am supposed to know. I don't know what it is I don't know, and yet am supposed to know, and I feel I look stupid if I seem both not to know it and not know what it is I don't know. Therefore, I pretend I know it. This is nerve-wracking, since I don't know what I must pretend to know. Therefore, I pretend to know everything. I feel you know what I am supposed to know, but you can't tell me what it is, because you don't know that I don't know what it is. You may know what I don't know, but not that I don't know it, and I can't tell you. So you will have to tell me everything. (Unknown)

This confusing quote reflects what many therapeutic recreation students and professionals think about research. It is something you think you should know, but don't know if either you want to know it or if you can understand it. This quote also speaks to the issue of seeking knowledge and the ability to understand what is known and what is not known. Research can help professionals determine what is known, as well as what needs to be learned in the field of therapeutic recreation. It can give practitioners new program ideas and confirm old ones that ultimately will help meet the client's goals.

To understand the status of therapeutic recreation research today, the first question is "What are the goals of research in therapeutic recreation?" As with most research, therapeutic recreation research should benefit our clients, fellow healthcare professionals (both in and outside of therapeutic recreation), and society as a whole. Methods for how these outcomes are accomplished, however, can take several shapes.

Goals of Therapeutic Recreation Research

Driver (1989) proposed four applications of scientific knowledge that can be easily related to therapeutic recreation research. The four areas of scientific knowledge are: (a) use of knowledge for its own sake, (b) promotion of additional scientific inquiry, (c) advancement of professional bodies of knowledge, and (d) resolution of real-world problems, including evaluation of programs. For the field of therapeutic recreation, each of these areas is important to pursue.

To students and new practitioners in therapeutic recreation, it may seem that research involves a lot of fancy words and complicated techniques and has no relevance to their personal or professional lives. Actually, the contrary is true. The fancy words are just labels, and there are many useful research techniques that are simple to conduct. In fact, most practitioners are working with research data daily through assessments, progress notes, and evaluation information. In addition, much of the knowledge and skills that have made the field of therapeutic recreation function today was generated by various forms of research in the past. Many research articles are written each year that can inform the Therapeutic Recreation Specialist's (TRS's) practice with innovative and effective interventions, new assessment techniques, or ways to address professional issues. Being a good consumer of research is just as important and useful as being able to conduct the research studies.

Use of Knowledge for Our Own Sake

Reading and understanding research studies for the mere sake of learning something new can bring both personal and professional benefits. The results, implications, and recommendations from research studies in fields including, but not limited to therapeutic recreation can be interesting as well as informative to professionals in the field. Knowledge from all types of sources is invaluable to the therapist who interacts directly with clients. An individual's breadth of knowledge and information will facilitate conversations and help make connections with clients and participants in all aspects of the APIE (assessment, plan, implementation, evaluation) process. Although much of the published research might not apply to the population with whom each therapist works, the information can be useful for merely building rapport, thus worthy and merits recognition.

Promotion of Additional Scientific Inquiry

Another goal of research is to provide the foundational information with which a therapeutic recreation professional can initiate additional research and study. Research is not a one-shot project. It should build over time. The recommendations of published studies should serve as a starting point for new studies. Being a good consumer of research allows students and future professionals to make informed decisions in assessment, programming, evaluation, and advocacy for people with disabilities. In addition, it helps the TRS raise new questions for future research. This constantly growing body of knowledge of new and innovative techniques, skills, and programs, in turn, helps practitioners to help their clients meet their rehabilitation goals.

In addition, practitioners in therapeutic recreation must be resourceful in generating funding for their programs and services. Basic research and evaluation can provide groundwork for soliciting funding for much-needed resources and programs. Baseline data from a simple survey or evaluation study can provide sufficient rationale and reason for administrators as well as external funders (e.g., community foundations) to fund equipment, new service opportunities, additional staff, more space/equipment, or larger research projects. In turn, these new acquisitions can be used to test new techniques, methods, and interventions.

Therefore, research results and conclusions can benefit programs beyond mere information for the practitioner.

Advancement of the Body of Knowledge

Currently, in the midst of healthcare reform and managed-care agendas, the field of therapeutic recreation is very concerned with demonstrating its worth. The field must not lose sight, however, of the importance of conceptual development as well. Carruthers (1997/98) stressed the importance of TRSs being able to conduct research in the field to "contribute to its development and sophistication as well as the demonstration of its effectiveness" (p. 29). In addition, as society, and subsequently, its populations change, so too do its healthcare needs. In the last decade, we have seen the morphing of therapeutic recreation services to non-traditional settings and "new" populations such as people who are homeless, youth at risk, and family caregivers. It is critical, then, that the field of therapeutic recreation uses research to advance its understanding of new consumers, services, and service providers as well. In essence, research should be used to find ways to contribute to the scientific body of knowledge and theory development as well as demonstrate the effectiveness of TR programs and interventions.

Resolution of Real-World Problems and Program Evaluation

According to Driver (1989), the fourth use of research is to provide the information necessary to address real-world problems in the field. Although the word "research" strikes fear in the hearts of some, published research that addresses real-world problem-solving and program evaluation can be very helpful to all therapeutic recreation professionals. Driver stated that these types of studies can "...offer more efficient ways of meeting an objective, evaluate the effectiveness of particular programs, provide new options that might promote greater public acceptance, evaluate the consequences of alternative policies, and expand choice options for the users of particular goods and services" (p. 602).

Understanding and using the conclusions and recommendations of research articles in areas of health, education, nursing, gerontology, occupational therapy, as well as therapeutic recreation can provide specific information for program development as well as modification. For example, studies in psychology have helped to understand stress, and research in public health has shown a relationship between leisure-time physical activity and quality of life. It is important that conclusions and recommendations from all fields be applied to the practice of therapeutic recreation to improve services.

Program evaluation research is another form of research that has multiple benefits, especially for the area of therapeutic recreation. Again, knowledge from studies from all health and related fields can help disprove "old" assumptions (programmatic, philosophical, interventive) that may limit the scope of practice. For example, animals were considered just pets until fairly recently, when research on the therapeutic benefits of animals in meeting rehabilitation goals was conducted. Prior to this research, animals were only used for diversion, if at all, in medical arenas. Now hospitals are establishing animal-assisted therapies as part of the interventions available in therapeutic recreation.

Another real-world challenge requiring problem-solving is the fact that therapeutic recreation is in a constant struggle for survival. Managed care and other fiscal impacts, as seen in Thompson's chapter 19, have consistently forced the field to prove itself to avoid reduction in staff and resources. Theoretical or sophisticated efficacy research is not usually feasible in a therapist's daily tasks. Simple program evaluation can help out significantly, however, in identifying program strengths and weaknesses.

We've Come a Long Way … but There's Still Work to be Done

To have direction for the future, it is important to know what has been accomplished in the area of research over the last few decades. Over the last 25 years, many educators and practitioners have identified strengths, weaknesses, and priorities for research in therapeutic recreation (e.g., Bedini & Wu, 1994; Carruthers, 1997/98; Compton & Dieser, 1997; Coyle, Kinney, Riley, & Shank, 1991; Iso-Ahola, 1988; Malkin, 1993; Mannell, 1983; Wilhite, Keller, Collins, & Jacobson, 2003; Witt, 1988). Some of the significant weaknesses identified included: (a) poor quality of research studies, (b) lack of innovative approaches, (c) lack of theoretical bases,(d) lack of efficacy research, (e) lack of funding for therapeutic recreation research, (f) lack of preparation of entry-level practitioners to understand research studies, and (g) lack of collaboration between agencies and between practitioners and educators. The following section will address these criticisms and determine if and how each weakness has been resolved today.

Quality of Research Studies

In 1993, Malkin noted that the "perceived lack of meaningful research [in the field of therapeutic recreation] is reported widely" (p. 13). Meaningful research should contribute to the body of knowledge as well as to the body of efficacy for the field of therapeutic recreation. For research to be truly meaningful, then, it is essential that the results can be trusted through "tightness" or rigor of the study's methods.

An equally important measure of quality is the usefulness of the study to the reader. Unfortunately, until recently, the results of research were rarely presented so that other researchers and practitioners could benefit from the results. Often, articles would end with a short conclusion section after the report of results with no implications or recommendations for practice or future research. For example, Jordan and Roland (1999) found that many leisure academics thought it was "perfectly acceptable to publish research for the sake of sharing complex information without application to practice" (p. 169). Also, Bedini and Wu (1994) found that 41% of research articles published in the major therapeutic recreation journal between 1986 to 1990 offered no recommendations to either practitioners or researchers. Today, however, Bedini and Magnes (2007) found that of the 81 research articles published in *Therapeutic Recreation Journal* and *Annual in Therapeutic Recreation* from 2001 through 2005, over 85% included recommendations for practitioners, and over 90% offered recommendations for researchers.

Limitations are also important to note in research studies because these help identify weaknesses in design and application of these concepts that should be considered in their practice. Stating limitations also gives future researchers ideas for how to make these studies better and gives them "warnings" as to weaknesses that might exist in a study. Compared to only 28% of those published from 1986 to 1990, 69% of recent research studies provided useful discussion of limitations (Bedini & Magnes, 2007).

Innovative Approaches

Reviews of therapeutic recreation research from the 1970s and 1980s (e.g., Mannell, 1983; Iso-Ahola, 1988; Witt, 1988) noted that research in therapeutic recreation used little diversity of methods. Later, Bedini and Wu (1994) found that 87% of therapeutic recreation research published in the *Therapeutic Recreation Journal (TRJ)* from 1986 to 1990 used only quantitative methods. Only 4% used qualitative approaches and only 9% used both approaches in triangulation. The recent review of therapeutic recreation research, however, found that of the 81 research articles published in TRJ and the *Annual in Therapeutic Recreation (ATR)*, there were 10 different research designs, including descriptive survey designs (36%), experimental designs (including single-subject design) (23.5%), and qualitative designs (23.5%) such as observation, in-depth interview, and case study (Bedini & Magnes, 2007). In addition, therapeutic recreation research in the early 2000s grew slightly in its use of triangulation, where a single problem was studied using several methods in 12% of the studies. As Mitra and Lankford (1999) noted, "a multi-method approach leads to better data for improved decision making" (p. 97).

Theoretical and Conceptual Bases

The absence of theoretical and conceptual bases to underlie research studies has been a concern in the field of therapeutic recreation for quite some time as Caldwell's Chapter 26 notes. Theories and conceptual frameworks are important, especially in therapeutic recreation research, because not only do they help guide the study, as Devine and Wilhite (1999) noted, but are also useful in the development of interventions as well as service accountability.

In the late 1980s, only 26% of the 46 articles reviewed used any type of theoretical or conceptual framework (Bedini & Wu, 1994). In 1999, Devine and Wilhite still lamented the lack of use of theoretical frameworks in the field. In 2007, however 46% of the research articles in the two major therapeutic recreation journals published between 2001-2005 presented a conceptual or theoretical basis for their studies (Bedini & Magnes, 2007). This trend contributes to stronger research and programs in the future.

Efficacy Research

Driven by cuts in programs and services in healthcare, many healthcare services have needed to prove their worth to survive; therapeutic recreation is no different. As noted earlier, the need to prove the efficacy of therapeutic recreation service has been one of the major foci in the field in the last decade. Malkin (1993) described a "paucity of research on the efficacy of TR interventions" (p. 13). Similarly, Compton and Dieser (1997) noted that "there is little change in the production of empirical research in therapeutic recreation" (p. 304).

The field of therapeutic recreation has not been without attempts to determine efficacy needs and programs, however. In 1989, Coyle, Kinney, Riley, and Shank examined issues of efficacy research in therapeutic recreation by conducting a national conference entitled *The Benefits of Therapeutic Recreation: A Consensus View*. This gathering brought together 80 of the country's top researchers, educators, and practitioners in therapeutic recreation to discuss and examine literature about the benefits of therapeutic recreation interventions and experiences. From this meeting, a book with the same title (1991) was published. The results of this work identified six primary benefits of therapeutic recreation: (a) physical health and health maintenance, (b) cognitive functioning, (c) psychosocial health, (d) growth and development, (e) personal and life satisfaction, and (f) societal and healthcare systems.

Carruthers (1997/98) conducted a Delphi study to develop a research agenda for the field of therapeutic recreation. The results indicated that the field of therapeutic recreation should focus its research in six primary areas, all of which dealt with efficacy of therapeutic recreation. These areas focused on the effect of therapeutic recreation on: (a) community integration/reintegration, (b) recidivism/prevention of further illness, (c) independent functioning, and (d) hospital costs/lengths of stay. In addition, the effect of leisure functioning on health and increased efficacy/control through therapeutic recreation on rehabilitation outcomes were noted.

Recently, Wilhite, Keller, Collins, and Jacobson (2003) also conducted a Delphi study to re-examine important efficacy research areas. They identified that the top five research agenda items were: (a) effect of leisure functioning on various aspects of health (e.g., social, physical, emotional), (b) effect of leisure education on quality of life, (c) effect of TR on overall independent functioning, (d) effect of frequency and duration of contact with clients on TR outcomes, and (e) effect of TR on successful community integration. According to the study, these items were supported by both educators and practitioners and should be the focus of future research in therapeutic recreation.

A current review of research (Bedini & Magnes, 2007) found that almost 24% of therapeutic recreation studies tested an intervention or program. Now that agendas have been identified, each professional must accept the challenge of conducting studies, no matter how small, to begin to collect solid data to prove TR's efficacy.

Funding

Up until approximately 15 years ago, little, if any, funding existed for professionals to study therapeutic recreation issues specifically. In the last decade, however, funding has been made available on several levels, although in relatively small amounts. For example, each year the American Therapeutic Recreation Foundation provides funding through the Bernard E. Thorn Efficacy Research Fund awarded biannually.

Similarly, many state societies provide the opportunity for members to compete for funding for therapeutic recreation research. For example, the North Carolina Recreation Therapy Association and the Therapeutic Recreation Division of the North Carolina Recreation and Parks Association each offer funding awards every year to members researching therapeutic recreation practice outcomes, program effectiveness, or related issues. Finally, more and more individual practitioners have sought and received funds from community foundations. Gradually, as the field of therapeutic recreation becomes more recognized by outside entities, more sources of funding outside of the field should become available.

Preparation and Entry-Level Professionals

A commonly stated concern is that there is a lack of preparation of entry-level practitioners to understand or conduct simple research studies. Compton and Dieser (1997) suggested that some of the reasons TR lacks more empirical research in the field may be a reflection of the "failure of either higher education preparation programs or professional organizations to advance the skill level of their professionals" (p. 304). Today, however, research and evaluation skills are part of the accreditation standards of recreation programs by the NRPA Council on Accreditation. Specifically, standard 8.17 requires students to have the "Ability to apply basic principles of research and data analysis related to recreation, park resources, and leisure services" (NRPA/AAPAR, 2004).

Similarly, the 2007 NCTRC™ Job Analysis Report listed two job tasks that address research specifically: "support research programs and projects" (#52) and "enhance professional competence" (#6). This second standard refers to reading current research literature to keep up with new techniques and related implications for practice (National Council for Therapeutic Recreation Certification™).

The class of 2005 from the Leadership ATRA program (12-month program that focuses on leadership development in TR) conducted a small study to determine practitioners' views on participating in research. They found that 75% of the CTRSs™ surveyed stated that they would be interested in participating in research projects, but they stated several barriers to participating: (a) lack of time to do research and supervisor expectations, (b) lack of research knowledge, and (c) limited knowledge of funding monies. Respondents actually noted that although they learned research techniques in school, they did not think it was enough to conduct a study now (Carson, 2006). To this end, Caldwell and Weissinger (1993) recommended that students, practitioners, and educators who are interested in collaborating take the responsibility to become good consumers of research, becoming intimately familiar with the research process before beginning the journey. Therefore, it is incumbent upon all practitioners, new and experienced, to take advantage of the many opportunities to learn about the research process so they are ready when the opportunity to collaborate arises.

The Future is Now: Moving Forward with Therapeutic Recreation Research

Your Ethical Duty

Both NTRS and ATRA identify the use and pursuit of research as an ethical obligation of the TR professional. For example, the NTRS ethical standard, *Knowledge*, is defined as, "Professionals work to increase and improve the profession's body of knowledge by supporting and/or by conducting research" (NTRS Code of Ethics and Interpretive Guidelines, 2001). Being a good consumer of research can address the ethical standards of competence as defined by both ATRA and NTRS's Codes of Ethics. The NTRS standard, *Competence,* is defined as "Professionals continuously enhance their knowledge and skills through education and by remaining informed of professional and social trends, issues, and developments." Similarly, Principle 7 in the ATRA Code of Ethics (2001), *Competence,* states, "…The professional has the responsibility for contributing to changes in the profession through activities such as research, dissemination of information through publications and professional presentations, and through active involvement in professional organizations." Therefore, all professionals have an ethical obligation to keep up with research and to begin to get involved professionally to get more exposure and opportunities dealing with the research process.

Becoming a Good Research Consumer

As noted earlier, it is important for students and practitioners to be involved in research as good consumers if not actually conducting research. Unfortunately, this is a challenge for many practitioners. Jordan and Roland (1999) conducted a study that found that 65 to 96% of recreation practitioners do not read research journals.

Students and professionals in therapeutic recreation can meet this challenge in several ways. First, many beginning specialists will have taken an evaluation or a research course before graduation. It is important to take this course seriously to hone these consumer skills while in school. This course will serve as a foundation to become a good consumer of research studies later. In addition, each beginning therapist should review Caldwell and Weissinger's (1993) strategies for reading research literature. Often it is somewhat intimidating to take on reading a full research study in a major journal. Therefore, another approach to reading research is for students to begin with more "accessible" research reports that could enhance basic knowledge and practice. Several examples of alternatives to research journals include the "Research Update" section of *Parks and Recreation Magazine* or the *Journal of Applied Leisure Research.*

Finally, to be good consumers of research, it is important for students to branch out beyond therapeutic recreation research. Much of what can be used in a TR setting comes from other disciplines. For example, the *New England Journal of Medicine* published an article by Verghese et al. (2003) demonstrating a link between leisure activities and reduction of dementia. Rogers and Zaragoza-Lao (2003) published a study in the *American Journal of Public Health* that examined the relationship of art, entertainment, and recreation to happiness and children's health. Nelson and Gordon-Larsen (2006) published in *Pediatrics* findings that adolescents who participate in a wide variety of physical recreation activities had higher self-esteem and were at less risk for negative behaviors (e.g., drugs, violence). As professionals in healthcare, we would be remiss to ignore this wealth of information from other disciplines related directly to the benefits of recreation and leisure for people with disabling conditions.

On a personal level, honing one's research knowledge and skills, especially as a student, provides several benefits. First, having experience in actual research studies on a resumé increases marketability in the job arena. Employers will solicit competent therapeutic recreation specialists who can also conduct or facilitate a research study. Greater skills create greater demand. Second, the more students and practitioners know about the research process as well as how to read and interpret research studies, the more likely they are to be able to plan, implement, and evaluate innovative and effective programs for their clients. Knowing where to find answers to difficult problems encountered as an intern, new practitioner, or even a seasoned supervisor will improve programs, which is the goal of all CTRSs™.

Professionally, one real problem for therapeutic recreation practice is the acknowledgment and support from the administration. Being involved in research within an individual agency can contribute to the TR staff developing clout with administrators. Practitioners are involved with data every day. Involvement can range from comparing simple data summaries of the types of activities participants attended to engaging in complex analysis of the effects of a particular intervention on some construct of human behavior. By knowing how and then systematically collecting data from programs and clients, the TRs will be in the position to demonstrate the effectiveness of services. In turn, being able to defend the worth and value of interventions, staff, and programs can invaluable in this time of flux within managed care.

How to Develop Your Research Competence Checklist

Young professionals as well as seasoned students are not too new in the field to begin getting involved in the research process. The following are easy ways future professionals as well as new practitioners can get involved in research process.

1. Internship Research Project

A way of getting involved in the research process without getting in over your head is to design a small research study as part of the senior internship. This study can be a basic program evaluation to a more complex theoretical study. Find out if one of the TR practitioners at the sponsoring internship agency might be involved in a research study. If not, the faculty supervisor might guide you. Either way, the student could propose to be involved as part of the requirements of the internship.

2. Join the Research Committee

Another easy way to get involved but not get overwhelmed is to observe others who have experience conducting research. By joining the research committee of a state or national organization, students and beginning professionals can learn by watching and can gradually work into the process. Currently, each national organization, the American Therapeutic Recreation Association (ATRA) and the National Therapeutic Recreation Society (NTRS), has a Research Committee that would welcome a student and/or young professional. In addition, most states have a therapeutic recreation division or association. Often, these organizations have research committees as well. It is important that students know they are welcome to join these committees.

3. Attend a Research Institute and Symposium at State or National Conference

Each year, the two national therapeutic recreation organizations as well as many kindred organizations (e.g., Gerontological Association of America, Association for the Care of Children in Hospitals, Association for Experiential Education) have a conference at which they offer several sessions dealing with research for people with disabilities. Also, many agencies and institutions as well as colleges and universities offer in-services, workshops, and professional presentations that discuss results from, or the use of, research methods in healthcare. Attending these opportunities is another way to improve research knowledge. Students should know that it is not only okay but often encouraged for them to attend these research symposia at state and national conferences.

4. Ask to be Involved in a Professional Presentation

Often practitioners and educators who present at these conferences would welcome the help and participation of a student in the presentation. Consider asking the faculty as well as internship supervisors if they would like a "co-presenter." Also, many master's-level students often submit their theses or projects to the research tracks of these state and national conferences and get accepted to present. It is not only for educators.

5. Never Stop Questioning

The last and perhaps most important and significant way every person can be involved in the research process is to never stop asking questions. Always consider how therapeutic recreation programs could be better and ask what needs to be known in order to improve them. It is not necessary to have the ability to initiate methods to get the answers but to be alert regarding who can. As long as professionals are curious and ask the important questions, there is great potential to advance the field.

Summary

Although initially intimidating, research and evaluation should be an essential component for every student studying in the field of therapeutic recreation. The research knowledge and skills derived from class work, professional committees, projects, and the literature can make a student or new professional a better programmer, advocate, and practitioner in the field. Students must take responsibility, however, to learn as much as possible as well as take the initiative to get involved in challenging research experiences. In the field of therapeutic recreation, there are problems to be solved, decisions to be made, and barriers to be overcome. With the skills to address these problems, decisions, and barriers, the foundation is created to empower clients and participants to take the necessary steps to meet rehabilitation goals and embrace an independent leisure lifestyle.

Discussion Questions

1. Develop a five-year plan for your own involvement in research. This plan may include any activities ranging from reading more journals to going to research sessions at conference to conducting actual research.
2. Discuss Driver's concept of knowledge for its own sake. How does that fit into therapeutic recreation research, especially in light of the call for more efficacy research?
3. Identify and discuss methods to overcome the three barriers to practitioners pursuing research as stated by the Leadership ATRA study.
4. Exploring your own community/county, identify three local foundations that might fund research for people with disabilities.
5. Create an annotated bibliography of at least 10 journal articles (not including those in *Therapeutic Recreation Journal* or *Annual in Therapeutic Recreation*) that address the benefits of leisure or recreation for people with disabilities.
6. Predict the status of therapeutic recreation research in the year 2030. Back up your predictions. Consider that the conceptual as well as the practical content your therapeutic recreation courses came from the results and implications of previous research studies.

References

American Therapeutic Recreation Association. (2001, June). *Code of ethics*. Retrieved April 25, 2007 from http://www.atra-tr.org/ethics.html

Bedini, L. A., & Magnes, M. C. (2007). A methodological review of therapeutic recreation research in from 2001-2005. Unpublished manuscript.

Bedini, L. A., & Wu, Y. (1994). A methodological review of research in *Therapeutic Recreation Journal* from 1986 to 1990. *Therapeutic Recreation Journal, 28*, 87-98.

Caldwell, L. L., & Weissinger, E. (1993). A model for research utilization in therapeutic recreation. In M. J. Malkin, & C. Z. Howe, (Eds.), *Research in therapeutic recreation: Concepts and methods* (pp. 127-142). State College, PA: Venture.

Carruthers, C. (1997/98). Therapeutic recreation efficacy research agenda. *Annual in Therapeutic Recreation, 7*, 29-41.

Carson, K. (2006, March/April). Leadership ATRA. *ATRA Newsletter, 22*(2), 4-5.

Compton, D. M., & Dieser, R. (1997). Research initiatives in therapeutic recreation. In D. M. Compton (Ed.), *Issues in therapeutic recreation: Toward a new millennium* (2nd ed.) (pp. 299-326). Champaign, IL: Sagamore.

Coyle, C. P., Kinney, W. B., Riley, B., & Shank, J. W. (1991). *Benefits of therapeutic recreation: A consensus view*. Ravensdale, WA: Idyll Arbor.

Devine, M. A., & Wilhite, B. (1999). Theory application in therapeutic recreation practice and research. *Therapeutic Recreation Journal, 33*(1), 29-41.

Driver, B. (1989). Applied leisure research: Benefits to scientists and practitioners and their respective roles. In E. L. Jackson, & T. L. Burton (Eds.), *Understanding leisure and recreation: Mapping the past, charting the future* (pp. 597-612). State College, PA: Venture.

Iso-Ahola, S. E. (1988). Research in therapeutic recreation. *Therapeutic Recreation Journal, 22*(1), 7-13.

Jordan, D. J., & Roland, M. (1999). An examination of differences between academics and practitioners in frequency of reading research and attitudes toward research. *Journal of Leisure Research, 31*, 166-170.

Malkin, M. J. (1993). Issues and needs in therapeutic recreation research. In M. J. Malkin, & C. Z. Howe (Eds.), *Research in therapeutic recreation: Concepts and methods* (pp. 3-24). State College, PA: Venture.

Mannell, R. C. (1983). Research methodology in therapeutic recreation. *Therapeutic Recreation Journal, 17*(4), 9-16.

Mitra, A., & Lankford, S. (1999). *Research methods in park, recreation, and leisure studies*. Champaign, IL: Sagamore.

National Council for Therapeutic Recreation Certification.™ (2007). *2007 Job analysis report*. Retrieved April 25, 2007 from http://nctrc.org/documents/NCTRCJAReport07.pdf

National Therapeutic Recreation Society. (2001). *NTRS code of ethics and interpretive guidelines,* Retrieved April 25, 2007 from http://nrpa.org/content/default.aspx?documentId=867

National Recreation and Park Association/American Association of Physical Activity and Recreation. (2004). *Standards and evaluative criteria for baccalaureate programs in recreation, parks resources, and leisure services*. Alexandria, VA: Author.

Nelson, M. C., & Gordon-Larsen, P. (2006). Physical activity and sedentary behavior patterns are associated with selected adolescent health risk behaviors. *Pediatrics, 117*(4), 1281-1290.

Rogers, M. A. M., & Zaragoza-Lao, E. (2003). Happiness and children's health: An investigation of art, entertainment, and recreation. *American Journal of Public Health, 93*(2), 288–289.

Verghese, J., Lipton, R. B., Katz, M. J., Hall, C. B., Derby, C. A., & Kuslansky, G. (2003). Leisure activities and the risk of dementia in the elderly. *New England Journal of Medicine, 348*, 2508-2516.

Wilhite, B., Keller, M. J., Collins, J. R., & Jacobson, S. (2003). A research agenda for therapeutic recreation revisited. *Therapeutic Recreation Journal, 37*(3), 207-223.

Witt, P. A. (1988). Therapeutic recreation research: Past, present, and future. *Therapeutic Recreation Journal, 22*(1), 14-23.

CHAPTER 26

The Role of Theory in Therapeutic Recreation: A Practical Approach

Linda Caldwell, Ph.D.
Pennsylvania State University

The word "theory" can make people shudder. To many, theories seem grand and esoteric and not very practical. In the busy and hectic daily schedule, theories seem far removed from something that might be useful. Thus, the energy expended to understand what theory is and how it might be used in daily practice seems inefficient or wasted effort. The truth is, however, that theories can be very useful and practical.

Becoming skilled in using theories to develop therapeutic recreation (TR) assessments, programs, and evaluations can lead to many important outcomes, such as increased programmatic efficacy and the ability to better communicate with the individuals with whom you work, colleagues, and policy makers. Thus, the purpose of this chapter is to demystify theory and address how theory can, in fact, be an essential part of what TRSs do. To paraphrase Lewis Carroll, if you do not know exactly what you are trying to accomplish, then how do you know if you have done it? If you do not know exactly why you did what you did, then how can you justify success, or problem-solve failure? If you do not know exactly how the program or intervention worked or did not work, then how can you explain what you have done or improve it? Thus, theories provide the foundation for understanding TR programming, and as a result can become one of the most important tools a TRS can use.

Notice that the word "exactly" is used in the above questions. All competent TRSs can provide some reasoning behind what they do. Answers such as "I want to improve self-efficacy" or "The patient needs to increase anger-management skills" explains in general what the TRS's treatment goals might be. A good theory, however, will provide the tool to specify beforehand what might happen, and even more important, why and how it might happen.

It takes a little more work to incorporate theory into everyday programming, but once theoretical proficiency is established, theories will become indispensable. The focus of this chapter is on how practical theories and scholarly theories can assist TRSs in providing the best services to the people with whom they work.

Theory is a Tool

As implied in the previous discussion, a theory is a specific statement of the relationships among concepts and actions. For example, in general, self-efficacy theory suggests that if a TRS provides targeted and specific feedback to an individual about his or her skills in a specific leisure activity (e.g., rock climbing) that affirms his or her competence, the individual will perceive increased self-efficacy. Furthermore, if self-efficacy increases as a result of participation in the leisure activity, feelings of personal control in all daily situations might increase. In research terms, theory identifies the independent (cause) and dependent (effect or outcome) variables. In this example, the independent variable is self-efficacy in a specific leisure activity and the dependent variable is a feeling of personal control in daily life situations.

Not all theories apply to all people under all circumstances; however, many theories are general enough to provide guidance in many different contexts. Nevertheless, one also must consider under what conditions the theory might work. Some theories, for example, may work differently with younger persons, persons of a particular race or ethnicity, or persons with developmental disabilities. That is why researchers spend time and energy conducting studies on different population groups using the same theory. These researchers want to determine where and with whom theories are most appropriately applied.

Theory is a useful tool, because it specifically links intervention and program implementation with outcomes. Therefore, using theory encourages one to specify beforehand what might happen, how, and why. Doing this prompts one to think about daily actions and to become more deliberate in programming. An example of this will be described later in this chapter.

Where Theories Originate

Theories are formulated in three primary ways: using deductive, inductive, or user-focused approaches (Patton, 1997). Theories from deductive and inductive approaches involve data-based research studies and are formal and scholarly. In some cases, an existing theory is selected to provide the framework for answering a research question that a researcher might have. A researcher would state one or more hypotheses (an exact prediction of cause and effect between variables) or pose one or more research questions (a more general question that seeks to understand relationships between or among variables if an exact hypothesis cannot be stated). Using self-efficacy theory as an example, a hypothesis might be, "A high mean score on a leisure-related, self-efficacy scale will positively predict increased leisure participation in the community upon discharge." In this case, leisure-related self-efficacy is the independent variable, and leisure participation in the community is the dependent variable. That is, participation in the community depends on one's level of self-efficacy.

A research question might be, "Does the relationship between increased self-efficacy and increased community recreation participation differ based on one's sociodemographic characteristics (e.g., age and gender)?" Data then are collected to provide support (or not) to the hypotheses or to provide an answer to the research question. Based on the results, refinement of the theory occurs. This approach to research is called a deductive research process. The two examples presented later in this chapter come from a deductive research process.

An alternative research process begins with observations about human behavior (perhaps in the form of data collected from an interview). Patterns are discovered in the data (i.e., the words used by the participants) by the researcher, often with the help of study participants, and then tentative hypotheses might be stated.

Eventually this leads to the development of theory. This process is termed inductive research. An example of inductive research is a study done by O'Brien in 1995. She was interested in using adventure therapy as a TR intervention, but she was concerned that the existing theories and research on adventure really did not capture the true meaning of what adventure meant to all people, especially African American adolescents.

To answer her research questions and to give her better insight into developing an adventure-based program, O'Brien (1995) designed an inductive research study. One of her research questions was, "What meanings and understandings do young African American adolescents associate with the word 'adventure'?" She developed a rapport with a group of African American adolescents, gave them each a camera, and asked them to take pictures of what adventure meant to them. They also were asked to provide titles to their pictures. After the pictures were developed, O'Brien interviewed each young person individually. She asked them about the pictures they took and why the pictures represented adventure. The conclusions of her study were that the meanings of adventure for these African American youth were both similar and different to what is typically found in the literature. Being aroused and seeking novelty were part of their definition of adventure, as the existing literature would suggest. In addition, however, a unique finding was that youth defined some instances of adventure by the relationships they had with the environment. O'Brien concluded that both arousal and relationships with the world were important in understanding adventure for these particular youth. Thus, from her interviews (the data), she was able to develop some tentative hypotheses about relationships.

Both deductive and inductive research processes contribute to theory development as well as TR programming. Selecting and using scholarly theories for program development is based on the degree to which the theory seems useful to practice, a point that will be elaborated on later.

The user-focused approach to theory development is particularly salient to practitioners, especially when combined with theories that derive from a deductive or inductive approach. This user-focused approach produces a "theory of action" (TOA) and is based on the perceptions and experiences of the people who actually conduct the program. A theory of action is specific to a practitioner's program or department, thus it is more practical.

Patton (1990, 1997) discussed the importance of a theory of action to practice. A theory of action helps link intervention or program implementation with outcomes. That is, the theory of action is a concrete depiction of how what is done produces what happens. Doing this helps one think through the exact outcomes that are desired for the individual client in an individual session. A TOA also specifies what is expected to happen to the individual (or group) from a longer-term programmatic perspective. TOAs are based on people's explanations of and observations about how things work and why. Patton (1997) summarized the use of TOAs by stating:

> The purpose of thoroughly delineating a program's theory of action is to assist practitioners in making explicit their assumptions about the linkages between inputs, activities, immediate outputs, intermediate outcomes, and ultimate goals. (p. 225)

It is possible to have a good TOA that does not have a scholarly theory as its foundation, but the most useful and powerful TOA requires a scholarly theory. The naïve TOA (having no scholarly basis) is helpful for articulating the precise reason one does what one does; these TOAs are based on experience. The informed TOA uses both experience and scholarly theories to help articulate why certain actions take place (Patton, 1997).

There is an important relationship between scholarly theories and TOAs. Not only are TOAs more powerful if combined with scholarly theories, but also scholarly theories are often instigated by TOAs, thus increasing their practicality. In this case, empirical research (that which is observed) is gathered systematically to provide supportive evidence for the TOA. Thus, the relation of theory to research is an iterative one. TOAs are critical to keep research grounded in real life, and research is critical in helping to fine-tune both scholarly theories and TOAs.

To make the difference between scholarly theories and a TOA more concrete, consider the process of gardening. There are numerous scholarly theories about plant growth responses, carbon metabolism, photosynthesis, and soil composition, for example, that would be helpful to someone in structuring a garden. In addition to those scholarly theories, however, most gardeners have their own TOAs based on their own personal experience and wisdom as to how their particular garden works. For example, one section of a garden may be wetter than another section, and over time, the gardener realizes that peppers are not as happy there. My own garden is large enough that the amount of sun it gets at different places in the garden varies, and I have learned through experience that my dahlias prefer a sunnier spot than I had them in this past year. At the present time, my TOA is fairly naïve, because I do not know or use plant growth theories. If I did, and then applied them specifically to my garden and its unique characteristics, I would have an informed TOA on growing and, no doubt, a better garden. We will return to this garden metaphor a bit later in the chapter.

Determining Levels of Outcomes

Several points from the preceding paragraph need to be developed. First, a TOA can be thought of in two ways: what one thinks she or he is doing compared with what she or he is actually doing. Careful thought, as well as a good process or implementation evaluation, can help determine the congruence of the two. A second point is that a good TOA should help clarify outcomes on a number of different levels. What does the TRS hope to have happen as a result of each program's session? Should the individual be able to state how confident he or she feels in overcoming three constraints to his or her leisure? These are immediate outcomes; they happen as a direct result of the program, and the TRS has more control over influencing them.

As a side note, this chapter is touching on two "black boxes" of TR programming. First, and this is the focus of this chapter, is the black box of content: why you are doing what you are doing. Here I am advocating that theoretically based content is more powerful. The second black box is one of process. This addresses the issue of implementation—the operationalization of a program, actions taken, and all related processes. Although it is beyond the scope of this chapter, it is important to make it clear that the two black boxes (theory-based content and process) are inextricably intertwined in producing outcomes.

The next level of outcome relates to the overall goal of the entire program. One asks, "What is predicted to happen as a result of participation in the program as a whole, after the individual has all of the session?" Perhaps the goal is for the individual to develop an action plan of how he or she will deal with identified constraints upon discharge. These would be called intermediate outcomes. And, finally, what does the TRS think will happen "down the road" as a result of the program? This is a longer-term perspective, and these outcomes might take a year or so to happen. Thinking about this future orientation helps the TRS determine what his or her ultimate goal for the individual might be. These goals are called long-range or ultimate outcomes. In this example, an appropriate long-range goal might be that the person's chance of returning to the institution is decreased, and the chance that he or she will feel a part of his or her community is increased.

The further away in time the predicted outcome is, the less direct control the TRS will have in influencing the outcome due to many other factors that may intervene in the long run. Nevertheless, it is critical for the TRS to adopt this multilevel outcome perspective as it gives context to specific programs and helps the TRS connect to broader goals for the individual based on an interdisciplinary perspective. Determining which outcomes to target comes from scholarly and naïve TOAs.

Returning to the garden metaphor for a moment, an immediate outcome is that the gardener can go and pick a delicious tomato for dinner. An intermediate outcome is that she or he can prepare a quantity of tomato sauce for the upcoming year. The impact or ultimate goal might be that (a) it saves money in the budget for the upcoming year, and (b) if unexpected houseguests arrive, a meal can be ready quickly.

While immediate and intermediate goals are of critical importance to a TRS and reflect directly on daily efforts, the importance of impact, or ultimate goals, should not be overlooked, even though they may not seem directly linked to day-to-day operations. The TRS's job is to demonstrate a chain of events, linking the three levels of goals with the intervention. If this linkage is done successfully, it provides an important communication tool to use with other practitioners. It is likely that people in the treatment team will be working toward at least one common ultimate (impact) goal, and the extent to which the TRS can demonstrate that the intervention will (eventually) contribute to that ultimate goal will provide a great deal of relevancy in TR programming. Thus, TR outcomes are always in concert with the treatment team's outcomes. This is especially helpful if not all of the TR outcomes are functionally based but rather are more humanistic or leisure-oriented.

Finally, if the outcomes at all levels are based on theory, the TRS will make a knowledgeable and important contribution to the individual client's progress, as well as to the treatment team's efforts.

From Theory to Practice

In this section, how scholarly theories can lead to TOAs will be examined. To do so, two examples will be provided: one from the author's own research in progress (dealing with adolescents) and one that is based on a research study reported by Carruthers and Hood (2002) in the *Therapeutic Recreation Journal*.

Diagramming a theory is a particularly useful way to understand it. Many people use logic models to diagram their ideas. Logic models help one to think through what the important outcomes are and depict the chain of events that will demonstrate how to produce the outcomes. Logic models contain a description of the situation, assumptions, inputs, outputs, and outcomes. They also contain how the program will be evaluated, from a process and outcome perspective. Thus, logic models are excellent planning, evaluation, and communication tools.

Not only do logic models help depict one's TOA and what to evaluate, but also they are important communication tools. Showing others (e.g., team members, policy makers) a logic model is an excellent way to educate others about the how, what, and why of one's program, as well as the outcomes associated with the program. As an example of logic models in practice, in 2006, Fairfax County Virginia Department of Recreation and Community Services hired a consultant to help them develop a health and leisure logic model that will serve as the basis for programming across the department (including therapeutic recreation).

An abbreviated logic model will be provided in this chapter to illustrate an example of theory-based programming. It is beyond the scope of this chapter to more fully develop the discussion on logic models as tools to use theory to develop programs. Readers are encouraged to consult other sources about developing and using logic models based on theory. Some excellent sources will be provided at the end of the chapter.

Risk Reduction and Prevention: TimeWise Leisure Education Example

Preventing problem or risky behavior through health promotion has been a rapidly growing field in the last two decades (referred to as prevention science). Leisure and therapeutic recreation have a lot to contribute to prevention efforts. Conversely, TR could learn a lot from the way prevention interventions are developed and evaluated in other fields (e.g., public health, substance use, and mental health). In order to understand and demonstrate how TR can make a contribution, it is important to identify relevant theories and related outcomes.

One challenge is that risk prevention and health promotion are complex issues, and one theory is generally inadequate to explain human behavior. In our work in prevention, we have found it helpful to work with a combination of theories. From a practical perspective, however, the TRS will want to consider how a complex theory or grouping of theories is going to be useful for a TOA. We will return to this issue later in the chapter.

In Figure 26.1, several theories are combined to form an overall theory of preventing risk among adolescents. Because this is a complex model, it will be dissected to see how it can be useful. Being based on theory, numerous relations among variables are suggested; that is, relations among variables are hypothesized. The study reported here is an illustration is based on a larger study undertaken to prevent or reduce substance use among middle school adolescents and promote healthy use of leisure through a leisure education intervention. Our overall theory was based on a social ecological model, where various personal, social, and contextual factors were hypothesized to either promote healthy use of leisure (e.g., taking initiative to engage in prosocial activities) or promote unhealthy use of leisure that may lead to substance use (e.g., being bored in leisure). The leisure education program, TimeWise: Taking Charge of Leisure Time (Caldwell, 2004), was designed to mitigate the risk factors such as boredom in leisure and help youth learn leisure skills and behaviors to promote positive leisure (e.g., learning to restructure boring situations, leisure interests, leisure motivation, overcoming constraints, and planning and decision-making skills).

The design and evaluation of TimeWise used a logic model framework. An abbreviated logic model is presented in Figure 26.1 as an illustration for this example.

In this model, the ultimate or long-term outcome is to prevent or decrease substance use. It is based on more than one scholarly theory, although the "grand theory" is a social ecological model, as mentioned previously. The theories used to construct the TimeWise intervention suggested that if we were able to increase youth's intrinsic motivation and decrease amotivation (using Self-determination Theory, e.g., Ryan & Deci, 2000), and increase interest and decrease boredom (optimal arousal theory, e.g., Csikszentmihalyi,

Figure 26.1
Abbreviated Logic Model of Substance Use Prevention

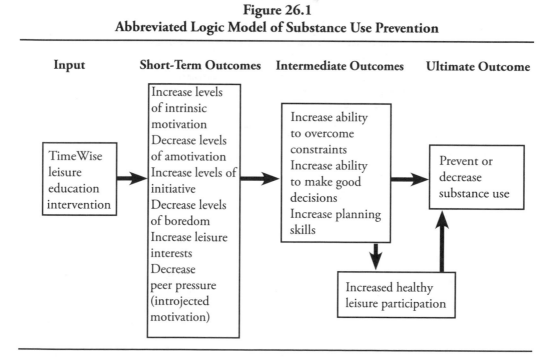

1990; Hunter & Csikszentmihalyi, 2003), we would influence youth's ability to make good decisions, plan, and overcome constraints. These were hypothesized to either prevent or decrease substance use. Thus, several TOA are suggested in this model.

The complexity of the relations in this overall model points to a challenge that will face the TRS. Although the TRSs informed TOA would be grounded in this overall theoretical framework, it may be difficult to focus the actual intervention program on the entire model (and theories) in Figure 26.1. Deciding on what to focus for the TOA and resulting TR program depends on suggestions from past research (if available) as well as what is practical and important in one's situation.

Hypothetically, imagine a TOA based on the model in Figure 26.1. An example is depicted in Figure 26.2 and demonstrates a possible chain of events implied by the general logic model. Note that that model is less complex, meaning that there are less outcomes on which the TRS would need to focus. This chain of events was determined by several theories (used to develop the logic model) that suggest that decreasing boredom and increasing motivation will decrease amotivation. The more motivated one is, the more likely one will be to act to overcome constraints to desired participation and be able to plan for one's leisure. This ability hypothetically leads to healthy leisure participation and eventually prevention or mitigation of substance use.

A TOA could be based on this model that would guide practice and provide a set of outcomes to target and evaluate. It would only be until the model is tested empirically (data are collected and analyzed), however, that one could have confidence that the hypothesized relations really do exist. Thus, research should inform practice. Suppose research shows that the strongest relationship in this model is from decreasing amotivation to healthy leisure, and that decreased amotivation does not really influence one's ability to plan, make decisions, and overcome constraints. Thus, one TOA might be to focus the leisure education

---

Figure 26.2
TOA of Substance Use Prevention

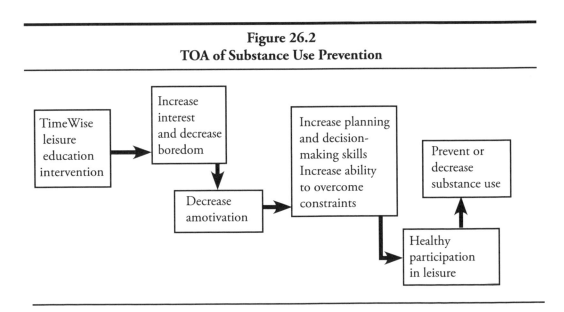

program decreasing boredom and increasing interest and decreasing amotivation because (a) it is the strongest relationship chain, (b) it is a practical one to address in a TR setting, and (c) by intervening at that point in the model, the TRS could prevent a chain of events from happening, ending with alcohol abuse.

The TOA should be coherent with other aspects of service delivery, so it would influence assessment (e.g., assess levels of boredom, interest, and amotivation in leisure), the intervention program, and evaluation of the program's success. Figure 26.3 represents one way that programming could be conceptualized based on this TOA. In this case, a leisure education program could be developed that focused on increasing an individual's ability and desire to determine his or her own interests and activities. The intervention should be developed specifically to decrease feelings of boredom and amotivation. The intervention activities used would be deliberately chosen because of their relevance to this TOA. For example, one activity might be for individuals in the program to construct a time diary to determine times during the day when they are bored or interested, identify who they are with, and what activity they are doing. This activity stems directly from the TOA.

Figure 26.3 also addresses levels of outcomes. Increasing interest, decreasing boredom, and amotivation are immediate outcomes that follow directly after the leisure education program. Increasing healthy leisure participation is an intermediate outcome, expected to happen some time after the leisure education program. The impact or ultimate outcome is avoidance or reduction of substance use, which may not be evident for some time after the program. It should be noted that to truly evaluate the success of this program, an experimental design would be needed. A process evaluation that examined the inputs (for example, implementation of the intervention) would also be very useful.

This is a simplified example. In reality, of course, practitioners often have multiple and competing client goals, each having its own theoretical (scholarly and TOA) basis. Often TRSs have to make choices about what services to provide and to whom. Having theoretical

---

Figure 26.3
TOA Connected to Service Delivery

Baseline Assessment of Targeted Outcomes	**Leisure Education Intervention**	**Evaluation**
Short Term: Boredom Interest Amotivation *Medium Term:* Healthy Use of Leisure *Long Term:* Substance Use	Activities specifically linked to outcomes	Measure Targeted Outcomes Post Intervention *Short Term:* Boredom Interest Amotivation *Medium Term:* Healthy Use of Leisure *Long Term:* Substance Use

underpinnings to what one does in practice allows the careful selection of interventions and targeted outcomes.

Risk Reduction and Prevention: Coping Skills Program Example

A second example of a program based on theory is a coping skills program for individuals with alcoholism. Carruthers and Hood (2002) have done an excellent job of developing this coping skills program developed on coping skills theory (Hood & Carruthers, 2002). They describe both the theoretical basis and the program in two articles in *Therapeutic Recreation Journal*. A brief description of the program will be provided here, but readers are encouraged to read both articles to get a fuller picture of the theory and the program.

Like the TimeWise intervention previously described, Carruthers and Hood based their coping skills program on a number of different coping theories. This is important, because it illustrates that often there is more than one theory about the same phenomenon from which to choose. At first, this might seem daunting, but in fact it is helpful, as often the theories were tested on different types of people, and the TRS can choose which theory might seem most useful for their needs based on the way the study was conducted and with whom it was conducted. Rather than combining elements from different theories, it is often best to stick with just one theory, although that is not always the best way to proceed if the reality of the practical situation suggests that elements of different theories could successfully be combined to form a TOA.

Carruthers and Hood (2002) used a conceptual framework from Wills and Shiffman (1985) as the basis of their program. This framework suggests that environmental demands lead to cognitions about those demands that are either ill-informed, accurate, or exaggerated. These cognitions can lead to physiological responses that are stress-enhancing or reducing, or that are neutral. These responses, in turn, lead to different types of stress reactions. Thus, this framework suggests a TOA based on the chain of events in an implied logic model. The TOA suggests focusing on helping the individual with various cognitive skills (e.g., distracting activities, learning to minimize the importance of the event, using willpower) and behavioral skills (e.g., direct action, pleasure seeking, relaxation) that helps one restore balance, which then reduces stress.

Based on this theoretical framework, Carruthers and Hood (2002) described the seven session goals of their coping skills program. Each session's goals and activities derived directly from the theory and also provided specific outcomes to target and evaluation. For example, in Session One, the two goals were (1) To recognize and change negative thoughts that might interfere with enjoying life, and (2) To focus on and enjoy the present. These two goals were directly related to shaping cognitions that were part of the Wills and Shiffman (1985) model.

What is unique and important to the Carruthers and Hood (2002) program is that they also integrated theories related to alcoholism. Thus, they combined two important theoretical perspectives. An example of this is in Session Seven. The two goals of Session Seven are (1) To identify leisure interests that promote enjoyment of chemically free lifestyle, and (2) To identify ways of overcoming barriers to involvement in satisfying leisure activities. The first goal is important and is based on a larger, grand theory of "positive hedonic." Using several specific theories, Carruthers and Hood discuss the importance of persons who are alcoholic having pleasurable experiences as lack of joy and ability to "indulge" are predictors of relapse.

Kicking it Up

Let us make things a little more interesting, or as Emeril, the TV chef, would say, "Let's kick it up a notch!" During the last two examples, certain questions can be posed. But don't these relationships depend on certain things? Under what conditions do these relationships occur? They are excellent questions. Answers would help develop even more effective treatment or intervention programs.

There are numerous other factors that will influence the hypothesized relations depicted in Figures 26.1 and 26.2. For example, amount of parental control or autonomy support would be an important consideration. Research has shown that perceptions of too much parental control by adolescents can actually lead to boredom and substance use. Conversely, parents who provide autonomy support for their youth with regard to their leisure pursuits actually may serve as a protective factor for substance use initiation. Perhaps the hypothesized relations do not hold for all adolescents. In particular, the relation between increasing interest and decreasing boredom and amotivation may not work for younger adolescents because their brains have not yet matured to the point where their executive functioning skills (the basis of planning and decision making) are fully developed. There also may be gender differences.

If the relationships just mentioned did depend on age or gender, it would mean that leisure education groups might need to be segregated by age or gender or that individualized assessment plans need to take into account the age and gender of the person. These complications are not meant to frustrate the reader but rather to encourage one to make sure he or she fully analyzes the situation, external factors, and assumptions, in addition to consulting current research. Then, one must make the best decision one can. TRSs excel at individualizing treatments and programming, so this kind of thinking is not new. This example demonstrates how theory and research can be used to help do a better job of developing assessments, goals, and program planning.

Theory-Based Coherent Programming in Therapeutic Recreation

It would be impossible to cover all of the theories that have relevance to TR in this chapter, but this next section will provide some ideas as a starting point. First, though, some important questions such as "How is a theory or (theories) chosen?" or "Which is decided first, the theory or the goals for the individual?" should be addressed.

There are some personal, contextual, and client-centered issues that help the TRS address these questions. For example, does the TR department have a pragmatic philosophy that guides one's activity? If so, is this philosophy based on producing behavioral or functional outcomes, existential outcomes, or developmental outcomes? If the TR department's philosophy is based on producing outcomes to increase functional ability, for example, the TRS will need to select theories that focus on producing a recognizable change in behavior or functional outcome. Self-efficacy theory might be useful. If one's philosophy is existentially oriented toward experience and self-expression, then theories of empowerment, for example, may be more useful. If one subscribes to a philosophy that focuses on human development and education, then there are theories that are more appropriate for that perspective, such as selective optimization with compensation (e.g., Baltes & Baltes, 1990) or action in context (Silbereisen et al., 1986). Often, however, these theories are not philosophically mutually exclusive, and their use depends on one's philosophical perspective and the perspective of the home department or agency. In the past, TRSs have not been very good at this consistency of philosophy-theory-assessment-intervention-outcome coherence, but it is a challenge that should be embraced.

The client-centered issue, related to theory use, asks one to think about the purpose of the theory (outcome) and whether it is suitable for the department's clientele. For example, theories that rely on abstract thinking are not as useful for individuals with cognitive and developmental disabilities. It is doubtful that a TRS would use the theory of selective optimization with compensation (Baltes & Baltes, 1990) to design a program for someone with Alzheimer's disease, because using that theory in practice assumes that the individual has intact decision-making and cognitive skills.

Although the coherence of philosophy-theory-assessment-intervention-outcome was previously presented as linear and hierarchical, these relationships are anything but, suggesting that there is no easy answer to the question of which to choose first: theory, outcome, or assessment. It is entirely possible, and in many cases even desirable, to articulate a theory of action based on experience before one can articulate a scholarly theory.

There are two important considerations in developing coherent theory-based TR programming. First, if one has articulated a clear TOA, its relationship to a scholarly theory(ies) must be analyzed. TRSs should be prepared to tweak their TOAs if needed, or conversely, if they have the opportunity to conduct research, they may be in a position to tweak the scholarly theory. The second important point is that TRSs should examine closely the content of assessments and client-centered goals to make sure they connect directly to both the theory and the outcomes. Stumbo makes this same point in chapters 1 and 17.

One way to link theory and practice is to develop a matrix similar to the one in Table 26.1. This will help in the specification and linking of treatment goals, theories, assessments, and outcomes. Remember, this is just an initial step. The important thing is to focus on the theory and understand precisely how it links with the intended outcome to develop a theory of action.

Table 26.1 identifies three theories that might be useful to TRSs and briefly provides examples of what a coherent approach to programming might look like. Despite the holes in this table, one can see congruence among client goals, assessments, and outcomes from a theoretical perspective. What is missing from this table, of course, is the process or action plan that is, how to deliberately develop the program based on these theories.

The first theory presented, self-determination theory (SDT; e.g., Deci & Ryan, 1985 Ryan & Deci, 2000), addresses intrinsic motivation, which is a hallmark of leisure as well as therapeutic recreation. Becoming familiar with the theory and its complexities could be very helpful to a TRS in developing a coherent and informed TOA. For instance, SDT helps one understand how extrinsically motivated behavior might be internalized by the individual such that the behavior eventually becomes intrinsically motivated. The next theory, self-efficacy (e.g., Bandura, 1986, 1997), is one often heralded as being useful in many TR contexts. Suppose one is working with an older group of individuals who are unable to overcome numerous intrapersonal, interpersonal, and structural (e.g., time) constraints to their leisure. If a TRS developed an intervention program specifically based on self-efficacy theory that assisted individuals in mastering one new activity (e.g., Tai Chi), the TRS could help the individuals see how they could transfer their mastery of Tai Chi into mastery of their personal constraints to leisure. Finally, the last example relates to youth and is based on a currently popular theory: resiliency (e.g., Cicchetti & Garmezy, 1993; Masten, Morison, Pellegrini, & Tellegen, 1990). Youth who are more resilient are thought to have a

Table 26.1
Linking Theory and Practice

Client Goal	Theory	Assessment Focus	Outcomes (level)
Increase ability to become self-determined	Intrinsic motivation (e.g., Deci & Ryan, 1985). You might also ask: What is the role of extrinsic motivation?	• Degree of internalization of behaviors • What makes something interesting to the person?	• Increase self-awareness (immediate) • Decrease stated need for external rewards (immediate) • Decrease recidivism (impact)
Increase belief in personal ability to control one's situation	Self-efficacy (Bandura, 1986, 1997)	• Level, strength, and generality of ability to negotiate through constraints to desired activity	• Increase in perceived level, strength, and abilities (immediate) • Increase in number and frequency of activity participation (intermediate) • Decrease in social isolation (impact) • Decrease in need for home visitation (impact)
Increase social competence	Resiliency/Protective Factors (e.g., Cicchetti & Garmezy, 1993; Masten, Morison, Pellegrini, & Tellegen, 1990)	• Social cognition • Humor • Divergent thinking	• Ability to deflect criticism (immediate and intermediate) • Ability to diffuse a situation with humor (immediate and intermediate) • Prevent school dropout (impact)

better chance of working their way through life's challenges. Learning a series of life skills is presumed to provide youth with protection (protective factors) against these challenges and provide them with positive coping skills (affordances).

Not All Theories Are Useful

Not all theories are good theories. Perhaps they haven't been empirically tested or are loosely used. Maslow's (1968) Hierarchy of Needs theory, while having served an important conceptual focus, is one of these theories. Some theories are not suitable for one's situation because of personal or agency philosophy, or they are inappropriate for clientele served, as described previously.

Remember, the best test of a theory from a practical perspective is whether or not it is useful. From there, the next question is its validity. Does it really produce the results that it should be producing? Although ultimately a question for outcome-based evaluation research, TRSs can address the issue of theoretical validity from a practical perspective through observation and documentation.

Many theories are tied ultimately to cause-and-effect relations, especially when used as the basis for interventions. Establishing cause and effect, however, is extremely difficult and requires methodological rigor and sophistication. Because of the difficulty in clearly establishing cause and effect, it is important to realize that (a) theories are not immutable; that is, as good as they are, fine-tuning is usually appropriate and ongoing, and (b) theories and related research do not prove something causes something else. Theories and related research simply provide evidence that the theory in question might work (or might not). Sorting out causal linkage is extremely difficult when dealing with human behavior. Finally, both qualitative and quantitative approaches are necessary in developing and testing theories.

Benefits of Theory in Therapeutic Recreation

To summarize, there are many benefits of using theory in TR practice. First, theory helps with treatment specification: that is, theory will allow one to identify exactly what about the program or intervention is supposed to bring about what effect. Theory helps one identify and think through exactly what independent variables (adding fertilizer every week) are supposed to bring about the outcome (more robust flowers) and why (increased nutrient intake).

Theory also helps one know exactly what to evaluate using both outcome and process evaluations. Thus, it helps the TRS be more deliberate in what she or he does. It also encourages reality testing. Is what you say you do, and what you think you do, really what you do?

Theory helps with instrument development. Building assessment and outcome instrumentation on theory is much more defensible and produces better results. This is particularly true if the TRS is willing to treat coherent programming as a work in progress.

Basing programming and activities on theory also can increase one's activity repertoire. Widmer (e.g., 1999) is fond of saying, "If you learn how to use a hammer, everything begins to look like a nail." In other words, TRSs often rely on a restricted set of activities, games, and interventions as their tools of intervention. Using theory to gain a deeper understanding about the program process will facilitate an expanded activity repertoire.

Finally, being fluent in using theories also is politically practical. Basing assessments, goals, and programs on theory will help to answer questions that seem to plague TRSs, such as how is TR unique and how does one justify services. If an administrator or colleague makes specific inquiries about a program and its goals, basing the answer on theory will no doubt advance their understanding of what is being done, why, and its importance in terms of intervention or prevention.

The Challenge—Tips to Achieve Theoretical Bliss

It may be apparent by now that theories are useful and important. Even so, TRSs may or may not use them. Why? Sometimes theories are written in ways that seem inaccessible. Some journals are more notorious than others for this practice because they are written in a scientific, formal language that attempts to speak more to other academics than to people who actually use the theory.

Here are some suggestions that might help one find and use theories.
- Learn some basic research terminology. There are many research textbooks that are helpful, and, increasingly, on-line materials over the Internet are available.
- Work with two or more colleagues to read a journal article and attempt to figure out together what it is saying.
- Practice. It is true that the more TRSs read and think this way, the easier it becomes.
- When developing a TOA, start from the right. Identify ultimate impact outcomes and work backward from there.
- Consult with someone one knows and trusts who can help to figure it out.
- Talk to a professor or someone who does research.
- Get rewarded for one's efforts. Build research into a job description, whether it is doing research or reading it. This will help to secure the time to devote to reading and thinking about how theory might be useful, and may even be helpful in doing some of one's own research. Going back to the example of the Fairfax County Department of Recreation and Community Services, the head of the Teen Services Division recently built into his staff's job description that they would not only be evaluated on developing theory-based programs, but that he would give them time and resources (including an intensive staff development workshop) to develop these programs (Braff, 2007).

Useful References

Following are some useful references that might help TRSs learn more about theory and its application and usefulness in TR. These books are not necessarily directly related to TR but contain useful theories that have implications for TR.

Baldwin, C. K., Hutchinson, S. L., & Magnuson, D. R. (2004). Program theory: A framework for theory-driven programming and evaluation. *Therapeutic Recreation Journal,* 38, 16-31. This journal article uses the Self-determination and Enjoyment Enhancement (SDEE) model by Dattilo, Kleiber, & Williams (1998) as an example of using a theory for therapeutic recreation programming.

Jackson, E. (Editor, 2005). *Constraints to leisure.* State College, PA: Venture. This book edited by Jackson provides a number of theoretical perspectives on various types of constraints to leisure participation and enjoyment. Although it is not directly related to TR, it promises to be a very useful resource in helping to conceptualize constraints and constraints negotiation.

Kleiber, D. (1999). *Leisure experience and human development: A dialectical interpretation.* New York: Basic Books. This is an excellent book for anyone who is interested in understanding leisure behavior from a lifespan perspective. Significant human development theories are covered. More importantly, Kleiber addresses issues of disability, rehabilitation, and relapse in portions of the book.

Mannell, R. C., & Kleiber, D. A. (1997). *A social psychology of leisure.* State College, PA: Venture. This book provides basic information on a number of theories that relate to therapeutic recreation from a social psychological perspective. The book also describes the relationship of the research process to understanding and examining theory. It is written in an accessible and interesting manner.

Witt, P. A., & Caldwell, L. L. (Eds.). (2005). *Recreation and youth development.* State College, PA: Venture. This book will be helpful to anyone interested in programming for youth. There is a chapter on using logic models for programming, as well as a chapter on risk and resiliency.

Helpful Internet resources for using logic models:
www.uwex.edu/ces/lmcourse
www.uwex.edu/ces/pdande
http://www.cdc.gov/eval/index.htm
http://ctb.ku.edu/
http://www.innonet.org/
http://www.eval.org/

Discussion Questions

1. Why are theories important in therapeutic recreation?
2. What are two types of a "theory of action?" How are both useful in therapeutic recreation?
3. Think about a program with which you are familiar. Diagram a theory of action that would explain the program, its theory, and its processes. Make sure to include various levels of outcomes. (Do not forget to work backwards from ultimate or impact outcomes.)
4. Describe how the theory of action that you developed in #3 can be used for coherent programming.
5. Identify scholarly theories with which you are familiar. What do these theories offer to therapeutic recreation programming?

6. What can you do to increase your skills in using theory to develop coherent programming?

References

Baltes, P. B., & Baltes, M. M. (1990). Psychological perspectives on successful aging: The model of selective optimization with compensation. In P. B. Baltes, & M. M. Baltes (Eds.), *Successful aging: Perspectives from the behavioral sciences* (pp. 1- 34). New York: Cambridge University Press.

Bandura, A. (1986). *Self-efficacy: The exercise of control.* New York: W. H. Freeman and Co.

Bandura, A. (1997). *Social foundations of thought and action: A social cognitive theory.* Englewood Cliffs, NJ: Prentice Hall.

Braff, E. (2007). Personal communication.

Caldwell, L. L. (2004). *TimeWise: Taking charge of leisure time curriculum for middle school students.* Scotts Valley, CA: ETR Associates.

Carruthers, C. P., & Hood, C. D. (2002). Coping skills program for individuals with alcoholism. *Therapeutic Recreation Journal, 36,* 137-153.

Cicchetti, D., & Garmezy, N. (1993). Prospects and promises in the study of resilience. *Development and Psychopathology, 5,* 497-502.

Csikszentmihalyi, M. (1990*). Flow: The psychology of optimal experience.* New York: Harper and Row.

Dattilo, J., Kleiber, D., & Williams, R. (1998). Self-determination and enjoyment enhancement: A psychologically-based service delivery model for therapeutic recreation. *Therapeutic Recreation Journal, 32,* 258-271.

Deci, E. L., & Ryan, R. M. (1985). *Intrinsic motivation and self-determination in human behavior.* New York: Plenum Press.

Hood, C. D., & Carruthers, C. P. (2002). Coping skills theory as an underlying framework for therapeutic recreation services. *Therapeutic Recreation Journal, 36,* 137-153.

Hunter, J. P., & Csikszentmihalyi, M. (2003). The positive psychology of interested adolescents. *Journal of Youth and Adolescence, 32,* 27-35.

Maslow, A. H. (1968). *Toward a psychology of being* (2nd ed.). Toronto, ON: Van Nos Reinhold.

Masten, A. S., Morison, P., Pellegrini, D., & Tellegen, A. (1990). Competence under stress: Risk and protective factors. In J. Rolf, A. S. Masten, D. Cicchetti, K. H. Nuechterlein, and S. Weintraub (Eds.), *Risk and protective factors in the development of psychopathology.* New York: Cambridge University Press.

O'Brien, A. J. (1995). Meanings of adventure: Images and voices of African American young people. Unpublished master's thesis, University of Georgia.

Patton, M. Q. (1990). *Qualitative evaluation and research methods* (2nd ed.). Thousand Oaks, CA: Sage.

Patton, M. Q. (1997). *Utilization-focused evaluation: The new century text* (3rd ed.). Thousand Oaks, CA: Sage.

Ryan, R. M., & Deci, E. L. (2000). Self-determination theory and the facilitation of intrinsic motivation, social development, and well-being. *American Psychologist, 55,* 68-78.

Silbereisen, R. K., Eyferth, K., & Rudinger, G. (Eds.). (1986). *Development as action in context: Problem behavior and normal youth development.* New York: Springer.

Widmer, M. (1999). ATRA pre-conference workshop on program evaluation. Portland, OR, September 30.

Wills, T. A., & Shiffman, S. (1985). Coping and substance abuse: A conceptual framework. In S. Shiffman, & T. A. Wills (Eds.), *Coping and substance abuse* (pp. 1-24). San Diego, CA: Academic Press.

CHAPTER 27

Methods for Outcome Research in Therapeutic Recreation

Mark A. Widmer, Ph.D., TRS
Brigham Young University

Neil R. Lundberg, Ph.D., TRS, CTRS™
Brigham Young University

Significant changes have come to the healthcare industry as managed-care organizations have taken over the administration and provision of healthcare services. Changes tend to focus on reducing the length of stay and eliminating unessential services in an effort to maintain or increase profits. The push to increase profits and provide cost-effective services places pressure on clinicians to demonstrate the efficacy of their services. Consequently, attention to and the need for outcome research have increased. Historically, outcome research was conducted in response to the concern for quality of care rather than cost-cutting or efficiency (Kendall & Norton-Ford, 1982). The aim was to identify the combination of interventions, therapist characteristics, and client characteristics that produced the best results or to determine what features of a program have the largest impact on treatment goals. Outcome research provides opportunities to obtain excellent information that can be used to improve the efficiency and effectiveness of services (Elkin, 1999).

It is becoming more common for therapeutic recreation (TR) practitioners to be held accountable and justify their services. This pressure may be undesirable to some, yet TR professionals should recognize the underlying opportunity to demonstrate the value of their services through outcome research. Consequently, both practicing TR professionals and prospective professionals may benefit from gaining a greater understanding of outcome research and the principles and challenges associated with conducting this research. Outcome research takes on a variety of forms, but one of the most important aspects for the TR professional focuses on quantifying changes in a patient's clinical status (Berman, Rosen, Hurt, & Kolarz, 1998). The purpose of this chapter is to a) highlight the TR process in discussing six basic steps used in conducting clinical outcome research, and b) to expose readers to the challenges and issues associated with conducting outcome studies.

Therapeutic Recreation Specialists (TRSs) unfamiliar with research may feel somewhat intimidated as they approach conducting outcome research. Although the TRS may not have been trained in the research process, he or she is trained in the TR process. In other words, the TRS is familiar with a system, if used properly, that identifies clinical and program outcomes, quantifies changes in a patients' clinical status, and measures effectiveness of intervention, all at the client level. Therefore, the six basics steps for conducting clinical outcome research will be discussed using the TR process to illustrate the similarities between the TR process and conducting outcome research.

Step One: Deciding to Begin

Deciding to begin is the first step in conducting clinical outcome research. Recreational therapists must recognize the critical need to demonstrate the clinical effectiveness as well as the cost effectiveness. Clinical outcome research is the process used to accomplish these goals. In order for this to occur, however, hesitation and reluctance must be set aside, replaced by a commitment to begin.

Deciding to begin outcome research should include at least two components: clarifying the purpose of the research and identifying available resources needed to conduct the research. Clarifying who will be using the findings of research and how the results will be put to use is critical. Sometimes the answers to these questions are not immediately apparent. The answers also may be highly political. Outcome research often is promoted by a variety of stakeholders who have different agendas. For example, one company interested in conducting outcome research initially indicated the results would be used to show the effectiveness of a group of agencies providing services for the state. It became clear that the data also would be used to determine which of the agencies in the group was most effective. The agencies that influenced the focus of the study knew that if it were tailored to the strengths of their own programs, the results would favor their agencies. As a result, those one or two agencies that influenced the study would get a bigger piece of the pie by obtaining larger contracts from the state at the expense of the agencies that had less input on the focus of the study.

Knowing who will use the data and how it will be used allows the TRS to ask the questions necessary to develop a sound basis for the study in order for the intended purpose of the study to be accomplished. Understanding the political implications and the values and needs of the stakeholders will help guide the development of a sound study. Acknowledging that various purposes exist for outcome research, clarifying who will be using the findings of research, and how the results will be put to use is a critical component of deciding to begin.

Determining the availability of resources is another critically important aspect of deciding to begin an outcome-based research project. Resources needed to conduct outcome research include: cooperation from staff members responsible for the research, availability of staff time, needed supplies, and basic agency approval. First and foremost, in order for outcome research to be done appropriately, cooperation from staff responsible for conducting the research is critical. Frequently the necessity for conducting research is only apparent to the administrator or the individual therapist who is most interested in the project. Outcome research, however, achieves best results when conducted as a team. It requires the commitment of other staff members.

Commitment from other staff members is also important to the thoroughness of the study and the results that are produced. Staff members who are not committed to the project often neglect small details that will ensure the accuracy and validity of information gathered. Conducting outcome research may also require extra effort on the part of staff; an uncommitted staff is unlikely to provide the needed effort to conduct an accurate and complete project with the pressures of their busy schedules.

Availability of staff time is another important resource needed to conduct outcome research. Simply put, research projects require time. Typically, this time is above and beyond the regularly scheduled activities and responsibilities of the TRS. Creating projects that minimize impact on staff will increase the likelihood of success. Administrators may also need to approve any projects that may require overtime hours on the part of their staff. Making sure that time is available, or will be approved by administrators, is an important step in deciding to begin.

Depending on the design, acquiring the appropriate supplies and resources is another important aspect in making the decision to begin a research project that may be important. Outcome research often requires additional paperwork, envelopes, postage, and a variety of general supplies. Research projects may also require additional programmatic items or equipment. In addition to supplies, research projects may also require additional space or additional time in using a scheduled activity space. These resources must be considered in advance and must be available where necessary in order for a research project to be appropriately conducted.

Finally, approval for conducting research will be needed prior to beginning. Agencies typically have a pre-established approval process for conducting research. Understanding the process and following the established guidelines is critical. Failure to do so could create unanticipated problems such as exposure to liability. Approval guidelines are established in order to protect all parties involved in a research project and must be followed. The approval process will also assist the researcher in determining how to inform individuals regarding their rights as a participant in research.

Deciding to begin outcome research is an interesting and exciting adventure but should be approached realistically. Understanding the purpose of research, who will use the results, getting cooperation from staff members responsible for the research, determining the availability of staff time, obtaining needed supplies, and understanding the process for getting agency approval are all important aspects of deciding to begin a research project.

Step Two: Conceptualizing a Study

The next step is to develop a conceptual foundation to serve as a basis for the study. This is done by identifying the outcomes of primary interest to the stakeholders and the associated interventions employed to bring about the outcomes. The researcher must know the principal diagnosis of the clients through careful assessment (Osberg, 1997). While this process can be very challenging, an appropriate and thorough assessment is the key to clearly identifying outcomes and establishing the conceptual foundation for research based on the needs of the client. Assessment is the systematic process of gathering and interpreting client information to make decisions regarding treatment. In order for the assessment to be used effectively in addressing client needs and conducting clinical outcome research, it must provide specific information regarding the client's deficiencies; generalities will not provide the detailed information needed to identify priorities for service and develop specific behavioral objectives, both of which are critical elements in identifying outcomes and conducting research. With the diagnosis in mind, clear treatment goals that focus on the problem must be established. In some instances, TR staff members may direct services on secondary symptoms or issues related exclusively to the clients' leisure behavior.

Assessing levels of client functioning in various domains, including physical, emotional, social, cognitive, and spiritual, provides the starting point for identifying outcomes important to both TR services and research. The International Classification of Function (ICF) (Dahl, 2002) and a model for functional assessment (Granger, 1998) provide an excellent framework by which client functioning can be assessed and outcomes determined. Assessment of body structure is done at the organ level, allowing the therapist to identify outcomes related to specific client impairment. Impairment is defined as a specific physiological or psychological deficit. Impairment may be related to a deficit in body tissue, range of motion, or in the function of a particular muscle group. As a specific impairment is identified through assessment, so too, is a medically oriented treatment, which focuses on the remediation of deficiencies caused by the impairment; and the result of the medically oriented treatment is the outcome. At the organ or body-structure level, accurate assessment of impairment is critical in selecting the appropriate intervention and identifying the intended outcome.

Assessment at the person level identifies specific activities or activity limitations affecting the individual. Assessment at this level, instead of focusing exclusively on the impairment, is intended to gather information on deficits related to the performance of activities due to an identified impairment. Person-level assessment identifies the effect of disability; in other words, how impairment negatively affects client functioning in activities considered essential for everyday life. Person-level assessment might also identify limitations related to participation, as identified by the ICF (Dahl, 2002). Participation limitations focus on client deficits in fulfilling social roles related to work, family, leisure, or living independently. As the effects of disability are identified in terms of activity and participation limitations, appropriate interventions are developed that focus specifically on the remediation of deficiencies; again, the intended result of the intervention selected is the outcome.

The influence of social, cultural, and environmental factors should also be considered in the assessment (Dahl, 2002). Assessment at this level identifies outcomes following the same process as mentioned above but focuses on deficits and limitations experienced due to negative social or cultural influences, such as stereotyping, discriminatory social policy, or social norms that inhibit functioning at optimal levels. As limitations and deficiencies are identified at the social, cultural, and environmental levels, appropriate interventions are developed, the results of which are considered outcomes of the intervention.

Consider this example of identifying outcomes and a conceptual foundation based on client assessment. One adolescent treatment center struggled to identify which outcomes were the most important to their agency and stakeholders. The adolescents they served had a variety of problems including substance abuse, truancy, status offenses, school failure, general rebellion, and promiscuity. In the social history and intake assessment conducted by the agency, most parents indicated a high level of conflict between their "problem" child and themselves. In a discussion about the desired outcomes of the program, the staff's suggestions ranged from simple behavior changes, such as reduction or elimination of substance abuse, to more abstract outcomes, such as reduction of conflict within the family. As the discussion progressed and the staff members continued to reflect on the goals of their program, they came to the conclusion that while their assessment had identified many important outcomes, the overarching goal was to diminish parent-child conflict and thus improve family functioning. Further discussion suggested they were using principles of Self-Determination Theory (Deci, 1995) as the theoretical foundation of their program. The theory provided principles they applied in their programs to bring about change. This theory provided a conceptual foundation for the program and also measures used to quantify outcomes.

If a formal theory is not being used as the conceptual basis of the program, the staff should be asked to articulate its theory of action (as described in Chapter 26 by Caldwell in this volume). Although outcome studies often focus directly on changes in clinical symptoms or conditions, other valuable outcomes may be important to stakeholders. The client's satisfaction with treatment is an important indicator of the perceived value of a particular program or service. For agencies interested in marketing their programs, client satisfaction with services may be as important as the reduction in clinical symptoms.

Once the outcomes have been established, the researcher may begin to make decisions about the measures to be used and the methodology of the study. The outcomes, if stated clearly, lead the researcher to select appropriate measures and methodologies. For example, if the outcome for a depressed client is to increase perceptions of control or freedom so she can enjoy leisure participation, specific measures related to perceived freedom (e.g., the Leisure Diagnostic Battery by Witt & Ellis, 1989) or perceptions of control (the Attributional Style Questionnaire by Peterson et al., 1982) would be selected. These measures and methods would probably be very different if the outcome were defined as a change in attitude or cognition such as attributions.

Step Three: Selecting Measures for Quantifying Outcomes

While some outcomes variables are measured easily, others are much more abstract and challenging to quantify. For example, if a program is designed to change or establish overt behaviors, measuring the outcome is usually more straightforward. The behavior is described so that it is clear to observers when the behavior occurs. For instance, in a rehabilitation center serving people with traumatic spinal-cord injuries, the goal or outcome may be to teach clients new leisure skills. Based on this goal, behavioral performance objectives are then developed identifying observable and measurable behavior. For instance, people with paraplegia may be taught to water ski using adaptive equipment such as a mono ski or to play tennis using a wheelchair. For the client learning to adapt to paraplegia, both of these activities are new and challenging. Clients who learn to ski or volley (the behavior) for a specified period of time (the measurable criteria) attain the desired outcome. Measurement of the outcome is done through establishing objective standards that are observed directly and then recorded.

The same rehabilitation center or TR staff may decide that the desired outcome for its patients is more abstract than overt behaviors. Perhaps the outcome is defined as a positive change in attribution style (Russell, 1982; Russell & McAuley, 1986) and perceived freedom in leisure (Witt & Ellis, 1989). While the outcome appears to be more abstract, the same process applies as when measuring overt behaviors. The important question now becomes, are there overt observable behaviors associated with changes in attribution style and perceived freedom? If the answer is yes, then those behaviors would be selected and measured to determine if the outcome was achieved. If the answer is no, then the therapist may need to create debriefing activities where clients discuss or write, therefore making hidden thoughts, perceptions, attitudes, or knowledge observable or known to the therapist. The same guidelines apply in that behavioral objectives should identify something the client does, says, or writes and a measurable criteria so that the outcome or goal can be evaluated.

For example, in the case of attributional style, the underlying theory suggests that specific steps may be taken to change how people explain success and failure (Seligman, 1991). Research indicates that using these steps while teaching the client to water ski or play tennis will facilitate the acquisition of the treatment goals or outcomes. In order for a therapist to evaluate changes in attribution style, a debriefing session could be created to evaluate the way a person verbally evaluates his or her experience. This verbal communication then becomes the data upon which the outcome is evaluated.

Further, social learning theory (Bandura, 1997) suggests that teaching clients to engage successfully in challenging (recreational) activities will have a positive effect on attribution style and perceived freedom in leisure. Knowing this, the staff uses attribution theory as the conceptual basis of its program. The principles of the theory are integrated into the process of teaching the client to ski or play tennis. Because the staff uses the theory, it can describe the mechanisms that bring about the desired changes in the clients. This allows staff members to explain to stakeholders what they do in treatment and why they do it. The logic behind the program may provide critical support for empirical outcome data. Describing the theory behind the program when presenting outcome data to stakeholders is particularly important when one considers how difficult it is to demonstrate through an outcome study that the treatment is the cause of the change.

Identifying observable behaviors, including words, related to more abstract outcomes such as attribution style and perceptions of freedom is only one way to quantify client change. Changes in a patients' clinical status with respect to constructs such as attribution style or perceptions of freedom can also be evaluated using psychometric tools. These are pencil and paper tests designed to measure specific constructs, like depression, perceived freedom in leisure, or coping skills. In the context of the rehabilitation center example, the researcher must find measures that have appropriate psychometric properties or evidence that valid and reliable inferences may be made from test scores about attribution style and perceived freedom in leisure. Most good theories have well-established measures, as is the case with attribution theory (e.g., Russell, 1982) or perceived freedom (Witt & Ellis, 1989). Or in the case of self-efficacy, excellent guidelines for creating measures are available (e.g., *Guide for Creating Self-Efficacy Scales*, Bandura, 2006). These measures allow the TRS to quantify the levels of the presenting problems, or constructs, at the beginning of the program. They can also be used after the program is completed to document changes in the client.

General outcome measures are difficult to find. Berman et al. (1998) suggested that in the mental health area there is a "dearth of outcome measures in any domain but symptomatology of psychiatric disorders, that are brief, reliable, valid across populations, sensitive to change, and minimally burdensome and reflect multiple perspectives" (p. 127). They go on to say that *SF-12* and *SF-36* are examples of the few existing outcome measures that are excellent in these areas (Ware & Sherbourne, 1992). In terms of patient satisfaction, some general measures have been developed and used effectively (Kane, 1997). These include the *Patient Satisfaction Scale* (Cryns, Nichols, Katz, & Calkins, 1989) and the *Client Satisfaction Questionnaire-8* (Granello, Granello, & Lee, 1999). With the current limits on good general pencil and paper tests, systematic observation and structured interviews may be used to measure general changes in attitudes and cognitions. This type of information complements the results of psychometric measures.

Other measurement procedures have been developed for use in outcome studies, such as in-depth semi-structured interviews (Sigrell, Cornell, Gyllenskoeld, Lindgren, & Stenfelt, 1998), goal attainment scaling (Kiresuk, Smith, & Cardillo, 1994), and multi-modal approaches (Munson, 1986, 1992). Most of these measurement techniques are associated directly with a particular research or treatment method. (Depending on the situation, this step (3) may occur as part of Step 5: Identifying Methods.)

Step Four: Selecting Subjects in Outcome Studies

Clients with different characteristics, or different levels of the same characteristic, may respond to treatment in diverse ways (Kendall & Norton-Ford, 1982). Deeply depressed patients may respond dramatically to an intervention that has little or no effect on moderately depressed patients. Therefore, it is important to ensure that groups included in outcome research are as homogeneous as possible with respect to the variable(s) of interest. To create homogeneous groups, it is critical that clients participating in outcome studies are diagnosed adequately (Osberg, 1997). Using a triangulated or multimethod approach to assessment will improve adequate diagnosis. This involves the use of valid and reliable psychometric instruments, interviews, observations, and carefully reviewing the client's family and treatment history.

Other pre-existing factors not related directly to the diagnosis may have an effect on how the client responds to treatment. For example, one study suggested that successful outcomes in a therapeutic wilderness program were related to levels of sensation-seeking, the number of prior treatments, and parental commitment (Weston, McGuire, & Shinew, 1995). For the same reasons, researchers need to be sensitive to ecological and cultural factors that may differ among the research participants and adversely affect outcomes (Bernal, Bonilla, & Bellido, 1994). Researchers should consider carefully pre-existing client factors that may cause varied responses to treatment. If the TRS/researcher is confident that the clients participating in the study are diagnosed properly and have similar pre-existing factors, then subjects may be selected for inclusion in the outcome study.

Step Five: Identifying Methods and Strategies
for Conducting Outcome Research

The primary limiting factor in conducting outcome research is the inability to control extraneous and confounding variables (e.g., history, maturation, testing, regression, mortality, and selection). The nature of outcome research makes it difficult to institute traditional research methods, such as homogeneous subject selection, factorial designs, and random assignment. Controlling variation from sources other than the treatment is extremely difficult. The factors that are out of the researcher's control when doing studies in treatment settings are innumerable. The unavoidable consequence is that almost all outcome studies contain threats to internal validity or influences other than the treatment effect being measured. In other words, it is difficult to demonstrate that change in a client is due solely to the effects of the treatment or intervention (that the independent variable is the only variable affecting the dependent variable). The goal of outcome research is to make every effort to limit threats to internal validity so the findings present a strong case that the treatment is causing the desired change or outcome.

Many different strategies have been employed to improve internal validity of outcome studies. One basic approach is to create randomly a control group (no treatment) and a treatment group (treatment) and then measure the differences between the groups (mean scores) on the desired outcomes. It is difficult or unethical, however, to recruit people with illnesses or disabling conditions and convince them to put off treatment so a study will have subjects for a control group. If an agency has a waiting list of people who are trying to get into the program, individuals on the waiting list may serve as the control group. Because subject assignment to groups is not randomized, steps must be taken to investigate the homogeneity of the waiting list (control) group and the group undergoing treatment. During certain times of the year, some therapeutic wilderness programs are unable to admit all of the adolescents who are seeking placement. Consequently, these agencies create waiting lists. If the researcher can determine that the adolescents on the waiting list are similar in terms of diagnosis, severity of presenting problems, and pre-existing factors, the waiting list is likely to be an acceptable control group.

Another approach is to provide a group of clients with the best alternative treatment. In this scenario, one group gets the best alternative treatment available while the other undergoes the treatment of interest (Kendall & Norton-Ford, 1982). One would expect to find that the treatment of interest is more effective than the alternative. The problem with this method is that most agencies offer what they believe is the best treatment. Developing an alternative treatment can be expensive and time-consuming. Finding an alternative at another agency is difficult, because competitors may be unwilling to participate in comparison research for fear of negative results. When agencies are willing to collaborate, however, this is an excellent approach to making comparisons between treatment programs. Programs that include multiple phases or stages of treatment may consider employing dismantling procedures to determine the effectiveness of individual phases or combinations of phases (Kendall & Norton-Ford, 1982; Krause & Howard, 1999). Dismantling is a technique of systematically eliminating a phase or phases treatment for groups of clients to determine if the elimination has an impact on outcomes. Dismantling is effective in determining what parts or phases of a program have the greatest or least impact on clients.

This allows stakeholders to eliminate less effective phases to shorten the length of treatment and streamline costs. This type of outcome study has the potential to benefit both the client and the service provider.

In a program where treatment takes place in phases, each phase may be viewed as an independent treatment program. For example, in a five-phase program, the staff may believe that one or two phases are not essential in facilitating the acquisition of client treatment goals. The phases thought to be unnecessary are identified and then eliminated systematically for certain groups of clients. The results are compared with the original program. As illustrated in Table 27.1, a group completes the original program. A second group (experimental group 1) receives program with the exception of phase 2, a phase that some staff believe may not be necessary. A third group (experimental group 2) completes the program with the exception of stage 3, which other staff members believe is a waste of time. A fourth group (experimental group 3) completes stages one, four, and five. When data are collected on the outcome measures, the extent to which the outcomes where achieved for each group may be compared. If none of the experimental groups had outcomes similar to the original group, then the researcher would recommend leaving the program intact. If any of the experimental groups had similar outcomes to the original program, then the recommendation might be to eliminate phases that do not appear to have an important effect.

An alternative to conducting outcome studies with comparison groups is to establish or use existing normative data. Healthcare and governmental agencies collect data regarding general issues such as average length of stay for particular diagnoses, recidivism, school performance, and legal involvement. As with all comparisons, it is important to determine if the groups being compared are similar in terms of the critical characteristics (e.g., diagnosis, severity of presenting problems, duration of symptoms). Once comparable norms have been established, the norms may be used as a benchmark for determining whether or not the desired outcomes have been reached on a client-by-client basis.

Step Six: Implementation and Evaluation

With a sound conceptual foundation, subjects selected, good measures, and an appropriate design in place, the study is ready to be implemented. One of the most important

Table 27.1
Example of Dismantling Design for Outcome Research

Treatment Phases	1	2	3	4	5
Original Program	X	X	X	X	X
Experimental group 1	X		X	X	X
Experimental group 2	X	X		X	X
Experimental group 3	X			X	X

factors in successfully implementing an outcome study is enlisting the commitment of the staff to ensure that interventions are completed correctly and the measures administered appropriately. The staff is more likely to be committed if they have a vested interest in the successful completion of the study. Often this can be accomplished by ensuring that the staff understands the purpose of the study and how it will provide information to improve the programs and services the staff offers.

As the study is implemented, some aspects may not go as planned. For example, subjects will relocate, become disenchanted, or drop out for other reasons. The resulting attrition can pose serious problems for the study (Kendall & Norton-Ford, 1982). In our research in wilderness adventure programs, we continually struggle with staff training to properly implement interventions. Because of attrition and other problems that are likely to arise while conducting outcome research, it is important that the individual responsible for overseeing the study track all aspects of the study in order to catch problems early and make the changes necessary for the study to continue. Careful monitoring and open communication with the staff implementing the interventions will allow for fine-tuning of the study as it progresses. When the study is complete, the staff should meet to evaluate if the study was implemented as designed, and if not, determine what impact the changes had on the findings. Based on the evaluation, recommendations for future studies could be identified. Finally, the findings may be presented to the stakeholders.

Challenges and Issues in Conducting Outcome Research

A number of challenges and issues are associated with conducting outcome studies. The issues range in nature from methodological to political to ethical. While some issues are obvious, others are more subtle. Consulting or collaborating with researchers at universities is one way to obtain a helpful perspective from someone with experience.

The complex nature of the issues and challenges associated with outcome research may be illustrated through a personal example. For us, many of these issues came to light when we, along with some colleagues, conducted an outcome study for a therapeutic wilderness program. We responded to a request for proposals and were selected by an agency to conduct the study. The agency serves adolescents with emotional and behavioral problems. Participants in the program come from around the U.S. The youth are brought, sometimes against their will, to the main office where they are admitted and assessed. They are then taken into the wilderness for eight weeks. During this time, students learn survival skills and other outdoor activities. Each student receives the bare necessities, such as a blanket, knife, and basic food items. While in the wilderness, they go through a process that includes living, hiking, and working closely with other youth, field staff, and clinical staff.

Licensed therapists visit the youth weekly for counseling sessions. At the same time, the program requires parents of the students to attend a seminar on building healthy relationships. Near the end of the program, each student goes on a three-day, solo survival trip. The final phase of the program has the youth take their parents on a three-day survival trip. During this trip, the students use the survival skills learned during the previous weeks to care for their parents. They build shelters, find food, and build fires to cook the food for their parents. On our first visit to the main office, a student and his parents came in just off their survival experience. His mother, a wealthy urbanite, proudly displayed a walking stick they had carved during the survival trip. A rattlesnake skin, with the rattle still attached, was neatly wound around the stick. The mother enthusiastically told the staff how they had killed and eaten the snake.

It became clear that a variety of aspects of this program could have therapeutic benefits that would affect outcomes. To complicate matters even more, the youth participating in the program came from diverse backgrounds and presented a variety of emotional and behavioral problems. We learned later that the diagnoses of the students included such things as anorexia nervosa, depression, poly-substance abuse, and wide-ranging disorders such as opposition defiant, obsessive-compulsive, anxiety, and adjustment. A majority of the students came to the program with a history of substance abuse and school failure. A few had committed serious crimes. Some of the youth had been in numerous forms of treatment prior to admission into the therapeutic wilderness program. Each of these factors could influence the possible outcomes associated with the therapeutic wilderness program's treatment goals.

As we tried to clarify who would be using the findings and how the results would be put to use (Step 1) the political nature of outcome research became obvious. One administrator indicated that the findings would be used to determine the overall effectiveness of the program. Another administrator wanted us to measure a specific construct that he thought was central to the program's purpose. We learned that funding for the study came from outside donors who wanted data to use for marketing and to persuade third parties to pay for the services. The dietician who planned menus was convinced that eating patterns had the biggest impact on behavior. He believed that most of the problems the students faced were the result of eating poorly and that a strict, healthy diet produced positive behavioral outcomes. Another staff member felt that the emphasis on a higher power and spirituality was the most important part of the program and had the biggest impact. Still another suggested that the wilderness itself brought about the change in the participants. From our perspective, it was possible they were all partially correct. But how would one investigate the influence of each of these variables?

We worked with the staff to develop a clear picture of what they wanted and to determine the best way to help them. We focused on limiting the study to a few outcomes that most of the staff agreed upon. With many competing interests and a number of stakeholders, it was difficult to develop a sound conceptualization (Step 2). First, an attempt was made to identify the most important treatment goals of the agency. We then asked the administrators and staff to explain the mechanisms behind their program that produced the desired outcomes. Interestingly, they seemed to agree on the general principles. They had their own theory of action, but they had never tried to articulate it or write it down. Once the conceptual basis or theory of their program was clear and the treatment goals had been identified, measures to quantify the outcomes could be selected (Step 3). Unfortunately, one of the primary stakeholders was in a hurry to get the results of the study. Consequently, they asked if we would use existing data from the intake assessment as a baseline. The assessment had a number of problems that brought the reliability and validity of the measure into question.

In this study, the methods (Step 5) directly influenced the subject selection (Step 4). For example, if we chose to do a comparison, we would need a control or comparison group. This could have been accomplished by employing a waiting-list control group or even by using adolescents in a traditional psychiatric residential treatment center. We also considered doing a longitudinal or repeated measure study to track the outcome variables from admissions to five years post-discharge. A variety of dismantling techniques were discussed to evaluate different aspects of the program and identify ways to improve outcomes. This would have allowed us to randomly assign students in the program to different groups and avoid the use of external control groups. In the end, the program administrators decided to use the available intake assessments as a baseline, and we created a parallel follow-up measure to obtain outcome data.

Issues and Related Questions for Discussion

Understanding the effectiveness of a TR program may be complicated, because the program may be part of a larger intervention, it may use recreation and traditional therapy, and the therapist may have an additional effect. When TR programs are in the context of larger treatment programs, ferreting out the TR effect is an interesting and difficult challenge. Within the TR effect is the question about the effect of recreation vs. therapy. Programs that use recreation as a modality for a clinical intervention may need to find methods to address this question. Some programs use recreation as the intervention or a means to an end. In these cases, the research is much less complicated. Another issue is determining the "therapist effect" in achieving outcomes; that is, how much of the change is a result of the therapist over the recreation and the clinical component? (Elkin, 1999).

From an ethical perspective, professionals should consider if the need for outcome information justifies doing anything less than the best for the client. Under what circumstances is placing clients in a control group justified? Another ethical issue has to do with conflicts of interest. Who should conduct outcome studies when the results will be used to promote a program? Is it appropriate for agencies to conduct internal studies and then use the results to market their program, or should the agencies provide funding for grants that are competitive among researchers in an effort to answer key questions? It is not uncommon for agencies or professional organizations to hire researchers to gather outcome data to promote their agency or industry. Ultimately, the issue deals with eliminating bias and increasing objectivity. No research is without bias, and few studies approach complete objectivity. What guidelines would help promote objectivity in outcome research?

Summary

With the current demands of the healthcare industry, therapeutic recreation will continue to be asked to justify its services and demonstrate the effectiveness of programs. Consequently, both practicing TR professionals and prospective professionals will benefit from gaining a greater understanding of outcome research and the principles and challenges associated with conducting outcome research. This chapter discusses the basic steps for conducting clinical outcome research and attempts to expose readers to some of the challenges and issues associated with conducting sound outcome studies. Thoughtful persons will realize that conducting outcome research is a complex task. But well-developed studies can provide valuable information that can demonstrate the effectiveness of programs, promote the profession, and most importantly, improve the quality of client care.

Discussion Questions

1. How can the TR process be used in conducting outcome research? As a class, consider the different TR agencies where you have worked or volunteered.
2. What are the most difficult challenges to overcome when conducting outcome research?
3. Identify strategies that were not discussed in this chapter that might address the challenges identified in question 2.
4. Is outcome research in therapeutic recreation more important in clinical settings than in community-based settings? Explain your answer.
5. Identify some reasons why outcome research would be valuable in community-based settings.
6. How might existing, published outcome research be used by a TRS?
7. What steps might be taken by a researcher to increase the confidence in the results of an outcome study?
8. Discuss what outcomes would be of greatest interest for each of these agencies. Can you identify one or two common outcomes that would be of value in all of the agencies you discussed? Pick a specific population and develop a hypothetical study following the steps outlined in this chapter.

References

Bandura, A. (1997). *Self-efficacy: The exercise of control.* New York: Freeman and Co.

Bandura, A. (2006). Guide for creating self-efficacy scales. In Pajares, & Urdan (Eds.), *Self-efficacy beliefs of adolescents.* Greenwich, CT: Information Age.

Berman, W., Rosen, C., Hurt, S., & Kolarz, C. (1998). Toto, we're not in Kansas anymore: Measuring and using outcomes in behavioral healthcare. *Clinical Psychology: Science and Practice,* 5(1), 115-133.

Bernal, G., Bonilla, J., & Bellido, C. (1994). Ecological validity and cultural sensitivity for outcome research: Issues for the cultural adaptation and development of psychosocial treatments with Hispanics. *Journal of Abnormal Child Psychology,* 23(1), 67-82.

Coyle, C., Kinney, W., Riley, B., & Shank, J. (1991). *Benefits of therapeutic recreation: A consensus view.* Philadelphia, PA: Temple University.

Cryns, A., Nichols, R., Katz, L., & Calkins, E. (1989). The hierarchical structure of geriatric patient satisfaction: An older patient satisfaction scale designed for HMOs. *Medical-Care,* 27(8), 802-816.

Dahl, T. (2002). International classification of functioning, disability and health: An introduction and discussion of its potential impact on rehabilitation services and research. *Journal of Rehabilitation Medicine,* 34(5), 201-204.

Deci, E. (1995). *Why we do what we do: Understanding self-motivation.* NY: Penguin.

Elkin, I. (1999). A major dilemma in psychotherapy outcome research: Disentangling therapists from therapies. *Clinical Psychology: Science and Practice,* 6(1), 10-32.

Evans, H. (1981). Psychiatric patient participation in goal setting as related to goal attainment. Dissertation Abstracts International, 41, 4658B. (University Microfilms No. 1111691).

Granello, H., Granello, P., & Lee, F. (1999). Measuring treatment outcomes and client satisfaction in a partial hospitalization program. *The Journal of Behavioral Health Services and Research, 26*(1), 50-63.

Granger, C. (1998). The emerging science of functional assessment: Our tool for outcome analysis. *Archives of Physical Medicine and Rehabilitation, 79*(3), 235-240.

Kane, R. (1997). *Understanding healthcare outcomes research.* Gaithersburg, MD: Aspen.

Kendall, P., & Norton-Ford, J. (1982). Therapy outcome research methods. In P. Kendall, & J. Butcher (Eds.), *Handbook of research methods in clinical psychology* (pp. 429-460). New York: Wiley & Sons.

Kiresuk, T., Smith, A., & Cardillo, J. (1994). *Goal attainment scaling: Applications, theory, and measurement.* Hillsdale, NJ: Lawrence Erlbaum.

Krause, M., & Howard, K. (1999). "Between-group psychotherapy outcome research and basic science" revisited. *Journal of Clinical Psychology, 55*(2), 159-169.

Munson, W. (1986). Multimodal leisure counseling with older people. *Activities, Adaptation, and Aging, 9*(1), 1-15.

Munson, W. (1992). Therapeutic recreation for handicapped youth offenders: A multimodal approach. In G. L. Hitzhusen, & J. R. Gigstad (Eds.), *Abstracts from the International symposium on Therapeutic Recreation* (Nottingham, England).

Osberg, T. (1997). Teaching psychotherapy outcome research using a research-based checklist. *Teaching of Psychology, 24*(4), 271-274.

Pajares, F., & Urdan, T. (Eds). (2006). *Self-efficacy beliefs of adolescents.* Greenwich, CT: Information age.

Peterson, C., Semmel, A., Bryer, C., Abramson, L., Melalsky, G., & Seligman, M. (1982). The attributional style questionnaire. *Cognitive Therapy and Research, 6*(3), 287-300.

Russell, D., & McAuley, E. (1986). Causal attributions, causal dimensions, and affect reactions to success and failure. *Journal of Personality and Social Psychology, 50*(6), 1174-1185.

Russell, D. (1982). The causal dimension scale: A measure of how individuals perceive causes. *Journal of Personality and Social Psychology, 42*(6), 1137-1145.

Seligman, M.E.P. (1991). *Learned optimism.* New York: Knopf.

Sigrell, B., Cornell, A., Gyllenskoeld, K., Lindgren, I., & Stenfelt, P. (1998). Psychoanalytic psychotherapy and outcome research: A qualitative study. *Psychoanalytic Psychotherapy, 12*(1), 57-73.

Touchstone, W. (1984). A personalized approach to goal planning and evaluation in clinical settings. *Therapeutic Recreation Journal, 18*(2), 25-31.

Ware, J. E. Jr., & Sherbourne, C. (1992). The MOS 36-item short form health survey: Conceptual framework and item selection. *Medical Care, 34*(3), 473-483.

Weston, R., McGuire, F., & Shinew, K. (1995). The relationship between selected social/psychological input variables and success in a therapeutic wilderness program for at-risk youth. *Abstracts from the Symposium on Leisure Research, National Congress for Recreation and Parks.* Arlington, VA: NRPA.

Witt, P., & Ellis, G. (1989). *The leisure diagnostic battery users' manual.* State College, PA: Venture.

CHAPTER 28

Research into Practice: Building Knowledge Through Empirical Practice

Bryan P. McCormick, Ph.D., CTRS™
Indiana University
Youngkhill Lee, Ph.D., CTRS™
Calvin College
Marieke Van Puymbroeck, Ph.D., CTRS™
Indiana University

Everybody talks about the weather, but nobody does anything about it.
—Mark Twain

Over the past 20 years, there have been a number of discussions about therapeutic recreation research (Compton, 1984; Compton & Dieser, 1997; Coyle, Kinney, & Shank, 1991; Shank & Coyle, 2002; Witt, 1988). Unfortunately, the consensus of these reviews and commentaries has been uniformly critical of the quality and volume of therapeutic recreation research. At times, it seems as if research in therapeutic recreation is somewhat akin to the weather in the above quote by Mark Twain. Yet over the same time period, there has been an increasing demand from society, healthcare payers, and healthcare institutions for accountability in the provision of health and human services. These demands have been noted both from within therapeutic recreation, characterized as "efficacy research" (Malkin, Coyle, & Carruthers, 1998; Russoniello, 2003), and from the healthcare environment, characterized as "outcomes research" (Joint Commission on Accreditation of Healthcare Organizations, 1997; Katz & Green, 1998).

Although there have been repeated calls for increasing research production in the field, at the same time, we seem to be faced by a variety of barriers. As noted in previous chapters, these barriers have included such things as the lack of resources (including time and money), a lack of competence and confidence, a lack of institutional/administrative support, and a perceived lack of relevance. However, it may be argued that one of the greatest obstacles to research in therapeutic recreation is the conceptual separation of research from practice. In virtually all presentations of therapeutic recreation practice, research and evaluation receive minimal attention. In other presentations (cf. Compton, 1997), issues of research are identified as issues of "professionalization" as opposed to issues of "practice." As a result, examining the effects or impacts of our interventions is seen as an "add on" to practice. However, this separation is not unique to therapeutic recreation. For example, Lindsey and Kirk (1993) characterized social work's history as having favored "action over theory, practice insight over scientific research, and good intentions over effective outcomes; this has led to a de-emphasis on research" (p. 378). Such a characterization is arguably just as applicable to the history of therapeutic recreation. If we are to increase the knowledge base of our profession, we must begin to address, as a profession and as individual practitioners, the fact that research and evaluation are valuable tools for demonstrating accountability and can no longer be viewed as "add-ons" to therapeutic recreation practice. That is, they must be part and parcel of therapeutic recreation practice. The purpose of this chapter is to identify how research may be integrated as a component of therapeutic recreation practice.

Empirical Practice: Integrating Practice and Research

The difficulty of integrating research and practice is not unique to therapeutic recreation. This same issue can be seen in fields such as nursing (McSkimming, 1996), education (Jacobson, 1998), speech-language pathology (Ratner, 2006), clinical psychology (Kazdin, 2006), and social work (Reid, 1994; Siegel, 1984). In addition, many of the same forces as those affecting therapeutic recreation noted above have affected other professions. For example, Witkin (1996) identified that the social and political climate of the early 1970s created a scarcity of resources for social programs. This scarcity increased competition among helping professions and led to the need for social work to legitimize its claims as a profession worthy of public and financial support. In addition, internal questions were being raised by social workers regarding the efficacy of social work practice (cf. Fisher, 1973). One model for addressing such concerns sought to increase the knowledge base of the profession through encouraging the use of research methods in practice. This model came to be identified as "empirical practice." Siegel (1984) cited the following as requirements for empirically based practice:

1. Practitioners maximize use of research findings.
2. Data are systematically collected to monitor interventions.
3. The effectiveness of interventions is empirically demonstrated.
4. Problems, interventions, and outcomes are specified in concrete, measurable terms.
5. Practitioners use research methods and models in the conceptualization of clients' problems, the formulation of questions for practice, the collection of assessment data, and the evaluation of the effectiveness of interventions.
6. Research and practice are viewed as part of the same problem-solving process.
7. Research is seen as a tool to be employed in practice. (p. 330)

In essence, the concept of empirical practice implies that practice is developed, modified, and examined according to standards of empirical evidence. Empiricism implies that evidence must be concrete, observable, and measurable. Although this model has not been without criticism (cf. Witkin, 1996), it has provided a structure through which techniques of practice and research may be integrated (Blythe & Tripodi, 1989; Reid, 1994). In addition, the adoption of such a model in therapeutic recreation practice might aid in addressing two pressing concerns of practice. First, the use of empirically based practice would increase the accountability of therapeutic recreation services through systematic examination of the effectiveness of interventions. Second, empirically based examinations of service effectiveness have the potential to contribute to the knowledge base of the profession through the identification of effective services across a variety of practice settings (Gabor & Grinnell, 1994; Straus, Richardson, Glasziou, & Haynes, 2005; Widmer, Zabriskie, & Wells, 2003).

Based on Siegel's (1984) characterization of empirical practice, there are three principal areas of activity to enact this model. First, therapeutic recreation practitioners must be intelligent consumers of research. That is, practitioners must maximize the use of research findings. Theories, practices, and techniques generated through research on therapeutic recreation should provide a foundation of our program of services. In other words, accountable therapeutic recreation practice is research-based practice. Second, therapeutic recreation specialists must be able and willing to use research techniques in examining, verifying, and refining their practice. In essence, our profession, through the collective actions of practitioners and researchers, must expand our production of practice-based research. Finally, the methods and concepts of research must be integrated into professional preparation of therapeutic recreation practitioners.

Research as a Basis for Practice

It appears that practitioners and researchers live in two different worlds. A practitioner might make the following statement: "Therapeutic recreation research, per se, does not guide me one bit. I read occasionally, but this offers little help for my practice. My clinical experience is the only thing that has helped me in my practice." Still other practitioners might say: "Researchers do not address the needs of real-life situations of practitioners and clients." They often believe that researchers offer too little, are consumed by irrelevant questions, and fail to appreciate the knowledge that arises from practice. In contrast, researchers might say: "Practitioners do not read and apply what we have produced. They primarily use their experience and awareness of a number of immediate situational factors to facilitate therapeutic process." Researchers might further charge that practitioners are poorly equipped to use research and are uninformed about current scientific information.

This researcher-practitioner gap indicates a lack of integration between research and practice. Perhaps one of the important reasons for the research-practice gap is due to a lack of understanding and awareness rather than any justifiable division between these two activities. In other words, each of us has a tendency to view the world through our own lenses. Through our own lenses, it is easy to see our activities as the most important. Consequently, it is no surprise that divisions between practice and research have arisen. Yet, this is not to say that all practitioners are ignorant of research and all researchers are ignorant of practice realities. The best practitioners, as we argue in this chapter, are informed by research, just as the best researchers' studies are informed by the constraints of practical settings. What is lost by the myopic view is that practice and research are linked mutually in two important ways. First, these activities share the same primary goal—provision of effective services for clients. Second, they should be informed by the same body of knowledge.

Underutilization of Research

How do both researchers and practitioners consume current research? Jordan and Roland (1999) empirically examined the utilization of research among practitioners and academicians including both TR and recreation and leisure professionals. Among their respondents consisting of 71.8% of practitioners and 28.2% academicians who do some research, they found that both practitioners and academicians generally do not read research journals.[1] While between 72% of all respondents reported that they rarely or never read research journals, this proportion was higher among practitioners (86%).

As Jordan and Roland's (1999) study demonstrated, underutilization of research is problematic for the field. Although respondents did not provide reasons for the underutilization of research, there may be several important reasons of underutilization of therapeutic recreation research among practitioners. They include: (a) many irrelevant research questions, (b) poor reflection of actual clinical contexts in the treatments and measures utilized in research, (c) an overemphasis on technical matters (e.g., statistical analysis), and (d) too little discussion of integrating research findings to clinical applications. One important implication of underutilization of research is that it hinders our ability to effectively serve clients.

Need for Integration of Research into Practice

There is an imperative need for integrating research into practice. Practitioners must be capable of identifying pertinent and relevant evidence and integrating it into practice. While this may be easier said than done, one of the major impediments to the integration of research into practice may be the lack of an integrated conceptual model that unites the activities of practice and research.

Research can aid practitioners in thinking critically by basing decisions on rules of empirical observation and by the pursuit of realistic therapeutic goals. The importance of integration of research into practice is not a new concept. Flexner (1925), in a landmark report that revolutionized medical education, emphasized the intimate relationship between research and practice:

> At bottom, the intellectual attitude of the two are—or should be—identical: neither investigator nor practitioner should be blinded by prejudices or jump at conclusions; both should observe, reflect, conclude, try, and watching results, continuously reapply the same method until the problem in hand has been solved or abandoned. (Flexner, 1925, p. 4)

---

[1] *Therapeutic Recreation Journal* was noted as the most frequently read of the research journals.

Perhaps the ideal approach might be that practitioners apply the findings of research in order to understand and address the problems presented by their clients.

Exclusive reliance on intuition or clinical experience might prove problematic. The problem is that through the exclusive use of the logic and reason of clinical experience, the profession's body of knowledge will never progress beyond what Witt (1988) characterized as the "social philosophy" stage of knowledge. At the same time, it should be noted that exclusive reliance on research evidence may be problematic. Empirical practice requires that good therapists use both clinical evidence based on clinical experience and the best available research evidence and that neither alone is enough (c.f., Brown, 1999; Perkins, Simnett, & Wright, 1999).

Stricker (1992) introduced different levels of integrating research into practice. At one level, utilization of research refers to an awareness of research. He argued that this might be the most common type of utilization of research. This level is the least that should be expected of any active practitioner. A more advanced level of utilization involves the active consideration of the implications of research for practice. However, the contemplation of research implications is still only a partial integration of research. The highest level of utilization, posited by Stricker, is to integrate research into practice. We strongly advocate for the integration of research and practice in therapeutic recreation. The key word is integration. We firmly believe that both research knowledge and practical experience are necessary for therapeutic recreation practice.

Current Context That Demands Integration of Research into Practice

The integration of research into practice is paramount. As mentioned previously, the world of healthcare is increasingly being judged based on accountability and research evidence (Shank & Coyle, 2002). For practitioners to be credible providers of therapeutic recreation services, we must put the best of our systematic research knowledge at the center of therapeutic recreation practice. Practitioners are being asked currently to provide accountability information and documentation that the services they provide are effective. Clients, third-party payers, and healthcare administrators are only a few of those who may want data-based information concerning the rationale and effectiveness of therapeutic recreation interventions. Consequently, it may be to the practitioner's advantage to be an intelligent research consumer.

Moving Toward Evidence-Based Practice

Having addressed the importance of integrating research into practice, it is a logical next step to move on to introduce a conceptual "map" that may help to integrate research into practice. A starting point can be identified through the adoption of "evidence-based practice" (DeJong, 1999). Evidence-based practice implies that scientific evidence, not tradition or conventional wisdom, should ultimately govern the selection of interventions and the delivery of our health service (see chapters 15 and 16 in this text). Evidence can be any data that were created through the systematic process of scientific examination. With evidence, the foundation or rationale for our interventions may be more convincingly articulated to outside parties.

It is important that evidence is recognized by relevant stakeholders, but it is also important that there is open, scientific evidence that appeals to rational criteria rather than other evidence that might appeal to subjective criteria which practitioners might employ. In other words, the claims can be acceptable when they meet objective scientific criteria, rather than subjective, emotional ones. However, it is not to say that experience is an unimportant source of information for clinical practice. Instead, we argue that experience should not overrule the findings of logic presented in research.

In evidence-based practice, therapeutic recreation practice is a pragmatic activity grounded on the evolving knowledge base that is derived from the broad range of scientific findings. As a pragmatic, problem-solving activity, the choice of interventions would depend on the particular client problem rather than on interventions that are commonly used or most preferred. Systematic research would be an integral part of clinical decision making. Because this knowledge base constantly evolves, clinicians would need to continually use it to remain informed.

Practitioners can ask two general questions about their clinical practice: (a) What about my work is helpful in producing successful client outcomes? and (b) How can my work be further enhanced? The practitioner can turn to qualitative and quantitative (meta-analytic) reviews of the research to determine if what they do has been consistently found to be effective. In this evidence-based model, a practitioner should know which outcomes are appropriate targets for therapeutic recreation intervention. Advanced theoretical knowledge of therapeutic recreation outcomes with specific populations serves as a foundation. One resource for identifying potential outcomes can be found in the International Classification of Functioning Disability and Health (ICF; World Health Organization, 2001). As presented in chapter 4, Van Puymbroeck, Porter, McCormick, and Singleton report that the ICF identifies a number of elements of functioning that are potential areas of intervention. It is imperative for practitioners to become skilled in comprehensive awareness and knowledge of the therapeutic recreation outcomes; otherwise, the results can only happen by chance. We cannot afford to leave outcomes to the laws of chance but must purposefully create outcomes by design based on a foundation of empirical knowledge of therapeutic recreation outcomes.

Finally, evidence-based practice implies a constant evolution. That is, there is a need for constantly updating information. The body of knowledge that should underlie interventions continuously evolves. Rather than providing definitive answers and ultimate truths, the body of knowledge is constantly changing as new findings, interpretations, and questions are developed. Today's conclusions are quite naturally replaced by tomorrow's findings.

Research and the Examination of Practice

Although there have been repeated calls for research on the efficacy of therapeutic recreation interventions, the development and production of such research has been characterized as "glacier-like" (Ferguson, 1997). Although many authors have identified barriers to the production of research, one of the most consistently identified is a lack of research skills. This should not be particularly surprising as the principal practice degree in therapeutic recreation is the bachelor's degree. Should we expect bachelor's-level practitioners to be competent to conduct research in the field? This seems a tall order. Another avenue has been proposed through the use of collaboration between practitioners and researchers (Savell, Huston, & Malkin, 1993). Although this model represents a possibility for increasing the participation of practitioners in the production of research, there are an estimated 24,000 therapeutic recreation practitioners in the U.S. (U.S. Department of Labor, Bureau of Labor Statistics, 2007). If only partially implemented, collaboration would overwhelm researchers/educators. Possibly what is needed is to examine how research can be integrated into practice and how empirically based examinations of practice might contribute to the body of knowledge of therapeutic recreation. In this sense, techniques of research, employed in the examination of therapeutic recreation interventions, may provide a venue through which a much larger number of members of the therapeutic recreation profession may participate in contributing to our body of knowledge.

Patrick (1997, and chapter 29 in this volume) suggested that practice-based research may be advanced through the use of outcome evaluation. The use of outcome evaluation may provide a good starting point since it is increasingly mandated in health and human service organizations as a means for both increasing accountability and providing a basis for service improvement (Sluyter, 1998). In addition, research and evaluation have been characterized as following similar processes, and evaluation processes may be transferred to the research process (Caldwell & Weissinger, 1993). In order to use program evaluation as a beginning for practice-based research, an understanding of the similarities and differences of the two is in order. In addition, for practitioners to be producers of knowledge, programs must be designed in such a way that they lend themselves to empirical evaluation.

Research and Evaluation

Bedini and Wu (1994) stated that "the ultimate purposes of research [are] testing and building theory to contribute to the body of knowledge" (p. 96). Although research is typically presented as the method through which knowledge is generated, it is not the only empirically based process that can be used to examine practices and generate knowledge. Program evaluation has also been presented as a method for the generation of professional knowledge (Gabor & Grinnell, 1994). Caldwell and Weissinger (1993) characterized research as "concerned with relationships—not as they are unique to a specific program, but as they are generalizable to other programs, settings, and populations" (p. 130). In contrast, they noted that program evaluation is "concerned with evaluating the effectiveness of specific interventions or programs" (p. 129). Bloom (1997) has also identified the relationship of research and evaluation noting that "classical" research is a knowledge-generating activity whereas evaluation is a knowledge-testing activity. Thus, in both of these characterizations, research and evaluation appear as related activities, however, research is seen as broader in scope, typically more rigorous in method and the findings are more universally applicable than in evaluation. In this way, although research can be used to develop and test broadly applicable theories and practices, evaluation may be used to develop knowledge of the effectiveness and impact of practices in specific service contexts (see also Bedini's chapter 25).

Techniques in Empirically Based Practice

Ferguson (1997) noted that although efficacy research moves rather slowly, this should not necessarily hinder the development of practice. Instead, he argued that existing research could be used to develop "standard, outcome-oriented protocols" (p. 406). This is consistent with the concept noted above of empirically based practice. Siegel (1984) cited as one of the bases for empirical practice the ability to identify problems, interventions, and outcomes in measurable terms. The use of treatment protocols, developed with concrete descriptors of client need (problems), intervention activities, and predicted outcomes, aids in the empirical examination of practice. Although treatment protocols would be characterized most appropriately as being part of the "planning" phase of the process used in therapeutic recreation, the use of empirically based techniques should guide activities in (a) assessment of clients' need and baseline status, (b) the selection and identification of interventions, and (c) the evaluation of client progress and intervention effectiveness (Blythe, Tripodi, & Briar, 1994). However, one of the keys to understanding and applying empirically based practice is the concept and techniques of measurement.

Measurement in practice

Blythe and Tripodi (1989) defined measurement as "a process that results in the consistent assignment of properties of people or objects so they can be classified, ordered, or counted. It enables one to identify and compare observations that pertain to the description and relationship of phenomena that are vital for work" (p. 27). Measurement is a useful technique that enables the translation of many otherwise unobservable phenomena into observable indicators. For example, a widely used measurement in physical rehabilitation is the Functional Independence Measure (FIM; Uniform Data System for Medical Rehabilitation, 1995). As implied by its title, this measure records a client's ability to function independently through indicators of self-care, sphincter control, mobility transfers, locomotion, communication, and social cognition. In other words, a client's level of functioning on each of these subdomains are indicators of the client's overall functional ability. Furthermore, functioning on each of the subdomains is measured through indicators stated as behavioral competencies. One should remember that measurement is a process that uses indicators as a means for identifying properties of clients and that the worth of a measurement is directly related to the quality of indicators. In addition, indicators are not identical with the phenomenon being measured. It is a necessary approximation, and practitioners are wise to remember that qualities such as functional independence cannot be wholly captured by measurement.

Translating a phenomenon into a measure is accomplished through four steps. First, concepts to be measured must be identified (Blythe & Tripodi, 1989). For example, Klosek and Crilly (1997) identified "leisure competence" as a concept that is appropriate for measurement within therapeutic recreation practice. The second step in measurement is to specify an indicator of the concept. In the case of more complex concepts, such as leisure competence, multiple indicators are likely to be required. According to Klosek and Crilly, leisure competence is indicated by competencies in (a) leisure awareness, (b) leisure attitude, (c) leisure skills, (d) cultural/social behaviors (e) interpersonal skills, (f) community integration skills, (g) social contact, and (h) community participation.

Once the concept has been identified and indicators have been specified, the third step is to operationally define data required to record the indicator's presence and/or level. In other words, what data are considered as evidence that the indicator is present, and, if appropriate, what is the degree of its presence? For example, a client's response to a specific question (or series of questions) may be considered as evidence of an indicator such as leisure needs (cf., Witt & Ellis, 1987). Another approach to operationalizing indicators has been to use behavioral descriptors, which are compared to observed client behavior. Based on these descriptors, clients are classified according to the indicator and concept. The final step in measurement is to determine the validity and reliability of the measurement. Blythe and Tripodi (1989) stated that measures that are inconsistent (poor reliability) and/ or are irrelevant to the concept being measured (poor validity) are at best useless and, at worst, misleading in practice. Thus, establishing validity and reliability of measures is a final, critical step to the use of measurement in practice.

Empirically based assessment

Although there are a variety of definitions of assessment within therapeutic recreation, most definitions include a few key similarities. First, virtually all definitions include a component related to the collection of information. In addition, this information is collected systematically as opposed to haphazardly. Second, most definitions indicate that information is collected for the purposes of decision making based on client characteristics. One result of this process is the identification of prioritized client need (Austin, 1998). However, in order for assessment to provide a basis for empirical practice, the information collected must be measurable, as noted above. The use of valid and reliable measurement in the assessment process affords the practitioner the ability to use the assessment information as a basis for not only intervention but also for the purposes of comparison to outcomes. Assessment measures allow the practitioner to compare a client against other clients on the same measure, and the assessment measurement may be compared to intervention outcomes (these issues are discussed in more depth in chapter 17).

Empirically based interventions

As with assessment, interventions can be measured. Blythe et al. (1994) suggested that interventions can be made available for measurement through the specification of five basic components. First, the intervention must specify the person or persons involved in providing the intervention itself. Second, specification of the content of the intervention is necessary. Specifying the content of the intervention enhances empirical practice by providing a basis for (a) consistent application of the intervention, and (b) measuring the fidelity of an intervention against its specifications. The next key component for specification is the target of the intervention. In this sense, interventions should specify who is to receive the intervention and may include the extent to which individuals are to participate (Blythe et al., 1994). The fourth component to identify is the location(s) of the intervention. Finally, empirically based interventions specify the purpose of the intervention in terms of resultant outcomes. For those familiar with treatment protocols, this level of specification or "proceduralization" should not be new. Thomas (1984) indicated that through this level of specification of the intervention, the empirical practitioner can measure the extent to which the intervention was implemented as planned (treatment integrity) and the degree to which the intervention is consistently applied in repeated applications (procedural reliability).

Empirical evaluation of results

One of the hallmarks of empirically based practice is the use of measurable data in the examination of the results of services. Two general classes of results can be examined empirically. First, as noted above, there is increased demand on practitioners to demonstrate accountability through demonstration of the effectiveness of their services. Effectiveness, most simply, denotes that an intervention achieved its intended results. Empirically based practice uses measurable data to make such determinations. Through the comparison of a client's measured state at service termination versus service initiation, differences may be seen. In addition, the degree of attainment of treatment goals also may provide a basis for measurable effectiveness (cf., Kiresuk, Smith, & Cardillo, 1994; see Widmer and Lundberg's Chapter 27). However, the sensitivity of the measurement instrument will relate directly to the ability to detect differences. Another examination of the results of services is possible through examining the impact of services (Schalock, 1995). In examining the impact of services, a practitioner compares the results of his or her interventions to either (a) no intervention, or (b) another intervention. For example, Finnell, Card, and Menditto (1997) found that a therapeutic recreation program had a greater impact in producing appropriate social behaviors among people with mental illness than a vocational training program. Through the planned and careful use of empirical measurement, conclusions regarding the results of the intervention can be based on observable data.

Brief Example of Empirically Based Practice

The first step in empirically based practice is to determine intervention outcomes based on knowledge of existing research and theory. The following provides a brief example of empirical practice for clients with schizophrenia.

Foundation

At the inpatient psychiatric facility, a recreational therapist (RT) keeps noting that the patients she sees who have schizophrenia have trouble dealing with stressful situations. As the RT ponders this, she wonders what can be done about it. First, she lays the foundation by searching the existing literature. The RT finds that people with schizophrenia often show a pattern of vulnerability to stress, such that the symptoms of the disorder are exacerbated by stressful life events (Lukoff, Snyder, Ventura, & Neuchterlein, 1984; Zubin, 1986). Since people with schizophrenia have been found to experience greater amounts of unoccupied (free) time (Delespaul & deVries, 1987), the ability to cope with stressors during this time has implications for TR in working with this population. One intervention that has been demonstrated empirically to be effective in working with people with schizophrenia has been coping-skills training (Kopelowicz & Liberman, 1995; Liberman & Kopelowicz, 1995; Tarrier et al., 1993). Furthermore, the ability of clients to develop coping skills has been found to be important in both substance-abuse treatment (Moggi & Crosby, 1999; Moggi, Ouimette, Finney, & Moos, 1999) and mental-health rehabilitation (Bradshaw, 1996). Specifically, greater use of approach coping (the use of strategies to directly address stressors) and less reliance on avoidance coping (the use of strategies to avoid stressors) have been found to be related to better adaptation to life stress in the general population (Holahan, Moos, & Schaefer, 1996), as well as in psychiatric populations (Swindle, Cronkite, & Moos, 1989).

Assessment

Based on this information, the first step is to identify an assessment instrument that (a) could be used to identify the different coping strategies, (b) has demonstrated validity and reliability, and (c) has been used with the population in question. *The Coping Responses Inventory* (CRI; Moos, 1993) is an example of an instrument that is designed to measure people's use of approach versus avoidance coping. When the RT looks at studies using the *CRI*, she reads that this instrument has demonstrated appropriate psychometric qualities (validity and reliability) and has been used with people with schizophrenia (cf., Moggi, Ouimette, Finney, & Moos, 1999).

Intervention

The next step in empirically based practice is to specify the intervention. First, this intervention is to be provided by a staff that is credentialed at the professional level as a Certified Therapeutic Recreation Specialist™ (CTRS™). Second, the intervention content for a coping-skills intervention might include such components as (a) identification of stressors/stressful situations, (b) managing physiological arousal, (c) cognitive-coping strategies, and (d) behavioral-coping strategies. In addition, processes for delivery of the content (lecture, modeling, exercises, practice) and locations for the delivery of content are also specified. Finally, specific outcomes of the intervention would be identified. These outcomes would be directly related to the purpose and content of the intervention (which in turn is based on empirical support). For example, one outcome statement might be that clients can demonstrate at least two relaxation techniques to manage physiological arousal.

Evaluation

As with assessment and intervention, the empirically based practitioner bases evaluation on measurable phenomena. In examining the results of an intervention for any one individual, the practitioner would first evaluate treatment integrity. This is done by examining the documentation from the implementation of the intervention and comparing it against the intervention as it was designed. Second, the practitioner would evaluate the effectiveness of treatment. If outcome statements are written in measurable terms, these statements provide a natural means for measuring treatment effectiveness. In addition, goal-attainment scaling (Kiresuk et al., 1994) can be used to measure the degree of attainment of outcomes. So to use the above outcome statement, if the client is able to demonstrate two relaxation techniques, the goal has been achieved. This outcome would be recorded along with other outcomes to evaluate the effectiveness of the coping-skills intervention. In addition, the original assessment instrument may be appropriate for retesting upon completion of the intervention. While these data can be used in a variety of ways, an easy and appropriate manner to use this information is to compare pre- and post-scores to evaluate improvement in empirical terms. Collecting pre- and postscores on the same intervention with numerous patients and then examining the mean change from pre-test to posttest can provide the therapist a base understanding of changes that may be due to the intervention.

Another easy and valid way to compare pre- and posttest changes is to measure the percent change that occurred during the intervention period. To do this, the therapist would collect the pre- and postdata. Then, the therapist would find the mean score of the pretest,

---

Figure 28.1
Formula to Determine Percent Change

$$\frac{(\text{Mean Pretest} - \text{Mean Posttest})}{\text{Mean Pretest}} = \% \text{ Change}$$

---

and the mean score of the posttest. Mean scores are found by adding up all of the total numbers for all patients and then dividing the total score by the total number of patients whose data were entered into the score. The formula in Figure 28.1 gives the process for determining percent change.

By collecting the percent change over the intervention period, the therapist is able to demonstrate changes in client functioning. This serves two important purposes: 1) It documents the effect the treatments are having, allowing the therapist to either continue or discontinue treatment, and 2) It provides empirical evidence to the facility administrators on the effects of therapeutic recreation treatment interventions.

Empirically Based Practice and Contribution to Knowledge

Although research often is seen as the preeminent technique through which knowledge is created, it is not the only method for the generation of knowledge. The use of empirical practice has the potential to contribute to the practical and technical knowledge base of therapeutic recreation interventions. Gabor and Grinnell (1994) suggested that the empirical examination of services can be a source of knowledge in that over a series of examinations of an intervention at a variety of practice sites, knowledge of the interventions most likely to be effective with different types of clients can be gained. They also cited that empirical examinations of practice can be "used to increase knowledge both about social problems and about the ways in which human-service programs address these problems" (p. 9). Finally, one of the most important areas of knowledge that can be gained through empirical practice is the testing of treatment interventions in practice settings. Although empirical practice will generate information for practitioners and stakeholders at a particular site, in order for it to contribute to a professional body of knowledge, it must be publicly presented. Without presentation and/or publication of the results of empirical practice, the knowledge created in one practice setting will not be transmitted to other members of the profession.

Empirical Practice and Professional Preparation

One of the final, and possibly most critical, issues in the integration of research in therapeutic recreation practice is related to professional preparation. As Witt (1988) indicated over two decades ago, the failure to socialize students of therapeutic recreation to the concepts and practices of research will result in practitioners who feel unqualified to consume or contribute to therapeutic recreation's body of knowledge. Compton and Dieser (1997) also echoed this sentiment, noting that the most important step to facilitate research in therapeutic recreation "is to cultivate research literacy across the profession" (p. 319).

Entry-level practitioners should possess the basic concepts and understandings of research; however, they are much more likely to be required to develop and examine interventions in specific practice settings. As a result, they should have competencies related to (a) interpreting research findings (including theory) as a basis for practice and (b) using empirical techniques for the examination of the effectiveness and impact of their interventions. If we are to prepare entry-level practitioners for these tasks, then research techniques and findings must be taught and viewed as an integral part of practice, not an "add-on" to working with clients.

In addition, we should not expect research skills to be evenly distributed across all levels of education within the field of therapeutic recreation. Graduate-level education should develop different research competencies for the doctoral and master's degree. First, the doctorate should be considered a research degree. Students should enter doctoral programs with the understanding that, upon completion of their degree, they will have the training and expectation of participating in research. By comparison, master's-trained personnel should be able to intelligently consume and use published research in services and should be able to independently examine those services through empirical methods.

Challenges and Opportunities with Evidence-Based Practice

While the aforementioned information is quite important to the advancement of the field, there are some challenges (and corresponding opportunities) that may be encountered when deciding to undertake evidence-based practice. Among the challenges may be the perception by administrators that using research in practice is time consuming and is hence too costly to undertake. While this does take time at the outset, the reward of gathering data on the effectiveness of interventions speaks to ensuring that the clients are receiving treatments that are producing measurable outcomes.

Another potential challenge is that such empirical practice may create a narrow understanding of the multiple factors that might influence changes in client outcomes. As in our example above, we focused on stress coping as a beginning point, and these findings were based on averages of experience among people with schizophrenia. It should be recognized that there are a number of variables that may affect how people cope with stress that were not examined. Such weaknesses in breadth can be addressed when the therapist collects data from a number of patients over time. Using such an aggregated patient data set, outcomes can be explored by looking at the influence of different factors on the change in the measure (e.g., diagnosis, age, socioeconomic status, gender, etc.).

Finally, a challenge may be raised to question the ability of bachelor's-prepared practitioners to conduct research. Although the research training included in the typical bachelor's degree is limited, professional associations continue to provide valuable continuing education opportunities to develop the skills necessary for practitioners to participate in research.

Summary

Without question, our field is in need of the continued production of research to build professional knowledge. However, calls for increased research production over this period have not resulted in significant increases in the volume of research being produced. We have argued that through the use of empirically based practice, practitioners may begin to integrate both the findings and techniques of research as an integral component of practice. In addition, through the use of these methods, practitioners may be able to contribute to the knowledge base of therapeutic recreation. However, empirical practice will not inherently contribute to the knowledge base of a profession.

As noted above, evaluation techniques are context- and program-specific. In order for the specific findings of program evaluation to contribute to the knowledge base of therapeutic recreation, they must be presented (i.e., at conferences or workshops). In addition, the contextual nature of such examinations of services can only contribute to therapeutic recreation's body of knowledge through replication. Knowing that a leisure education program conducted at a particular agency is effective in increasing leisure competence is very important for that agency; however, by itself, this knowledge is of marginal value for the profession. Only through replication and accumulation can evaluation findings contribute to a professional body of knowledge.

Finally, our argument is not intended to be a plea for the replacement of research with evaluation. Instead, what we are suggesting is that empirical practice, drawing on concepts of evaluation, might be a realistic avenue through which practitioners, most of whom have bachelor's degrees, will be able to meaningfully participate in the creation of therapeutic recreation's body of knowledge.

Discussion Questions

1. Compare research and evaluation. How are they alike? How do they differ?
2. What is meant by empiricism?
3. Identify an outcome that would be appropriate for therapeutic recreation intervention.
    a.   What are some indicators of this outcome?
    b.   Identify operational specifications of the indicator.
    c.   What data would you need to find to determine the presence or level of the   indicator?
4. How can empirically based practice contribute to the knowledge base of therapeutic recreation?
5. What challenges exist to implementing empirically based practice?

References

Austin, D. R. (1998). *Therapeutic recreation: Processes and techniques* (4th ed.). Champaign, IL: Sagamore.

Bedini, L., & Wu, Y. (1994). A methodological review of research in *Therapeutic Recreation Journal* from 1986 to 1990. *Therapeutic Recreation Journal, 28*, 87-98.

Bloom, M. (1997). The scientist-practitioner concept, revisited. *Social Work Research, 21*, 190-194.

Blythe, B. J., & Tripodi, T. (1989). *Measurement in direct practice*. Newbury Park, CA: Sage.

Blythe, B. J., Tripodi, T., & Briar, S. (1994). *Direct practice research in human service organizations.* New York: Columbia University Press.

Bradshaw, W. (1996). Structured group work for individuals with schizophrenia: A coping skills approach. *Research on Social Work Practice, 6,* 139-155.

Brown, S. J. (1999). *Knowledge for healthcare practice: A guide to using research evidence.* Philadelphia, PA: W.B. Saunders Company.

Caldwell, L. L., & Weissinger, E. (1993). A model for research utilization in therapeutic recreation. In M. J. Malkin, & C. Z. Howe (Eds.), *Research in therapeutic recreation* (pp. 127-142). State College, PA: Venture.

Compton, D. M. (1984). Research priorities in recreation for special populations. *Therapeutic Recreation Journal, 18*(1), 9-17.

Compton, D. M. (Ed.). (1997). *Issues in therapeutic recreation: Toward the new millennium* (2nd ed.). Champaign, IL: Sagamore.

Compton, D. M., & Dieser, R. (1997). Research initiatives in therapeutic recreation. In D. M. Compton (Ed.), *Issues in therapeutic recreation: Toward the new millennium* (2nd ed.), (pp. 299-325). Champaign, IL: Sagamore Publishing.

Coyle, C. P., Kinney, W. B., & Shank, J. (1991). A summary of benefits common to therapeutic recreation. In C. P. Coyle, W. B. Kinney, B. Riley, & J. Shank, (Eds.), *The benefits of therapeutic recreation: A consensus view* (pp. 353-385). Ravensdale, WA: Idyll Arbor.

DeJong, G. (1999). Toward an evidence-based rehabilitation: The role of values, outcomes disclosure, and stakeholder groups. *Rehabilitation Outlook, 4*(2), 1-11.

Delespaul, P. A. E. G., & deVries, M. W. (1987). The daily life of ambulatory chronic mental patients. *Journal of Nervous and Mental Disease, 175,* 537-544.

Ferguson, D. D. (1997). Protocols in therapeutic recreation: Dancing on the bubble. In D. M. Compton (Ed.), *Issues in therapeutic recreation: Toward the new millennium* (2nd ed.), (pp. 403-417). Champaign, IL: Sagamore.

Fisher, J. (1973). Is casework effective? A review. *Social Work, 1S,* 5-20.

Finnell, A., Card, J., & Menditto, A. (1997). A comparison of appropriate behavior scores of residents with chronic schizophrenia participating in therapeutic recreation services and vocational rehabilitation services. *Therapeutic Recreation Journal, 31,* 10-21.

Flexner, A. (1925). *Medical education: A comparative study.* New York: MacMillan.

Gabor, P. A., & Grinnell, R. M., Jr. (1994). *Evaluation and quality improvement in the human services.* Boston: Allyn & Bacon.

Holahan, C. J., Moos, R. H., & Schaefer, J. A. (1996). Coping, stress resistance, and growth: Conceptualizing adaptive functioning. In M. Zeidner, & N. S. Endler (Eds.), *Handbook of coping: Theory, research and application* (pp. 24-43). New York: Wiley.

Jacobson, W. (1998). Defining the quality of practitioner research. *Adult Education Quarterly, 48,* 125-139.

Joint Commission on Accreditation of Healthcare Organizations. (1997). *Using outcomes to improve performance in long-term care and sub-acute settings.* Oakbrook Terrace, IL: Author.

Jordan, D., & Roland, M. (1999). An examination of differences between academics and practitioners in frequency of reading research and attitudes toward research. *Journal of Leisure Research, 31,* 166-170.

Kazdin, A. E. (2006). Arbitrary metrics: Implications for identifying evidence-based treatments. *American Psychologist, 61*, 42–49.

Katz, J. M., & Green, E. (1998). *Managing quality: A guide to system-wide performance management in healthcare* (2nd ed.). St. Louis, MO: Mosby.

Klosek, M., & Crilly, R. G. (1997). *Leisure competence measure.* London, Ontario, Canada: Leisure Competence Measure Data System.

Kopelowicz, A., & Liberman, R. P. (1995). Biobehavioral treatment and rehabilitation of schizophrenia. *Harvard Review of Psychiatry, 3*(2), 55-64.

Kiresuk, T. J., Smith, A., & Cardillo, J. E. (Eds.). (1994). *Goal attainment scaling: Applications, theory, and measurement.* Hillsdale, NJ: Erlbaum & Associates.

Liberman, R. P., & Kopelowicz, A. (1995). Basic elements in biobehavioral treatment and rehabilitation of schizophrenia. *International Clinical Psychopharmacology, 9* (Suppl 5), 51-58.

Lindsey, D., & Kirk, S. A. (1993). The continuing crisis in social work research: Conundrum or solvable problem? *Journal of Social Work Education, 28*, 370-383.

Lukoff, D., Snyder, K., Ventura, J., & Neuchterlein, K. (1984). Life events, familial stress, and coping in the developmental course of schizophrenia. *Schizophrenia Bulletin, 10*, 258-292.

Malkin, M. J., Coyle, C. P., & Carruthers, C. (1998). Efficacy research in recreational therapy. In F. Brasile, T. K. Skalko, & j. burlingame (Eds.), *Perspectives in recreational therapy* (pp. 141-164). Ravensdale, WA: Idyll Arbor.

McSkimming, S. A. (1996). Creating a cultural norm for research and research utilization in a clinical agency. *Western Journal of Nursing Research, 18*, 606-611.

Moggi, F., & Crosby, P. (1999). Dual diagnosis patients in substance-abuse treatment: Relationship of general coping and substance-specific coping to 1-year outcome. *Addiction, 94*, 1805-1817.

Moggi, F., Ouimette, P. C., Finney, J. W., & Moos, R. H. (1999). Dual diagnosis patients in substance-abuse treatment: Relationship of general coping and substance-abuse coping to 1-year outcome. *Addiction, 94*, 1805-1817.

Moos, R. H. (1993). *Coping responses inventory.* Odessa, FL: Psychological Assessment Resources.

Patrick, G. (1997). Making clinical research happen. In D. M. Compton (Ed.), *Issues in therapeutic recreation: Toward the new millennium* (2nd ed.) (pp. 327-345). Champaign, IL: Sagamore.

Perkins, E. R., Simnett, I., & Wright, L. (1999). Creative tensions in evidence-based practice. In E. R. Perkins, I. Simnett, & L. Wright (Eds.), *Evidence-based health promotion* (pp. 1-22). New York: John Wiley & Sons.

Ratner, N. B. (2006). Evidence-based practice: An examination of its ramifications for the practice of speech-language pathology. *Language, Speech, and Hearing Services in Schools, 37*, 257–267.

Reid, W. J. (1994). The empirical practice movement. *Social Service Review, 68*, 165-184.

Russoniello, C. V. (2003). The efficacy of therapeutic recreation: Back to the future. In N. J. Stumbo (Ed.), *Client outcomes in therapeutic recreation service* (pp. 111-126). State College, PA: Venture.

Savell, K. S., Huston, A. D., & Malkin, M. J. (1993). Collaborative research: Bridging the gap between practitioners and researchers/educators. In M. J. Malkin, & C. Z. Howe (Eds.), *Research in therapeutic recreation* (pp. 77-96). State College, PA: Venture.

Schalock, R. L. (1995). *Outcome-based evaluation.* New York: Plenum.

Shank, J., & Coyle, C. (2002). *Therapeutic recreation in health promotion and rehabilitation.* State College, IL: Venture.

Siegel, D. H. (1984). Defining empirically based practice. *Social Work, 29,* 325-331.

Sluyter, G. V. (1998). *Improving organizational performance.* Thousand Oaks, CA: Sage.

Straus, S. E., Richardson, W. S., Glasziou, P., & Haynes, R. R. (2005). *Evidence-based medicine: How to practice and teach EBM* (3rd ed). Edinburgh: Churchill-Livingstone.

Stricker, G. (1992). The relationship of research to clinical practice. *American Psychologist, 47*(4), 543-549.

Swindle, R. W., Cronkite, R. C., & Moos, R. H. (1989). Life stressors, social resources, coping, and the 4-year course of unipolar depression. *Journal of Abnormal Psychology, 98,* 468-477.

Tarrier, N., Sharpe, L., Beckett, R., Harwood, S., Baker, A., & Yusopoff, L. (1993). A trial of two cognitive behavioral methods of treating drug-resistant residual psychotic symptoms in schizophrenic patients II. Treatment-specific changes in coping and problem-solving skills. *Social Psychiatry and Psychiatric Epidemiology, 28,* 5-10.

Thomas, E. J. (1984). *Designing interventions for the helping professions.* Beverly Hills, CA: Sage.

Uniform Data System for Medical Rehabilitation. (1995). *Guide for the use of the uniform data set for medical rehabilitation (Adult FIM), Version 4.0.* Buffalo, NY: State University of New York at Buffalo.

U.S. Department of Labor, Bureau of Labor Statistics. (2007). Occupational outlook handbook, 2006-07 edition, Recreational Therapists, on the Internet at http://www.bls.gov/oco/ocos082.htm (visited March 18, 2007).

Widmer, M. A., Zabriskie, R. B., & Wells, M. S. (2003). Program evaluation: Collecting data to measure outcomes. In N. J. Stumbo (Ed.), *Client outcomes in therapeutic recreation service* (pp. 201-220). State College, PA: Venture.

Witkin, S. L. (1996). If empirical practice is the answer, then what is the question? *Social Work Research, 20,* 69-76.

Witt, P. A. (1988). Therapeutic recreation research: Past, present, and future. *Therapeutic Recreation Journal, 22*(1), 14-23.

Witt, P. A., & Ellis, G. D. (1987). *The leisure diagnostic battery users manual.* State College, PA: Venture.

World Health Organization. (2001). *International classification of functioning, disability, and health.* Geneva, Switzerland: World Health Organization.

Zubin, J. (1986). Implications of the vulnerability model for the DSM-IV with special reference to schizophrenia. In T. Millon, & G. L. Klerman (Eds.), *Contemporary directions in psychopathology: Toward the DSM-IV* (pp. 473-494). New York: Guilford Press.

CHAPTER 29

Perspective: Clinical Research Methods and Mandates

George Patrick, Ph.D., CTRS™

The idea that science can provide important information for making medical decisions has only recently become a reality. The first double-blind experiment in the history of medicine was done in 1835 (Jonas, Linde, & Walach, 1999). Clinical trials are a more recent event. The first randomized controlled trial occurred only 61 years ago. The scientific basis for approving drugs for medical use by the U.S. Food and Drug Administration is only 27 years old. Only in the past 17 years has a serious emphasis on evidence-based medicine (EBM)—the use of published research findings to guide decisions in patient care—occurred (Evidence-Based Medicine Working Group, 1992).

In conventional medicine, an evidence-based approach to medical decision making has been needed for a long time. In medical practice, the introduction, adoption, and abandonment of procedures had been influenced predominantly by social prestige, power, or potential profit rather than by evidence of public benefit (Collins, 1982; DiGiacomo, 1987; McKinlay, 1981). Because the relatively new profession of therapeutic recreation (TR) is quite a latecomer, adjunct to medical treatments, a similar need is even more acutely evident. TR has relatively little social prestige, power, or potential for profit. TR finds itself seeking legitimacy in a culture that is embracing an evidence-based model; thus, it is thrust into the somewhat uncomfortable role of providing evidence of efficacy for much, if not all, of its treatments.

On the other hand, the last two decades have witnessed a wave of specialty medicine that has been less personal and more costly. To counteract the drastic rise in the cost of medical treatment, cost-containment efforts (managed care among them) have resulted in billing by procedures done, rather than focusing upon alleviation of troublesome chronic symptoms, improved function, or increased quality of life in satisfied patients (Ornish, Schweritz, & Billings, 1998). Only in the last several years has there been a countershift to more general medical practice that has opened up the concept of customized care with more patient input and personal choice. Another wave of complementary and alternative medical (CAM) practices has been hard to ignore in that 62% of adult patients have sought out nontraditional health practitioners at a recently estimated $47 billion per year, non-insured, out-of-pocket expense (Barnes, Powell-Griner, McFann, & Nahin, 2004).

The recent interest in complementary and alternative medicine (CAM) provides useful and meaningful parallels for TR. Some of the CAM modalities include acupuncture, massage, chiropractic, herbal medicines, meditation and prayer, electromagnetics, diet and nutrition, and mind-body interventions. Both CAM and TR only recently came into the view of modern medical treatment. Both CAM and TR claim to have special benefits not met by conventional medicine. Both CAM and TR usually emphasize a holistic approach. For patients, this means that the psychosocial aspects of their illness are attended to. Indeed, TR practitioners, much like CAM practitioners, spend more time addressing "high-touch, low-tech" psychosocial needs, which TR specialists do through leisure activities, and thus leave their patients more satisfied than with their visits to conventional practitioners (Ernst, Resch, & Hill, 1997).

CAM and TR share a perspective that emphasizes using health enhancement in the treatment of disease and teaching patients to be proactive and self-responsible in addressing early warning and lifestyle factors that put them at risk. Both CAM and TR are more focused on healing than cure. Both CAM and TR are not only more likely to spend more time per session but also require more sessions, recognizing that behavior and lifestyle change are rarely the effect of one-trial learning. Both CAM and TR look to evaluate patient outcomes rather than count procedures. CAM and TR goals are stated in terms that respond to patient complaints and symptoms rather than offering specific procedures and evaluating treatment in terms of biomarkers (such as increased arterial flow, tumor reduction, reduced white blood cell count, etc.).

One of the more troublesome issues shared by CAM and TR is measurement of treatments that purport to affect the broad complexity of disease often by supporting the equally complex power of the body to heal itself. Measurements of clinical medicine are difficult, especially so in evaluating the outcome of chronic disease. Thomas (1994) demonstrated that nearly 80% of those who seek medical care get better no matter what the treatment. Jonas (1994) called this the "80% rule," meaning that data collected on novel therapies delivered in an enthusiastic clinical environment typically yield positive outcomes in nearly 80% of patients so treated. When studied rigorously, our most accepted treatments, apparently effective under the 80% rule, are not scientifically validated "due to factors unrelated to treatment, such as the ability of the body to heal (often enhanced by expectation), statistical regression to the mean (a measurement problem), and self-delusion (sometimes called bias)" (Jonas, 1994, p. 6). Jonas and Levine (1999) continued:

> The methods of clinical research—especially blinding [the participant and/or the clinician not knowing the treatment regimen] and the randomized controlled trial—have emerged as powerful approaches to better identifying to what extent the outcome can be attributed to the treatment. These methods must be used rigorously, however, if we wish to examine both the social and statistical forces that shape our perception of reality. (Jonas & Levine, 1999, p. 6)

It is very unlikely that even most TR treatment (like CAM) can be examined by large, rigorous, randomized trials. Current methods for examining TR practices or, for that matter, chronic disease, are not adequately measured by reductive science. Other methods must be developed. Among these are observation and outcomes research as methods for obtaining acceptable evidence for the use of low-risk therapies in treatment of chronic disease (Pincus, 1997).

Evidence-Based Practice as a Survival Tool

To state the obvious, every health-related profession has the responsibility to develop evidence-based practices as much as possible and within ethical boundaries. Without evidence-based practices, survival within traditional medicine is threatened. Stumbo (2003) stressed the importance of evidence-based practice in TR as improving "the predictability and causality of service outcomes and provides regulators, payers, and consumers increased assurance of quality care" (p. 25-26). Systematic collection of data from quality-improvement studies, program evaluations, retrospective and/or concurrent chart reviews, cost analyses, and studies of patient compliance with crucial lifestyle changes are all valuable sources for developing evidence-based practice. This can be accomplished by a TR service providing practice validation for its immediate customers (patients, physicians, and administrators), but eventually such evidence-based practice will have to be replicated with an acceptable number of cases to form a body of empirical research, publication with rigorous peer review in order to be valued by the healthcare industry.

Regardless of the relatively low cost and the low risk of TR services, patients, other medical personnel, and third-party payers (public and private insurers) rightfully want to know the probability of benefit from these TR practices. This information can be obtained from either randomized clinical trials or systematic observational outcome studies. Three evaluative criteria should be employed:

1. Carefully diagnosed (both disease and functional status) participants;
2. Clinical relevance and reliability of the outcome measures; and
3. The number of participants entered in and then analyzed at the end of the study.

How can TR improve the health-related quality of life for individuals with illness or impairment? To fail to answer this question with data from clinical research is to ensure professional irrelevance and risk annihilation as an allied-health provider. A scientific basis for clinical practice is a necessity. No longer is it just a question of whether clinical research is valuable, important, or necessary. It is also a matter of survival. We need to get clinical research underway as a part of ordinary business.

The Practice of Evidence-Based TR

Some of the minimal requirements for practicing evidence-based treatment were chronicled by Jonas and Levine (1999) in Table 29.1. No TR program should be proposed without a serious search of the research literature for support. In addition to searching through TR-related journals such as *Therapeutic Recreation Journal, Annual in Therapeutic Recreation, American Journal of Recreation Therapy*, and texts such as *Benefits of Therapeutic*

Recreation: A Consensus View (Coyle, Kinney, Riley, & Shank, 1991), TR clinicians can make evidence-based decisions though the internet from sources such as MEDLINE at www.medline.nlm.nih.gov, PSYCH ABSTRACTS at www.apa.org/psychinfo/pa.html, Best Evidence Selection at www.webcom.com/mjljweb/jrnlclb/index.htm, and Agency for Healthcare Research and Quality at www.ahrq.gov/clinic/epicix.htm. Where no evidence is found, one can reasonably assume that there is little or no clinical evidence for the intervention/therapy considered. A clinician's skill and ability to search for and evaluate quality data can assist both the clinician and patient in making treatment decisions.

Acceptable evidence of healthcare quality comes essentially from patient outcomes. In patient terms, health-related quality of life is the crucial outcome. Health-related quality of life is, at least in part, measurable. Insofar as it is quantifiable and replicable, it is amenable to scientific investigation. The remainder of this chapter addresses how program evaluation (quality assessment) can be translated into clinical research. Abbreviated case studies are offered as examples as steps toward the development of evidence-based practice that can occasionally lead to clinical research.

Begin with Your Mission

When I began (1992) as the new chief of what was then called the Patient Activities Department of the Clinical Center for the National Institutes of Health, I initiated a process to determine the TR staff perception of what our program services are and what was the relative importance of each component. We served an extremely diverse set of research patient diagnoses with 24 staff, about half of whom were CTRSs™. Our department services were about half treatment (physician referral) and half open (drop in/special events) recreation. When the TR staff was asked to rate the relative value of the various program offerings, the treatment components were rated more highly. It became obvious that both staff clinical training and program rebalancing were needed. Still, there were considerable conceptual changes that had to be made. This chapter will present a number of case studies of how we moved from program evaluation projects to outcome research. The case studies below became an important part of revising the mission of our program.

Case Study #1: What Symptoms Are Patients Presenting?

This study involved the entire department. We collected a retrospective (chart reviews over the previous six months) by each of our 14 patient care units (representing different admitting institutes and diagnostic groups). A simple tally (frequency count) of symptoms mentioned in patient assessments or treatment plans indicated that our TR staff was not clinically oriented toward symptom management or reduction. We then collected patient symptoms addressed in treatment plans for the following six months. In this period, our staff became keenly aware of what we were measuring, and the next tally done at three months was far more robust.

Commentary: Our therapists initially were not treating symptoms associated with disease or loss of function. This project began what could be called the symptom reduction movement within our Patient Activities Department (a title soon to be more appropriately re-labeled in the ensuing years). Furthermore, we observed that one symptom, pain, was

Table 29.1
Minimum Guidelines for Assessment of Study Validity (Jonas & Levine, 1999)

Purpose of Study	Sample	Validity	Reliability
Therapy	Was there concealed random allocation to comparison groups?	Were outcome measures of known or probable clinical importance?	Were there few patients lost to follow-up compared with the number of bad outcomes (<20%)?
Diagnosis	Were the patients those to whom you would want to apply the test in practice?	Was an objective or reproducible diagnostic standard applied to all participants?	Was a blinded assessment of the test and diagnostic standards ("gold standard") done?
Prognosis	Was the group being assessed (the inception cohort) gathered early in the course of the study?	Was there an objective or reproducible assessment of clinically important outcomes?	Were there few lost to follow-up compared with the number of bad outcomes (<20%)?
Etiology	Was there a clearly defined comparison group, or those at risk for or having the outcome of interest?	Was there blinding of observers to the status of the exposure to the outcome of interest?	
Reviews	Were there explicit criteria for selecting articles and rating?	Was there a comprehensive search for all relevant articles? Were negative and unpublished articles found?	
Observational	Were there outcome measures of known or probable clinical importance?	Were there few lost to follow-up compared with the number of bad outcomes (<20%)?	Was the probability of benefit reported worth the inconvenience, risk of side effects, and costs of the treatment?	Were confidence intervals reported, and were they narrow?

almost ubiquitous with our medical-surgical research patients regardless of diagnosis. Realizing that many of our TR staff did not have the necessary clinical skills to relieve or reduce symptoms, we embarked on a four-month relaxation training course that included meditative breathing, guided imagery, progressive relaxation, progressive muscle relaxation, autogenic training, and both focused and mindfulness meditation. Furthermore, the TR staff took the lead in developing a cross-disciplinary team to address pain management with our rehabilitation colleagues. When we merged our department with rehabilitation, we adopted a new name more appropriate to our mission: "Recreation Therapy." In the ensuing decade, the recreation therapy section moved from 25% therapy and 75% recreation to 75% therapy and 25% recreation in gradual steps.

In mid-1999, the NIH instituted a new pain management service. In December 1999, a mandate came from the Joint Commission on Healthcare Organizations (JCAHO) that pain would be treated as the fifth vital sign (Yadgood, Miller, & Matthews, 2000). All patients were to be assessed for pain (documentation of that assessment was required). The Rehabilitation Medicine Department, led by RT, was already providing services that became an integral part of the pain management team. RT staff provided pain reduction service through relaxation training, biofeedback, light exercise, yoga, meditation, and a wide variety of distraction and/or focus activities.

Next, Introduce Program Evaluation

Professional standards of practice, codes of ethics, healthcare administrations, and accreditation bodies such as the Commission on Accreditation of Rehabilitation Facilities (now called the Rehabilitation Accreditation Commission) and JCAHO required therapeutic recreation specialists to do some program evaluation in the form of quality assessment (QA). What is not required is to evaluate all health-related outcomes nor are there prescribed outcomes. A clinician may choose from myriad possible outcomes to assess program quality. In that freedom resides a fair amount of room to take risks. The author's experience with a large number of therapeutic recreation specialists has revealed a wide range in their willingness to take conceptual risks. Will we only measure that which will affirm what we already know? Or will we be willing to risk finding out what we don't know, especially if there is a chance that a negative finding could occur?

QA appears to be the best entree for clinical research, since every clinical program must have some form of evaluation study. Furthermore, the recent emphasis on measuring patient outcomes provides a fertile field for extending some of these evaluation studies into research on clinical effectiveness by increasing the scientific rigor. When quality assessment is inconsequential, as when the data affirm what is already well documented or fails to measure important health-related outcomes, such as symptom reduction or improvements in function, then a clinical research agenda gains naught. What needs nurturance is the willingness to risk an investigation into the unknown or less well-documented areas of knowledge.

Case Study #2: The Effects of Animal-Assisted Therapy (AAT) on Pediatric Anxiety

A significant portion of our staff and volunteer time was spent in frequent dog visits. While AAT is not a unique program offering in TR services, it is not well supported by a body of literature. A treatment versus control (delayed treatment) measured state anxiety (STAI-C) in 76 pediatric patients. Statistical analysis showed no significant difference between those patients who received AAT versus the controls. Only when the patients were split by diagnostic group did the children with HIV show greater benefit over controls compared to the larger group of children with cancer. Since the data were planned to be scored cumulatively and the numbers were small, we did not hold this one finding with strong confidence.

Commentary: We did learn to randomize patients without depriving any of AAT, but this was a program evaluation project rather than an outcome research. We had little control over many intervening variables, including the period of time that passed between the end of the AAT intervention and the administration of the posttest, because children often were whisked to their next procedure before the post STAI-C could be administered until perhaps an hour later. This project exceeded the ordinary bounds of program evaluation by its use of a standardized test, not an ordinary part of our standard assessment tools. Such use would have to gain administrative approval as a regular and ordinary assessment or go through the research process via an Institutional Review Board (IRB) approval. A related research protocol was approved some six years later by the National Cancer Institute IRB. It included separate randomized treatment and control groups and is using cortisol as a biomarker. *Source: Holly Parker, CTRS™, Kristin Johnsen, CTRS™, and Linda Wheeler, CTRS™*

Clinicians need to find valid, reliable, and usable measurement tools and to learn their psychometric properties by carefully reading the manuals and journal articles in which the tool is used and, finally, will need to practice using the tool with patients. Making time for this while carrying on the expected direct patient care requires both vision and discipline. The choice of measurement tools (formal assessment, questionnaire, scale, or behavioral observation) is one of the most challenging issues in program evaluation. While research standards exist by which to select valid and reliable measurement tools, the standards for program evaluation need not be as stringent as evidence-based science. Quality assessment standards require only that each clinical site set and meet their own standards. Measurement tools never seem to be totally suited to the patient population of a particular facility or brief enough to administer easily to patients. Finding an appropriate measurement tool usually requires a literature review of more than one's own discipline. Again, the Internet sources previously cited can provide the convenience and speed of a desktop search.

Case Study #3: Evaluation of a Pediatric Assessment Tool

The Draw a Person in the Hospital (DPH) was presented as an intriguing diagnostic tool at an ATRA Annual Conference in Colorado. Under a departmental screening protocol, 15 drawings were collected and analyzed according to the test manual. Participants were outpatients ranging in diagnoses of HIV, rhabdomyosarcomas, leukemia, glioma brain tumor, and a bone marrow donor. The information gained from the scoring yielded what was considered to be diagnostically valuable in revealing patient concerns worthy of being addressed by the TR and entire psycho-social treatment team. All 15 pediatric patients positively received the DPH. No child uttered a grumble about his/her willingness to participate in the drawing. Qualitatively, the value added by the completion and analysis of the drawings according to the manual of instructions was judged significant enough to warrant utilization of the pediatric assessment tool.

Commentary: Standardized tests need to be "trialed" by a small number of patients to determine their clinical usefulness in a particular setting. DPH standardized drawings were shown to be an effective measure of self-expression for diagnostic purposes in this setting; therefore, the DPH was placed in the pediatric TR assessment toolbox. It should be noted that many assessment tools require specialized training and/or specific professional credentials. *Source: Karen Perkins, CTRS*™

To boldly choose a QA topic that has a chance to generate meaningful clinical research means that the results are in question (and could possibly be negative). A good example of this kind of risk-taking can be found in Caldwell, Adolph, and Gilbert (1989), who questioned the long-term effect of leisure counseling and found results contrary to their expectation (leisure education, in this setting, did not help the clients overcome negative outcomes such as boredom). They used this negative finding to reconsider and modify their leisure education program. Embracing risk is an inherent aspect of clinical research.

Case Study #4: The Relationship between Boredom, Depression and Leisure Satisfaction in the Recovery from Alcohol Dependence

Two symptoms exhibited by those in recovery from alcohol dependence include boredom and depression. This program evaluation examined the effect of a structured recreation therapy program on adult patients' perception of boredom, depression, and leisure satisfaction. As part of the TR program contract with an alcoholic treatment inpatient unit, *Free Time Boredom Measurement* (FTBM), *Hamilton Depression Rating Scale* (HAM-D) (administered by specially trained nurses), and *Leisure Satisfaction Scale-Short Form* (LSS) were administered to 55 patients as a TR program evaluation at three intervals during their 28-day treatment regimen. In all four scales of the *FTBM* (physical involvement, mental involvement, meaningfulness, and speed of time), positive changes were noted in the first two weeks of treatment but leveled off in the final two weeks. Similar changes were mirrored in the LSS and HAM-D. The usefulness of this triad of assessment was clinically helpful. The TR recognized that the first two weeks were crucial in developing treatment "traction," and while the chart plotting the relationship between this triad of assessments provided visual evidence of close correlation, no analysis could be done to determine which of the three variables had the most influence.

Commentary: This program evaluation was used as a stepping-stone to a formal clinical research protocol currently awaiting data analysis and write up. *Source: Michael Duquette, CTRS*™*, Mark Mattiko, CTRS*™*, and George Patrick, CTRS.*™

Program evaluation can be done individually or in teams. The former works better when the individual has sole control over the program to be evaluated. The latter has appeal in that teams can provide the social support to carry on through individual discouragement (Williamson & Stroot, 1994). In either case, an outside coworker can provide data collection without bias caused by patients trying to please their resident therapist. This author has seen both work and does not recommend one exclusively over the other.

A dangerous misconception is that a program must be perfect and theoretically sound before one dares evaluate it. All programs have less-than-perfect circumstances, making program outcomes less than generalizable. Bloom, Hastings, and Madaus (1971) suggested that imperfect programs provide the greatest opportunity to improve effectiveness. Before improving effectiveness, program results need to be measured. Answering the question "What do we want our patients to get from of this program?" also tells us what needs to be measured.

Case Study #5: The Effect of Medical Play on Patient Retention

A program evaluation was done to determine the effects of pediatric medical play on research study drop-out rates. Children's anxiety and fear of research medical procedures on a multi-institute (all pediatric research protocols except diagnoses of cancer and HIV) inpatient care unit had not yet received routine medical play (explaining, modeling, and acting out roles of nurse, anesthesiologist, surgeon) using gowns, masks, play medical instruments such as intravenous drip poles, simulated blood draws, full-body MRI, or other specific medical procedures that each child would be experiencing. The NIH pediatric cancer and HIV program has a long, successful history of using TR-led medical play. It was deemed unethical to randomly deny some children of this service to provide a comparison of treatment/no treatment. However, the newly formed multi-institute pediatric unit did not yet have a medical play program. The TR service proposed a trial of medical play comparing the drop-out rate of previous patients (19 of 60 dropped out during the non-medical play period) with the next consecutive 60 child patients receiving medical play (only one of 60 dropped out). The attending physician attributed the reduction in dropouts due to reduced anxiety and fear (crying/screaming) in the children and their parents' relative comfort over their considerably less emotionally distressed children. Medical play was enthusiastically accepted as a required modality both prior to and after medical procedures, saving expensive staff hours and reduction of lost data.

Commentary: The patient care unit's Attending Physician and Research Nurse stated that each patient who failed to complete the protocol cost thousands of dollars in medical tests and researcher time, not including standard medical care, a substantial savings of time and money. Their support during a proposed administrative reduction in staff allowed the TR service to maintain its staffing level. This program evaluation was not allowed to become a randomized clinical trial because the demonstration of medical play was so effective that it was seen as unethical to withhold it from a control group. *Source: Elvera Sales and Frances Byrd, CTRS*

Program evaluation is an expected part of offering a TR patient service (ATRA Standards of Practice, Standard 4, 1993; ATRA Code of Ethics, Principle 7, 1998).

At NIH, program evaluation does not need administrative approval, nor does it require approval of a human subjects protection committee (Institutional Review Board), as provided for in the Code of Federal Regulations (45 CFR 46, 1983). The evaluation can be ongoing, with points along the way selected to collate the data. But data alone do not complete an evaluation report. The data must be analyzed and interpreted clearly. A QA analysis requires a discussion of improving the program; and, finally, a forthright statement about the perceived limitations of the evaluation (usually lack of generalizability).

Case Study #6: Fitness Program Impact on Psychosis

This outcome project measured the effect of a fitness program on 11 common symptoms associated with psychosis for 14 adult patients diagnosed with schizophrenia. Patients rated their perceived intensity of symptoms using a visual analogue scale anchored at zero, "not at all," and 100, "very much," in a prepost format. Data were collected over an 18-week period. The 11 symptoms measured were the most frequently reported by these patients before the data collection and fitness program began: low energy, hearing voices, depression, visual hallucinations, boredom, paranoia, lack of motivation, inability to focus on an activity, withdrawal, irritability, and anxiety. Of the 14 participants in this program evaluation, nine had statistically significant symptom reduction, supporting the concept that the fitness program helped these patients manage their schizophrenia-related symptoms. Mean combined pre scores = 36.0; mean post scores = 20.3.

Commentary: The self-reporting of patients with schizophrenia raised questions of report reliability because of various cognitive deficits associated with this condition. Specifically, "low energy" was interpreted differently from the therapist's intention (lethargy) versus whether the patient participant felt energized or exhausted after the fitness group activity. The recreation therapist felt that "bored" might need to be changed to "feeling bored." If this program evaluation were to be repeated, the recreation therapist/fitness instructor suggested that she would clarify the meanings of each symptom prior to beginning such a study. Furthermore, the symptoms of "withdrawal" and "lack of motivation" could be removed from the rating list because, if the patients attended, there was little or no opportunity to express or feel these emotions. In a follow-up program evaluation, data more convincingly showed a reduction in symptom burden as a result of the fitness group. Medical staff (psychiatrists, nurses, psychologists, and a social worker) were appreciative of not only the positive results for their patients, but also for the effort and skill of the recreation therapist in doing this program evaluation. The results of these outcome projects were shared via several professional conference presentations. *Source: Marcia D. Smith, MA, CTRS™, H/FI and Mark J. Mattiko, MS, CTRS™*

Program evaluations and their resulting program improvements are then shared with peers and administration. This sharing demonstrates the value of QA and can enhance the perception of the evaluator's professional competence. Practitioners have little problem using program evaluation results to improve their programs; however, most evaluations yield more questions than they answer. Such questions provide a rationale for further study. At this point, one can either proceed to investigate the spin-off question(s) or consider doing a more sophisticated kind of clinical research. The latter will frequently require additional resources, often attainable only from collaboration from outside the clinical setting, often an academic (university) institution.

Collaborative Research Agreements

Collaboration in clinical research is critical because of the multiple domains, many of which are beyond the scope of TR. Furthermore, sophisticated statistical support is occasionally important to address the complexities of clinical research. Such support may not be available at a clinical site. Program evaluation findings provide a rich source of information to a potential research collaborator, giving that researcher the variables of interest to the clinician, a sense of the clinical team's capacity to collect data, other possible research questions, patient selection, and other issues related to the work site.

First, let's look at why a researcher (academic or clinician with research skills) would want to assist a therapeutic recreation specialist to conduct clinical research. A research collaborator might ask what seems to be a selfish question: "What's in it for me?" Few, if any, professionals can afford to get nothing in return for countless hours of investment. The clinician will have to give the researcher reason to make such an investment. Be prepared to make a sales pitch by offering not only cooperation but the agency's blessing by getting prior administrative approval for such a discussion.

Next, package the initial evaluation study in such a way that it might entice the researcher to follow up. Share not only the findings, but also the secondary questions considered from the initial evaluation study. Intellectual curiosity and investment in the study will weigh heavily in the decision process of the researcher. They are signs of the probability that the clinical side of the bargain will be kept.

While the remainder of this chapter is devoted to clinician/academician collaboration, working with an associate from another clinical discipline also can be mutually beneficial. One multidisciplinary example is provided by an evaluation of the effectiveness of a stress-reduction course. Beyond use of patient self-reports, measuring biological markers to demonstrate effectiveness could be impressive. A study on the effects of a two-day stress-management course for healthcare workers (N=94) with weekly support groups was conducted by Orth-Gomer, Ericksson, Moser, Theorell, and Fredlund (1994). Eight months later, the stress management group showed a six-percent decline in the ratio of LDL/HDL over a randomized, no-treatment control group (N=35), a clearly beneficial reduction in a significant health-risk factor.

Such a course and support group for patients under extraordinary stress might well have a similar effect on blood chemistry. But the researcher might need collaboration with another discipline to develop a strong enough design to control for many of the potentially confounding variables (not to mention the collection of blood samples). Working together, physicians, psychologists, various rehabilitation therapists, and nurses can optimize the treatment, design, or data collection to ensure a better study.

The Collaborative Research Model developed by Savell, Huston, and Malkin (1993) recognized the contributions that both clinicians and researchers make to the research process. "Through this model, the abilities and resources of practitioners and researchers are optimized, and each group comes to perceive the centrality and interdependence of its own, as well as the other's role" (p. 84).

This model involves a nine-stage process. An outline of the Collaborative Research Model is given in Figure 29.1. The involvement of the educator/researcher may not begin until Stage 5. Some stages are practitioner-driven, other stages are the responsibility of the researcher, and in some stages both are responsible for implementation. In a discussion with M. Malkin (personal communication, January 20, 2000), it was revealed that the authors collectively now believe that stages 4 and 5 could well be transposed, effectively bringing the researcher in earlier in the process.

A cooperative research agreement should be a formally written document that recognizes the commitment of time, energy, and resources needed for the project. Using the Collaborative Research Model as an outline, the agreement should explain the enterprise from the point of entry of the researcher (stage 4 or 5) to the criteria for authorship.

Preparing to Conduct Research

Since most healthcare facilities are geared to provide clinical service, separate resources for research may be rare and limited. Authorization to do clinical research does not come easily. Chief executive officers or even clinical department directors are not usually trained to approve research protocols, and thus the easiest answer is "No." As plans are considered, try to identify and anticipate the "sticking points" for the administrators; plan to adjust or modify them, avoid them, or accept some limitation in the pace of the study's progress.

This author recommends a solid way to enter a clinical research project is through program evaluation, because such behavior is within the accepted norm of clinical practice. A chief executive officer should receive written program evaluation reports from therapeutic recreation staff as they are completed (again as an ordinary practice). An oral review will ensure that this administrator is aware that the evaluation is taken seriously. This history of evaluation reporting establishes credibility, generates researchable questions-hypotheses, and may allow taking the next step toward clinical research.

The Research Hypothesis and the Role of Theory

Most clinical research projects require a testable research hypothesis. It is true, however, that some clinical studies consist of simple observation over extended periods, and much is learned without hypothesis. Yet the most productive clinical research is generated when a hypothesis is based upon known facts embellished by creative conjecture as to operational mechanisms. "If-then" prediction is the key to hypothesis creation. An example of a hypothesis is: if disoriented nursing-home residents improved their measured reality orientation due to a music-based reality-orientation program, at the same time that randomly assigned controls who received a standard reality orientation program showed no improvement, then music stimulation may enhance the outcome of other similar cognitive functions.

There are many factors and much hard work hidden in such a simple hypothesis. Literature support or personal experience is a prerequisite to expect that music could enhance cognitive function. Considerable study of cognitive function as it is related to reality orientation is also needed. Other factors need consideration, too. What level of intensity or duration (dosage) of music is sufficient to get an effect? What number of patients is required (power analysis) to answer the research question? Can that number of patients be recruited? How will the control group be treated? Are the resources (space, time, money, etc.) required for the study available?

Hypotheses are traditionally stated in the null (negative), i.e., music has no effect on reality orientation. Terms such as "null hypothesis" and "statistical significance" are part of the technical jargon of research that can be a barrier for clinicians. So let's take a no-nonsense look at hypothesis generation.

Even before hypothesis development, research questions should be offered in generous numbers. Research questions are much easier to generate because they are phrased in the

---

Figure 29.1
The Collaborative Research Model

Stage 1
Problem Formulation—identify the topic/issue/concern/need

Stage 2
Review of existing, relevant literature

Stage 3
Hypothesis/Research Question Development—based upon
your interest and the review of the literature

Stage 4
Variable Definition—define the variables you are interested in researching
and operationalize the independent and dependent variables

Stage 5
Collaborative Relationship—with agency researcher
and/or with university TR researcher

Stage 6
Research Design—identify the research design and the
associated data-collection and analysis procedures

Stage 7
Implementation—implement the study

Stage 8
Data Analysis and Interpretation—best conducted by agency or
university researcher with access to computer resources

Stage 9
Disseminating of Results—involves both the dissemination
of findings and implications for service delivery

From Savell, K., Huston, A., & Malkin, M. (1993). Collaborative research: Bridging the gap between practitioners and researchers/educators. In M. Malkin, & C. Howe (Eds.), *Research in therapeutic recreation* (p. 84). State College, PA: Venture.

way we usually think, for example, "Will music improve reality-orientation outcomes?" To turn them into hypotheses and then null hypotheses is best done long after the most worthy research questions are generated, because (null) hypotheses are often phrased in formal language that precludes thoughtful analyses, for example, "Music therapy does not improve reality orientation."

Not only is grounding the research question in theory one of the most practical things to do, it is a crucial criterion for publication acceptance. After a theoretical basis for the research question is identified, a careful reading of that theory and research articles that theory has generated will provide a conceptual map to address threats to the meaningfulness of the results. It is also a way to interpret results in light of either supporting or questioning that theory. Sometimes more than one theory underlies the research question. In that case, the research design might do well to ask sub-questions to test one theory over another (see chapter 26).

The practicality of theory-grounded research, however, does not allay most clinicians' distrust of theory. The sticking point is that practitioners and researchers have different purposes for doing research (Henderson & O'Neill, 1995). Practitioners want to know what treatment works best, and researchers typically want to learn how it works. While collaborative research has great potential, this disparate view of the role of theory is a sticking point that probably needs to be addressed explicitly so that a working understanding of both perspectives can be accommodated.

Scientists/academicians are taught to write in specific technical ways with rigorous discussions of methodology. "Although the traditional ways of teaching [research] writing are being criticized today, the jargon and complex explanations are appropriate for getting research published in the top journals" (Henderson & O'Neill, p. 19). While research "bilingualism" is a desirable trait, it is not necessarily a given in collaborative research between scientist/academician and therapist/clinician.

Research Protocol

The first major task for a clinical research project should be the creation of a research protocol. This document will provide a road map for the performance of the study. The development of a research protocol forces the collaborative research team (or individual investigator) to anticipate problems and facilitate communication between those who will have a part or interest in the investigation. The research protocol provides a template to write for publication (Decker, 1992).

The research protocol should give the background and rationale for the study and a concise statement of a research plan; for example: "A prospective non-concurrent study of health-related quality of life in patients with metastatic lung cancer who receive stress management and relaxation training compared with similar patients receiving only standard hospital care" or "A retrospective study of the role of leisure activities in coping responses of adult patients during hospitalization of periods exceeding seven days." As adapted from Decker (1992), the research protocol scrupulously states its methods including:

1. Definition of patient population for both treatment and control
   a. Inclusion criteria—usually disease or condition diagnostic criteria, age, gender, and medications permitted
   b. Exclusion criteria—conditions making study difficult or impossible such as inability to communicate, expectation to leave before study is completed, list of prohibited medications
2. Outcome definition
   a. Standard clinical definitions
   b. Textbook description of outcomes
   c. Previously recognized study outcomes
3. Specify treatment/intervention
   a. Plan for unforeseen occurrences by submitting cases to unbiased experts
4. Data collection
   a. Specify what, by whom, and how
   b. Timetable, including follow-up
5. Informed consent

A written informed consent document is a requirement for the research protocol (Office for Protection from Research Risks, 1983). In ordinary language, it must simply explain the goal of this research study, the risks and benefits (if any) to the participants, and the principal investigator's name and contact information. Furthermore, it must state that the participant may withdraw at any time without prejudice. The reading level of the consent document in general must not exceed that of the ninth grade and usually is improved if it can be written at a lower level. Consent is not a static process; oral discussion and careful listening to a prospective patient's answers to the question, "What do you understand about your participation in this research study?" will provide a better chance for fully informed consent. Children (minors) have special rules that must be scrupulously followed for obtaining consent by parents and for obtaining assent of children.

6. Participant recruitment
   a. Estimate patient availability
   b. Determine general recruitment approach
   c. Secure commitment and enthusiasm of recruiting staff

Institutional Approval

The research protocol is the document submitted to obtain Institutional Review Board (IRB) approval. No human research project can go forward without such administrative approval. Research approval is required legally (federal) and ethically. An IRB is in an academic (university), clinical research facility, and a clinical setting. In collaborative research between a university researcher and a clinical agency, both the agency and the university must give approval. This conjoint approval is absolutely necessary before the research project begins. This approval is required even before "pilot projects" are initiated.

IRBs have been known to impose sanctions on researchers for beginning research without approval and to rule invalid any data collected before approval. Coyle, Kinney, and Shank (1993) have chronicled the necessity for obtaining institutional support in field-based research. They give the clinician a good idea of what some of the issues (trials and tribulations) are which need to be faced. Coyle, Kinney, and Shank also give a strong rationale for the irreplaceability of field-based (clinical) research in determining the future of TR in the twenty-first century.

The difference between clinical research and quality assessment or quality improvement projects (program evaluation) are worthy of mention again, because program evaluation can be the logical precursor of clinical research. Quality assessment is standard practice for some clinical settings and does not require research approval or patient consent (other than the consent to be treated).

Clinical research ideas can (and do) spring from program evaluations, but as long as information is gathered to evaluate the standard program of care, no research approval is required. The use of existing program evaluation data can provide retrospective information valuable to the profession (Shank, Coyle, Kinney, & Lay, 1995). But whenever information is gathered, either retrospectively or prospectively on experimental or nonstandard treatment in order to answer a research question, IRB research approval is prerequisite regardless of how small a sample is used.

This preparatory period is the best time to determine who the potential co-authors will be and their order on the finished product. There have been recent concerns about the meaning of authorship. For instance, the concept of "honorary co-author" is definitely not in favor. One feature of authorship is the ability to describe and defend the study and manuscript as a whole; the other is the amount of substantive work in the conceptualization or interpretation (not merely the data collection) of the study.

Williamson and Stroot (1994) have discussed collaborative research projects' benefits, limitations, and implications. It is instructive that they recommend a formal agreement laying out ownership of data, access, and publication, and authorship criteria in advance of the study. The use of criteria for authorship may make possible the postponement of the actual authorship decision until the project's end, when the objective criteria can be used to determine which names are listed and in what order.

Conclusion

Conducting quality clinical research in TR is necessary to learn what is effective in providing patients with good health and functions. Such positive results can help ensure that this newly blooming profession manages to survive the healthcare crises over the next decade. We have agendas and models from the 1991 Temple University project on efficacy research and from the Research Agenda for the National Center for Medical Rehabilitation Research (NIH, 1993). We have evidence that practitioners of clinical therapeutic recreation have become increasingly interested in pursuing research as a survival strategy. For example, TR clinician O'Dea-Evans' (1992, p. 1) newsletter message listed 10 priorities for action by therapeutic recreators to ensure the survival of TR. Note that all 10 focus on research:

1. Read and collect effectiveness research (inside and outside TR).
2. Develop quality assurance plans that systematically collect effectiveness data.
3. Investigate your facility's policy on human-subject research.
4. Develop questions on leisure functioning to include on your facility's follow-up surveys or your own department survey.
5. Volunteer your agency as a site for graduate and doctoral student research.

6. Find a research mentor.
7. Develop a research project for your agency.
8. Take a research methods or statistics class.
9. Publish your results.
10. Set a goal with a deadline to complete at least one item on this list.

Developing a clinical research agenda is a facility-by-facility effort. The time to do such often comes in the hours after clinical care and documentation are completed. If we build the momentum from solid program evaluation (QA or QI), the logic, effort, and support to mount a clinical research project flows more naturally. At that point, an invitation for collaboration with the academic community or from other clinical disciplines seems most appropriate.

Collaborative clinical research is probably the best opportunity to develop an empirically based therapeutic recreation efficacy knowledge bank. Without it, "others will determine when and how we practice and will control whether we are compensated for the services we deliver" (Seibert, 1991, p. 7). When the clinician drives the research project (initiating collaborative research with the academic community or other clinical disciplines from the work done in program evaluation), a mutually beneficial relationship is likely. Clinical research can be a promising reality if it is an "inside job." If we believe that TR makes a real difference in our patients' lives, then you and I ought to design and conduct increasingly rigorous studies that have a chance of verifying the full range of our effectiveness.

Discussion Questions

1. Why should TR clinicians do research?
2. Who should clinicians go to for assistance in doing research? Why?
3. Why does Patrick suggest doing program evaluation as a first step before considering a research protocol?
4. How does a clinician go about assuring fully informed consent from a patient to participate in research?
5. What are some of the features that complementary and alternative medicine shares with TR as far as the needs for and kinds of research?
6. Patrick shared six case studies. Which would you most be interested in following up as a clinical research topic? Why? What would be your first several (5-7) steps?

References

American Therapeutic Recreation Association. (2000). *Standards for practice of therapeutic recreation*. Alexandria, VA: Author.

American Therapeutic Recreation Association. (1998). *Code of ethics*. Hattiesburg, MS: Author.

Barnes, P., Powell-Griner, E., McFann, K., & Nahin, R. (May 27, 2004). Complementary and alternative medicine use among adults: United States, 2002. Advance data from vital and health statistics. *Centers for Disease Control, 343*, 1-4.

Bloom, B., Hastings, J., & Madaus, G. (1971). *Handbook on formative and summative evaluation of student learning.* New York: McGraw-Hill.

Caldwell, L., Adolph, S., & Gilbert, A. (1989). Caution! Leisure counselors at work: Long-term effects of leisure counseling. *Therapeutic Recreation Journal, 23*(4), 41-49.

Collins, H. (1982). *Sociology of scientific knowledge: A source book.* Bath, England: Bath University Press.

Compton, D. (1989). Epilogue: On shaping a future for therapeutic recreation. In D. Compton (Ed.), *Issues in therapeutic recreation: A profession in transition* (pp. 484-500). Champaign, IL: Sagamore.

Coyle, C., Kinney, W., Riley, B., & Shank, J. (Eds.). (1991). *Benefits of therapeutic recreation: A consensus view.* Ravensdale, WA: Idyll Arbor.

Coyle, C., Kinney, W. & Shank, J. (1993). Trials and tribulations in field-based research in therapeutic recreation. In M. Malkin, & C. Howe (Eds.), *Research in therapeutic recreation* (pp. 207-232). State College, PA: Venture.

Decker, J. (1992). *Protomechanics.* Washington, D.C.: U.S. Department of Health and Human Services (NIH publication no. 92-2499).

DiGiacomo, S. (1987). Biomedicine as a cultural system: An anthropologist in the kingdom of the sick. *Encounters with Biomedicine, 14,* 315-346.

Evidence-Based Medicine Working Group. (1992). Evidence-based medicine: A new approach to teaching the practice of medicine, *JAMA, 268,* 2420-2425.

Ernst, E., Resch, K., & Hill, S. (1997). Do complementary practitioners have a better bedside manner than physicians? *Journal of Research in Sociology of Medicine, 90,* 118-119.

Henderson, K., & O'Neill, J. (1995). Has research contributed to the advancement of professional practice? *Parks and Recreation, 30*(1), 17-20.

Jonas, W. (1994). Therapeutic labeling and the 80% rule. *Bridges, 5*(1), 4-6.

Jonas, W., & Levine, J. (1999). Introduction: Models of medicine and healing. In W. Jonas, & J. Levine (Eds.), *Essentials of complementary and alternative medicine.* Philadelphia: Lippincott, Williams, & Wilkins.

Jonas, W., Linde, K., & Walach, H. (1999). How to practice evidence-based complementary and alternative medicine. In W. Jonas, & J. Levin (Eds.), *Essentials of complementary and alternative medicine.* Philadelphia, PA: Lippincott, Williams, & Wilkins.

McKinlay, J. (1981). From "promising report" to "standard procedure": Seven stages in the career of a medical innovation. *Health and Society, 59,* 374-411.

National Institutes of Health. (1993). *Research plan for the National Center for Medical Rehabilitation Research.* Washington, D.C.: U.S. Department of Health and Human Services (NIH Publication No. 93-3509).

National Therapeutic Recreation Society. (2004). *Standards of practice for therapeutic recreation service.* Arlington, VA: National Recreation and Park Association.

O'Dea-Evans, P. (1992, Spring). President's message. *Therapeutic Recreators for Recovery* Newsletter.

Ornish, D., Schweritz, L., & Billings, J. (1998). Intensive lifestyle changes for reversal of coronary heart disease. *JAMA, 280,* 2001-2007.

Office for Protection from Research Risks. (1983). Title 45 Code of Federal Regulations Part 46. Washington, D.C.: U. S. Government Printing Office.

Orth-Gomer, K., Ericksson, I., Moser, V., Theorell, T., & Fredlund, P. (1994). Lipid lowering through work stress reduction. International *Journal of Behavioral Medicine, 1* (3), 204-214.

Patrick, G. (1994). Making clinical research happen. In D. Compton (Ed.), *Professional issues in therapeutic recreation* (pp. 144-165). Champaign, IL: Sagamore.

Pincus, T. (1997). Analyzing long-term outcomes of clinical care without randomized controlled clinical trials: The consecutive patient questionnaire database. *Advances, 13,* 3-31.

Savell, K. (1991). Notes from the ATRA Publications Committee. In B. Riley (Ed.), *Quality management: Applications for therapeutic recreation* (p. vii). State College, PA: Venture.

Savell, K., Huston, A., & Malkin, M. (1993). Collaborative research: Bridging the gap between practitioners and researchers/educators. In M. Malkin, & C. Howe (Eds.), *Research in therapeutic recreation.* State College, PA: Venture.

Shank, J., Coyle, C., Kinney, W. & Lay, C. (1995). Using existing data to examine therapeutic recreation services. *Annual in Therapeutic Recreation, 5.*

Seibert, M. (1991). Keynote. In C. Coyle, W. Kinney, B. Riley, & J. Shank (Eds.), *Benefits of therapeutic recreation: A consensus view* (pp. 5-15). Philadelphia: Temple University Press.

Stumbo, N. (2003). The importance of evidence-based practice in therapeutic recreation. In N. Stumbo (Ed.), *Client outcomes in therapeutic recreation services.* State College, PA: Venture.

Thomas, K. (1994). The placebo in general practice. *Lancet, 344,* 1066-1067.

Williamson, K., & Stroot, S. (1994). Benefits, limitations, and implications of collaborative research. *The Physical Educator, 51*(4), 170-178.

Yadgood, M., Miller, P., & Matthews, P. (2000). Relieving the agony of the new pain management standards. *American Journal of Hospital Palliative Care, 17,* 333-3341.

Authors

Leandra A. Bedini is a professor and the director of Graduate Study in the Department of Recreation, Tourism, and Hospitality Management at the University of North Carolina at Greensboro. She received her Ph.D. from the University of Maryland in 1986, her M.S. from Michigan State University in 1980, and her B.S. from East Carolina University in 1975. She has served as associate editor for the *Therapeutic Recreation Journal*, as well as coordinator of the American Therapeutic Recreation Association's Research Institute. Bedini was awarded the ATRA Scholarly Achievement Award in 2000, the National Therapeutic Recreation Society Research Award in 1997, and is an HSG (University of St. Gallen) Fellow of the World Demographic Association.

Charles (Chuck) W. Bloom received a B.S. and M.S. degree in Therapeutic Recreation from Illinois State University. He worked as a Certified Therapeutic Recreation Specialist at Oak Forest Hospital until May 2008 and has 18 years of experience working in the area of physical rehabilitation.

Linda L. Buettner is a professor at the University of North Carolina at Greensboro and a gerontologist and recreational therapist who specializes in therapeutic programs for persons with dementia. She received her Ph.D. from Penn State University in 1994 and is the author of *Therapeutic Recreation in the Nursing Home*, co-author of *Dementia Practice Guidelines for Recreational Therapy*, and the *N.E.S.T.* (needs, environment, stimulation, and techniques) *evidence-based behavioral approach for dementia*. She has served as a board member for the American Therapeutic Recreation Association, Alzheimer's Association, the U.S. Senate Alzheimer's Study Group, and the Alzheimer's Association Early Stage Task force and is the editor for the *American Journal of Recreational Therapy*. She is on the editorial board of the *American Journal of Alzheimer's Disease*, a fellow of the Gerontological Society of America, and the Association of Gerontology in Higher Education.

Linda Caldwell is a professor of Recreation, Park, and Tourism Management and Human Development and Family Studies at Penn State University. She is co-author of *Recreation and Youth Development* and has served as the guest editor for a number of journals with special issues devoted to youth and leisure. She is the developer of TimeWise: Learning

Lifelong Leisure Skills and co-developer of HealthWise South Africa: Life Skills for Young Adults.

Marcia Jean Carter has a Ph.D. from Indiana University. She initiated the process to create the National Council for Therapeutic Recreation Certification, Inc. and was its first president. She has chaired and been a member of the Council on Accreditation of the National Recreation and Park Association. Carter received the Distinguished Fellow Award from the American Therapeutic Recreation Association and the Distinguished Service Award from the National Therapeutic Recreation Society.

Peg Connolly is an associate professor and director of Recreational Therapy at Western Carolina University. She was the first executive director of the National Council for Therapeutic Recreation Certification, where she served for 16 years. Connolly served on the National Therapeutic Recreation Society Board of Directors, and is the founding president of the American Therapeutic Recreation Association. She is a Certified Therapeutic Recreation Specialist and a Licensed Recreational Therapist in the state of North Carolina.

Suzanne Fitzsimmons is a geriatric nurse practitioner with a certificate in recreational therapy. She is an adjunct instructor for Florida International University in Miami and the University of North Carolina at Greensboro. Fitzsimmons co-authored the *Dementia Practice Guidelines for Recreational Therapy: Treatment of Disturbing Behaviors* and has been honored with awards from both nursing and recreational therapy with Binghamton University Award for Nursing Excellence in April 2000 and the Achievement award in September 2002 from the American Therapeutic Recreational Association.

Jean Folkerth received her doctorate from Indiana University and served for five years on the board of directors of the National Council for Therapeutic Recreation Certification and was president of NCTRC for two of those years. Folkerth was the American Therapeutic Recreation Association's representative to the Alliance Taskforce on Higher Education and has received the Scholarly Achievement Award from the American Therapeutic Recreation Association for her many contributions. Folkerth recently retired from the University of Toledo.

Mary Ann Keogh Hoss is an associate professor and program director for Health Services Administration in the College of Business and Public Administration at Eastern Washington University in Spokane. She has a Ph.D. from Gonzaga University and is certified nationally as a therapeutic recreation specialist. She has fellow status in the American College of Healthcare Executives and the American Therapeutic Recreation Association. Keogh Hoss served as the director of Rehabilitation Services at Eastern State Hospital in Medical Lake, Washington, as the chief operating officer for St. Luke's Rehabilitation Institute in Spokane, and as an interim CEO for Western State Hospital in Ft. Steilacuum, Washington. She is published in *Advancing Women in Leadership, Encyclopedia of Health Information, International Journal of Small Business and Entrepreneurship,* and *Annual in Therapeutic Recreation.* She currently serves as a board member and officer for the Friends of Eastern, a nonprofit organization attempting to meet the unmet needs of patients at Eastern

State Hospital. She has served as a board member at large for the American Therapeutic Recreation Association and is currently the president. She is also on the Medical Tourism Advisory Board.

Susan Hutchinson was one of the first graduates of the Therapeutic Recreation program at Douglas College in Vancouver, British Columbia, in 1984. She worked as a recreation therapist for approximately 10 years in both long-term care and rehabilitation before returning to graduate school under the mentorship of Colleen Hood at Dalhousie University for her master's degree and Douglas Kleiber at the University of Georgia for her doctorate degree. She is currently associate professor, cross-appointed in the leisure studies and health promotion program area at Dalhousie University, in Halifax, Nova Scotia.

Kari Kensinger is assistant professor of therapeutic recreation at Grand Valley State University in Allendale, Michigan. Kensinger earned her B.S. and M.S. degrees in Therapeutic Recreation from the University of Nebraska at Omaha and her Ph.D. from the University of Florida. She is a past president of the Nebraska Association of Recreation Therapists and the Michigan Therapeutic Recreation Association.

Judy S. Kinney received her B.S. degree in Therapeutic Recreation from Virginia Commonwealth University, her M.S. in Therapeutic Recreation from Southern Illinois University, and her Ph.D. in Educational Psychology from Temple University. Kinney teaches part-time at the University of North Carolina at Wilmington and works as a statistical and evaluation consultant in the School of Nursing as well as other departments. She spent a combination of five years as an evaluator on Minnesota and North Carolina's Safe Schools Healthy Students grants.

Walter B. (Terry) Kinney is chairperson of Health and Applied Human Sciences at the University of North Carolina at Wilmington. Kinney received his B.S.E. degree in Recreation from the State University of New York at Cortland, his M.S. in Recreation and Leisure Studies from the University of Illinois, and his Ph.D. from New York University. Kinney was the first recipient of the American Therapeutic Recreation Association's Scholarly Achievement Award, received ATRA's Organization Award for Outstanding Research, National Therapeutic Recreation Society's National Research Award, and Pennsylvania Therapeutic Recreation Association's Award for Outstanding Research.

Peggy Holmes-Layman received her M.S. and Ph.D. from the University of Illinois. She is an associate professor in the Department of Recreation Administration at Eastern Illinois University. She has taught in therapeutic recreation for several years and has practitioner experience in long-term care, physical disabilities, and psychiatric settings. She has presented and written on many aspects of the therapeutic recreation field and leisure behavior.

Youngkhill Lee is a faculty member at Calvin College teaching therapeutic recreation as well as some general core courses in recreation. He is currently the Spoelhof Teacher and Scholar Chair at Calvin College. He is also an Associate Editor for *Therapeutic Recreation*

Journal and *The Open Rehabilitation Journal*. His research interests include posttraumatic growth, everyday life of people with physical disabilities, and Christian faith of people with disabilities.

Neil Lundberg is an assistant professor of Therapeutic Recreation at Brigham Young University. He is the former program director at the National Ability Center in Park City, Utah, where he provided leisure education and therapeutic programming for individuals with disabilities for nearly a decade. He specializes in adaptive sports, including skiing, waterskiing, cycling, and outdoor recreation and is currently a fully certified adaptive and alpine ski instructor. His current research focuses on quality of life and health benefits due to sports participation for individuals with disabilities. Neil enjoys spending time outdoors with his wife, Melanie, and five daughters.

Marjorie Malkin has been involved with therapeutic recreation/recreation therapy for over 20 years. She completed her M.S. in Recreation Administration and Ed.D. in Therapeutic Recreation at the University of Georgia. Dr. Malkin served as consultant to the Illinois Office of Mental Health for seven years while a faculty member at Southern Illinois University, Carbondale. She currently is a professor at Southern Illinois University and has numerous national and international presentations and publications, including conferences and workshops in England, Costa Rica, Russia, and Ireland. She is a former board member and committee chair of ATRA. Dr. Malkin serves as a co-leader of the International Relations Team at ATRA.

Bryan P. McCormick is an associate professor of Recreation, Park, and Tourism Studies at Indiana University and serves as a member of the Public Health-World Health Organization for the American Therapeutic Recreation Association. McCormick's research has focused on the social and community functioning of individuals with severe mental illness cross culturally.

Nancy H. Navar is a professor and director of Therapeutic Recreation at the University of Wisconsin-La Crosse. Navar served on the board of directors for the American Therapeutic Recreation Association, National Therapeutic Recreation Society, state associations, and the National Council for Therapeutic Recreation Certification committees. Navar designed a community focused service project in La Crosse through the Leisure Lifestyle Center.

Sharon Nichols is a clinical specialist in Therapeutic Recreation for the Northeast Area of Genesis Healthcare Corporation and the chair of the Recreation Therapy Governing Board, which is a division of the New Hampshire Office of Licensed Allied Health Professions. Nichols has held numerous professional leadership positions, including president of the American Therapeutic Recreation Association, president of the New England Therapeutic Recreation Association, chair of the American Therapeutic Recreation Foundation, chair of the Standards Hearing Committee for the National Council for Therapeutic Recreation Certification, and member of the board of directors of the National Therapeutic Recreation Society. She is a graduate of Northeastern University with a degree in Therapeutic Recreation.

Nichols has been recognized as a distinguished fellow by the American Therapeutic Recreation Association.

George Patrick retired from his position as chief of the National Institutes of Health Clinical Center, Recreation Therapy Section, Rehabilitation Medicine Department in mid-2006. Patrick wishes to thank Mark J. Mattiko, who served as evaluation and research coordinator for mentoring and in most cases doing literature reviews, data analysis, as well as writing drafts for over 30 program evaluations and several research protocols. Recreational Therapy Section staff members mentioned in the text of this chapter provided sample case studies of outcome projects. Patrick abbreviated, re-summarized, and provided commentary on aspects of these case studies. He is responsible for leaving out details in order to encourage the thoughtful reader to consider the circumstances under which these case studies might be improved or crafted into outcome research.

John Henry Pommier received his Ph.D. from Texas A&M University and is a professor in the Department of Recreation Administration at Eastern Illinois University. He is president of the Paradise Equestrian Therapy Center, treasurer for Rho Phi Lambda —National, and chair of the Charleston Park & Recreation Foundation. He worked for Hurricane Island Outward Bound School (1988-1994), based mainly in Florida, serving individuals with conduct disorder and offender status. He serves on the National Therapeutic Recreation Society Internship and Fieldwork, and Outdoor/Adventure Experimental Therapy Committees.

Heather Porter is an adjunct instructor and Ph.D. candidate in the Health Studies program at Temple University, a member of ATRA's Public Health-World Health Organization team, and primary author of Recreational Therapy Handbook of Practice: ICF-Based Diagnosis and Treatment.

Marieke Van Puymbroeck is an assistant professor of Recreation, Park, and Tourism Studies at Indiana University and serves as a member of the Public Health-World Health Organization for American Therapeutic Recreation Foundation. Van Puymbroeck's professional interests include incorporating the International Classification of Functioning, Disability, and Health (ICF) into research and education, and her research focuses on examining the efficacy of physical activity and mind-body interventions for informal caregivers. Her professional experience includes working as a recreational therapist in inpatient psychiatry and skilled nursing. Van Puymbroeck teaches therapeutic recreation classes at the graduate and undergraduate levels and believes in incorporating her research experiences into teaching.

Nancy E. Richeson is employed as an associate professor at the University of Southern Maine, College of Nursing and Health Professions. Richeson is a gerontologist, a certified therapeutic recreation specialist, a Reiki Master/Teacher, and is registered as a therapy dog tester and observer through Therapy Dogs, Inc. She completed a semester-long research projected testing the effects of an adult education course for the Osher Lifelong

Learning Institute, developed by Fitzsimmons and Buettner, titled *Health Promotion for the Mind, Body, and Spirit*. She has authored over 25 publications related to these research interests. Richeson is a member of the American Therapeutic Recreation Association, the Gerontological Society of America, the Maine Alzheimer's Association, and Therapy Dogs, Inc.

Jo-Ellen Ross received her Ph.D. in Leisure Studies from the University of Illinois and is a Certified Therapeutic Recreation Specialist. She has been a presenter at state, regional, and national conferences and was the co-editor for the Practice Perspective Section of *Therapeutic Recreation Journal* for six years. She has been active in both the American Therapeutic Recreation Association and the National Therapeutic Recreation Society, particularly in relationship to technology.

Janet R. Sable is chair and professor in the Department of Recreation Management and Policy within the College of Health and Human Services at the University of New Hampshire. She has served on the National Council for Therapeutic Recreation Certification and was actively involved in the process that led to the state of New Hampshire's licensure of Recreation Therapists.

Candace Ashton-Shaeffer received her Ph.D. in Leisure Studies at the University of Illinois, Urbana-Champaign. She is a professor and program coordinator at the University of North Carolina at Wilmington. She is a past president of the National Therapeutic Recreation Society and has received numerous service awards from both NTRS and the American Therapeutic Recreation Association. Along with being a Certified Therapeutic Recreation Specialist, she is a Licensed Recreational Therapist in North Carolina.

John W. Shank is professor and chair of the Therapeutic Recreation Department, College of Health Professions at Temple University. He earned a B.S. degree from Springfield College, an M.S. degree from the Pennsylvania State University, and an Ed.D. from Boston University. In 1984, Shank founded and chaired the Legislative Coalition of the American Therapeutic Recreation Association, National Therapeutic Recreation Society, and the Negros Center for People Empowerment and Rural Development. Shank has served on the board of directors for the NTRS and the National Council for Therapeutic Recreation Certification and has done extensive committee work for the ATRA, NTRS, and the NCPERD. He is a member of ATRA's Public Health-World Health Organization team. He is co-author, with Catherine Coyle, of the text, *Therapeutic Recreation in Health Promotion and Rehabilitation*. Shank has received awards for his research and scholarship from NTRS, ATRA, and the Pennsylvania Therapeutic and Recreation Society. He is a Distinguished Fellow of the American Therapeutic Recreation Association.

Jerome Singleton has been employed by the School of Health and Human Performance at Dalhousie University since 1981. Singleton is cross-appointed to the School of Nursing, Sociology, and Anthropology at Dalhousie University, the École de Kinésiologie et Récréologie, Université de Moncton, the Department of Health at the University of Toronto, and the School of Social Work at the University of Toronto. Singleton has published articles in *Canadian Association on Gerontology, Activities Adaptation and Aging, Journal of Leisurability, Leisure Today, Journal of Occupational Science Australia, World Leisure and Recreation Journal*, and the *Journal of Leisure Research*. He has made presentations on his work in a variety of professional conferences ranging from the Recreation Association of Nova Scotia, Leisure Research Symposium, Canadian Congress on Leisure Research, National Therapeutic Recreation Society Institute, Gerontological Society of America, Canadian Association on Gerontology, and the World Demographic Association. He was made a fellow of the World Demographic Association in 2006. The Canadian Therapeutic Recreation Association in 2007 recognized his contribution to Therapeutic Recreation by naming him the Therapeutic Professional of the Year.

Charlsena F. Stone is an associate professor in the Department of Recreation, Tourism, and Hospitality Management at the University of North Carolina at Greensboro. She received her B.S. degree from North Carolina A&T State University and her M.S. and Ph.D. degrees from the University of North Carolina at Chapel Hill. Stone maintains active involvement professionally through work with the American Therapeutic Recreation Association and state associations.

Norma J. Stumbo recently retired from the University of Illinois. She was director of the National Science Foundation-funded Midwest Alliance in Science, Technology, Engineering, and Mathematics, from 2005 to 2008. From 1984 to 2005, she was a professor of therapeutic recreation and associate dean of undergraduate studies at Illinois State University. She has authored a number of texts in the field, including: *Therapeutic Recreation Program Design: Principles and Procedures* (with Carol Peterson), *Client Assessment in TR Services, Client Outcomes in TR Services, Professional Issues in TR Services*, and the five-part *Leisure Education* manual series. Stumbo received her Ph.D. from the University of Illinois and her M.S. and B.S. degrees from the University of Missouri-Columbia.

G.T. Thompson was, in November 2008, elected to represent Pennsylvania's fifth district as a member of Congrss. In the 11th Congress, he serves on the Agriculture, Small Business, and Education/Labor Committees. Prior to that, he had been a recreational therapist and rehabilitation services manager with the Susquehanna Health System in north-central Pennsylvania. He has a B.S. degree in Therapeutic Recreation from Penn State University and M.S. degree from Temple University. He has served the American Therapeutic Recreation Association as Coverage and Reimbursement Committee Chair and in the Office of External Affairs. His duties have included working as the liaison to the Healthcare Finance Administration. Most recently he was appointed to an HCFA Technical Expert Panel on the Rehabilitation Prospective Payment System. Currently Thompson serves as the treasurer and Public Policy Co-Team Leader for the American Therapeutic Recreation Association.

Ray E. West has an M.S. degree from Penn State University and a B.S. degree from Lock Haven University of Pennsylvania. He is currently in private practice as a consultant.

He retired from his former position as the director of the Department of Recreational Therapy at the University of North Carolina Hospitals-Chapel Hill in 2005 after serving as department director for 25 years. He held an adjunct appointment and taught in the Curriculum in Leisure Studies at UNC-Chapel Hill from 1981 until 1994. He served as instructor in Recreation and Parks at Penn State University and as chief recreational therapist at the Williamsport Hospital and Rehabilitation Center in Pennsylvania. West is a member of the North Carolina Board of Recreational Therapy Licensure, a founder and member of the board of directors and past chair of the Southeast Therapeutic Recreation Symposium, and serves as an American Therapeutic Recreation Association organization liaison to the Coalition of Rehabilitation Therapy Organizations for the Hospital Accreditation Program, Professional Technical and Advisory Committee of the Joint Commission. He is a founder and past-president of ATRA and the North Carolina Board of Recreational Therapy Association and a past-president of the Pennsylvania Therapeutic Recreation Society.

Mark A. Widmer is a professor of therapeutic recreation at Brigham Young University in Utah. Widmer spent a number of years designing and operating theory-based wilderness adventure research programs where youth participate in survival, whitewater rafting, mountain biking, rock climbing, and other outdoor activities. Mark also conducts outcome research and consults with a number of therapeutic wilderness and adventure programs.

Jeff Witman is an associate professor in the Behavioral Science Department at York College of Pennsylvania and is coordinator of the Recreation Program. Witman also taught at the University of New Hampshire, Kent State University in Ohio, and Lock Haven University in Pennsylvania. He spent nine years as director of Occupational Therapy and Therapeutic Recreation at Hampstead Hospital in New Hampshire, five years as director of Activity Therapy at Philhaven Behavioral Healthcare in Pennsylvania, and five years as a program director at several camps. Witman works part time as a trainer for Teambuilders, Inc., leading adventure experiences for a variety of groups. He has served as president of the National Therapeutic Recreation Society and had membership on the State Boards for Special Olympics and for Very Special Arts. Witman is the president of the Pennsylvania Therapeutic Recreation Society. His publications include *Special Education Naturally* (Indiana University), *Guidelines for Curriculum Planning in Therapeutic Recreation: A Tool for Self-Assessment,* and *Taking The Initiative.*

Heewon Yang was born in South Korea, where he worked at mental health hospitals, nursing homes, orphanages, shelters for the homeless, and a private company as a recreation program consultant. Yang came to the United States in 1995, and received his M. S. degree at the University of Tennessee, Knoxville. He received a Ph.D. from Indiana University in leisure behavior with an emphasis on therapeutic recreation. After finishing his doctoral degree, he taught at Kent State University in Ohio, where he served as a program director for a weekend Respite and Recreation Program for Adopted Children with special needs. Currently, Yang is an associate professor in the department of Health Education and Recreation at Southern Illinois University. Yang teaches both general recreation and therapeutic recreation courses. He is a co-leader of the International Relations Team at the American Therapeutic Recreation Association and a chair of the Exam Maintenance Committee at the National Council for Therapeutic Recreation Certification.

Ramon B. Zabriskie has a Ph.D. from Indiana University. He has actively served in capacities related to professional quality in local and national professional organizations, credentialing bodies, and licensure boards as a licensed and certified practitioner and later as an educator and scholar. He has written and presented extensively on issues related to accreditation. He is currently on faculty in the Department of Recreation Management & Youth Leadership at Brigham Young University in Utah.

INDEX